HARRISES OF CONNECTICUT

HARRISES OF CONNECTICUT
SCATTERED DESCENDANTS

Gale Ion Harris, J.D., Ph.D.
Fellow of the American Society of Genealogists

Printed by
McNaughton & Gunn, Inc.
Saline, Michigan

2012

ISBN 978-1-4675-5690-3
Library of Congress Control Number: 2012922172

PREFACE

In 1904, Henry R. Stiles presented sketches of eighteenth- and nineteenth-century Harris families in his *History of Ancient Wethersfield, Connecticut*. In 1947, Donald Lines Jacobus, who is generally regarded as having provided the main impetus for modern standards in American genealogy, remarked in a brief article on Harrises in the western part of Connecticut that Stiles had given "an impossible account of the origin of this family." Jacobus did not elaborate, but it is clear from context he meant that the connection Stiles had made between the families in Wethersfield with earlier Harrises in nearby Middletown was false. Later publications clearly showed that Jacobus was right, but revealed also that the true origin of the Wethersfield Harrises was an elusive matter indeed.

But Stiles left an important clue well hidden away in a footnote, easily ignored and obviously discounted by Stiles himself as of little consequence, which, nonetheless, eventually provided a basis for a better understanding of what really took place in the prior century. Stiles acknowledged that much of his information was provided by Nathaniel H. Morgan of Hartford and Miss Mary J. Harris of Wethersfield. From context, one may deduce that Morgan's contribution probably was the "impossible" connection to the unrelated Middletown family, while Miss Harris obviously was his source for the discounted clue:

Miss Harris states that . . . a family tradition says that the first of the name here were two brothers, John and Thomas by name, who came up from New London in a boat, as far as Middletown and traded their boat for land in Wethersfield.

Stiles buried her "tradition" in the footnote, no doubt because it conflicted with the account he had from Morgan—although he did allow: "still there may be a kernel of truth in the story." As a more systematic study of earlier Harrises in Connecticut advanced, a growing realization developed that the tradition, though perhaps distorted in detail, was essentially correct. There were in fact two Harris men, John and Thomas, who left traces of their presence in ancient Wethersfield after about 1664. I have presented elsewhere a fuller discussion of the tradition and the historical elements underlying a determination that it does indeed preserve a late memory of early facts.

The available contemporary evidence, however, does not prove that these two men actually were brothers—we have only the tradition for that. Thus, since it follows that we also cannot say who their parents were, an assumption that they were in fact related is avoided in this book by starting its account with one of the pair, John, whose trace in the records, although dim, is enough for us to be reasonably confident that he was the ancestor of Harris families who remained in Wethersfield and many others who scattered out across America. The early generations of the other one of the pair, Thomas, are presented as Appendix I. Sketches for other Harris families in Connecticut before 1700, whose relationship, if any, is unknown, are presented in Appendix II.

This book might not have been possible without the prior work of two early Fellows of the American Society of Genealogists, Donald Lines Jacobus and Walter Lee Sheppard Jr., and their collaborators, whose work on this subject appeared in the decade following the end of World War II. Jacobus focused his attention mainly on Harrises in and around Wethersfield, while Sheppard and his collaborators concentrated on Harrises in New Jersey and their royal descent through a maternal line. Yet, there is no clear evidence that they ever believed they were working on branches of the same family.

Most of the foundation work showing that they were indeed of the same family has appeared in several research articles published since their time. They are cited at appropriate places in this book; its objecttive is to bring it all together.

Gale Ion Harris
East Lansing, Michigan
November 2012

CONTENTS

HARRISES OF CONNECTICUT

SCATTERED DESCENDANTS

John Harris presents an extreme example of a man who managed to leave few traces of his presence, yet enough to allow us to discern circumstances sufficient to place him at the head of the large group of descendants covered in this book. Traditionally, he appeared in Wethersfield with a brother Thomas; they "came up from New London in a boat, as far as Middletown and traded their boat for land in Wethersfield."[1] Indeed, we know that a Thomas Harris did come up the Connecticut River from the direction of New London in the mid-1660s, settled on the east side of the River, and built a sawmill in the north part of what is now the town of Glastonbury (formed from Wethersfield in 1690). Before arrival, he had married about 1664 Sarah Wright, a daughter of Capt. Richard Wright downriver at Twelve-Mile Island (now East Haddam). Their descendants, reported elsewhere,[2] are summarized in Appendix I of this book.

John Harris is not so well documented, yet no less real than Thomas. The earliest direct reference to him is the record in Boston, Massachusetts, of his marriage there on 10 September 1657 to fifteen-year-old Hannah Briggs,[3] daughter of the tailor William Briggs and wife Mary of Boston.[4] He appears there again in the record of the birth of their son John on 8 August 1658.[5]

Circumstances make it apparent that John, with his young bride and new son, preceded by several years her parents' move in the mid-1660s to Wethersfield on the Connecticut River below Hartford. The Briggses sold their Boston property on 23 June 1665[6] and were in Wethersfield before 11 June

---

[1] Henry R. Stiles, *The History of Ancient Wethersfield, Connecticut*, 2 vols. (New York: Grafton Press, 1904), 2:412n. For a more complete discussion, see Gale Ion Harris, "Enigmas #26, Early Harrises of Wethersfield, Connecticut: Analysis of a Tradition," *The American Genealogist* [TAG] 83 (2009):249-57.

[2] Gale Ion Harris, "Thomas Harris, Sawmiller of Hartford, Connecticut," *National Genealogical Society Quarterly* 78 (1990):182-203, including at pp. 186-87 a map of the relevant Hockanum-Naubuc neighborhood in East Hartford and Glastonbury; Gale Ion Harris, "Robert Harris of Connecticut and Descendants in the Hudson Valley," *New York Genealogical and Biographical Record* [NYGBR] 130 (1999):183-96, 269-82.

[3] *Boston Births, Baptisms, Marriages, and Deaths, 1630–1699, [Ninth] Report of the Record Commissioners of the City of Boston* (Boston, 1883), 62.

[4] Gale Ion Harris, "William[1] and Mary Briggs of Boston and the Connecticut Valley: With Notes on their Sons-in-Law John Harris and Wolston Brockway," *New England Historical and Genealogical Register* [NEHGR] 151 (1997):87-101.

[5] *Boston Births, Baptisms, Marriages, and Deaths*, 65.

[6] *Suffolk Deeds*, 14 vols. (Boston, 1880–1906), 13:464-65.

1666, when John Winthrop Jr. entered a prescription for him in his medical journal.[7] Their Harris son-in-law may have been there early enough to be the John Harris who was chosen as constable for the east side of the Connecticut River in March 1659/60,[8] where a few years later Thomas Harris erected his saw mill. In any case, John died before September 1664, by which time his widow Hannah had married Wolston Brockway in the Wethersfield locality and with him settled farther downriver in Lyme, Connecticut.[9] After a few years in Wethersfield and Middletown, Hannah's father, William Briggs, joined them in Lyme.[10]

John Harris's marriage in Boston in 1657 to young Hannah Briggs apparently was not his first, but no specific evidence of an earlier wife's identity has been found. Her existence is inferred from a close study of Harrises who appear at the right times and places to have been children of John, but with an earlier wife. The clearest example is the appearance of Walter Harris as an 11 or 12 year-old boy in the Hockanam neighborhood in November 1664,[11] a plain indication that—following a common practice of the time—he had been placed in another family (Edwards) there upon his stepmother's remarriage about that time to Wolston Brockway. Walter surely was a son of John Harris, but too old to be Hannah's son. Similarly, on the basis of associations, chronology, and the name itself, the Thomas Harris who appeared in Killingworth, Connecticut, and East Hampton, Long Island, is best placed as another son of John and the earlier wife.[12] The relationships are more fully set out in the following genealogical summary.

FIRST GENERATION

1 JOHN[1] HARRIS, parentage unknown, born say 1627 (assuming he was about 25 at the birth of his first identifiable child), died by 1664, probably in Wethersfield (or modern Glastonbury), Connecticut. He probably had an early, unidentified wife by 1652, the mother of his apparent sons Walter and Thomas. John married in Boston on 10 September 1657, presumably as his

---

[7] Medical Records of John Winthrop [Jr.], MS, Massachusetts Historical Society, 660.

[8] Connecticut Colonial Court Records, 2:186. The only reason for any doubt about this record is the possibility that it could have been intended for John *Harrison*, a known inhabitant of Wethersfield at that time. There was no other John *Harris* in Wethersfield to whom it could refer.

[9] Gale Ion Harris, "Wolston[1] Brockway of Lyme, Connecticut: With Further Analysis of His Associations," NEHGR 162 (2008):37-46, 140-48, 301.

[10] Harris, "William[1] and Mary Briggs," NEHGR 151 (1997):88.

[11] Medical Records of John Winthrop, 576.

[12] Gale Ion Harris, "The Origins of Thomas Harris of East Hampton, Long Island, and Killingworth, Connecticut," NYGBR 128 (1997):11-24.

second wife, **HANNAH BRIGGS**, born there on 28 August 1642, who died in Lyme, Connecticut, on 6 February 1687[/8], daughter of William[1] and Mary (___) Briggs of Boston, and later of Wethersfield, Middletown, and Lyme.[13] Hannah married second, probably at Wethersfield by September 1664 (birth of first child), Wolston Brockway, with whom she settled at Lyme.[14] Hannah and Wolston Brockway, who was described in at least one record as a cooper,[15] were the parents of ten children born from 1664 to about 1684 and recorded in Lyme: Hannah, William, Wolston, Mary, Bridget, Richard, Elizabeth, Sarah, Deborah, and John.[16]

It is inferred from the circumstances that when Hannah married Brockway in the Wethersfield locality, she followed common practice by placing her oldest stepson Walter Harris with the Thomas Edwards family in what is now Glastonbury and probably took the younger stepson, Thomas Harris, and her own son John Harris [Jr.] with her to Lyme.

Probable children of John[1] and ____ (___) Harris:

2 i WALTER[2] HARRIS, b. ca. 1652 or 1653; m. (1) MARY (HALE) BENJAMIN, (2) MARY HOLLISTER.
3 ii THOMAS HARRIS, b. say 1654; m. RUTH JAMES.

Child of John[1] and Hannah (Briggs) Harris:

4 iii JOHN HARRIS, b. Boston 8 Aug. 1658; m. MEHITABLE DANKS.

SECOND GENERATION

2 WALTER[2] HARRIS (*John[1]*), born about 1652 or 1653 (age "about 11 or 12 years" in 1664),[17] died intestate in Wethersfield, Connecticut, on 1 December 1715, the date given in the inventory of his estate filed at Hartford.[18] Walter and his first wife, **MARY (HALE) BENJAMIN**, were married "some considerable time before" January 1686/7[19] probably in that part of Wethersfield on the east side of the Connecticut River later set off as the town of Glastonbury. Soon afterward, on 25 February 1686/7, the court at Hartford fined them 40 shillings "for incontinence before marriage."[20] Mary, a

---

[13] Harris, "William[1] and Mary Briggs," NEHGR 151 (1997):91-92.
[14] Harris, "Wolston[1] Brockway of Lyme," NEHGR 162 (2008):140.
[15] Lyme, Conn., Deeds, 3:3.
[16] Harris, "Wolston[1] Brockway of Lyme," NEHGR 162 (2008):141-48.
[17] Medical Records of John Winthrop, 576.
[18] Hartford District Probate Files, no. 2592.
[19] Hartford District Probate Files, no. 447 (estate of Caleb Benjamin).
[20] Hartford County Court Records, 4:123.

daughter of Samuel and Mary (Smith) Hale born in Wethersfield on 29 April 1649 and died "probably by 1700," was the widow of Caleb Benjamin who died at Wethersfield on 8 May 1684, son of John and Abigail (Eddy) Benjamin. With Caleb Benjamin, Mary had seven children born in Wethersfield from 1671 to 1684: Mary, Abigail, Sarah, John, Samuel, Martha, and Caleb.[21]

While single and still at home with her parents, Mary gave evidence in 1669 regarding her "cat" experience in the night with the voice of Katherine Harrison, the widow of John Harrison of Wethersfield, who recently had been imprisoned and indicted for witchcraft. It provides an exceptional glimpse into the period and her young life, so her deposition is presented below as it has been preserved.

MARY HALE'S TALE

Mary Hale aged about 20 years testifieth that about the latter end of November: being the 29 day 1668 the said Mary Hale lying in her bed a good fire giving such light that one might see all over that room we heard the said Mary then was the said Mary heard a noise and presently some things fell on her legs with such violence that she feared it would have broken her legs, and then it came upon her stomach and oppressed her so as if it would have pressed the breath out of her body then appeared an ugly shaped thing like a dog, having a head such that I clearly and distinctly know to be the head of Katherine Harrison who was lately imprisoned upon suspicion of witchcraft, Mary saw it walk to and fro in the chamber, and went to her father's bedside then came back and disappeared: that day seven night next after at night lying in her bed something came upon her in like manner as is formerly related first on her legs and feet and then on her stomach crushing and oppressing her very sore, she put forth her hand to feel (because there was no light in the room so as clearly to discern), Mary aforesaid felt a face which she judged to be a woman's face, presently then she had a great blow on her fingers which pained her 2 days after which she complained of to her father and mother, and made her fingers black and blue, during the former passages Mary called to her father and mother but could not wake them till it was gone. After this the 19: day of December in the night (the night being very windy) something came again and spoke thus to her saying to Mary aforesaid you said that I would not come again, but are you not afraid of me, Mary said no, the voice replied I will make you afraid before I have done with you, and then presently Mary was crushed and oppressed very much then Mary called often to her father and mother, they lying very near, the voice said though you do call they shall not hear, till I am gone, then the voice said you said that I preserved my cart to carry me to the gallows, but I will make it a [death?] cart to you (which said words Mary remembered she had only spoke in private to her sister a little before, and to no other)[.] Mary replied she feared her not, because God had kept her, and would keep her still[.] The voice said she had a commission to kill her, Mary asked who gave you the commission, the voice replied God gave

[21] Details of these children and Walter Harris's administration of the Benjamin estate may be found in Donald Lines Jacobus and Edgar Francis Waterman, *Hale, House and Related Families, Mainly of the Connecticut River Valley* (Hartford: Connecticut Historical Society, 1952), 8-11.

me the commission, Mary replied the devil is a liar from the beginning for God will not give commission to murder, therefore it must be from the devil, then Mary was again pressed very much then the voice said you will make known these things abroad when I am gone, but if you will promise me to keep these aforesaid matters secret, I will come no more to afflict you. Mary replied I will tell it abroad, whereas the said Mary mentioneth divers times in the former writing that she heard a voice, the said Mary affirmeth that she did and doth know that it was the voice of Katherine Harrison aforesaid, and also Mary aforesaid affirmeth that the substance of the whole relation is the truth.

Sworn in court May 25, 1669 attests John Allyn Secretary about the cat.[22]

The death of Walter Harris's wife Mary (Hale) (Benjamin) is unrecorded; she was living as late as 10 February 1692/3, when she testified that she had heard the Indian, Nanico, say that he was sick about a week before he was "said to be Hurtt by Samuel Cirkome."[23] Walter married another Mary about 1700, **MARY HOLLISTER**, who was born probably by 1670[24] and was living in Wethersfield as late as 22 April 1740,[25] a daughter of Thomas and Elizabeth (Lattimer) Hollister of Wethersfield.[26] After Walter's death, she married secondly sometime after 19 April 1716 Peter Blinn, a widower of Wethersfield, born about 1741, who died there on 7 March 1724/5.[27]

After Walter Harris's first appearance in 1664 as an 11- or 12-year-old "servant" [in the sense of employee or ward][28] in Thomas Edwards's home in that part of Wethersfield on the east side of the Connecticut River that later became the Town of Glastonbury, he grew up in the neighborhood known as Hockanum, which extended across the present town line between Glastonbury and East Hartford. At the county court in Hartford on 15 December 1671, Walter and three other young fellows were fined 10s. each "for unseasonable nightwalking and stealing watter mullions from Richard Smith," who had property in the Hockanum neighborhood. In addition, they

---

[22] David D. Hall, *Witch-Hunting in Seventeenth-Century New England: A Documentary History, 1638–1692* (Boston: Northeastern University Press, 1991), 181-82, citing Willis Papers, The Annmary Brown Memorial Library, Brown University. After one trial where the jurors could not agree, and another from which the magistrates dissented, Katherine was ordered to leave the colony; she was in New York by 1670.

[23] Connecticut Archives: Crimes and Misdemeanors, 1:190, Connecticut State Library, Hartford.

[24] Jacobus estimated that Mary Hollister was born "say 1678" (*Hale, House*, 619), but I have reviewed elsewhere (Gale Ion Harris, "Walter Harris of Wethersfield, Connecticut," NEHGR 142 [1988]:329-30) circumstances showing that she probably was born earlier and likely was the third person in the Thomas Hollister household at Wethersfield in 1670 ("List of Families in Wethersfield with Quantity of Grain in Possession of Each," *The Wyllys Papers*, Coll. Conn. Hist. Soc. 21 [Hartford, 1924]:197-99, at 199).

[25] Wethersfield Deeds, 8:93 (Mary Blin, widow, to "my son" Thomas Harris of Wethersfield.)

[26] Jacobus and Waterman, *Hale, House*, 619.

[27] Gale Ion Harris, "Walter Harris's Widow and the Blinns of Wethersfield, Connecticut," NEHGR 143 (1989):303-24, at 305.

[28] Medical Records of John Winthrop, 575.

were sent "to prison and there to continue in Durance the Courts pleasure."[29] The record does not show how long that lasted.

On 6 January 1681/2, at age about 30, Walter purchased from John Hunnewell a "sorol horse 5 y[rs] old with a blaze in y[e] forehead."[30] At that time, Hunnewell had a sawmill and brick kiln south of Wethersfield village where he had "set his house" and kept an inn.[31] Next year, Walter was owed £15 5s.—probably unpaid wages—as a creditor of the estate of his former master Thomas Edwards, who had died at Wethersfield on 27 July 1683.[32]

Walter Harris was chosen as a fence viewer in Wethersfield—probably for the east side of the River—on 23 December 1690.[33] Two years later, soon after the east side gained its separate status as a town, Walter was described as "of Glasenbury" when his wife testified about Nanico's death, and he was residing there on 29 December 1693 when Glastonbury's first town meeting was held. Walter Harris and Thomas Brewer were chosen as fence viewers. At the next meeting, held 26 December 1694, Walter was elected constable, and in 1704 he was again elected, with Joseph Hills, as fence viewer.[34] On 25 December 1695, Samuel Hale [Jr.], Samuel Smith, Joseph Smith, Samuel Gaines, John Hubbard, and Walter Harris purchased property in Glastonbury on which to build a corn mill "for the benefit of the town."[35]

By a note dated 9 July 1698, Jonathan Colefax of Wethersfield promised to repay £3 5s. that he had "borrowed of Mr. Walter Harris of Glasinbury." Walter sued on the debt and a summons for Colefax's appearance was issued on 19 February 1698/9. The outcome of the case is not stated,[36] but this litigation might in some way explain Walter's ownership before 1703 of a 14-acre parcel in the 2nd Tier in Wethersfield that originally had been granted to Cole-

---

[29] Connecticut Colonial Court Records, 1663–1677, 3:117, Connecticut State Archives.

[30] Wethersfield, Conn., Deeds, 2:44.

[31] Stiles, *History of Ancient Wethersfield,* 1:279; *Willis Papers,* 278. Later that spring, Allumchoyce, an Indian from Farmington stopped by Hunneywell's inn and, "being much in drink," proceeded up Broad Street to the house of the Randalls, where neighbor Abiah (Kimberly) Boardman, sitting at her door, saw him stab Goodwife Randall, for which he was executed on 28 June 1682 (Gale Ion Harris, "John Edwards of Wethersfield, Connecticut, NEHGR 145 (1991):340-41).

Incidentally, the day after Allumchoyce's hanging, Abiah gave birth to Eunice Boardman, later the wife of Abraham Williams with whom she had a daughter Rebecca Williams who became the wife of Walter Harris's son Daniel (Gale Ion Harris and Norman W. Ingham, "Thomas[1] and Rebecca (Waterhouse) Williams of Wethersfield, Connecticut," TAG 79 [2004]:55).

[32] Hartford District Probate Records, 4:78, 157, Connecticut State Library.

[33] Wethersfield Town Votes, 1646-1783, 1:215, Town Clerk's Office.

[34] Glastonbury, Conn., Deeds, 1:25, 27, 63.

[35] Glastonbury, Conn., Deeds, 2:3.

[36] Connecticut Archives: Private Controversies, 5:86a, 87, Connecticut State Library.

fax in 1693. No grantee deed for it to Walter appears, but he sold it to John Wright in February 1711.[37]

Colefax's note is of interest today because at the bottom of it is the only known example of Walter Harris's signature:

Mr Stel if the [*illegible*] of this bill be payed with the tim[e] that we concluded on then deliver this bill to Jonethan Colefax and in so doeing you will oblige your frend *Walter Hares.*

The addressee probably was Capt. James Steele of Wethersfield. The note shows that Walter could write and sign his name, although after 1710 his recorded deeds all indicate that he signed them by mark.[38]

On 9 December 1701, Walter Harris of Glastonbury and John Williams of Wethersfield became sureties for the estate of Lt. Thomas Hollister who had died in November, the father of Walter's second wife Mary. Soon after, on 9 March 1701/2, Joseph Hollister, Mary's brother, chose Walter Harris as his guardian.[39]

Also in 1702, Walter apparently had in his home Lydia Colt, age probably about 24, daughter of John and Hester (Edwards) Colt of East Hartford and Windsor, Connecticut. Lydia, whose mother was a half-sister of Walter's former master Thomas Edwards of Hockanum, soon married in March 1704/5 Richard Fox Jr. of Glastonbury.[40]

On 7 May 1703 and still described as "of Glastonbury," Walter sold two acres in the common meadow in Wethersfield, which had been distributed to his wife, Mary, from Thomas Hollister's estate. The property was bounded by the Great [Connecticut] River on the east, by Walter's own land on the north, by Jonathan Hollister's land on the south, and by a highway on the west.[41] On 20 December 1709, Walter Harris of Glastonbury, husbandman, with his wife Mary's consent, sold to George Stillman about one acre of meadow on the Great River near the south end of Wethersfield, which Mary had also received from her father's estate.[42]

At this period of Walter's life, he seems to have been in more affluent circumstances than he was later. In addition to the above, on 4 April 1699, he

---

[37] Wethersfield, Conn., Deeds, 4:52, 8:165.

[38] This note appears to be in the same hand as in an account in 1697 of Walter's debts incurred in the handling of the estate of his first wife's former husband, Caleb Benjamin.

[39] Charles William Manwaring, *A Digest of the Early Connecticut Probate Records*, 3 vols. (Hartford: R. S. Peck & Co., 1904–6), 2:80–81.

[40] Gale Ion Harris, "John[1] Colt of Hartford and Windsor, Connecticut: Review and Reconciliation," TAG 80 (2005):92, citing Benjamin Talcott Account Book, 1699–1725, Connecticut Historical Society.

[41] Wethersfield, Conn., Deeds, 3:130, 4:194.

[42] Wethersfield, Conn., Deeds, 4:52.

loaned £14 15*s*. to Moses Goffe, who secured it by giving him a mortgage on about 13 acres, including a house and barn, at Rocky Hill on the west side of the Connecticut River in Wethersfield.[43] This transaction resulted in a dispute between them, evidence of which is scattered through the county court records until March 1710/11. Walter eventually won a foreclosure action and gained possession of the Rocky Hill property on 6 June 1710.[44]

Walter moved right away across the River onto this Rocky Hill property. He was still residing in Glastonbury on 7 March 1709/10, but on 13 June 1710 he was referred to as "Walter Harris Sen[r] now residing in Wethersfield."[45] In the absence of contrary evidence, it is presumed that he continued to reside on that place for the remainder of his life.

Between April 1707 and April 1713, Walter was frequently involved as a party in Hartford County civil actions. They can be summarized briefly:

Richard Edwards of Hartford, plaintiff, a prominent attorney (8 April 1707).

Aaron Goffe of Wethersfield, defendant (8 April 1707), also on 2 Sept. 1707 when Walter did not appear because "he was sick."

Jonathan Hollister of Wethersfield, Walter's brother-in-law, defendant, Walter failing to prosecute (8 Nov. 1707).

Elizabeth Blackleach of Wethersfield, plaintiff (18 Nov. 1707), executor of her husband John Blackleach's will in an action for a debt of £5 "partly for goods taken up since the decease of said John Blackleach."

Thomas Morely Sr. of Glastonbury, plaintiff, Walter failing to prosecute his appeal (2 March 1709/10 and 5 Sept. 1710).

Ebenezer Kilbourn of Glastonbury, plaintiff, sueing Walter for "unjustly seizing and detaining . . . a certain black cow taken out of the meadow in Glassenbury about the beginning of November last," Walter unsuccessfully answering that "said cow was then his own Proper estate," Walter appealing but failing to prosecute (? March 1709/10 and 5 Sept. 1710).

Thomas Kimberly of Glastonbury, plaintiff, several items related to a debt and bonds, the "action commenced by attachment served on a certain red cow belonging to said Harris," Walter unsuccessfully appealing (13 June and 5 Sept. 1710).

Aaron Goffe of Wethersfield, again, defendant, Walter successful in a debt action (5 Sept. 1710).

---

[43] Wethersfield, Conn., Deeds, 3:5. The property was described as having a house and barn, and adjacent to the brook, the highway to Middletown, and lands of Mr. Wolcott and Philip Goffe.

[44] Hartford Co. Court Records, Record Group 3, 1:111, 116, 146, 183, Connecticut State Library.

[45] Hartford Co. Court Records, Record Group 3, 1:132.

Thomas Brewer Sr. of Glastonbury, defendant in a debt action, Brewer appealing and Walter failing to defend, so non-suited (5 Sept. 1710, 5 Dec. 1710, 6 March 1710/11).

Robert Loveland of Glastonbury, defendant, action on a debt due by book, Walter winning judgment (9 March 1713/4).

William Whiting of Hartford, plaintiff, action on a book debt, Walter successfully defending (probably 6 March 1713/4).[46]

Apparently vexed by some of these actions, Walter, "being before this court [on 13 June 1710] pleading to a case wherein he was concerned amongst other things in a reflecting manner several times said to the judge, 'you always catch me up and will not suffer me to speak'." Walter was assessed a fine of 5s. for contempt, which he paid in court.[47]

This was not the last of Walter's troubles with that court; less than a year later he was arrested on a complaint by deputy sheriff John Stedman and brought before court on 6 March 1710/11 on the charge that he "did unpeaceably behave himself towards the said Sheriff." Walter was required to give a bond of £10 for his appearance in court "in September next," but no further reference to the matter appears in the court records.[48]

Land records, however, reveal the inconvenience Walter was put to in order to meet his bond. On 31 March 1711, Nathaniel Hooker of Hartford assigned to Lt. John Coleman of Wethersfield a mortgage which Hooker had obtained on four acres of Walter's land in Wethersfield on 1 November 1710. On the same date as Hooker's assignment, Walter bound two acres of the four-acre meadow to Coleman "untill next September court" in consideration of the bond posted to secure his appearance. The other two acres were to stand as security for a £10 loan to Walter.[49] Richard Smith Sr. and Walter Harris Jr. witnessed, a rare instance in which the records directly associate Walter with one of his own family.

Walter's land dealings after moving over into Wethersfield all involve mortgages or sales of his Wethersfield properties, apparently to raise cash. The five deeds not already mentioned were dated between 27 February 1712/3 and 5 April 1715, the last of these being eight months before he died, a sale of half of the four-acre piece forfeited to Walter by his wife's uncle,

[46] Hartford Co. Court Records, Record Group 3, 1:6, 18, 23, 32, 35, 41, 100, 111, 117, 132-33, 140, 142, 146-47, 167, 171, 316-17.

[47] Hartford Co. Court Records, Record Group 3, 1:133.

[48] Hartford Co. Court Records, Record Group 3, 1:185. The dates involved prompt a guess that Walter had not viewed with equanimity the attachment of his red cow by Thomas Kimberly.

[49] Wethersfield, Conn., Deeds, 3:411, 4:53.

Lazarus Hollister. The buyer was Nathaniel Hale, nephew of his earlier wife Mary (Hale) Benjamin.[50]

Walter died intestate in Wethersfield on 1 December 1715. His widow Mary was granted administration on 7 February 1715/6 with George Stillman, a Wethersfield merchant, and John Austin of Hartford, creditors of the estate. The inventory, taken on 5 March 1715/6 by John Lattimer and James Treat and valued at £38 15s. 11d., included livestock, personal items, household goods, tools and "3 old bibles," revealing that Walter was then of modest means. A slip of paper included with the inventory and bond lists nine items totaling £39 due from the estate. In addition to those already mentioned, the creditors included Mrs. Asford [sic: probably Alford], Walter Harris Jr., Mrs. Wilson, Capt. Joseph Whiting, and Deliverance Blinn.[51] No other reference to his children appear in the file. Deliverance Blinn was soon to become a stepson of Walter's widow; the other names can be identified with prominent merchant families of Hartford and Boston.

On 19 April 1716, Walter's widow, "Mary Harris," released by quitclaim deed to Elizabeth Hollister, widow of Jonathan Hollister, whatever interest she still had in the two acres that Walter had conveyed to her brother Jonathan on 7 May 1703. The adjoining land on the north was held then by "heirs of Walter Harris."[52] No children of Mary (Hollister) Harris are mentioned in this deed, nor in any records created during Walter's lifetime.

Years later, however, after becoming the wife of Peter Blinn and again a widow after his death in Wethersfield in March 1724/5, Mary executed a deed on 22 April 1740 as follows:

I Mary Blin of Wethersfield . . . widow in consideration of 11 pounds rec'd to my satisfaction of *my son* Thomas Harris of Wethersfield quit claim all right . . . I now have in or to Common and undivided lands lying within the bounds of the township of Wethersfield. . . .[53]

This deed has provided the basis for the identification of this Mary as the mother of the brothers Thomas, Daniel, and Abraham Harris, and their sister Mary of Wethersfield.[54]

Children of Walter[2] and Mary (Hale) (Benjamin) Harris:

5   i   WALTER[3] HARRIS, b. probably between March 1686/7 and Aug. 1688; m. (1) ABIGAIL RANNEY, (2) ELIZABETH WHEELER, (3) DEBORAH (BOOTH) PRINDLE.

---

[50] Wethersfield, Conn., Deeds, 4:82, 87, 130-31, 160.
[51] Hartford District Probate File 2592, Connecticut State Library.
[52] Wethersfield, Conn., Deeds, 4:194.
[53] Wethersfield, Conn., Deeds, 8:93.
[54] Harris, "Walter Harris's Widow and the Blinns of Wethersfield," NEHGR 143 (1989):303-24.

Children of Walter[2] and Mary (Hollister) Harris:

6   ii   THOMAS HARRIS, b. ca. 1702; m. ANNE NOTT.
7   iii   DANIEL HARRIS, b. ca. 1705; m. REBECCA WILLIAMS.
8   iv   MARY HARRIS, b. say 1707; m. JOHN TAYLOR.
9   v   ABRAHAM HARRIS, b. ca. 1709; m. (1) ANNE BLINN, (2) RUTH (HART) BECK-
          LEY, (3) ABIGAIL (WETMORE) (BURT) GEER.

3 THOMAS[2] HARRIS (*John[1]*), born say 1654 (assuming he was in his 20s when he married), was a cooper and died "by his owne hand" at Killing-worth, Connecticut, before 11 July 1697 (date of his inventory discussed below). He married in East Hampton, Long Island, on or soon after 9 March 1682/3 **RUTH JAMES**,[55] born in New Haven, Connecticut, about 1664, daughter of Rev. Thomas and Ruth (Jones) James of East Hampton.[56] Ruth married secondly at East Hampton on 26 October 1704, as his second wife, Joseph Moore of Southampton,[57] and with him had children Abigail and Ruth.[58] The Reverend Thomas James had settled in East Hampton in 1651 as that town's first minister; his will dated there on 5 June 1696 names his daughter Ruth and son-in-law Thomas Harris.[59]

Thomas Harris apparently never owned real estate in East Hampton or across Long Island Sound at Killingworth. He was present in East Hampton by 1680,[60] however, and it appears that he and his wife Ruth lived there until some time not long before his death at Killingworth in 1697. On 27 December 1680, while still single, Thomas witnessed in East Hampton when Thomas Dyment gave property to his son James Dyment.[61] James had married in 1677

---

[55] Their marriage date is closely established from the age of their first child (13 in June 1697) and the fact that while still unmarried they jointly witnessed at East Hampton on 9 March 1682/3 a release by Ruth's brother-in-law James Dyment (Thomas W. Cooper, *The Records of the Court of Sessions of Suffolk County in the Province of New York, 1670–1688* (Bowie, Md., 1993), 134.

[56] Donald Lines Jacobus and Clarence Almon Torrey, "James, Mellows and Ingoldsby Connections," TAG 11 (1934):29.

[57] *Records of the Town of East Hampton, Long Island, Suffolk Co., N.Y.*, 9 vols. (Sag-Harbor: J. H. Hunt, 1887–1957), 5:521.

[58] Effingham P. Humphrey Jr., "Descendants of Edward Howell of Westbury Manor . . . and South-ampton, Long Island, New York," *The Genealogist* 5 (1984):14.

[59] William S. Pelletreau, *Early Long Island Wills of Suffolk County, 1691–1703* (New York: F. P. Harper, 1897), 123-27.

[60] It is possible that he was the Thomas Harries [*sic*] who witnessed an agreement at Southampton on 7 April 1675 whereby Richard Howell and Joseph Raynor hired seven native Americans to "whale for the season" (*Records of the Town of Southampton, L.I., New York*, 6 vols. [Sag Harbor, 1877–1915], 2:60). For a discussion of some wrong guesses and brief notes of other Harris families, see Harris, "Thomas Harris of East Hampton," NYGBR 128 (1997):11-24 at 14n.

[61] Cooper, *Court of Sessions of Suffolk County*, 130.

Thomas James's daughter Hannah.[62] His father, Thomas Dyment (Diament, Deming), was a ship carpenter earlier in Wethersfield, Connecticut.[63] Thus, his association with the Dyment/Deming family from Wethersfield appears to have led Thomas to meet his wife, Ruth James.

With John Merideth, Thomas Harris witnessed a deed on 25 July 1687 from the Indians to the trustees of East Hampton. On 25 May 1693, Thomas and his father-in-law Thomas James witnessed when Joseph Hand Sr. of Guilford, Connecticut, quitclaimed to James Dyment a parcel "originally John Millers Sr. lott."[64] Thomas also was an executor of his father-in-law's will in 1696. His widow appears on the East Hampton church list in September 1699.[65]

Thomas Harris's inventory in July 1697, valued at £118 13*s.* 6*d.*, was taken at Killingworth by Henry Crane, William Stevens, and John Griswold. It included household items, cooper's tools, some books, and "by information upon Longisland 1 ox: 2 three year old heaifers: 1 cow: 23 sheep," and "by information at Winsor [Windsor, Connecticut] about fiftye: 50 sidar barrels." Also listed were the children: Mary, age 13; Thomas, age 8; Nathaniel, age 3; and Samuel, age 8m. Mrs. Ruth Harris, relict and widow, was allowed her third; a double portion was set off to the eldest son and single portions to the "rest of ye Children." An allowance of £15 was provided for the education "of ye younger Children."[66]

The inventory is a key document for this family. It serves to further associate this Thomas Harris with the Wethersfield family. The cooper's tools are consistent with an earlier but unrecorded presence in the home of Wolston Brockway in nearby Lyme, Connecticut, a cooper whom his presumed stepmother, Hannah (Briggs) Harris, had married in the Wethersfield locality in the early 1660s. More tellingly, the fifty cider barrels stored upriver at Windsor, the shipping point for John Pynchon's cider production venture ("rossin designe"), solidly associates him with the activities of his half-brother John Harris (no. 4), who certainly was raised in

[62] Jacobus and Torrey, "James, Mellows and Ingoldsby Connections," TAG 11 (1934):29.

[63] Stiles, *Ancient Wethersfield*, 2:272; George R. Howell, *The Early History of Southampton, L.I., New York*, 2nd ed. (Albany, N.Y.: Weed, Parsons and Co., 1887), 32, 282.

[64] *Records of the Town of East Hampton*, 2:213-14, 291.

[65] *Records of the Town of East Hampton*, 5:420.

[66] Walter Lee Sheppard Jr., "Inventory of Thomas Harris of Killingworth, Conn.," TAG 183-84, citing New Haven Probate Paper no. 4700.

the Brockway home and who had been working under contract for Pynchon since 1692 or before.[67]

Thomas and Ruth Harris's sons Thomas, Nathaniel, and Samuel Harris first appear in Salem (now Cumberland) County, New Jersey, in 1715, when on 16 November their names appear on the muster roll of Capt. Joseph Seeley's company of the South Side of the Cohansey.[68] They settled in Fairfield and Hopewell Townships in the part of Salem County set off as Cumberland County in January 1747/8, where they headed large families in New Jersey. Through their mother, Ruth James, they share a royal descent from William Longespée, natural son of Henry II of England.[69]

Children of Thomas[2] and Ruth (James) Harris (father's inventory):

    i   MARY[3] HARRIS, b. ca. 1684 (age 13 in 1697), m. East Hampton 3 June 1702/3 JOHN MOORE, the Rev. Nathaniel Huntting presiding.[70]

10 ii THOMAS HARRIS, b. ca. 1689 (age 8 in 1697); m. ANNA ____.

11 iii NATHANIEL HARRIS, b. 8 Oct. 1693; m. (1) MIRIAM BROOKS, (2) ELIZABETH ____.

12 iv SAMUEL HARRIS, b. ca. Oct. 1696 (age 8m in June 1697), (1) SARAH JOHNSON, (2) RACHEL (____) HOOD.

4 JOHN[2] HARRIS (*John[1]*), born in Boston on 8 August 1658,[71] a carpenter, died probably in or near Springfield, Massachusetts, before 1703 (when his widow remarried). He married by 26 February 1691/2 **MEHITABLE DANKS**,[72] born say 1673, died in Westfield, Massachusetts, in November 1744,[73] daughter of Robert and Elizabeth (Swift) (Webb) Danks of Northampton, Massachusetts.[74] Mehitable married second at Westfield on 17 May 1703, as his

---

[67] For details, see Gale Ion Harris, "John[2] and Mehitable (Danks) Harris of Northampton and Springfield, Massachusetts: Probable Parents of Mary Harris, the Deerfield 'Indian Captive,'" TAG 72 (1997): 333–43.

[68] *New York Colonial Muster Rolls, 1664–1775: Second Annual Report of the State Historian of New York*, 2 vols. (Albany, 1897), 1:538.

[69] Walter L. Sheppard, Jr., "Noble Ancestry of the Harris Family of Cumberland County," *The Vineland Historical Magazine* [VHM] 35 (1951):88-90, and "Royal Ancestry of the Harris Family: Further Notes," 41 (1956): 367-69.

[70] *Records of the Town of East Hampton*, 5:520.

[71] *Boston Births, Baptisms, Marriages, and Deaths*, 65.

[72] The will of Robert Danks, dated at Northampton on 26 Feb. 1691/2, gave a two-acre parcel to "my daughter Harris" (Hampshire Co., Mass., Court Records in Deed Book A:16).

[73] Westfield, Mass., Births, Marriages, Deaths, 1669–1765, Westfield City Hall, p. 23, Family History Library [FHL] microfilm 185474.

[74] Harris, "John[2] and Mehitable (Danks) Harris," TAG 72 (1997):341–42.

second wife, John Sackett Jr., and with him had five children recorded there from 1704 to 1715.[75]

This John Harris, born in Boston, was taken by his parents to Wethersfield about 1660 and after his mother's remarriage was taken by her and his stepfather, Wolston Brockway, to Lyme, Connecticut. At age 22, John appears to have gotten into some unspecified situation. At a meeting of the Lyme townsmen on 1 March 1680/1, they considered "the disposeall of John Harris according to an order of a Towne court held in Lyme the 22th [*sic*] day of February 1680." John appeared before them and declared "that hee had made choice of his Uncle John Briggs and Lt. Abram Brunson for his guardians as also by a wrighting under his hand. . . ." The townsmen approved, but required a bond of £20 from Isaac Watrous "to secure them from all and every charge or damage which shall or may accrue unto them by the said John Harris by reason of his sickness, lameness, or any other inability . . . during the time he may have access unto the Towne for relief.[76]

Entries in the Lyme town records indicate that John was in town until 1685. The above bond was declared by the townsmen "null and void" on 25 June 1686, and on 5 March 1687/8 John's stepfather Brockway was "allowed for John Haris one pound seven shillings."[77]

John had been upriver near Springfield and Northampton, Massachussets, long enough to have married Mehitable Danks there before 1692. He had been working for John Pynchon at Springfield for some time before 15 April 1692, when Pynchon agreed with him

for 7 months service upon the Rossin designe to worke about it where we carry it on about 7 Mile of[f] & be constant in the Imploym[en]t, to begin about the worke on Munday Come seven night the 25[th] of April for which Service of his I am to allow & pay him 42s. per Mo in corne Dld: Pease & some wt Rye & Porke at current price he opting hims[elf] w[hi]ch he [*illegible*] rath[e]r than 30s. & also to Let him have the use of my house (at the street by Mr. Glovers during the terme of the 7 Mos).[78]

[75] Westfield, Mass., Births, Marriages, Deaths, p. 23; Charles H. Weygant, *The Sacketts of America . . . 1630–1907* (Newburgh, N.Y., 1907), 24.

[76] Jean Chandler Burr, ed., *Lyme Records, 1667–1730* (Stonington, Conn.: Pequot Press, 1968), 41-42.

[77] Burr, *Lyme Records*, 42, 64. In May 1679, the town had adopted a rule of division for the town lands providing "that every male child in the Towne . . . shall be allowed the rate of 18th [*sic*] per annum for every year they have lived in the Towne—since it was a towne" (ibid., 33). If a rate of 18*d.* per annum was intended, the rule would mean that Brockway was allowed compensation for his stepson for 18 years since the town was formed in 1667, or through 1685.

[78] Carl Bridenbaugh and Juliette Tomlinson, eds., *The Pynchon Papers*, 2 vols., Colonial Soc. Mass. Pubs., 60-61 (Boston, 1982–85), 2:238-39.

Pynchon's "rossin designe" was a venture pursued at a camp about seven miles out of Springfield "in the midst of a stand of the best turpentine-producing pines. . . . Many forty-gallon barrels of rosin were produced at the camp," for which "there was a good market, especially for making varnish and soap."[79] The compensation recited in the employment agreement, especially the use of Pynchon's house near the Rev. Pelatiah Glover's house in Springfield, indicates that John Harris had a family in April 1692, certainly his wife Mehitable and probably infant daughter Sarah.

One other record shows John Harris's presence in Springfield. On 24 November 1694, John Pynchon examined "John Buck the Indian" on a complaint that he had stolen houses and other items from several persons. Buck had been caught

at Chickkuppy House and brought . . . back with several things which are as followeth[:] besides the Horse of James Warrinars a Saddle and Bridle of Joseph Willistons a Halter of James Muns .3. yards of [*illegible*] Homemade linen of Mary Perrys a lace neck Handchercheife and a Muslene neckcloth of John Harris his a kettle of Mr. Pynchon besides several fowles about 10 etc a Loafe of Bread etc and other provisions etc the al[l] which were delivered to the several owners.[80]

At Lyme on 20 April 1702, Wolston Brockway complained that "John Harris and his daughter Sarah [were] left out of the last Distribution," But the committee "concerning the fourth Division" of Lyme lands could not "find anything due to goodman Brockway for John Harris and Sarah was not of agge."[81] From this, we may deduce that John's daughter Sarah had been sent down to Lyme after he died at Springfield. Despite the committee's finding, land was laid out to Brockway in June 1710 "upon the account of his fourth division for his own right and John Haresons [*sic*] Right."[82] In September 1716, Brockway gave his son John Brockway land, including some "taken up by me upon the account of my son John Harises head right in the fourth division." Finally, in February 1720/1, land laid out in that division to John Brockway included parcels in right of his deceased father Wolston, his brother Richard Brockway, and "on the Right of John haris."[83]

---

[79] *Pynchon Papers*, 2:212.

[80] Joseph H. Smith, ed., *Colonial Justice in Western Massachusetts (1639–1702): The Pynchon Court Record . . .* (Cambridge, Mass.: Harvard University Press, 1961), 341.

[81] Lyme, Conn., Grants and Earmarks, 1665–1948, in Lyme Deeds, 39:43. Indeed, as shown above the town had already compensated Brockway £1 7s. in March 1687/8 for the 18-year period John was in the town.

[82] Lyme, Conn., Deeds, 2:346.

[83] Lyme, Conn., Deeds, 3:2-3.

Children of John[2] and Mehitable (Danks) Harris:[84]

    i   SARAH[3] HARRIS, b. say 1692, "not of agge" in April 1702 when the land com-
        mittee at Lyme, Conn., declared that nothing was due her step-grandfather
        Wolston Brockway for her head right in the fourth division.[85] She probably
        had been sent down to Lyme relatives from Northampton or Westfield,
        Mass., after her father died. No further mention of her is found unless she
        was the Sarah Harris who, by mark, witnessed with Mary Macky the will of
        John Seymour at Hartford on 12 Dec. 1712.[86]

13 ii MARY HARRIS, b. say 1694; had at least one INDIAN HUSBAND.

    iii JOHN HARRIS, b. Northampton, Mass., 20 June 1696.[87] If he survived, it is pos-
        sible that he was with his sister Sarah at Hartford and, despite his youth, the
        otherwise unplaced John Harris who witnessed there on 7 April 1710 the
        will of Timothy Hide, a young single man.[88]

14 iv PHILLIP HARRIS, b. say 1698; m. (1) ____ ____, (2) ELIZABETH (DEMOND)
        GLEASON.

    v THOMAS HARRIS, b. say 1700; m. ELIZA ____, and lived at Saybrook, just across
        the Connecticut River from Lyme, his father's former home. In July 1736,
        Thomas Harris of Saybrook purchased property near that of his apparent
        brother Phillip in Simsbury, Conn., bounded by land of Joshua Moses on the
        north and heirs of Josiah Alford on the south.[89] Later that year, in Nov. 1736,
        Thomas Harris of Saybrook, who signed deeds by mark, *H*, bought 100 acres
        with a dwelling house in Simsbury,[90] but no evidence is seen that he actually
        resided there. No later history of this family been learned.

        Children of Thomas[3] and Eliza (____) Harris, recorded in Saybrook:[91]
        1 *John[4] Harris*, b. 9 April 1733, presumably named for his grandfather.
        2 *Desire Harris*, b. 12 March 1735.
        3 *Abner Harris*, b. 2 Feb. 1736/7.
        4 *Elizabeth Harris*, b. 10 June 1738.

---

[84] Harris, "John[2] and Mehitable (Danks) Harris," TAG 72 (1997):341–42; Gale Ion Harris, "Phillip Harris of Simsbury, Connecticut: With Notes on His Humphrey and Hinman Descendants," TAG 78 (2003):47–54.

[85] Lyme Grants and Earmarks, in Lyme, Conn., Deeds, 39:43.

[86] Manwaring, *Early Connecticut Probate Records*, 2:290. For further discussion, see Harris, "John[2] and Mehitable (Danks) Harris," TAG 72 (1997):342. Cases are known of witnesses as young as 14.

[87] Town Record, Corbin Manuscript Collection (Reel 14), 50.

[88] Manwaring, *Early Connecticut Probate Records*, 2:222-23. Timothy's father, Timothy Hide [Sr.], b. in Boston in 1644, resided at Wethersfield and Hartford after 1675.

[89] Simsbury Deeds, 6:118, 156. Not long before, in Dec. 1733 and Jan. 1734/5, Phillip Harris and Joshua Moses had jointly purchased property nearby (ibid., 6:121-22, 125).

[90] Simsbury, Conn., Deeds, 6:119, 181.

[91] *Vital Records of Saybrook, 1647–1834* (Hartford: Connecticut Historical Society and Connecticut Society of the Order of Founders and Patriots of America, 1948), 85.

THIRD GENERATION

5 WALTER³ HARRIS (*Walter²*, *John¹*), born about 1687, probably in that part of Wethersfield that soon became the town of Glastonbury, was living at Lebanon, Connecticut, in April 1747[92] and probably as late as 17 March 1759, when his land there was mentioned as adjoining a parcel owned by John Woodward, which was sold on that date to Walter's son Nathaniel.[93] He married first in Middletown, Connecticut, on 21 January 1713/4 **ABIGAIL RANNEY**,[94] daughter of Thomas and Mary (Hubbard) Ranney.[95] Abigail "departed this life by death" on 15 December 1714,[96] soon after the birth of an infant daughter on 20 November, and Walter married there secondly on 23 January 1717/8 **ELIZABETH WHEELER**,[97] born at Concord, Massachusetts, on 8 August 1690, who died in Middletown on 13 September 1718,[98] a daughter of Joseph and Mary (Power) Wheeler of Fairfield and Stratford, Connecticut, and of Concord and Stow, Massachusetts.[99] Walter married there third on 1 November 1720 **DEBORAH (BOOTH) PRINDLE** "of Stratford,"[100] born "say 1688,"[101] who was living at Lebanon in 1747. She was a daughter of Ebenezer and Elizabeth (Jones) Booth of Stratford and widow of John Prindle of Derby, Connecticut, who died there on 4 October 1712.[102]

Walter Harris Jr. first appears in Wethersfield records on 11 Mary 1711, when he witnessed a mortgage deed for his father.[103] On 7 December 1711, Walter Harris Jr., Thomas Ranney, and Francis Willcock witnessed James Scovill's will at Middletown.[104] And a list of debts due from Walter Harris's estate in Wethersfield in 1716 includes an item owing to Walter Harris Jr.

---

[92] Petition by the heirs of Richard Jones of Haddam, which mentions Walter Harris and wife Deborah as "living" in Lebanon, TAG 11 (1935):190-91.

[93] Lebanon, Conn., Deeds, 9:411.

[94] Barbour Collection, Connecticut Vital Records, citing Middletown LR2:27.

[95] Charles Collard Adams, "Descendants of Thomas Ranney," *Middletown Upper Houses* (New York: Grafton Press, 1908), 151.

[96] Barbour Collection, citing Middletown LR2:27.

[97] Barbour Collection, citing Middletown LR2:27.

[98] Barbour Collection, citing Middletown LR2:27.

[99] Homer W. Brainard, "Captain Thomas Wheeler and Some of his Descendants," TAG 12 (1935–36):138).

[100] Barbour Collection, citing Middletown VR1:4.

[101] Donald Lines Jacobus, *The Genealogy of the Booth Family* (Pleasant Hill, Mo.: E. C. Booth, 1952), 4.

[102] Donald Lines Jacobus, *History and Genealogy of the Families of Old Fairfield*, 1 (1930): pt. 1, 89.

[103] Wethersfield, Conn., Deeds, 4:53.

[104] Manwaring, *Early Connecticut Probate Records*, 2:289-90.

Two days before his first marriage, Walter, "now Rezident in . . . Middle-town," bought from his prospective bride's brother John Ranney five acres of the Thomas Ranney estate in East Middletown, now Portland. In May 1715, he purchased an adjacent 5-acre parcel from John's brother Ebenezer Ranney, the £15 purchase price secured in part by a gray mare "if it is now alive." Meanwhile, Walter witnessed on 2 April 1714 when Joshua Gill of Middletown conveyed 17 acres to his brother Ebenezer Gill.[105]

Walter owned the Covenant on 14 January 1721/2, was chosen as collec-tor for a mister's rate in 1723, and in 1728 was a member of the school committee at the East Society in Middletown.[106] On 10 March 1729/30, he sold the two Ranney estate parcels, including his dwelling house, to Ebene-zer Lyman of Lebanon, Connecticut.[107]

In Lebanon on the same date, Ebenezer Lyman conveyed to Walter Harris a 55-acre tract there adjoining Henry Woodward and the "County Road leading to Hartford" with a "dwelling house [and] all the fixed work standing. . . ."[108] In October 1728, Walter had purchased from John Ranney Sr. a 6½-acre parcel on the east side in Middletown, which he sold on 4 September 1730 to Nathaniel White as his last deed in Middletown. Al-though still called "of Middletown," Walter acknowledged the deed the same day at Hartford.[109]

Walter had settled at Lebanon, in the part of it now called Columbia, by November 1732, when he was mentioned in the will of his wife's father Ebenezer Booth at Stratford, Connecticut.[110] He was among those listed in the rate bill for the North Parish of Lebanon for the year 1741; his assess-ment was £2 9s.[111] On 27 November 1746, Walter and Deborah Harris made an arrangement in Lebanon with their son-in-law Ebenezer Buck of Hebron, Connecticut, whereby they conveyed their 55-acre homestead to Buck on condition that he "take the special care of them to maintain and provide for them . . . fitting and suitable for their old age." A few months later, in Mary 1747, Buck assigned his interest in this property to Nathaniel Harris for £600, but no transfer of the obligation is mentioned.[112]

---

[105] Middletown, Conn., Deeds, 3:91, 208, 225-26.
[106] Portland First Congregational Church Records, 1:22, 25, 5:2.
[107] Middletown, Conn., Deeds, 2:545.
[108] Lebanon, Conn., Deeds, 4:257.
[109] Middletown, Conn., Deeds, 5:265, 428.
[110] Jacobus, *Genealogy of the Booth Family*, 4.
[111] "Rate Bill for the North Parish of Lebanon (now Columbia), Conn., for the year 1741," NEHGR 20 (1866):46.
[112] Lebanon, Conn., Deeds, 7:51, 52, 9:196.

Child of Walter³ and Abigail (Ranney) Harris:

    i   ABIGAIL⁴ HARRIS, b. 29 [*blank*] 1714, d. Middletown, Conn., 20 Nov. 1714.[113]

Children of Walter³ and Deborah (Booth) (Prindle) Harris, all recorded in Middletown[114] and bp. East Middletown (Portland) Church:[115]

    ii ABIGAIL HARRIS (again), b. Middletown, Conn., 11 Dec. 1721; m. there 7 May 1740 ROBERT DIXON "of Colchester."[116] They owned the Covenant at East Middletown (Portland) Church on 22 Feb. 1741.[117]

        Children of Robert and Abigail⁴ (Harris) Dixon, bp. Portland Church:[118]

        1 *Charles Dixon*, bp. 1 Dec. 1746.
        2 *Edward Dixon*, bp. 25 April 1751.
        3 *Rebeckah Dixon*, bp. 23 Sept. 1753.

    iii DEBORAH HARRIS, b. Middletown 13 Aug. 1723, d. Lanesboro, Mass., 17 Oct. 1798.[119] She was "of Lebanon" when she m. in Middletown 16 Nov. 1743 EBENEZER BUCK of Middletown,[120] b. there 11 Nov. 1717,[121] d. Lanesboro 13 Nov. 1805, son of Thomas and Sarah (Judd) Buck.[122]

        Children of Ebenezer and Deborah⁴ (Harris) Buck, the first recorded at Middletown and the others at Hebron:[123]

        1 *Deborah Buck*, b. Middletown 18 Oct. 1744; m. Hebron 13 Nov. 1764 Ebenezer Root Jr., both of Hebron.[124]
        2 *Sarah Buck*, b. Hebron 13 Oct. 1745; m. Hebron 20 May 1767 Peter Robinson, both of Hebron.[125]
        3 *Mary Buck*, b. Hebron 25 Feb. 1748, d. 23 Aug. 174[ ].
        4 *Ebenezer Buck*, b. Hebron 23 Feb. 1750.
        5 *Cyble Buck*, b. Hebron 28 May 1752.
        6 *Mary Buck* (again), b. Hebron 6 April 1755.

15 iv NATHANIEL HARRIS, b. Middletown 13 June 1725; m. GRACE LYMAN.
    v ELIZABETH HARRIS, b. Middletown 14 April 1728.

6 THOMAS³ HARRIS (*Walter²*, *John¹*), born about 1702,[126] probably in Glastonbury, Connecticut, died in Wethersfield in the spring of 1774.[127] He

---

[113] Barbour Collection, citing Middletown LR2:27.
[114] Barbour Collection, citing Middletown VR1:4.
[115] Barbour Collection, citing Middletown VR1:4; Portland, Conn., Church Records, 5:2-6.
[116] Barbour Collection, citing Middletown VR1:119.
[117] Portland, Conn., Church Records, 5:15.
[118] Portland, Conn., Church Records, 5:19, 29, 31.
[119] Harris, "Walter Harris of Wethersfield," 336.
[120] Barbour Collection, citing Middletown VR2:40.
[121] Barbour Collection, citing Middletown LR2:14.
[122] Stiles, *Ancient Wethersfield*, 2:147.
[123] Barbour Collection, citing Middletown VR2:40 and Hebron VR:1:55, 2:146, 147.
[124] Barbour Collection, citing Hebron VR2:96.
[125] Barbour Collection, citing Hebron VR2:96.

married there on 18 December 1729 **ANNE NOTT**, born 29 July 1699, who died there on 9 October 1769, daughter of John and Patience (Miller) Nott of Wethersfield.

Donald Lines Jacobus pointed out in 1947 that Henry R. Stiles had given "an impossible account of the origin" of this Thomas Harris by identifying him as a son of the unrelated Daniel Harris of Middletown.[128] Subsequent work, already mentioned, definitely places him in Walter Harris's family.

The first record of Thomas's presence in Wethersfield is on 5 May 1724, when his younger brother Daniel chose him as his guardian.[129] Soon afterward, Thomas purchased from John Hurlbut Jr. 53 acres nearby in Middletown, part of an allotment "originally David Sages" in the "west most Range or Teer of Lotts." In July 1726, Thomas traded this property to Ziba Tryon for a parcel in Wethersfield and appears not to have had any further dealings in Middletown.[130] Thomas had purchased from John Wiard in Wethersfield on 24 August 1724 a lot with a house, which in March 1726 he reconveyed to John's widow Phebe Wiard.[131]

Thomas bought or sold land 87 times in Wethersfield in the period 1724–1774, including a sale in May 1737 of an acre in the meadow to his brother Daniel Harris. In addition, in January 1734/5, he purchased 65½ acres in Eastbury Parish, Glastonbury, on the Hebron bounds, which he sold five months later to Elisha Coleman of Wethersfield.[132] Thomas built a house on South Hill in Wethersfield in 1755, which was reported to be still standing "in a good state of preservation" in 1904.[133]

In June 1752, Hezekiah Hart, Thomas Harris, and Elisha Williams Jr. witnessed a codicil to the will of William Blinn [Thomas's step-brother]. In 1759 Blinn's 16-year-old grandson William chose Thomas as his guardian, but it was Thomas's brother Abraham Harris who accepted the trust. In April 1758, Jacob Hollister, a 15-year-old son of Thomas's cousin Jonathan Hollister, chose Thomas as his guardian, but in September 1759 Thomas

---

[126] Donald Lines Jacobus, "Early Harris Families of Western Connecticut," TAG 23 (1947):159. Jacobus's date, "about 1702," for Thomas's birth is in better agreement with available evidence than is the date, 1695, printed in Stiles, *Ancient Wethersfield*, 2:413, and apparently followed in the carving of a modern gravestone in Wethersfield Village Cemetery.

[127] Stiles, *Ancient Wethersfield*, 2:413.

[128] Jacobus, "Early Harris Families of Western Connecticut," TAG 23 (1947):160.

[129] Manwaring, *Early Connecticut Probate Records*, 2:519.

[130] Middletown, Conn., Deeds, 3:483, 5:113.

[131] Wethersfield, Conn., Deeds, 5:57, 156.

[132] Glastonbury, Conn., Deeds, 4:171-72.

[133] Stiles, *Ancient Wethersfield*, 2:413.

"desire[d] to be freed" from Jacob's guardianship and the court allowed his mother, Susannah Hollister, to assume the responsibility.[134]

Thomas Harris's own will, dated at Wethersfield on 14 December 1773, names his sons Hosea and Thomas, daughters Sarah Robbins, Anne Willard, and Mehitabel Robbins, and granddaughter Mehitabel Robbins, "only child of daughter Mehitabel." The estate was appraised at £885.3*s.* 5*d.*[135]

Children of Thomas[3] and Anne (Nott) Harris, recorded Wethersfield:[136]

   i   ANNA[4] HARRIS, b. 29 Nov. 1730, d. 29 Jan. 1731.
   ii ANNE HARRIS (again), b. 20 March 1732, d. 28 May 1736.
   iii SARAH HARRIS, b. 18 Feb. 1733/4; m. 8 Sept. 1755 ELISHA ROBBINS b. 20 June 1729, d. 27 Oct. 1756, son of Samuel and Lucy (Wolcott) Robbins.
           Child of Elisha and Sarah[4] (Harris) Robbins:[137]
           1 *Sarah Robbins*, b. 29 March 1756; m. 26 April 1784 Elisha Wells.
16 iv   HOSEA HARRIS, b. 11 Feb. 1736; m. EUNICE (BOARDMAN) KING.
   v   MEHITABEL HARRIS, b. 28 April 1738; m. Wethersfield 14 Oct. 1756 HEZE-KIAH ROBBINS,[138] b. there 20 Sept. 1733, d. 18 Dec. 1776, son of Daniel and Prudence (Griswold) Robbins.[139] In 1777, "Wido Hezi[a] Robbins" had a child enrolled at the Broad Street schoolhouse.[140]
   vi   ANNA HARRIS (again), b. 8 April 1740, d. 1 June 1824, age 83; m. 24 March 1768 STEPHEN WILLARD, b. 9 Feb. 1739/40, d. 29 April 1817, son of Ephraim and Lydia (Griswold) Willard.
           Children of Stephen and Anna[4] (Harris) Willard, b. Wethersfield:[141]
           1 *Stephen Willard*, b. 30 Jan. 1770, d. 16 Sept. 1849, age 86 [*sic*]; m. (1) 20 June 1793 Martha Robbins, b. ca. 1767, d. 9 May 1813, age 46, (2) 17 April 1814 Rhoda Latimer, b. ca. 1786, d. 22 April 1859, age 73.[142]
           2 *Anne Willard*, b. 28 Sept. 1771; m. 30 Sept. 1794 Capt. Ebenezer Riley of Berlin, Conn.
           3 *Mary/Polly Willard*, b. 11 Aug. 1773, d. 18 Jan. 1808.
           4 *Wealthy Willard*, b. 13 April 1775, d. 12 July 1777.
           5 *John Willard*, b. 24 July 1777, d. at sea.
           6 *William Willard*, b. 2 Oct. 1779, drowned, bur. 19 Sept. 1781.
           7 *Thomas Willard*, b. 11, d. 23 Aug. 1781.

---

[134] Hartford District Probate Records, 16:231-32, 262, 18:10, 70.
[135] Hartford District Probate Records, 22:18, 73.
[136] Stiles, *Ancient Wethersfield*, 2:413.
[137] Barbour Collection, citing Wethersfield VR2:92; Stiles, *Ancient Wethersfield*, 2:553-54.
[138] Barbour Collection, citing Wethersfield VR2:12, Rev. James Lockwood presiding.
[139] Barbour Collection, citing Wethersfield VR1:9; Stiles, *Ancient Wethersfield*, 2:552.
[140] Stiles, *Ancient Wethersfield*, 1:384.
[141] Stiles, *Ancient Wethersfield*, 2:795.
[142] Stiles, *Ancient Wethersfield*, 2:796.

8 *William Willard* (again), b. 21 Nov. 1783, d. 8 March 1832; m. 28
Aug. 1804 Hannah Wolcott, b. April 1785, d. 14 Nov. 1864.[143]
9 *Wealthy Willard* (again), bp. 18 June 1786, d. 29 Oct. 1842, age 57.

17   vii   THOMAS HARRIS, b. 7 May 1743; m. ABIGAIL ROBBINS.

7 DANIEL[3] HARRIS (*Walter[2]*, *John[1]*), born about 1705 (age 19 in 1724),[144]
probably in Glastonbury, Connecticut, was living in Goshen, Connecticut,
on 30 August 1774, when he sold the last of his land to his son Jeremiah.[145]
He married by 1737 (birth of first child) **REBECCA WILLIAMS**, daughter of
Abraham and Eunice (Boardman) Williams, born in Wethersfield on 25
April 1706,[146] who was living in March 1748/9 (birth of last child).

Daniel probably resided in Wethersfield after 1716 with his mother and
elderly stepfather, Peter Blinn, before choosing his brother Thomas as guardian in 1724. In August 1733, Daniel was one of the witnesses to Martha
Burnham's will.[147] In May 1737, two months before the birth of his first
child, Daniel purchased from his brother Thomas an acre in the Great
Meadow in Wethersfield. He subsequently bought and sold small parcels in
that meadow, but his first homestead may have been a half-acre parcel with
improvements on "the highway from Wethersfield to Hartford," which he
bought on 1 November 1740 from his brother Thomas's brother-in-law John
Nott of Fairfield. In 1744, Daniel sold the half acre on the highway to David
Wolcott and bought a lot with a house from Benjamin Stillman in Wethersfield village, described as on "the northwest corner of Broad Street facing
the meadows." Daniel sold the Broad Street property to Samuel Rose in
1752, and in 1753 he sold all of his Great Meadow and rights in commons to
Elisha Williams Jr. and Reverend James Lockwood.[148]

These deeds show that Daniel was still in Wethersfield on 17 April 1753,
but "late of Wethersfield, now of Goshen," two months later on 29 June
when he sold to Rev. Lockwood. While still "of Wethersfield" on 25 October 1752, he had purchased 50 acres from Joseph Brunson in the northwest part of Goshen.[149] This lot was on the Goshen-Cornwall town line
across from Cornwall Hollow in the northeast corner of Cornwall, and near
the four corners of Goshen, Cornwall, Canaan, and Norfolk.[150]

---

[143] Stiles, *Ancient Wethersfield*, 2:796.

[144] Manwaring, *Early Connecticut Probate Records*, 2:519.

[145] Goshen, Conn., Deeds, 6:15.

[146] Harris and Ingham, "Thomas[1] and Rebecca (Waterhouse) Williams," TAG 79 (2004):55.

[147] Manwaring, *Early Connecticut Probate Records*, 3:18.

[148] Wethersfield, Conn., Deeds, 6:278, 360, 8:33, 171, 176, 390-91, 9:35, 69, 89, 171.

[149] Goshen, Conn., Deeds, 3:165.

[150] A short distance south of this place was the property of another, unrelated, Daniel Harris who had
come there from Middletown, and, of course, the two Daniels sometimes have been confused.

Daniel later added nearby parcels to his 50-acre lot in Goshen. He disposed of all his properties—except a five-acre parcel on the Goshen-Cornwall town line—by deeds of gift dated 24 January 1772 to his sons Jeremiah and John, with son Daniel Harris Jr. as a witness. Two years later, on 30 August 1774, in the last record found of him, Daniel sold the remaining five-acre parcel to son Jeremiah.[151] Daniel probably moved in with Jeremiah and may have died there not long after; no administration of his estate has been found.

Children of Daniel[3] and Rebecca (Williams) Harris, recorded in Wethersfield:[152]

    i   ELISHA[4] HARRIS, b. 29 July 1737, served from 13 Sept. to 2 Dec. 1755 in Capt. Samuel Pettibone's company of the 4th Regiment (from Goshen, Conn.) during the French and Indian War.[153] No other record of him has been found.

    ii EUNICE HARRIS, b. 17 Jan. 1739[/40]; m. at Goshen, Conn., 7 April 1757 Dr. ELIAS DEMING,[154] b. Wethersfield 7 Nov. 1721, son of Benjamin and Mary (Wickham) Deming,[155] who was living at Hillsdale, Columbia Co., N.Y., in 1800.[156] A physician, Elias Deming purchased land in Goshen in 1754, later moved to Columbia Co., N.Y., and was residing at Hillsdale in 1791.[157]

        Children of Dr. Elias and Eunice[4] (Harris) Deming, recorded at Goshen:[158]

          1 *Wait Deming*, b. 9 May 1758, d. Hillsdale, N.Y., 5 July 1787 leaving two sons who were brought up by his father. He m. in Goshen in 1779 Ruth Ingraham. He served in the Revolution in Capt. Chapman's company, 7th Regiment, Continental Line, and in Capt. Ephraim Chamberlain's company, 2nd Regiment.[159]

          2 *Elisha Harris Deming*, b. 20 July 1759, d. Salisbury, Conn., in June 1821. He m. (1) Mary Bailey, (2) Catharine Dutcher, b. 2 July 1774, d. 1836, dau. of Gabriel and Christine (White) Dutcher. He resided in the southern part of Salisbury, also in Sheffield, Mass., and Green River N.Y.[160] He witnessed a deed for his uncle John Harris at Hillsdale, N.Y., on 29 July 1794.[161]

---

[151] Goshen, Conn., Deeds, 5:126-27, 6:15.

[152] Barbour Collection, citing Wethersfield VR2:67a.

[153] *Rolls of Connecticut Men in the French and Indian War, 1755–1762*, Coll. Conn., Hist. Soc., vols. 9-10 (Hartford, 1903, 1905), 9:57-58.

[154] Barbour Collection, citing Goshen VR1:269.

[155] Barbour Collection, citing Wethersfield VR1:28; Judson Keith Deming, *Genealogy of the Descendants of John Deming of Wethersfield, Connecticut* (Dubuque, Iowa; Press of Mathis-Mets Co., 1904), 23.

[156] 1800 U.S. Census, Hillsdale, Columbia Co., N.Y., p. 7.

[157] Deming, *Descendants of John Deming*, 45-46.

[158] Barbour Collection, citing Goshen VR1:262, 273.

[159] Deming, *Descendants of John Deming*, 93.

[160] Deming, *Descendants of John Deming*, 93-94.

[161] Goshen, Conn., Deeds, 9:432.

18   iii   DANIEL HARRIS, b. 23 Dec. 1741; m. SUBMIT JOHNSON.
19   iv   JEREMIAH HARRIS, b. 30 April 1743; m. ESTHER COWLES.
       v   ABIGAIL HARRIS, b. 25 Sept. 1745, living at Goshen, Conn., in May 1767 but
            d. soon after. She m. ca. 1764, probably in Goshen, as his 1st wife, SAMUEL
            OVIATT JR., b. Milford, Conn., 22 Feb. 1741, d. Braceville, Trumbull Co.,
            Ohio, 18 April 1818, son of Samuel and Keziah (Plumb) Oviatt of Milford
            and Goshen. Samuel Jr. m. (2) before 1779 Sarah (Cooke) Preston, b.
            Windsor, Conn., 2 May 1753, d. Braceville, 7 Sept. 1823, widow of Hacke-
            liah Preston of Waterbury and Goshen, with whom he had eight children.[162]
               Children of Samuel and Abigail⁴ (Harris) Oviatt, b. prob. Goshen:
               1 *Eunice Oviatt*, b. 19 Jan. 1765, d. Goshen 1 Jan. 1845; m. Julius Beach,
                  b. ca. 1764, d. Goshen 7 Nov. 1848, age 84, both bur. Beach Ceme-
                  tery in Goshen.[163]
               2 *John Oviatt*, b. 5 May 1767, d. 1 Aug. 1827, bur. Old Hudson Town-
                  ship Burying Ground, Hudson, Ohio;[164] m. (1) ____ ____, (2) 1817
                  Polly Kellogg.
20   vi   JOHN HARRIS, b. 23 March 1748/9; m. (1) PHEBE HILL, (2) OLIVE ____.

8 MARY³ HARRIS (*Walter²*, *John¹*), born say 1707, probably in Glastonbury, Connecticut, died in Wethersfield on 3 December 1738.[165] She married
there on 11 May 1732, as his second wife, **JOHN TAYLOR**,[166] born in Wethersfield on 20 March 1701[/2], son of John and Sarah (Scone) Taylor of
Rocky Hill, then part of Wethersfield.[167] John had married first on 8 March
1721/2 Deborah Wolcott, who died in 1731; he married third on 8 March
1739/40 Lydia (Boardman) Goffe, widow of David Goffe.[168]

Children of John and Mary³ (Harris) Taylor, recorded Wethersfield:[169]

       i   JONATHAN TAYLOR, b. 25 Aug. 1733; m. 29 March 1759 ABIGAIL PERCY "of
            Pontoosuck" as recorded in Becket, Mass., church records.[170]
       ii DAVID TAYLOR, b. 20 Aug. 1735, d. Waterbury, Conn., 19 Aug. 1801, a mer-
            chant and Revolutionary War soldier. He m. (1) 14 July 1760 JEMIMA JUDD,
            who d. 12 May 1761, dau. of John and Mercy (Bronson) Judd, and (2) 24

---

[162] Susan Woodruff Abbott and Jacquelyn L. Ricker, *Families of Early Milford, Connecticut* (Baltimore: Genealogical Publishing Co., 1979), 506-8. It was known in 1892 by Oviatt descendants in Ohio
that Samuel Oviatt had a first wife Abigail Harris with whom he had two children (Truman D. Oviatt,
MS dated 24 Feb. 1892 at Warren, Ohio, Oviatt File, Hudson Public Library, Hudson, Ohio.)

[163] Gravestone photo online at <www.findagrave.com>, accessed Aug. 2012.

[164] Gravestone photo online at <www.findagrave.com>, accessed Aug. 2012.

[165] Barbour Collection, citing Wethersfield VR1:103.

[166] Barbour Collection, citing Wethersfield VR1:103, Daniel Russell presiding.

[167] Gale Ion Harris, "William¹ Taylor of Wethersfield and New London, Connecticut," TAG 76 (2001):
180-81.

[168] Stiles, *Ancient Wethersfield*, 2:699-700.

[169] Barbour Collection, citing Wethersfield VR1:103.

[170] Stiles, *Ancient Wethersfield*, 2:699-700.

June 1762 HULDA (PORTER) FAIRCHILD, b. ca. 1733, d. 1 March 1823, dau. of Dr. James Porter of Middlebury, Conn., and widow of Joseph Fairchild.[171]

9 ABRAHAM[3] HARRIS (*Walter[2], John[1]*), born about 1709 (age 17 in January 1726/7), probably in Glastonbury, was buried in Middletown, Connecticut, on 11 November 1792.[172] He married first about 1734, his step niece **ANNE BLINN**, daughter of William and Anna (Coultman) Blinn of Wethersfield, born there on 4 February 1712/3, who died on 23 April 1767 and buried in a Berlin, Connecticut cemetery.[173] Abraham married second in Newington Parish, Wethersfield, on 24 November 1767 **RUTH (HART) BECKLEY**,[174] born in Kensington (now New Britain), Connecticut, on 1 November 1726, who died there on 4 March 1760. She was a daughter of Hezekiah and Martha (Beckley) Hart and widow of Daniel Beckley. Abraham married third, before 4 October 1781, **ABIGAIL (WETMORE) (BURT) GEER**, born 18 September 1729, who died in Middletown before 5 October 1789, when her will was proved. Abigail, a daughter of Jeremiah and Abigail (Butler) Wetmore of Middletown, had married first, 25 July 1752, Jonas Burt, and second, about 1760, Samuel Geer.[175]

On 3 January 1726/7, at age 17, Abraham chose his brother Thomas as his guardian.[176] At age about 25, near the time of his first marriage, he witnessed on 29 August 1734 the will of Samuel Wolcott at Wethersfield.[177] On 23 March 1741/2, jointly with his wife Anne, he traded Wethersfield properties with Joseph Dickinson;[178] both properties adjoined land of Anne's father, William Blinn, who also was Abraham's stepbrother.

On 8 October 1740, Anne's brother William Blinn Jr. had given Abraham a quitclaim deed for a small parcel adjoining the above properties. Later, in March 1754, Anne's brother Peter Blinn also quitclaimed to Abraham his interest in a one-acre parcel in Tier 3.[179] In February 1749/50 and May 1750,

---

[171] Sarah J. Prichard and Joseph Anderson, *The Town and City of Waterbury, Connecticut*, 3 vols. (New Haven: Price & Lee Co., 1896), 2:235-36.

[172] Jacobus, "Early Harris Families of Western Connecticut," TAG 23 (1947):160.

[173] Harris, "Walter Harris's Widow and the Blinns of Wethersfield," NEHGR 143 (1989):314-15.

[174] Roger Welles, *Early Annals of Newington* (Hartford: Case, Lockwood & Brainard Co., 1874), 108.

[175] Harris, "Walter Harris of Wethersfield," 344-45.

[176] Manwaring, *Early Connecticut Probate Records*, 2:520.

[177] Manwaring, *Early Connecticut Probate Records*, 3:212.

[178] Wethersfield, Conn., Deeds, 6:98, 7:102, 133. The deeds were witnessed by John Taylor, husband of Abraham's sister Mary.

[179] Wethersfield, Conn., Deeds, 8:32, 10:328.

respectively, Abraham took inventory of the estates of Joseph Steele of Farmington and of Daniel Collins at Middletown.[180]

In his will at Wethersfield dated 6 August 1750, William Blinn gave 20s. to "my daughter Anne . . . she having already received her portion." On 3 September 1754, the court ordered distribution of his estate to heirs, including "Ann Blin alias Harriss."[181] On 3 October 1759, Anne's 16-year-old nephew, William Blinn, chose "Thomas Harriss of Wethersfield" as his guardian, but the record continues: "the *said Abraham* Harriss acknowledged himself bound. . . ."[182]

Abraham and his wife Anne were among the early settlers of Canaan, Connecticut, but they did not stay long. The first town meeting for Canaan was held in Wethersfield on 22 February 1737/8 and settlement commenced next June. Abraham Harris was admitted as an inhabitant in April 1743 by vote of the town.[183] While still at Wethersfield on 7 April 1742, Abraham had purchased a 7-acre parcel "on the plain" from Josiah Walker of Canaan. Abraham and Anne had traded their Wethersfield property on 23 March 1741/2, thus they probably moved to Canaan that spring or summer and had been there about a year before the town's vote. On 9 November 1743, Abraham Harris "of Canaan" purchased two more lots from Augustine Bryan containing a total of about 34 acres, 17 acres of which he sold to Zebulon Deming 20 days later.[184]

By 21 February 1744/5, Abraham was again of Wethersfield when he traded the Canaan properties to Jonathan Russell of Wethersfield for four acres with a dwelling house, bar, orchard, etc., at Beckley's Farm.[185] Abraham's last deed in Wethersfield was recorded on 12 June 1780.[186] He and his third wife, Abigail, sold land in Middletown on 4 October 1781.[187]

Abigail Harris's will at Middletown, dated 3 June 1789 and proved 5 October 1789, leaves five shillings each to grandchildren Rachel Sage, Josiah Sage, and Abigail Sage, children of "my daughter Lucretia," with the remainder to go to "my son Hezekiah Geer, he to provide for my affectionate husband, Abraham Harris, in his advanced age."[188]

---

[180] Manwaring, *Early Connecticut Probate Records*, 3:527, 656.
[181] Hartford District Probate Records, 15:232, 17:39.
[182] Hartford District Probate Records, 16:231, 17:39, 18:70.
[183] *History of Litchfield County*, Connecticut (Philadelphia: J. W. Lewis & Co., 1881), 268.
[184] Canaan, Conn., Deeds, 1:46, 129, 158.
[185] Canaan, Conn., Deeds, 1:177; Wethersfield, Conn., Deeds, 7:255.
[186] Wethersfield, Conn., Deeds, 16:129.
[187] Middletown, Conn., Deeds, 32:401.
[188] Jacobus, "Early Harris Families of Western Connecticut," TAG 23 (1947):160, citing Middletown Files, no. 1674.

Child of Abraham³ and Ann (Blinn) Harris:

    i   Lois⁴ Harris, b. say 1734, m. Newington Parish, Wethersfield, 7 Nov. 1751 David Sage,¹⁸⁹ of Middletown, b. there 29 June 1732, d. 25 Feb. 1779, son of David and Bathsheba (Judd) Sage of Middletown and Berlin, Conn.¹⁹⁰
        Children of David and Lois⁴ (Harris) Sage, all recorded in Middletown:¹⁹¹
            1 *Lois Sage*, b. 9 Nov. 1752, d. 27 Oct. 1773.
            2 *Abraham Sage*, b. 30 July 1754.
            3 *David Sage*, b. 30 May 1756, d. 7 Oct. 1756.
            4 *Ann Sage*, b. 30 July 1757, d. 30 May 1758.
            5 *Harris Sage*, b. 18 March 1759, d. 18 March 1776.
            6 *David Sage* (twin), b. 12 April 1761, d. 7 Oct. 1775.
            7 *Jonathan Sage* (twin), b. 12 April 1761.
            8 *Ann Sage* (again), b. 9 May 1763.
            9 *Mehitabel Sage*, b. 20 Nov. 1765.
            10 *Barsheba Sage*, b. 18 Feb. 1768.
            11 *Seth Sage*, b. 1 Oct. 1770, d. 9 July 1771.
            12 *Ruth Sage*, b. 13 June 1772, d. 6 July 1775.
            13 *David Sage* (again), b. 5 May 1778.

10 Thomas³ Harris (*Thomas²*, *John¹*), born about 1689 (age 8 in 1697), probably in East Hampton, Long Island, died in Fairfield Township, Cumberland County, New Jersey, between 24 October and 19 December 1749, the dates of his will and its proof.¹⁹² He married by November 1710 (birth of first child) **Anna** ____, who died there between 13 and 21 December 1750, the dates of her will and its proof, see below.

In 1714, Thomas Harris and Levi Preston, and their wives, appeared for baptism at the Cohansey Baptist Church in Hopewell Township, Cumberland County, but returned their own [Presbyterian] Church.¹⁹³ Thomas was a private in Capt. Joseph Seeley's company of militia on the south side of the Cohansey in November 1715,¹⁹⁴ and served as collector for that district in 1732, surveyor of highways in 1743, and a freeholder in 1746-47. He had land in Deerfield, where he resided.¹⁹⁵

---

¹⁸⁹ Welles, *Annals of Newington*, 106; also recorded in Middletown VR2:292.

¹⁹⁰ Harold Kenneth Sage, "David Sage, of Middletown, Connecticut, His Children, and Grandchildren," NEHGR 106 (1952):215; Harris, "Walter Harris of Wethersfield," 346.

¹⁹¹ Barbour Collection, citing MiddletownVR2:293.

¹⁹² *Calendar of New Jersey Wills*, 13 vols., *New Jersey Archives, First Series*, vols. 23,30, 32-42, at 30:222.

¹⁹³ Walter Lee Sheppard Jr. and Lewis D. Cook, "Harris of Cumberland County, New Jersey," *Pennsylvania Genealogical Magazine* [PGM] 17 (1949):79-109, at 79-80, citing Morgan Edwards, *Materials Towards a History of the Baptists in New Jersey* (Philadelphia: Thomas Dobson, 1792), 2:31.

¹⁹⁴ *New York Colonial Muster Rolls*, 1:538.

¹⁹⁵ H. Stanley Craig, *Cumberland County, New Jersey, Genealogical Data* (Merchantville, N.J.: By the author, 19—), 194. The earlier generations in the "Harris" sketch are unreliable.

The will in 1749 of Thomas Harris of Fairfield Precinct, Cumberland County, names wife Anna; son Caleb; son Thomas; son Isaac, deceased (who had sons Isaac and Thomas both under 21); son Jeremiah; Anna, Mercy, Mary, and Esther Harris, daughters of my late son Isaac; and daughter Sarah Ogden; executors sons Thomas and Jeremiah. His inventory, dated 19 December 1749, including a negro man, cattle, sheep, and hogs, was valued at £298 2s.[196]

The will of Thomas's widow Anna of Fairfield Precinct in 1750 names sons Thomas, Caleb, and Jeremiah, granddaughter Anna Harris, and "children in my house and family with me all that woolen cloth already made for clothing, each child to have as intended by me known to my daughter Sarah Ogden and Granddaughter Anna Harris." Daughter Sarah Ogden, wife of Thomas Ogden to have residue of estate; son-in-law Thomas Ogden executor. Her inventory, dated 21 December 1750, was valued at £148 17s. 9d.[197]

Children of Thomas[3] and Anna (____) Harris:[198]

21   i   THOMAS[4] HARRIS, b. ca. Nov. 1710; m. (1) SARAH DAYTON, (2), SUSANNA (____) (ELMER) WESTCOTT.

     ii   ISAAC HARRIS, d. Salem Co., N.J., before 22 May 1745, when his wife MAREY ____, was appointed administratrix, with Henry Seeley and David Stratton, bondsmen. His inventory, valued at £94 2s. 5d., includes cattle and horses.[199]

       Children of Isaac[4] and Marey (____) Harris, all named in grandfather Harris's 1749 will:[200]

         1 *Isaac[5] Harris*, living 1749, then under 21.
         2 *Thomas Harris*, living 1749, then under 21.
         3 *Anna Harris*; m. (license dated 3 March 1757) Joseph Bishop.[201]
         4 *Mercy Harris*, bp. Pittsgrove Presbyterian Church, 7 June 1740.[202]
         5 *Mary Harris*, bp. 7 June 1741.
         6 *Hester Harris*, bp. there 3 Aug. 1743.[203]

   iii   JEREMIAH HARRIS, b. ca. 1721, d. Fairfield Twp. 22 Feb. 1755 in his 35th year; m. ABIGAIL STRATTON, b. 25 Feb. 1726, who d. 4 April 1759, dau. of Benjamin and Abigail (Preston) Stratton. Abigail m. (2) ____ Bradway.[204] By his father's will, Jeremiah was to share land at Deerfield with his brother Thomas.

[196] Sheppard and Cook, "Harris of Cumberland County," PGM 17 (1949):79-80, citing West New Jersey Will Book 6:295.
[197] *New Jersey Archives*, 30:221-22.
[198] Sheppard and Cook, "Harris of Cumberland County," PGM 17 (1949):81.
[199] *New Jersey Archives*, 30:222.
[200] Sheppard and Cook, "Harris of Cumberland County," PGM 17 (1949):83.
[201] Craig, *Cumberland County Genealogical Data*, 194.
[202] Craig, *Cumberland County Genealogical Data*, 194.
[203] Craig, *Cumberland County Genealogical Data*, 194.
[204] Craig, *Cumberland County Genealogical Data*, 23.

Jeremiah d. intestate in Fairfield, Cumberland Co. Bond was set to his widow Abigail Harris as administratrix on 5 April 1755; his inventory was valued at £297 16*s*.[205]

Children of Jeremiah[4] and Abigail (Stratton) Harris:[206]

1 *Jeremiah*[5] *Harris*, b. 1748, d. 23 Jan. 1812, bur. "Old Stone" Churchyard near Fairton; m. (1) Rachel Dare, b. ca. 1750, d. 20 Nov. 1788 in her 39th year, dau. of William and Freelove (Preston) Dare; (2) Jane ____, b. ca. 1761, who d. 9 April 1795 in her 35th year; (3) 15 July 1795 Rhoda Fithian; (4) 30 Aug. 1797 Susannah (____) Bateman, b. ca. 1758, d. 27 July 1808 in her 51st year, widow of Burgin Bateman; (5) 16 Jan. 1809 Ruth DuBois of Salem Co., who survived him.

2 *Abigail Harris*, living 1759.

3 *Reuben Harris*, living 1767.

iv   SARAH HARRIS, b. ca. 1722, d. 23 March 1760, age 38; m. before 1743, as his 1st wife, THOMAS OGDEN SR., b. ca. 1720, d. 23 Dec. 1785, age 65. Thomas m. (2) (license 6 Aug. 1760) Violetta (Lorance) Harris, widow of Sarah's nephew Thomas Harris Jr. (no. 21 i), (3) (license 21 March 1761) Sarah Westcott, (4) Sarah (Austin) Stratton.[207]

Children of Thomas and Sarah[4] (Harris) Ogden:[208]

1 *Thomas Ogden Jr.*, b. ca. 1743, d. Fairfield Twp. 10 Jan. 1768, age 25; m. in 1761 Abigail Dare, b. ca. 1741, who d. 24 Oct. 1793, age 52. She had m. (2) Ephraim Buck, and (3) Abiel Shaw.

2 *Sarah Ogden*; m. her 1st cousin Samuel Ogden.

v   CALEB HARRIS, b. after 1728, living 1749 still a minor. By his father's will, Caleb was to share with his mother "the improvements within Beller's Survey," he to improve his part "under conduct of executors."

11 NATHANIEL[3] **HARRIS** (*Thomas*[2], *John*[1]), born on 8 October 1693, probably in East Hampton, Long Island, died in Hopewell Township, Cumberland County, New Jersey, on 2 November 1775.[209] He married first by 1716 (birth of first child) **MIRIAM BROOKS**, born on 16 August 1698, who died on 13 February 1722, and secondly **ELIZABETH** ____, who died apparently before 1770. Nathaniel was a private with his brothers Thomas and Samuel in Capt. Joseph Seeley's company of militia on the south side of the Cohansey in November 1715.[210]

Nathaniel's will, dated in Hopewell Township on 27 June 1770 and proved on 14 November 1775, gave £10 each to sons Nathaniel, John, Jona-

[205] *New Jersey Archives*, 32:146.

[206] Sheppard and Cook, "Harris of Cumberland County," PGM 17 (1949):84.

[207] Sheppard and Cook, "Harris of Cumberland County," PGM 17 (1949):84-85.

[208] Sheppard and Cook, "Harris of Cumberland County," PGM 17 (1949):85.

[209] Sheppard and Cook, "Harris of Cumberland County," PGM 17 (1949):91, citing Bible record of Nathaniel Harris family in possession of the Vineland Historical Society.

[210] *New York Colonial Muster Rolls*, 1:538.

than, and Noah, to son Josiah "the plantation where I dwell," and bequests to grandson Ebenezer Harris, grandson David Harris son of David, David's widow, daughter Hannah Ewing, daughter Ruth Whittacar, daughters Abigail Alderman and Elizabeth Bowen, and son Noah Harris; friend Thomas Read executor. The inventory, taken on 8 November 1775, was valued at £196 8*s.* 7*d.*[211]

Children of Nathaniel[3] and Miriam (Brooks) Harris:[212]

    i   MARY[4] HARRIS, b. 12 June 1716, living 1786; m. SAMUEL MOORE, who d. ca. 1772.

        Children of Samuel and Mary[4] (Harris) Moore; "the rest still live [1786]":

        1 *David Moore*, who wrote a letter from Deerfield, N.J., on 25 July 1786 as "Capt." David Moore to his "Dear Aunt" (unidentified) with news of family members.[213] He added that he was "in the war several years" [where he was wounded at the Battle of Brandy-wine], had a wife and three children (unnamed), and, "ten years past, I bought the Plantation in Deerfield on which Captain Charles Clark lived."

        David was the father of Dr. Samuel Moore, b. Deerfield in 1774, U.S. Congressman three terms beginning 1818, appointed Director of the U.S. Mint by President Monroe in 1824, and was presiding officer of the Hazleton Coal Company.[214]

        2 *Samuel Moore*, in 1786 "my brother Sam died many years past."

        3 *Elizabeth Moore*, d. ca. 1777, "my sister Betsy has been dead nine years [in 1786]."

        4 *Israel Moore*, "died on board the British prison ship in 1780."

   ii MIRIAM HARRIS, b. 20 Feb. 1717/8.

  iii ABIGAIL HARRIS, b. 26 March 1720, d. Duplin Co., N.C., 1771; m. ca. 1740 DANIEL ALDERMAN, b. 1711, d. Duplin Co. by Oct. 1785 (proof of will), son of Thomas and Mary (Seagrave) Alderman of Cohansey, earlier from Simsbury, Conn. They moved from N.J., to Duplin Co., N.C., in 1755.[215]

      The will of Daniel Alderman Sr., carpenter, dated 19 Dec. 1782 and proved in Duplin Co. in October Court, 1785, gives his wife Abigail a third of his cleared ground, orchard, furniture, and livestock, his son David "the

[211] Sheppard and Cook, "Harris of Cumberland County," PGM 17 (1949):91-92.

[212] Sheppard and Cook, "Harris of Cumberland County," PGM 17 (1949):92, citing Bible record.

[213] Letter of David Moore, 25 July 1786. A copy of this letter was made available in 1996 by Kathryn Harris Hines of Nacogdoches, Tex., with comment that Moore's "Aunt" is supposed to have been at her home in North Carolina. The provenance of the letter is unknown to me.

[214] "Obituary Notice of [his son] Dr. Samuel Moore," *Proceedings of the American Philosophical Society* 8 (1861):53-56.

[215] William Alderman Parker, *Aldermans in America* (Raleigh, N.C.: By the author, 1957), 39-42. Parker somehow confused Abigail's stepmother Elizabeth with Elizabeth Hazen who resided in Rowley, Mass., and married a different Nathaniel Harris (Walter Goodwin Davis, *The Ancestry of Bethia Harris, 1748-1833* . . . [Portland, Maine: Southworth Press, 1934], 14).

plantation whereon I now live," and 5*s.* each to "all my [other] sons and daughters." Sons Daniel and David were appointed executors.[216]
Children of Daniel and Abigail[4] (Harris) Alderman, prob. all b. Deerfield, N.J.:[217]

>1 *John Alderman*, b. 1742; d. Duplin Co., N.C., in Aug. 1822; m. 1770 Mary Cashwell.
>2 *Rachel Alderman*, b. 1744; m. Charles Bland.
>3 *Mary Alderman*, b. 1746; m. Elijah Bowen.
>4 *Daniel Alderman*, b. 11 March 1748, d. Duplin Co. 8 Aug. 1824; m. Sarah Newton.
>5 *David Alderman*, b. 1749, d. Bulloch Co., Ga., 23 Oct. 1831; m. Duplin 1773 Jemima Hall, b. Duplin Co. 1753, d. Statesboro, Bulloch Co., Ga., 21 March 1832.
>6 *Hannah Alderman*, b. 1751; m. [James Bland?].
>7 *Abigail Alderman*, b. 1753; m. William James.

iv ELIZABETH HARRIS, b. 16 Jan. 1721/2; m. CLIFTON BOWEN.

Children of Nathaniel[3] and Elizabeth (____) Harris:

v NATHANIEL HARRIS, b. 27 May 1723, d. Hopewell Twp., Cumberland Co., 3 Dec. 1797, bur. Broad Street Cemetery; m. 12 Nov. 1746 ABIGAIL PADGETT, b. 28 June 1727, d. 1 Nov. 1810, dau. of Thomas and Dorothea (Sayre) Padgett of Cumberland Co.[218]
Children of Nathaniel[4] and Abigail (Padgett) Harris:[219]

>1 *Mary[5] Harris*, b. 3 Nov. 1747, d. 3 Sept. 1814, unm.
>2 *Rachel Harris*, b. 2 Sept. 1750, d. 24 Sept. 1825; m. (license 7 Aug. 1778) George Ewing of Cumberland Co.
>3 *John Harris*, b. 14 Feb. 1753, d. 19 Jan. 1830; m. 8 April 1783 Elizabeth Bacon, b. 3 May 1760, d. 17 Dec. 1851.
>4 *Noah Harris*, b. 25 April 1755, d. 28 March 1821; m. (license 18 April 1781) Sarah Carle.
>5 *Hannah Harris*, b. 26 Jan. 1758, d. 23 Sept. 1773.
>6 *Thomas Harris*, b. 9 May 1760, d. Hopewell Twp. 1 Dec. 1799; m. Pamela ____.
>7 *Nathaniel Harris*, b. 14 Jan. 1763, d. Trenton, N.J., 1811; m. Trenton 9 March 1802 Catharine (Cox) Stockton, dau. of Col. John Cox and widow of Samuel William Stockton. Nathaniel was a clergyman.
>8 *Abijah Harris*, b. 2 Jan. 1765, d. 7 July 1848.
>9 *Abigail Harris*, b. b. 26 Oct. 17[68], d. 19 July 1838; m. 5 April 1790 Mark Riley.

vi JOHN HARRIS, b. 29 Sept. 1725, d. Abbeville Co., N.C., between the 1790 census date and before 5 April 1791 (proof of will);[220] m. in Md. in 1759

---

[216] Full transcription in Parker, *Aldermans in America*, 41-42.
[217] Parker, *Aldermans in America*, 42-47.
[218] Theodore M. Banta, *Sayre Family: Lineage of Thomas Sayre, a Founder of Southampton* (New York: De Vinne Press, 1901), 70, 126-27, which, however, makes Nathaniel a son of his father's first wife.
[219] Sheppard and Cook, "Harris of Cumberland County," PGM 17 (1949):93.

MARY HANDY, b. Somerset Co., Md., 8 Nov. 1733, d. Abbeville Co. 6 July 1801, dau. of Col. Isaac and Ann (Dashiell) Handy of Somerset Co., Md.[221] John received the A.B. degree from Nassau Hall (now Princeton University) in 1753, served as minister to several churches in Delaware, Virginia, and Maryland, before arriving in Ninety Six (later Abbeville) District, S.C., in Nov. 1772. There, he established the Fort Boone, Bull Town, and Long Cane Congregations. Through grants in the period 1774–1787, he obtained some 1,709 acres in Ninety Six District. He served in the Second Provincial Congress in 1775 and 1776, and in the First and Second General Assembly's in 1776–1778, where he voted for ratification of the federal Constitution.[222]

Children of Rev. John[4] and Mary (Handy) Harris:[223]

1 *Handy[5] Harris*, b. 7 Jan. 1760, a surgeon during the Revolutionary War. His household near that of his father in Abbeville Co., S.C., in 1790 consisted of one male 16 or over and one white female.[224]

2 *John Harris*, b. 6 Dec. 1762, d. 26 April 1845; m. Mary Pickins, dau. of Gen. Andrew Pickens, remained in S.C.

3 *Anna Harris*, b. 10 Feb. 1765, d. 1830; m. Elijah McCurdy of Charleston, S.C.

4 *Thomas Harris*, b. 11 May 1768, d. 12 Aug. 1851, moved to DeKalb Co., Ga., where he was active in establishing several churches.

5 *Elizabeth Harris*, b. 15 Feb. 1769, d. 1827; m. Joseph Irving and moved to Jackson Co., Ga.

6 *Nathaniel Harris*. The youngest of this family, Nathaniel was ill at their home when it was invaded by Tories during the Revolutionary War. They took all the family's valuables and stripped Nathaniel of his clothing, leaving him to die in his youth.

vii DAVID HARRIS (twin), b. 16 July 1727, d. Hopewell Twp., Cumberland Co., N.J., before 26 Oct. 1770 (date of administrators' bond); m. MARY ____, who survived him.[225]

viii JONATHAN HARRIS (twin), b. 16 July 1727, d. between 8 June and 11 Aug. 1802. He m. (1) 14 June 1753 ABIGAIL LEEK, bp. Easthampton, L.I., 17 Jan.

---

[220] 1790 U.S. Census, Abbeville Co., S.C., p. 456; *Biographical Directory of the South Carolina House of Representatives*, 5 vols. (Columbia, S.C.: University of South Carolina Press, 1974–92), 3:321. This biography of John Harris, a Presbyterian minister, gives his birth date as 29 Sept. 1725, an exact match for the date given in the Bible of Nathaniel Harris in New Jersey for his son John, yet the writers of the biography clearly did not know his parentage.

[221] Isaac W. K. Handy, *Annals and Memorials of the Handys and their Kindred* (Ann Arbor, Mich.: William L. Clements Library, 1992), 17, 49. The name *Ruth* given for this John Harris's wife in Sheppard and Cook, "Harris of Cumberland County," PGM 17 (1949):92, apparently resulted from some confusion with the wife, Ruth Test, of another man of the same name, a Quaker of Salem Co., N.J. (ibid., 102).

[222] *Biographical Directory of the South Carolina House of Representatives*, 3:321.

[223] *Handys and their Kindred*, 49-50.

[224] 1790 U.S. Census, Abbeville Co., S.C., p. 456.

[225] Sheppard and Cook, "Harris of Cumberland County," PGM 17 (1949):92, 108n.

1731, d. 30 March 1759, dau. of Recompense Leek, (2) MARTHA ____, b. 3
Jan. 1736, d. Deerfield Twp., Cumberland Co., 26 Nov. 1815, age 79.[226]
   Child of Jonathan[4] and Abigail (Leek) Harris:
      1 *Ruth[5] Harris*; m. ____ Garrison, who d. before 1806.
   Children of Jonathan[4] and Martha (____) Harris:
      2 *Jonathan Harris* (possibly by Abigail); m. 1788 Catharine Costo.
      3 *Josiah Harris*, b. 4 April 1765, d. 1833; m. Hannah Brown, b. 3 Nov.
         1764, dau. of Mark and Mary (____) Brown.
      4 *Amos Harris*.
      5 *Philip Harris*, d. 1828; m. Rebecca Edwards.
      6 *Sarah Harris*, bp. 6 Dec. 1772, living 8 Feb. 1806; m. Daniel Brooks.
      7 *Joel Harris*, bp. 29 Jan. 1775.
      8 *Elizabeth Harris*, bp. 22 Sept. 1776.
   ix NOAH HARRIS, b. 16 July 1729, d. in camp of smallpox in March 1777.[227] He
      had two unknown wives before he m. (3) (N.J. license 23 July 1761) MARY
      APPLIN, dau. of Joseph Applin of Woolwich Twp., Gloucester Co., N.J.,
      who was living in Aug. 1777.[228]
      Children of Noah[4] Harris and unknown first wife, both living 1777:
         1 *Elizabeth[5] Harris*.
         2 *Tamsen Harris*.
      Child of Noah[4] Harris and unknown second wife, living 1777:
         3 *Susannah Harris*.
      Children of Noah[4] and Mary (Applin) Harris:
         4 *Hannah Harris*, living 1777; m. ____ Kates.
         5 *Meriam Harris*, living 1777; prob. m. (1) Isaac Smith, (2) David Shep-
            pard.
         6 *Mary Harris*; m. 8 Oct. 1813 James Flanagan.
         7 *Phebe Harris*; m. 8 April 1812 Henry Mulford.
         8 *Abigail Harris*, living 1777; m. John Mulford of Woodstown.
         9 *John Applin Harris*, bp. 23 June 1771, d. 31 Oct. 1772.
         10 *Noah Harris*, bp. 11 April 1773, chose Henry Mulford as guardian,
            bond dated 28 June 1788.
   x JOSIAH HARRIS, b. 16 Nov. 1732, d. Hopewell Twp., Cumberland Co., 18 June
      1776. He married, but the name of his wife (or wives) is not known. His
      will, dated Hopewell Twp. 16 June 1776 and proved 5 July 1776 mentions
      his wife (unnamed) and the five children listed below.[229]
      Children of Josiah[4] and ____ (____) Harris:[230]
         1 *Enos[5] Harris*, b. 1769, d. 23 April 1795.
         2 *Israel Harris*, living 1776.
         3 *John Harris*, bp. 11 April 1773.
         4 *Hannah Harris*, living 1776.

---

[226] Sheppard and Cook, "Harris of Cumberland County," PGM 17 (1949):93-94.
[227] Letter of David Moore, 26 July 1786.
[228] Sheppard and Cook, "Harris of Cumberland County," PGM 17 (1949):94-95.
[229] *New Jersey Archives*, 34:230.
[230] Sheppard and Cook, "Harris of Cumberland County," PGM 17 (1949):95.

            5 *Elizabeth Harris*, bp. 3 March 1776.

  xi   RUTH HARRIS, b. 10 June 1734, d. 5 Oct. 1772; m. AMBROSE WHITTACAR.

  xii HANNAH HARRIS, b. 5 Sept. 1738, living 1786; m. JOSHUA EWING, d. Greenwich Twp., Cumberland Co., between 11 July 1784 and 15 Aug. 1785, the dates of his will and its proof; wife Hannah to be executrix.[231] Joshua served as a member of the New Jersey Assembly 1781–1783.[232]

        Children of Joshua and Hannah[4] (Harris) Ewing, named in will:

          1 *Palmis Ewing.*
          2 *Joshua Ewing.*
          3 *James Ewing.*
          4 *Robert Ewing.*
          5 *Elizabeth Ewing.*
          6 *Anna Ewing.*

12 SAMUEL[3] HARRIS (*Thomas[2], John[1]*), born about October 1696 (age 8m in June 1697), died in Hopewell Township, Cumberland County, New Jersey on 16 January 1773 in his 77th year, a weaver, buried in Old Cohansey Baptist Cemetery. He married first **SARAH JOHNSON**, born in 1697, who died on 16 June 1761, age 64y, daughter of Nicholas Johnson of Cohansey, and second (New Jersey license 25 August 1761) **RACHEL (___) HOOD**, apparently the widow of Robert Hood of Hopewell Township who died on 10 March 1761 in his 71st year.

    Samuel was a private with his brothers Thomas and Nathaniel in Capt. Joseph Seeley's company of militia on the south side of the Cohansey in November 1715.[233] He was Deacon of the Cohansey Baptist Church in 1757.[234]

    Samuel's will, dated 4 January 1773 and proved on 30 January 1773, names wife Rachel, sons Samuel, Abraham, Benjamin, and Silas, daughter Hannah Thompson, and "my grandson Jacob Harris son of Jacob Harris deceased. Sons Daniel and Silas were to receive the two looms. The inventory was valued at £196 10s.[235]

    Children of Samuel[3] and Sarah (Johnson) Harris:[236]

    i   SAMUEL[4] HARRIS JR., bp. July 1765, living 1773 (father's will).

    ii ABRAHAM HARRIS, b. ca. 1724, d. Alloways Creek Twp., Salem Co., N.J., 14 Feb. 1776 in his 53rd year; m. ESTHER LANGLEY.

        Children of Abraham[4] and Esther (Langley) Harris:

---

[231] *New Jersey Archives*, 35:140.

[232] Craig, *Cumberland County Genealogical Data*, 58.

[233] *New York Colonial Muster Rolls,* 1:538.

[234] Sheppard and Cook, "Harris of Cumberland County," PGM 17 (1949):96.

[235] *New Jersey Archives*, 34:231.

[236] Sheppard and Cook, "Harris of Cumberland County," PGM 17 (1949):97-101.

1 *Abraham*[5] *Harris*, living 1776.

2 *Isaac Harris*, living 1776.

3 *Jacob Harris*, "died February 13, 1797, and left a widow and 6 children, one name Polly is since dead [in 1806]."[237]

4 *John Harris*, b. 10 Sept. 1753, d. Lower Alloways Twp., Salem Co., N.J., 29 March 1814; m. 12 Jan. 1785 Lydia Smith, b. 11 Feb. 1764, d. 28 Oct. 1824, dau. of Capt. William and Sarah (Stretch) Smith of Salem Co.[238]

5 *Nicholas Harris*, living Cumberland Co., N.J., 1798.

6 *Parmenas Harris*, d. Lower Alloways Creek Twp., Salem Co., N.J., 1798. "Parmenas [Brother Abram's] youngest son, died about the same time that son Andrew died and left a widow and six children. Sophia, his daughter, is dead [in 1806], five sons living. Sister Ruth has but one here, that is, Joel Sheppard's wife, two sons. Daniel and Nathaniel Jenkins we expect is at Nova Scotia. Amy Jenkins is married to Nathan Davis and is gone beyond the Genesee country several years ago. Thomas Jenkins moved with his family over Delaware Bay 5 or 6 years ago."[239]

7 *Zerviah Harris*, living 1776.

iii Benjamin Harris, d. Hopewell Twp., Cumberland Co., between 14 Nov. and 26 Nov. 1776 (dates of his will and an inventory of his personal estate).[240] He m. (1) Priscilla Ogden, who d. 6 Dec. 1772, dau. of Daniel and Mary (Dixon) Ogden of Deerfield Twp., and (2) Rachel (Shepherd) Bacon, dau. of Enoch and Rachel (Watson) Shepherd of Hopewell Twp. and widow of Jeremiah Bacon of Stow Creek Twp.

"Brother Benjamin has five children living [in 1806], namely, Anne Perry, Phebe Ryley, Johnson Harris, Priscilla Strathorn, and Rachel Bacon. Moses Perry died about 19 years ago and left Anne with 4 children, namely, Phebe, Ann Mary, Hosea Harris Perry, and Eunice. The girls are all married, Hosea not. Phebe is married to Noah Bowen and moved out last spring to Warren in the Ohio state. Mary is married to Mark Westcott, Eunice to John Tomkins (?)."[241]

Children of Benjamin[4] and Priscilla (Ogden) Harris:

1 *Phebe*[5] *Harris*, living 1806; m. ____ Ryley.

2 *Ogden Harris*, a minor in 1776.

3 *Benjamin Harris*, a minor in 1776.

4 *Johnson Harris*, living 1806.

5 *Alvah Harris*, a minor in 1776.

6 *Ann Harris*, living 1806; m. Moses Perry, d. ca. 1787.

---

[237] Letter dated Cohansey, N.J., 10 Sept. 1806, from Silas Harris to his son Jones Harris in Cincinnati, Ohio ("Harris Letter," NYGBR 53 [1922]:131-33, at 132).

[238] Sheppard and Cook, "Harris of Cumberland County," PGM 17 (1949):100-1, citing Bible record in Rogers Collection, A-K-316, Genealogical Society of Pennsylvania. Eight children.

[239] "Harris Letter," NYGBR 53 (1922):131.

[240] *New Jersey Archives*, 34:229.

[241] "Harris Letter," NYGBR 53 (1922):132.

       7 *Priscilla Harris*, under 14 in 1779, living 1806; m. _____ Strathom.

    Child of Benjamin[4] and Rachel (Shepherd) (Bacon) Harris:

       8 *Rachel Harris*, living 1806; m. _____ Bacon.

iv JACOB HARRIS, b. ca. 1728, d. Hopewell Twp., Cumberland Co., 8 June 1761 in his 34th year; m. ca. 1750 RACHEL CROSLEY, dau. of Moses and Sarah (_____) Crosley of Fairfield Twp, who survived him. "Brother Jacob has but two children living [in 1806], namely, Moses and Elizabeth. Elizabeth is married to Joseph Young at Alloway's Creek."[242]

    Children of Jacob[4] and Rachel (Crosley) Harris:

       1 *Jacob[5] Harris*, b. ca. 1751, d. 13 Feb. 1797 in his 47th year; m. (N.J. license 29 Feb. 1780) Rachel Bacon, who d. "1808-11."

       2 *Moses Harris*, b. 26 April 1754 (calc.), d. 8 Sept. 1823, age 69y 4m 13d; m. (N.J. license 26 Nov. 1779) Phebe Brooks.

       3 "supposed" *Rachel Harris*; m. (N.J. license 18 Feb. 1771) Elijah Bowen.

       4 *Elizabeth Harris*, living 1806; m. Joseph Young "at Alloway's Creek."

v DANIEL HARRIS, d. Hopewell Twp., Cumberland Co., in June 1776. He m. (1) MARY HOOD, who d. ca. Feb 1769, "probably" dau. of Robert Hood (2) (N.J. license 28 Feb. 1779) MARTHA OGDEN, dau. of Daniel Ogden. Martha m. (2) Lewis Westcott, son of Henry Westcott of Fairfield Twp. Daniel Harris and wife Mary joined the Cohansey Baptist Church in Dec. 1765.

    "Brother Daniel has 4 children living here [in 1806], namely Robert, Daniel, Eunice and Joel. Robert has a son that is a Baptist preacher: he preaches up in East Jersey in Amwell by the name of Samuel Harris . . . I forgot Mary Fithian, brother Daniel's daughter. She has 7 or 8 children, and her sister Eunice has been married to William Davis as much as 18 or 19 years and never had any children."[243]

    Children of Daniel[4] and Mary (Hood) Harris:

       1 *Robert[5] Harris*, living 1806; m. (1) 2 Jan. 1776 Mary Berryman, (2) 1 March 1800 Mrs. Hannah Bacon.

       2 *Daniel Harris*, b. ca. 1777; bur. 26 May 1846; m. 9 Nov. 1784 Mary (Vickers) Worthington, dau. of Philip and Sarah (Sheppard) Vickers and widow of John Worthington.

       3 *Hosea Harris*, d. before 1806.

       4 *Joel Harris*, b. 12 Dec. 1764, living 1806.

       5 *Eunice Harris*, living 1806; m. 24 Dec. 1787 William Davis.

       6 *Mary Harris*, b. 25 Aug. 1767, living 1806; m. Jonathan Fithian.

    Child of Daniel[4] and Martha (Ogden) Harris:

       7 *Amos Harris*, b. 1770, d. before 1806.

vi HANNAH HARRIS; m. JACOB THOMPSON. "Sister Hannah has two children living here [in 1806], namely, Jacob Thompson and Phebe Finley."[244]

---

[242] "Harris Letter," NYGBR 53 (1922):131-32.

[243] "Harris Letter," NYGBR 53 (1922):132.

[244] "Harris Letter," NYGBR 53 (1922):132.

vii   MARY HARRIS, d. apparently before her father's 1773 will; m. _____ WALLING. In
       1806, "Sister Mary has one living by the name of David Walling. Jonathan,
       his twin, died last fall."[245]

viii   SILAS HARRIS, d. Stow Creek Twp., Cumberland Co., N.J., 26 Sept. 1820, bur.
       Baptist Churchyard at Roadstown; m. (1) _____ _____, (2) MARY _____, who
       d. 15 July 1808.
          Silas was a weaver in N.J., in 1806 when he wrote the letter quoted above
       to his son Jones Harris in Cincinnati. It indicates that his present wife was his
       son Jones's "stepmother." In addition to Jones, he mentions his children Silas
       (no letter in "this 4 years"), Andrew, deceased (3 ch: Peggy Jones Harris,
       Lydia Harris, Andrew Harris), Jeremiah (down to see me last June, 2 sons
       George and Jeremiah), and Sarah (has sons Moses and Eli in Philadelphia).[246]
       The will of Silas Harris of Stow Creek Twp., dated 6 July 1818, probed 10
       Sept. 1820, names children James, Silas, and Margaret wife of Daniel Noble,
       and grandchildren Andrew Harris, Mary Tullis, and Margaret Noble.[247]
          Children of Silas[4] and Mary (_____) Harris (order assumed):
          1 *Jones*[5] *Harris*, living Cincinnati, Ohio, 1806.
          2 *Andrew Harris*, deceased in 1806.
          3 *Jeremiah Harris*, living 1806.
          4 *Sarah Harris*; in 1806 had sons "Moses and Eli in Philadelphia."
          5 *James Harris*, living 1818 (father's will).
          6 *Silas Harris*, living 1818 (father's will).
          7 *Margaret Harris*; m. 14 Dec. 1813 Daniel Noble.
          8 *Samuel Harris*.

13 MARY[3] **HARRIS** (*John*[2-1]), born probably at Springfield, Massachusetts,
say 1694 (estimated age 9 or 10 in February 1703/4), was living at Kahnawake, near Montreal, Canada, in 1756 and was "still absent from [her]
native country" in 1758."[248] She had married by about 1714 (a "son" was
aged about 30 in 1744) probably at Kahnawake and perhaps the **INDIAN
HUSBAND** who was with her at White Woman's Creek near Coshocton in
(present) Ohio in January 1751.[249]

Again following a practice common in this family, after her father's death
and mother's remarriage Mary apparently had been placed with Simon
Beaman's family at Deerfield, Massachusetts. The Beamans were from
Springfield, where the family had been employed by John Pynchon.[250] Mary

---

[245] "Harris Letter," NYGBR 53 (1922):132.

[246] "Harris Letter," NYGBR 53 (1922):132-33.

[247] Sheppard and Cook, "Harris of Cumberland County," PGM 17 (1949):100.

[248] Rev. John Williams, *The Redeemed Captive Returning to Zion, Taylor Edition* (1795; repr. Springfield, 1908), 171-72.

[249] George F. Smythe, "Mitchner's 'Legend of the White Woman, and Newcomerstown'," *Ohio Arch.
and Hist. Soc. Pubs.*, 33 (1924):283-300.

[250] Richard I. Melvoin, *New England Outpost: War and Society in Colonial Deerfield* (New York and
London: Norton, 1989), 136.

was most likely the "servant girl" with Beaman and his wife when all three were captured in the infamous 29 February 1703/4 raid on Deerfield and carried with other captives to Canada.[251]

Mary was at Kahnawake, near Montreal, in 1744. Her fellow captive Capt. Joseph Kellogg interviewed her two sons at his home in Suffield, Massachusetts (now Connecticut) that fall. In a letter to the Governor of Massachusetts on 3 December, Kellogg wrote,

Two young men Mary Harrises children have been with me twice, which have lodged at my house[;] one of them is a very Intellegable man about thirty years of age and from them I have indeavored critically to examine them about the affairs of Canada.[252]

Mary seems to have accompanied her sons at least part way on their trip to New England. Their travel may have been prompted in part by the impending death of her mother that November in Westfield—the town laying next north of Suffield. In October 1744, Mary appeared at a trading post kept by John Henry Lydius at Fort Edward below Lake Champlain. On 24 October, he wrote,

I have used my indeavour to perswade Mary Harris who was made a captive at Dearfield to goo and see her parents. It is my humbel opinion that in case her parents are not in a capacity to pass them in cuntery [it] would not do a miss to ead and and [sic] assist them in it for it is [as good?] a barier as a hundred men on the front and that charge would far excead this.[253]

Taken together, the sense of these two letters appears to be that Mary could not be persuaded to set foot again in New England, although her two sons went ahead on the journey.

In 1751, while traveling as agent for the Ohio Company of Virginia, Christopher Gist stopped at the place called White Woman's Creek near Coshocton in (present) Ohio, which was frequented by the Iroquois, principally Mohawks, from Kahnawake. During his brief visit, he recorded:

[T]his white woman was taken away from New England, when she was not above ten years old, by the French Indians; She is now upwards of fifty, and has an Indian Husband and several Children—Her name is Mary Harris, she still remembers they used to be very

[251] Many accounts of this historic event in New England are available; one reference is George Sheldon, *A History of Deerfield, Massachusetts*, 2 vols. (Deerfield: E. A. Hall & Co., 1895–96), 1:293-316.

[252] Letter, Joseph Kellogg, Interpreter, to the Governor of Massachusetts, 3 Dec. 1744, Massachusetts Archives Collection, 31:518-20; John Demos, *The Unredeemed Captive: A Family Story from Early America* (New York, 1994), 215.

[253] Letter, John Henry Lydius to Col. John Stoddard, 24 Oct. 1744, Massachusetts Archives Collection, 31:510-11.

religious in New England, and wonders how the White Men can be so wicked as she has seen them in these woods.[254]

Sometime in 1756, a British army soldier, Robert Eastman, was captured at Oswego, New York, and taken to Canada, where he wrote that he had lodged at Kahnawake "with the French captain's mother (an English woman named Mary Harris, taken captive when a child from Deerfield, in New England), who told me she was my grandmother and was kind."[255]

It is possible that Mary was back in the Ohio country later that year and was the person mentioned by James Smith, who had been captured near Bedford, Pennsylvania, in 1755 and carried away by the Indians. At "the mouth of the little lake" [Sandusky Bay in present Ohio] in October 1756, he and his companion—his "brother" Tecaughretanego—joined a company of Caughnewagas and Ottawas, and "was introduced to a Caughnewaga sister, and others I had never before seen. My sister's name was Mary, which they pronounced *Maully*." Smith asked his companion "how it came that she had an English name; he said that he did not know that it was an English name; but it was the name the priest gave her when she was baptized." The group was still travelling together in northeastern Ohio that December, when Smith mentioned "my sister Molly's husband" who was a Jibewa [Chippewa] and could understand Caughnewaga, so acted as interpreter. Also with them was Molly's father-in-law, Manetohcoa, an infirm old man they had to carry on a litter but much respected as a "great conjurer."[256]

Children of Mary[3] Harris with unknown Indian husband; the two unnamed sons who visited Capt. Kellogg in 1744 and "several" at White Woman's Creek in 1751:

i A son[4] b. ca. 1714 (age about 30 in 1744).
ii A son, probably younger, who also visited Kellogg in 1744. One of these sons might have been the "French captain" at Kahnawake in 1756.

---

[254] For this journal entry and a critique of facts and fiction concerning this "first white woman settler in Ohio," see Smythe, "Mitchner's 'Legend of the White Woman and Newcomerstown'," 283-300. Kenneth P. Bailey misdates the "massacre at Deerfield" as 1738, but places this journal entry in the wider context of Gist's travels (*Christopher Gist: Colonial Frontiersman, Explorer, and Indian Agent* [Hamden, Conn.: Archon Books, 1976], 40-41).

[255] Sheldon, *History of Deerfield*, 1:344; Emma Lewis Coleman, *New England Captives Carried to Canada Between 1677 and 1760 During the French and Indian Wars*, 2 vols. (Portland, Maine: Southworth Press, 1925), 2:42-44, 87-88.

[256] James Smith, *An Account of the Remarkable Occurrences in the Life and Travels of Col. James Smith . . .* (Lexington, Va.: John Bradford, 1799), 52, 65, 68-69.

14 PHILLIP³ HARRIS (*John²⁻¹*), born say 1698, probably in Springfield, Massachusetts, died at Simsbury, Connecticut, on 3 September 1758.[257] The mother of his son Phillip, born in 1721, has not been identified. He married subsequently, after 8 May 1745 (death of her prior husband), **ELIZABETH (DEMOND) GLEASON**, born at Simsbury in the summer of 1700 and living as Phillip's widow in April 1769, the illegitimate daughter of Mary (Case) (Alderman) Hillyer of Farmington and Simsbury, and widow of Thomas Gleason of Enfield and Simsbury, whom she had married in Simsbury on 21 February 171[6/]7 and had six children.[258]

On 3 April 1769, Elizabeth Harris, widow, exhibited an account of her administration and moved for an order of distribution of the estate of Phillip Harris late of Simsbury, deceased. The probate court directed distribution of one-third part of the estate to Elizabeth as widow, and the remaining part equally "to Mary Hinman the wife of Asher Hinman and to Elizabeth Harris, granddaughters of the said deceased, being the only heirs to [the] estate."[259]

Child of Phillip³ and ____ (____) Harris:

22   i   PHILLIP⁴ HARRIS, b. Simsbury 6 Aug. 1721;[260] m. RHODA ____ (prob. RHODA ALFORD).

FOURTH GENERATION

15 NATHANIEL⁴ HARRIS (*Walter³⁻², John¹*), born in Middletown, Connecticut, on 13 June 1725,[261] was living in Lebanon, Connecticut, on 1 October 1760,[262] but died before 3 February 1761, when his widow was granted administration on his estate.[263] He married probably before 1750 **GRACE LYMAN**, born in Lebanon on 6 December 1730,[264] died there before 6 May

---

[257] Date stated in his inventory, Hartford District Probate Records, 18:31, 61.

[258] George E. McCracken, FASG, "Two Mary Cases and Some of their Early Descendants named Alderman, Gleason and Phelps," NEHGR 122 (1968):38-40; Albert C. Bates, *Simsbury, Connecticut, Births, Marriages, and Deaths* (Hartford: Case, Lockwood & Brainard Co., 1898), 37, 44, 151, 157; John Barber White and Lillian May Wilson, *Genealogy of the Descendants of Thomas Gleason of Watertown, Mass., 1607–1909* (Haverhill, Mass.; Press of the Nichols Print, 1909), 42.

[259] Hartford District Probate Records, 21:170.

[260] Bates, *Simsbury Births, Marriages, and Deaths*, 152.

[261] Barbour Collection, citing Middletown VR1:4.

[262] Lebanon, Conn., Deeds, 9:233.

[263] Windham District Probate Records, Special Series, 3:257.

[264] Barbour Collection, citing Lebanon VR1:178.

1776, daughter of Ebenezer and Lydia (Wright) Lyman of Lebanon (now Columbia).[265]

Children of Nathaniel[4] and Grace (Lyman) Harris:

    i DEBORAH[5] HARRIS, "eldest daughter," a "minor" in Oct. 1765, was living in Lebanon, N.H., in 1800, age 45 or over;[266] m. there 10 June 1774 SAMUEL SPRAGUE,[267] b. Lebanon, Conn., 6 July 1748, d. ca. 1799, son of Elijah and Demaris (Clark) Sprague.[268] They moved to Lebanon, N.H., before 13 June 1774, when they conveyed to Benjamin Lyman the 10-acre parcel in Lebanon, Conn., that had been laid out to Deborah from her father's estate.[269] On 20 Feb. 1799, a bond at Lebanon, N.H., mentions widow Deborah Sprague, son Elijah, eldest daughter Amelia Hall, and daughter Deborah.[270]

        Children of Samuel and Deborah[5] (Harris) Sprague, b. Lebanon, N.H.:[271]

        1 *Elijah Sprague*, b. 7 March 1775; m. Lebanon, N.H., 24 Sept. 1797 Polly Simmons,[272] who d. a widow before 7 March 1821.

        2 *Amelia Sprague*, b. 12 Dec. 1776; m. Lebanon, N.H., 1 Sept. 1796 Orley Hall,[273] son of Nathaniel. Their household in Lebanon, N.H., in 1800 consisted of a male 26-44, two females 16-25, and a boy and two girls under 10.[274]

        3 *Zeruiah Sprague*, b. 12 April 1778, d. 3 May 1782.

        4 *Deborah Sprague*, b. 12 April 1779, living 1799.

        5 *Polly Sprague*, b. 3 June 1782, d. 20 Aug. 1782.

        6 *Samuel Sprague*, b. 3 May 1784, d. 11 June 1786.

   ii REBECCA HARRIS, "second daughter," a "minor" in Oct. 1765; m. Columbia, Conn., Church 5 May 1774 BENJAMIN GARY.[275]

  iii TAMAR HARRIS, b. ca. 1755, "third daughter," a "minor" in Oct. 1765, d. 29 May 1800;[276] m. before 29 Aug. 1778, prob. at Sharon, Conn., ELIJAH PARDEE, b. Sharon 31 Oct. 1753,[277] d. Richfield Springs, N.Y., 22 Dec.

[265] Lyman Coleman, *Genealogy of the Lyman Family in Great Britain and America* (Albany, N.Y.: J. Munsell, 1872), 88.

[266] 1800 U.S. Census, Lebanon, Grafton Co., N.H., p. 692 (Deborah Sprague household).

[267] New Hampshire Marriage Records, 1637–1977, image online at <www.FamilySearch.org>.

[268] Warren Vincent Sprague, *Sprague Families in America* (Rutland, Vt.; Tuttle Co., Printers, 1913), 28, 43.

[269] Lebanon, Conn., Deeds, 12:360.

[270] Sprague, *Sprague Families*, 43, citing Woodsville, N.H., probate records.

[271] Sprague, *Sprague Families*, 43, 61.

[272] New Hampshire Marriage Records, 1637–1977, image online at <www.FamilySearch.org>.

[273] New Hampshire Marriage Records, 1637–1977, image online at <www.FamilySearch.org>.

[274] 1800 U.S. Census, Lebanon, Grafton Co., N.H., p. 690.

[275] Frederic W. Bailey, *Early Connecticut Marriages as Found on Ancient Church Records Prior to 1800*, 7 vols. (New Haven: Bureau of American Ancestry, 1896–1906), 7:74, misprinting his surname as *Gay*.

[276] Donald Lines Jacobus, ed., *The Pardee Genealogy* (New Haven: New Haven Colony Historical Soc., 1927), 187. Jacobus was unaware of Tamar's family name.

[277] Barbour Collection, citing Sharon LR3:413.

1832, bur. Wiltwyck Cemetery, Kingston, Ulster Co., N.Y.,[278] son of Jehiel and Ann (Clark) Pardee of Sharon. Elijah and Tamar acknowledged a deed at Sharon in Aug. 1779.[279]

Children of Elijah and Tamar[5] (Harris) Pardee, b. at Sharon:[280]

1 *Erastus Pardee*, d. before 1850; m. Deborah Hanchett, b. Conn. 28 July 1782, d. Marshall, Mich., 12 Dec. 1865, dau. of Sylvanus and Sarah (Stoddard) Hanchett. Eight children.[281] In 1850, Deborah Pardee, age 68, b. Conn., was residing with her son Erastus Pardee, a 30-year-old tailor in St. Joseph Co., Mich.[282]

2 *David Pardee*, b. 1777, d. in Ohio 1848; married and had a daughter.

3 *Miranda Pardee*, b. 1784, d. Amenia, N.Y., 23 March 1825; m. Elijah H. Williams.

4 *Irwin Pardee*, b. 11 Sept. 1786, b. 11 Sept. 1786, d. Kingston, N.Y., 17 Dec. 1850; m. (1) Amenia, N.Y., 31 Oct. 1812 Emily Hamlin, b. Sharon 19 March 1790, d. Richfield Springs, N.Y., 29 Aug. 1837, dau. of Darling and Elizabeth (Doty) Hamlin of Sharon, Conn., and Afton, N.Y., (2) Ann (Roggen) Holmes, b. 5 July 1782, d. 15 March 1857, dau. of Petrus and Anna (Masten) Roggen and widow of ____ Holmes. Irwin served as a member of the New York Assembly from Ulster Co. in 1845. Three children.[283]

5 *Almira Pardee*, b. 1789, d. 20 June 1847; m. Lewis Lockwood.

6 *Julia Pardee*, d. young.

iv NATHANIEL HARRIS, "eldest son," a "minor" in Oct. 1765, d. "lately" without issue before 21 Aug. 1778, when the court ordered distribution of his estate to his sisters and brother. He is said to have been "shot down" at the side of his brother Walter in the Revolutionary War.[284]

23 v WALTER HARRIS, "youngest son," b. Lebanon, Conn., 8 June 1761;[285] m. (1) JEMIMA FISHER, (2) ELIZABETH (EVANS) CLEVELAND, (3) JANE (AIKEN) AIKEN.

16 HOSEA[4] HARRIS (*Thomas[3], Walter[2] John[1]*), born in Wethersfield on 11 February 1736, died 11 April 1792, age 56.[286] He married in Wethersfield 11 December 1760 **EUNICE (BOARDMAN) KING**, born there on 11 November 1733, who died on 2 April 1813, aged 80, daughter of Joseph and Mary

[278] Gravestone photo online at <www.findagrave.com>, accessed Aug. 2012.
[279] Lebanon, Conn., Deeds, 12:448.
[280] Jacobus, *Pardee Genealogy*, 187.
[281] Jacobus, *Pardee Genealogy*, 263.
[282] 1850 U.S. Census, Nottawa Twp., St. Joseph Co., Mich., p. 366.
[283] Jacobus, *Pardee Genealogy*, 263-64.
[284] Edmund J. and Horace G. Cleveland, *The Genealogy of the Cleveland and Cleaveland Families*, 3 vols. (Hartford: Case, Lockwood & Brainard Co., 1899), 1:355.
[285] *Cleveland and Cleaveland Families*, 1:355.
[286] Stiles, *Ancient Wethersfield*, 2:413, citing Wethersfield church record.

(Belden) Boardman of Wethersfield, and widow of David King of Sandisfield, Massachusetts, who died in 1759.[287]

Children of Hosea[4] and Eunice (Boardman) (King) Harris:[288]

    i   MEHITABLE[5] HARRIS, b. 11 June 1761, d. 1 Feb. 1819, age 58;[289] m. THOMAS BELDEN of Hartford, b. 7 July 1761, d. 19 Nov. 1841, son of Joseph and Lois (Curtis) Belden of Wethersfield. Thomas's father, Joseph Belden, graduate of Yale and commander of the sloop *Betsy*, d. soon after Thomas's birth (inventory dated Dec. 1762).[290]

        Children of Thomas and Mehitable[5] (Harris) Belden:[291]

           1 *Elizabeth Belden*, b. ca. 1782; m. Hartford 7 Sept. 1806 Isaac Perkins, Esq.[292]

           2 *Joseph Belden*, b. ca. 1784, d. Hartford 29 Oct. 1817, age 33, consumption.[293]

           3 *Infant Belden*, d. 6 March 1790, bur. Center Church Cemetery, Hartford.

           4 *Thomas Belden Jr.*, living Hartford 1830, age 30-39:[294] m. Simsbury, Conn., 5 April 1821 Marianna Phelps,[295] b. there 10 March 1795, d. Hartford as his widow in May 1863, dau. of George R. and Charlotte (Griswold) Phelps.[296]

           5 *Infant Belden*, d. 15 April 1800, bur. Center Church Cemetery.

   ii EUNICE HARRIS, b. 29 June 1763, d. 5 April 1841, age 77, bur. Wethersfield Village Cemetery;[297] m. Capt. MOSES MONTAGUE, b 22 Nov. 1763, d. 15 Aug. 1804 in his 41st year, bur. same cemetery, son of Richard and Olive (Nott) Montague.[298] Moses "was a captain of a sailing vessel and was taken by the French, carried to France, and was absent a long time from his family."[299]

        Children of Capt. Moses and Eunice[5] (Harris) Montague:[300]

---

[287] Charlotte Goldwaithe, *Boardman Genealogy, 1525–1895* (Hartford: Case, Lockwood & Brainard Co., 1895), 263.

[288] Stiles, *Ancient Wethersfield*, 2:413, citing Wethersfield church record.

[289] Edwin Pond Parker, *History of the Second Church of Christ in Hartford* (Hartford: Belknap & Warfield, 1892), 399 ("Mehitabel, wife of Thomas Belden, Chronic.")

[290] Franklin Bowditch Dexter, *Biographical Sketches of the Graduates of Yale College, Vol. II, May 1745–May 1763* (New York: Henry Holt and Co., 1896), 248.

[291] Lucius Barnes Barbour, *Families of Early Hartford* (Baltimore: Genealogical Pub. Co., 1982), 48.

[292] Parker, *History of the Second Church*, 364.

[293] Parker, *History of the Second Church*, 398.

[294] 1830 U.S. Census, Hartford, Hartford Co., Conn., p. 56.

[295] Barbour Collection, citing Simsbury TM4:492.

[296] Oliver Seymour Phelps and Andrew T. Servin, *The Phelps Family of America and Their English Ancestors*, 2 vols. (Pittsfield, Mass.: Eagle Publishing Co., 1899), 352, 620.

[297] Gravestone photo online at <www.findagrave.com>, accessed Aug. 2012.

[298] Stiles, *Ancient Wethersfield*, 2:509-10.

[299] George W. Montague, *History and Genealogy of the Montague Family of America* (Amherst, Mass.: Press of J. E. Williams, 1886), 106-7.

[300] *Montague Family*, 107; Stiles, *Ancient Wethersfield*, 2:510.

1 *William Montague*, b. 12 April 1787.

2 *Gurdon Harris Montague*, b. 24 April 1789; m. 5 May 1812 Martha Robbins.

3 *Richard Montague*, b. 13 April 1791, d. Brooklyn, N.Y., 13 June 1822, age 29, unmarried.

4 *Julia Ann Montague*, b. 10 Sept. 1793; m. 23 Dec. 1813 William Bradley of Hartford.

5 *Moses Montague*, b. 28 March 1796, d. Louisville, Ky., 31 Oct. 1821, unmarried.

6 *Eunice Montague*, b. 29 April 1798, d. 3 April 1846; m. 11 May 1820 Horace Welles.

7 *Huldah Montague*, bp. 4 Nov. 1798.

8 *Noble Montague*, bp. 9 April 1801.

9 *Noble Montague* (again), b. 29 Dec. 180[1], d. 9 Aug. 1838, age 37; m. 23 Oct. 1827 Julia Ann Robbins, b. ca. 1803, d. 27 Feb. 1852, age 49.

iii   MARY HARRIS, b. 10 Sept. 1765; m. THOMAS WELLES 2nd.

iv   HOSEA HARRIS, b. 18 Nov. 1768, d. W.I. in Feb. 1794, age 23 [*sic*].

24   v   JOHN HARRIS, b. 13 July 1770; m. MARTHA RUSSELL.

vi   ANNA HARRIS, b. ca. 1772, bp. 4 Sept. 1774, d. 11 Oct. 1831, age 59, bur. Leeds Graveyard, Darien, Conn.;[301] m. Stamford, Conn., 17 May 1793 CARY LEEDS Jr.[302] of Stamford, ca. 1771, d. 12 Feb. 1841, bur. same cemetery.

Children of Cary Jr. and Anna[5] (Harris) Leeds, recorded Stamford:[303]

1 *Joseph Harris Leeds*, b. 4 March 1799, d. 6 May 1872, age 73y; m. Mary Elizabeth Weed, b. 22 May 1803, d. Stamford 13 Sept. 1867, both bur. Leeds Graveyard, dau. John and Hannah (Knapp) Weed.

2 *Lucy Leeds*, b. 4 April 1801.

3 *Gideon Leeds*, b. 29 May 1803.

4 *Lavina Leeds*, b. 1811, d. April 1863, bur. Leeds Graveyard.

25   vii   JOSEPH HARRIS, b. 15 Feb. 1774; m. ELIZABETH HANMER

viii   LUCY HARRIS.

17 THOMAS[4] HARRIS (*Thomas[3], Walter[2], John[1]*), born in Wethersfield on 7 May 1743,[304] died there 27 December 1774 from an injury received during a barn raising; married 26 July 1770 **ABIGAIL ROBBINS**,[305] born 29 April 1749, died 8 August 1796, daughter of Joshua and Mary (Welles) Robbins of Wethersfield.[306] She married second 25 or 27 March 1778, as his second wife, Dr. Josiah Hart, with whom she had three children.[307]

---

[301] Gravestone photo online at <www.findagrave.com>, accessed Aug. 2012.

[302] Barbour Collection, citing Stamford VR2:91.

[303] Barbour Collection, citing Stamford VR2:91.

[304] Barbour Collection, citing Wethersfield VR2:60a.

[305] Stiles, *Ancient Wethersfield*, 2:413, citing Wethersfield church record.

[306] Stiles, *Ancient Wethersfield*, 2:553.

[307] Stiles, *Ancient Wethersfield*, 2:413, 417-18.

Children of Thomas[4] and Abigail (Robbins) Harris, b. Wethersfield:[308]

26 i THOMAS[5] HARRIS, b. 8 Feb. 1771; m. SARAH CRANE.

   ii ABIGAIL HARRIS, b. 6 June 1773, d. 27 Jan. 1874, bur. Wethersfield Village Cemetery; m. (1) 25 Feb. 1793 JOSIAH GRISWOLD, b. ca. 1771, d. Wethersfield 16 Sept. 1802 in his 32nd year,[309] son of Daniel and Jerusha (Gibbs) Griswold,[310] (2) by 1813 Dr. SAMUEL BROADBENT, b. 29 March 1759, d. 2 April 1828, bur same cemetery.[311]

   Josiah Griswold was a sea captain and navigator. The distribution of his estate in 1809 mentions Abigail Broadbent, his late widow, Jerusha, Jacob, and Harris Griswold.[312] In 1870, Abigail Broadbent, age 97, was in the Wethersfield household of her daughter, Rowena Morgan, age 56.[313]

   Children of Josiah and Abigail[5] (Harris) Griswold:[314]

   1 *Jacob Griswold*, b. 26 Aug. 1794, d. 14 May 1854, age 59, bur. Wethersfield Village Cemetery; m. Elizabeth R. ____, b. ca. 1795, d. 29 Jan. 1888, age 93.[315]

   2 *Thomas Harris Griswold*, b. 30 Aug. 1796, d. 9 Jan. 1801.

   3 *Jerusha Griswold*, b. 8 Feb. 1799.

   4 *Harris Griswold*, b.20 Oct. 1801, d. 21 July 1852, age 52; m. Delia R. Blinn.[316]

   Child of Dr. Samuel and Abigail[5] (Harris) (Griswold) Broadbent, recorded Wethersfield:

   5 *Rowena Broadbent*, b. 13 Nov. 1813, d. 3 April 1897; m. Wethersfield 17 June 1832 Stephen Morgan,[317] b. 28 Feb. 1809, d. 17 Oct. 1865, both bur. Wethersfield Village Cemetery.[318]

   iii SARAH HARRIS, b. 26 April 1775, d. 22 Dec. 1850, bur. Center Cemetery, South Windsor, Conn.;[319] m. 5 Jan. 1800 CHESTER WOLCOTT of South Windsor,[320] b. 23 Jan. 1775, d. 25 March 1842, bur. same cemetery, son of Benjamin and Abigail (Pinney) Wolcott.[321]

[308] Stiles, *Ancient Wethersfield*, 2:414.

[309] Barbour Collection, citing Wethersfield VR2:177a (marriage and Josiah's death).

[310] Stiles, *Ancient Wethersfield*, 2:400.

[311] Stiles, *Ancient Wethersfield*, 2:135; gravestone photo online at <www.findagrave.com>, accessed Aug. 2012.

[312] Glenn E. Griswold, *The Griswold Family: England—America*, 4 vols. (Cleveland: Griswold Family Assn., 1935), 2:234.

[313] 1870 U.S. Census, Wethersfield, Newington P.O., Hartford Co., Conn., p. 24.

[314] Barbour Collection, citing Wethersfield VR2:177a.

[315] Gravestone photos online at <www.findagrave.com>, accessed Aug. 2012.

[316] Gravestone photo online at <www.findagrave.com>, accessed Aug. 2012.

[317] Barbour Collection, citing Wethersfield VR3:21 (birth and marriage).

[318] Gravestone photos online at <www.findagrave.com>, accessed Aug. 2012.

[319] Gravestone photo online at <www.findagrave.com>, accessed Aug. 2012.

[320] Stiles, *Ancient Wethersfield*, 2:414.

[321] Henry R. Stiles, *History and Genealogies of Ancient Windsor, Connecticut*, 2 vols. (Hartford: Case, Lockwood & Brainard Co., 1892), 2:829.

Children of Chester and Sarah[5] (Harris) Wolcott:[322]

1 *Harris Hart Wolcott*, b. 27 Oct. 1800; m. 1825 Eliza Loring, dau. of David Loring of Boston, Mass. They were in New York City in 1849.

2 *John Wolcott*, b. 8 Oct. 1802, d. 10 Oct. 1802.

3 *Ralph Hart Wolcott*, b. 3 Feb. 1804, d. 19 Jan. 1834.

4 *Henry Wolcott*, b. 20 Oct. 1806, d. 26 Dec. 1831.

5 *Julia Ann Wolcott*, b. 25 April 1809; m 13 March 1833 Warren Skinner of Vernon.

6 *Truman Wells Wolcott*, b. 8 May 1812; m. 14 Sept. 1842 Mary M. Studley, dau. of Walter Studley of Hartford, Conn. They were in Hartford in 1849.

7 *Cynthia Newbury Wolcott*, b. 10 July 1814; m. 4 April 1838 Warren Skinner of Vernon.

8 *John Nelson Wolcott*, b. 15 April 1817; m. 29 Nov. 1843 Sarah Kelsey, dau. of Ezra Kelsey of Haddam, Conn. They lived in South Windsor, Conn.

9 *Mary Robbins Wolcott*, b. 23 Oct. 1819.

18 DANIEL[4] HARRIS (*Daniel[3], Walter[2], John[1]*), born in Wethersfield on 23 December 1741,[323] was living in Cornwall, Connecticut, on 8 December 1798, when he and his wife Submit sold their property there.[324] He married at Canaan, Connecticut, on 23 February 1764 **SUBMIT JOHNSON**,[325] baptized in Middletown (Cromwell), Connecticut, on 21 February 1741/2,[326] daughter of Isaac and Thankful (Cowles) Johnson of Canaan.[327]

Daniel served from Goshen, Connecticut, in the 1759 and 1762 campaigns of the French and Indian War,[328] and in the Revolutionary War from Canaan in 1776.[329] He had settled in Canaan on property that his wife Submit received in 1761 from her brother Isaac Johnson's estate.[330] They lived there until 5 March 1794, when they sold their property and moved over the town line into Cornwall.[331]

---

[322] Chandler Wolcott, *Wolcott Genealogy: The Family of Henry Wolcott* (Rochester, N.Y.: Genesee Press, 1912), 267-68, 241-42.

[323] Barbour Collection, citing Wethersfield VR2:67a.

[324] Cornwall, Conn., Deeds, 7:162.

[325] Barbour Collection, citing Canaan VR:A4, Rev. Mr. Farrand presiding.

[326] Cromwell First Congregational Church Records, 1715–1809, MS, 1:15, 36.

[327] Calvin Duvall Cowles, *Genealogy of the Cowles Families in America*, 3 vols. (New Haven; Tuttle, Morehouse & Taylor Co., 1929), 1:42; Jennie Henderson Porter, *Hannah Johnson and Polly Palmer* (Kansas City: Lowell Press, 1930), 12.

[328] *Rolls of Connecticut Men in the French and Indian War, 1755–1762*, Coll. Conn., Hist. Soc., vols. 9-10 (Hartford, 1903, 1905), 10:160-62, 337-39.

[329] *History of Litchfield County,* 308.

[330] Canaan, Conn., Deeds, 2:194, 212.

[331] Canaan, Conn., Deeds, 5:114; Cornwall, Conn., Deeds, 6:531.

Children of Daniel[4] and Submit (Johnson) Harris, recorded at Canaan:[332]

    i LUCY[5] HARRIS, b. 16 April 1765, d. Saratoga Co., N.Y., 27 Feb. 1849 in her 84th year, bur. Hoesville Road Cemetery, Fulton Co., N.Y.[333] She m. JAMES LOWREY, b. Farmington, Conn., 30 March 1759,[334] d. Lorraine, Jefferson Co., N.Y., 18 July 1833, son of John and Elida (Scott) Lowrey.[335]

        Children of James and Lucy[5] (Harris) Lowrey (prob. others):

        1 *Hannah Lowrey*, b. Conn. 1786, d. Galway, Saratoga Co., N.Y., 16 Jan. 1877; m. Saratoga Co., N.Y., 1 Jan. 1809 Ichabod Seabury, son of Constant and Susannah (Gray) Seabury, b. Little Compton, R.I., 18 Nov. 1786, d. Galway 6 Sept. 1859.

        2 *Daniel Lowrey*, b. Galway 1788, d. Lorraine, Jefferson Co., N.Y., 1835; m. by 1810 Hannah/Anna Grinnell, b. Saybrook, Conn., 1793.

        3 *Esther Lowrey*, b. N.Y. ca. 1799, d. 21 March 1817 in her 19th year, bur. beside her mother.

        4 *James Lowrey*, b. Saratoga Co., N.Y., 14 April 1801, d. Boylston, Oswego Co., N.Y., 27 June 1873; m. 31 March 1828 Lydia Gardner, b. Mass. 1810, d. Boylston 1878.

    ii ANNE HARRIS, b. 21 Nov. 1766.

19 JEREMIAH[4] HARRIS (*Daniel[3], Walter[2], John[1]*), born in Wethersfield on 30 April 1743,[336] was living in Goshen, Connecticut, on 4 February 1777, when he sold all of his property there to Major (later General) John Sedgwick, his neighbor across the town line in Cornwall Hollow.[337] He married probably about 1764 (first child born about 1765) **ESTHER COWLES**, born at Canaan, Connecticut, on 30 September 1744,[338] eldest child of Joseph and Ruth (Woodruff) Cowles of Southington and Canaan.[339] No records of Jeremiah and Esther's deaths have been found. Jeremiah probably died between 1785 (conception of last known child) and before the 1790 U.S. census was taken in Canaan,[340] where some of his children—and probably Esther—can be accounted for in the household of his father-in-law, Joseph Cowles.[341]

[332] Barbour Collection, citing Canaan VR:A27.
[333] Gravestone photo online at <www.findagrave.com>, accessed Aug. 2012.
[334] Barbour Collection, citing Farmington LR11:585.
[335] "Willstaedt Simpson Families," Rootsweb WorldConnect Project, accessed Nov. 2006.
[336] Barbour Collection, citing Wethersfield VR2:67a.
[337] Goshen, Conn., Deeds, 6:144.
[338] Barbour Collection, citing Canaan LR1:425.
[339] Cowles, *Genealogy of the Cowles Families*, 1:61-62.
[340] 1790 U.S. Census, Litchfield Co., Conn., p. 356.
[341] For discussion of this point, see Gale Ion Harris and Margaret Harris Stover, "The Second Daniel Harris of Goshen, Connecticut, and His Descendants in New York and Other States," *New York Genealogical and Biographical Record*, 122 (1991):16n4.

At age 19, Jeremiah served from Goshen with his brother Daniel in the 1762 campaign of the French and Indian War.[342] He built a house in Goshen before September 1772 on property that his father had given him that January, located near the Goshen-Cornwall town line and just north of his father's home.[343] In 1772 and 1774, Jeremiah sold parts of this land to his brother-in-law Samuel Oviatt Jr. and bought the remaining part of his father's property.[344]

Children of Jeremiah[4] and Esther (Cowles) Harris:[345]

i EUNICE[5] HARRIS, b. ca. 1765, d. 6 July 1843, age 78, bur. Cowles Cemetery, Smithville, Chenango Co., N.Y.[346] She m. Canaan, Conn., 6 Jan. 1785 JEREDIAH BROWN JR.,[347] b. there 26 Oct. 1764,[348] d. 19 March 1813 and bur. same cemetery, son of Jerediah and Phebe (Way) Brown of Canaan, neighbors of Eunice's grandfather Joseph Cowles.[349]

Jerediah Brown, Elisha and Woodruff Harris, and their cousins Bela and Sylvester Cowles were among a group of settlers in Smithville "as early as 1808."[350] Jedediah [*sic*] Brown had a household of seven persons at Greene, N.Y., in 1810.[351] Letters of administration on Jerediah Brown's estate were issued to Leonard Livermore in April 1813.[352]

Children of Jerediah and Eunice[5] (Harris) Brown, 1–7 recorded Canaan:[353]

1 *Dorothy Brown*, b. 17 Nov. 1785, d. 6 April 1790.
2 *Hannah Brown*, b. 11 May 1787.
3 *Mary Brown*, b. 12 March 1789.
4 *Emma Brown*, b. 18 Aug. 1791.
5 *Chauncey Brown*, b. 26 June 1794, d. 10 Jan. 1854, age 59, bur. Cowles Cemetery, Smithville Center, Chenango Co., N.Y.;[354] m. Emma Cowles, b. Canaan, Conn., 7 Dec. 1798, d. 24 Sept. 1851,

---

[342] *Connecticut Men in the French and Indian War*, 10:337-39.

[343] Goshen, Conn., Deeds, 5:126, 6:108.

[344] Goshen, Conn., Deeds, 5:170, 172, 6:14, 15.

[345] For identification of these children, see discussion in Harris and Stover, "Second Daniel Harris of Goshen," 122 (1991):16-17.

[346] "Cemetery Records of Greene, N.Y., and Vicinity," Greene Public Library, Greene, N.Y. Cowles Cemetery takes its name from Timothy Cowles (1746–1831), Eunice's uncle and Revolutionary War veteran who is buried there. The cemetery is located near the Smithville-Greene town line and adjacent to property possessed by Eunice's brothers Elisha and Joseph Harris between 1811 and 1817.

[347] Barbour Collection, citing Canaan VR:A46.

[348] Barbour Collection, citing Canaan VR:A5.

[349] Harris and Stover, "Second Daniel Harris of Goshen," 122 (1991):17.

[350] James H. Smith, *History of Chenango and Madison Counties, New York* (Syracuse: D. Mason & Co, 1880), 298.

[351] 1810 U.S. Census, Greene, Chenango Co., N.Y., p. 340.

[352] Chenango Co., N.Y., Letters of Administration, 1811–1813, Norwich, N.Y.

[353] Barbour Collection, citing Canaan VR:A46.

[354] Gravestone photo online at <www.findagrave.com>, accessed Aug. 2012.

bur. same cemetery, dau. of Bela and Aurelia (Trall) Cowles.[355]
They were living in Greene, N.Y., in 1850; he was a farmer.[356]

6 *Amanda Brown*, b. 25 Aug. 1797.

7 *Phebe Brown*, b. 26 Nov. 1800.

8 perhaps a boy b. 1800-1810, accounted for in the Brown household at Greene, N.Y., in 1810.

ii REBECCA HARRIS, b. ca. 1771, d. 3 May 1798, age 27, bur. Under Mountain Cemetery, Canaan, Conn.[357] She m. at Canaan 13 Oct. 1791 LEMUEL DEMING, b. there 17 Sept. 1751,[358] d. there 28 Oct. 1810, son of Hezekiah and Hannah (Warren) Deming. Lemuel m. (2) 16 June 1805 Jerusha Abel.[359]

Children of Lemuel and Rebecca⁵ (Harris) Deming, born Canaan:[360]

1 *Hannah Deming*, b. 3 May 1793, d. 4 Feb. 1883; m. 2 Feb. 1820 Darius Howe.

2 *Rhoda Deming*, b. 28 April 1795; m. 1 Dec. 1814 Jabez Howe.

3 *Lovisa Deming*, b. 6 Sept. 1796, d. 6 July 1880; m. 7 May 1815 John Lowrey.

4 *Joel Harris Deming*, b. 15 March 1798, d. Canaan 16 May 1877; m. there 11 Dec. 1821 Hepsibah Benedict, b. 22 April 1799, d. 7 Aug. 1895, dau. of Francis Knapp and Phebe (Northrop) Benedict.[361]

27 iii ELISHA HARRIS, b. Goshen, Conn., Aug. 1773; m. (1) SUSAN MALLORY, (2) DOROTHEA (SMITH) PURPLE.

28 iv JOSEPH HARRIS, b. Conn. say 1775; m. JULIA TOWSLEY.

v ALANSON HARRIS, b. say 1780, may have been the man of that name, aged 26-44, with a household of three persons in Warsaw, Genesee Co., N.Y., in 1820.[362] He had been with his brothers earlier in Chenango Co., N.Y., where he had judgments entered against him in Oct. 1806 and in Feb. 1813.[363] He m. prob. ca. 1805 ____ ____, as suggested by the 1810 census in Smithville, Chenango Co., showing that his household then consisted of a male age 26-44 [Alanson], a female 16-25 [unknown wife], and two boys and a girl under 10.[364] In 1807, he was appointed as ensign in Lt. Col. Thomas Lyon's Chenango Co. militia regiment. Two years later, he was lieutenant, and in 1810 he was appointed captain of "a new Company." In 1812, as vice captain of Levi Benedict's company, he "removed out of beat."[365]

In Sept. 1814, Alanson and [his brother] Woodruff Harris had "summons served on them" by Warren Gray, a Justice of the Peace in Greene, Che-

[355] Cowles, *Genealogy of the Cowles Families*, 1:245, 517.
[356] 1850 U.S. Census, Greene, Chenango Co., N.Y., p. 350.
[357] Hale Collection, Connecticut Cemetery Inscriptions, vol. 8.
[358] Barbour Collection, citing Canaan LR2:232.
[359] *Descendants of John Deming*, 38, 82, incorrectly stating that Rebecca was daughter of a *Joel* Harris.
[360] *Descendants of John Deming*, 82.
[361] *Descendants of John Deming*, 154.
[362] 1820 U.S. Census, Warsaw, Genesee Co., N.Y., p. 310.
[363] Chenango Co., N.Y., Judgment Docket, 1798–1821, Norwich, N.Y.
[364] 1810 U.S. Census, Smithville, Chenango Co., N.Y., p. 345.
[365] *Military Minutes of the Council of Appointment of the State of New York, 1782–1867*, 4 vols. (Albany: J. B. Lyon, state printer, 1901–02), 1:889, 2:1037, 1156, 1291.

nango Co.[366] Although he had an earmark recorded for him in Smithville in 1816, the same earmark recorded to his brother Joseph in 1804,[367] Alanson may by that time have moved to Scipio, Cayuga Co., where he was residing in July 1816 when a notice was given to his creditors to "show cause why an assignment of his estate should not be made, and he be discharged pursuant to the act in such case made and provided."[368]

29   vi   WOODRUFF HARRIS, b. Goshen, Conn., 10 April 1786; m. (1) FRANCIS/FANNY PURPLE, (2) PHEBE (ORTON) CULVER.

20 JOHN[4] HARRIS (*Daniel[3]*, *Walter[2]*, *John[1]*), born in Wethersfield on 23 March 1748/9, died probably in Salisbury, Connecticut, between the 1810 census date,[369] and 12 July 1814 when Olive Harris, his widow, released her dower interest in a deed for property in Egremont, Massachusetts.[370] He married first, probably about the time that he received a gift of property in Goshen, Connecticut, from his father in 1772, **PHEBE HILL**, who was living in 1794, daughter of Jonathan and Mary (___) Hill of Waterbury and Goshen. On 29 July 1794, as heirs of Jonathan Hill "late of Goshen, deceased," John and Phebe Harris "of Hillsdale, Columbia County, New York, conveyed to Mary Hill of Goshen their claim to her dower rights and their separate interest in land on the west side of Goshen. John's nephew Elisha Harris Deming witnessed. John and Phebe acknowledged that deed in Paris, Herkimer (now Oneida) County, New York, on 18 August 1794, but there is no evidence that they actually established a residence there.[371] John married second, before 18 August 1803, **OLIVE ____**, as shown below.

In January 1801, while he was a blacksmith in Hillsdale, New York, John bought several parcels of land in adjoining Egremont, Massachusetts. He moved into Egremont before 18 August 1803, when he and his wife Olive sold 120 acres there to Isaac Beach of Kent, Connecticut.[372] In January 1807, John Harris and John Harris Jr. of Egremont jointly conveyed two tracts there to Octavius Joyner and Elijah King. Appended to the deed is a release of dower and discharge dated 12 July 1814, signed by Olive Harris,

---

[366] Mildred English Cochrane, *From Raft to Railroad, A History of Greene, Chenango County, New York, 1792–1867* (Ithaca, N.Y.: Cayuga Press, 1967), 93.

[367] Smithville Town Minute Book, extracts provided by Philip M. Rogers, Smithville Town Clerk, Greene, N.Y., 1983, pp. 4, 9, 25, 33, 48.

[368] *The Albany Argus*, 23 July 1816, p. 4.

[369] 1810 U.S. Census, Salisbury, Litchfield Co., Conn., p. 200.

[370] Berkshire Co., Mass., Deeds, Southern District, 43:443.

[371] Goshen, Conn., Deeds, 9:432. Mary Hill sold her interest in this property to her son Lemuel Hill of Alford, Mass., on 15 Dec. 1795 (ibid., 10:450).

[372] Berkshire Co., Mass., Deeds, Southern District, 38:839, 841, 40:485.

"widow and relict of . . . John Harris," and by "Aesenath Harris wife of . . . John Harris Junr." Milo Harris, one of John's younger sons, witnessed.[373]

As discussed elsewhere, John can be traced by deeds and census records from Goshen to Salisbury in 1774 (when he sold his Goshen land to his brother-in-law Samuel Oviatt Jr.), to Hillsdale, New York, about 1793, to Paris, Oneida County, New York, by August 1794 and back to Salisbury by May 1799, to Hillsdale again by the 1800 census date, to the adjoining town of Egremont, Massachusetts, by August 1803, and finally back to Salisbury between January 1807 and the 1810 census date.[374]

Children of John[4] and Phebe (Hill) Harris:[375]

30   i   JOHN[5] HARRIS, b. say 1773; m. AESENETH WRIGHT.
31   ii   ELISHA HARRIS, b. Salisbury, Conn., ca. 1775; m. (1) MARY SARDAM, (2) JANE BOGHROUGH/JACOBS.
     iii (prob.) POLLY HARRIS, received in the church in Salisbury 1 Sept. 1816, presumably the Polly whose death on 17 Jan. 1833 was recorded there.[376]
32   iv   DANIEL HARRIS, b. Salisbury ca. 1787; m. (1) JERUSHA JONES, (2) LAURA BOWEN.
33   v   MYLO HARRIS, b. Salisbury, Conn., ca. 1789; m. (1) ABIGAIL (COMEGIN) JONES, (2) LOIS R. (DEMORANVILLE) DUNBAR.
34   vii LUTHER HARRIS, b. Conn. ca. 1795; m. REBECCA____.

21 Capt. THOMAS[4] HARRIS (*Thomas[3-2]*, *John[1]*), born about November 1710, died on 27 April 1783, age 72y 5m, and buried in Presbyterian Churchyard, Fairfield Township, Cumberland County, New Jersey. He married first **SARAH DAYTON**, born about 1713, who died on 2 April 1774 in her 62nd year, daughter of Ephraim and [Hannah (Sayre)?] Dayton of Cohansey, New Jersey, and secondly, as her third husband, **SUSANNA (___) (ELMER) WESTCOTT**, born about March 1720, who died 14 November 1784, age 64y 8m,[377] widow of Rev. Daniel Elmer and David Westcott. She survived Thomas Harris and is buried with Daniel Elmer.[378]

Thomas was assessor for the south side of Cohansey in 1733 and surrogate in 1770. In 1750 he had been sent to England on behalf of the people of Fairfield, New Jersey, to secure a better title to land in the south part of the township, but was not successful. He served as a surgeon in rank of captain

---

[373] Berkshire Co., Mass., Deeds, Southern District, 43:443.
[374] Harris and Stover, "Second Daniel Harris of Goshen," 122 (1991):96-97.
[375] These children are identified in Harris and Stover, "Second Daniel Harris of Goshen," 122 (1991): 98, where it is suggested that they possibly had three additional girls and a boy unidentified.
[376] Salisbury Congregational Church Records, 1:77, 2:199.
[377] Inscription, Old Cohansey Cemetery.
[378] Walter Lee Sheppard, Jr., "The Daytons of South Jersey," TAG 22 (1946):135-37.

with New Jersey troops in the Revolutionary War.[379] He was for many years an Elder in the Church in Fairfield.[380]

The will of Thomas Harris of Fairfield Township, dated 6 February 1781 and proved 17 March 1784, names wife Susannah, eldest son Ephraim Harris ("the plantation where he lives"), grandson Isaac Harris ("the plantation whereon his father lived and died, he paying to his 4 sisters Ruth, Sarah, Abigail, and Bathsheba" £5 each), son James Harris ("the plantation I live on which was left to me by my father Thomas Harris"), son Amariah Harris ("the plantation where he lives"), daughter Judith Harris (£30). He gave personal estate to "five daughters now living": Ruth Bower, Sarah Clark, Abigail Stratton, Barsheba Brooks and Judith Harris; sons Ephraim, James, and Amariah Harris executors.[381]

Children of Thomas[4] and Sarah (Dayton) Harris:[382]

     i   THOMAS[5] HARRIS, b. ca. 1730, d. 6 Feb. 1759, age 29y;[383] m. by 1754 VIO-LETTA LORANCE, b. ca. 1735, dau. of Nathan Lorance. She d. 9 Nov. 1760, age 25, after marrying (2) Thomas Ogden (see no. 10 iv). The inventory of the personal estate of Thomas Harris Jr. late of Fairfield Twp., made 6 March 1759, was appraised at £345 19s. 1d.[384]

          Children of Thomas[5] and Violetta (Lawrence) Harris:

             1 *Thomas[6] Harris*, b. ca. 1754, d. 15 Feb. 1759, age 5.

             2 *Violetta Harris*, b. ca. 1756, d. 5 Feb. 1759, age 3.

    ii EPHRAIM HARRIS, b. Fairfield Twp., Cumberland Co., 14 June 1732, d. 2 Nov. 1794, in his 63rd year, "statesman and approved magistrate";[385] m. (1) 30 Jan. 1755 JANE PIERSON, b. 21 Oct. 1731, who d. 27 March 1778, and (2) 9 Aug. 1779[386] REZINE (LOVELL) ANDERSON "of Maidenhead, Hunterdon Co.," who d. Bordentown, N.J., 3 Oct. 1803,[387] dau. of John and Patience (Townsend) Lovell of Bordentown and widow of Ephraim Anderson of Trenton, N.J. Ephraim Harris was appointed as a justice of the peace in Cumberland Co. in 1772, a justice of the court of pleas in 1774, served as representative in the council of the state meeting at Trenton in 1778 and as

---

[379] Craig, *Cumberland County Genealogical Data*, 195.

[380] Walter Lee Sheppard Jr. and Charles M. Jones, "Memoir of a Revolutionary Soldier," VHM 41 (1956):302-8, 317-19, 362-67, at 319.

[381] *New Jersey Archives*, 35:179.

[382] Sheppard and Cook, "Harris of Cumberland County," PGM 17 (1949):82.

[383] Inscription, Old Cohansey Cemetery.

[384] *New Jersey Archives*, 32:146.

[385] Inscription, Presbyterian Churchyard, Fairfield.

[386] Sheppard and Jones "Memoir," VHM 41 (1956):318.

[387] Walter L. Sheppard, Jr., "Noble Ancestry of the Harris Family of Cumberland County," VHM 35 (1951):88-90, with transcription of Ephraim Harris Bible at 89-90.

speaker pro tempore of the house of assembly; he was one of the leaders in the adoption of the state constitution.[388]

Children of Ephraim[5] and Jane (Pierson) Harris:[389]

1 *Ephraim[6] Harris Jr.*, b. 13 Feb. 1756, d. 19 Feb. 1805; m. ca. 1776 Sarah [Ireton?].

2 *Thomas Harris*, b. 9 Sept. 1759, d. 3 March 1825; m. 16 July 1778 Elizabeth Lawrence, who d. 5 May 1844. Both are bur. in the churchyard of the "Old Stone Church" (Presbyterian) at Fairton.[390] Thomas, who served during the Revolutionary War, was the writer (about 1821–1825) of the memoirs of his family and service, edited by Walter Lee Sheppard Jr., F.A.S.G., and Charles M. Jones, cited several places in the present account.

3 *John Harris*, b. 11 Dec. 1761,[391] d. 2 Dec. 1805; m. his cousin Hannah Ogden, who d. 12 Nov. 1805.[392]

4 *Pierson Harris*, b. 18 April 1764, d. 4 April 1803, age 39y;[393] m. Judith Nixon, dau. of Jeremiah and Hannah (____) Nixon.

5 *Allen Harris*, b. 29 April 1766, d. 5 Feb. 1767, age 7m 9d.

6 *Jane Harris*, b. 22 Feb. 1768, d. 16 July 1803; m. (1) Henry Westcott, son of Ebenezer Westcott, (2) Isaac Sheppard.[394]

7 *Hannah Harris*, b. 3 April 1771, d. 21 Aug. 1819; m. (1) Allen Whitacar, (2) Thomas Roork.[395]

iii RUTH HARRIS, b. 1734, d. 17 March 1782; m. JOHN BOWER. "They lived together about 30 years in Sayres Neck, they had no children."[396]

iv SARAH HARRIS, b. ca. 1738, d. 6 June 1802 in her 65th year; m. (1) "in youth" DAVID OGDEN, b. ca. 1731, d. Fairfield Twp. 4 April 1767, son of John Ogden Esq., (2) (license 20 June 1769) JAMES CLARK, b. ca. 1735, d. 3 June 1789 in his 55th year, son of Stephen Clark.

Children of David and Sarah[5] (Harris) Ogden:[397]

1 *Norton Ogden*, "his mother changed his name to David and he d. at age 17 in service in the Revolutionary War.

2 *Mary Ogden*; m. Silas Whitacar and d. without children.

3 *Sarah Ogden*; m. Joseph Ogden, son of Joseph and Abigail (____) Ogden.

4 *Hannah Ogden*, d. 12 Nov. 1805; m. John Harris, "her cousin, my brother," b. 11 Dec. 1761,[398] d. 2 Dec. 1805.

[388] Sheppard and Cook, "Harris of Cumberland County," PGM 17 (1949):86-87.
[389] Sheppard and Jones "Memoir," VHM 41 (1956):362-63; Bible record, in Sheppard, "Harris Family of Cumberland County," VHM 35 (1951):89-90.
[390] Sheppard and Jones "Memoir," VHM 41 (1956):366.
[391] Craig, *Cumberland County Genealogical Data*, 195.
[392] Sheppard and Jones "Memoir," VHM 41 (1956):306.
[393] Inscription, Presbyterian Churchyard, Fairfield.
[394] Sheppard and Jones "Memoir," VHM 41 (1956):362.
[395] Sheppard and Jones "Memoir," VHM 41 (1956):363.
[396] Sheppard and Jones "Memoir," VHM 41 (1956):307.
[397] Sheppard and Jones "Memoir," VHM 41 (1956):305.
[398] Craig, *Cumberland County Genealogical Data*, 195.

Children of James and Sarah[5] (Harris) (Ogden) Clark:

  5 *James Clark*; m. 8 Oct. 1789 Sarah Dayton, dau. of Joseph and Freelove (____) Dayton.

  6 *David Clark*; m. Mary Potter, dau. of Mathew Potter, a blacksmith of Bridgeton.

  7 *Ruth Clark*; m. (1) Rev. Nathaniel Ogden, son of Joseph and Abigail (____) Ogden, (2) Rev. Abijah Davis of Deerfield.

  8 *Bathsheba Clark*; m. 6 Dec. 1797 Theophilus Parvin, "both died quite young."

v JAMES HARRIS, Esq., b. 7 May 1739 (calc.), d. intestate 29 Sept. 1803, age 64y 4m 22d.[399] He "lived with his father until about 40 years old [and] marryd nine months before his death" [26 Oct. 1802] ABIGAIL HUSTED, dau. of Samuel Husted. No issue.[400]

vi ABIGAIL HARRIS, b. ca. 1742, d. 18 Dec. 1785 in her 44th year; m. (1) DANIEL POWELL of Fairfield Twp., b. ca. 1735, d. 24 April 1772 in his 38th year "the morning of the great earthquake," (2) by 1774 LEVI STRATTON, b. ca. 1744, d. 16 Feb. 1792 in his 49th year. Levi m. (2) Elizabeth ____.

  Children of Daniel and Abigail[5] (Harris) Powell:[401]

    1 *Violetta Powell*, living 1772, d. young.

    2 *Abigail Powell*, living 1772.

  Children of Levi and Abigail[5] (Harris) Stratton:[402]

    3 *Levi Stratton*, d. "in his youth."

    4 *Daniel Powell Stratton*, who lived at Bridgeton.

    5 *Abigail Stratton*; m. Reuben Buck and "went westward."

vii ISAAC HARRIS, b. ca. 1745, d. 17 Oct. 1775, age 30; m. RUTH OGDEN, dau. of Joseph and Abigail (Pierson) Ogden of Fairfield Twp. Ruth m. (2) Daniel Lawrence, who d. 1792.

  Children of Isaac[5] and Ruth (Ogden) Harris:[403]

    1 *Isaac[6] Harris*, b. ca. 1767, d. 25 Dec. 1788, age 21y;[404] m. when "very young" Mary Bowen of Hopewell.

    2 *Ruth Harris*; m. (1) Jonathan Diament, son of Nathaniel "of Jones Island," who "drowned in the Delaware," and (2) Thomas Hampton of Pittsgrove.

    3 *Sarah Harris*; m. Dr. Henry Hampton of Pittsgrove, brother of her sister Ruth's 2nd husband.

    4 *Abigail Harris*; m. Daniel Burt of Cedarville.

    5 *Bathsheba Harris*; m. 3 Aug. 1797 Daniel Reed of Downes.

viii BATHSHEBA HARRIS, b. in Jan. 1747, d. 6 July 1814 in her 67th year [*sic*]; m. HENRY BROOKS of Jones Island, b. ca. 1739, d. 19 Sept. 1774. They lived at Jones Island.

---

[399] Inscription, Presbyterian Churchyard, Fairfield.

[400] Sheppard and Jones "Memoir," VHM 41 (1956):303.

[401] Sheppard and Cook, "Harris of Cumberland County," PGM 17 (1949):89.

[402] Sheppard and Jones "Memoir," VHM 41 (1956):307.

[403] Sheppard and Jones "Memoir," VHM 41 (1956):304.

[404] Inscription, Presbyterian Churchyard, Fairfield, "son of Isaac and Ruth."

Children of Henry and Bathsheba[5] (Harris) Brooks:[405]

1 *Henry Brooks*, b. 6 June 1765, d. 9 Oct. 1829; m. 5 June 1786 Amy Pierson, b. 14 March 1769, d. 4 May 1834. They lived on Jones Island.

2 *Josiah Brooks*; m. Mary Reed, dau. of Daniel Reed, and moved west.

3 *Harris Brooks*, b. 1733, d. 1813 "in the late war [War of 1812] with Great Britain and died in the service upon the frontiers near Canada."[406]

ix AMARIAH HARRIS, b. ca. 1750, d. 28 March 1793, age 43; m. (1) LYDIA MYARS who d. "soon," (2) MARY LAWRENCE, b. ca. April 1756, d. 22 March 1815, age 58y 11m, dau. of Jonathan and Abigail (Ogden) Lawrence. Mary m. (2) ____ McNight.[407] Amariah served as a Lieutenant of Cumberland Co. militia in the Revolutionary War.

Child of Amariah[5] and Lydia (Myars) Harris:[408]

1 *Dayten[6] Harris*, d. young.

Children of Amariah[5] and Mary (Lawrence) Harris:[409]

2 *Lydia Harris*; m. 16 Jan. 1798 Jonathan Sheppard, dau. of Jonadab [*sic*] Sheppard of Downs.

3 *James Harris*, b. March 1781, drowned in Delaware River 15 Dec. 1805 "on his way home from Philadelphia"; m. Sarah Diament, dau. of James and Theodosia (____) Diament. She m. (2) John Elmer, and (3) Robert Alderman.

4 *George Harris*, b. Dec. 1784, drowned 19 Nov. 1835; m. Hannah Nixon dau. of William and Sarah (____) Nixon.

5 *Mary Harris*; m. 27 Nov. 1805 Isaac Alderman of Pittsgrove, a tanner.

6 *Violetta Harris*, b. 28 Feb. 1796 (calc.), d. 19 Sept. 1818, age 22y 6m 22d "of consumption"; m. Ebenezer Westcott.

7 *Bathsheba Harris*; m. William D. Barrett of Downs.

x JUDITH HARRIS, b. ca. 1753, d. 21 Dec. 1805 in her 53rd year,[410] unm. Administration of her estate was set to her brother-in-law Henry Brooks.

22 PHILLIP[4] HARRIS (*Phillip[3], John[2-1]*) was born in Simsbury, Connect-icut, on 6 August 1721,[411] and died in New Hartford, Connecticut, between 14 February and 15 April 1755, the dates of his last deed and inventory.[412] He married by about 1752 (birth of first child) **RHODA —**, born about 1726, who died in West Simsbury (now Canton) soon before 13 November 1799,

---

[405] Sheppard and Cook, "Harris of Cumberland County," PGM 17 (1949):90.

[406] Sheppard and Jones "Memoir," VHM 41 (1956):307.

[407] Inscription, Presbyterian Churchyard, Fairfield.

[408] Sheppard and Jones "Memoir," VHM 41 (1956):304.

[409] Sheppard and Jones "Memoir," VHM 41 (1956):304-5.

[410] Inscription, Presbyterian Churchyard, Fairfield.

[411] Bates, *Simsbury Births, Marriages, and Deaths*, 152.

[412] New Hartford, Conn., Deeds, 1:178; Hartford District Probate Records, 17:152.

aged 73.[413] She was probably **RHODA ALFORD**, born in Simsbury on 28 December 1726,[414] daughter of Nathaniel and Experience (Holcomb) Alford/Alvord of Simsbury.[415] Rhoda married second in Simsbury on 13 October 1757,[416] as his second wife, Ezra Wilcox(son), son of Joseph and Abigail (Thrall) Wilcoxson, with whom she had children Giles, born about 1759, John, Hezekiah, Rhoda, and Zeruiah.[417]

While still single, Rhoda Alford, signing by mark, witnessed the will of Joseph Case in Simsbury on 17 February 1742/3.[418] The will of Nathaniel Alford of Simsbury, dated 9 September 1768 and proved on 6 June 1769, names son Nathaniel and five daughters (without surnames) Hannah, Rhoda, Susannah, Lydia (who had daughter Sarah Case), and Mary.[419]

On 28 December 1742, for "love and goodwill," Phillip Harris [Sr.] conveyed lands in Simsbury and in the adjacent town of New Hartford to "my son Phillip Harris Jr. of Simsbury."[420] Phillip Jr. bought adjoining parcels in November 1745 separated by the line dividing Simsbury and New Hartford, then another adjoining parcel in New Hartford from Jonathan Steel of Hartford in November 1747. As his last deed, Phillip Harris Jr. "of New Hartford" sold 20 acres of the latter tract to William Lurvey on 14 February 1755, with his father, Phillip Harris [Sr.], as a witness.[421] On 12 September 1770, Asher Hinman of Simsbury [son-in-law of Phillip Harris Jr.] purchased that property, then described as 20 acres bounded "east on land belonging to Phillip Harris's Heirs," from William Lurvey Jr. "of Kenderhook," Albany County, New York.[422]

---

[413] Hale Collection, Connecticut Newspaper Notices, 64:38, citing *Litchfield Weekly Monitor*, 13 Nov. 1799 (Mrs. Rhoda Wilcox, Widow, date of death not stated).

[414] Bates, *Simsbury Births, Marriages, and Deaths*, 142. A search for Rhoda births in Simsbury yields only one match, this Rhoda Alford b. 28 Dec. 1726. No marriage record is found for her, but her father's will shows that she was alive in 1768, surname not stated. Unsuccessful attempts have been made to learn the source for statements posted online that she m. ca. 1747 one Philip "Jarvis." This claim obviously suggests the existence of some unfound document that names her husband as a Philip whose surname "Jarvis" easily could be a misreading of "Harris" in the script of the period.

[415] Bates, *Simsbury Births, Marriages, and Deaths*, 151 (marriage of the parents, 3 July 1724).

[416] Bates, *Simsbury Births, Marriages, and Deaths*, 159.

[417] Reynold Webb Wilcox, *Wilcoxson-Wilcox, Webb, and Meigs Families* (New York: National Historical Society, 1938), 49; Frederick Humphrey, *The Humphreys Family in America*, 2 vols. (New York: Humphrey, 1883–86), 1:256.

[418] Manwaring, *Early Connecticut Probate Records*, 3:522.

[419] Hartford District Probate Records, 20:375-76. Nathaniel Alford d. 6 Feb. 1769 and Experience, his widow, d. 15 Dec. 1774 (Bates, *Simsbury Births, Marriages, and Deaths*, 213, 241). No probate was found for widow Experience Alford.

[420] Simsbury, Conn., Deeds, 7:41.

[421] New Hartford, Conn., Deeds, 1:70, 99, 178. Phillip Harris [Sr.] apparently signed his name as witness; he had witnessed at least one earlier deed by mark, P (Simsbury, Conn., Deeds, 6:158).

[422] New Hartford, Conn., Deeds, 2:109.

The inventory of the estate of Phillip Harris Jr., certified on 15 April 1755 by Joseph Mills and Ephraim Wilcocks and valued at £153 2*s.* 11*d.*, included livestock, a Bible, and 105 acres with a dwelling house and barn. Administration was granted on 10 June 1755 to Rhoda Harris, "widow of Philip Harris Jr. late of Symsbury." On 2 October 1758, "Rhoda Wilcocks *alias* Harris" exhibited her account.[423]

Sixteen months later, in March 1760, the Hartford Probate Court appointed Rhoda's husband, "Ezra Wilcocks of Symsbury," to be guardian to Elizabeth Harris, aged about 8 years, and Mary Harris, aged about 6 years, "children of Philip Harris of Symsbury deceased."[424] In February 1765, Jonah Case of Goshen, Connecticut, gave a quitclaim deed to Ezra Wilcocks as guardian to the children of Phillip Harris "late of New Hartford," and heirs to the estate "of Philip Harris the Elder late of Simsbury." The deed released a Simsbury mortgage given in 1742 by Jonah's father, Jonah Case, "since deceased," to Phillip Harris the Elder.[425]

On 2 March 1770, on motion of Asher Hinman "in right of his wife Mary ... Daughter to Phillip Harris Jun[r] of New Hartford Dec[ease]d," the probate court at Hartford ordered distribution of Phillip's estate "to Rhoda Wilcocks alias Harriss Relict of the s[ai]d Dec[ease]d [one third of personal and real property, and] to Mary Hinman and Elizabeth Harriss children of the s[ai]d Deceased to each an equal share."[426]

Children of Phillip[4] and Rhoda (Alford) Harris:

    i   ELIZABETH[5] HARRIS, b. ca. 1752 (age 8 in March 1760), living 1823;[427] m. Simsbury, 24 Nov. 1774, AMAZIAH HUMPHREY, b. there 28 Jan. 1754,[428] d. 26 Feb. 1822, aged 68y, and bur. as "Captain" Amaziah in Hop Meadow Cemetery, Simsbury, a son of Benajah and Caroline (Humphrey) Humphrey.[429] On 30 April 1771, Amaziah Humphrey, aged 16 [*sic*], "having neither parents nor guardian nor Master," chose Mr. Silvanus Humphrey of Simsbury as his guardian.[430] Amaziah was with Sgt. Joseph Goodwin's Company who arrived in N.Y. on 24 Aug. 1776 with the 18th Regiment of

[423] Hartford District Probate Records, 17:70, 152; 18:31.
[424] Hartford District Probate Records, 18:88.
[425] Hartford District Probate Records, 18:88.
[426] Hartford District Probate Records, 21:5.
[427] *Humphreys Family*, 1:184, citing Simsbury probate records.
[428] Bates, *Simsbury Births, Marriages, and Deaths*, 273 (Amaziah's birth and their marriage).
[429] *Humphreys Family*, 1:138-39, 184, giving details of the settlement of Amaziah's estate in 1822 and 1823. A more recent transcription of his gravestone inscription incorrectly states the year of his death as 1829 (Hale Collection, Connecticut Headstone Inscriptions, 44:2).
[430] Simsbury District Probate Records, 1:141.

Connecticut Militia.[431] On 17 Jan. 1778, Amaziah and Elizabeth Humphrey of Simsbury conveyed to [her brother-in-law] Asher Hinman 20 acres in New Hartford adjoining Asher's own land and "the Widows Thirds."[432]

Children of Amaziah and Elizabeth[5] (Harris) Humphrey, b. Simsbury:[433]

1 *Elizabeth Humphrey*, b. 28 Aug. 1775, living 1823; m. Elijah Wilcox.
2 *Caroline Humphrey*, b. 10 Aug. 1777, d. 13 Aug. 1850; m. Simsbury 3 April 1796 Philander Case.
3 *Amaziah Humphrey*, b. 4 Oct. 1779, d. 20 Oct. 1779.
4 *Hepzibah Humphrey*, b. 25 Feb. 1781, d. before 1823; m. 28 June 1804 James Wilcox.
5 *Dianthe Humphrey*, b. 27 Nov. 1782, d. before 1823; m. Calvin Case.
6 *Dorcas Humphrey*, b. 30 March 1785, d. before 1823; m. Grandison Case.
7 *Rhoda Humphrey*, b. 27 Oct. 1787, d. 10 Sept. 1864, aged 77, unm.

ii   JOHN HARRIS, "son of Philip and Rhoda," b. New Hartford, 12 Oct. 1753,[434] d. before April 1769 (no share with his sisters in grandfather Harris's estate).

iii   MARY HARRIS, b. ca. 1754 (age 6 in March 1760), d. 1821;[435] m. by 3 April 1769 ASHER HINMAN,[436] b. ca. 1741, d. 22 March 1809, aged 68y, and bur. Dyer Cemetery, Canton, Conn., as "Sergeant," where his inscription credits him with service in the Revolutionary War at the time of the Lexington Alarm.[437] The farm of Phillip and Rhoda Harris "became the property of Asher Hinman and wife and from them passed into the hands of Thomas Bidwell, Jun." About 1786, they "removed to the west side of the river, where they lived the remainder of their lives."[438]

Hinman deeds in New Hartford include one from Asher Hinman of Simsbury in May 1803 to [his son] Arad Hinman for 10 acres abutting "east on my own land,"[439] one from Asher and his wife Mary of Simsbury in Jan. 1806 "for love and goodwill" to "our son Amasa Hinman of New Hartford" (16 acres, reserving "a convenient passway to get to and from my large orchard west [of my] dwelling house),[440] and one from Asher Hinman "of

---

[431] Henry P. Johnston, ed., *The Record of Connecticut Men in the Military and Naval Service During the War of the Revolution, 1775–1783* (1889; repr. Baltimore, 1997), 474.

[432] New Hartford, Conn., Deeds, 6:231. The widow presumably was Elizabeth's mother, Rhoda Wilcox.

[433] Bates, *Simsbury Births, Marriages, and Deaths*, 273-74; *Humphreys Family*, 1:184-85.

[434] Barbour Collection, citing New Hartford VR1:42.

[435] The date, 1821, is given without source in Abiel Brown, *Genealogical History . . . of the Early Settlers of West Simsbury, now Canton, Conn.* (Hartford; Case, Tiffany and Co., 1856), 72.

[436] Hartford District Probate Records, 21:170.

[437] Hale Collection, Connecticut Headstone Inscriptions, 8:160. An entry in *DAR Patriot Index* (Washington, D.C., 1966), 331, gives Asher's birth date as 13 March 1742 and death as 8 March 1809.

[438] Brown, *Early Settlers of West Simsbury, now Canton*, 70, 72. A New Hartford deed shows that on 11 Oct. 1787 Asher Hinman of Simsbury and his wife Mary (she signing by mark) sold to Thomas Bidwell a 2¾-acre parcel in New Hartford "about one mile and a half southerly from the great Bridge across Farmington River" (New Hartford, Conn., Deeds, 5:147).

[439] New Hartford, Conn., Deeds, 8:111.

[440] New Hartford, Conn., Deeds, 9:206.

Canton" in April 1807 "for love and goodwill" to "my son Amasa Hinman of New Hartford" (about one acre northeast of Amasa's dwelling house).[441]

On 13 Jan. 1809, Asher Hinman, Mary Hinman, Arad Hinman, and Asher Hinman Jr. of Canton, for $2380, conveyed to Zerah Hinman of New Hartford "the whole of the lands that we own . . . in New Hartford," being "about 140 acres with a barn and cider mill . . . reserving however the use and improvement of said land and buildings a sufficiency for the accom-modation and comfortable support of us the said Asher Hinman and Mary Hinman during our natural lives."[442] Asher's son Zera Hinman was ap-pointed administrator of his estate at Canton on 9 May 1809. On 14 Nov. 1809, the probate court set aside $117.20 to "Mrs. Mary Hinman, widow and relict."[443]

Children of Asher and Mary[5] (Harris) Hinman:[444]

1 *Amasa Hinman*, b. 1768, living New Hartford in April 1807;[445] m. Polly Hinman.

2 *Zera Hinman*, b. ca. 1771, d. Canton 11 Oct. 1848, aged 77; m. Can-ton 8 Nov. 1793 Anna Mills, b. 4 March 1773, d. Canton 14 April 1859, age 86, bur. Dyer Cemetery.

3 *Eliza Hinman*; m. Uriah Beach.

4 *Philip Harris Hinman*, residing New Hartford 14 Jan. 1811, when he and [his brother] Arad Hinman jointly sold 63 acres there with im-provements to William Battell of Torrington, Conn.[446]

5 *Rhoda Hinman*; m. Canton 27 Aug. 1797 Moses Mills, b. New Hart-ford 12 Sept. 1768, bur. Canton 1 June 1846, aged 78.

6 *Arad Hinman*, residing New Hartford 14 Jan. 1811 (see brother Philip Harris Hinman); m. Polly Richards.

7 *Asher Hinman*, b. ca. 1786, d. 26 Aug. 1851, aged 65; m. Eunice Alderman, b. ca. 1787, d. 18 Jan. 1884, aged 97, both bur. Village Cemetery, Canton, Conn.[447]

8 *Cretia/Lucretia Hinman*, b. ca. 1786, d. Canton 27 Sept. 1817, aged 31; m. ca. 1801 Ebenezer Mills, b. New Hartford 5 Oct. 1777, d. there Dec. 1810, aged 32.

FIFTH GENERATION

23 REV. WALTER[5] HARRIS (*Nathaniel[4] Walter[3-2]*, *John[1]*), born in Lebanon, Connecticut, on 8 June 1761,[448] died at Dunbarton, New Hampshire, on 25

---

[441] New Hartford, Conn., Deeds, 9:211. Canton was formed from the west part of Simsbury in 1806.

[442] New Hartford, Conn., Deeds, 9:110.

[443] Simsbury District Probate Records, 6:140, 333.

[444] Brown, *Early Settlers of West Simsbury, now Canton*, 72; Helen Schatvet Ullmann, *Descendants of Peter Mills of Windsor, Connecticut* (Camden, Maine: Penobscot Press, 1998), 86, 212, 216.

[445] New Hartford, Conn., Deeds, 9:211.

[446] New Hartford, Conn., Deeds, 9:191 (called "Harris Hinman" in this deed).

[447] Hale Collection, Connecticut Headstone Inscriptions, 8:66.

[448] *Cleveland and Cleaveland Families*, 1:355.

December 1843.[449] He was "of Lebanon" when he married first in Dunbarton on 22 September 1789 **JEMIMA FISHER** of Franklin, Massachusetts,[450] daughter of Nathaniel Fisher. He married second at Wrentham, Massachusetts, on 27 December 1815 **ELIZABETH (EVANS) CLEVELAND**,[451] widow of Rev. John Cleaveland—she died in Dunbarton in 1829,[452] and third in Goffstown, New Hampshire, on 11 April 1831 **JANE (AIKEN) AIKEN**, widow of James Aiken,[453] born 12 February 1776 (calc.), died of "old age" in Manchester, New Hampshire, on 16 January 1866, age 89y 11m 4d.[454] Jane was residing in Manchester in June 1855 when she applied for bounty land based on Walter's service. Lewis F. Harris and Mary P. Harris, residents of Manchester, deposed that Jane had resided in their family for the past eight years.[455]

Walter enlisted at Lebanon on 28 April 1777 as a fifer in Capt. Jude Alden's company of Col. Samuel B. Webb's regiment of the Continental Line. He served three full years in the Revolutionary War and was discharged on 28 April 1780. He gave his age as 71y and was residing at Dunbarton, New Hampshire on 24 July 1832 when he applied for a pension.[456]

Walter graduated from Dartmouth in 1787, studied theology with Dr. Emmons of Franklin, Massachusetts, and was settled over the Congregational church at Dunbarton on 25 August 1789. The D.D. was conferred by Dartmouth in 1826; he resigned his pastorate on 7 February 1830.[457]

Children of Rev. Walter[5] and Jemima (Fisher) Harris, b. Dunbarton, N.H.:[458]

   i   CLARISSA[6] HARRIS, b. 17 June 1790.
   ii   JEMIMA HARRIS, b. 12 Feb. 1792.
   iii   NATHAN FISHER HARRIS, b. 4 Feb. 1794.
   iv   ELIJAH LYMAN HARRIS, b. 18 Nov. 1798.
   v   LEWIS FISHER HARRIS, b. 16 May 1801, d. of dysentery in Cincinnati, Ohio, 29 June 1861, age 60y 1m 13d, and bur. Manchester, N.H.[459] He m. at

---

[449] Revolutionary War Pension File W2106 (Walter Harris), NARA M804, online at fold3.com.

[450] New Hampshire Marriage Records, 1637–1947, images online at <www.FamilySearch.org>.

[451] Thomas W. Baldwin, comp., *Vital Records of Wrentham, Massachusetts, to the Year 1850*, 2 vols. (Boston: F. H. Gilson Co., 1910), 2:315.

[452] *Cleveland and Cleaveland Families*, 1:355.

[453] James Aiken of Goffstown had m. Jane Aiken of Bedford in Bedford, N.H., on 17 Nov. 1807 (New Hampshire Marriage Records, 1637–1947, images online at <www.FamilySearch.org>).

[454] New Hampshire Death Records, 1654–1947, images online at <www.FamilySearch.org>.

[455] Pension File W2106 (Walter Harris).

[456] Pension File W2106 (Walter Harris).

[457] *Cleveland and Cleaveland Families*, 1:355.

[458] New Hampshire Birth Records, Early to 1900, images online at <www.FamilySearch.org>.

[459] New Hampshire Death Records, 1654–1947, images online at <www.FamilySearch.org>.

Bedford, N.H., 12 July 1830 MARY PARKER,[460] b. N.H. ca. 1806, who was living with him in Manchester in 1860.[461]

vi WALTER HARRIS, b. 26 Nov. 1803, living Newark, N.J., 1850; m. New Boston, N.H., 27 May 1829 SERENA CALDWELL, both of Dunbarton, she b. N.H. ca. 1808 and living with Walter in 1850.[462] Walter was listed next before [his father] Walter Harris in Dunbarton, N.H., in 1830 with a household consisting of two males 20-29, a female 20-29, and a girl under 5.[463] They had moved to Newark, N.J., before 1844, where he was a bookkeeper at the time of the 1850 census.[464]

Children of Walter[6] and Serena (Caldwell) Harris, 1st two b. Dunbarton, N.H.:[465]

1 *Elizabeth C.[7] Harris*, b. 17 April 1830.
2 *Lewis Fisher Harris*, b. 1 June 1832, with parents 1850.
3 *Frederick W. Harris*, b. N.J. ca. 1844, with parents 1850.

24 JOHN[5] HARRIS (*Hosea[4], Thomas[3], Walter[2], John[1]*), born in Wethersfield on 13 July 1770,[466] died 4 April 1858, buried Wethersfield Village Cemetery;[467] married 21 November 1790 **MARTHA RUSSELL**, born on 14 August 1769, who died on 31 March 1853, daughter of Major William Russell.[468]

John and Martha were residing in Wethersfield in 1850 with three adult children—Timothy R., Martha, and Delia—at home.[469]

Children of John[5] and Martha (Russell) Harris:[470]

35 i JOHN[6] HARRIS, b. 30 April 1791; m. SARAH CRANE.

ii CLARISSA HARRIS, b. 14 March 1794, d. 5 April 1871; m. 10 March 1818 Capt. HUMPHREY WOODHOUSE, bp. 3 April 1797, d. 19 Aug. 1872, son of Capt. Humphrey and Rebecca (Adams) Woodhouse. They were residing in Wethersfield in 1850, where he was a pilot.[471]

Children of Capt. Humphrey and Clarissa[6] (Harris) Woodhouse:[472]

1 *Clarissa H. Woodhouse*, bp. 1 April 1821, d. 2 Sept 1824.

---

[460] New Hampshire Marriage Records, 1637–1947, images online at <www.FamilySearch.org>.

[461] 1860 U.S. Census, Ward 4, Manchester, Hillsborough Co., N.H., p. 93. The household included Jane A. Harris, age 84.

[462] New Hampshire Marriage Records, 1637–1947, images online at <www.FamilySearch.org>.

[463] 1830 U.S. Census, Dunbarton, Merrimack Co., N.H., p. 111.

[464] 1850 U.S. Census, South Ward, Newark, Essex Co., N.J., p. 298.

[465] New Hampshire Birth Records, Early to 1900, images online at <www.FamilySearch.org>.

[466] Barbour Collection, citing Wethersfield VR2:68a.

[467] Gravestone for John and wife Martha, photo online at <www.findagrave.com>, accessed Aug. 2012.

[468] Stiles, *Ancient Wethersfield*, 2:414.

[469] 1850 U.S. Census, Wethersfield, Hartford Co., Conn., p. 79/157.

[470] Stiles, *Ancient Wethersfield*, 2:414.

[471] 1850 U.S. Census, Wethersfield, Hartford Co., Conn., p. 133.

[472] First child from Stiles, *Ancient Wethersfield*, 2:849, citing Wethersfield church record, others based on 1850 U.S. Census.

2 *Francis Woodhouse*, b. Conn. ca. 1828, with parents 1850.
3 *Cornelius Woodhouse*, b. Conn. ca. 1830, with parents 1850.
4 *Caroline Woodhouse*, b. Conn. ca. 1837, with parents 1850.
5 *Ellen Woodhouse*, b. Conn. ca. 1840, with parents 1850.

iii MARY HARRIS, b. 20 Aug. 1796, d. 25 May 1888; m. 28 April 1844, as his 2nd
wife, CHAUNCEY APPLETON WOLCOTT, bp. 26 July 1795, d. 11 Sept. 1853,
son of Elisha and Mary (Welles) Wolcott. Chauncey had m. (1) 4 March
1829 Abigail Wells, who d. 13 Oct. 1832.[473] Chauncey and Mary were in
Wethersfield in 1850; he was a farmer.[474] In 1880, widow Mary Wolcott,
age 83, and her "sister" Cordelia Harris, age 53, were sharing a house in
Wethersfield.[475]

36 iv HOSEA HARRIS, b. 22 July 1799; m. SARAH FRANCIS.

v TIMOTHY RUSSELL HARRIS, b. 15 March 1802, d. 20 Feb. 1853; m. 25 Nov. 1824
JULIA ROBBINS,[476] dau. of Robert Robbins. Timothy was with his elderly
parents in Wethersfield in 1850. Timothy R. Harris and his sister Mary A.
Wolcott share the same gravestone in Wethersfield Village Cemetery.[477]

37 vi WALTER HARRIS (twin), b. 24 Aug. 1805; m. CAROLINE M. ORCUTT.

vii WILLIAM HARRIS (twin), b. 24 Aug. 1805.

38 viii HENRY HARRIS, b. 8 May 1808; m. FRANCES ROBBINS.

ix MARTHA HARRIS, b. 19 April 1811, d. 1 Feb. 1876, bur. Wethersfield Village
Cemetery; m. JOHN BLINN, b. 31 Jan. 1813, d. 2 May 1853.[478]

x CORDELIA/DELIA HARRIS, b. 8 Oct. 1815, d. 11 May 1893; her gravestone in
Wethersfield Village Cemetery includes inscriptions for her sister Martha
and Martha's husband John Blinn.[479] She was single, age 64, and residing in
1880 with her sister Mary Wolcott in Wethersfield.

25 JOSEPH[5] HARRIS (*Hosea[4], Thomas[3], Walter2, John[1]*), born in Wethersfield on 15 February 1774, died on 16 September 1832;[480] married 19 June 1800 **ELIZABETH HANMER**,[481] born in Wethersfield on 13 July 1780, who died on 9 September 1860, daughter of Samuel and Sarah (Willis) Hanmer.[482] Elizabeth was head of a household in Hartford in 1850 and 1860.[483]

[473] Stiles, *Ancient Wethersfield*, 2:844.
[474] 1850 U.S. Census, Wethersfield, Hartford Co., Conn., p. 133.
[475] 1880 U.S. Census, Wethersfield, Hartford Co., Conn., E.D. 39, p. 11.
[476] Barbour Collection, citing Wethersfield VR2:247.
[477] Gravestone photo online at <www.findagrave.com>, accessed Aug. 2012.
[478] Gravestone photo online at <www.findagrave.com>, accessed Aug. 2012.
[479] Gravestone photo online at <www.findagrave.com>, accessed Aug. 2012.
[480] Stiles, *Ancient Wethersfield*, 2:414.
[481] Barbour, *Families of Early Hartford*, 294, citing Wethersfield Church record.
[482] Stiles, *Ancient Wethersfield*, 2:410, 414.
[483] 1850, 1860 U.S. Census, City of Hartford, Hartford Co., Conn., pp. 574, 975, respectively.

Children of Joseph[5] and Elizabeth (Hanmer) Harris:[484]

  i   Child[6] of Joseph Harris, d. 18 Oct. 1801, age 1y, bur. Center Church, Hartford.[485]

  ii   JOSEPH HARRIS, b. 29 July 1802, d. Nov. 1844.

  iii   EDWARD HARRIS, b. 8 Nov. 1806, d. 17 Nov. 1868. He was a pump maker residing with his mother in Hartford in 1850 and 1860.

  iv   HENRY HARRIS, b. 8 Jan. 1809, d. 6 Jan. 1873.

39   v   GEORGE HARRIS, b. July 1810, bp. 1st Church, Hartford, 1818;[486] m. EVELINA MADEN.

  vi   ELIZABETH HARRIS, b. 5 Nov. 1812, d. 8 April 1899. She was with her mother in Hartford in 1850.

40   vii   SAMUEL HARRIS, b. 8 June 1814; m. JANE C. WOOD.

26 THOMAS[5] HARRIS (*Thomas[4-3]*, *Walter[2]*, *John[1]*), born in Wethersfield on 8 February 1771, died on 2 February 1829, age 58, buried Wethersfield Village Cemetery;[487] married 8 February 1797 **SARAH CRANE**, born 7 May 1772, who died on 7 February 1829, "both of typhoid," and buried beside Thomas, a daughter of Hezekiah and Mary (Dix) Crane.[488]

Children of Thomas[5] and Sarah (Crane) Harris:[489]

  i   SARAH[6] HARRIS, b. 25 Dec. 1797, d. 12 Nov. 1828, age 31; m. 21 Jan. 1819 SYLVESTER WOODHOUSE, b. 1793, bp. Wethersfield 23 March 1794, d. 27 Aug. 1838, son of Samuel and Abigail (Goodrich or Goodwin?) Woodhouse of Wethersfield. Sylvester m. (2) 9 Feb. 1835 Emily Crane.[490]

  ii   THOMAS HARRIS, b. 20 Aug. 1799, d. 4 Sept. 1857, unmarried.

  iii   MARY HARRIS, b. 21 Feb. 1801, d. 1 April 1872; m. Wethersfield 10 Feb. 1833 WASHINGTON HATCH,[491] b. Winchester, Conn., 14 March 1797, d. there in March 1872, son of Capt. Moses and Abigail (Loveland) Hatch of Wethersfield and Winchester.[492] The Hatch household in Winchester in 1850 included Washington's mother, Abigail Hatch, age 87.[493]

  iv   ABIGAIL HARRIS, b. 28 Nov. 1802, d. 8 March 1876, unmarried.

  v   HEZEKIAH CRANE HARRIS, b. 18 June 1804, d. 12 June 1812.

---

[484] Stiles, *Ancient Wethersfield*, 2:414.

[485] Barbour, *Families of Early Hartford*, 294, citing Wethersfield Church record.

[486] Barbour Collection, citing Hartford VR1:S (by Rev. Joel Hawes).

[487] Gravestone photo online at <www.findagrave.com>, accessed Aug. 2012.

[488] Stiles, *Ancient Wethersfield*, 2:414.

[489] Stiles, *Ancient Wethersfield*, 2:849, citing Wethersfield church records and inscriptions.

[490] Stiles, *Ancient Wethersfield*, 2:414.

[491] Barbour Collection, citing Wethersfield VR3:33.

[492] John Boyd, *Annals and Family Records of Winchester, Conn.* (Hartford: Case, Lockwood & Brainard, 1873), 191.

[493] 1850 U.S. Census, Winchester, Litchfield Co., Conn., p. 205.

vi ELIZABETH HART HARRIS, b. 10 April 1806, d. 31 March 1883, bur. Wethersfield Village Cemetery;[494] m. Wethersfield 12 May 1830 Col. WILLIAM TALCOTT,[495] b. 22 Sept. 1806, d. 14 March 1886, also bur. there, son of William and Amelia (Hanmer) Talcott of Wethersfield. Col. Talcott was a house builder, a representative to the Connecticut Legislature in 1847.[496]

Children of Col. William and Eliza Hart[6] (Harris) Talcott:[497]

1 *William Hanmer Talcott*, b. 17 Feb. 1831; m. 5 Nov. 1861 Charlotte F. Church, dau. of Charles Church of Hartford, b. 31 Jan. 1836. William was a bookbinder in Hartford, where he served on the city council, was commander of the governor's foot guards, and was a member of the Connecticut Historical Society.[498]

2 *Francis Hanmer Talcott*, b. 3 March 1833, d. Hartford 30 Oct. 1893; m. 15 June 1856 Ellen Sophia Prudden of Hartford, dau. of Nathaniel Prudden. Francis worked as a partner with his brother William in Hartford as a bookbinder.

3 *Thomas Harris Talcott*, b. 23 May 1835, d. 11 Jan. 1909, bur. Wethersfield Village Cemetery.[499] He resided in New York City, unm.

4 *Elizabeth Amelia Talcott*, b. 3 Feb. 1838, d. Wethersfield 14 April 1902; m. 23 Nov. 1864 James T. Smith of Wethersfield, b. 4 May 1833, d. Dec. 1901.

5 *Marshall Decatur Talcott*, b. 3 Oct. 1840; m. Alice Benedict of Marshall, Mich. They resided in Chicago.

6 *Dewitt Clinton Talcott*, b. 3 June 1842, d. 25 Aug. 1886, bur. Wethersfield Village Cemetery.[500] He resided in New York City.

7 *Cecilia Augusta Talcott*, b. 5 Nov. 1845, d. 14 Nov. 1910, bur. Wethersfield Village Cemetery;[501] m. George Smith of Wethersfield.

8 *Harriet Ella Talcott*, b. 3 March 1849, d. 28 Jan. 1913, unm., bur. Wethersfield Village Cemetery.[502]

vii EMILY HARRIS, b. 29 March 1808, d. 15 Jan. 1829, unmarried.

viii JANE HARRIS, b. 3 Oct. 1810, d. 24 July 1896, unmarried. In 1880, Jane, "sister," was keeping house in Wethersfield for her brother Hezekiah.[503]

ix HEZEKIAH HARRIS, b. 7 July 1814, d. 9 Aug. 1894, unmarried.

41 x CHAUNCEY HARRIS, b. 21 Sept. 1816; m. EMELINE WELLS.

27 ELISHA[5] HARRIS (*Jeremiah[4]*, *Daniel[3]*, *Walter[2]*, *John[1]*), born in Goshen, Connecticut, in August 1773, died at Hiram, Portage County, Ohio, on 2

---

[494] Grave monument photo online at <www.findagrave.com>, accessed Aug. 2012.

[495] Barbour Collection, citing Wethersfield VR3:91.

[496] Stiles, *Ancient Wethersfield*, 2:698-99.

[497] Stiles, *Ancient Wethersfield*, 2:699.

[498] Stiles, *Ancient Wethersfield*, 2:699.

[499] Gravestone photo online at <www.findagrave.com>, accessed Aug. 2012.

[500] Gravestone photo online at <www.findagrave.com>, accessed Aug. 2012.

[501] Gravestone photo online at <www.findagrave.com>, accessed Aug. 2012.

[502] Gravestone photo online at <www.findagrave.com>, accessed Aug. 2012.

[503] 1880 U.S. Census, Wethersfield, Hartford Co., Conn., E.D. 39, p. 12.

July 1841, age 69 [*sic*], and buried in Chester Cemetery in Geauga County, Ohio.[504] He married first on 17 May 1795 **SUSAN MALLORY**, who died in 1809,[505] and second at Whitestown, Oneida County, New York, on 5 October 1809 **DOROTHEA (SMITH) PURPLE**,[506] born in Plainfield, Hampshire County, Massachusetts, on 7 October 1779, who died at the home of her son Henry Harris in Chester Township, Geauga County,[507] on 25 March 1851, age 72, and buried beside Elisha. Dorothea was a daughter of Dr. Ephraim and Abigail (Higgens) Smith of Whitestown,[508] and widow of Ansel Purple whom she had married at New Hartford, New York on 19 February 1798.[509] The manuscript papers of Ansel and Dorothea's grandson, Dr. Samuel Smith Purple, have been an important source for Elisha Harris and his brother Woodruff Harris and their families.

Elisha was somewhere in New York by 1796, where his eldest child was born, and in Smithville, Chenango County, New York by 1804, when he and his brother Joseph Harris had earmarks recorded in the Town Minute Book.[510] He was a "settler" there as "early as 1808" with his brother Woodruff, brother-in-law Jerediah Brown,[511] and their Cowles relatives. He was an overseer of highways there in 1809, 1810, 1811, and 1814. His household there in 1810 was listed sequentially with that of his brother Joseph and near brother Alanson.[512] In October 1817, he bought and sold property in Lots 46 and 51, which had been leased by his brother Joseph in 1811.[513] Later that month, he moved to Parkman, Geauga County, Ohio.

In Parkman on 5 July 1819, Elisha purchased 400 acres from Samuel Parkman, the town's founder, and built a log house on it.[514] In 1832, he

---

[504] Gravestone photo online at <www.findagrave.com>, accessed Sept. 2012.

[505] Samuel S[mith] Purple, "Manuscript notes, correspondence, wills, etc., on the descendants of Edward Purple who was an inhabitant of Haddam, Connecticut, in May 1674 (manuscript file: Purple Family, NYG&B Collection, 1880, 200 pages). For discussion of this manuscript, parts of which wee prepared by Dr. Purple about 1870, see Gale Ion Harris, "The Edward¹ Purple Family of Connecticut and New York: An Overdue Account," NYGBR 137 (2006):3 n3.

[506] New Hartford Church Records, Vosburgh Collection of New York Church Records.

[507] *Pioneer and General History of Geauga County* (Burton, Ohio: Geauga County Historical Society, 1880), 699.

[508] Henrietta Elizabeth Savery Smith, *Anderson, Perrine, Barbour-Smith, Howell-Clark, Porter and Savery Families* (Detroit: Perrine Press, 1902), 88-90, which interchanges the marriages of Dorothea and her sister.

[509] Harris, "Edward¹ Purple Family" 137 (2006):214. Ansel and Dorothea Purple were the grandparents of Dr. Samuel Smith Purple, a New York genealogist and early editor of the *Record*.

[510] Courtesy of Philip M. Rogers, Smithville Town Clerk, Greene, N.Y., in 1983.

[511] Smith, *History of Chenango and Madison Counties,* 298.

[512] 1810 U.S. Census, Smithville, Chenango Co., N.Y., p. 1072.

[513] Chenango Co., N.Y., Deeds, W:513, 515.

[514] Geauga Co., Ohio, Deeds, 6:335; *History of Geauga County,* 699.

moved over the county line into Hiram, Portage County. By 1838, he had disposed of his land there by conveyances to his sons John Sheldon, Philo, Hiram, and Henry. On 8 August 1838 in Nelson, the town adjoining Hiram on the east, Elisha and his brother Joseph were co-makers of a $338 note, which was found by Elisha's administrators in 1841. His son Henry was appointed administrator on 23 September 1841, and his nephew Erwin Harris, Joseph's son, was one of the appraisers.[515]

Children of Elisha[5] and Susan (Mallory) Harris:

42   i   HIRAM[6] HARRIS, b. N.Y. ca. 1796, m. (1) ANNA WALKER, (2) AURELIA MILLS.
43   ii   HARVEY HARRIS, b. N.Y., ca. 1797; m. ALMIRA HOWARD.
      iii WILLIAM HARRIS, b. say 1800, d. young.
      iv   BETSEY HARRIS, b. say 1802, d. young.
44   v   JOHN SHELDON HARRIS, b. N.Y. 15 July 1804; m. (1) RACHEL ANN JONES, (2) LUCELIA YOUNG.
      vi   RUBY HARRIS, b. N.Y. 12 Sept. 1806, d. 28 Aug. 1888, bur. Grove Cemetery, Troy, Geauga Co., Ohio. She m. in Geauga Co. 27 Nov. 1823 MINOR DAVIS,[516] b. N.Y. in 1803, d. Benton Co., Iowa, 15 April 1859, age 55y 6m.[517] Ruby's father had been appointed guardian of Minor and Fanny Davis, "minor heirs of Isaiah Davis, deceased," by Nov. 1822.[518]
            Children of Minor and Ruby[6] (Harris) Davis, from 1850 census, b. Ohio:[519]
            1 *Alva Davis*, b. ca. 1824.
            2 *Minerva Davis*, b. ca. 1826; m. Geauga Co., Ohio, 25 Oct. 1849 Hercules Carrolle.[520]
            3 *Robert W. Davis*, b. ca. 1828; m. Geauga Co., Ohio, 25/27 June 1858 Mary Cook.
            4 *Emeline C. Davis*, b. ca. 1831; m. Portage Co., Ohio, 4/7 April 1851 Joab Austin.
            5 *Mary Davis*, b. ca. 1833.
            6 *Edward Davis*, b. ca. 1837.
            7 *Newton Davis*, b. ca. 1844.
      vii HOSEA HARRIS, b. 1809, "being a few days old when his mother died";[521] m. Portage Co., Ohio, 8 March 1830 CAROLINE SKINNER,[522] b. 1811–1815. He last appears in the 1835 census of males over age 21 in Mantua, Portage Co.[523]

[515] Estate papers in custody of the Portage County Chapter, Ohio Genealogical Society, Mansfield, Ohio, Betty J. Widger, custodian in 1977.

[516] Ohio County Marriages, 1789–1994, online at <www.FamilySearch.org>.

[517] Portage County Newspaper Deaths, 1825–1860, courtesy of Betty J. Widger, Ravenna, Ohio.

[518] Geauga Co., Ohio, Probate Records, B:69.

[519] 1850 U.S. Census, Hiram, Portage Co., Ohio, p. 6.

[520] Ohio County Marriages, 1789–1994, online at <www.FamilySearch.org>.

[521] Purple, "Manuscript Notes."

[522] Ohio County Marriages, 1789–1994, online at <www.FamilySearch.org>.

[523] Merrible E. Meyers, "Portage County Tax Lists," typescript (Ravenna, Ohio: Old Northwest Chapter, NSDAR, 1976), Ohio State Library, Columbus, Ohio.

Children of Elisha[5] and Dorothea (Smith) (Purple) Harris:

35 viii PHILO HARRIS, b. Smithville, Chenango Co., N.Y., 5 Oct. 1810; m. (1) PAMELIA K. HALL, (2) HARRIET CORNELIUS GRIDLEY.

    ix SALLY ANN HARRIS, b. Smithville, Chenango Co., N.Y., 18 May 1813, d. Nevada City, Mo., 25 Sept. 1868, bur. McMullin Cemetery, Vernon Co., Mo.;[524] m. Geauga Co., Ohio, 19 April 1831 SILAS NEWTON HOWARD of Parkman, Ohio,[525] b. N.Y. 18 Nov. 1806, who d. in Nevada City 5 Nov. 1869, bur. same cemetery.[526] Sally's half brother Harvey Harris deposed for their license at Chardon, Ohio, on 14 April 1831 that "he saw Elisha Harris who is the father of said Sally, age under 18, sign a certificate of consent to said marriage." Silas and Sally were in Sandusky Co., Ohio, in 1850,[527] where he was a hotel keeper; by 1860 they had moved to Olmsted Co., Minn., where he was a farmer.[528]

        Children of Silas Newton and Sally Ann[6] (Harris) Howard:[529]

        1 *Orange L. Howard*, b. Ohio ca. Aug. 1832, d. Worthington, Minn., 19 Oct. 1907, age 75y 2m, bur. Worthington Cemetery;[530] m. Lucas Co., Ohio, 15 April 1858 Sarah Ann Crissey,[531] b. N.Y. 26 Oct. 1831, d. Worthington 17 Nov. 1907, dau. of David and Mary (Phillips) Crissey.[532]

        2 *Cecelia A. Howard*, b. Fremont, Ohio, 28 March 1833, d. Dubuque, Iowa, 29 Nov. 1866, bur. Linwood Cemetery;[533] m. Mansfield, Ohio, 30 July 1847 Delose E. Lyon, b. Franklinville, Cattaraugus Co., N.Y., 14 Nov. 1832, d. Dubuque 10 April 1913, a prominent attorney, son of Jonathan and Harriet (Perkins) Lyon. Delose m. (2) 8 Jan. 1868 Eunice Ann Taylor.[534]

        3 *Minnie Calista Howard*, b. Ohio 30 April 1839, d. St. Louis, Mo., 5 Jan. 1905, bur. Gatewood Gardens Cemetery;[535] m. Albert James Howland, b. N.Y. 1832, d. Sept. 1898, bur. Leavenworth National Cemetery, Leavenworth, Kans.[536]

        4 *Silas Newton Howard*, b. Ohio ca. 1846, with parents 1850, 1860.

46 x WILLIAM SMITH HARRIS, b. Smithville 19 Sept. 1816; m. (1) LOUISA EGGLESTON, (2) LOUISA RUSSELL.

---

[524] Gravestone photo online at <www.findagrave.com>, accessed Aug. 2012.

[525] Geauga Co., Ohio, Marriage Records, Chardon, Ohio.

[526] Gravestone photo and obituary online at <www.findagrave.com>, accessed Aug. 2012.

[527] 1850 U.S. Census, Washington Twp., Sandusky Co., Ohio, p. 14.

[528] 1860 U.S. Census, Marion Twp., P.O. Marion, Olmsted Co., Minn., p. 71.

[529] Named in Purple, "Manuscript Notes."

[530] Death notice, *Worthington [Minn.] Advance*, 25 Oct. 1907, p. 1.

[531] Ohio County Marriages, 1789–1994, online at <www.FamilySearch.org>.

[532] Gravestone photo and obituary online at <www.findagrave.com>, accessed Aug. 2012.

[533] Gravestone photo and death notice online at <www.findagrave.com>, accessed Aug. 2012.

[534] Gravestone photo and obituary online at <www.findagrave.com>, accessed Aug. 2012.

[535] Memorial photo and obituary online at <www.findagrave.com>, accessed Aug. 2012.

[536] Gravestone photo online at <www.findagrave.com>, accessed Aug. 2012.

xi HENRY HENDERSON HARRIS, b. Parkman, Geauga Co., Ohio, 1 May 1818, d. 5 July 1869, probably at Hiram, Portage Co., Ohio. He m. (1) Geauga Co., Ohio, 12 Nov. 1839 ELIZABETH IRENE BALDWIN,[537] b. N.Y. 10 July 1818, d. 20 Aug. 1860, (2) Geauga Co. 25 May 1861 LYDIA AINGER (BALDWIN) DAVIS,[538] b. N.Y. 19 July 1820, sister of his first wife and widow of James Wilson Davis of Parkman, Ohio, merchant. Their parents were Augustus Russell and Mary (Angier) Baldwin of Whitestown, N.Y., and Parkman. Henry had "no children."[539]

xii ELIZABETH MINERVA HARRIS, b. Parkman, Ohio, 7 Feb. 1821, d. at the home of her son Professor Thomas McKean at Berea, Cuyahoga Co., Ohio, 26 Nov. 1904, bur. Woodvale Cemetery, Middleburg Heights;[540] m. Sandusky, Ohio, 28 Oct. 1850 Rev. JOHN MCKEAN[541] of the Northern Ohio Conference, b. Sandesbury, Cumberland (now Perry) Co., Pa., 29 Sept. 1817, d. Berea 31 July 1898, bur. same cemetery. They were residing at Berea in 1880;[542] Elizabeth was in her son Thomas's home there in 1900.[543]

Children of Rev. John and Elizabeth Minerva[6] (Harris) McKean:[544]

1 *Joseph McKean*, b. Shannon (or Bluffton), Allen Co., Ohio, 17 July 1851, d. Long Beach, Pacific Co., Wash., 7 Sept. 1925, bur. Ilwaco Cemetery;[545] m. ca. 1879 Emma Jane Darling, b. Lapeer Co., Mich., 1 Jan. 1858, d. Long Beach 8 Aug. 1924, bur. same cemetery, dau. of Henry and Lydia (___) Darling. Joseph and Emma were in Grundy Co., Mo., in 1880,[546] in Oregon in 1888, and in Washington by 1891.[547]

2 Infant son, b. Adrian, Ohio, 17 April 1853, d. 20 April 1853.

3 *William McKean*, b. Ohio ca. 1854, d. before 1900, a "law student" living with his brother Joseph in Mo. in 1880, age 26.

4 *Minnie J. McKean*, b. Ohio ca. 1858; m. Cuyahoga Co., Ohio, 6 June 1878 Howard F. Parminter. Minnie was residing with her parents in 1880 with a child, Ethel Parminter, age 1.

5 *John Spencer McKean*, b. Ohio in Nov. 1859, d. Alva, Woods Co., Okla., 15 Nov. 1912, bur. Alva Municipal Cemetery;[548] m. ca. 1890

---

[537] Ohio County Marriages, 1789–1994, online at <www.FamilySearch.org>.

[538] Ohio County Marriages, 1789–1994, online at <www.FamilySearch.org>.

[539] Charles Candee Baldwin, *Baldwin Genealogy Supplement* (Cleveland: Cleveland Leader, 1889), 1069.

[540] Inscription data online at <www.findagrave.com>, accessed Sept. 2012.

[541] Ohio County Marriages, 1789–1994, online at <www.FamilySearch.org>.

[542] 1880 U.S. Census, Village of Berea, Cuyahoga Co., Ohio, E.D. 68, p. 9.

[543] 1900 U.S. Census, Village of Berea, Cuyahoga Co., Ohio, E.D. 224, sheet 5B, the record showing that she was the mother of nine children, six then living.

[544] First two from Purple, "Manuscript Notes" others from census records.

[545] Inscription data online at <www.findagrave.com>, accessed Sept. 2012.

[546] 1880 U.S. Census, Myers Twp., Grundy Co., Mo., E.D. 205, p. 6, their household then including "brother" William McKean, age 26, "law student."

[547] Based on children's birth places stated in 1900 U.S. Census, Long Beach Precinct, Pacific Co., Wash., E.D. 141, sheet 7B.

[548] Inscription data online at <www.findagrave.com>, accessed Sept. 2012.

Laura V. ____, b. Ill. in Oct. 1848, d. 18 Nov. 1943, bur. same cemetery. They were in Kiowa, Kans., in 1900.[549]

6 *Emma May McKean*, b. Melmore, Seneca Co., Ohio, 3 March 1864, d. Dorchester Co., Md., 7 June 1960, age 96, unm., bur. Woodvale Cemetery, Middleburg Heights, Ohio.[550]

7 *Thomas Lincoln McKean*, b. Ohio in April 1866, d. Berea, Ohio, 10 Jan. 1942, bur. Woodvale Cemetery, Middleburg Heights, Ohio;[551] m. Cuyahoga Co., Ohio, 12 June 1890 Emma Marie Brown,[552] b. Ohio in May 1867, d. Beria 12 March 1931, bur. same cemetery. He was a school teacher in Beria in 1900.[553]

8-9 Two children who d. before 1900.

28 JOSEPH[5] HARRIS (*Jeremiah[4]*, *Daniel[3]*, *Walter[2]*, *John[1]*), was born about 1775, probably in Goshen, Connecticut.[554] He was living near Durand in Winnebago County, Illinois, on 2 November 1840, when he voted for the Whig ticket of five presidential electors including "Abe Lincoln" and a sheriff.[555] He probably died there not long after that election. Most likely, he was buried in Hulse Cemetery in Pecatonica Township,[556] but no marker for him has been found there or in other cemeteries in the vicinity. He married, probably in Salisbury, Connecticut, about 1803 (first child born in 1804), **JULIA TOWSLEY**, born there on 7 September 1784,[557] a daughter of Samuel Towsley and his wife Anna (Owen) of Salisbury.[558] Julia died apparently in Smithville, Chenango County, New York, soon after the birth of her son Edgar Eggleston Harris in September 1828.

---

[549] 1900 U.S. Census, Kiowa Twp., Barber Co., Kans., E.D. 6, sheet 10A.

[550] Inscription data and obituary online at <www.findagrave.com>, accessed Sept. 2012.

[551] Inscription data and obituary online at <www.findagrave.com>, accessed Sept. 2012.

[552] Ohio County Marriages, 1789–1994, online at <www.FamilySearch.org>.

[553] 1900 U.S. Census, Village of Berea, Cuyahoga Co., Ohio, E.D. 224, sheet 5B, the record showing that she was the mother of nine children, six then living.

[554] Harris and Stover, "Second Daniel Harris of Goshen," 122 (1991):152.

[555] Copy of an 1840 poll book included with a letter dated in June 1876 from John Herring to the editor of the *Durand Patriot*, courtesy of Barbara Winchester of Durand.

[556] On the township line four miles south and two miles west of Durand. It is probable that Joseph was buried in a space just north of the graves of his eldest son Edwin and Edwin's infant daughter Polly.

[557] *Historical Collections of the Salisbury Association, Inc.*, 2 vols. (New Haven: By the Association, 1913–16), 2:110. Joseph's wife is identified as Julia Towsley in marriage and death records of their sons Elisha and Erastus Harris, and in a biography of their grandson Henry E. Harris in *Portrait and Biographical Record of Winnebago and Boone Counties, Illinois* (Chicago: Biographical Publishing Co., 1892), 652-53.

[558] Julia was an orphan before age seven. A discussion of her ancestry, in particular the identification of her mother as Anna Owen, not Ann Peck as sometimes claimed, has been presented elsewhere (Gale Ion Harris, "Michael[1] and Mary (Husse) Towsley of Suffield in Massachusetts," *The Genealogist* 23 [2009]: 34-72, 177-202, at 185-88).

Joseph's parents were living in Goshen as late as 1777, but they probably died before 1790, when Joseph and other children can be accounted for in their maternal grandfather Joseph Cowles' household nearby in Canaan, Connecticut.[559] Joseph first appears on record in 1804, however, when he and his brother Elisha Harris recorded livestock earmarks at Smithville.[560] His brothers Alanson and Elisha were residing there at that time,[561] but Joseph apparently was a non-resident and only grazing some cattle or sheep there with Elisha's herd. Census and gravestone inscription data show that Joseph's two eldest children, Edwin and Erwin, were born in Connecticut in August 1804 and about 1806, respectively.

Joseph was engaged in "trade" in Connecticut in 1806. On 25 March that year, Joseph Harris and William Porter, "both of Canaan," leased "the Old Meadow" from the estate of Deacon Elisha Beebe.[562] The lease was to be effective from 1 September 1805 to 28 May 1813.[563] However, as shown by the following newspaper item, their venture did not last that long:

TAKE NOTICE

HARRIS AND PORTER, having dissolved their Partnership in Trade, earnestly request all those who have unsettled accounts with them, to turn their attention to the same without further notice. —All Accounts and Notes which have become due, must be paid by the First of January next, to prevent our entering into the general practice of placing them in the hands of an Attorney for collection. Joseph Harris, William Porter
     Canaan, Nov. 5, 1806.[564]

Soon afterward, by certificate dated 2 December 1806, Joseph Harris declined to join the Congregational Church in Canaan, stating that his views "differ in sentiment from the worship and ministry . . . now under the care of

---

[559] Harris and Stover, "Second Daniel Harris of Goshen," 16-17n4, 152. Joseph Cowles died at Canaan on 20 April 1806, aged 90 (Cowles, *Genealogy of the Cowles Families*, 1:61).

[560] Smithville Town Minute Book.

[561] Harris and Stover, "Second Daniel Harris of Goshen," 122 (1991):99, 156.

[562] Canaan, Conn., Deeds, 7:60.

[563] William Porter married Sally Bunnal at the Canaan church on 5 Sept. 1805, where they recorded the deaths of two children in 1807 and 1810. Porter moved to Greene, Chenango Co., N.Y., where by about 1815, with "____ Taylor, [he] did business in company until about 1820 when they removed from the Town." With Asa Whitney and Warren Gray, he "commenced business under the name of Whitney, Porter and Gray about 1822, and continued about a year." (Smith, *History of Chenango and Madison Counties*, 203, 204.) In 1820, Asa Whitney and William Porter were residing nearby in Lisle, Broome Co., N.Y. (U.S. Census, pp. 216, 222). Warren Gray (1784–1869) had lived in Egremont, Mass., before settling in Greene, Chenango Co., about 1805 (M. D. Raymond, *Gray Genealogy* [Tarrytown, N.Y., 1887], 80-81).

[564] *The Litchfield Monitor*, 19 Nov. 1806, also appearing in the issue of 17 Dec. 1806.

the Rev. Charles Prentice and that I choose to join myself to and support the Denomination of Christians called Episcopalians."[565]

If statements in later census entries are correct, Joseph's third child, Eli, was born in New York before about 1810. Joseph seems to have moved from Canaan to Smithville near the time that his uncle Timothy Cowles moved there from Canaan in 1809.[566] In any case, Joseph was residing in Smithville in the summer of 1810, when his household there was listed in sequence with those of his brother Elisha Harris and his brother-in-law Eli Towsley.[567] The Smithville Town Minute Book shows that Joseph Harris was the Town Clerk there from 1810 to 1812. On 23 November 1811, Joseph "contracted" (leased) from John Hornby 120 acres in Lots 46 and 51 in Smithville.[568]

Joseph apparently was engaged in some undetermined business in Smithville and neighboring Greene until about the time his wife Julia died. The Smithville Town Minute Book preserves motions that he introduced at Town Board meetings in 1810 and 1820, the latter proposing "that we raise fifty dollars for the support of the poor [and] that the poor money now on hand be put out at interest." In 1818, Joseph was "among the members of the Eastern Light Lodge [in Greene] either by being made Masons or by affiliation."[569] Recorded as age 45 or over and engaged in "agriculture," Joseph had a household in Smithville in 1820 including his wife, seven children, and an extra female aged 45 or over.[570] In March 1825, Joseph

[565] Canaan First Ecclesiastical Society and Congregational Church Records, 1741–1842, 3:38.

[566] Cowles, *Genealogy of the Cowles Families*, 1:108-109; Timothy Cowles' Revolutionary War pension file, W16546, National Archives, Washington, D.C.

[567] 1810 U.S. Census, Smithville, Chenango Co., N.Y., p. 1073. Eli Towsley, b. at Salisbury on 23 Jan. 1777, m. about 1802 Melinda Hurlbut, b. at Cornwall, Conn., on 20 March 1781, daughter of Joab Hurlbut (Henry H. Hurlbut, *The Hurlbut Genealogy* [Albany; J. Munsell's Sons, 1888], 100, 438). Joab Hurlbut's land in Cornwall, on the town line, was close to or possibly adjacent to land of Joseph Harris's father and grandfather in Goshen (Cornwall, Conn., Deeds, 5:128).

[568] This lease is mentioned in a later deed, dated 6 Oct. 1817, by which Joseph's brother Elisha Harris bought some of the same property from Hornby, then sold it seven days later to George Alizon "late of New York City and now of Smithville" (Chenango Co., N.Y., Deeds, W:513, 515). These later deeds also show that Joseph had land adjoining Elisha in 1817, but no deeds are recorded in Chenango Co. by this Joseph Harris. Lots 46 and 51 adjoin each other in the extreme south-central part of Smithville, such that Lot 51 abuts the Smithville-Greene town line north and slightly east of Greene Village. Along their east side is the Cowles Cemetery where Joseph's uncle Timothy Cowles (1746–1831), his elder sister Eunice (Harris) Brown (1765–1843), and his son Elmore Harris (1825–1899) are buried.

[569] Mildred English Cochrane, *From Raft to Railroad, A History of the Town of Greene, Chenango County, New York, 1792–1867* (Ithaca, N.Y., 1967), 88.

[570] 1820 U.S. Census, Smithville, Chenango Co., N.Y., p. 207. The unidentified female in 1820 possibly was Joseph's mother Esther, who, if living, would have been aged 75. In Smithville's 1810 census, an unidentified female aged 45 or over was in the household of Joseph's elder brother Elisha Harris, who, before 1820, had moved on to Geauga Co., Ohio.

Harris and Benjamin Birdsall Jr. (a merchant in Greene), "both of Chenango County," were named executors in Andrew Ackhorn's will in Oxford, the town next east of Smithville.[571] In March 1826, Joseph Harris, Charles Squires, Anthony Squires (the latter two were merchants in Greene), and (attorney) Robert Monell had a judgment of $187.26 entered against them by "The President and Directors of the Bank of Chenango." Some months later, in June 1826, a judgment of $103.42 was entered against Joseph Harris by Reuben Hunt.[572] Joseph's property in Smithville was noted in April 1827 as a point in a survey for a school lot.[573]

No further mention of Joseph Harris is found in Chenango County sources, but he probably was still residing in Smithville in September 1828, as his youngest child, Edgar, reportedly was born then in "New York." This boy's mother, Julia, apparently died at or soon after his birth. The obituary at Durand, Illinois, in 1900 of Edgar's older brother Elisha Harris, born in Smithville in 1817, states: "[Elisha's] mother dying when he was quite young the family was scattered and the younger children [were] put out to other families."

The infant Edgar apparently was placed with the Eggleston family nearby in Lisle (later called Triangle) in Broome County. Elisha and his older brothers Erwin and Eli Harris probably went to their mother's Towsley relatives; they later show up in Steuben County, New York, where their cousins Susan (Towsley) Cowles and Samuel Towsley had moved from Smithville before 1840. Susan and Samuel were children of Julia's brother Eli Towsley, who, as late as 1832, owned property at Smithville in Lot 51,[574] the lot that had been under lease to Joseph Harris in 1817.

Joseph does not appear by name in the 1830 census, but it is reasonably certain that by that time he had moved to Auburn, Geauga County, Ohio, where he was the male aged 50-59 in his brother Woodruff Harris's household.[575] The adjacently-listed household was that of Nelson Brooks, who shortly before had married Joseph's daughter Rebecca Harris, then about seventeen. Next year, in 1831, Joseph and his son-in-law Brooks were recorded in a tax census for the Town of Mantua in Portage County, just over the county line from Auburn.[576] On 6 September 1836, Joseph Harris

---

[571] Chenango Co., N.Y., Wills, B:97.
[572] Chenango Co. Supreme Court, Docket of Judgments, 1819–1847, Norwich, N.Y.; Smith, *History of Chenango and Madison Counties*, 205.
[573] Smithville Town Minute Book, 156.
[574] Smithville Town Minute Book, 183.
[575] 1830 U.S. Census, Auburn, Geauga Co., Ohio, p. 261.
[576] Meyers, "Portage County Tax Lists."

and Alva Udall witnessed in Portage County when Joseph's brother Elisha Harris conveyed land in Hiram Township to his (Elisha's) son Hiram Harris. On the same day, they witnessed when Calvin Tyler "of Hiram" conveyed land to Joseph's son Erwin Harris, then "of the town of Ervin in the County of Steuben in New York."[577] In August 1838, Joseph signed a note at Nelson in Portage County, cosigned by his brother Elisha Harris, promising to "pay James Knowlton or order $338 one year from date, $65 of which is to be on interest and the remainder without interest." The note was deemed "doubtful" when it was found among Elisha's papers by the administrators of his estate in 1841.[578]

Sometime between August 1838 and 1840, Joseph followed his sons Edwin and Elisha to Winnebago County, Illinois. Probably he was the male aged 60-69 in Edwin's household when the first U.S. census was taken there in 1840.[579] No probate or other settlement of his estate has been found.

Children of Joseph[5] and Julia (Towsley) Harris:

47	i	EDWIN[5] HARRIS, b. in Conn. 3 Aug. 1804; m. IRENE W. E. STEVENS.
48	ii	ERWIN HARRIS, b. in Conn. ca. 1806; m. LAURA A. JOHNSON.
49	iii	ELI HARRIS, b. in N.Y. between 1807 and 1810; m. MARY MULFORD.
	iv	JESSE HARRIS, b. prob. after the census date in 1810; m. in Geauga Co., Ohio, on 8 Dec. 1834 SARAH MORSE "of the Township of Auburn," by Austin Richards, J.P. Jesse d. apparently before 9 May 1841, when Sarah m. (2) in Geauga Co. Leonard Gilson "of Auburn."[580] Jesse is accounted for as one of two boys under age 10 in Joseph Harris's household at Smithville in 1820, and was perhaps the male aged 15-19 with Joseph in Woodruff Harris's household at Auburn in 1830. Jesse appears with Edwin Harris (no. 47) in the 1835 tax census of adjoining Mantua, Portage Co., where their father, Joseph, had appeared in 1831. No children are found.
50	v	REBECCA A. HARRIS, b. in N.Y. ca. 1813; m. (1) NELSON BROOKS, (2) SYLVESTER REED.
51	vi	ELISHA HARRIS, b. Smithville, N.Y., 20 July 1817; m. (1) CALISTA CHRISTINA ROBB, (2) MARIA LOUISA (FASSETT) HARRIS.
52	vii	ERASTUS HARRIS, b. Chenango Co., N.Y., 13 July 1822; m. MARIA BETSEY WARREN.
53	viii	ELMORE HARRIS, b. Smithville, N.Y., in 1825; m. OLIVE CARTRIGHT.
54	ix	EDGAR EGGLESTON HARRIS, b. in N.Y. 4 Sept. 1828; m. MARIA LOUISA FASSETT.

---

[577] Portage Co., Ohio, Deeds, 24:355; 36:465, Ravenna, Ohio.

[578] Portage Co. Probate Records, found in 1977 by Betty J. Widger of Ravenna, Ohio, among 50 boxes of unindexed material placed in her custody as President of the Portage County Chapter of the Ohio Genealogical Society, Mansfield, Ohio.

[579] 1840 U.S. Census, Howard Twp., Winnebago Co., Ill., p. 431.

[580] Geauga Co. Marriage Records, Chardon, Ohio.

29 WOODRUFF[5] HARRIS (*Jeremiah[4], Daniel[3], Walter[2], John[1]*), born in Goshen, Connecticut, on 10 April 1786,[581] died as a resident of Geauga County, Ohio, on 14 June 1837,[582] reportedly in a boating accident on St. Lawrence River, as discussed below. His unusual name presumably came from his maternal grandmother, Ruth (Woodruff) Cowles, of Southington and Canaan, Connecticut.[583] Woodruff's father, Jeremiah, apparently had died in Goshen or adjoining Canaan before 1790, when Woodruff can be accounted for as one of four boys under age 16 in the household in Canaan of his maternal grandfather, Joseph Cowles.[584]

By 1808, while still single, Woodruff had migrated with his older brother Elisha and some Cowles relatives to Smithville.[585] He was "of Smithville" on 19 August 1813, when he married, as his first wife, **FRANCES/FANNY PURPLE**, born in East Hampton, Connecticut, on 9 October 1793, who died at Parkman, Geauga County, Ohio, on 26 September 1827 [*sic*: probably 1825 or 1826], daughter of Edward and Lydia (Cowdrey) Purple.[586]

Little notice of Woodruff appears in Chenango County records except that he had four debt judgments entered against him in court there on 15 February 1817, totaling $735.62.[587] He had moved to Hiram, Portage County, Ohio, by 1820, when his household consisted of a male and a female ages 26-44, and a girl and two boys under 10.[588] Woodruff and his brother Elisha were assessed for taxes nearby in Parkman, Geauga County, in 1825.[589]

Woodruff married secondly in Geauga County on 4 March 1827 **PHEBE (ORTON) CULVER**,[590] born in Litchfield, Connecticut, on 16 August 1800,

---

[581] Birth date and place from Purple, "Manuscript Notes."

[582] Date from Purple, "Manuscript Notes," p. 119.

[583] Cowles, *Genealogy of the Cowles Families*, 1:61-62.

[584] 1790 U.S. Census, Litchfield Co., Conn., p. 356 (Joseph Cowls, 34400). The household apparently included several of Woodruff's older siblings and probably their mother, Esther (Cowles) Harris (Harris and Stover, "Second Daniel Harris of Goshen," 122 (1991):16-17n4).

[585] Smith, *History of Chenango and Madison Counties*, 298.

[586] Harris, "Edward[1] Purple Family," 137 (2006):212, citing "Purple Manuscript," p. 119. Dr. Samuel Smith Purple was a first cousin, once removed, of Woodruff's wife Frances Purple. The year in Purple's notes for this death conflicts with the recorded date of Woodruff's second marriage (4 March 1827), see below.

[587] Chenango Co., N.Y., Judgment Docket, Norwich, N.Y.

[588] 1820 U.S. Census, Hiram, Portage Co., Ohio, p. 40.

[589] Harris and Stover, "Second Daniel Harris of Goshen," 122 (1991):157. Elisha's second wife, Dorothea (Smith) Purple, had been the widow of Ansel Purple of East Haddam, Conn., and Whitestown, N.Y., an uncle of Woodruff's wife Frances Purple and grandfather of Dr. Samuel Smith Purple (Harris, "Edward[1] Purple Family," 137 [2006]:214).

[590] Geauga Co., Ohio, Marriage Records, B:60. The application for their license was made at Chardon on 2 March 1827 by Woodruff's nephew, John Sheldon Harris of Parkman, son of Elisha. Phebe's maiden name is from the Michigan death certificate of her son Erwin Alanson Harris.

daughter of Hezekiah and Hannah (___) Orton.[591] Phebe was formerly the wife of Nathan Culver whom she had married in Burlington, Connecticut, on 16 September 1816 and divorced in Geauga County on 14 August 1826. Nathan had "threatened to cut off Phebe's head with an axe, burned her clothing, [and] many other acts of extreme cruelty."[592] Phebe survived Woodruff also and died in Campbell, Ionia County, Michigan, on 23 September 1872, age 72y 1m 7d.[593]

Woodruff was residing in Auburn, Geauga County, in 1830, when his household consisted of a male age 50-59 [presumably his older brother Joseph Harris],[594] a male 40-49 [Woodruff], a female 30-39 [Phebe], a male 15-19, three girls and a boy 10-14, a boy 5-9, and two boys under 5.[595] On 8 March 1832, Woodruff's wife Phebe purchased a 40-acre parcel nearby in Nelson Township, Portage County,[596] where they were residing in 1834.[597] Woodruff and Phebe, "both of Nelson Township," sold that parcel on 7 January 1835[598] and moved back over the line into Geauga County, where, by a deed recorded on 7 April 1835, Phebe purchased 40 acres in Lot 4, Troy Township.[599]

Woodruff Harris is reported to have died in 1837 in a "boating accident on St. Lawrence River."[600] Nothing further has been learned of the circumstances of his death. He is called "late of Troy" in his inventory, dated in Geauga County 30 October 1837. His wife Phebe had been appointed as administratrix with Ira Webster and William Crafts as sureties, and Silas Herrick, William Mumford, and Daniel G. Converse as appraisers. His estate included carpenters tools, 33 bushels of wheat, oats in bundles, one hog, all valued at

---

[591] Barbour Collection, citing Litchfield VR1:153. Phebe's older brother Morgan Orton had settled nearby in Auburn by 1820 (U.S. Census, Auburn, Geauga Co., Ohio, p. 95; Edward Orton, *An Account of the Descendants of Thomas Orton of Windsor, Connecticut, 1641* [Columbus, Ohio: Nitschke Brothers, 1896], 134, 160-61).

[592] Frances N. Slack, trans., "Geauga County Supreme Court Divorces, 1806–1839," *Lakelines: Newsletter of the Lake County [Ohio] Genealogical Society* (Jan.–April, 1989), including marriage place and date (not found in Conn. vital records), and naming two children: Hanna, age 7, and Lucy, age 5.

[593] Michigan Deaths 1867–1897, images online at <www.FamilySearch.org>.

[594] Harris and Stover, "Second Daniel Harris of Goshen," 122 (1991):153.

[595] 1830 U.S. Census, Auburn, Geauga Co., Ohio, p. 261.

[596] Portage Co., Ohio, Deeds, 15:124.

[597] William Cumming Johnson, *Enumeration of Youth and Partial Census for School Districts in Portage County, Ohio* (Kent, Ohio: American History Research Center, 1982).

[598] Portage Co., Ohio, Deeds, 20:39. A witness, Hannah Culver, probably was Phebe's daughter with her first husband, Nathan Culver.

[599] Geauga Co., Ohio, Deeds, 20:114.

[600] The manner and place of his death is from Barbara Purple LaViers, letter of 19 Nov. 1999, citing records of her grandfather, Ivan Clinton Purple, publisher of a local newspaper in Newark Valley, Tioga Co., N.Y., and grandson of Woodruff's brother-in-law Thomas Seldon Purple.

$52.06. The estate was deemed "not sufficient for the support of the widow and children for 12 months and had there been property we would have given more, but as it is, we give the widow the property specified in this inventory." On 26 June 1839, Phebe reported: "no debts due decedent or other property except as set off by the appraisers for support of the administrator and family for one year. Estate wholly insolvent."[601]

By 1840, Phebe had moved to Auburn Township, just west of Troy, when her household consisted of a female age 40-49 [Phebe], two females 20-29 [her two Culver daughters], a boy 10-14, and two girls 5-9.[602] On 30 June 1848, Phebe sold the 40-acre farm in Troy to Voltimond D. Davis and purchased a half-acre lot in Bainbridge, next west of Auburn.[603] In 1850, Phebe Harris, age 50, born in Connecticut, was residing in the J. H. Stafford household in Bainbridge, a merchant, with [her son] Alanson Harris, age 20, and [daughter] Betsey P. Harris, age 15.[604] On 4 November 1856, Phebe sold to Samuel Wagoner the half-acre lot in Bainbridge that she had purchased in 1848.[605] In 1860, Phebe, age 60, was residing with her son Erwin A[lanson] Harris in Johnstonville, Trumbull County, Ohio.[606] By 1870, Phebe, then aged 70, had moved to Michigan with Erwin and his family.[607]

Children of Woodruff[5] and Frances/Fanny (Purple) Harris:[608]

    i MONELL[6] HARRIS, b. Smithville, Chenango Co., N.Y., 17 April 1815, was a photographer living in Fremont, Sandusky Co., Ohio, in 1870;[609] m. Mt. Vernon, Knox Co., Ohio, 17 April 1840 MARY A. T. NYE, b. there 18 Nov. 1818, living with Monell in Fremont 1870. They were in Fredericktown, Ohio, in 1860, his occupation then listed as "M.D."[610] No children.

55 ii LYMAN PURPLE HARRIS, b. Greene, Chenango Co., N.Y., 12 Aug. 1817; m. ELVIRA A. LANE.

   iii ESTHER ALMIRA HARRIS, b. Hiram, Portage Co., Ohio, 2 Oct. 1819, b. Hiram, Portage Co., Ohio, 2 Oct. 1819,[611] was living in Solon, Cuyahoga Co.,

---

[601] Geauga Co., Ohio, Probate Records, D:587, E:276, Chardon, Ohio.

[602] 1840 U.S. Census, Auburn Twp., Geauga Co., Ohio, p. 145.

[603] Geauga Co., Ohio, Deeds, 39:467, 42:307.

[604] 1850 U.S. Census, Bainbridge Twp., Geauga Co., Ohio, p. 303.

[605] Geauga Co., Ohio, Deeds, 52:453. Her son Erwin Alanson Harris witnessed.

[606] 1860 U.S. Census, Johnston Twp., P.O. Johnstonville, Trumbull Co., Ohio, p. 122 (Ervin A. Harris, cooper).

[607] 1870 U.S. Census, Campbell, P.O. West Campbell, Ionia Co., Mich., p. 390 (Erwin A. Harris, farmer).

[608] Purple, "Manuscript Notes," pp. 119-20, unless otherwise noted.

[609] 1870 U.S. Census, City of Fremont, 2nd Ward, Sandusky Co., Ohio, p. 24.

[610] 1860 U.S. Census, Fredericktown, Knox Co., Ohio, p. 138.

[611] Purple, "Manuscript Notes," p. 120.

Ohio, in 1870, age 50.[612] She m. 27 Feb. 1848 Dr. WILLIAM THOMPSON "of Bainbridge, Ohio," b. Ireland 19 Nov. 1819, who d. 9 July 1861.[613] Census entries for their household show that he was a "physician" in Solon in 1850,[614] and a "Doctor" there in 1860.[615]

Children of Dr. William and Esther Almira[6] (Harris) Thompson (from census entries):

1 *Samuel H. Thompson*, b. Ohio ca. 1848, a "R.R. Agent" in Arcadia, Hancock Co., Ohio, in 1880; m. Defiance Co., Ohio, 30 Dec. 1875 Mary Dell Parrott,[616] b. Ohio ca. 1854, living in 1880.[617]

2 *Florence M. Thompson*, b. Ohio ca. Jan. 1850 (age 9m in Oct. 1850), with parents in 1850 and 1860, and her mother in 1870.

3 *Robert E. Thompson*, b. Ohio ca. 1852, with parents in 1860 and his mother in 1870.

4 *William P. Thompson*, b. Ohio ca. 1854, a "R.R. employee" in Cleveland in 1880;[618] m. (license Cuyahoga Co., Ohio, 19 Aug. 1878) Hattie Brown,[619] b. England in July 1860, living as a widow in Cleveland in 1900.[620]

iv WILLIAM DEWEL HARRIS, b. Hiram 2 April 1823, d. Calif. 1 May 1858. He was perhaps the otherwise unplaced William Harris, age 22 [*sic*], cabinet-maker, b. Ohio, residing at the time of the 1850 census with his cousin Elisha Harris in Howard (later Durand), Winnebago Co., Ill.[621] Nothing further has been learned of William's life or of his experience in California.

v FANNY M. HARRIS, b. Parkman, Geauga Co., Ohio, 1 Sept. 1827 [*sic*: prob. 1825 or 1826], d. 1 June 1828.

Children of Woodruff[5] and Phebe (Orton) (Culver) Harris (the 1840 census included a second female child age 5-9):

56 vi ERWIN ALANSON HARRIS, b. Ohio 2 June 1830; m. MARY HOGLE.

vii BETSEY P. HARRIS, b. Ohio ca. 1835, living with her mother in 1850, age 15.

30 JOHN[5] HARRIS (*John[4], Daniel[3], Walter[2], John[1]*), born say 1773, probably in Goshen, Connecticut, was living in Salisbury, Connecticut, in 1820, age 45 or over, when his household was listed in a cluster including his brothers Daniel, Mylo, and Luther.[622] He married by 1799 **AESENETH**

[612] 1870 U.S. Census, Solon Twp., P.O. Solon, Cuyahoga Co., Ohio, p. 4.
[613] Purple, "Manuscript Notes," p. 120, his birthplace from census entries.
[614] 1850 U.S. Census, Town of Solon, Cuyahoga Co., Ohio, p. 410.
[615] 1860 U.S. Census, Solon Twp., P.O. Solon, Cuyahoga Co., Ohio, p. 47.
[616] Defiance Co., Ohio, Marriage Records, 2:305.
[617] 1880 U.S. Census, Washington Twp., Hancock Co., Ohio, E.D. 176, p. 42.
[618] 1880 U.S. Census, Cleveland, Cuyahoga Co., Ohio, E.D. 41, p. 61.
[619] Cuyahoga Co., Ohio, Marriage Records, 21:523, marriage return not entered.
[620] 1900 U.S. Census, 31st Ward, Cleveland, Cuyahoga Co., Ohio, E.D. 155, sheet 21A.
[621] 1850 U.S. Census, Howard, Winnebago Co., Ill., p. 317; Harris and Stover, "Second Daniel Harris of Goshen," 122 (1991):154-55.
[622] 1820 U.S. Census, Salisbury, Litchfield Co., Conn., p. 374.

WRIGHT, daughter of James and _____ (Hyde) Wright of Sheffield, Massachusetts.

In Canaan, Connecticut, on 7 October 1799, "John Harris Jr. and his wife Aeseneth Harris of Salisbury, which s[ai]d Aeseneth is Granddaughter and one of the Heirs at Law to the estate of Mr. Nathaniel Hyde the Elder late of Lebanon [Connecticut]" released their interest to Hyde's executor. Acknowledging in Canaan, Aeseneth signed her name and John made his mark. On the same day, Nathaniel Hyde's "grandson" James Wright Jr. of Sheffield released his interest.[623] In 1800, the households of James Wright and James Wright Jr. were adjacently listed in Sheffield.[624] In June 1815, Aeseneth Harris was a major creditor of the estate of James Wright Jr. at Sheffield.[625]

John Harris Jr. was in Hillsdale, Columbia County, New York, in 1800,[626] where his household was listed in sequence with that of his father, but he was back in Salisbury in time for the 1810 census.[627] John Jr., his father, and brother Elisha were jointly engaged in farming and blacksmithing in Egremont, Massachusetts, in the period 1804–1807. On 12 July 1814, Aeseneth Harris, with her brother-in-law Mylo Harris as witness, released her interest in an 1807 joint conveyance of Egremont property by her husband, John Harris Jr., and his father John Harris.[628]

Children of John[5] and Aeseneth (Wright) Harris:[629]

    i   _____ [6] HARRIS, b. 1795–1800, a female who appears in John's household in 1800, 1810, and 1820, perhaps the POLLY HARRIS who was received in church in Salisbury in 1816 and d. in 1833, although she could as well have been a younger sister of John Jr. (see no. 20 iii).

    ii   _____ HARRIS, b. 1791–1800, a male who appears only in John's home at Hillsdale, N.Y., in 1800.

    iii   JAMES HARRIS, b. Conn. ca. 1804, d. Salisbury, Conn., 9 Feb. 1855, age 50, bur. in Chapinville Cemetery.[630] In 1850, James Harris, age 46, was a blacksmith residing in David Foley's home in Salisbury.[631] James' uncle Mylo Harris was appointed as his administrator on 14 Feb. 1855. The inventory, valued at $497.99, included a house, blacksmith ship with tools, barn, household goods, and three small parcels of land. Debts were owing

---

[623] Lebanon, Conn., Deeds, 12:142-43.
[624] 1800 U.S. Census, Sheffield, Berkshire Co., Mass., p. 229.
[625] Berkshire Co., Mass., Probate Records, file no. 3232.
[626] 1800 U.S. Census, Hillsdale, Columbia Co., N.Y., p. 10 (10010-10010).
[627] 1810 U.S. Census, Salisbury, Litchfield Co., Conn., p. 200 (20010-01010).
[628] Berkshire Co., Mass., Deeds, Southern District, 40:547, 41:329, 524, 42:112, 258, 262, 43:199, 433.
[629] Harris and Stover, "Second Daniel Harris of Goshen," 122 (1991):224-25.
[630] *Historical Collections of the Salisbury Association*, 1:87.
[631] 1850 U.S. Census, Salisbury, Litchfield Co., Conn., p. 36.

to seven persons, including his cousins Joseph and Harlow P. Harris.[632] In April 1856, James's remaining real estate was distributed "to and among the legal heirs thereof": Elisha Harris, the "legal heirs of Luther Harris, deceased," Daniel Harris, and Milo Harris, i.e. his uncles or their heirs. Thus he had no surviving issue or siblings as next-of-kin.

James' real estate was described as the "homestead," perhaps the otherwise unrecorded home of his deceased parents, John and Aeseneth Harris. Elisha Harris and the heirs of Luther Harris received in common four acres with the "dwelling house thereon and the blacksmith shop" adjoining David Foley's land and the Great or North Pond. Similarly, Daniel and Milo Harris received six acres with the barn at the North End, also adjoining the pond and bounded east on the highway to Chapinville.[633]

iv EDWARD HARRIS, b. ca. 1810, d. 23 Nov. 1846, bur. Chapinville Cemetery in north Salisbury.[634] No evidence appears that he married or had children. At the request of next-of-kin in Dec. 1846, the court appointed Frederick Plumb, a local attorney, as administrator of Edward's estate. Valued at $1690 and including military clothing, 57½ acres of land, and a horse, it was distributed to his uncle Luther Harris and others. Expenses were listed for a "Journey to New Hartford" and for another "to New York."[635] Edward's land transactions in Salisbury in the 1830s, which confirm his place in this family, have been discussed elsewhere.[636]

21 ELISHA[5] HARRIS (*John[4], Daniel[3], Walter[2], John[1]*), born in Salisbury, Connecticut,[637] about 1775,[638] was presumed alive somewhere in 1856, when he received a share of his nephew James Harris's estate, but his residence after 1822 is unknown. He married first, soon before the 1800 census date, **MARY SARDAM**, born in Salisbury on 26 November 1776, daughter of Tunis Sardam 2nd and wife Abigail ____.[639] Sardam's will in 1810 mentioned his "grandson" Hymen Harris, and Himen [*sic*] Harris of Salisbury mentioned "my father Elisha Harris" and "my Grandfather Tunis Sardam" in an 1823 deed.[640]

Mary died apparently following Hymen's birth soon after the 1800 census date, and Elisha married second by 1802 **JANE BOGHROUGH** *alias* **JACOBS**, born in Salisbury on 15 September 1771, who died on 12 or 13 March 1841

---

[632] Salisbury District Probate Records, 1:433-34, 498-501, 512.

[633] Salisbury District Probate Records, 2:14.

[634] Inscription data online at <www.findagrave.com>, accessed Sept. 2012.

[635] Sharon District Probate Records, V21:534, 539, W22:114, 119, 120, 132.

[636] Harris and Stover, "Second Daniel Harris of Goshen," 122 (1991):225.

[637] The death record in 1876 of their son John Harris in a Richmond, Mass., town record states that his father, Elisha Harris, and mother, Jane Harris, were both born in Salisbury, Conn.

[638] According to notes prepared by a descendant.

[639] Salisbury, Conn., Vital Records, 2:8.

[640] Sharon District Probate Records, file no. 3173; Salisbury, Conn., Deeds, 16:269.

and buried in Center Cemetery at Richmond, Massachusetts,[641] daughter of Hyman Jacob Bagrough and his second wife, Hannah Sardam.[642]

Elisha's placement is John Harris's family is established by the distribution of his nephew James Harris's estate, and by land records in Salisbury and in Egremont, Massachusetts, discussed elsewhere.[643] In February 1805, Elisha bought from his father-in-law Tunis Sardam 2nd property in Salisbury "at the edge of North Pond . . . where his dwelling house now stands." He conveyed property to his brother Mylo Harris in April 1814 and in January 1815, the latter a mortgage. In September 1821, he purchased George Comegin's interest in two parcels in the "northerly part of town," one near the scythe manufactory and the other on the side of Toconnock Mountain, which had descended to George from his grandfather Tunis Sardam and brother Jonathan Comegin. Elisha gave back a mortgage deed to secure the $85 purchase price.[644]

On 1 March 1822, Elisha sold land to Levi Mason on Toms Hill adjoining Mylo Harris for $85, just the amount needed to pay off his mortgage to Comegin. Next August, the month he left town and family, "having taken with him the wife of a neighbor,"[645] he sold the "land on which my dwelling house now stands" to his son Hymen for $350. That December, Hymen obtained a judgment against his father for $307.50. When the constable enforced it in February 1823, execution was levied on the interest that Elisha had from Comegin in the parcels mentioned above. Elisha was "late of Salisbury" in March 1823, when the sheriff attempted to enforce a judgment on behalf of Levi Mason for $13.92. Also that March, Hymen sold to James Harris for $75 the interest he had obtained from his father. In December 1825, James paid Abel Starks $85 for a quitclaim of interest in these two parcels.[646]

On 18 December 1823, Elisha Harris was separated by vote of the Church for "scandalous misconduct" and disappears thereafter.[647] On 25 October

---

[641] *Vital Records of Richmond, Massachusetts, to the Year 1850* (Boston: NEHGS, 1913), 99.

[642] Judith Miner Hine Luedemann, "Hyman Jacob Bagrough and His First Wife, Jane Dutcher," NYGBR 122 (1991):75-83. Elisha's wife was called "Jane (Jacobs or Jacups)" in *Cleveland and Cleaveland Families*, 1:612.

[643] Harris and Stover, "Second Daniel Harris of Goshen," 122 (1991):225-26.

[644] Salisbury, Conn., Deeds, 11:341, 14:59, 108, 16:41, 88.

[645] Salisbury Congregational Church Records, 1:52.

[646] Salisbury, Conn., Deeds, 16:69, 87, 121, 306, 545-46. The James Harris involved in these transactions apparently was not Elisha's 19-year-old nephew, but instead an unrelated James Harris who operated after 1812 a nearby business variously called the "Iron Works," "scythe manufactory" and "Harris Works" in Salisbury deeds. For discussion, see Harris and Stover, "Second Daniel Harris of Goshen," 122 (1991): 226n8.

[647] Salisbury Congregational Church Records, 1:52.

1835, Jane, Sarah, and John Harris were "dismissed to Richmond," Massachusetts. Elisha and Jane had been admitted the Salisbury church on 1 September 1816, and next month they had six children including Sarah baptized there, but John's name is not in the list.[648]

Child of Elisha[5] and Mary (Sardam) Harris:

  i   HYMEN/HIMEN[6] HARRIS, b. prob. soon after the 1800 census date, but bp. at Salisbury 4 Oct. 1816, was named as a grandson in Tunis Sardam's will in 1810. He referred to Elisha Harris as his father and Tunis Sardam his grandfather in Sept. 1823, when he sold land he had from both of them to [his half-brother] William Harris.[649] No further record found.

Children of Elisha[5] and Jane (Boghrough *alias* Jacobs) Harris:

57   ii   WILLIAM JAY HARRIS, b. ca. Jan. 1802; m. SARAH GROAT.
     iii HANNAH HARRIS, b. say 1804, bp. Salisbury 4 Oct. 1816.
     iv   MARY HARRIS, b. Salisbury, Conn., ca. March 1806, d. Richmond, Mass., 15 Sept. 1876, age 70y 6m;[650] m. Salisbury 12 Oct. 1825 SAMUEL D. GROAT "of Mt. Washington, Mass.," b. Copake, N.Y., ca. May 1802, d. Richmond 21 Aug. 1885, age 83y 3m., son of Philip and Lydia (___) Groat.[651] They resided in Richmond, Mass., for some time before moving to Adams, Mass., where they were living in 1850 and 1860,[652] and returned to Richmond before 1870.[653] Samuel was in Richmond in 1880, age 77, a widowed farmer.[654]
          Children of Samuel D. and Mary[6] (Harris) Groat:
          1 Child, b. ca. 1827, d. Richmond, Mass., 5 March 1832, age 5.[655]
          2 *Mary Jane Groat*, b. Salisbury in Jan. 1829, living Richmond, Mass., 1900, widow, age 71;[656] m. Richmond at age 17 on 14 Oct. 1845 John Sherrill 2nd,[657] who d. there 25 March 1877 of heart disease, age 50, son of Lewis C. and Nancy (Andrews) Sherrill.[658]
          3 *Charles W. Groat*, b. Richmond, Mass. in March 1831, d. there 25 Nov. 1901 of acute cystitis, single, age 70y 9m.[659] He was in Richmond in

---

[648] Salisbury Congregational Church Records, 1:77, 146, 2:199, 200.

[649] Salisbury, Conn., Deeds, 16:259.

[650] Massachusetts Vital Records, 1841–1910, 283:60.

[651] Massachusetts Vital Records, 1841–1910, 364:65.

[652] 1850, 1860 U.S. Census, Adams, Berkshire Co., Mass., p. 60, 184, respectively.

[653] 1870 U.S. Census, Richmond, Berkshire Co., Mass., p. 4.

[654] 1880 U.S. Census, Richmond, Berkshire Co., Mass., E.D. 37, p. 1.

[655] *Vital Records of Richmond,* 97.

[656] 1900 U.S. Census, Richmond, Berkshire Co., Mass., E.D. 79, sheet 2B, the record showing that she was the mother of six children, all living.

[657] *Vital Records of Richmond,* 65.

[658] Massachusetts Vital Records, 1841–1910, 238:55.

[659] Massachusetts Vital Records, 1841–1910, 516:121.

1880, age 77, a widowed farmer,[660] and living there near his sister Mary Jane Sherrill in 1900, age 69 and single.[661]

4 *Frances Mariah Groat*, b. Mass. in Jan. 1834, m. Richmond, Mass., 16 June 1879, as his 3rd wife, Daniel J. Mickle, of New York City, "deputy marshal," age 59, son of John and Elizabeth (___) Mickle.[662] He d. before 1900, when Frances was residing with her brother Charles in Richmond, age 66, a widow with no children.

5 *Martha Matilda Groat*, b. Mass. ca. 1838, d. Richmond, Mass., 1 Oct 1898, single, age 62, heart failure.[663] She was keeping house for her father in 1880.

6 *Ellen Groat*, b. Mass. ca. 1838, with parents 1850.

7 *Adaline Groat*, b. Mass. ca. 1843, with parents 1850, 1860, prob. the *Amelia* Beckley, "sister," b. Nov.1842, a widow, in her brother Charles Groat's household in Richmond in 1900.[664]

v   LUCY JANE HARRIS, b. 7 Oct. 1810 [*sic*, perhaps 1809], bp. as "Jane" 4 Oct. 1816, d. Hannibal, Cayuga Co., N.Y., 24 Aug. 1851; m. at Wolcott, Wayne Co., N.Y., in 1827 BEZALEEL FARNUM CLEAVELAND, b. Salisbury, Conn., 28 Aug. 1804, who d. at Sterling or Martville, Cayuga Co., 10 April 1848, age 43, son of Bradford and Eunice (Farnum) Cleaveland. He "dwelt at Salisbury in 1827, South Britain, New Haven County, Conn., Wolcott to 1840, Martville afterwards, miller."[665]

Children of Bezaleel Farnum and Lucy Jane[6] (Harris) Cleaveland:[666]

1 *Lucy Jane Cleaveland*, b. Wolcott, N.Y., 1832, d. Martville 17 Sept. 1747.

2 *Mary Elizabeth Cleaveland*, b. East Wolcott, N.Y., 28 July 1834, d. Sennett, N.Y., 25 Sept. 1882; m. Lysander, Onondaga Co., N.Y., 8 Nov. 1854 Edward Drake, liveryman, b. Cato, N.Y., 9 Dec. 1833, son of James and Sophia (Habeer) Drake.

3 *Recepha Ann Cleaveland*, b. Wolcott, N.Y., 25 July 1835; m. Sterling, N.Y., 6 Jan. 1857 John Augustus Doud, merchant, b. Camillus, N.Y., 2 Feb. 1834, s. of Zenas and Sally Clark (Jones) Doud.

4 *Isadore Mariah Cleaveland*, b. Wolcott 22 June 1837/1838; m. Martville, N.Y., 6 Feb. 1855 Henry Niver Whitman, farmer, b. Canaan, N.Y., 27 Jan. 1832, son of Samuel and Elizabeth (Niver) Whitman.

5 *Bradford Franklin Cleaveland*, b. Martville, N.Y., 22 Aug. 1840; m. Sennett, N.Y., 31 March 1868 Ellen Gertrude Remington, b. Sennett 18 Dec. 1844, dau. of Rufus and Elizabeth (Donoven) Remington. Bradford was a farmer in Holt Co., Nebr. in 1883.

---

[660] 1880 U.S. Census, Richmond, Berkshire Co., Mass., E.D. 37, p. 1.

[661] 1900 U.S. Census, Richmond, Berkshire Co., Mass., E.D. 79, sheet 2B, the record showing that she was the mother of six children, all living.

[662] Massachusetts Vital Records, 1841–1910, 307:61.

[663] Massachusetts Vital Records, 1841–1910, 481:121.

[664] The Charles W. Groat household in 1900 also included a "niece", Lizzy B. Leitch, b. Dec. 1865, a widow with no children.

[665] *Cleveland and Cleaveland Families*, 1:612.

[666] *Cleveland and Cleaveland Families*, 1:612, 2:1217-18.

6 *Clarissa Antoinette Cleaveland*, b. Martville 6 Aug. 1844; m. Hannibal, N.Y., 18 Dec. 1864 Rev. Horatio Yates, Methodist Episcopal clergyman, b. Mentz, Cayuga Co., N.Y., 13 Dec. 1841, son of Jacob Peter and Marilla (Woodruff) Yates.

58   vi   JOHN HARRIS, b. Salisbury, Conn., 11 Feb. 1811; m. CAROLINE MARKHAM.

     vii   SARAH HARRIS, b. Conn. say 1813, bp. 4 Oct. 1816, a widow living Williamsburg, Mass., 1880;[667] m. NATHAN RISLEY, b. Mass. ca. 1817, a butcher with whom she was living in Williamsburg in 1860.[668] Sarah was admitted to the Salisbury church on 17 July 1831 and dismissed "to Richmond" with her mother and brother John on 25 Oct. 1835. No evidence is found that she had children.

32 DANIEL[5] HARRIS (*John[4], Daniel[3], Walter[2], John[1]*), born Salisbury about 1787, was living there in 1870.[669] He married first **JERUSHA JONES**, born in Copake, Columbia County, New York,[670] probably the female aged 16-25 in his household at Salisbury in 1810.[671] He married second, apparently by 1813, **LAURA BOWEN**, born in Sheffield, Massachusetts, on 13 October 1789,[672] who died of typhoid fever in Salisbury on 23 October 1863, age 74y 10d,[673] daughter of Joseph and Mary (Elton) Bowen.[674] Laura Harris, "wife of Daniel," was admitted to the Salisbury Congregational Church in January 1816.[675]

Daniel's household appears in all the census enumerations taken in Salisbury from 1810 to 1870, always near [his brother] Mylo Harris. He had no real estate or livestock in the 1819 tax assessment,[676] but in March 1838, Daniel acquired by quitclaim deed from Eliphalet Whittlesey a half-acre 'about 40 rods north of Mylo Harris' dwelling house" in the north part of Salisbury, which "is the same land on which the said Daniel Harris' house now stands."[677] Next 16 August, Daniel, signing by mark, mortgaged this property "together with all buildings" for $27, it being "all the land owned by said Harris" in Salisbury.[678]

[667] 1900 U.S. Census, Williamsburg, Hampshire Co., Mass., E.D. 39, p. 27.
[668] 1880 U.S. Census, Williamsburg, Hampshire Co., Mass., p. 31.
[669] 1870 U.S. Census, Salisbury, Litchfield Co., Conn., p. 9.
[670] Jerusha's name and birth place are from the death record of her son Harvey Harris, mentioned below.
[671] 1810 U.S. Census, Salisbury, Litchfield Co., Conn., p. 200.
[672] Sheffield, Mass., Town Records, 2:26.
[673] Salisbury Death Record.
[674] Harris and Stover, "Second Daniel Harris of Goshen," 123 (1992):40.
[675] Salisbury Congregational Church Records, 1:72.
[676] Salisbury, Conn., Deeds, 15:484.
[677] Salisbury, Conn., Deeds, 22:376.
[678] Salisbury, Conn., Deeds, 22:260.

Daniel and his brother Elisha Harris both had children baptized in the Salisbury Congregational Church on 4 October 1816, and it appears that two other children were born before 1820. Then, after a long hiatus, sons born about 1829 and 1833 were baptized at the same church, the latter when their mother Laura was about age 45.

Child of Daniel[5] and Jerusha (Jones) Harris:

59   i   HARVEY[6] HARRIS, b. Salisbury say 1806, m. (1) ELIZA ____, (2) MARY ____.

Children of Daniel[5] and Laura (Bowen) Harris (possibly the first two were by Jerusha):

ii   JULIAN HARRIS, b. say 1808, bp. Salisbury 4 Oct. 1816, presumably the second male under age 10 in Daniel's home in 1810.

iii   MARY HARRIS, b. say 1810, bp. Salisbury 4 Oct. 1816 and accounted for as the female child b. 1805–1810 in Daniel's home in 1820 and 1830. She was admitted to the Salisbury church on 4 Sept. 1831 and m. there 11 Oct. 1832 WILLIAM HALL, "both of Salisbury."[679]

Child of William and Mary[6] (Harris) Hall:
1 *Alexander Hall*, bp. Salisbury 8 April 1835.[680]

iv   LAURA ELIZA HARRIS, b. Conn. ca. 1813 (age 57 in 1870), bp. Salisbury 4 Oct. 1816 and accounted for as the female child b. 1810–1815 in Daniel's home in 1820 and 1830, was recorded as his "sister" Laura "Harris," her age grossly understated as 52y, and "keeping house" for her half brother Harvey Harris in Salisbury in 1880 (see above).

Laura had at least three husbands and a divorce. Laura Harris "of Salisbury, Conn.," m. (1) at New Lebanon, Columbia Co., N.Y., 16 Oct. 1838, prob. as his 2nd wife, HIRAM H. BIDWELL of Barrington, Mass.,[681] b. Mass. ca. 1804 (age 46 in 1850). They apparently divorced before 1840; Hiram's subsequent marriages in the 1840s are discussed elsewhere.[682] Laura E. Bidwell "of Salisbury" m. there (2) 3 March 1846, as his 2nd wife, FREDERICK C. LANDON,[683] b. there 1 Oct. 1797, son of David and Johannah (____) Landon.[684] Their household in 1850 was near that of her father, Daniel Harris, in Salisbury.[685] Laura m. (3) by 1865 (birth of son Charles) ____ HINMAN. As "Laura Hinman, age 57, she was "keeping house" for her elderly father in Salisbury in 1870.

Child of ____ and Laura[6] (Harris) Hinman:
1 *Charles Hinman*, b. Conn. ca. 1865, was with his mother in 1870, age 5, and with his uncle Harvey Harris in 1880, age 15.

---

[679] Salisbury Congregational Church Records, 2:210, 265.
[680] Salisbury Congregational Church Records, 2:249.
[681] Olive R. Hand, "Records of Marriages by Ira Hand, J.P., New Lebanon, N.Y., 1832–1851," p. 12.
[682] Harris and Stover, "Second Daniel Harris of Goshen," 123 (1992):41.
[683] Salisbury, Conn., Town Records.
[684] Salisbury, Conn., Town Records.
[685] 1850 U.S. Census, Salisbury, Litchfield Co., Conn., p. 36.

60   v   JOSEPH HARRIS, b. Salisbury, Conn., 30 Aug. 1816; m. MARY ANN SEELEY.
      vi   (prob.) a female child, b. 1811–1820, presumably after the other children
           above were bp. in 1816, appears in Daniel Harris's household only in 1820.
      vii ELIZA HARRIS, b. Salisbury, Conn., ca. 1820, living in Monterey, Mass., in 1856.
           Eliza Harris "of Salisbury, Conn.," m. at New Lebanon, N.Y., 25 Sept. 1838
           JOHN MORRISON of Tyringham, Mass.,[686] b. North East, Dutchess Co., N.Y.,
           ca. 1815. Eliza is accounted for as a female in her father's home in 1820 and
           1830. John and Eliza Morrison recorded children in Monterey (adjoining
           Tyringham) between 1847 and 1856. The record of their household in 1850
           the names of three other children b. in Mass.[687]
               Children of John and Eliza[6] (Harris) Morrison:
               1 *Maria Morrison*, b. ca. 1841.
               2 *Mary Morrison*, b. ca. 1845.
               3 *Henry Morrison*, b. ca. 1847.
               4 *William H. Morrison*, b. 31 May 1847.[688]
               5 *E. Jenny Lind Morrison*, b. 29 Nov. 1850.[689]
               6 *Unnamed female child*, b. 27 Dec. 1856.[690]
61   viii ALBERT HARRIS, bp. Salisbury 3 July 1829;[691] m. MARY A. ____.
62   ix   HENRY ULYSSES HARRIS, b. Salisbury ca. 1833; m. MARY ____.

33 MYLO[5] **HARRIS** (*John*[4], *Daniel*[3], *Walter*[2], *John*[1]), born in Connecticut
about 1789, died 6 October 1875, age 87, and buried in Salisbury Center
Cemetery. He married first at Salisbury on 3 April 1810 **ABIGAIL (COMEGIN)**
JONES, born there 27 January 1791,[692] who died on 10 March 1873 and
buried in same cemetery, daughter of Jonathan and Susannah (Sardam)
Comegin of Salisbury and widow of ____ Jones.[693] Mylo married secondly in
Great Barrington, Massachusetts, on 2 March 1867 **LOIS R. (DEMORAN-**
VILLE) DUNBAR, born in Middleborough, Massachusetts,[694] about 1810,
daughter of Lewis and Naomi (Pierce) Demoranville and widow of Thaddeus
Dunbar, a Methodist clergyman who died in New Marlborough, Massachu-

---

[686] "Records of Marriages by Ira Hand," p. 12.
[687] 1850 U.S. Census, Monterey, Berkshire Co., Mass., p. 161.
[688] Massachusetts Vital Records, 1841–1910, 28:32.
[689] Massachusetts Vital Records, 1841–1910, 42:38.
[690] Massachusetts Vital Records, 1841–1910, 96:48.
[691] Salisbury Congregational Church Records, 2:247.
[692] Salisbury, Conn., Town Records.
[693] For discussion of Abigail's identity, see Harris and Stover, "Second Daniel Harris of Goshen,"
122 (1991):43n11.
[694] Massachusetts Vital Records, 1841–1910, 199:43. The record gives Mylo's age as 70y, understating
it by about 8 years, and his parents as "John and Olive." A double fiction clearly was involved, as the age
stated would have him about age 13 at his first marriage, and his father's first wife, Phebe (Hill) Harris, was
still alive and living with him in 1794 (Goshen, Conn., Deeds, 9:432).

setts, on 8 January 1866.[695] Lois was with Mylo in 1870 and was his widow in 1875.

By September 1823 Mylo and Abigail were residing in Canaan "on the Great Mountain near the Pond" when they mortgaged their Canaan property in the "northerly part of Salisbury."[696] One of these parcels, "70 acres with all buildings," had been given to Abigail by Tunis Sardam. A judgment against Mylo's lands in April 1824 also refers to the "farm late owned by Tunis Sardam dec'd and by him given to the said debtor's wife."[697]

Although he was residing in Canaan in 1823 and 1824, Mylo appears in all of the censuses taken at Salisbury from 1820 through 1870. In 1814, he had witnessed when his stepmother, Olive Harris, and his brother John's wife Aeseneth released their interest in Egremont, Massachusetts, land. Mylo's tax assessment of $86.10 in 1819 for buildings, land (66 acres), and livestock was the highest among the Harris households in that list.[698] Mylo was one of the business and professional men who purchased pews in the Episcopal Church in Salisbury, and some of his children attended and were married there.[699] A biographical sketch in 1881 of Mylo's son Harlow Peck Harris lists for them eleven children without dates of birth, all said to have been born in Salisbury except Mylo and Susan, born at Canaan.[700]

Children of Mylo[5] and Abigail (Comegin) (Jones) Harris:

i ELEANOR[6] HARRIS, b. Conn. ca. 1810, d. Salisbury in Sept. 1889, age 79.[701] She m. there 21 Dec. 1831 CALVIN SPARKS of Sheffield, Mass.,[702] b. Conn. ca. 1808, who d. in the 1870s. They were in Richmond, Mass., by 1836, when a daughter was born,[703] but they returned to Salisbury before the census of 1840,[704] when they were listed next to their father.

Except for a brief residence in Sheffield in the 1840s, where Eleanor was admitted and baptized as an adult on 7 Sept. 1845,[705] they were in Salisbury

---

[695] Massachusetts Vital Records, 1841–1910, 192:43; 1860 U.S. Census, Becket, Berkshire Co., P.O. West Becket, Mass., p. 26 (household of Thaddeus Dunbar, Methodist clergyman, including wife Lois, age 50, and her father, Lewis Demoranville, age 87).

[696] Salisbury, Conn., Deeds, 16:573-74.

[697] Salisbury, Conn., Deeds, 17:491.

[698] Salisbury, Conn., Deeds, 15:395, 484.

[699] Salisbury Episcopal Church Records, 2:58.

[700] *History of Litchfield County,* 558. Although unreliable for earlier generations, that account correctly identifies Harlow's own siblings.

[701] Salisbury Congregational Church Records, 3:272.

[702] Salisbury Congregational Church Records, 2:265.

[703] George Leander Randall, *Tripp Genealogy: Descendants of James, son of John Tripp* (New Bedford, Mass.: Vining Press, 1924), 162.

[704] 1840 U.S. Census, Salisbury, Litchfield Co., Conn., p. 269.

[705] Sheffield Congregational Church Records, 13, 33.

also for the censuses of 1850, 1860, and 1870. In 1880, widow Ellen Sparks, age 70, was residing with Lucy Sparks, "daughter-in-law," age 55, in a home near her brother Martin Harris.[706]

Children of Calvin and Eleanor⁶ (Harris) Sparks, the first from *Tripp Genealogy* and the others from census and Chapinville Cemetery records:

1 *Francis Augusta Sparks*, b. Richmond, Mass., 14 Aug. 1836, living 1900; m. Sheffield, Mass., 21 Dec. 1853 Hiram Tripp, b. 24 Nov. 1830, d. Waltham, Mass., 30 March 1918, son of Daniel I. and Damaris (Myers) Tripp of Dutchess Co., N.Y.[707] They were in Goshen, Conn., in 1900.[708]

2 *Miles H. Sparks*, b. ca. 1838, d. 9 Dec. 1841, age 3.

3 A boy, one of two males under 5 in the household in 1840.

4 *Robert Sparks*, b. Mass. ca. 1843 (census), d. 9 Aug. 1850, age 7.

5 *Sarah P. Sparks*, b. Mass. ca. 1845.

6 *Walter C. Sparks*, b. Conn. ca. 1847.

ii ORRA HARRIS, b. Conn. 16 Oct. 1811, d. 11 Feb. 1886, bur. Kinsman Cemetery, Kinsman, Trumbull Co., Ohio;[709] m. Salisbury 15 March 1837 LUCIUS HOLCOMB "of Johnston, Ohio,"[710] b. Conn. 16 May 1813, d. 7 Nov. 1899, bur same cemetery. They were in Johnston, Trumbull Co., Ohio, in 1850,[711] and in Vernon, Trumbull Co., in 1860,[712] where they were still residing on a farm in 1880.[713]

Children of Lucius and Orra⁶ (Harris) Holcomb:

1 *Milo H. Holcomb*, b. Ohio ca. 1838; m. Trumbull Co., Ohio, 8 March 1861 Sarah I. De Wolf.[714]

2 *Henry C. Holcomb*, b. Ohio ca. 1842; m. Trumbull Co. 7 Dec. 1864 Mary J. Simpkins.[715]

63 iii MILES HARRIS, b. Conn. ca. 1816; m. (1) ELIZA JANE AMES, (2) MATILDA COOKINGHAM.

iv MARTIN HARRIS, b. Conn. ca. 1818, 3 July 1891, age 73, bur. Salisbury Center Cemetery. He m. (1) HETTY ____, b. 8 Nov. 1825 (calc.) the "wife of Martin Harris," who d. 30 Jan. 1848, age 22y, 2m, 22d, and bur. Hillside Cemetery in adjoining Sharon, Conn. He m. (2) in Sharon 4 Dec. 1848 MARY E. BIERCE, "both of Sharon,"[716] b. in Jan. 1826, d. 15 Oct. 1906, bur. beside Martin. She appears as "Mary C. Harris" in census records, so she probably was the Mrs. Mary Clark Harris who was admitted and baptized as

---

[706] 1880 U.S. Census, Salisbury, Litchfield Co., Conn., p. 15.

[707] Randall, *Tripp Genealogy*, 89-90, 162.

[708] 1900 U.S. Census, Goshen Town, Litchfield Co., Conn., E.D. 236, sheet 5B.

[709] Gravestone photo online at <www.findagrave.com>, accessed Sept. 2012 (birth and death dates inscribed).

[710] Salisbury Town Records.

[711] 1850 U.S. Census, Johnston Twp., Trumbull Co., Ohio, p. 324.

[712] 1850 U.S. Census, Vernon Twp., Trumbull Co., Ohio, p. 60.

[713] 1880 U.S. Census, Vernon Twp., Trumbull Co., Ohio, E.D. 405, p. 11.

[714] Ohio County Marriages, 1789–1994, online at <www.FamilySearch.org>, accessed Sept. 2012.

[715] Ohio County Marriages, 1789–1994, online at <www.FamilySearch.org>, accessed Sept. 2012.

[716] Barbour Collection, citing Sharon LR27:551.

an adult in the Salisbury church on 3 July 1887.[717] Martin was a "merchant" in 1860, was appointed to a building commission in 1877,[718] and was an insurance agent in 1880. His widow, Mary C. Harris, was living alone in Salisbury in 1900, the record indicating that she never had children.[719]

v   ABIGAIL HARRIS, b. 14 June 1819, d. 2 Sept. 1895, bur. Pleasant Plains Cemetery, Dutchess Co., N.Y.;[720] m. Salisbury 22 Nov. 1848 MICHAEL COOKINGHAM, "of Hyde Park, N.Y.,"[721] b. N.Y. 3 June 1823, d. 3 Feb. 1901, bur. same cemetery. As a widower, Michael was living with his son John in Clinton, Dutchess Co., in 1900.[722] Michael and Abigail were in Hyde Park in 1850,[723] but in Clinton by 1860,[724] where they stayed.

Children of Michael and Abigail[6] (Harris) Cookingham:

1 *Harris L. Cookingham*, b. ca. 1850.

2 *John Calvin Cookingham*, b. Aug. 1842, d. 1930; m. Mary A. Carpenter, b. 1858, d. 1935, both bur. Pleasant Plains Cemetery.[725]

3 *[Orellia?] Cookingham*, b. ca. [1860?], name and age nearly illegible on the 1870 census.

vi   MILO HARRIS, b. "in Canaan" 29 Sept. 1821, d. 30 Nov. 1865, bur. Salisbury Center Cemetery as "Milo Harris Jr." He m. Salisbury 27 June 1853 JANE A. SWIFT,[726] b. 23 Aug. 1834, dau. of Ward and Statira (Green) Swift.[727] In 1860, Milo Harris Jr. was a retail merchant in Salisbury village with no children.[728]

vii SUSAN HARRIS, b. "in Canaan" 13 April 1824, d. Ypsilanti, Mich., 28 July 1864; m. at Salisbury 3 Jan. 1849, as his 1st wife, FREDERICK WESTON CLEAVELAND,[729] b. Sharon, Conn., 2 Dec. 1824, who d. at Ypsilanti 4 Sept. 1896, age 71, son of John and Mary (Ingraham) Cleaveland.[730] He m. (2) South Egremont, Mass., 15 Jan. 1871 Mary Jane Gardner.[731] The Cleaveland household at Salisbury in 1850 was adjacently listed with that of Susan's brother Luther Harris.[732] According to the *Cleaveland Genealogy*, Frederick is said to have resided in Chapinville, Conn., until 1853, afterwards at Ypsilanti where he was a carriage dealer and a "U.S. City Marshall."

---

[717] Salisbury Congregational Church Records, 3:207, 239.

[718] *Historical Collections of the Salisbury Association*, 2:27.

[719] 1900 U.S. Census, Salisbury, Litchfield Co., Conn., E.D. 250, p. 4.

[720] Gravestone photo online at <www.findagrave.com>, accessed Sept. 2012.

[721] Salisbury Episcopal Church Records, 1:89.

[722] 1900 U.S. Census, Clinton, Dutchess Co., N.Y., E.D. 3, p. 1.

[723] 1850 U.S. Census, Hyde Park, Dutchess Co., N.Y., p. 223.

[724] 1860 U.S. Census, Clinton, Dutchess Co., N.Y., p, 947.

[725] Gravestone photo online at <www.findagrave.com>, accessed Sept. 2012.

[726] Salisbury Episcopal Church Records, 1:96.

[727] Bible record, *The Detroit Society for Genealogical Research Magazine* 7 (1943):24.

[728] 1860 U.S. Census, Salisbury, Litchfield Co., Conn., 979.

[729] Salisbury Episcopal Church Records, 1:89.

[730] *Cleveland and Cleaveland Families*, 1:606, 2:1212.

[731] Egremont Congregational Church Records, 234, 317.

[732] 1850 U.S. Census, Salisbury, Litchfield Co., Conn., p. 37.

Children of Frederick Weston and Susan[6] (Harris) Cleaveland (*Cleaveland Genealogy*):

1 *Susan Orphelia Cleaveland*, b. Salisbury, Conn., 3 Aug. 1850.

2 *Carrie Calista Cleaveland*, b. Ypsilanti, Mich., 19 Sept. 1856. After her mother's death in 1864, Carrie went to her uncle Miles Harris and was in his household in Lansing, Mich., in 1870 at age 13.

viii CELESTA E. HARRIS, b. April 1826, was living in Hyde Park, N.Y., in 1900, age 74.[733] She m. in Salisbury 28 Oct. 1846 Albert T. Jones of Poughkeepsie, N.Y.,[734] b. N.Y. ca. 1819, d. in 1860s. "Bushnell Tavern was run after 1850 by Albert Jones who married a sister of Martin and Harlow P. Harris."[735] Albert and Celesta were managing a boarding house and inn in Salisbury in 1850, their home including a boy Albert Jones, age 2, b. N.Y.[736] In 1860, they were farming in Hyde Park, N.Y., the boy Albert then age 12.[737] In 1870, Celesta Jones, age 43, and her son Albert, age 22, were residing in Pine Plains, N.Y.[738] She was in her brother Martin Harris's household in Salisbury in 1880 as "sister" Celesta Jones, a widow.[739] By 1900, she was back in Hyde Park with her son Albert and his wife Minerva. Celesta and her husband Albert had "for a number of years kept the Pine Plains Hotel," which, after his death she "kept for a while before becoming 'housekeeper for the late Richard Peck.'"[740]

Child of Albert T. and Celesta E.[6] (Harris) Jones:

1 *Albert T. Jones*, b. N.Y. in Aug. 1847,[741] d. Hyde Park, N.Y., 28 June 1923,[742] bur. Poughkeepsie Rural Cemetery; m. ca. 1875 Minerva Mackay, b. N.Y. in March 1850, d. April 1825, bur. same cemetery, dau. of John Moore and Orinda S. (Platt) Mackay.[743]

ix LLEWELLYN HARRIS, "son of Milo and Abigail," b. ca. 1828, d. 12 Aug. 1848, age 20, bur. Salisbury Center Cemetery.[744]

64 x HARLOW PECK HARRIS, b. 30 July 1830; MARGARETTA A. SWEET.

xi HANNAH D. HARRIS, b. ca. 1833, is mentioned as Mylo Harris' youngest child in the biography of her brother Harlow Peck Harris. She is accounted for in Mylo's home in 1840 and appears there in 1850 at age 17.

34 LUTHER[5] HARRIS (*John[4]*, *Daniel[3]*, *Walter[2]*, *John[1]*), born in Connecticut about 1795 (age 55 in 1850), died soon after January 1856, when "land owned

---

[733] 1900 U.S. Census, Hyde Park, Dutchess Co., N.Y., E.D. 11, sheet 8A, the record showing that she was the mother of one child, who was living.

[734] Salisbury, Conn., Town Records.

[735] *Historical Collections of the Salisbury Association*, 2:23.

[736] 1850 U.S. Census, Salisbury, Litchfield Co., Conn., p. 27.

[737] 1860 U.S. Census, Hyde Park, Dutchess Co., N.Y., p. 856.

[738] 1870 U.S. Census, Pine Plains, Dutchess Co., N.Y., p. 24.

[739] 1880 U.S. Census, Salisbury, Litchfield Co., Conn., p. 16.

[740] Obituary of son Albert T. Peck, *Pine Plains Register*, 5 July 1923.

[741] 1900 U.S. Census, Hyde Park, Dutchess Co., N.Y., E.D. 11, sheet 8A.

[742] Obituary, *Pine Plains Register*, 5 July 1923.

[743] Data online at <www.findagrave.com>, accessed Sept. 2012.

[744] Salisbury Episcopal Church Records, 1:133.

by Luther Harris Heirs" was mentioned as adjoining property sold by his brother Mylo as administrator of their nephew James Harris's estate. He married, apparently before 1820, **REBECCA** ____, born in Connecticut, whose age given as 46y in the 1850 census at Salisbury appears to be understated.[745] Luther was assessed in Salisbury for one cow in 1819.[746] The 1820 through 1840 enumerations at Salisbury imply that he had married by 1820, and consistently indicate that his wife was born in the period 1795–1800.

Luther and Rebecca lived near the North Pond, close to Chapinville in the north part of Salisbury, where he was most closely associated with his oldest brother John's sons James and Edward. In January 1829, Luther leased from Polly Dutcher a quarter-acre parcel there "for and during the term of his natural life and the natural life of his wife Rebecca Harris," with Edward Harris and Daniel Dutcher witnessing.[747] In April 1832, he leased from Edward another quarter-acre next to the "piece said Luther bought of Polly Dutcher and on which Luther now lives."[748]

Children of Luther[5] and Rebecca (____) Harris:

    i   A female[6], b. 1816-1820, in Luther's home in 1830.[749]

    ii   A female, b. 1821-1825, also in Luther's home in 1830.

    iii CHARLES HARRIS, b. Salisbury, Conn., ca. 1832 and accounted for in Luther's home in 1840 and 1850,[750] was residing in Lee, Mass., on 5 Jan. 1860 when he m. there JULIA ANN BONSEY (age 15), b. Otis, Mass., ca. 1845.[751] They were residing in Lee in July 1860.[752]

SIXTH GENERATION

35 JOHN[6] HARRIS (*John[5], Hosea[4], Thomas[3], Walter[2], John[1]*), born in Wethersfield on 30 April 1791, died on 3 February 1869 and buried in Wethersfield Village Cemetery.[753] He married in Wethersfield **SARAH CRANE**, born 29 December 1792, who died on 1 October 1858 and buried beside him, daughter of Joseph and Abigail (Dix) Crane.[754]

---

[745] 1850 U.S. Census, Salisbury, Litchfield Co., Conn., p. 36.

[746] Salisbury, Conn., Deeds, 15:484.

[747] Salisbury, Conn., Deeds, 19:483.

[748] Salisbury, Conn., Deeds, 19:130.

[749] 1830 U.S. Census, Salisbury, Litchfield Co., Conn., p. 490.

[750] 1840, 1850 U.S. Census, Salisbury, Litchfield Co., Conn., pp. 270, 36, respectively.

[751] Massachusetts Vital Records, 1841–1910, 135:44 (b. Salisbury, son of Luther and Rebecca).

[752] 1860 U.S. Census, Lee, P.O. South Lee, Berkshire Co., Mass., 98 (married "within the year").

[753] Gravestone photo online at <www.findagrave.com>, accessed Aug. 2012.

[754] Stiles, *Ancient Wethersfield*, 2:258, 414.

Children of John[6] and Sarah (Crane) Harris:[755]

     i   ABIGAIL[7] HARRIS, b. ca. 1821, d. 2 April 1890, age 69, bur. Wethersfield Center Cemetery;[756] m. Capt. JUSTUS G. CHURCHILL, b. ca. 1817, d. 22 Aug. 1874, age 57, bur. beside Abigail. Justus was a butcher in Wethersfield in 1860,[757] and a farmer there in 1870.[758]

          Children of Justus G. and Abigail[7] (Harris) Churchill:

           1 *Charles N. Churchill*, b. ca. 1846, with parents in 1860.

           2 *Clarissa H. Churchill*, b. ca. 1847, with parents in 1860.

           3 *Stephen Frank Churchill*, b. ca. 1852, with parents in 1860 and 1870.

           4 *Prudence W. Churchill*, b. ca. 1858, with parents in 1860 and 1870.

           5 *William Churchill*, b. ca. 1861, with parents in 1870.

           6 *Lillie Bell Churchill*, b. ca. Oct. 1865, d. 15 Feb. 1868, age 2y 5m, bur. with parents.

    ii   CLARISSA HARRIS, b. ca. 1821, d. 3 Nov. 1831, age 10, bur. Wethersfield Village Cemetery.[759]

   iii   SARAH HARRIS, b. Conn. ca. 1822; m. HENRY KING, b. Conn. ca. 1820. They were residing in Wethersfield in 1850,[760] but not found in later censuses.

          Child of Henry and Sarah[7] (Harris) King, perhaps others b. later:

           1 *Alice King*, b. Conn. ca. 1848, with parents in 1850.

    iv   LUCY HARRIS, b. Conn. in Sept. 1824, d. 30 July 1903; m. FRANCIS C. WIL-COX, b. Jan. 1827. They were in Berlin, Conn., in 1900, the record showing that Lucy had no children.[761]

    v   JOHN HARRIS, b. 29 June 1826, d. 15 Feb. 1870; m. 6 June 1853 ROXANNA LOSEY, b. ca. 1832. John Harris, carriage trimmer, age 32 [*sic*], and wife Anna, age 28, and son William E., age 5, were residing in Wethersfield in 1860 with his father, John Harris, age 70.[762]

          Children of John[7] and Roxanna (Losey) Harris:[763]

           1 *William E.[8] Harris*, b. 4 Feb. 1855; m. 6 Sept. 1882 Helena Wein-garten.

           2 *Frank Harris*, b. 20 March 1857, d. 24 Sept. 1859.

           3 *James H. Harris*, b. 22 Feb. 1863.

36 HOSEA[6] HARRIS (*John[5], Hosea[4], Thomas[3], Walter[2], John[1]*), born in Wethersfield on 22 July 1799, died on 16 October 1874 and buried in Wethersfield Village Cemetery.[764] He married **SARAH FRANCIS**, born in

---

[755] Stiles, *Ancient Wethersfield*, 2:258, 414.

[756] Gravestone photo online at <www.findagrave.com>, accessed Aug. 2012.

[757] 1860 U.S. Census, Wethersfield, Hartford Co., Conn., p. 34.

[758] 1870 U.S. Census, Wethersfield, Hartford Co., Conn., p. 21.

[759] Gravestone photo online at <www.findagrave.com>, accessed Aug. 2012.

[760] 1850 U.S. Census, Wethersfield, Hartford Co., Conn., p. 80.

[761] 1900 U.S. Census, Berlin, Hartford Co., Conn., E.D. 116, sheet 12A.

[762] 1860 U.S. Census, Wethersfield, Hartford Co., Conn., p. 34.

[763] Stiles, *Ancient Wethersfield*, 2:258, 416.

[764] Gravestone photo online at <www.findagrave.com>, accessed Aug. 2012.

Wethersfield on 30 July 1801, died 27 December 1854 and buried beside Hosea, daughter of Charles and Sarah (Adams) Francis.[765]

Children of Hosea[6] and Sarah (Francis) Harris:[766]

     i   CHARLES[7] HARRIS, b. 22 Feb. 1822, d. 1828.

    ii   EVELINA H. HARRIS, b. 3 Oct. 1824; m. Wethersfield 24 July 1844 Capt. JOHN NEWTON FRANCIS, b. there 11 Jan. 1822, d. at sea of yellow fever 6 June 1867, captain of the *Swanee*, son of Daniel and Mehitable (Goodrich) Francis.[767]

        Children of Capt. John Newton and Evelina H.[7] (Harris) Francis:[768]

        1 *Albert Newton Francis*, b. Wethersfield 10 June 1845; m. 16 Jan. 1878 Emma A. Shepard and resided in Hartford.

        2 *Henry Harris Francis*, b. Wethersfield 24 Oct. 1847; m. 24 Oct. 1876 Sarah Alice Bidwell, dau. of Samuel W. Bidwell, resided Hartford.

        3 *John Francis*, b. New Haven 10 April 1850, d. 30 May 1850.

        4 *Harriet Evelina Francis*, New Haven 25 Sept. 1851, d. Galesburg, Ill., 17 Sept. 1890; m. Marcus E. Robinson.

        5 *Mary Elida Francis*, b. New Haven 21 July 1854, lived in Hartford, unm.

        6 *Daniel Francis*, b. Chatham Ill., 31 May 1857, d. Wethersfield 11 March 1865.

        7 *John Newton Francis*, b. Wethersfield 2 April 1860, d. there 2 Oct. 1861.

        8 *William Hanmer Francis*, b. Wethersfield 12 June 1862; m. 11 April 1887 Kate G. Karey and resided in Hartford.

65   iii   FRANCIS HOSEA HARRIS, b. 24 Jan. 1829; m. EMELINE WILLOUGHBY BRADLEY.

    iv   HENRY H. HARRIS, b. 9 Sept. 1834, d. 28 July 1914, age 80, unm., bur. Wethersfield Village Cemetery, his gravestone inscribed "Co. H., 11 Inf., Conn. Vols."[769]

     v   SARAH A. HARRIS, b. 29 Oct. 1837; m. by 1858 Dr. H. H. SPRAGUE, b. Ohio 14 July 1827, d. 4 Feb. 1888, bur. Deepwood Cemetery, Nevada, Vernon Co., Mo.[770] They were in Sangamon Co., Ill., in 1860 with two-year-old daughter Mary, b. Ill.[771] The household of widow Sarah A. Sprague in Vernon Co. in 1900 included her recently married daughter Edna J. Gwinn, b. Kans. in Aug. 1876, and son-in-law Oliver H. Gwinn, b. Mo. in April 1877.[772]

        Children of Dr. H. H. and Sarah A.[7] (Harris) Sprague:

        1 *Mary Sprague*, b. Ill. Ca. 1858, with parents in 1860.

---

[765] Stiles, *Ancient Wethersfield*, 2:414.

[766] Stiles, *Ancient Wethersfield*, 2:414.

[767] Stiles, *Ancient Wethersfield*, 2:345.

[768] Stiles, *Ancient Wethersfield*, 2:345. 348-49.

[769] Gravestone photo online at <www.findagrave.com>, accessed Aug. 2012.

[770] Gravestone photo online at <www.findagrave.com>, accessed Aug. 2012 ("H. H. Sprague, M.D.").

[771] 1860 U.S. Census, Dist. 16, P.O. Chatham, Sangamon Co., Ill., p. 45. They have not been located in 1870 and 1880.

[772] 1900 U.S. Census, Clay Twp., Vernon Co., Mo., E.D. 125, sheet 7A, the record showing that Sarah was the mother of three children, all then living.

2 A child living in 1900.

3 *Edna J. Sprague*, b. Kans. in Aug. 1876; m. ca. 1900 Oliver H. Gwinn, b. Mo. in April 1877. They were with Edna's mother in 1900.

vi   MARY L. HARRIS, b. 19 March 1844, living Rocky Hill, Conn., 1900, the record showing that she was the mother of seven children, all living;[773] m. ca. 1865 FREDERICK MORTON a farmer of Rocky Hill, b. Conn. in Sept. 1843, living with Mary in 1900. They had been enumerated there also in 1880.[774]

Children of Frederick and Mary L.[7] (Harris) Morton, from the census:

1 *Frederick A. Morton*, b. Conn. ca. 1866, with parents 1880.

2 *Emma L. Morton*, b. Conn. ca. 1868, with parents 1880.

3 *Cora A. Morton*, b. Conn. ca. 1872, d. 1903, bur. Center Cemetery, Rocky Hill, Conn.[775]

4 *Ethel F. Morton*, b. Conn. in Dec. 1876, with parents 1880, 1900.

5 *Florence E. Morton*, b. Conn. in May 1878, with parents 1880, 1900.

6 *Harriet Morton*, b. Conn. in Sept. 1882, with parents 1900.

7 *Mary Morton*, b. Conn. in Feb. 1887, with parents 1900.

37 WALTER[6] HARRIS (*John[5], Hosea[4], Thomas[3], Walter[2], John[1]*), born in Wethersfield on 24 August 1805,[776] died in Elizabeth, New Jersey, on 8 April 1880, age 75;[777] married in First Church, Hartford, Connecticut, 15 August 1836 **CAROLINE M. ORCUTT**,[778] born in New York on 25 August 1818, died in Elizabeth, New Jersey, on 22 March 1898, age 82 [*sic*], widowed.[779]

Walter and Caroline were in Hartford in 1850, when their household included all the children listed below.[780] They all were in New York City by 1860, where Walter was an "importer";[781] and still there in 1870, when he was a "retired merchant."[782] By 1880, they had moved to Elizabeth, New Jersey, where he was then a retired merchant and invalid.[783]

---

[773] 1900 U.S. Census, Rocky Hill, Hartford Co., Conn., E.D. 216, sheet 7B.

[774] 1880 U.S. Census, Rocky Hill, Hartford Co., Conn., E.D. 56, p. 22.

[775] Gravestone photo online at <www.findagrave.com>, accessed Aug. 2012.

[776] Barbour Collection, citing Wethersfield VR2:189.

[777] New Jersey Deaths and Burials, 1720–1988, online at <www.FamilySearch.com>.

[778] Barbour Collection, citing Hartford VR1:171 (by Rev. Joel Hawes, a Hartford minister). Stiles *Ancient Wethersfield*, 2:415, states without explanation that this marriage was performed in Schoharie, N.Y.

[779] New Jersey Deaths and Burials, 1720–1988, online at <www.FamilySearch.com>.

[780] 1850 U.S. Census, City of Hartford, Hartford Co., Conn., p. 589/295.

[781] 1860 U.S. Census, Ward 20, New York City, New York Co., N.Y., p. 262

[782] 1870 U.S. Census, Ward 20, New York City, New York Co., N.Y., p. 563.

[783] 1880 U.S. Census, 6th Ward, Elizabeth, Union Co., N.J., E.D. 174, p. 22. Among those included in the household was a granddaughter Anneta Harris, age 10, b. N.Y.

Children of Walter[6] and Caroline M. (Orcutt) Harris:[784]

    i   GEORGINE CAROLINE[7] HARRIS, b. Conn. 17 June 1837, d. 19 July 1898; m. STEPHEN CHESTER, b. N.Y. ca. 1836; they were residing with her parents in New York in 1870, and Elizabeth, N.J., in 1880, when Stephen's occupation was "civil engineer" and "telegraph instrument," respectively."[785]
           Child of Stephen and Georgine Caroline[7] (Harris) Chester:
             1 *Clifford Chester*, b. N.Y. in Feb. 1868; m. ca. 1899 Catharine ____, b. Mo. March 1868. They were "boarders" in Elizabeth, N.J., in 1900, when he was an insurance agent.[786]

    ii FRANCES A. HARRIS, b. Conn. 13 Feb. 1839, d. 13 Feb. 1877.

    iii WALTER CLIFFORD HARRIS, b. Conn. 14 April 1841, d. in Mexico 1883. He was living with his parents in 1880, widower and a broker.
           Probable child of Walter Clifford[7] and ____ (____) Harris:
             1 *Anneta*[8] *Harris*, b. N.Y. ca. 1870, listed as granddaughter age 10, in Walter and Caroline Harris household in Elizabeth, N.J., in 1880.

    iv ALBERT W. HARRIS, b. Conn. 11 Feb. 1843, living Manhattan, N.Y., 1900, "oil merchant;" m. ca. 1873 MARY R. ____, b. Wis. In June 1859, with Albert in 1900.[787] Two of their children were b. in N.J. before they appear in New York City in 1880, where he was an oil merchant.[788]
           Children of Albert W.[7] and Mary R. (____) Harris, from censuses cited:
             1 *Caddie J.*[8] *Harris*, b. N.J. ca. 1874, with parents 1880.
             2 *Albert T. Harris*, ("Tudor R." in 1900), b. N.J. Aug. 1875, with parents in 1880 and 1900.
             3 *Maize T. R. Harris*, b. N.Y. June 1886, with parents 1900.

    v HENRY TUDOR B. HARRIS (recorded as "Philip" in 1860, age 14), b. Conn. 19 March 1845; m. ca. 1874 SARAH L. G. ____, b. Md. in Sept. 1856. They were residing near his parents in Elizabeth, N.J., in 1880, when he was a paymaster for the U.S. Navy. They were still there in 1900, childless, where he still had the same job.[789]

38 HENRY[6] HARRIS (*John*[5], *Hosea*[4], *Thomas*[3], *Walter*[2], *John*[1]), born in Wethersfield on 8 May 1808, died 7 January 1872 and buried in Cedar Hill Cemetery in Hartford, Connecticut;[790] married by 1835 (birth of first child) **FRANCES ROBBINS**, born about 1813, who died on 17 April 1898, age 85, and buried beside Henry, daughter of William and Rebecca (Crane) Robbins

[784] Stiles *Ancient Wethersfield*, 2:415.
[785] 1880 U.S. Census, 6th Ward, Elizabeth, Union Co., N.J., E.D. 174, p. 22.
[786] 1900 U.S. Census, 8th Ward 8, Elizabeth, Union Co., N.J., E.D. 108, sheets 8A-9B.
[787] 1900 U.S. Census, Manhattan, City of New York, New York Co., N.Y., E.D. 469, sheet 4A.
[788] 1880 U.S. Census, City of New York, New York Co., N.Y., E.D. 504, p. 14.
[789] 1900 U.S. Census, 11th Ward, Elizabeth, Union Co., N.J., E.D. 115, sheet 15A.
[790] Gravestone photo online at <www.findagrave.com>, accessed Aug. 2012.

of Wethersfield.[791] Henry, a farmer, and Frances were living in Wethersfield in 1870,[792] and Frances was there in 1880.[793]

Children of Henry[6] and Frances (Robbins) Harris:

    i   MARSHALL H.[7] HARRIS, b. Conn. 29 July 1835, d. 27 Sept. 1901; m. ca. 1860 HONOR/NORA G. WOODHOUSE, b. Conn. 14 May 1834, d. 21 Feb. 1906, age 72, dau. of Manna and Honor (Goodrich) Woodhouse of Wethersfield.[794] Honor was living with Marshall in Wethersfield in 1900;[795] they are bur. in Cedar Hill Cemetery at Hartford.[796]

        Children of Marshall H.[7] and Honor/Nora G. (Woodhouse) Harris:[797]

         1 *Carrie T.*[8] *Harris*, b. Conn. 31 Jan. 1864; m. George Royce.

         2 *Henry Alfred Harris*, b. Conn. 28 Oct. 1868; m. ca. 1898 Annie Griswold, b. Conn. in Oct. 1868. They were in Wethersfield in 1900.[798]

         3 *Annie L. Harris*, b. 11 Dec. 1872; m. F. W. Weildon.

         4 *Luther R. Harris*, b. Conn. 11 Feb. 1874, with parents in 1900.

    ii FANNIE A. HARRIS, b. Conn. ca. 1841, d. 7 July 1876, bur. Cedar Hill Cemetery, Hartford;[799] m. by 1870 EDWIN R. CURTIS of Glastonbury,[800] b. Conn. ca. 1844. They were residing at Naubuc in Glastonbury in 1870 with Joseph and Celia (____) Curtis, presumably his parents. Edwin and Joseph were described as agents.[801]

    iii LUTHER D. HARRIS, b. Conn. ca. 1845, d. Lerado, Tex., 6 May 1888, age 43,[802] unm.

    iv MARTHA R. HARRIS, b. ca. 1855, d. 18 March 1885, bur. Cedar Hill Cemetery, Hartford;[803] m. FRANK YOUNG.[804] He is probably the Frank Young who was working "in a machine shop" in Hartford in 1881, age 25, his household including his wife, "Mrs. Young," age 35 [*sic*], and son Frank Jr., age 1.[805]

---

[791] Stiles *Ancient Wethersfield*, 2:415.

[792] 1870 U.S. Census, Wethersfield, P.O. Newington, Hartford Co., Conn., p. 8.

[793] 1880 U.S. Census, Wethersfield, Hartford Co., Conn., E.D. 40, p. 8.

[794] 1860 U.S. Census, Wethersfield, Hartford Co., Conn., p. 10 (Manny Woodhouse household).

[795] 1900 U.S. Census, Wethersfield, Hartford Co., Conn., E.D. 225, sheet 9B, the record showing that Honor was the mother of four children, all living.

[796] Gravestone photo online at <www.findagrave.com>, accessed Aug. 2012.

[797] Stiles *Ancient Wethersfield*, 2:416.

[798] 1900 U.S. Census, Wethersfield, Hartford Co., Conn., E.D. 225, sheet 9B (household listed after that of his parents).

[799] Gravestone photo online at <www.findagrave.com>, accessed Aug. 2012.

[800] Stiles *Ancient Wethersfield*, 2:415.

[801] 1870 U.S. Census, Glastonbury, P.O. Naubuc, Hartford Co., Conn., p. 36.

[802] As inscribed on his sister Fanny A. (Harris) Lewis's monument in Cedar Hill Cemetery, Hartford.

[803] As inscribed on her sister Fanny A. (Harris) Lewis's monument in Cedar Hill Cemetery, Hartford.

[804] Stiles *Ancient Wethersfield*, 2:415.

[805] 1870 U.S. Census, Glastonbury, P.O. Naubuc, Hartford Co., Conn., p. 36.

39 GEORGE⁶ HARRIS (*Joseph⁵, Hosea⁴, Thomas³, Walter², John¹*), born July 1810, died 16 September 1858; married **EVELINA MADEN** of Cuba.[806] They are not found in the 1850 U.S. Census.

Children of George⁶ and Evelina (Maden) Harris:

    i   JOSEPH⁷ HARRIS.
   ii   ELLEN HARRIS.
  iii   GEORGE HARRIS.

40 SAMUEL H.⁶ HARRIS (*Joseph⁵, Hosea⁴, Thomas³, Walter², John¹*), born 8 June 1814, died 6 July 1897; married by 1845 (birth of first child) **JANE C. WOOD** of New York, born 24 August 1824, died 3 February 1873.[807] Samuel and Jane were in New York City in 1850, where he was a "ship joiner."[808] They were back in Hartford by 1860, when his occupation was entered in the census as "car builder."[809]

Children of Samuel H.⁶ and Jane C. (Wood) Harris:

    i   WILLIAM A.⁷ HARRIS, b. N.Y. ca. 1845, with parents 1850 and 1860.
   ii   ELIZABETH E. HARRIS, b. N.Y. ca. 1847, with parents 1850 and 1860; m. W. R. PIERCE.[810]

41 CHAUNCEY⁶ HARRIS (*Thomas⁵⁻⁴⁻³, Walter², John¹*), born 21 September 1816, died in Wethersfield on 12 February 1875 and buried in Cedar Hill Cemetery in Hartford.[811] He married in Wethersfield on 6 May 1846 **EMELINE WELLES**,[812] born there on 7 March 1820,[813] who died on 23 November 1912 and was buried in Chauncey's lot at Hartford, daughter of George W. and Prudence (Deming) Welles.[814] Emeline was residing in Wethersfield in 1900 at age 80.[815]

While a child, Chauncey lost most of the fingers on his right hand. He taught school in Bristol and Meriden, Connecticut; Hempstead, Long Island;

---

[806] Stiles *Ancient Wethersfield*, 2:414.
[807] Stiles *Ancient Wethersfield*, 2:414.
[808] 1850 U.S. Census, 11ᵗʰ Ward, City of New York, New York Co., N.Y., p. 481.
[809] 1860 U.S. Census, Hartford, Hartford Co., Conn., p. 149.
[810] Stiles *Ancient Wethersfield*, 2:414.
[811] Grave monument photo online at <www.findagrave.com>, accessed Aug. 2012.
[812] Barbour Collection, citing Wethersfield VR2:127 (both of Wethersfield, Rev. Mark Tucker presiding).
[813] Albert Welles, *History of the Welles Family in England and Normandy* (New York: By the author, 1876), 287.
[814] Stiles, *Ancient Wethersfield*, 2:415.
[815] 1880 U.S. Census, Hartford, Hartford Co., Conn., E.D. 6, p. 96B.

and at Rock Island, Illinois, before becoming prominent as Superintendant of Schools and the Orphan Asylum in Hartford.[816] He was a "teacher" in Hartford in 1850, when his household included Emeline and the first two children below.[817] In 1860, his occupation in Hartford was "Superintendant of Orphan Asylum."[818] By 1870, the family had returned to Wethersfield, where Chauncey was again called "teacher."[819]

Children of Chauncey[6] and Emeline (Welles) Harris:[820]

    i GEORGE WELLS[7] HARRIS, b. 25 March 1847, d. 1942, bur. Cedar Hill Cemetery, Hartford;[821] m. (1) 12 Jan. 1871 ALICE JOSEPHINE ROWE of Baltimore, dau. of Henry Rowe, (2) 28 Sept. 1876 ELIZABETH S. MILLS of West Hartford,[822] b. Conn. Sept. 1854, d. 1940, bur. Cedar Hill Cemetery, dau. of Charles Mills. George and Elizabeth and their four children were residing in Wethersfield in 1900.[823] They were still there in 1940.[824]

        Child of George Wells[7] and Alice Josephine (Rowe) Harris:

        1 *Alice J. Rowe[8] Harris*, b. 17 March 1872, d. 1 July 1872.

        Children of George Wells[7] and Elizabeth S. (Mills) Harris:

        2 *Chauncey Karl Harris*, b. Conn. 1 Feb. 1879, living Hollister, Calif., 1940, age 60, implement salesman; m. ca. 1907 Bertha W. ____, b. Calif. ca. 1887, with Chauncey in 1940.[825] They were in San Jose, Calif., in 1910,[826] and had moved to Hollister by 1920.[827]

        3 *George Mills Harris*, b. Conn. 3 Feb. 1883, living Wethersfield 1940, age 57; m. Beatrice ____, b. Conn. ca. 1895, with George 1940.[828]

        4 *Marjorie Stillman Harris* (twin), b. 6 June 1890.

        5 *Rodney Wells Harris* (twin), b. Conn. 6 June 1890, living Wethersfield 1940, age 49; m. Ruth ____, b. Conn. ca. 1895, with Rodney 1940.[829]

   ii FANNY ESTELLE HARRIS, b. 1 Oct. 1849; m. 17 Oct. 1877 E. NEWTON LOVELAND,[830] b. Conn., in July 1844. They were residing in Wethersfield in 1900 with no children; he was a farmer.[831]

---

[816] Stiles, *Ancient Wethersfield*, 2:415 (including signed portrait of Chauncy Harris; Welles, *History of the Welles Family*, 287.
[817] 1850 U.S. Census, City of Hartford, Hartford Co., Conn., p. 265/529.
[818] 1860 U.S. Census, Third District, Hartford, Hartford Co., Conn., p. 52.
[819] 1870 U.S. Census, Wethersfield Hartford Co., Conn., p. 43.
[820] Stiles, *Ancient Wethersfield*, 2:415-16.
[821] Gravestone and monument photo online at <www.findagrave.com>, accessed Aug. 2012.
[822] Stiles, *Ancient Wethersfield*, 2:415.
[823] 1900 U.S. Census, Wethersfield Town, Hartford Co., Conn., E.D. 225, sheet 21A.
[824] 1940 U.S. Census, Wethersfield, Hartford Co., Conn., E.D. 2-258, sheet 19B.
[825] 1940 U.S. Census, Hollister City, San Benito Co., Calif., E.D. 35-1, sheet 6A.
[826] 1910 U.S. Census, Ward 3, San Jose, Santa Clara Co., Calif., E.D. 102, sheet 11A.
[827] 1920 U.S. Census, Hollister, San Benito Co., Calif., E.D. 32, sheet 3A.
[828] 1940 U.S. Census, Wethersfield, Hartford Co., Conn., E.D. 2-258, sheet 19B.
[829] 1940 U.S. Census, Wethersfield, Hartford Co., Conn., E.D. 2-258, sheet 20A.
[830] Stiles, *Ancient Wethersfield*, 2:415.
[831] 1900 U.S. Census, Wethersfield Town, Hartford Co., Conn., E.D. 225, sheet 10B.

iii MARY J. HARRIS, b. 25 Oct. 1854, d. 1935, bur. Cedar Hill Cemetery, Hartford.[832] She was with her mother in Wethersfield in 1900, unmarried. bur. Cedar Hill Cemetery, Hartford.[833]

iv EMMA L. HARRIS, b. 31 July 1857, d. 1921, bur. Cedar Hill Cemetery, Hartford.[834] She was with her mother in Wethersfield in 1900, unmarried.

v CHARLES EDWARD HARRIS, b. 23 Oct. 1859, d. 29 March 1861, bur. Cedar Hill Cemetery, Hartford.[835]

vi CHARLES CHAUNCEY HARRIS, b. 14 Jan. 1863, d. 1940, bur. Cedar Hill Cemetery, Hartford;[836] m. 11 Dec. 1889 CARRIE R. ADAMS, b. Conn. in April 1866, d. 1929, dau. of Josiah G. and Ellen (Warner) Adams.[837] They were residing in Wethersfield in 1900 with son Burton A.[838]

Child of Charles Chauncey[7] and Carrie R. (Adams) Harris:

1 *Burton Adams[8] Harris*, b. 2 July 1891, d. Wethersfield in Nov. 1974;[839] m. ca. 1917 Inez Wilcox, b. Conn. 30 April 1896, d. Wethersfield in Nov. 1983.[840] She was with Burton in Wethersfield in 1940.[841] On 5 June 1917, Burton Adams Harris, age 25, b. Wethersfield, single and working on his father's farm, registered for the World War I draft.[842]

42 HIRAM[6] HARRIS (*Elisha[5], Jeremiah[4], Daniel[3], Walter[2], John[1]*), born in New York about 1796, died in Hiram, Ohio, on 8 September 1873. He married first **ANNA WALKER**, born in New York on 13 October 1799, who died on 15 February 1877 and buried in Fairlawn Cemetery at Hiram. She had married second in 1848 William Riley Bates. Hiram and Anna were divorced by 1847 and he married secondly in Portage County, Ohio, on 19 November 1855 **AURELIA MILLS**,[843] born in Vermont on 14 September 1806, who died on 5 January 1876. Hiram and Aurelia are buried in Fairlawn Cemetery.

In 1850, the William and Anna Bates household in Hiram Township included Caroline Harris, age 17, Cordelia Harris, age 9, and Alphelde Harris, age 18, the latter unidentified but the first two from Anna's marriage

[832] Monument photo online at <www.findagrave.com>, accessed Aug. 2012.
[833] About that time, Mary J. Harris gave information to Henry R. Stiles about the Harris family in Wethersfield, which became a featured item in a discussion by the present writer, "Enigmas #26: Early Harrises of Wethersfield, Connecticut: Analysis of a Tradition," *The American Genealogist* 83 (2009): 249-57.
[834] Monument photo online at <www.findagrave.com>, accessed Aug. 2012.
[835] Monument photo online at <www.findagrave.com>, accessed Aug. 2012.
[836] Monument photo online at <www.findagrave.com>, accessed Aug. 2012.
[837] Stiles, *Ancient Wethersfield*, 2:416.
[838] 1900 U.S. Census, Wethersfield Town, Hartford Co., Conn., E.D. 225, sheet 21A.
[839] Social Security Death Index, SSN 043-30-2685.
[840] Social Security Death Index, SSN 043-38-8964.
[841] 1940 U.S. Census, Wethersfield, Hartford Co., Conn., E.D. 2-258, sheet 20A.
[842] World War I Draft Registration Cards, 1917–1918, no. 145, image online at <www.Ancestry.com>.
[843] Ohio County Marriages, 1789–1994, online at <www.FamilySearch.org>.

with Hiram Harris. At that time, Hiram, age 54, was residing in the adjacently listed household of M. B. Quimby.[844]

Hiram Harris was "one of the elder sons of Elisha Harris" who made the first settlement "on the road leading west" from Parkman [Geauga County] in 1820, and which he sold in 1822,[845] and does not appear again in Geauga County records until 1836. Hiram and Anna probably resided during the intervening period in Oxford, Chenango County, New York, where his household was enumerated in 1830.[846]

By 6 September 1836, however, they had returned to Ohio when he paid his father $100.00 for 10 acres in Hiram Township. Their household in Hiram in 1840 consisted of a male and female 40-49, two girls between 5 and 15, and an unidentified male 30-40.[847] In the following six years, Hiram purchased additional property in Hiram Township from Milo Porter, Charles Walker, and Warren Henry, parts of which he sold in 1844 and 1846.

Apparently as part of Hiram and Anna's divorce settlement, on 8 February 1848 they sold most of the remaining portion of the land to Alva Udall and Abner Harris [unrelated]. Hiram retained at least a half-acre, which he sold on 4 April 1853 to [his-son-in-law] George Bates. Hiram Harris, a farm laborer, and his second wife were enumerated sequentially with William and Anna Bates in Hiram Township in 1860 and 1870.[848]

Hiram's will, dated 4 April 1873 and proved in Portage County on 1 October 1873, mentions his "present wife" Aurelia and "my three children" (unnamed); William Allen executor, witnesses W. E. and M. Hank.

Children of Hiram[6] and Anna (Walker) Harris:

    i   JANE M.[7] HARRIS, b. N.Y. ca. 1827; m. Portage Co. 21 Feb. 1849 WILLIAM A. HINKLEY,[849] b. Ohio ca. 1823. They were in Mantua Twp., Portage Co., in 1850, when he was a jailor, and in 1860 when he was a hotel keeper.[850]
       Child of William A. and Jane M.[7] (Harris) Hinkley:
       1 *Clara D. Hinkley*, b. Ohio ca. 1856, with parents 1860.
    ii CAROLINE HARRIS, b. N.Y. ca. 1833, d. 1904; m. Portage Co. 2 July 1852 GEORGE BATES,[851] b. ca. 1830, d. 2 July 1856. They are bur. Fairlawn Ceme-

---

[844] 1850 U.S. Census, Hiram Twp., Portage Co., Ohio, p. 4.

[845] *History of Geauga County*, 699.

[846] 1830 U.S. Census, Oxford Twp., Chenango Co., N.Y., p. 68 (male and female 30-39 and a girl under 5).

[847] 1840 U.S. Census, Hiram Twp., Portage Co., Ohio, p. 187.

[848] 1860, 1870 U.S. Census, Hiram Twp., Portage Co., Ohio, pp. 64, 331, respectively.

[849] Ohio County Marriages, 1789–1994, online at <www.FamilySearch.org>.

[850] 1850, 1860 U.S. Census, Mantua Twp., Portage Co., Ohio, pp. 57, 62, respectively.

[851] Ohio County Marriages, 1789–1994, online at <www.FamilySearch.org>. In 1850, 20-year-old George Bates was residing in Hiram in the household of Abner Harris. Despite their close association in

tery in Hiram, her stone inscribed "mother," but no children have been identified. In 1860, widow Caroline Bates was residing in Hiram with her
mother and stepfather; in 1870 she was keeping house there for her mother,
Anna Bates, age 71.[852]

    Iii   CORDELIA H. HARRIS, b. Hiram Twp., Portage Co., Ohio, 15 Sept. 1841, d.
there 30 June 1909.[853] She m. Portage Co. 3 July 1861 GILBERT D. WEST-
LAND,[854] b. Ohio in 1828, d. 1901, son of William and Nancy (___) Westland of Hiram. Cordelia and Gilbert are bur. Fairlawn Cemetery, Hiram.

    They appear in the census for Hiram in 1870 and 1880; he was a car-
penter and joiner.[855] The *Garrettsville Journal* of 8 July 1909 reported that
"after an illness of nearly two years, Mr. Cordelia Westland died at home of
her daughter, Mrs. John Everhard, Wednesday, June 30th," and "save for a
brief two years [her entire life] was passed in the town of her birth. Her
lengthy illness was due to an accident which confined her for more than a
year. A son Vernon, and a daughter, Mrs. Ida Everhard, blessed the home.
Her husband died eight years ago."

    Children of Gilbert D. and Cordelia H.[7] (Harris) Westland:

    1 *Vernon C. Westland*, b. Ohio ca. 1862, with parents 1870, 1880.
    2 *Ida May Westland*, b. Ohio ca. 1866, d. 1942, bur. Fairview Ceme-
tery, Hiram, Ohio;[856] m. Portage Co., 8 Aug. 1889 John Henry
Everhard,[857] b. 1865, d. 1941, bur. same cemetery.

43 HARVEY[6] HARRIS (*Elisha[5], Jeremiah[4], Daniel[3], Walter[2], John[1]*), born in
New York about 1797, died in Allegan County, Michigan, of typhoid fever
in August 1869.[858] He married by 1820, probably in Broome or Chenango
County, New York, **ALMIRA HOWARD**,[859] born in New York about 1797,
who was living in her son Silas's home in Allegan County in 1870, age 73.

    Harvey apparently remained in New York for some time after his parents
moved to Geauga County, Ohio. Their first child was born in New York
about 1820, but he had had rejoined his parents by 20 May 1823, when they
gave him, "for love and affection," 50 acres in Parkman Township, Geauga
County.[860] The deed stipulated that his father was to retain rights to "erect
mills on the stream which runs through the land." On 4 April 1825, Harvey

Ohio (e.g., Abner bought land from Hiram Harris in 1847), Abner, b. 6 Feb. 1804 in Plainfield, Conn.,
was a son of the unrelated William[6] Harris (*Abner[5], Jonathan[4], Richard[3], Thomas[2-1]*) from Smithfield,
R.I., who arrived in Hiram from Conn. in 1818.

[852] 1860, 1870 U.S. Census, Hiram Twp., Portage Co., Ohio, pp. 64, 331, respectively.
[853] Obituary of Cordelia Westland, *Garrettsville [Ohio] Journal*, 8 July 1909.
[854] Ohio County Marriages, 1789–1994, online at <www.FamilySearch.org>.
[855] 1870, 1880 U.S. Census, Hiram Twp., Portage Co., Ohio, pp. 18, E.D. 121, p. 17, respectively.
[856] Data online at <www.findagrave.com>, accessed Sept. 2012.
[857] Ohio County Marriages, 1789–1994, online at <www.FamilySearch.org>.
[858] 1870 U.S. Census, Mortality Schedule, Heath Twp., Allegan Co., Mich.
[859] Purple, "Manuscript Notes."
[860] Geauga Co., Ohio, Deeds, 10:141, Elisha Purple and Sheldon Harris witnessed.

and Almira sold this land to Albon C. Garner for $400.00, but with the mill rights retained.[861] They continued to live nearby, however, as Hiram was listed near his father in 1840.[862]

On 14 April 1831, Harvey appeared at the court house in Chardon, the county seat, to make application for a marriage license for his underage sister Sally Harris "of Parkman" and Silas N. Howard, stating that he "saw Elisha Harris who is the father of the said Sally sign a certificate of consent."[863] On 9 July 1835, Harvey purchased from Martin Nash 40 acres of Section 14 in Troy Township.[864] It is reported elsewhere that in 1835, "Harvey Harris located on Section 6, next to the county line."[865] Harvey mortgaged the Section 14 property on 9 February 1836, then sold it to John Weston for $350.00 on 16 January 1838.

In the early 1840s, Harvey moved his family from Troy, Geauga County, to Troy, Wood County, also in Ohio, where, on 3 June 1844, he purchased from Elijah Huntington and wife Susan 80 acres in Section 11, Township 6, for $80.00.[866] Next September, he bought part of Tract no. 42 from Shibnah and Mary Ann Spink for $42.[867] Their household was enumerated in Troy Township, Wood County, in 1850, when he was a carpenter; and again in 1860, when he was a farmer.[868] After 1853, a sequence of deeds shows that Harvey and Almira Harris, at various times, conveyed land to their children and others until they were left with one acre in the northeast corner of Tract 42.[869] The latter was sold on 10 April 1866 by "Harvey Harris and Almira Harris of Troy Township" to Henry P. Buckland for $350.00;[870] that is probably about the time they moved to Michigan.

Children of Harvey[6] and Almira (Howard) Harris:[871]

>   i   ELISHA[7] HARRIS, b. N.Y. ca. 1820; m. Wood Co., Ohio, 4 July 1843 LUCINA POWERS,[872] b. ca. 1823 (age 37 in 1850), Ezra Howland, M.G., presiding. In

---

[861] Geauga Co., Ohio, Deeds, 10:259.

[862] 1840 U.S. Census, Hiram Twp., Geauga Co., Ohio, p. 187.

[863] Marriage licenses on file in Chardon, Ohio.

[864] Geauga Co., Ohio, Deeds, 21:189.

[865] *History of Geauga County*, 614, sub. Troy Township. Possibly, Harvey and Almira may have been somewhere in N.Y. between 1831 and 1835. Their son Ransom, b. July 1832, is shown in his Civil War disability discharge as b. in Troy, Geauga Co., Ohio, but his death record and several census entries all show his birthplace as in "New York."

[866] Wood Co., Ohio, Deeds, N:447.

[867] Wood Co., Ohio, Deeds, N:446.

[868] 1850, 1860 U.S. Census, Troy Twp., Wood Co., Ohio, pp. 212, 33, respectively.

[869] Wood Co., Ohio, Deeds, N:448, P:307, U:509-10.

[870] Wood Co., Ohio, Deeds, 30:34.

[871] Harris and Stover, "Second Daniel Harris of Goshen," 122 (1991):100.

1850, they were in Oregon Twp., Lucas Co., Ohio, where his occupation was given as "hunter."[873] By 1860, however, they had moved back into Wood Co., now listed as a "farmer."[874]

Children of Elisha[7] and Lucina (Powers) Harris, from census, all b. Ohio:

1 *Philenda*[8] *Harris*, b. ca. 1845. A Phinnie D. Harris m. Wood Co. 20 Dec. 1869 Thomas R. Trombla.[875]

2 *Henry H. Harris*, b. ca. 1847.

3 *Asahel A. Harris*, b. ca. 1849.

4 *Harvey H. Harris*, b. ca. 1851.

5 *Sarah A. Harris*, b. ca. 1852.

ii MARIA HARRIS, b. Ohio ca. 1825, living Allegan Co., Mich., 1870; m. Wood Co., Ohio, 4 July 1843 HIRAM POWERS,[876] b. Ohio ca. 1823 (age 37 in 1850), evidently a brother of Elisha's wife Lucina, their ages indicating they probably were twins. They appear in the 1850 and 1860 census for Freedom, Twp., Wood Co.[877] By 1870, they had moved into Allegan Co., Mich.[878]

Children of Hiram and Maria[7] (Harris) Powers, from census, all b. Ohio:

1 *Orange H. Powers*, b. ca. 1844; m. by 1867 Sarah ____, b. N.Y. ca. 1848. Their household was enumerated next after his parents in Allegan Co., Mich., in 1870, but they were in Van Buren Co., Mich. in 1880.[879]

2 *Melissa Powers*, b. ca. 1846, with parents 1870.

3 *Alice Powers*, b. ca. 1848, prob. d. before 1860.

4 *Howard Powers*, b. June 1851, d. Heath, Allegan Co., Mich., 29 Aug. 1925;[880] m. ca. 1869 Sophia Harnden, b. N.Y. July 1850, living with Howard in Allegan, Mich., in 1900, their household including father-in-law Simon Harnden, age 82, b. N.Y.[881]

5 *Celia Powers*, b. ca. 1854, with parents 1870.

iii SILAS HOWARD HARRIS, b. Ohio ca. 1829; m. before Dec. 1854 Melinda [Hatch?], b. Ohio or Pa. ca. 1836. On 5 Sept. 1853, he received from his parents a part of Tract 42 in Troy Twp., Wood Co.; Melinda Harris and J. Chappell, J.P., witnessed.[882] On 18 Dec. 1854, Silas H. Harris and wife Melinda sold land (prob. the same) in Tract 42 to Nathan F. Hatch.[883] On 12 Nov. 1855, Howard Harris was the mortgagor of land in Tract 42 that

---

[872] Ohio County Marriages, 1789–1994, online at <www.FamilySearch.org>.

[873] 1850 U.S. Census, Oregon Twp., Lucas Co., Ohio, p. 90.

[874] 1860 U.S. Census, Lake Twp., Wood Co., Ohio, p. 327.

[875] Ohio County Marriages, 1789–1994, online at <www.FamilySearch.org>.

[876] Ohio County Marriages, 1789–1994, online at <www.FamilySearch.org>.

[877] 1850, 1860 U.S. Census, Freedom Twp., Wood Co., Ohio, pp. 187, 440, respectively.

[878] 1870 U.S. Census, Heath Twp., Allegan Co., Mich., pp. 6-7.

[879] 1880 U.S. Census, Columbia, Van Buren Co., Mich., E.D. 209, p. 14.

[880] Michigan, Deaths and Burials Index, 1867–1995, online at <www.Ancestry.com>.

[881] 1900 U.S. Census, Allegan Village, Allegan Co., Mich., E.D. 1, p. 12A.

[882] Wood Co., Ohio, Deeds, N:448.

[883] Wood Co., Ohio, Deeds, N:449.

Franklin Hatch sold to Howard's father, Harvey Harris.[884] Howard was head of a household in Troy Twp. in 1860, a farmer.[885] On 26 Sept. 1862, he purchased from his parents 40 acres of Section 11 in Troy Twp. for $400.00; his brother Ransom Harris witnessed. By about 1865, they had moved to Allegan Co., Mich., where their household is found in 1870; his mother, Almira Harris, age 73, was living with them.[886]

 Children of Silas Howard[7] and Melinda [Hatch?] Harris (1860, 1870 census):

 1 *Mary*[8] *Harris*, b. Ohio ca. 1854.

 2 *Sherburn R. Harris*, b. Ohio ca. 1859.

 3 *Orange Harris*, b. Mich. Ca. 1865.

 4 *Ida Harris*, b. Mich. in Oct. 1869.

66 iv RANSOM ADDISON HARRIS, b. Troy, Geauga Co., Ohio, 9 July 1832; m. SUSANNAH M. SANDERS.

 v (prob.) SANFORD F. HARRIS; m. Wood Co., Ohio, 27 Nov. 1860 MELISSA FINCH.[887] In 1862, Sanford witnessed deeds for his presumed parents, Harvey and Almira Harris, to their son Ransom, and for Sanford and his wife Susannah back to their parents. No further information found.

 vi SHERBURN A. HARRIS, b. Nov. 1836, living Wood Co., Ohio, 1900; m. Wood Co., Ohio, 3 Aug. 1861 ELIZABETH CRAMER,[888] b. Ohio in Jan. 1839, living with Sherburn in 1900. In 1866, Sherburn purchased land from Peter Aultiman in Wood Co.[889] On 12 Feb. 1897, at age 61, he signed an affidavit in Wood Co. in support of his brother Ransom's widow's pension claim.

 Child of Sherburn A.[7] and Elizabeth (Cramer) Harris:

 1 *Emma S.*[8] *Harris*, b. Ohio in Feb. 1867, with parents 1870, 1880, 1900.

 vii HENRY H. HARRIS, b. Wood Co., Ohio, 10 March 1842, d. of "consumption" in Webster Twp., Wood Co., 15 Sept. 1870;[890] m. Wood Co., Ohio, 2 Nov. 1868 CHARLOTTE ELIZABETH ALLMAN,[891] b. Ohio in Aug. 1851. Their household in Webster Twp., Wood Co., in 1870 included two male children (names illegible) ages 2 and 3m, both b. Ohio. Charlotte m. (2) Wood Co. 22 Jan. 1872 Obediah C. Craiglow,[892] b. Ohio in June 1836. They were residing in Ottawa Co., Ohio, in 1880 and 1900.[893]

 Children of Henry H.[7] and Charlotte (Allman) Harris:

 1 A boy[8], age 2 in 1870.

 2 *Horace Harris*, b. Ohio in May 1870 (age 3m on 1870 census date), living with his mother ("Lottie E") and stepfather in 1880, age 10.

---

[884] Wood Co., Ohio, Deeds, N:450.

[885] 1860 U.S. Census, Troy Twp., Wood Co., Ohio, p. 33.

[886] 1870 U.S. Census, Heath Twp., P.O. Hamilton, Allegan Co., Mich., p. 2.

[887] Ohio County Marriages, 1789–1994, online at <www.FamilySearch.org>.

[888] Ohio County Marriages, 1789–1994, online at <www.FamilySearch.org>.

[889] Wood Co., Ohio, Deeds, 27:308.

[890] Wood Co., Ohio, Court of Common Pleas, no. 63.

[891] Ohio County Marriages, 1789–1994, online at <www.FamilySearch.org>.

[892] Wood Co., Ohio, Marriage Returns, 5:348.

[893] 1880, 1900 U.S. Census, Clay Twp., Ottawa Co., Ohio, E.D. 62, p. 42, and E.D. 128, sheet 19B, respectively.

44 JOHN SHELDON⁶ HARRIS (*Elisha⁵, Jeremiah⁴, Daniel³, Walter², John¹*), born in New York on 15 July 1804, died in Portage County, Ohio, on or about 3 May 1893.[894] He married first in Portage County on 1 January 1828 **RACHEL ANN JONES**, born in New York in 1809, who died at Hiram, Portage County, on 19 September 1859, and secondly in Geauga County, Ohio, on 20 March 1861 **LUCELIA YOUNG**, born in New York in 1822, who died in 1906. John and his two wives are buried side-by-side in Overlook Cemetery, Parkman, Ohio.

About six months after his first marriage, on 5 July 1828, John purchased from his parents a tract of 100 acres in Parkman Township. He conveyed it back to his father two months later, the reason unstated.[895] In 1830, "Sheldon" was in Shalersville Township,[896] southwest of Hiram in Portage County, but by 1831 he had moved to Hiram Township, where he purchased from his father 106 acres in lot 14.[897] On 12 November 1835, he sold 20 acres of this tract to William R. Bates (who later married his brother Hiram's ex-wife).[898] On 14 March 1861, he sold another 15 acres of this land to his son Albert S. Harris.[899]

Children of John Sheldon⁶ and Rachel Ann (Jones) Harris, born Ohio:

67   i   ALBERT S.⁷ HARRIS, b. Ohio 14 Oct. 1828; m. MARIAN E. CANFIELD.

       ii   LEWIS J. HARRIS, b. ca. 1830, appears in 1860 as a clerk for James Hereck, a merchant in Mantua, Portage Co.

       iii SOPHIA A. HARRIS, b. Ohio in Feb. 1836, d. 1914; m. Portage Co. 25 Dec. 1856 JOHN FRANK WELLS,[900] b. Ohio in May 1835, d. 1900, both bur. Park Cemetery, Garrettsville, Ohio.[901] Their household was in the Village of Garrettsville, Portage Co., in 1900, his occupation entered as "capitalist."[902]
            Child of John Frank and Sophia A.⁷ (Harris) Wells:
            1 *Jennie A. Wells*, b. Ohio in Feb. 1859; m. Portage Co. 11 April 1882 Jacob M. Ruedi,[903] b. Ohio in Jan. 1857. They were in Hiram Twp., Portage Co., in 1900, the record showing that Jennie had no children.[904]

---

[894] *Ravenna Republican*, 3 May 1893 ("Sheldon Harris, one of our oldest and most respected citizens is lying at the point of death as a result of paralytic shock; he is nearly 90 years old").

[895] Geauga Co., Ohio, Deeds, 12:278, 14:422.

[896] 1830 U.S. Census, Shalersville Twp., Portage Co., Ohio, p. 252.

[897] Portage Co., Ohio, Deeds, 17:431.

[898] Portage Co., Ohio, Deeds, 23:484.

[899] Portage Co., Ohio, Deeds, 77:287.

[900] Ohio County Marriages, 1789–1994, online at <www.FamilySearch.org>.

[901] Data online at <www.findagrave.com>, accessed Sept. 2012.

[902] 1900 U.S. Census, Garrettsville Village, Portage Co., Ohio, E.D. 83, sheet 6A.

[903] Ohio County Marriages, 1789–1994, online at <www.FamilySearch.org>.

[904] 1900 U.S. Census, Garrettsville Village, Portage Co., Ohio, E.D. 83, sheet 6A.

iv CHARLES GRANDERSON HARRIS, b. ca. 1850; m. Portage Co. 24 Dec. 1878 MARION ISABELLE COOPER,[905] b. Ohio 14 Jan. 1856, dau. of Jeremiah and Laura (Foote) Cooper of Streetsboro, Ohio.[906]

> Children of Charles Granderson[7] and Marion Isabelle (Cooper) Harris:
>> 1 *Lewis Guy*[8] *Harris*, b. Hiram, Ohio, 4 Jan. 1880; m. 28 July 1899 Minnie L. Gunn of Troy, Ohio, b. 17 June 1880.
>> 2 *Paul Sheldon Harris*, b. Hiram, Ohio, 22 Dec. 1886.

45 PHILO[5] HARRIS (*Elisha[5], Jeremiah[4], Daniel[3], Walter[2], John[1]*), born in Smithville, Chenango County, New York, on 5 October 1810, died in Cleveland, Ohio, on 18 September 1852. He married first in Portage County, Ohio, on 12 February 1835 **PAMELIA K. HALL**,[907] born in Tolland, Massachusetts, in 1815, who died on 8 February 1839, and secondly in Portage County on 17 January 1840 **HARRIET CORNELIUS GRIDLEY**,[908] born in New York about 1822.[909] Philo and Pamelia are buried in Chester Cemetery, Geauga County, Ohio, alongside his parents.

On 6 November 1832, Philo purchased from his father 96 acres of Lot 14 in Hiram Township, Portage County.[910] He appears in the 1835 census of Hiram for males over age 21,[911] and again there in the 1840 U.S. census.[912] In 1850, he was enumerated there at age 40, a farmer, with wife Cornelia, age 28, son Lucius, age 13, and Amanda Rogers, age 18, born Massachusetts.[913] On 30 March 1852, Philo sold the 96 acres in Hiram to Henry Hart,[914] and appears to have moved to Chester in Geauga County, where he died.

Child of Philo[6] and Pamelia K. (Hall) Harris:[915]

68 i LUCIUS O.[7] HARRIS, b. Hiram, Ohio, 25 June 1837; m. ESTHER C. HICKCOX.

46 WILLIAM SMITH[6] HARRIS (*Elisha[5], Jeremiah[4], Daniel[3], Walter[2], John[1]*), born in Smithville, New York, on 19 September 1816,[916] died in Mansfield,

---

[905] Ohio County Marriages, 1789–1994, online at <www.FamilySearch.org>.

[906] Abram W. Foote, *Foote Family* . . . , 2 vols. (Rutland, Vt.: Marble City Press, The Tuttle Co., 1907–32), 1:280.

[907] Ohio County Marriages, 1789–1994, online at <www.FamilySearch.org>.

[908] Ohio County Marriages, 1789–1994, online at <www.FamilySearch.org>.

[909] 1850 U.S. Census, Hiram Twp., Portage Co., Ohio, p. 6.

[910] Portage Co., Ohio, Deeds, 17:430.

[911] Meyers, "Portage County Tax Lists."

[912] 1840 U.S. Census, Hiram Twp., Portage Co., Ohio, p. 187.

[913] 1850 U.S. Census, Hiram Twp., Portage Co., Ohio, p. 6.

[914] Portage Co., Ohio, Deeds, 57:358.

[915] Civil War Pension File, certificate nos. 723419, WC748482, National Archives, Washington, D.C.

[916] Purple, "Manuscript Notes."

Ohio, on 10 May 1885 and buried in Mansfield Cemetery.[917] He married first in Portage County, Ohio, on 2 August 1846 **LOUISA EGGLESTON**,[918] born in Ohio about 1827, who died in 1861 and buried in same cemetery. He married secondly in Richland County, Ohio, on 17 October 1868 **LOUISA RUSSELL**,[919] born in Mansfield on 23 April 1846, died there on 7 January 1939 and buried in same Cemetery. William and his first wife, with son William, were in Mansfield in 1860, when he was a merchant.[920] He was still there, but with his second wife, in 1870 and in 1880.[921]

Children of William Smith[6] and Louisa (Eggleston) Harris:

  i   WILLIAM C. B.[7] HARRIS, b. Ohio ca. 1856; m. Richland Co. 11 June 1896 MARY E. HETLER.[922]

  ii WINIFRED LOUISE HARRIS, b. Mansfield 7 Feb. 1861, d. 29 Jan. 1939, bur. Fairview Cemetery, Galion, Ohio;[923] m. Richland Co., Ohio, 6 Sept. 1892 MINOR M. HOWARD,[924] b. 7 Jan. 1866, d. 2 Nov. 1932, bur. same cemetery, son of John E. and Ellen Arelia (Russell) Howard.

Child of William Smith[6] and Louisa (Russell) Harris:

  iii ALBERTA BEATRICE HARRIS, b. Richland Co., Ohio, 3 Nov. 1881, d. Mansfield, Ohio, 26 April 1948, bur. Mansfield Cemetery, unm.[925]

47 EDWIN[6] HARRIS (*Joseph[5], Jeremiah[4], Daniel[3], Walter[2], John[1]*), born in Connecticut, probably Canaan, on 3 August 1804 (calc.), died near Durand, Winnebago County, Illinois, on 12 March 1850, and buried in Hulse Cemetery, age 45y 7m 9d.[926] He married in Geauga County, Ohio, on 15 August 1833 **IRENE W. E. STEVENS** "of Montville,"[927] born in Ohio on 26 August 1816, who died near Durand on 28 April 1870[928] and was buried in Howard Union Cemetery.[929] She was a daughter of Roswell and Polly (King)

---

[917] Gravestone photo online at <www.findagrave.com>, accessed Sept. 2012.

[918] Ohio County Marriages, 1789–1994, online at <www.FamilySearch.org>.

[919] Ohio County Marriages, 1789–1994, online at <www.FamilySearch.org>.

[920] 1860 U.S. Census, Mansfield City, 2nd Ward, Richland Co., Ohio, p. 18.

[921] 1870, 1880 U.S. Census, Mansfield, Richland Co., Ohio, p. 8 and E.D. 208, p. 7, respectively.

[922] Ohio County Marriages, 1789–1994, online at <www.FamilySearch.org>.

[923] Inscription data online at <www.findagrave.com>, accessed Sept. 2012.

[924] Ohio County Marriages, 1789–1994, online at <www.FamilySearch.org>.

[925] Gravestone photo online at <www.findagrave.com>, accessed Sept. 2012.

[926] Tombstone inscription, Hulse Cemetery, Pecatonica Twp., Winnebago Co., Ill. (viewed 19 July 2007).

[927] Geauga Co. Marriage Records, Chardon, Ohio.

[928] Mortality Schedule, 1870 U.S. Census, Durand, Winnebago Co., Ill., unpaged.

[929] One mile north and a half mile west of Edwin's burial place in Hulse Cemetery.

Stevens of Montville, Geauga County.[930] Irene married secondly, in Stephenson County, Illinois, on 12 May 1853, Harrison P. Elliott,[931] a widower of Durand Township, born in Clark County, Ohio, on 10 December 1815, who died near Emporia, Kansas, on 23 November 1894. He had moved there in the fall of 1880 after having married third, on 9 May 1873, Eleanor A. Dale, born in New York about 1824. With her second husband, Irene had children Mary Elliott, born about 1855, and Zelia Elliott, born in February 1858, who were living "in Iowa" in 1894.[932]

Edwin Harris's place in this family is established in a letter by his son Joseph Roswell Harris, dated 9 June 1880 at Durand, Illinois, which refers to his "uncle" Elisha Harris of Durand (no. 51).[933] Edwin probably came with his father to Ohio from Smithville, New York, soon before 1830, but the first known record of him is his Geauga County marriage to a Montville girl in 1833. His sister Rebecca (no. 50) and husband had settled in Montville a year or two before, so it is likely that Edwin had been living with them. By 1835, however, he had moved to Mantua, Portage County, where his father is known to have been residing in 1831. Edwin appears there in the 1835 tax census of males over age 21; his younger brother Jesse Harris and cousin Hosea Harris also were there. Mantua adjoins the west side of Hiram Township, where Edwin was District Clerk for Hiram School District no. 5 in 1836.[934]

Edwin had moved to Howard (now Durand) Township, Winnebago County, Illinois, by 1840, where his household included himself (aged 30-39), his wife (20-29), and daughter Polly (under five).[935] Two extra persons in his household were probably his father, Joseph Harris (60-69), and his

---

[930] *History of Geauga County*, under "Montville Township"; Gertrude Van Rensselaer Wickham, ed., *Memorial to the Pioneer Women of the Western Reserve*, 5 pts. in 2 vols. (Cleveland, 1896–1924), 512.

[931] Stephenson Co., Ill., Marriage Records, license no. 422. Stephenson is the next county west of Winnebago County.

[932] Obituary of Harrison P. Elliott, Emporia, Kansas, *Daily Republican*, 29 Nov. 1894, which differs slightly in some dates from his sketch in William G. Cutler, *History of the State of Kansas* (Chicago: A. T. Andreas, 1883), under Lyon County, Biographical Sketches. In 1880, Harrison Elliott's household consisting of himself, age 64, wife Eleanor, 56, and daughter Mary, 24, was enumerated in Lanark, Carroll Co., Ill. (1880 U.S. Census, p. 536B). Daughter Zelia had m. in Winnebago Co., Ill., 29 March 1876 William A. Crowley (license no. 41), a hardware merchant with whom she was living in Pecatonica, Winnebago Co., in 1880 (1880 U.S. Census, p. 97B). In 1900 Zelia Crowley, then a widow, was residing in Galva, Ida Co., Iowa (1900 U.S. Census, E.D. 45, sheet 5A). She d. there on 12 Jan. 1933 (1933 Ida County Pioneer Record Newspaper Index, online <http://www.iagenweb.org/ida/News1933.htm>, accessed Nov. 2009).

[933] Copy provided by descendant R. Wesley Harris of Heber Springs, Ark.

[934] William Cumming Johnson, "Enumeration of Youth and Partial Census for School Districts in Portage County, Ohio, 1832–1838" (Kent, Ohio: American History Research Center, 1982).

[935] 1840 U.S. Census, Howard Twp., Winnebago Co., Ill., p. 431.

brother Elisha (20-29), who had arrived there in 1837. Since Edwin died shortly before the 1850 census date, his surviving family could be expected to be enumerated then in Winnebago County, but no trace of them is found in that census. In 1860, however, the Harrison P. Elliott household included Edwin's remarried widow Irene Elliott, her two Elliott daughters Mary and Zelia, and Beakey A. Harris, aged 17, and George Harris, aged 13.[936] On 6 April 1875, Harrison P. Elliott, Mary Elliott, and Zelia Elliott of Durand, Joseph R. Harris and wife Maria H. Harris of Smith County, Kansas, and Allen W. Tunks and wife Beckah A. Tunks of Linn County, Iowa, all "heirs at law of Irene E. W. [*sic*] Elliott late of the County of Winnebago," conveyed Lots 1 and 2 in Block 61 in Durand to Oscar Norton.[937]

Children of Edwin[6] and Irene W. E. (Stevens) Harris:

    i   POLLY I.[7] HARRIS, b. 24 June 1839, d. 17 July 1841.[938]
69 ii JOSEPH ROSWELL HARRIS, b. in Ill. 17 Nov. 1840; m. RACHEL HANNAH MARIA PUTNEY.
    iii BECKAH ANN HARRIS, b. in Ill. 16 Aug. 1843, d. in Linn Co., Iowa, on 11 Sept. 1891, where she is buried in Lafayette Cemetery near Cedar Point. She m. Monroe, Greene Co., Wis., 24 Aug. 1871, ALLEN W. TUNKS, b. Union Co., Ohio, 27 Dec. 1839, d. in Linn Co. on 2 Oct. 1917, son of Levi and Sarah (Alexander) Tunks of Durand, Ill.

        During the Civil War, Allen served in the 74th Regiment, Illinois Infantry, where in Nov. 1864 he was wounded in the foot by a "minnie ball or musket ball . . . while falling back toward Nashville."[939] According to his pension file, Allen and Beckah Ann Tunks moved to Decatur Co., Iowa, in 1872, and to Linn Co. in 1874, where they were living in 1880.[940] Allen's household there in 1900 included himself, a widower, and six children.[941] He was still there at age 70 in 1910 with dau. Eva and son Ellis still at home.[942]

        Children of Allan W. and Beckah Ann[7] (Harris) Tunks, from pension file, 1880 and 1900 census, and Lafayette Cemetery inscriptions:

        1 *Walton W. Tunks*, b. Wis. 7 May 1872, d. 2 Oct. 1880, bur. Lafayette Cemetery.

        2 *Lewis Oscar Tunks*, b. Iowa 8 July 1874, d. 1952, bur. Lafayette Cemetery. He m. Marion, Iowa, 15 July 1903 Neva/Minerva Ferguson, dau. of Isaac and Lorenda (Bramer) Ferguson, b. Benton Co., Iowa, ca. 1883,[943] with whom he was living in Cedar Point in

---

[936] 1860 U.S. Census, Howard Twp., Winnebago Co., Ill., house 2882, fam. 2895.
[937] Winnebago Co. Deeds, 93D:449-51, Rockford, Ill.
[938] Tombstone by her father's stone in Hulse Cemetery, Pecatonica Twp.
[939] Civil War pension certificate no. 738780, National Archives, Washington, D.C.
[940] 1880 U.S. Census, Center Point, Linn Co., Iowa, p. 395C.
[941] 1900 U.S. Census, Washington Twp., Linn Co., Iowa, E.D. 104, sheet 15B.
[942] 1910 U.S. Census, Cedar Point, Linn Co., Iowa, E.D. 122, sheet 6B.
[943] Iowa Marriages, 1809–1992, online at FamilySearch.org, accessed Aug. 2011.

1910.[944] He registered there on 12 Sept. 1918 for the draft during World War I, giving his occupation as carpenter and son Glen Tunks as nearest relative.[945]

   3 *Forrest Levi Tunks*, b. Iowa 19 July 1876, living Linn Co., Iowa, 1920; m. Cedar Point, Iowa., 27 Dec. 1905 Elsie Hunter, b. Linn Co. 1887, dau. of James B. and Emma Luisa (Dennison) Hunter.[946] Elsie was living in 1920.[947] On 12 Sept. 1918, Forrest registered for the draft during World War I, giving his address as Cedar Point, occupation as farmer, and [wife] Elsie Tunks as nearest relative.[948]

   4 *Eva Etta Tunks*, b. Iowa 7 April 1878, d. 1919, bur. Lafayette Cemetery, unm.

   5 *Ida A. Tunks*, b. Iowa 20 Oct. 1879, d. 1926, bur. Center Point Cemetery, Linn Co., Iowa;[949] m. Marion, Iowa, 24 Feb. 1910 Fred Hunter, son of James B. and Emma Luisa (Dennison) Hunter,[950] b. Center Point 1883, d. 1977, bur. Center Point Cemetery.

   6 *Ella A. Tunks* (twin), b. 1 July 1883, d. 1980, bur. Greens Grove Cemetery, Linn Co., Iowa;[951] m. Toddville, Iowa, 12 March 1902 William T. Newman, son of Aquilla and Ruth (Hoff) Newman,[952] b. Linn Co. 1882, d. 1918, bur. Greens Grove Cemetery.

   7 *Ellis Allan Tunks* (twin), b. 1 July 1883, d. 1965, bur. Lafayette Cemetery. When he registered for the draft on 12 Sept. 1918, he gave his occupation as day laborer and [brother] Forrest Tunks as nearest relative.[953] In 1920 he was single and living at age 37 with his brother Forrest.

iv ELI F. HARRIS, b. in Ill. ca. 1845 (aged 15 in 1860), d. Dalton, Ga., 13 March 1865 while in service during the Civil War. He and [his brother] George E. Harris had enlisted together at Pecatonica, Ill., in Feb. 1865 in Company G., 147th Illinois Infantry Regiment.[954] In June 1860 Eli was residing with J. H.

---

[944] 1910 U.S. Census, Cedar Point, Linn Co., Iowa, E.D. 122, sheet 6B.

[945] World War I Draft Registration Card, no. 1267-A1559.

[946] Iowa Marriages, 1809–1992, online at FamilySearch.org, accessed Aug. 2011.

[947] 1910 U.S. Census, Cedar Point, Linn Co., Iowa, E.D. 122, sheet 2B; 1920 U.S. Census, Washington Twp., Linn Co., Iowa, E.D. 146, sheet 12B.

[948] World War I Draft Registration Card, no. 1248-A1923.

[949] Gravestone photo online at <www.findagrave.com> (Ida and husband Fred on same stone).

[950] Iowa Marriages, 1809–1992, online at FamilySearch.org, accessed Aug. 2011.

[951] Gravestone photo online at <www.findagrave.com> (Ella and husband William on same stone).

[952] Iowa Marriages, 1809–1992, online at FamilySearch.org, accessed Aug. 2011.

[953] World War I Draft Registration Card, no. 3181-A2923.

[954] *Report of the Adjutant General of the State of Illinois*, 7 (Springfield, 1867):452. A descendant of Joseph Roswell Harris (no. ii. above) writes that he had a brother and cousin, George and Eli, "one of whom died while imprisoned at Andersonville" during the Civil War (letter of Beulah Balsters, Tulsa, Okla., 8 Aug. 1981). This statement obviously expresses some knowledge of these two Harrises, but as is the case with many such family traditions it is wrong in some details. The available evidence shows that they joined the same military unit at Pecatonica and that they both soon died while on garrison duty at Dalton, Ga. (neither one in prison at Andersonville). The "cousin" tradition for Eli has not been verified; it might have roots in some confusion with Joseph Roswell Harris's cousin Erastus P. Harris (no. 51 ii), son of Elisha Harris of Durand) who d. in service at Murfreesboro, Tenn., in March 1863.

Churchill, a farmer at Ridott across the county line from Durand in Stephenson Co., Ill.[955] Eli could be the "Elisha" Harris whose name is listed in sequence with George Harris on the Durand War Memorial.

v   GEORGE E. HARRIS, b. in Ill. ca. 1847 (aged 13 in 1860), d. Dalton, Ga., 14 Aug. 1865 while in service during the Civil War. He had enlisted with Eli F. Harris above at Pecatonica in Feb. 1865 in Company G., 147th Illinois Infantry Regiment.[956] In 1860 he was residing in Durand (then Howard) Twp. with his mother, Irene, and stepfather, Harrison P. Elliott. George is listed on the Durand War Memorial.

48 ERWIN[6] HARRIS (*Joseph[5]*, *Jeremiah[4]*, *Daniel[3]*, *Walter[2]*, *John[1]*), born in Connecticut about 1806, probably in Canaan, died of "general debility" in Hiram Township, Portage County, Ohio, on 8 May 1879, aged 73, and buried in Park Cemetery at Garrettsville.[957] He married, probably in Chenango County, New York, 16 April 1834, **LAURA A. JOHNSON**, born in New York about 1809, who died on 28 June 1876 and is buried in Park Cemetery. The date, but not place, of their marriage is from a Bible record quoted in the Civil War pension file of their son Melvin Johnson Harris.[958] Laura was a daughter of Rufus and Mary (Beadle) Johnson of Smithville, New York,[959] whose household there in 1810 was near that of Erwin's father, Joseph Harris. Rufus died about 1815 and his widow Mary appears there in 1820 with children. About 1829, she married secondly, Simeon Andress, and before 1850 they had moved to Ohio to live with her daughter Laura Harris and family.

Erwin came to Ohio from Steuben County, New York, where he probably had been living with Towsley relatives. The 1900 obituary of Elisha Harris (no. 51) relates that "at the age of nineteen" (about 1836), Elisha came from Steuben County "to Portage County, Ohio, where his elder brother Erwin had settled." On 26 December 1835, Erwin Harris "of Steuben County," New York, bought 65 acres in Lot 7, Hiram Township, Portage County, from Reuben and Christiana Ryder of Hancock County, Ohio. Several months later, in September 1836, Erwin Harris "of the Town of Ervin, County of Steuben in New York," bought a parcel in Lot 6, Hiram Township, from Calvin and Emma Tyler of Hiram; his father Joseph Harris witnessed. Then, in August 1838, Erwin witnessed at Hiram when his uncle

---

[955] 1860 U.S. Census, Town of Ridott, P.O. Ridott, Stephenson Co., Ill., p. 21.

[956] *Report of the Adjutant General of the State of Illinois*, 7 (Springfield, 1867):452.

[957] Portage Co., Ohio, Probate, Ravenna, Ohio.

[958] File no. 610663, National Archives, Washington, D.C.

[959] Obituary of Mary Andress, *Garrettsville Journal*, 7 March 1872, Hiram College Library, Hiram, Ohio.

Elisha Harris conveyed ninety acres to his son Henry, Erwin's cousin.[960] About that time, Erwin's father and elder brother Edwin Harris were leaving for Winnebago County, Illinois, where his younger brother Elisha had already gone, but Erwin stayed in Ohio.

The 1840 through 1870 census enumerations for Hiram, Portage County, show that Erwin settled there as a farmer in close association with his uncle Elisha Harris and children. In 1840, for example, Erwin's household was in the middle of a cluster of Harrises including his uncle Elisha and Elisha's sons Philo, John Sheldon, and Hiram.[961] In October 1841, Erwin Harris, Peter Cooper, and Calvin Tyler were appointed to appraise Elisha Harris's estate in Hiram.[962] The proximate census listings persist through 1870, when Laura's mother Mary Andress, then aged 94, was still in their home.[963]

Children of Erwin[6] and Laura A. (Johnson) Harris:

    i   CHAUNCY B.[7] HARRIS, b. in Ohio ca. 1838, d. at age 21 on 26 Aug. 1859 and is buried in the lot at Garrettsville with his parents and grandmother Mary J. Andress.

    ii   JULIA E. HARRIS, b. at Hiram, Ohio, 6 July 1842, d. Garrettsville, Ohio, 15 June 1918,[964] "the last of a family of four children of Erwin and Laura Johnson Harris and an only daughter."[965] She m. (1) in Portage Co., 20 Dec. 1865, FREDRICK MOWBRAY, b. in England ca. 1839, who d. in Kans. after 1870, son of Fredrick and Francis (____) Mowbray of Nelson, Portage Co., and (2) in Portage Co., 1 May 1876, LEONARD A. GRIDLEY, b. in N.Y. 1 Jan.

---

[960] Portage Co., Ohio, Deeds, 24:355; 31:380; 36:187.

[961] 1840 U.S. Census, Hiram Twp., Portage Co., Ohio, p. 187; for Erwin's uncle Elisha Harris, see Harris and Stover, NYGBR 122 (1991):98-101. In addition to this related group of Harrises in Hiram, there was living nearby the unrelated family of William[6] Harris (*Abner[5], Jonathan[4], Richard[3], Thomas[2-1]*), b. Smithfield, R.I., 11 Sept. 1767, who d. at Hiram on 12 Aug. 1852 (see, e.g., *American Ancestry*, 12 vols. [Albany, 1887–99], 4:120). William m. at Smithfield 24 Dec. 1789 Barbara Allen, b. 18 Jan. 1767, who d. at Hiram in Oct. 1863. They came to Hiram in 1818 after several years in Plainfield, Conn. They recorded six children at Smithfield and Plainfield between 1790 and 1804. At least the two youngest— William Brown Harris and Abner Harris—came to Hiram with them. These two unrelated Harris families lived very near each other, possibly owning adjacent land along Norton Road about one mile north and a half mile east of Hiram Village. In 1847, Erwin's cousin Hiram Harris (son of Elisha) conveyed property in Lot 9 to the unrelated William Harris's son Abner, and in 1853 a half acre in Lot 8 to George Bates (Portage Co., Ohio, Deeds, 47:548; 64:107). George Bates, age 21, was in Abner Harris's household in 1850 and in July 1852 married Hiram Harris's daughter Caroline, born ca. 1833 (Harris and Stover, NYGBR 122 [1991]:99-100).

[962] Portage Co., Ohio, Probate, records in custody of Betty J. Widger of Ravenna in 1977.

[963] 1870 U.S. Census, Hiram Twp., Portage Co., Ohio, house 178, fam. 175.

[964] Certificate of Death, State of Ohio, Bureau of Vital Statistics, file no. 39564 (informant, Mrs. M. Harris of Garrettsville).

[965] Obituary, undated and without name of newspaper, found "pasted in a scrapbook" by Betty J. Widger, Ravenna, Ohio, 1979.

1930, d. Garrettsville, Portage Co., Ohio, 25 Dec. 1910, son of Leonard and Mercy (Finney) Gridley.[966]

In 1870 Fredrick Mowbray, farmer, and his wife Julia were residing in Leavenworth, Kans.[967] In 1910 Julia was living with her second husband in Garrettsville, the census entry stating that she had no children.[968] Julia's obituary states that she attended Hiram Eclectic Institute (now Hiram College) and went to Kansas with her first husband. She returned to Hiram, then lived for some time in Chicago with her second husband before finally returning to Hiram. Many surviving relatives are mentioned.

   iii   MELVIN JOHNSON HARRIS, b. at Hiram, Ohio, 29 Sept. 1843, d. "suddenly [of heart failure] at his winter home of Tarpon Springs, Florida," on 10 Dec. 1915.[969] He m. in Portage Co., 5 Nov. 1867, JULIA ALICE WILLIAMS, b. in Garrettsville, Ohio, 15 Aug. 1840, d. there on 16 Aug. 1923, dau. of Jefferson and Adeline (Cooley) Williams.[970] Melvin J. Harris served during the Civil War in the 177th Regiment, Ohio Infantry, in Tenn. and N.C.[971] His pension file shows that he had lived in or around Garrettsville most of his life except for a year in California about 1882, and that he had no children "living or dead." His will, dated 10 Dec. 1912 in Portage Co., names his wife Julia A. Harris and "my sister Julia E. Gridley." His widow Julia's 1916 pension application was supported by affidavits of Melvin's brother Floyd Harris, aged 69, Floyd's wife Ellen H. Harris, and by Julia's sister Ann Eliza King, aged 78.

  70   iv   FLOYD O. HARRIS, b. in Ohio 4 April 1846; m. ELLEN H. PAINE.

49 ELI[6] HARRIS (*Joseph[5], Jeremiah[4], Daniel[3], Walter[2], John[1]*), born probably in New York about 1807–1810,[972] died at Lindley, Steuben County, New York, after 28 June 1847 but before the 1850 census date. He married by 1833 (first child), probably in Steuben County, **MARY MULFORD**, born in New York on 31 July 1816 (calc.), who died at Lindley on 2 December 1849 [*sic*: more likely 1850], where she is buried in the Lindley-Mulford Cemetery.[973] She was a daughter of Jeremiah Mulford of Lindley, born on 1

---

[966] Certificate of Death, State of Ohio, Bureau of Vital Statistics, file no. 68833 (informant, Leonard C. Gridley of Cleveland).

[967] 1870 U.S. Census, Leavenworth Co., Kans., Leavenworth P.O., p. 521.

[968] 1910 U.S. Census, Garrettsville Village, Portage Co., Ohio, E.D. 100, sheet 11B. I have not found them in 1900.

[969] Obituary, *Garrettsville Journal*, 16 Dec. 1915; and Florida Death Certificate.

[970] Certificate of Death, State of Ohio, Division of Vital Statistics, file no. 51182 (informant, Mrs. Eva W. Smith of Cleveland).

[971] Pension File 610663, National Archives, Washington, D.C.

[972] The early census data place Eli's birth between 1805 and 1810; his son Edward W. Harris claimed in the 1900 census that his father was born in New York. Eli's father, Joseph Harris, was still in Connecticut in Dec. 1806, but had arrived in Smithville, N.Y., before the 1810 census date.

[973] Mary Mulford is named as Edward W. Harris's mother in his 1913 death record in Hubbard Co., Minn. A printed record of her tombstone shows that she died on 2 Dec. 1849, aged 33y 4m 2d (NYGBR

April 1786 in New Jersey, who died at Lindley on 14 April 1860. His will, dated there on 28 June 1847, names his wife Anna and several children, including "Mary, wife of Eli Harris."[974]

Several factors combine to identify Eli as one of Joseph and Julia (Towsley) Harris's children. They include his own name (probably for his uncle Eli Towsley) and those of his children Joseph and Julia. But most significantly, after Eli and his wife Mary died in Lindley, their orphaned son Edward W. Harris, while still a boy, went to Durand, Illinois, where he was closely associated over a forty-year period with (his uncle) Erastus Harris (no. 42) in Durand and in Iowa and Minnesota.

After Eli's mother died at Smithville, New York, in the late 1820s, he probably went to live with her Towsley relatives in Steuben County. The first record of him is in the 1835 state census for Ervin, Steuben County, where his brother Erwin Harris was residing (see no. 48). The census entry for Eli, "2-2-0-1," indicated males, females, militia duty, and voters, respectively. However, Eli's residence at other times during the 1830s is difficult to determine. His son Joseph and daughter Julia are shown in later census records as having been born in "Ohio" in 1833 and about 1837, but his daughter Laura is said to have been born about 1840 in Lindley. Some migration back and forth between relatives in Steuben County and Geauga or Portage Counties, Ohio, is indicated. The 1840 census places him in Lindley, lists him two names from his father-in-law Jeremiah Mulford, and credits his household with one male aged 30-39, one female 20-29, one male 5-9, and two females under 5.[975] Nearby in Lindley were his cousin Samuel Towsley, Hiram Cowles (also a cousin, who married Samuel Towsley's sister Susan), and Hiram Cowles' brother Luther, all from Smithville, Chenango County.

Eli Harris was tax collector for Lindley in 1846,[976] but the last known reference to him as alive is in his father-in-law Jeremiah Mulford's will in June 1847. In July 1860, after Mulford died in Lindley the preceding April, his son Charles Mulford obtained a release of interest in his real estate from Joseph E. Harris, Julia A. Whitney, and Laura Whitney, "children and heirs of Mary Harris now deceased who was one of the children of Jeremiah Mulford now deceased."[977] The younger son Edward W. Harris was not

---

85 [1954]:223). Some error is evident, however, as Mary Harris, aged 33, appears at Lindley in her father's household at the time of the 1850 census.

[974] Steuben Co., N.Y., Wills, 7:437.

[975] 1840 U.S. Census, Town of Lindley, Steuben Co., N.Y., p. 21.

[976] W. Woodford Clayton, *History of Steuben County, New York* (Philadelphia, 1879), 352.

[977] Steuben Co., N.Y., Deeds, 89:542.

included in the release, probably because he was still a minor at age seventeen; but in any case, he was by that time in Illinois with his Harris uncles.

Children of Eli[6] and Mary (Mulford) Harris:[978]

71   i   JOSEPH E.[7] HARRIS, b. Ohio in Sept. 1833; m. (1) EMELINE AMANDA WHITNEY, (2) FRANCIS ____, (3) JENNIE ____.

      ii   EDWARD H. HARRIS, b. 5 Aug. 1835 (calc.), d. 22 Aug. 1836, aged 11m 14d.[979]

      iii   JULIA A. HARRIS, b. Ohio ca. 1837, was living in Chippewa Falls, Wis., in 1870. She m. in 1852 JAMES LEWIS WHITNEY, b. Danby, N.Y., 28 March 1834, who was living in Eau Claire, Wis., in Dec. 1875, a brother of Joseph E. Harris's wife Emeline above.[980] In 1850 Julia Harris, aged 13, b. Ohio, was in the Melvin H. Brant household in Lindley,[981] whose wife Jerusha was Julia's aunt, a daughter named in Jeremiah Mulford's will. Julia was living in Wellsville, Allegheny Co., N.Y., in July 1860 when she released her interest in her grandfather Mulford's estate.[982] In 1870 Julia, listed as a dressmaker, age 33, was living in Chippewa Falls with her husband James Whitney, age 36, "filer in saw mill."[983] No children are found.

      iv   LAURA HARRIS, b. N.Y. ca. 1840, apparently before the census date, was living in Morris, Otsego Co., N.Y., in 1880.[984] She has been described as "daughter of Eli and Mary (Mulford) Harris of Lindleytown, N.Y., where she was born."[985] She m. Wellsville, Allegheny Co., N.Y., 16 May 1859, as his second wife, EDGAR MORTIMER WHITNEY, b. Newfield, Tompkins Co., N.Y., 20 July 1828, and living in Morris in 1880, styled "Clergyman," a brother of Emeline Amanda and James Lewis Whitney above. Edgar had married previously, in 1850, Harriett Westcott.

           In 1850, Laura Harris, aged 10, b. in N.Y., and her mother were in her grandfather Mulford's household in Lindley.[986] Laura was "of Howard, Steuben County," in July 1860 when she released her interest in the Mulford estate. Edgar M. Whitney, "Clergyman," aged 41 and born in N.Y., is found in the Henry Sage household at Pekin, Ill., on 29 June 1870, but Edgar's family was not with them.[987] The Whitney Genealogy explains that Edgar was a minister of the Universalist Church who "dwelt at Charleston, Pa., from 1852 to 1856; at Wellsville, N.Y., till 1860; at South Danville, N.Y., till 1864; at Pekin, Ill., till 1870; at Ottawa, Ill., till 1874; then moved to Susquehanna Depot, Pa., and was living there in January, 1876."

---

[978] Possibly there was another child, one of the two females with unstated ages enumerated in Eli's household in 1835; but if she was a child of this family, she must have died young.

[979] Tombstone, Lindley-Mulford Cemetery, Lindley, N.Y.

[980] S. Whitney Phoenix, *The Whitney Family of Connecticut*, 3 vols. (New York, 1878), 2:1551-52.

[981] 1850 U.S. Census, Town of Lindley, Steuben Co., N.Y., p. 73.

[982] Steuben Co., N.Y., Deeds, 89:542.

[983] 1870 U.S. Census, 2nd Ward, City of Chippewa Falls, Chippewa Co., Wis., p. 393.

[984] 1880 U.S. Census, Morris, Otsego Co., N.Y., p. 249A (Edgar M. Whitney household).

[985] *Whitney Family of Connecticut*, 2:1551-52.

[986] 1850 U.S. Census, Town of Lindley, Steuben Co., N.Y., p. 74.

[987] 1870 U.S. Census, Pekin Twp., Tazewell Co., Ill., pp. 39-40.

Children of Edgar Mortimer and Laura[7] (Harris) Whitney, b. Pekin, Ill.:[988]
1 *Mary Frances Whitney*, b. 19 May 1865, at home in 1880.
2 *Edgar Mortimer Whitney*, b. 19 April 1868, a dry goods salesman living Milford, Otsego Co., N.Y., 1900; m. ca. 1893 Nellie ____, b. N.Y. in Jan. 1874.[989]
72   v   EDWARD W. HARRIS, b. Steuben Co., N.Y., 4 June 1843; m. MERCY JANE ROBERTS.

50 REBECCA A.[6] **HARRIS** (*Joseph*[5], *Jeremiah*[4], *Daniel*[3], *Walter*[2], *John*[1]), born in New York, probably at Smithville, Chenango County, about 1813, was living at Mantua, Portage County, Ohio, in 1880, aged 67.[990] She married first, not long before the 1830 census date, **NELSON BROOKS**, born in New York 10 August 1807 (calculated), died at Chardon, Geauga County, Ohio on 13 March 1850, where he is buried.[991] Nelson Brooks was named as his father in the 1912 death record of Rebecca's son Erwin H. Brooks in Winnebago County, Illinois. Rebecca married secondly in Portage County, 11 May 1856, as his second wife, **SYLVESTER REED**,[992] born in Connecticut in 1795, who died at Mantua on 25 September 1880, where he is buried in Eastlawn Cemetery beside his former wife, Mary, who died in 1855. He was a long-time resident of Mantua, having arrived from Connecticut "with twelve other young men in 1816."[993]

Among the factors that place Rebecca as a child of Joseph and Julia (Towsley) Harris is the migration of her son Erwin Brooks to Durand, Illinois, in 1867, where relatives had been collecting for thirty years, and where he was called "cousin" by children of Elisha Harris (no. 51) and Edgar Eggleston Harris (no. 54).[994]

In 1830, the household of Nelson Brooks, including a female presumed to be his wife Rebecca, was listed in Auburn, Geauga County, adjacent to her uncle Woodruff Harris[995] with whom, as discussed above, her father, Joseph Harris, apparently was living. Next year, Nelson Brooks and Joseph Harris

---

[988] *Whitney Family of Connecticut*, 2:1551-52.

[989] 1900 U.S. Census, Milford Village, Otsego Co., N.Y., E.D. 128, sheet 6.

[990] 1880 U.S. Census, Mantua Twp., Portage Co., Ohio, house 99, fam. 99.

[991] Tombstone, Village Cemetery, Chardon, Ohio, from Violet Warren and Jeannette Grosvenor, *Inscriptions and Interments in Geauga County, Ohio, through 1983* (Evansville, Ind., 1985), 137.

[992] Portage Co., Ohio, Marriage Records, Ravenna, Ohio.

[993] *History of Portage County, Ohio* (Chicago: Warner, Beers, 1885), 479.

[994] From remarks in a letter by Edgar Eggleston Harris's grandson Guy Earl Wescott, provided by Mrs. Katherine Fassett Schuster of Binghamton, New York: "[T]here was a cousin—evidently a son of a sister of the Harris boys—whose name was Irvin Brooks" (Letter postmarked Alma, Nebr., 6 March 1937, to Mrs. Fred Fassett of Stevensville, Pa.).

[995] 1830 U.S. Census, Auburn Twp., Geauga Co., Ohio, p. 261.

both appear in the census of males over age 21 in Mantua, the town next south across the county line in Portage County.

By 5 December 1832, Nelson and Rebecca Brooks were in Montville, Geauga County, where, according to his death record, their son Erwin was born, and where Rebecca's elder brother Edwin (no. 47) married in 1833. They were still there in 1840, when their household enumeration accounts for Nelson, Rebecca, and their two elder children, but also includes two males—one aged 20-29 and the other 15-19.[996] The younger one of these extra males may be Rebecca's brother Erastus Harris (no. 42), born in 1822, who appears shortly afterward in Durand, Illinois. Nelson Brooks was remembered in Montville as "working in 1834 at the carpenter and joiner business; a first class workman; a good, and a kind hearted man. After some years [he] moved to Chardon."[997]

Nelson and Rebecca Brooks were in Chardon, Geauga County, by January 1848, when they conveyed land in Lot 9 on the Hamben-Chardon town line to Horton Smith.[998] They conveyed more property there in March 1849, when their son Erwin H. Brooks witnessed.[999] Their last deeds were dated there on 23 February 1850, apparently in anticipation of Nelson's death three weeks later. Nelson Brooks "of Chardon" conveyed a half-acre there to Rebecca's brother Erwin Harris (no. 48) "of Hiram, Portage County." On the same day, Erwin Harris and his wife Laura conveyed it back to "Rebbecca A. Brooks of Chardon," her son Erwin H. Brooks again witnessing.[1000] The intent of these transactions apparently was to sever Nelson's interest in the title, an action to avoid probate and suggesting a possibility that he had potential heirs by a now unknown prior marriage. A few months later, on the 1850 census date, Rebecca and her three known children were residing at Chardon with the "L. C." and "C. L." Earl family.[1001]

In each of the 1860 through 1880 censuses, Rebecca appears with her second husband in Mantua, Portage County. His adopted daughter, Sarah Ewers, born in Ohio about 1827, was living with them. Sarah died on 8 December 1887.[1002]

[996] 1840 U.S. Census, Montville Twp., Geauga Co., Ohio, p. 118.
[997] *History of Geauga County*, 787.
[998] Geauga Co. Deeds, 42:650.
[999] Geauga Co. Deeds, 39:606; the records fail to show when or how they obtained these properties.
[1000] Geauga Co. Deeds, 41:665.
[1001] 1850 U.S. Census, Chardon Twp., Geauga Co., Ohio, p. 240.
[1002] Tombstone, Eastlawn Cemetery, Portage Co.

Children of Nelson and Rebecca A.**⁶** (Harris) Brooks:[1003]

    i ERWIN H. BROOKS, b. at Montville, Geauga Co., Ohio, 5 Dec. 1832, d. at Durand, Winnebago Co., Ill., 6 Oct. 1912.[1004] He m. Ashtabula, Ohio, 14 Sept. 1859 ALIPHINE SINES,[1005] b. in N.Y. 29 Nov. 1843, d. at Durand on 21 March 1932, daughter of Amos B. and Elizabeth P. (Hitt) Sines, both b. in N.Y.[1006] Erwin and his wife Aliphine are buried in Durand Cemetery.

        At the time of the 1860 census, Erwin Brooks, a "carpenter," and his wife Aliphine were living with his sister Laura A. Wood and family, and near their mother and stepfather, in Mantua, Portage Co., Ohio.[1007] They "moved to Durand October 15, 1867."[1008] Erwin was a carpenter at Durand in 1877,[1009] and his household is found there in the censuses of 1880, 1900, and 1910, the latter census showing that Aliphine was the mother of one child, then living.[1010] In 1880, their daughter Alice and Aliphine's "sister," Olivia Sines, b. in Ohio ca. 1850, a "dressmaker," were living with them. In 1920, widow Aliphine Brooks, aged 76, was living next to her widowed daughter Alice Nelson in Durand, where Aliphine was "dressmaking."[1011]

        Child of Erwin H. and Aliphine (Sines) Brooks:

        1 *Alice E. Brooks*, b. in Mantua, Ohio, 13 March 1862, d. at Durand 25 March 1928; m. (1) in Winnebago Co., Ill., 3 Feb. 1887 Edward Nelson, who d. in 1917, and (2) in 1924 John M. Geary, b. Ill. ca. 1858, an "undertaker," who survived her.[1012] In 1920, Alice's widowed "daughter" Hazel Baker, aged 27, was living with her in Durand.

   ii LAURA A. BROOKS, b. Montville, Ohio,[1013] in 1835, was living in Chagrin Falls, Cuyahoga Co., Ohio, in 1880.[1014] She m. in Geauga Co., Ohio, 24 April 1853, WARREN S. WOOD, b. in N.Y. ca. 1831 and living in 1880, "stone cutter." At marriage, Laura was "of Chardon Township, age over 18."[1015] Her brother Erwin H. Brooks and wife were living with them at Mantua, Portage Co., in 1860; Warren and Laura were still there in 1870.[1016]

        Children of Warren S. and Laura A. (Brooks) Wood, from the 1860, 1870, and 1880 censuses, all b. Ohio:

[1003] Another child may be the female, "S.C." Earl, born in Ohio ca. 1831, with whom Rebecca and the following children were residing in 1850.

[1004] Winnebago Co., Ill., Death Record, Rockford, Ill.

[1005] Ohio Marriages, 1800–1958, online at <www.FamilySearch.org>, assessed Aug. 2011.

[1006] Winnebago Co., Ill., Death Record, Rockford, Ill.

[1007] 1860 U.S. Census, Mantua Twp., Portage Co., Ohio, p. 57.

[1008] Obituary of their daughter Alice Geary, *The Durand Gazette*, 29 March 1928.

[1009] *Durand Directory*, 1877.

[1010] 1910 U.S. Census, Durand Village, Winnebago Co., Ill., E.D. 142, sheet 13B.

[1011] 1920 U.S. Census, Durand Village, Winnebago Co., Ill., E.D. 162, sheet 1B.

[1012] Obituary of Alice Geary.

[1013] Birthplace from her son William's death record, cited below.

[1014] 1880 U.S. Census, Chagrin Falls, Cuyahoga Co., Ohio, p. 64B.

[1015] Geauga Co. Marriage Records, Chardon, Ohio.

[1016] 1870 U.S. Census, Mantua Twp., Portage Co., Ohio, house 50, fam. 47.

1 *Algernon S. Wood*, b. ca. 1854, at home 1870.

2 *Stella J. Wood*, b. ca. 1857, at home 1860, not there 1870.

3 *William A. Wood*, b. Mantua, Ohio, 20 Sept. 1858, d. East Cleveland, Ohio, 2 Nov. 1931; m. Harriet L. ____.[1017]

4 *George McClelland Wood*, b. Mantua, Ohio, 6 Aug. 1863, d. Ravenna, Ohio, 14 April 1939, merchant; m. Margaret Fair.[1018]

5 *James H. Wood*, b. ca. 1866, at home 1880.

   iii ELMER C. BROOKS, b. Chardon, Ohio, in 1848, d. 1 April 1886, aged 37, and was buried in Kent, Ohio.[1019] He was at home with his mother at the time of the 1850 and 1860 censuses.

51 ELISHA[6] HARRIS (*Joseph[5], Jeremiah[4], Daniel[3], Walter[2], John[1]*), was born in Smithville, Chenango County, New York, on 20 July 1817, and died at Durand, Winnebago County, Illinois, on 12 December 1900, where he is buried.[1020] He married first in Winnebago County on 4 August 1842, **CALISTA CHRISTINA ROBB**, born in Ohio on 22 July 1822, who died on 19 August 1883 and is buried in the same cemetery lot. She was a daughter of Scott and Lovina (Preston) (Root) Robb of Durand, whose grave markers are nearby. In May 1836, "Salisbury Lowe and Scott Robb came with their families as far as the Pecatonica River where they camped for about a week while the men helped Alva Trask finish his ferry boat. On May 17 they crossed as his first passengers."[1021] Elisha Harris married secondly, at Spencer, Clay County, Iowa, on 28 September 1884 **MARIA LOUISA (FASSETT) HARRIS**, ex-wife of his brother Edgar Eggleston Harris who had moved from Durand to Spencer several years before (see no. 54). Elisha and Maria Louisa separated about 1893, when she went to Orleans, Nebraska, and died there on 25 January 1898.

Elisha's parents, Joseph Harris and Julia Lawley [*sic*], are named in the record of his second marriage at Spencer, Iowa. Joseph and Julia Harris, "natives of Connecticut," are mentioned as grandparents in a biography of Elisha's son Henry E. Harris.[1022] Julia's correct surname, Towsley, is confirmed by the 1903 death record of Elisha's brother Erastus Harris (no. 42) at Park Rapids, Hubbard County, Minnesota. Elisha's obituary does not name his parents, but it states that "the family was scattered and the younger

---

[1017] Ohio Deaths, 1908–1953, online at <www.FamilySearch.org>, accessed Aug. 2011.

[1018] Ohio Deaths, 1908–1953, online at <www.FamilySearch.org>, accessed Aug. 2011.

[1019] Tombstone, Standing Rock Cemetery, Kent, Ohio.

[1020] Tombstone, Oakland Cemetery; Winnebago Co. Death Record, Rockford, Ill.

[1021] *Changing Ways, A History of Durand, Harrison, and Laona Townships* (Durand: North Central Associated Publishers, 1976), 5. For the Robb family, see Katherine E. Rowland, *The Pioneers of Winnebago and Boone Counties, Illinois, Who Came Before 1841* (Baltimore, 1990), 367-68.

[1022] *Portrait and Biographical Record of Winnebago and Boone Counties*, 652-53.

children [were] put out to other families" when his mother died while "he was quite young," and that he "was reared by a Mr. Smith [unidentified] who lived in Steuben County, New York."

While a young single man, Elisha Harris was the first of this "scattered" family to migrate to Winnebago County, Illinois. In 1836, at "age 19" according to his obituary, he followed his elder brother Erwin Harris (no. 48) from Steuben County to Hiram, Portage County, Ohio. Next year, he "walked" to Michigan City, La Porte County, Indiana, with "four other young men," but after a few months he drove a flock of sheep "on foot" in 1837 to Winnebago County for William Shimmin. Mr. Shimmin of La Porte County later settled in Seward Township, Winnebago County, where he died in 1861, aged 70.[1023] By the 1840 census date, Elisha's father and brother Edwin (no. 47) had arrived in Durand (then Howard) Township. No doubt Elisha and their father Joseph Harris were the extra males of appropriate ages then in Edwin's household.

Elisha and Calista Harris's first child, Henry Edward, born in November 1842, is said to have been born "in the old log house on the home farm" near Durand Village (see no. 73). Perhaps so, but original deeds dated at Galena, Illinois, on 25 August 1843, 4 December 1844, and 5 July 1845, show that Elisha then acquired title to three forty-acre tracts in Sections 14 and 24 a short distance southeast of Durand Village,[1024] where he died fifty-five years later. The 1850 census for Howard (Durand) shows Elisha Harris, aged 33, born in New York, with his wife Calista, four sons, and one William Harris, aged 22 [*sic*], "cabinet maker," born in Ohio.[1025] William apparently was a cousin, probably the son of Elisha's uncle Woodruff Harris of Geauga County, Ohio.[1026] Although the file is missing, the Winnebago County Civil Docket Index at Rockford shows that Elisha was a codefendant in an 1859 civil action with one Martin Harris, who remains unidentified.

Elisha Harris appears in all of the existing U.S. censuses for Durand Township through 1900, and in the 1865 Illinois State Census. In 1900, then aged 82 and "widowed," he was residing on his home farm with his married sons Elmer and Jessie and their families.[1027]

[1023] Tombstone, Twelve Mile Road Cemetery, south of Pecatonica, Winnebago Co. See also Rowland, *Pioneers of Winnebago and Boone Counties*, 388.

[1024] *Changing Ways*, 61, 63.

[1025] 1850 U.S. Census, Howard Twp., Winnebago Co., Ill., fam. 118.

[1026] Harris, "Woodruff[4] Harris of Connecticut, New York, and Ohio," NYGBR 141 (2010):184 (William Dewel Harris, b. Hiram, Ohio, 2 April 1823, d. Calif. 1 May 1858).

[1027] 1900 U.S. Census, Durand Twp., Winnebago Co., Ill., E.D. 121, sheet 7.

Children of Elisha[6] and Calista Christina (Robb) Harris:[1028]

73   i   HENRY EDWARD[7] HARRIS, b. Durand, Ill., 27 Nov. 1842; m. (1) ANN CECELIA FRITZ, (2) FREDERICA ANNA (JACKSON) REA.

        ii   ERASTUS P. HARRIS, b. in Ill., 25 Jan. 1844, d. "of disease" in the Civil War at Murfreesboro, Tenn., 11 March 1863. Stating his age as 19 years, he had enlisted at Durand on 7 Aug. 1862 as a private in Company H, 74th Regiment, Illinois Infantry.[1029]

    iii, iv   "Twin Infants, Children of C. C. and E. Harris," d. 22 Oct. 1846.[1030]

74   v   WILLIAM EUGENE HARRIS, b. in Ill. 14 May 1847; m. CORA A. HURD.

75   vi   LEWIS FREDERICK HARRIS, b. in Ill. 10 Oct. 1848; m. MYRA AMINA TURNEY.

        vii   JULIA L. HARRIS, b. in Ill. 11 April 1851, d. at Durand, Ill., 6 Nov. 1869.[1031]

        viii   CHARLES E. HARRIS, b. in Ill. 19 March 1853, d. unm. before 1916.[1032] He was living with his father in 1880 and 1892, but he was at Bartonville, Peoria Co., Ill., by 1905,[1033] and a "patient" in the Peoria State Hospital in 1910.[1034]

        ix   JOSEPH SCOTT HARRIS, b. in Ill. 19 Jan. 1858, d. 2 Feb. 1892 and buried in his parents' lot.[1035] He was at home with his parents in 1880, age 22.

        x   WILLIS SPENCER HARRIS, b. in Ill. 18 Feb. 1860, d. in 1936 and buried at Durand.[1036] He m. (license, Winnebago Co. 13 March 1884) ESTELLA J. HUNT,[1037] b. Ill. in July 1863, d. in 1936 and buried by her husband. They were living in Sycamore, DeKalb Co., Ill., by 1892,[1038] where the census in 1900 shows that he was working for the railroad and that they had no children.[1039] By 1905, they had moved to Geneva, Kane Co., Ill.[1040]

76   xi   ELMER E. HARRIS, b. Winnebago Co., Ill., 23 July 1862; m. (1) EVA A. PLACE, (2) LOIS M. INGEBRITSON.

        xii   JESSIE F. HARRIS, b. in Ill. 13 July 1867, d. in 1922 and is buried in Durand Cemetery. He m. in Rock Co., Wis., 28 Feb. 1899 FLORENCE M. BREN-

---

[1028] Except for the twins who died young, these children are named in Elisha's obituary and the county histories cited.

[1029] Civil War Muster Rolls and Casualty Sheet, National Archives, Washington, D.C.

[1030] Tombstone, Oakland Cemetery, near Durand. Possibly the year is a misreading of 1845, as it conflicts with the birth date of the next child.

[1031] Tombstone, Oakland Cemetery; Mortality Schedule, 1870 U.S. Census, Durand.

[1032] Biography of his brother Jessie F. Harris, in Newton Bateman, Paul Selby, and Charles A. Church, eds., *Historical Encyclopedia of Illinois and History of Winnebago County*, 2 vols. (Chicago: Munsell Publishing Co., 1916), 2:1081.

[1033] Biography of his brother Elmer E. Harris, in Charles A. Church, ed., *Past and Present of the City of Rockford and Winnebago County, Illinois* (Chicago: S. J. Clarke Pub. Co., 1905), 291-92.

[1034] 1910 U.S. Census, Peoria Co., Ill., E.D. 66, sheet 14B.

[1035] Tombstone, Oakland Cemetery.

[1036] Tombstone, Durand Cemetery.

[1037] Winnebago Co. Marriage Records, license no. 79.

[1038] Biography of his brother Henry E. Harris, in *Portrait and Biographical Record of Winnebago and Boone Counties*, 653.

[1039] 1900 U.S. Census, Sycamore Twp., DeKalb Co., Ill., E.D. 20, sheet 4.

[1040] Biography of his brother Elmer E. Harris, in Church, *City of Rockford and Winnebago County*, 291-92.

TON,[1041] b. Wis. in May 1867, daughter of Dr. and Mrs. Joseph L. Brenton of Beloit, Wis. He attended State Normal School at Normal, Ill., and then taught school at Durand for five years. In 1902, he became cashier at a bank in Durand, a position that he held until at least 1916 except for a six-month period in 1913 at Grand Junction, Colo.[1042] The 1910 census for Durand shows that they had no children.[1043]

42 ERASTUS[6] HARRIS (*Joseph[5], Jeremiah[4], Daniel[3], Walter[2], John[1]*), was born in Chenango County, New York, on 13 July 1822, and died of "La Grippe" at Hubbard, Hubbard County, Minnesota, on 15 January 1903.[1044] He married in Winnebago County, Illinois, on 3 July 1843 **MARIA BETSEY WARREN**,[1045] born in New York on 22 October 1827, who died at Hubbard of "Brights Disease" on 11 May 1909, daughter of Pliney P. and Betsey W. (Willis) Warren of Durand, Winnebago County. Erastus and Maria are buried in the Shell City Cemetery a few miles southeast of Hubbard near the site of now-vanished Shell City village.[1046]

Erastus was no doubt one of the younger Harris children "put out to other families" after his mother died at Smithville, New York, in the late 1820s. He may have been the unidentified male of the right age group in his sister Rebecca A. Brooks' home in Geauga County, Ohio, in 1830 and 1840 (no. 50); in 1846, Erastus gave the name *Rebecca Ann* to his first child. In any case, he had arrived in Durand, Illinois, by the "winter of 1844 and 1845," when he was working for the Websters who had farms near his brother Elisha Harris.[1047]

The 1850 census for Durand (then Howard) lists Erastus's family twice, once with his wife's parents and again as a separate household.[1048] Birth places for their children stated in later censuses show that they were some-

---

[1041] Wisconsin Marriages, 1836–1930, online at <www.FamilySearch.org>, accessed Aug. 2011.

[1042] Biography of Jessie F. Harris, in *Historical Encyclopedia of Illinois and History of Winnebago County*, 2:1081.

[1043] 1910 U.S. Census, Durand Twp., Winnebago Co., Ill., E.D. 142, sheet 9B.

[1044] Hubbard Co., Minn., Death Records, Park Rapids, Minn., which names his parents "Jas. Harris and Julia Tousley."

[1045] A date 3 July 1845 is given in a typescript of Winnebago Co. marriage records at Rockford. Erastus's Civil War pension file gives the year as 1843, however, and his widow Maria stated in 1903 that she was "only" age 15 when they were married.

[1046] This cemetery was found in good condition on a visit in 1978, but only a few depressions were observed where the village of Shell City once stood. They were indicated by markers placed by Mr. Bill Branham of Hubbard, who kindly offered his recollections of Shell City and members of the Harris families who once lived nearby.

[1047] Undated affidavit of Miner A. Webster of Shell City, Minn., in Erastus Harris's Civil War pension file, Certificate no. 339630, National Archives, Washington, D.C.

[1048] 1850 U.S. Census, Howard Twp., Winnebago Co., Ill., families 88 and 155.

where in Iowa about 1856–1858, but by 1860 they were back in Durand Village, where he was a "laborer" with eight children.[1049]

On 26 September 1864, at age 42, Erastus enlisted in the 2nd Regiment, Illinois Light Artillery, and was mustered out at Montgomery, Alabama, on 3 June 1865. He got home in time to be enumerated with his large family in the State census taken at Durand [Howard] on 3 July 1865.[1050] The various documents in his pension file show that within a year after he returned to Durand he moved his family to Mindoro, LaCrosse County, Wisconsin, where they appear in 1870.[1051] They were in Riverton, Floyd County, Iowa, in 1879, where Erastus filed for his disability pension, but by June 1880 Erastus Harris, farmer, and his wife "Betsey M." had moved to Illyria Township, Fayette County, Iowa, where they appear with four of their younger children.[1052] By 1885 they were in Eden Township in that county, where Erastus filed a supporting pension affidavit.

Erastus had arrived in Hubbard County, Minnesota, before 13 January 1887, when he witnessed a conveyance to Robert L. Keyes of 160 acres by his son Plinn E. Harris, a "single man." Plinn had purchased the property from Angus R. Macfarlane of Duluth four months before.[1053] Erastus and Maria were residing nearby in Shell River Township, Wadena County, in 1895.[1054] On 29 June 1898, Erastus bought from John Coleman a lot in Brighton (now Hubbard Village),[1055] where he died four years later. In 1904, Maria was awarded a widow's pension of $8.00 per month, which was increased to $12.00 in 1908. The 1900 census for Hubbard Township states that Erastus's wife "Betsey" was the mother of fourteen children, eight then living.[1056]

Children of Erastus[6] and Maria Betsey (Warren) Harris:

    i   Rebecca Ann[7] Harris, b. at Howard (now Durand), Winnebago Co., Ill., 4 March 1846, was living in Hubbard Co., Minn., in Jan. 1900, when her second husband transferred 40 acres to her by a straw transaction through her

---

[1049] 1860 U.S. Census, Durand Village, Winnebago Co., Ill., house 2718.

[1050] 1865 Ill. State Census, Howard, Winnebago Co., Ill., p. 44 (one male 40-49, one female 30-39, two males and four females 10-19, one male and two females under 10).

[1051] 1870 U.S. Census, Mindoro Twp., LaCrosse Co., Wis., p. 83.

[1052] 1880 U.S. Census, Illyria Twp., Fayette Co., Iowa, outside Village of Wadena, E.D. 202, sheet 11.

[1053] Hubbard Co., Minn., Deeds, D2:237, 262.

[1054] 1895 Minnesota State Census, Shell River Twp., Wadena Co., p. 5, online at <www.FamilySearch.org>.

[1055] Hubbard Co., Minn., Deeds, D11:188.

[1056] 1900 U.S. Census, Hubbard Twp., Hubbard Co., Minn., E.D. 72, sheet 10; which states that "Betsey" was b. in N.Y. in "Oct. 1829," that she was aged 70, and that they had been married 57 years. See remarks above concerning inconsistent statements of their marriage date and her age.

parents.[1057] She m. (1) in Winnebago Co., 6 July 1865, as his third wife, SIMEON LUTHER DOWNER, b. Livonia, Mich., 14 Dec. 1834, d. Menahga, Minn., 4 Sept. 1893, and is buried in the Shell City Cemetery. He was a son of Milo and Eliza J. (Worden) Downer of Mindoro, Wis.[1058] Simeon had one child with each of his two former wives. Rebecca Ann m. (2) in Hubbard Co., 22 Oct. 1894, WILLIAM H. HOISINGTON.[1059] Simeon and Rebecca Downer were residing next to her parents in LaCrosse Co., Wis., in 1870. About 1878, they moved to Iowa, where they appear in Fayette Co. in 1880,[1060] and after May 1886 to Shell City, Minn.

Children of Simeon Luther and Rebecca Ann[7] (Harris) Downer, the first five or six b. Farmington, Wis., no. 7 in Butler Co., Iowa, and the last three at Eden, Iowa:[1061]

> 1 *Julia Edith Downer*, b. 6 Oct. 1868; m. Stoten Delos Warren.
> 2 *Vietta Maria Downer*, b. 16 Feb. 1870; m. Charles V. Wynn.
> 3 *Mary E. Downer*, b. 27 Oct. 1871, d. 14 Dec. 1878.
> 4 *Elsie L. Downer*, b. 16 Feb. 1873, d.y.
> 5 *Effie Alice Downer*, b. 16 June 1875; m. Burton F. Richards.
> 6 *Hill E. Downer*, b. 1 Dec. 1877, d.y.
> 7 *Nettie W. Downer*, b. 23 May 1879; m. George W. Evans.
> 8 *Martha E. Downer*, b. 5 Aug. 1881.
> 9 *Milo H. Downer*, b. 18 Feb. 1884.
> 10 *Fayette S. Downer*, b. 18 May 1886.

ii   (prob.) ALVIRA HARRIS, b. Ill. ca. 1847. She appears in the Erastus Harris household in 1860 at age 13, but inexplicably not in 1850, nor in 1870. It is possible that this girl was, instead, a daughter of Erastus's brother Edwin Harris (no. 47) who d. at Durand in the spring of 1850.

iii MELISSA J. HARRIS, b. Ill. ca. 1848, was still living with her parents in 1870.

iv GEORGE WARREN HARRIS, b. Ill. in Feb. or March 1850, was still living with his parents in 1870.

v   MARILLA (M.?) HARRIS, b. ca. 1851 or 1852, "Daughter of E. and M. Harris, died Aug. ___ ____, age 7y 4m 15d."[1062]

vi EMILY W. HARRIS, b. Ill. ca. 1854, was with her parents in 1860 and 1870; m. ____ PETERS. As Emily W. Peters, she witnessed a deed in Hubbard Co., Minn., in Jan. 1900 from her father to her sister Rebecca A. Hoisington. Her husband may have been John H. Peters, b. Pa. ca. 1853, a widower who in 1920 had a house in the Village of Hubbard adjoining the home of Emily's

---

[1057] Hubbard Co., Minn., Deeds, D11:417, 418.

[1058] David R. Downer, *The Downers of America* (Newark, N.J.: Baker, 1900), 176-77.

[1059] Hubbard Co., Minn., Marriage Records, Park Rapids.

[1060] 1880 U.S. Census, Eden Twp., Fayette Co., Iowa, E.D. 197, fam. 136.

[1061] More information about children and grandchildren may be found in Downer, *The Downers of America*, 177.

[1062] Gravestone, Oakland Cemetery, Durand, Ill., broken through date of death. Her age, the fact of her burial in this cemetery, and her absence from the 1850 and 1860 censuses indicate that she was born about 1851 or 1852.

sister Julia B. Wynn. He had a "son" living with him: Guy Peters, b. Minn. ca. 1902.[1063]

vii CALISTA A. HARRIS, b. Ill. in May 1855, was living at Hubbard, Minn., in 1900. She m. ca. 1886, possibly not as her first husband, WILLIAM STOM-BAUGH, b. Wis. in Dec. 1856, a "blacksmith" in Hubbard in 1900,[1064] prob. the widower of Calista's sister Dora. In 1887 "Willie" Stombaugh witnessed the marriage in Hubbard Co. of Calista's brother Plinn Erastus Harris. William and Calista Stombaugh witnessed the marriage of her sister Rebecca Ann to William H. Hoisington there in Oct. 1894. The 1900 census for Hubbard states that Calista was mother of five children, three then living, but none is listed in their household.

77 viii CHAUNCY E. HARRIS, b. Iowa in 1856; m. (1) LOUCIA A. (STOMBAUGH) CARTER, (2) SUSAN (____) SMITH.

78 ix PLINN ERASTUS HARRIS, b. Iowa or Ill. 3 Nov. 1858; m. MARY MUNISTER.

    x ELLA HARRIS, b. Ill. ca. 1860, was with her parents in 1870, aged 10.

  xi JULIA BETSEY HARRIS, b. Ill. ca. 1862, d. Hubbard Co., Minn., 7 Nov. 1948;[1065] m. Wadena Co., Minn., 16 May 1883 JESSIE EDWARD WYNN,[1066] b. Ind. in 1852, d. Hubbard Co. 29 April 1931,[1067] and bur. Shell City Cemetery. "Jess" and Julia Wynn, and two children, were residing in Shell River, Twp., in Wadena Co. in 1895.[1068] "Mrs. Julia Wynn of Hubbard" was "attending Physician" at her father's death there in 1903 and as "Betsy" Wynn she filed for expenses related to her mother's death there in 1909. Jesse E. and Julia B. Wynn were residing in Hubbard in 1910, where he was doing "Odd Jobs" and she was recorded as mother of three children, only one then living.[1069] They were there also in 1920 and in 1930.[1070]

    Children of Jessie Edward and Julia Betsey[7] (Harris) Wynn, one other died young:

    1 *Josie Wynn*, b. Minn. ca. 1885, with parents in 1895, age 10.

    2 *Jesse E. Wynn Jr.*, b. Hubbard, Minn., 23 Aug. 1888, living with his parents in 1910. He was a "farm laborer" and had a "wife and two children" on 4 June 1917, when he registered at Hubbard for the draft in World War I.[1071]

[1063] 1920 U.S. Census, Hubbard Village, Hubbard Co., Minn., E.D. 142, house 18.

[1064] 1900 U.S. Census, Hubbard Twp., Hubbard Co., Minn., E.D. 72, sheet 9.

[1065] Death Certificate Index, Minnesota Historical Society, online at <http://people.mnhs.org/bci/Results.cfm>.

[1066] Wadena Co., Minn., Marriage Records.

[1067] Wadena Co., Minn., Marriage Records.

[1068] 1895 Minnesota State Census, Shell River Twp., Wadena Co., p. 4, online at <www.FamilySearch.org>.

[1069] 1910 U.S. Census, Hubbard Village, Hubbard Co., Minn., E.D. 78, sheet 4B.

[1070] 1920, 1930 U.S. Census, Hubbard Village, Hubbard Co., Minn., E.D. 142, house 19, and E.D. 29-16, sheet 4B, respectively.

[1071] World War I Draft Registration Card, no. 238-7.

xii [ROSELIA?] HARRIS, "Daughter of E. and M. B. Harris, died Dec. 29, 1864, aged 2m 3d."[1072]

xiii DORA E. HARRIS, b. Farmington, LaCrosse Co., Wis., 1 May 1866, d. Shell City, Minn., 7 April 1884, aged 17y 11m 6d.[1073] She had m. six months before, in Park Rapids, Hubbard Co., Minn., 3 Oct. 1883, "both of Shell City," WILLIS S. STOMBAUGH, Justice Buck presiding.[1074] Willis possibly was the William Stombaugh who subsequently m. Dora's sister Calista.

79 xiv ERWIN EUGENE HARRIS, b. Wis. in Oct. 1868; m. ALIDA S. BENHAM.

53 ELMORE[6] HARRIS (*Joseph[5], Jeremiah[4], Daniel[3], Walter[2], John[1]*), sometimes "J. Elmer," born at Smithville, Chenango County, New York, in 1825, died there on 3 August 1899, aged 74, and buried in Cowles Cemetery.[1075] He married after the 1850 U.S. census date and before the 1855 New York State census, **OLIVE CARTRIGHT**, born in Delaware County, New York, in July 1830, who died on 7 January 1904, aged 74 [*sic*], and buried in the same cemetery. Olive was a daughter of Almon (or Almeron) and Phebe (Morse) Cartright of Delaware County, who moved to Smithville shortly before the 1850 census date, when she was still in their household. Their neighbors in 1850—Sylvester Cowles and Miles Hubbard—indicate that the Cartrights were residing on or near the property that Elmore's father, Joseph Harris, had in his possession from 1811 to 1817 or later. The 1855 state census for Smithville (no. 260) shows that Elmore Harris, "farmer," aged 29, born in Chenango County, had been living in that county for 29 years, and that his wife Olive aged 25, born in Delaware County, had been living in Chenango County for six years. They are not yet found in the 1860 or 1880 census, but they were in Smithville in 1865 (Elmore, age 39, Olive, age 34), and in 1870 (ages 44 and 40), without children.[1076]

The Smithville Town Clerk in 1899 was uninformed of the names of Elmore's parents, but the record of his death shows that he was born in Smithville at a time when no Harrises except Joseph and his family were residing there. No doubt Elmore was one of Joseph's younger children "put out" to other families after his wife Julia's death there in the late 1820s.[1077]

[1072] Gravestone, Oakland Cemetery, Durand, Ill., broken through inscription of her name. This daughter was born about the time that her father was "taken sick" on his way to his military unit at Springfield, Ill. (pension file).

[1073] Obituary, *Park Rapids Enterprise*, 11 April 1884, stating that she had come to "Shell City in 1882."

[1074] *Park Rapids Enterprise*, 4 Oct. 1883.

[1075] Gravestone, Cowles Cemetery, Smithville, N.Y.; "Smithville Book of Vital Records" (Smithville Town Clerk, Greene, N.Y.), which state: "Parents not known."

[1076] 1865 N.Y. State Census, First Election District, Smithville, p. 1567; 1870 U.S. Census, Smithville, Chenango Co., N.Y., p. 502.

[1077] Obituary of Elisha Harris, no. 51.

Elmore's presence after 1850 near Joseph's relatives, the Cowles, and his later burial in Cowles Cemetery suggest that he was reared with them after Joseph moved on to Ohio and Illinois. Apparently, Elmore was the only one of Joseph's children to stay in Chenango County.

Elmore apparently resided for some time in Missouri in the 1870s; in 1900, his widow Olive was living in Smithville with their only child:

> i BERT[7] HARRIS, b. Mo. in Jan. 1873; m. ca. 1893 MERTIE L. NORTON, b. N.Y. in Oct. 1874, dau. of Walter and Maria (___) Norton. Bert and Mertie Harris were living in Smithville in 1900 and 1905, when he was listed as a farmer.[1078] By 1910 they had moved to nearby Fenton Twp. in Broome Co.,[1079] where in 1920 he was a mail carrier and Mertie's parents were residing with them.[1080] No children in 1900, 1905, 1910, or 1920.

54 EDGAR EGGLESTON[6] HARRIS (*Joseph[5], Jeremiah[4], Daniel[3], Walter[2], John[1]*), born in New York on 4 September 1828,[1081] died in Kansas City, Missouri, on 29 June 1900, age 71.[1082] He married not long after the 1850 census date, most likely at Forkston, Wyoming County, Pennsylvania, **MARIA LOUISA FASSETT**, born there on 18 November 1832, who died of pneumonia at Orleans, Harlan County, Nebraska, on 25 January 1898, daughter of Gordon and Elizabeth (Bowman) Fassett of Forkston.[1083] Edgar and Maria Louisa were divorced at Spencer, Clay County, Iowa, on 25 September 1882,[1084] and she married second, at Spencer, on 28 September 1884, Edgar's brother Elisha Harris (no. 51). She lived with Elisha at Durand, Illinois, until about 1893, when she went to Orleans.

Joseph Harris's younger children were "put out" to other families in the late 1820s after his wife died at Smithville, New York. His infant son Edgar seems to have been placed with members of the Seth Eggleston family in adjoining Triangle, Broome County, who bestowed his middle name. Edgar Harris, "laborer," born in New York, first appears at age 21 in the 1850

[1078] 1900 U.S. Census, Town of Smithville, Chenango Co., N.Y., E.D. 82, fam. 154; 1905 N.Y. State Census, Smithville, Election Dist. 2, Chenango Co., p. 9.

[1079] 1910 U.S. Census, Fenton Twp., Broome Co., N.Y., E.D. 44, dwelling 21.

[1080] 1920 U.S. Census, Town of Fenton, Broome Co., N.Y., E.D. 74, sheet 3A.

[1081] Birthplace from later census records and death notice; date from 1900 census and notes provided by descendants of Edgar's daughter Addie Arvilla Wescott.

[1082] Record of Deaths–Kansas City, Mo., no. 4134; death notice, *Kansas City Star*, 30 June 1900.

[1083] Katherine Fassett Schuster, *The Fassett Genealogy* (Binghamton, N.Y.; By the author, 1974), 202. Maria's gravestone, inscribed "mother" and with these birth and death dates, stands in Orleans Cemetery between stones for her sister Sebrena D. Fassett and her (Maria's) daughter Addie A. Wescott.

[1084] Clay Co., Iowa, Circuit Court Records, I:571, Case no. 595.

census for Triangle in the home of Horace Eggleston,[1085] a son of Seth (1787–1829) and his wife Anna (Whitney), and grandson of John Eggleston of Triangle.[1086] Nearby neighbors included several other children and grand-children of John Eggleston.[1087] Also nearby was David Bowman, black-smith, uncle of Edgar's later bride Maria Louisa Fassett. About 1849, David's parents Elijah and Nancy (Burger) Bowman—Maria Louisa's grandparents—had moved up from Forkston, Pennsylvania, and in 1855 were residing in David's home.[1088]

Birthplaces of Edgar and Maria Louisa Harris's children reveal that they were residing in Pennsylvania in the early 1850s and at Binghamton, Broome County, New York, in April 1856. By 17 July 1857, they were in Durand, Winnebago County, Illinois, about twenty years after his father and elder brothers had arrived there. On that date, Edgar E. Harris "of Winne-bago County" bought three lots in Durand village from John Steeves, two of which he sold to Alexander G. Stewart next October.[1089] By 1860, Edgar was a deputy sheriff of Winnebago County, in which capacity he was defendant in a replevin action brought that December by Duncan J. Stewart for 1300 bushels of wheat raised on the Otis Webster farm near Durand.[1090]

[1085] 1850 U.S. Census, Town of Triangle, Broome Co., N.Y., house 346.

[1086] Gale Ion Harris, "John[5] Eggleston of Watertown, Connecticut, and Broome County, New York" (to be published in *American Ancestors Journal*).

[1087] Horace Eggleston, with whom Edgar Harris was residing in 1850, was only a child when Edgar's mother died. Circumstances outlined below indicate that Edgar probably had been placed with Horace's parents, Seth and Anna (Whitney) Eggleston of Lisle (later renamed Triangle); then, when Seth died in July 1829, Edgar was taken in by their eldest son Ransom Eggleston (b. ca. 1809) who had married Rhoda Blakesly about that time.

• Edgar's father, Joseph Harris, was closely associated with William Porter in Canaan, Conn. Porter moved to Lisle, N.Y., where in the early 1820s he was a merchant in company with Asa Whitney of Lisle, apparently a close relative of Seth Eggleston's wife Anna (Whitney) of Lisle.

• The first child of Seth's son Ransom Eggleston was born in 1832, yet, in the 1830 census for Lisle, Ransom's household included, in addition to himself and his young wife, three young males aged 15-19, 5-9, and under 5. The elder one of these young males may be his younger brother Ruloff, then about 19. The other two are not explainable as Eggleston relatives, but their ages are correct for Joseph Harris's youngest sons Elmore (b. 1825) and Edgar (b. 1828).

• Ransom Eggleston named daughters Adeline in 1845 and Arvilla in 1846. Edgar Eggleston Harris named a daughter Addie Arvilla in 1863, neither name appearing among his wife's Fassett relatives.

• By 1850, Ransom Eggleston had moved to Tioga Co., Pa., but, in the census of that year, Edgar Harris appears for the first time in the family of Ransom's younger brother Horace Eggleston in Triangle. In 1853 Horace named a daughter Ida. In 1856 Edgar Harris named a daughter Ida, again not a name appearing in the Fassett family.

[1088] 1855 New York State Census, Town of Triangle, Broome Co.

[1089] Winnebago Co., Ill., Deeds, 41D:284, 41E:67.

[1090] 1860 U.S. Census, Durand Village, Winnebago Co., Ill., house 2638; Winnebago Co. Circuit Court, Writ of Replevin, Rockford, Ill., 5 Dec. 1860.

The household of E. E. Harris in Howard, Winnebago County, in 1865 consisted of a male and a female age 30-39, two females 10-19, and two females under 10.[1091] In 1869, "E. E. Harris" advertised his business in Durand on "East Side Public Square" as Agent for the "Rockford, Rock River and Chicago Life Insurance Companies," and "House, Sign, Ornamental and Carriage Painting, Paper Hanging & Glazing," with "Paints, and Oils, Sash, Doors and Blinds kept constantly on hand."[1092]

Apparently responding to opportunities as the railroads pushed on west, Edgar and Maria Harris sold their Durand properties to Martha E. Wise in July 1873 and June 1874.[1093] They arrived in Spencer, Clay County, Iowa, before 18 September 1874, when Edgar bought two lots there from A. L. Lovewell. Six days later, Maria bought two lots there in her own name.[1094] Numerous later deeds there, in their names both jointly and separately, and Powers of Attorney granted to one another, show that they were active property traders in Spencer. In 1875, Edgar ran for the office of Clay County Coroner, but lost to J. Rood who received 292 votes, beating Edgar's 152 votes.[1095] Edgar's listed occupation there in 1880 was "house painter."[1096]

A regional history of western Iowa, published in 1882, contains this brief biographical notice:

E. E. Harris, painter, came to Spencer in 1874, from Ill. and engaged in the hotel business at the Metropolitan, now called Commercial. He afterwards opened the Central house now called the Gregory, after three years he rented the hotel and began working at his trade, that of painter. He worked at painting one year in the Black Hills. He is also agent for the Cedar Rapids Ins. Co.[1097]

[1091] 1865 Ill. State Census, Howard, Winnebago Co., Ill., p. 44.

[1092] *Rockford City Directory and Gazetteer, 1869*, 43.

[1093] Winnebago Co., Ill., Deeds, 93D:113, 225.

[1094] Clay Co., Iowa, Deeds, A:139, 403, Spencer, Iowa.

[1095] Samuel Gillespie and James E. Steele, *History of Clay County, Iowa, from its Earliest Settlement to 1909* (Chicago: S. J. Clarke Pub. Co., 1909), 100.

[1096] 1880 U.S. Census, Village of Spencer, Clay Co., Iowa, E.D. 57, sheet 6. Years later, it was said that Maria Louisa Harris "seemed to be engaged in many businesses—a hotel at Spencer, Iowa, a millinery shop and a dress maker, and as a side line bought several old houses—fixed them up and sold them—a very resourceful and capable woman." (Letter of her grandson Guy Earl Wescott, postmarked Alma, Nebr., 6 March 1937, to Mrs. Fred Fassett of Stevensville, Pa.) It seems that Maria handled the business and that Edgar was in charge of fixing and painting.

[1097] *History of Western Iowa: Its Settlement and Growth* (Sioux City: Western Pub. Co., 1882), 437. This sketch contains the only known mention of Edgar's presence in the Black Hills during the heyday of the gold rush in Deadwood and development of the Homestake mining operation at Lead.

The Commercial Hotel, mentioned in this sketch, was operated by Edgar's wife, Maria L. Harris, with her children's help.[1098] Several deeds dated in 1882 appear to be rearrangements of title associated with Edgar and Maria's divorce in Spencer that September.

In September 1884, Maria married at Spencer Edgar's older brother Elisha Harris of Durand (no. 51). That marriage lasted until about 1893, when she left him and went to Orleans, Nebraska, to join her sisters, her son Ernest Victor Harris, and uncle Calvin Bowman who had settled there in the early 1870s.[1099]

After his divorce in Iowa in September 1882, Edgar resided for some time in Orleans, Nebraska, where he is found in 1885 as "E. E. Harris," age 55 [sic], born in New York, single, and working as a "clerk in hotel."[1100] By 1889, however, Edgar was in Kansas City, Missouri, when a city directory lists him as residing at Bernard Place, no occupation given.[1101] In the census of 1900, taken that 2 June, Edgar E. Harris was recorded as a "patient" in "Kansas City Hospital."[1102] His eldest daughter and son-in-law Jacob Drumm had settled there some years before. The census further indicates that he was born in "N.Y." in September 1828, that he was "widowed," and that his home address was 224 W. 12th Street in Kansas City.[1103] He died of

---

[1098] Letter of Maria's son-in-law Judge Leander M. Pemberton, ca. 1928, provided by Miss Bess V. Gleason of Manhattan, Kans. Pemberton was residing in Maria's hotel in Spencer when he met her daughter Ida M. Harris and married her in 1879.

[1099] Schuster, *Fassett Genealogy*, 202. The statement included there that Elisha Harris of Durand was a "half brother to Edgar Eggleston Harris" has been given much attention, but a diligent effort has produced no evidence to support the implication that they had different mothers. The statement apparently has roots in some confusion revealed, for example, in remarks by Edgar's grandson Guy Earl Wescott: "I have talked to mother [Addie Arvilla (Harris) Wescott] and she tells me that there was quite a family [of Harrises] at Durand [Illinois], but they seemed to be half brothers of Edgar" (Letter postmarked 6 March 1937 at Alma, Nebr., to Mrs. Fred Fassett of Stevensville, Pa., mother of Mrs. Schuster, compiler of *The Fassett Genealogy*). Guy and his mother apparently used the term "half-brother" in reference to the unusual relationships created by the marriage of Elisha Harris to Edgar Eggleston Harris's ex-wife Maria. Only two weeks before, in a letter dated 19 Feb. 1937, Guy had informed Mrs. Fred Fassett of his intention to write to Elmer Harris, "this half brother and cousin of mother's in Colorado to find out what I can of the Harrises." Elmer Harris of Colorado, Elisha's son, was instead a *step*brother and cousin of Guy's mother (see no. 17). It is not known whether a response was received from Elmer; he could have clarified the matter for Guy and incidentally relieved much of the effort in later decades to disentangle the confusion.

[1100] 1885 Nebraska State Census, Orleans Village, Harlan Co., E.D. 392, p. 12.

[1101] *Hoyt's City Directory of Kansas City, Missouri, 1889–1890*, alphabetically arranged. His residence is listed as "Bernard Place east of Exposition," presently the site of the downtown Kansas City Marriott Hotel.

[1102] 1900 U.S. Census, Kansas City, Jackson Co., Mo., E.D. 112, sheet 15.

[1103] Site now [in 2012] of the downtown Kansas City Marriott Hotel.

"chronic nephritis" at the "City Hospital" on the 29th of that month, his death record also showing that he was a widower.[1104]

Children of Edgar Eggleston[6] and Maria Louisa (Fassett) Harris:

i   ALICE A.[7] HARRIS, b. in Pa. 14 May 1852 (family record), or 1854 (1900 census), or 1855 (death certificate), d. at her home at 1812 East 38th Street in Kansas City, Mo., 7 Feb. 1913, but buried at Beatrice, Gage Co., Nebr.[1105] She m. at Beatrice 13 Oct. 1883, as his third wife, JACOB DRUMM, b. near Tarlton, Ohio, 2 Oct. 1838, who d. at Urbana, Ill., 2 Feb. 1919. Jacob, who had five children with his prior wives, had served in the 107th Illinois Infantry Regiment during the Civil War in Georgia, Tennessee, North Carolina, and New York.[1106] Alice is said to have resided some time with her aunt Almeda (Fassett) Hull in Meshoppen, Wyoming Co., Pa., and that "she was a milliner there and in N.Y. City."[1107] According to his pension file, Jacob Drumm came to Beatrice in 1871, where he and Alice were residing at 500 Sixth Street in 1885, his occupation recorded as "postmaster."[1108] Jacob and Alice lived in Beatrice until 1892, when they moved briefly to Olathe and Lewisburg, Kans., before finally settling in Kansas City, where they were residing at 1812 East 38th Street in 1900 and 1910.[1109] In 1900, their household included Alice's "nephew" Guy E. Wescott and "niece" Maud B. Wescott, children of her sister Addie. A professional painter, Alice was a teacher of "art" in 1910, some of her works surviving. She had no children.

ii IDA M. HARRIS, b. at Binghamton, Broome Co., N.Y., 8 April 1856, d. at Beatrice, Nebr., 3 Sept. 1903, where she is buried in Evergreen Home Cemetery.[1110] She m. at Spencer, Clay Co., Iowa, 30 April 1879, LEANDER MUNSELL PEMBERTON,[1111] b. near Paris, Edgar Co., Ill., 12 Nov. 1845, who d. at Beatrice 23 April 1929, son of Harvey Guilford and Clarissa C. (King) Pemberton of Edgar Co.[1112] While single in 1874, Leander was living at the

---

[1104] Record of Deaths–Kansas City, Mo., no. 4134. In March 1937, Edgar's grandson Guy Earl Wescott (b. 1891) wrote: "Edgar Harris died in Kansas City; I can remember as a small boy visiting him in a hospital there" (letter postmarked Alma, Nebr., to Mrs. Fred Fassett, Stevensville, Pa.).

[1105] Death Certificate, Bureau of Vital Statistics, Kansas City, Mo.

[1106] Pension Cert. no. 80042, National Archives, Washington, D.C.

[1107] Letter, 19 Feb. 1937, Guy Earl Wescott, Route 1, Alma, Nebr., to Mrs. Fred Fassett, Stevensville, Pa.

[1108] 1885 Nebraska State Census, City of Beatrice, Gage Co., E.D. 349, p. 25, probably understating Alice's age as 29 years (see her sister Ida's stated age in that census). Nebraska census entries were provided by Leaman Don Harris of Chantilly, Va., 1979.

[1109] 1900 U.S. Census, 1812 38th St., Ward 12, Kansas City, Jackson Co., Mo., E.D. 127, sheet 4; 1910 U.S. Census, 4th Ward, Kansas City, Jackson Co., Mo., E.D. 170, sheet 2B.

[1110] Beatrice Vital Records, City Clerk's Office.

[1111] Clay Co., Iowa, Marriage Records, Spencer, Iowa.

[1112] Letter and autobiographical notes of L. M. Pemberton, ca. 1928, provided by Miss Bess V. Gleason of Manhattan, Kans. In a published biographical sketch for Leander M. Pemberton, his mother is called "Caroline C. King" (*Portrait and Biographical Album of Gage County, Nebraska* [Chicago: Chapman Brothers, 1888], 364).

Commercial Hotel in Spencer, the year it was purchased by his future mother-in-law, Maria Louisa Harris. As a Notary Public, his name appears on her deeds. Next year, he was Auditor of Clay County.[1113] By the 1880 census date, Leander and Ida had moved to Beatrice, Nebr.,[1114] where they were residing at 100 Grant Street in 1885, his occupation listed as "lawyer."[1115] In Sept. 1882, L. M. Pemberton "of Gage County, Nebraska," acted as strawman at Spencer in one of Ida's parents' property transactions related to their divorce that month. By 1885, Ida's younger sister Marietta Elnora ("Margaret") Harris had come from Spencer to live with her. Leander became "a prominent lawyer, judge, political figure, and member of the Nebraska Legislature."[1116] By 1900, the Pembertons and their five children had moved to 522 7th Street in Beatrice.[1117] Leander was listed as a District Court Judge, a widower, in Beatrice in 1910 and 1920.[1118] He had been elected in 1902 as a state senator from Gage County, and in 1907 as one of the judges of the old First Judicial District of Nebraska.[1119]

Children of Leander Munsell and Ida M.[7] (Harris) Pemberton, the first born in Iowa and the rest in Nebr.:

1 *Zulu L. Pemberton*, b. Jan. 1880, a school teacher, age 30, unmarried, living with her father in 1910, and "a highly respected teacher in the public schools of Seattle, Washington" in 1918.[1120] She was still a public school teacher there in 1930, single, age 49, and a lodger in a hotel.[1121]

2 *Pauline A. Pemberton*, b. Feb. 1882; m. (1) by 1918 Wyley B. Mayer, "a successful business man" of Beatrice,[1122] b. Iowa ca. 1882,[1123] (2) "a judge."

3 *Louisa M. Pemberton*, b. Oct. 1884; m. by 1918 Lee W. Johnson, b. Nebr. ca. 1888, both living with her father in 1920, Lee then a "court reporter."

4 *Frederick King Pemberton*, b. Beatrice in March 1887; m. Miles City, Custer Co., Mont., 13 Jan. 1910 Gertrude Vigoren, b. Bergen,

---

[1113] *Historical Atlas of the State of Iowa* (Chicago: Andreas Atlas Co., 1875).

[1114] 1880 U.S. Census, Beatrice, Gage Co., Nebr., E.D. 347, sheet 86A. Their household then included daughter Zulu, age 6m, and "bro in law" Ernest Harris, age 14.

[1115] 1885 Nebraska State Census, City of Beatrice, Gage Co., Nebr., E.D. 340, p. 34, stating Ida's age as 29 years.

[1116] Obituary of L. M. Pemberton, date and name of newspaper missing, provided by Miss Bess V. Gleason.

[1117] 1900 U.S. Census, Beatrice, Gage Co., Nebr., E.D. 39, sheet 6.

[1118] 1910 and 1920 U.S. Census, Beatrice, Gage Co., Nebr., E.D. 41, sheet 6, and E.D. 46, sheet 6A, respectively.

[1119] Biography of Leander M. Pemberton in Hugh J. Dobbs, *History of Gage County, Nebraska* (Lincoln, Nebr.: Western Pub. and Engraving Co., 1918), 587-91, at 590-91.

[1120] Dobbs, *History of Gage County*, 591.

[1121] 1930 U.S. Census, City of Seattle, King Co., Wash., E.D. 17-409, sheet 8A.

[1122] Dobbs, *History of Gage County*, 591.

[1123] 1920 U.S. Census, Beatrice, Gage Co., Nebr., E.D. 56, sheet 11B.

Norway, ca. 1890, dau. of Lase and Rachel (Ellingson) Vigoren.[1124] In April 1910 Frederick and Gertrude were in Miles City, where he was a railroad surveyor.[1125] They returned to Beatrice by 1920,[1126] where he was the proprietor of a shoe shop in 1930.[1127]

5 *Guilford H. Pemberton*, b. Beatrice 21 Jan. 1893, living Carversville, Bucks Co., Pa., in 1942, age 49.[1128] He was still single and gave his home address as 522 North 7th, Beatrice, Nebr., when on 12 June 1917 at age 24 he registered by mail for the draft for World War I while a teacher at the Urban Academy in Los Angeles, Calif.[1129] He soon became "a cadet in the signal corps of the aviation service now preparing for service in France, at Ellington Field, Texas."[1130]

iii   FRANK F. HARRIS, "Son of E. E. and M. L. Harris," b. 15 March 1857, d. 6 Oct. 1857.[1131] This child was born apparently a few months before his parents came to Durand from Binghamton, N.Y., no doubt on the railroad that reached Durand as its western terminus that June.[1132]

iv   JULIA ALVERETTE HARRIS, b. Durand, Ill., 1 July 1858, d. in Sacramento, Calif., on 17 March 1956, aged 97, last residing at 2201 Gunn Road, Carmichael, Calif.[1133] She m. at her parents' residence in Spencer, Iowa, 7 Sept. 1878, LINLEY S. MERRITT,[1134] b. in N.Y. 30 June 1857, who d. in Portland, Oreg., on 6 May 1929, son of Jacob and Sarah J. (Sutton) Merritt of Spencer. In 1880 Linley was a "clerk" in his father's dry goods store in Spencer.[1135] Family notes showing their children's birthplaces indicate that Linley and Julia Merritt were residing at Spencer in 1881, but by 1889 they had moved to Dubuque, Iowa, then to Des Moines by Oct. 1897, where they were living at 660 14th Street in June 1900.[1136] By 1910 they were in Baker City, Oreg., when Julia was recorded as being mother of five children, four then living.[1137] By Jan. 1920 they had moved to Seattle, where Linley, a "printer" for a newspaper, his wife Julia, and 12-year-old "grandson"

[1124] Montana, County Marriages, 1865–1950, images online at <www.FamilySearch.org>, accessed Aug. 2011.

[1125] 1910 U.S. Census, Miles City, Custer Co., Mont., E.D. 79, sheet 1A ("Mr. and Mrs. F. K. Pemberton," giving his birthplace as "Beatrice, Nebr.").

[1126] 1920 U.S. Census, Beatrice, Gage Co., Nebr., E.D. 52, sheet 4A.

[1127] 1930 U.S. Census, Beatrice, Gage Co., Nebr., E.D. 34-8, sheet 9A, showing them with two children, Munsell and Fred Pemberton, b. in "Montana" ca. 1912 and 1914, respectively.

[1128] World War II Draft Registration Card, no. U2445. He entered Bertrice Pemberton of Carversville, relationship unstated, as the "person who will always know your address."

[1129] World War I Draft Registration Card, no. 2435-178.

[1130] Dobbs, *History of Gage County*, 591.

[1131] Tombstone, Oakland Cemetery, Durand, Ill.

[1132] *Changing Ways*, 6.

[1133] Death Certificate, California State Registrar of Vital Statistics. The informant, Mrs. Louise Jenson, no doubt was Julia's youngest daughter.

[1134] Clay Co., Iowa, Marriage Records, Spencer, Iowa.

[1135] 1880 U.S. Census, Village of Spencer, Clay Co., Iowa, dwellings 7 and 8.

[1136] 1900 U.S. Census, Des Moines Twp., Polk Co., Iowa, E.D. 71, sheets 3-4.

[1137] 1910 U.S. Census, Depot Precinct, Baker City, Baker Co., Oreg., E.D. 4, sheet 11B.

Ronald Merritt [*sic*] were residing at 1807 East Elder St.[1138] Julia was living in Los Angeles in 1938.[1139]

Children of Linley S. and Julia Alverette[7] (Harris) Merritt:[1140]

1 *Goldie Alice Merritt*, b. Spencer, Iowa, 7 June 1879, d. Omaha, Nebr., 12 May 1904 but buried in Des Moines; m. there 6 Nov. 1897 Jerry Van Heusen, son of P. E. and Anna C. (Homrel/Honnel) Van Heusen,[1141] b. N.Y., July 1867. They were residing with Goldie's parents in Des Moines in 1900, at which time they had no children.

2 *Edgar Lindley Merritt*, b. Spencer 27 Sept. 1881, living in 1961; m. Caldwell, Idaho, 2 July 1915 Alice Jolley,[1142] b. Idaho 19 Feb. 1897, d. Lincoln City, Oreg., Feb. 1986,[1143] dau. of Thomas and Anna M. (___) Jolley.[1144] Edgar was single and residing as a "lodger" in Portland in 1910.[1145] On 12 Sept. 1918, Edgar was a "writer" for *New West Magazine* and residing at 70 East 7th Street in Salt Lake City when, at age 36, he registered for the draft during World War I.[1146] In Jan. 1920 Edgar, an "advertiser" for a newspaper, and his wife Alice were residing in Seattle with daughter Ariel D., age 2y 1m and born in Idaho.[1147] In April 1930 they were in Portland, where he was a newspaper editor and they had children Arial, age 12, b. Idaho, and Merilynn, age 8, b. Wash.[1148]

3 A child, named unknown, accounted for in the 1910 census.

4 *Marian Eliza Merritt*, b. Dubuque, Iowa, 5 Feb. 1889, d. Baker, Oreg., 21 March 1911;[1149] m. by 1908 ___ McLaughlin, b. N.Dak., whom she divorced.[1150] Marian and her two-year-old son Ronald D. Merritt [*sic*], b. Wash. ca. 1908, were residing with her parents in Baker in 1910.

5 *Ida Louisa Merritt*, b. Des Moines, Iowa, 4 Oct. 1897, d. Sacramento, Calif., 15 Jan. 1994;[1151] m. Salt Lake City 18 Nov. 1919 John W. Jensen, b. Richfield, Utah, 26 April 1892, son of John B. and Minnie (___) Jensen.[1152] John W. was a "pipe-fitter" for an oil

[1138] 1920 U.S. Census, Precinct 202, City of Seattle, King Co., Wash., E.D. 264, sheet 6A.

[1139] Obituary of her sister Addie Arvilla Wescott, no. 54 v.

[1140] From family notes and 1900 census at Des Moines.

[1141] Iowa Marriages, 1809–1992, online at <www,FamilySearch.org>, accessed Aug. 2011.

[1142] Canyon Co., Idaho, Marriages, 8:120.

[1143] Social Security Death Index, SSN 543-40-8968.

[1144] Alice's birth and parentage from 1900 U.S. Census, Franklin Twp., Oneida Co., Idaho, E.D. 96, sheet 10 (Thomas Jolley household).

[1145] 1910 U.S. Census, 7th Ward, Portland City, Multnomah Co., Oreg., E.D. 152, sheet 15B.

[1146] World War I Draft Registration Card, no. 117-710, stamped C43-1-18, in Salt Lake City. He gave the name Alice Merritt as nearest relative.

[1147] 1920 U.S. Census, 14th Precinct, City of Seattle, King Co., Wash., E.D. 78, sheet 4A.

[1148] 1930 U.S. Census, Election Precinct 446, Portland City, Multnomah Co., Oreg., E.D. 26-545, sheet 8A.

[1149] Oregon Death Index, 1903–98, citing certificate 1083.

[1150] Family data provided by Gwen Alice (Gleason) Haney, Concordia, Kans.

[1151] Social Security Death Index, SSN 553-72-6064.

[1152] Utah Marriages, 1887–1966, online at FamilySearch.org, accessed Aug. 2011.

refinery in Salt Lake City in Jan. 1920.[1153] In April 1940, J. W. and Ida Louise Jensen were residing in Richfield, where he was operator-manager of a filling station.[1154]

v　ADDIE ARVILLA HARRIS, b. Durand, Ill., 27 April 1863, d. at her home in Orleans, Harlan Co., Nebr., on 2 March 1938,[1155] and was buried adjacent to her mother and daughter "Margery" Wescott in Orleans Cemetery. She m. at Spencer, Iowa, 23 Aug. 1881, WILLIS SECOR WESCOTT, an "editor" of Sioux Rapids, Iowa,[1156] b. New Lisbon, Wis., 23 Aug. 1862, who d. in Minneapolis on 30 Dec. 1918, son of Lucius C. and Gertrude J. (Secor) Wescott. Willis and Addie Wescott resided for some time in Sioux Rapids, but moved before 1887 to Dubuque, Iowa, and by 1896 to Chicago. W. S. Wescott was in Durand, Ill., on 24 April 1890, however, when he witnessed a deed to his mother, Gertrude J. Wescott, from Elisha and Maria Louisa Harris of Durand, his wife Addie's stepfather and mother (no. 51). The property conveyed was in Spencer, Iowa.[1157] Willis and Addie separated at Chicago in 1897 and were subsequently divorced. Addie moved to Orleans, Nebr., in 1897 with four of her six children, leaving children Guy and Maude with their aunt Alice Drumm (no. 54 i) in Kansas City.[1158] She resided at first near Orleans with her brother Ernest Victor Harris who had been there since about 1883. She soon moved into Orleans Village where she was a "boarding house keeper" in June 1900.[1159] In 1907 she opened the Wescott Hotel in Orleans, which she operated for many years.[1160]

Children of Willis Secor and Addie Arvilla[7] (Harris) Wescott:

1 *Willis Selah Wescott*, b. Sioux Rapids, Iowa, 29 Sept. 1882, d. Kearney, Nebr., 6 Feb. 1960;[1161] m. ca. 1819 Esther Gwendolyn Anderson; they were divorced before 1930. He was a "cook," still single, and residing in Holdrege, Nebr., on 12 Sept. 1918, when at age 35 he registered for the draft for World War I.[1162] In 1920, Willis and his wife Esther G. were residing in his mother's home in Orleans,

---

[1153] 1920 U.S. Census, 5th Ward, Salt Lake City, Salt Lake Co, Utah, E.D. 169, sheet 7B.

[1154] 1940 U.S. Census, Richfield City, Sevier Co., Utah, E.D. 41-44, sheet 1A, no children indicated.

[1155] Obituary, *The Orleans Chronicle*, 10 March 1938; copy of Addie's birth certificate, with death date written in a later hand, provided by Gwen Alice Haney, Concordia, Kans.

[1156] Clay Co., Iowa, Marriage Records, Spencer, Iowa.

[1157] Clay Co., Iowa, Deeds, B:453.

[1158] 1900 U.S. Census, 1812 38th St., Ward 12, Kansas City, Jackson Co., Mo., E.D. 127, sheet 4 (Jacob Drum household). These children were in the Drum household in Kansas City on the census date there, 6 June 1900, but on 13 June 1900 they were listed with their mother in Orleans, Nebr. (1900 U.S. Census, Orleans Village, Orleans Twp., Harlan Co., Nebr., E.D. 99, sheet 11).

[1159] 1900 U.S. Census, Orleans Village, Orleans Twp., Harlan Co., Nebr., E.D. 99, sheet 11.

[1160] Obituary, *The Orleans Chronicle*, 10 March 1938. It is said by descendants that no cookies were served in this hotel because it was Addie's after-school job as a girl to bake the cookies for her mother's hotel in Spencer, Iowa. An undated photographic image shows the "hotel" in Orleans as a two-story frame structure with a sign on the front, "Wescott House" (online at <www.rootsweb.com/~neharlan/-pics/OrleansWescottHotel.JPG>, viewed 7 May 2006).

[1161] Family data provided by Gwen Alice (Gleason) Haney, Concordia, Kans.

[1162] World War I Draft Registration Card, no. 1159-A733. He listed his "mother, Ada Wescott" of Orleans as his nearest relative.

Nebr.[1163] In 1930, Willard [*sic*] S. Wescott, a lodger, age 47 and divorced, was working as a chef in an Omaha restaurant.[1164] In 1940, William [*sic*] Wescott, a painter, age 58 and divorced, was residing with his "brother" Guy E. Wescott in Orleans.[1165]

2 *Alice Bessie Leone Wescott*, b. Sioux Rapids 19 Nov. 1884, d. Concordia, Kans., 5 Dec. 1970;[1166] m. Orleans, Nebr., 16 June 1909 Olin Stanley Gleason,[1167] b. Vt. 1 April 1879, d. Concordia in Dec. 1968.[1168] On 12 Sept. 1918, Olin Stanley Gleason, age 39, photographer, registered for the draft, giving his address as 644 S. Ash, Casper, Wyo., and his nearest relative as his wife Bess Gleason at the same address.[1169] In 1940, Olin S. and Bess W. Gleason were residing in Concordia, where he was a photographer with his own studio.[1170] In 1953, Olin S. and Bess W. Gleason were owners of the Gleason Studio (photographers) at 127½ W. 6th Street in Concordia.[1171]

3 *Harry Clark Harris Wescott*, b. Dubuque, Iowa, 12 June 1887, d. 15 July 1950;[1172] m. Boise, Idaho, 22 June 1912 Edna R. Nebb,[1173] b. Idaho ca. 1895. On 5 June 1917, Harry C. Wescott, age 29, giving his address as Montour, Idaho, and married with a wife and child (unnamed), registered for the draft, the record adding that he had three years service as a corporal in the infantry.[1174] They were still in Montour in 1920, when he was a teamster.[1175] They were in Cascade Village, Valley Co., Idaho, in 1930, where he was a laborer for a lumber company.[1176] Harry was in Prineville, Oreg., in 1938.[1177]

[1163] 1920 U.S. Census, Orleans City, Harlan Co., Nebr., E.D. 126, sheet 2A. Parts of this record are faded beyond legibility.

[1164] 1930 U.S. Census, Omaha City, Douglas Co., Nebr., E.D. 28-32, sheet 12B.

[1165] 1940 U.S. Census, Orleans City, Harlan Co., Nebr., E.D. 42-11, sheet 10E. He had been living in the "same place" in 1935.

[1166] Family data provided by Gwen Alice (Gleason) Haney, Concordia, Kans.

[1167] Nebraska Marriages, 1855–1995, online at <www.FamilySearch.org>, accessed Aug. 2011. Alice Bessie Leone (Wescott) Gleason's daughters Bess Vera Gleason (1914–1980) and Gwen Alice (Gleason) Haney (b. 1917) provided invaluable early assistance with the elusive family of Edgar Eggleston Harris. By chance, Bess Vera Gleason and the writer were coworkers at the University of Kansas in 1955, long before either of us had any knowledge that we were related (2nd cousins).

[1168] Social Security Death Index, SSN 512-34-6542.

[1169] World War I Draft Registration Card, no. 2501, stamped A525.

[1170] 1940 U.S. Census, Concordia City, Cloud Co., Kans., E.D. 15-9, sheet 3A. They had been living in the "same house" in 1935.

[1171] *Concordia (Kansas) City Directory, 1953* (Colorado Springs, Colo.: Rocky Mountain Directory Co., 1953), 51.

[1172] Family data provided by Gwen Alice (Gleason) Haney, Concordia, Kans.

[1173] Idaho Marriages, 1888–1898, 1903–1942, online at <www.FamilySearch.org>, accessed Aug. 2012.

[1174] World War I Draft Registration Card, no. 1, stamped 11-2-16A.

[1175] 1920 U.S. Census, Montour, Gem Co., Idaho, E.D. 80, sheet 3A. Their daughter, Marjorie M. Wescott, age 5, b. Idaho, was with them.

[1176] 1930 U.S. Census, Cascade Village, Valley Co., Idaho, E.D. 43-4, sheet 1B.

[1177] Family data provided by Gwen Alice (Gleason) Haney, Concordia, Kans.

4 *Guy Earl Wescott*, b. Dubuque 27 Jan. 1891, d. Orleans, Nebr., 23 Nov. 1942, unm., and bur. near his mother in Orleans Cemetery. He served in a medical unit with the Rainbow Division in France in World War I, homesteaded in Wyoming, taught school in Nebraska, and subsequently traveled throughout the United States and Canada as an actor under the stage name "Don Don Carlos."[1178] In 1940, Guy and his "brother" William [*sic*] Wescott were residing together in Orleans.[1179]

5 *Maude Blanche Wescott*, b. Dubuque 26 Dec. 1893, d. Concordia, Kans., 3 Oct. 1954,[1180] bur. Alma Cemetery, Alma, Nebr.;[1181] m. Orleans, Nebr., 30 June 1914 Harry Monroe Mead, son of Howell Clarence and Angeline (McMustee) Mead,[1182] b. Alma 23 June 1893,[1183] d. 11 March 1936 and bur. same cemetery. He was a grocery merchant in Alma in 1920 and 1930.[1184] In 1940, Maude Mead, age 45 [*sic*], a widow, b. in Iowa, was the proprietor of a grocery in Alma.[1185]

6 *Marjorie Marie Wescott*, b. Chicago 19 Sept. 1896, d. Orleans, Nebr., 12 Aug. 1919, unm.[1186]

80   vi   ERNEST VICTOR HARRIS, b. Durand, Ill., 15 Aug. 1865 (possibly 1866); m. LAURA APALINE PIKE.

vii   MARIETTA ELNORA HARRIS, (also "Matie" and "Marjorie"), b. Durand, Ill., 27 June 1870, d. Milwaukee, Wis., 1 Oct. 1945.[1187] She m. Kansas City, Kans., 29 July 1910, FRANK MERCHANT YOUNG,[1188] b. Bedford, Iowa, 4 March 1880, who d. at Milwaukee on 19 July 1943, son of George Washington and Denah Temperance (Merchant) Young. Her age misstated as 13 years, Marjorie Harris was residing in 1885 with her sister Ida M. Pemberton at Beatrice, Nebr.[1189] She next appears at age 29, single, when she was residing in 1900 in Durand, Ill., with Henry E. Harris, son of her stepfather Elisha Harris (no. 51). Afterward, she moved to Chicago, her stated resi-

---

[1178] From Guy's letters about Harris and Fassett relatives, addressed to Mrs. Fred Fassett of Stevensville, Pa., cited several places in this account.

[1179] 1940 U.S. Census, Orleans City, Harlan Co., Nebr., E.D. 42-11, sheet 10E. Guy had been living in "Chicago" in 1935.

[1180] Family data provided by Gwen Alice (Gleason) Haney, Concordia, Kans.

[1181] Gravestone photo online at <www.findagrave.com>, accessed Aug. 2012.

[1182] Nebraska Marriages, 1855–1995, online at <www.FamilySearch.org>, accessed Aug. 2012.

[1183] Harry Monroe Mead World War I Draft Registration Card, no. 54, stamped 26-2-15-A. He registered in Alma on 5 June 1916, stating that he was married and was a merchant.

[1184] 1920, 1930 U.S. Census, Alma City, Harlan Co., Nebr., E.D. 120, sheet 10B, and E.D. 42-2, sheet 2A, respectively.

[1185] 1940 U.S. Census, Alma City, Harlan Co., Nebr., E.D. 42-2, sheet 7A. She had been living in the "same place" in 1935.

[1186] Family data provided by Gwen Alice (Gleason) Haney, Concordia, Kans.

[1187] Death Certificate, Wisconsin Bureau of Vital Statistics, stating her residence as 2636 N. 48th Street, Milwaukee.

[1188] Kansas City, Kans., Vital Records, understating her age by ten years.

[1189] 1885 Nebraska State Census, City of Beatrice, Gage Co., E.D. 340, p. 34.

dence prior to her marriage in Kansas City. In Jan. 1920 Frank, a machinery salesman, and Marjory Young were residing at 5631 Madison St. in Chicago.[1190] In 1940, they were in Milwaukee, where he was a salesman for Dodge Auto Manufacturing Co.[1191] She was a professional painter, one signed work in the writer's possession. She had no children.

viii MAUD LUELLA HARRIS, b. Durand, Ill., 30 Aug. 1872, d. in Los Angeles, Calif., 26 Dec. 1941.[1192] She m. at Orleans, Nebr., 11 Jan. 1899, ELMUS CLARK BENNETT,[1193] b. Nebr. 23 Dec. 1878,[1194] who survived her, son of Charles A. and Emma (___) Bennett of Orleans. They moved soon after 1900 from Orleans to Bismarck, N.Dak., then, by 1907, to Boise, Idaho, where, on 12 Sept. 1918, Elmus, age 39, registered for the draft during World War I, giving his address as 712 Frank St. in Boise, occupation "lumbering," and nearest relative "Mrs. Elmus Clark Bennett" at the same address.[1195] In 1920 their home was at 712 Franklin St. and Elmus was employed as a yardman for a lumber company.[1196] About 1922, they moved to Calif. and were residing in Los Angeles in 1930 while he was an "estimator" for a lumber mill.[1197] In 1940, Elmus was a salesman for a lumber yard in Los Angeles.[1198] The 1910 census shows that Maud was the mother of seven children, four living at that time.[1199]

Children of Elmus Clark and Maud Luella[7] (Harris) Bennett, from 1900, 1910, and 1920 censuses and family notes, all at home in 1920, not including three infants who d. before 1910:

1 *Grace P. Bennett*, b. Orleans in Nov. 1899.

2 *Bess G. Bennett*, b. Bismarck, N.D, ca. 1905.

3 *Phyllis O. Bennett*, b. near Boise, Idaho, ca. 1907, living with her parents in 1930 while working at a "Gas Co. Office."

4 *Basil Henry Bennett*, b. near Boise 14 March 1908, d. Spokane, Wash., 4 April 1973.[1200] By April 1936 he was in Klamath Falls, Oreg., where he was arrested, fined $100, and sentenced to a year and a day in the U.S. Penitentiary at McNeil Island, Wash., for

---

[1190] 1920 U.S. Census, 35th Ward, Chicago, Cook Co., Ill., 227, sheet 5B.

[1191] 1940 U.S. Census, Milwaukee City, Milwaukee Co., Wis., E.D. 72-501, sheet 1A.

[1192] Death Certificate, California State Register of Vital Statistics, stating her residence as 2208 W. Pico, Los Angeles, and that she had resided in Calif. for 19 years.

[1193] Harlan Co., Nebr., Marriage Records.

[1194] 1900 U.S. Census, Orleans Twp., Harlan Co., Nebr., E.D. 99, sheet 4, day from WWI draft Registration card.

[1195] World War I Draft Registration Card, no. 2065-2021, stamped 11-2-32-C.

[1196] 1920 U.S. Census, Boise City, Ada Co., Idaho, E.D. 12, sheet 8.

[1197] 1930 U.S. Census, Los Angeles City, Los Angeles Co., Calif., E.D. 459, sheet 5A.

[1198] 1940 U.S. Census, Los Angeles City, Los Angeles Co., Calif., E.D. 60-769, sheet 1A.

[1199] 1910 U.S. Census, Alpha Twp., Boise Co., Idaho, E.D. 67, sheet 5B.

[1200] Social Security Death Index, SSN 535-18-8669; Washington Death Index, 1940–1996, online at Ancestry.com.

"selling liq[uor] to Indians."[1201] He was still single and "without dependents" on 25 July 1942, when he enlisted as a private in the army at Spokane for the duration of World War II, giving his birthplace as Idaho, residence as Nez Perce, Idaho, and civil occupation as "production of beverages."[1202]

> 5 *Madeline/Matie Bennett*, b. near Boise, Idaho, 12 Sept. 1910, d. Riverside, Calif., 1 Jan. 1967;[1203] m. in 1930s Joseph W. Campbell, b. Utah 9 Feb. 1908, d. San Bernardino, Calif., 23 Jan. 1973,[1204] a deputy sheriff with whom she was living in Lancaster, Calif., in 1940.[1205] Matie was living with her parents in 1930 while a "typist in Oil Co. Office." Family notes state that she "danced in the movies," no date given.

55 LYMAN PURPLE[6] HARRIS (*Woodruff[5], Jeremiah[4], Daniel[3], Walter[2], John[1]*), born in Greene, Chenango County, New York, on 12 August 1817,[1206] died in Fort Wayne, Indiana, on 12 May 1896, age 78, and was buried beside his wife in Graceland Cemetery in Chicago.[1207] He married on 9 May 1841 **ELVIRA A. LANE** "of Frederickston, Ohio" [Fredericktown in Knox County], born there on 2 July 1821,[1208] who died at the residence of her daughter, Mrs. W. W. Wells, at No. 249 West Congress St. in Chicago on 4 January 1887, age 65, and buried in Graceland Cemetery.[1209]

Lyman P. Harris was a "teacher" in Miami County, Ohio, in 1850,[1210] a "Doctor" in Mansfield, Ohio, in 1860,[1211] a physician in Crestline, Crawford County, Ohio, in 1870,[1212] and a physician practicing in Fort Wayne in 1885.[1213] A Fort Wayne newspaper item in October 1877 announced: "Dr. L. P. Harris, of Crestline, Ohio, comes to us well recommended, not only as

[1201] McNeil Island, Washington, Penitentiary Records of Prisoners Received, 1887–1939, online at <www.Ancestry.com>, giving his "usual residence" as Klamath Falls, occupation laborer, and the only known source for his middle name, *Henry*.

[1202] U.S. World War II Army Enlistment Records, 1938–1946, online at <ww.Ancestry.com>, giving his height as 69 inches and weight 146 pounds.

[1203] California Death Index, 1940–1997, online at <www.Ancestry.com>.

[1204] California Death Index, 1940–1997, online at <www.Ancestry.com>.

[1205] 1940 U.S. Census, Lancaster, Antelope Twp., Los Angeles Co., Calif., E.D. 19-5, sheet 61B.

[1206] Purple, "Manuscript Notes," p. 120.

[1207] *The Fort Wayne Sentinel*, 13 May 1896, p. 1 (Dr. Lyman P. Harris, an old physician of this city . . . the remains will be shipped to Chicago for interment").

[1208] Purple, "Manuscript Notes," p. 120.

[1209] *The Chicago Tribune*, 4 Jan. 1887, p. 8.

[1210] 1850 U.S. Census, Washington Twp., Miami Co., Ohio, p. 363.

[1211] 1860 U.S. Census, 2nd Ward, Mansfield City, Richland Co., Ohio, p. 37.

[1212] 1870 U.S. Census, Crestline, P.O. Galion, Crawford Co., Ohio, p. 473. An entry in the "Purple Manuscript," p. 120, states that Lyman was "formerly of Crestline, Ohio, now of Toledo."

[1213] "The Doctors of the City and the Colleges They Hail From," *The [Fort Wayne] Daily Sentinel*, 29 Aug. 1885, p. 3, listing among them "Lyman P. Harris, Homeopathic Medical College of St. Louis, Mo."

a Physician of more than twenty-five years experience in the Homæopathic practice, but as a gentleman of fine culture and literary and scientific attainments. He may be found at No. 16 Chicago street until further notice."[1214]

Children of Lyman Purple[6] and Elvira A. (Lane) Harris:

    i   ERWIN R. ("ED")[7] HARRIS, b. Ohio ca. 1842, was living in Fort Wayne, Ind., in Sept. 1883, but d. before 1892 as shown below. He m. in Cleveland (but with a Huron Co., Ohio, license) 25 Dec. 1866 CELESTIA A. PICKARD,[1215] dau. of Reuben H. and Julia M. (_____) Pickard,[1216] b. Ohio in Dec. 1844,[1217] a widow living Omaha, Neb., in 1920, age 75, with her daughter Jessie A. Walkup, age 49, also a widow.[1218] Celestia had applied from there on 28 May 1892 for a widow's pension based on Erwin's Civil War service.[1219] He had served as a 2nd Lt. in the 3rd Regiment, Ohio Cavalry, organized at Monroeville, Huron Co., in 1861 and mustered out on 4 Aug. 1865. After some time in Tenn. (birth place of dau. Jessie), Erwin R. and "Lettie" A. Harris were enumerated in Muncie, Ind., in 1880, when he was a "commercial traveler."[1220]

       "Ed" R. Harris was in fact a widely traveled representative for the firm of Brown & Earl in New York, as we learn from lengthy accounts in the Fort Wayne newspapers in Sept. 1883 concerning the mental state of this "best tobacco salesman in the country . . . a son of Dr. Lyman P. Harris, the homeopathic physician now residing on West Wayne street." On 8 Sept., he had been "brought to his father's residence by a lady [unnamed], who stated that he was insane and needed treatment, that she was his wife, having been married in New York ten years ago, and that they had lived most of the time at Cleveland, and had recently been living in Chicago." She had not known that he was previously married, but, the writer continues, "sixteen years ago Mr. Harris was married to Miss Letia Pickard, daughter of Mr. C. [*sic*, R.] H. Pickard of Omaha, Nebraska. . . . The two ladies interested had a conference, and wife No. 2 returned to Chicago. . . . Harris can give no explanation owing to the unsettled condition of his mind." Ed was taken by the sheriff to Indianapolis, where he was committed to the state asylum, but wife No. 1 and her father soon arranged his release. On 28 Sept. 1883, he was "now at his home on Adams Street." The accounts suggest that he had

---

[1214] *Fort Wayne Daily News*, 30 Oct. 1877, p. 4.

[1215] Huron Co., Ohio, Marriage Records, 2:47 (no. 281), (S. M. Beatty, M.G., residing in Cuyahoga County, presiding).

[1216] She was in their home in Huron Co. in 1850 and 1860 (U.S. Census, Ridgefield Twp., Huron Co., Ohio, pp. 21, 344, respectively. They were in Neb. by 1880 (1880 U.S. Census, Douglas Precinct, Douglas Co., Neb., E.D. 25, p. 18B), consistent with newspaper accounts in 1883.

[1217] 1900 U.S. Census, Omaha City, Douglas Co., Neb., E.D. 4, sheet 2B (Andrew Walkup household).

[1218] 1920 U.S. Census, 5th Ward, Omaha City, Douglas Co., Neb., E.D. 47, sheet 9A.

[1219] Civil War Pension Index, Certificate No. 358538, images online at <www.Ancestry.com>.

[1220] 1880 U.S. Census, City of Muncie, Delaware Co., Ind., E.D. 184, p. 47. Their household included "daughter" Jessie Harris, age 10, b. Tenn.

become deranged by overwork, heavy losses in "Chicago speculations," and the loss (due to "erratic conduct") in July of his lucrative employment with Brown & Earl.[1221]

Child of Erwin R.[7] and Celestia A. (Pickard) Harris (1880, 1900 census):

> 1 *Jessie A.*[8] *Harris*, b. Tenn. in Jan. 1870, a widow living with her mother in Omaha in 1920; m. ca. 1889 Andrew C. Walkup, b. Iowa in Aug. 1868, living Omaha in 1910, an attorney.[1222]

ii EMMA M. HARRIS, b. Ohio in July 1846, d. Chicago 2 Oct. 1916;[1223] m. ca. 1866 WILLIAM W. WELLS, b. Ohio in Dec. 1846, living Chicago in 1920, a telegrapher.[1224] They were in Toledo in 1870,[1225] and in Chicago in 1880, 1900, and 1910.[1226] On 21 Sept. 1880, "Mrs. W. W. Wells of Chicago, who has been visiting her parents, Mr. and Mrs. Dr. L. P. Harris [in Fort Wayne] for the past month, returned to her home again this morning," and on 5 June 1887: "Died, in Chicago, at the residence of her daughter [249 West Congress Street], Mrs. W. W. Wells, Elvira A., wife of Dr. L. P. Harris."[1227]

Children of William W. and Emma M.[7] (Harris) Wells (from census):

> 1 *Nora Wells*, b. Ohio in Dec. 1867 [*sic*: prob. 1866]; m. Chicago 22 July 1891 Frank N. Walker,[1228] b. Ill. in Aug. 1867, he a "confectioner" there in 1900, she a school teacher.[1229]

> 2 *Frederick Wells*, b. Ohio in June 1868, living with parents 1910, widower; m. Cook Co., Ill., 23 Dec. 1893 Maria B. Goodlaxen,[1230] b. Wis. in June 1863. He was a railroad "baggage man" in Chicago in 1900,[1231] and a shipping clerk in 1910.

iii ELLA F. HARRIS, b. Ohio ca. 1851, with parents in 1860, 1870, and 1880, d. shortly before 21 Nov. 1906 (date of funeral), apparently at her sister Emma's home in Chicago.[1232] She had been in practice as a homeopathic physician for some time in Cleveland before returning to Fort Wayne in 1882 to join her father's practice, which she continued after his death.[1233] She had an office in Fort Wayne in 1897: "Dr. Ella F. Harris, Diseases of Females a Specialty. All

---

[1221] *Fort Wayne Daily Sentinel*, 11 Sept. 1883, p. 1; *The Fort Wayne Daily News*, 27 Sept. 1883, p. 1, 28 Sept. 1883, pp. 1, 7, citing in some instances "highly sensational" dispatches or items received from *The Chicago Times*.

[1222] 1910 U.S. Census, 1st Ward, Omaha City, Douglas Co., Neb., E.D. 4, sheet 3A (household included "mother-in-law" Celestia A. Harris, 65, widow).

[1223] Cook Co., Ill., Death Records, file no. 6027650.

[1224] 1920 U.S. Census, Ward 33, Chicago, Cook Co., Ill., E.D. 2602, sheet 9B ("grandfather" and widower in Edgar G. Wells household).

[1225] 1870 U.S. Census, 3rd Ward, City of Toledo, Lucas Co., Ohio, p. 54.

[1226] 1880, 1900, 1910 U.S. Census, City of Chicago, Cook Co., Ill., E.D. 116, p. 45, E.D. 150, p. 8B, and E.D. 1496, sheet 3A, respectively.

[1227] *Fort Wayne Daily News*, 21 Sept. 1880, p. 4; 5 Jan. 1887, p. 4; *The Fort Wayne Sentinel*, 3 Jan. 1887.

[1228] Illinois, Cook County Marriages 1871–1920, at <www.FamilySearch.org>.

[1229] 1900 U.S. Census, 12th Ward, City of Chicago, Cook Co., Ill., E.D. 354, sheet 14B.

[1230] Illinois, Cook County Marriages 1871–1920, at <www.FamilySearch.org>.

[1231] 1900 U.S. Census, 35th Ward, City of Chicago, Cook Co., Ill., E.D. 1131, sheet 18B.

[1232] *Chicago Daily Tribune*, 21 Nov. 1906, p. 14 ("Ella F. Harris, sister of Mrs. W. W. Wells").

[1233] *Fort Wayne Sentinel*, 8 Sept. 1882, p. 3; 8 Nov. 1887, p. 4.

chronic nervous troubles successfully treated. Magnetic and electric treatments given. Office, No. 148 Calhoun, Cor. Jefferson St. . . ."[1234]

56 ERWIN ALANSON[6] **HARRIS** (*Woodruff*[5], *Jeremiah*[4], *Daniel*[3], *Walter*[2], *John*[1]), born in Ohio on 2 June 1830, died in Campbell Township, Ionia County, Michigan, on 10 April 1907 and buried in Clarksville Cemetery.[1235] He married in Bainbridge, Geauga County, Ohio, on 3 July 1854 **MARY HOGLE**,[1236] born in New York on 20 April 1836, died in Ionia County on 11 March 1917 and buried in same cemetery,[1237] daughter of Hiram and Elizabeth (Hogle) Hogle of Genesee County, New York, and Fairport, Lake County, Ohio.[1238] Erwin and Mary, with his mother Phebe, moved from Ohio to Campbell, Michigan, after about 1863, where they appear in the census in 1870 and 1880.[1239] Erwin, age 69, was listed there in 1900 as "father-in-law" in the home of Noah and Eva R. Jepson.[1240]

Children of Erwin Alanson[6] and Mary (Hogle) Harris:

> i   EVA ROSELIA[7] HARRIS, b. Ohio in Jan. 1856,[1241] d. 8 April 1929;[1242] m. Ionia Co., Mich., 26 April 1881 NOAH K. JEPSON,[1243] a grocer, b. Mich. in April 1856, d. 1942 and bur. Clarksville Cemetery.[1244]
>
>> Child of Noah K. and Eva Roselia[7] (Harris) Jepson:
>>> 1 *Erwin B. Jepson*, b. Keene, Ionia Co., Mich., 12 July 1882.[1245]
>
> ii   HENRY S. HARRIS, b. Ohio in Oct. 1859,[1246] d. Ionia Co. 1947 and bur. Clarksville Cemetery; m. (1) ca. 1886 ARTIE T. LONGLEY, b. Mich. 16 Dec. 1858, d. 23 April 1906 and bur. Clarksville Cemetery, dau. of William and Esther (Murdock) Longley,[1247] (2) Saranac, Ionia Co., 1 Sept. 1909 ANNA (KRESBOUGH) DEAN, b. Mich. 1862, dau. of Joseph Kresbough.[1248]

[1234] *The Fort Wayne News*, 12 June 1897, p. 3.

[1235] Certificate of Death, State of Michigan, Registered No. 4, parents named as Woodruff Harris and Phebe Orton, Henry Harris of Clarksville, informant.

[1236] Geauga Co., Ohio, Marriage Records, E:108, Chardon, Ohio.

[1237] Certificate of Death, State of Michigan, Registered No. 3, Mrs. Noah Jepson of Clarksville, informant.

[1238] Margaret R. Waters and Donald D. Murphy, *Smith Family: Descendants of George and Barbara (Bash) Smith of Westmoreland County, Pennsylvania, and Coshocton County, Ohio* (Indianapolis: M. R. Waters, 1946), 75-76.

[1239] 1870 and 1880 U.S. Census, Campbell, Ionia Co., Mich., pp. 390 and 299D, respectively.

[1240] 1900 U.S. Census, Campbell, Ionia Co., Mich., E.D. 5, sheet 6B (Noah Jepson household).

[1241] 1900 U.S. Census, Campbell, Ionia Co., Mich., E.D. 5, sheet 6B.

[1242] Waters and Murphy, *Smith Family*, 76.

[1243] Ionia County Marriages, online at <http://ionia.migenweb.net/DibeanCol/dbean.html>.

[1244] Transcriptions online at <http://www.migenweb.net/ionia/cemetery/clarks.htm>.

[1245] Michigan Births 1867–1902, online at <www.FamilySearch.org>.

[1246] 1900 U.S. Census, Campbell, Ionia Co., Mich., E.D. 5, sheet 5a (Henry S. Harris household).

[1247] Certificate of Death, State of Michigan, Registered No. 10, H. S. Harris of Clarksville, informant.

[1248] Michigan Marriages 1868–1925, online at <www.FamilySearch.org>.

Children of Henry S.[7] and Artie T. (Longley) Harris:

1 *Loverne*[8] *Harris*, b. Campbell, Ionia Co., 8 March 1889.[1249]

2 *Charles Harris*, b. Mich. in Feb. 1893 (with parents 1900, 1910).

iii EUDORA ALMIRA HARRIS, b. Johnson, Trumbull Co., Ohio 1862, d. 20 July 1949 and bur. Clarksville Cemetery, Ionia Co.;[1250] m. (1) Bowne, Kent Co., Mich., 2 May 1882 OSCAR CHARLES KEMP, b. Howard, Canada, 1860,[1251] d. Campbell, Ionia Co., 12 Oct. 1886, son of William Kemp;[1252] (2) between 1924 (death of his 1st wife) and the 1930 census date,[1253] JOSEPH A. CLARK, b. 1859, d. 1946 and bur. Clarksville Cemetery.[1254]

iv NELLIE M. HARRIS, b. Campbell, Ionia Co., Mich., 7 March 1869,[1255] living Cleveland, Ohio, 1930, age 61;[1256] m. Clarksville, Ionia Co., Mich., 25 Aug. 1891 WILLIAM CHARLES WELLS,[1257] locomotive engineer, b. Jefferson, Ohio, 2 Nov. 1867, d. Cleveland 3 Dec. 1926, son of John and Sarah (McMurray) Wells.[1258] They had moved to Cleveland before the 1900 census.[1259]

Children of William Charles and Nellie M.[7] (Harris) Wells:

1 *Glen H. Wells*, b. Ohio in May 1892 (with parents 1900, 1910).

2 *Maude E. Wells*, b. Ohio in Feb. 1900; m. Charles Watkins, b. Ohio ca. 1897; they were residing with her mother in 1930.

57 WILLIAM JAY[6] HARRIS (*Elisha*[5], *John*[4], *Daniel*[3], *Walter*[2], *John*[1]), born about January 1802, baptized 4 October 1816, died in Lorain County, Ohio, on 9 May 1851, age 49y 4m, and buried in Garfield Cemetery.[1260] He married in Salisbury, Connecticut, on 19 December 1827 **SARAH GROAT**, "both of Salisbury," born in Massachusetts about 1808. She was admitted to the Salisbury church on 4 September 1829 "from Egremont by letter."[1261] She was living as William's widow in Oberlin, Ohio, in 1860.[1262]

Salisbury deeds show that they resided in or near Chapinville. Sarah Jane, daughter of William and Sarah Harris, was buried in Chapinville Cemetery.

[1249] Michigan Births 1867–1902, online at <www.FamilySearch.org>.

[1250] Transcriptions online at <http://www.migenweb.net/ionia/cemetery/clarks.htm>, birthplace from record of her first marriage.

[1251] Michigan Marriages 1868–1925, online at <www.FamilySearch.org>.

[1252] Michigan Deaths 1867–1897, online at<www.FamilySearch.org>.

[1253] 1930 U.S. Census, Saranac Village, Boston Twp., Ionia Co., Mich., E.D. 34-6, sheet 2A.

[1254] Transcriptions online at <http://www.migenweb.net/ionia/cemetery/clarks.htm>, also inscription for his 1st wife, Hyla M. Clark (1859–1924).

[1255] Michigan Births 1867–1902, online at <www.FamilySearch.org>.

[1256] 1930 U.S. Census, Cleveland City, Cuyahoga Co., Ohio, E.D. 18-468, sheet 5B.

[1257] Michigan Marriages 1868–1925, online at <www.FamilySearch.org>.

[1258] Ohio Certificate of Death, District No. 8116, File No. 10636, Nellie M. Wells informant.

[1259] 1900 U.S. Census, Collingwood Twp., Cuyahoga Co., Ohio, E.D. 212-5, sheet 28B.

[1260] Gravestone photo online at <www.findagrave.com>, accessed Sept. 2012.

[1261] Salisbury Congregational Church Records, 2:200, 264.

[1262] 1860 U.S. Census, Oberlin, Lorain Co., Ohio, p. 6 (record partly illegible).

Two boys and a girl under age 10 were in their home in 1840.[1263] They were dismissed from the Salisbury church by general letter dated 21 October 1849,[1264] and by the 1850 census date had moved to Lorain County, where their household then included six children.[1265]

> Children of William Jay[6] and Sarah (Groat) Harris, all except Sarah with their parents in 1850, all b. Conn.:
>
> i   SARAH JANE[7] HARRIS, bp. 6 Sept. 1829, d. 3 Jan. 1832, bur. Chapinville Cemetery.
> ii   ELIZABETH HARRIS, b. ca. 1830.
> iii   GRAHAM HARRIS, b. ca. 1832.
> iv   EDWARD HARRIS, b. ca. 1835.
> v   HIRAM HARRIS, b. ca. 1842.
> vi   ALICE HARRIS, b. ca. 1844.
> vii   WILLIAM HARRIS, b. ca. 1847.

58 JOHN[6] HARRIS (*Elisha[5], John[4], Daniel[3], Walter[2], John[1]*), born in Salisbury, Connecticut, on 11 February 1811, died of heart disease at Richmond, Massachusetts, on 30 August 1876, age 65y 6m.[1266] He was not baptized with his siblings, but the death record states that he was born at Salisbury, Connecticut, son of Elisha and Jane Harris. He married in New Lebanon, Columbia County, New York, on 6 July 1837 **CAROLINE MARKHAM**, "both from [Richmond]," Massachusetts, in presence of Samuel D. Gro[a]t and others, Rev. Hatch presiding.[1267] Caroline, a daughter of John and Lina (___) Markham of Egremont and Richmond, died on 6 October 1877, age 66, and buried in Cone Hill Cemetery at Richmond.[1268]

John Harris had been admitted to the Salisbury church on 4 September 1831 and dismissed "to Richmond" on 25 October 1835. John and Caroline were in Richmond in 1850 and 1860, a "furnace man,"[1269] and in Great Barrington, Massachusetts, in 1870.[1270]

[1263] 1840 U.S. Census, Salisbury, Litchfield Co., Conn., p. 269, 273 (enumerated twice).
[1264] Salisbury Congregational Church Records, 2:138.
[1265] 1850 U.S. Census, Carlisle Twp., Lorain Co., Ohio, p. 451.
[1266] Massachusetts Vital Records, 1841–1910, 283:60, online at <www.AmericanAncestors.org>, accessed Sept. 2012.
[1267] Harris and Stover, "Second Daniel Harris of Goshen," 122 (1991):228.
[1268] Gravestone photo online at <www.findagrave.com>, accessed Sept. 2012.
[1269] 1850, 1860 U.S. Census, Richmond, Berkshire Co., Mass., pp. 30, 304, respectively.
[1270] 1870 U.S. Census, Great Barrington, P.O. North Egremont, Berkshire Co., Mass., p. 2

Children of John[6] and Caroline (Markham) Harris, b. Richmond:[1271]

   i   SELENA AMELIA[7] HARRIS, b. 9 Sept. 1844, with parents 1860.

   ii HELEN E. HARRIS (twin), b. 15 Dec. 1847, d. 18 Feb. 1857.

   iii HERBERT M. HARRIS (twin), b. 15 Dec. 1847, with parents 1870; m. ca. 1871 SARAH ____, b. Conn. ca. 1852, with whom he was living in New Marlborough, Mass., in 1880.[1272]

        Children of Herbert M.[7] and Sarah (____) Harris, from 1880 census:

        1 *Ella*[8] *Harris*, b. Mass. ca. 1872.

        2 *Elizabeth Harris*, b. Mass. ca. 1876.

   iv JULIAN MARKHAM HARRIS, b. 21 July 1849; m. Richmond 20 Dec. 1880 LAURA REYNOLDS, b. Hudson, N.Y., ca. 1856, dau. of James Reynolds.[1273]

59 HARVEY[6] HARRIS (*Daniel*[5], *John*[4], *Daniel*[3], *Walter*[2], *John*[1]), born in Salisbury, Connecticut, say 1806, baptized as *Hervey* on 4 October 1816, probably one of the two males under 10 in Daniel's home in 1810 and presumably the Harvey Harris who died of typhoid fever at Salisbury on 17 September 1881, although his age was stated as 67y 10m.[1274] His death record states that he was born in Salisbury, married, and son of Daniel Harris born in Salisbury and Jerusha Jones born in Copake, New York.

A variety of ages are stated in records for this man, some obviously bogus; for example, in 1880 he was entered in the census at Salisbury as a 94-year-old day laborer with a 50-year-old wife.[1275] He had married by about 1847 (birth of son Lockwood) **ELIZA** ____, of whom no more is seen. His wife living with him in 1880 was **MARY** ____, born in Connecticut about 1830. He can be traced as the Harvey Harris, age 20-29, with a household in Salisbury in 1830 including a female 20-29 and female child under 5;[1276] the "farm laborer" in adjoining Canaan in 1870, age 49 [*sic*];[1277] and the "day laborer" in Salisbury in 1880. No record is found of him between 1830 and 1870 except for the birth of his son in Sheffield, Mass., about 1847. His household in Salisbury in 1880 included, in addition to wife Mary, his "sister" Laura "Harris," age 52 [*sic*], "cousin" Daisy Harris, age 12, and "nephews" Charles Hinman (Laura's son), age 15, and Frederick Webster, age 3.

[1271] *Vital Records of Richmond*, 27, and family record.

[1272] 1880 U.S. Census, New Marlborough, Berkshire Co., Mass., E.D. 34, p. 2

[1273] Massachusetts Vital Records, 1841–1910, 316:60, online at <www.AmericanAncestors.org>, accessed Sept. 2012.

[1274] Salisbury Town Records, p. 336.

[1275] 1880 U.S. Census, Salisbury, Litchfield Co., Conn., E.D. 2, p. 39. The stated age for Harvey, 94, is clearly written, but other circumstances indicate that age 74 is more likely.

[1276] 1830 U.S. Census, Salisbury, Litchfield Co., Conn., p. 497.

[1277] 1870 U.S. Census, Canaan, Litchfield Co., Conn., p. 3.

Apparent child of Harvey⁶ Harris by an unknown wife:

    i   Female child⁷, b. 1826–1830, in Harvey's home in 1830.

Child of Harvey⁶ and Eliza (___) Harris:

    ii   LOCKWOOD HARRIS, "son of Harvey and Eliza," b. Sheffield, Mass., ca. 1847, a "mechanic" on [20?] Aug. 1871 when at age 24 he m. there ELLEN COOPER, age 19, dau. of Milton Cooper.[1278]

60 JOSEPH⁶ HARRIS (*Daniel⁵, John⁴, Daniel³, Walter², John¹*), born in Salisbury, Connecticut on 30 August 1816 (calc.), baptized there 4 October 1816, died in Sandisfield, Massachusetts, of "kidney affection" on 10 July 1879.[1279] He married before 1840 **MARY ANN SEELEY**, born in Stephentown, New York, on 27 May 1823 (calc.), died in New Marlborough, Massachusetts, of "old age" on 24 December 1897, age 74y 6m 27d, daughter of James and Catherine (Button) Seeley.[1280]

In 1840, Joseph's household, listed next to that of his father in Salisbury, included himself, age 20-29, a female [Mary Ann], age 15-19, and a boy under 5.[1281] By 1850, they had moved across the town line into Canaan where, in February 1851, he bought eight acres with a house and barn, which he sold in April 1852.[1282] They were back in Salisbury by 1860 and residing again near his parents;[1283] by 1870 they had moved across the state line into Sheffield, Massachusetts.[1284] In 1880, widow Mary Ann Harris, age 57, was residing in Sandisfield as "mother-in-law" in the home of her daughter Marietta and husband Joseph Briggs.[1285]

Children of Joseph⁶ and Mary Ann (Seeley) Harris:

    i   A boy⁷, accounted for as the male under 5 in Joseph's home in 1840.
    ii   WILLIAM H. HARRIS, b. Mass. ca. 1843, with parents 1860.
    iii BETSEY A. HARRIS, b. Sheffield, Mass., ca. 1845; m. New Marlborough, Mass., 12 Dec. 1861 LEVI SNYDER, b. Salisbury, Conn., ca. 1838, son of Cornelius and Hannah (___) Snyder.[1286]

[1278] Massachusetts Vital Records, 1841–1910, 235:69. An unidentified Elizabeth Harris, b. Salisbury, age 32 and "married," d. of consumption at Sheffield on 17 May 1872, parents unknown. (ibid., 247:70).

[1279] Massachusetts Vital Records, 1841–1910, 310:57.

[1280] Massachusetts Vital Records, 1841–1910, 472:77.

[1281] 1840 U.S. Census, Salisbury, Litchfield Co., Conn., p. 270.

[1282] Canaan, Conn., Deeds, 16:369, 373, 407. The purchase money, $200, was secured by a mortgage with George Harris, unrelated, of Canaan.

[1283] 1860 U.S. Census, Salisbury, Litchfield Co., Conn., p. 9.

[1284] 1870 U.S. Census, Sheffield, Berkshire Co., Mass., p. 43.

[1285] 1880 U.S. Census, Sandisfield, Berkshire Co., Mass., E.D. 38, p. 3.

[1286] Massachusetts Vital Records, 1841–1910, 144:46.

    iv GEORGE H. HARRIS, b. Salisbury, Conn., ca. 1847; m. (1) Monterey, Mass., 28 Feb. 1872 EDITH DOWD, b. there ca. 1854, dau. of [*illegible*] and Mary (____) Dowd,[1287] (2) New Marlborough, Mass., 23 May 1895 JENNIE KNICKER-BOCKER, dau. of William and Rebeckah (Pulver) Knickerbocker.

    v EDWIN HARRIS, b. Canaan, Conn., 7 July 1848; m. New Marlborough, Mass., 18 May 1871 FLORENCE E. CRINE, b. there ca. 1856 (age 15 at marriage), dau. of Daniel and Amanda (____) Crine.[1288] They were residing in New Marlborough in 1880 and 1900.[1289]

         Child of Edwin[7] and Florence E. (Crine) Harris:

         1 *Nellie*[8] *Harris*, b. Mass. ca. 1874, with parents 1880.

    vi JOHN HARRIS, b. Salisbury, Conn., Dec. 1850, living New Marlborough, Mass., 1900;[1290] m. Sheffield, Mass., 5 Feb. 1873 MARY E. WILLIAMS, b. Salisbury in April 1848, dau. of John and Cornelia (____) Williams.[1291]

         Children of John[7] and Mary E. (Williams) Harris, recorded New Marlborough, Mass.):[1292]

         1 *Carrie*[8] *Harris* (twin), b. 5 Oct. 1873; m. New Marlborough 26 Sept. 1892 Frank Hull of Sheffield, b. ca. 1866, son of Alexander and Harriet (____) Hull.[1293]

         2 *Clara A. Harris* (twin), b. 5 Oct. 1873; m. New Marlborough 26 Dec. 1894 Charles E. Fellows, b. North Egremont ca. 1867, son of George H. and Anna D. (____) Fellows.[1294]

    vii JOSEPHINE HARRIS, b. Mass. ca. 1857; m. New Marlborough, Mass., 24 Jan. 1887 JAMES MOSELEY, b. there ca. 1855, son of Elijah and Margaret (____) Moseley.[1295]

    viii MARIETTA HARRIS, b. Sheffield, Mass., ca. 1858; m. Sandisfield, Mass., 2 March 1879 JOSEPH F. BRIGGS, b. New Marlborough, Mass., ca. 1857, son of Joseph and Ellen (____) Briggs.[1296] They were in Sandisfield, Mass., in 1880, their household then including "mother-in-law" Mary Ann Harris, age 57.[1297]

         Child of Joseph F. and Marietta[7] (Harris) Briggs:

         1 *Rolan Briggs*, b. Mass. ca. Dec. 1879, age 6m in June 1880.

[1287] Massachusetts Vital Records, 1841–1910, 244:56. George H. and Edith (Dowd) Harris had a dau. Susan b. at Sheffield on 1 Aug. 1873 (ibid., 250:71).

[1288] Massachusetts Vital Records, 1841–1910, 235:57.

[1289] 1880, 1900 U.S. Census, New Marlborough, Berkshire Co., Mass., E.D. 34, p. 19, and E.D. 46, sheet 3A, respectively, the record in 1900 showing that Florence was the mother of three children, only one then living.

[1290] 1900 U.S. Census, New Marlborough, Berkshire Co., Mass., E.D. 46, sheet 3A, the record showing that Mary was the mother of three children, all then living.

[1291] Massachusetts Vital Records, 1841–1910, 253:69.

[1292] Massachusetts Vital Records, 1841–1910, 250:56.

[1293] Massachusetts Vital Records, 1841–1910, 424:77.

[1294] Massachusetts Vital Records, 1841–1910, 442:73.

[1295] Massachusetts Vital Records, 1841–1910, 379:55.

[1296] Massachusetts Vital Records, 1841–1910, 307:62 (also recorded in Monterey VRs).

[1297] 1880 U.S. Census, Sandisfield, Berkshire Co., Mass., E.D. 38, p. 3.

61 ALBERT⁶ HARRIS (*Daniel⁵, John⁴, Daniel³, Walter², John¹*), "son of Daniel and Laura Harris," baptized in Salisbury, Connecticut, on 3 July 1829,[1298] was living in Burlington, Connecticut, in 1880, a laborer, age 51. He married by 1848 (birth of first child) **MARY A.** _____, born in Massachusetts about 1830, who was living with him in 1880.[1299] They moved often; their household was enumerated near that of his father in Salisbury in 1850,[1300] in Sheffield, Massachusetts, in 1860,[1301] in Norfolk, Connecticut, in 1870 (where he was working in a hoe shop),[1302] and in Burlington in 1880.

Children of Albert⁶ and Mary A. (_____) Harris:

    i   ADELBERT⁷ HARRIS, b. Conn., ca. 1848, was living in Morris, Conn., in 1920, a laborer, age 72, and single.[1303] He was with his parents in Norfolk in 1870, when he was working with his father in the hoe shop.

    ii   [ELEANORE?] HARRIS, age illegible in 1860, but attended school.

    iii   MINERVA HARRIS, b. Conn. ca. 1857, with parents 1860, 1870.

    iv   OSCAR HARRIS, b. Conn. ca. 1861, with parents 1870, 1880.

    v   CAROLINE HARRIS, b. N.Y. ca. 1867, with parents 1870, 1880.

    vi   JOHN STEVEN HARRIS, b. Conn. in May 1870, was living in Litchfield, Conn., in 1920, where he was a blacksmith.[1304] He m. ca. 1896 EMILY ALICE _____, b. Conn. in Nov. 1873 and living with him in 1920. John was with his parents in 1870 and 1880, and had settled in Litchfield by 1900.[1305]

        Children of John Steven⁷ and Emily Alice (_____) Harris:

        1 *Marion⁸ Harris*, b. Conn. in Feb. 1897, with parents 1900, 1910, 1920.

        2 *John Leslie Harris*, b. Conn. ca. 1906, with parents 1910, 1920.

62 HENRY ULYSSES⁶ HARRIS (*Daniel⁵, John⁴, Daniel³, Walter², John¹*), born in Salisbury, Connecticut, about 1833,[1306] was baptized there on 8 April 1835 as "son of D. & Laura Harris."[1307] He was living in Winchester, Connecticut, in 1880, age 46, farm laborer.[1308] He married **MARY** _____, born in Massachusetts about 1830, who was living with him in 1860 and 1870.

[1298] Salisbury Congregational Church Records, 2:247.

[1299] 1880 U.S. Census, Burlington, Hartford Co., Conn., E.D. 46, p. 7.

[1300] 1850 U.S. Census, Salisbury, Litchfield Co., Conn., p. 33.

[1301] 1860 U.S. Census, Sheffield, Berkshire Co., Mass., p. 149.

[1302] 1870 U.S. Census, Norfolk, P.O. Goshen, Litchfield Co., Conn., p. 299.

[1303] 1920 U.S. Census, Morris, Litchfield Co., Conn., E.D. 96, p. 4A.

[1304] 1920 U.S. Census, Litchfield, Litchfield Co., Conn., E.D. 195, sheet 15B.

[1305] 1900 U.S. Census, Litchfield Town, Litchfield Co., Conn., E.D. 240, sheet 6A.

[1306] Age given as 27 years in Oct. 1860 when his son Daniel's birth was recorded in Canaan.

[1307] Salisbury Congregational Church Records, 2:247.

[1308] 1880 U.S. Census, Winchester, Litchfield Co., Conn., E.D. 8, p. 41.

Henry was in his parents home at age 16 in 1850, in Canaan, Connecticut, in 1860 and 1870,[1309] and in Winchester by 1880.

Children of Henry Ulysses[6] and Mary (___) Harris:

 i   HENRIETTA[7] HARRIS, b. Canaan, Conn., ca. 1859; age 16 when she m. there 10 June 1875 CHARLES S. HOUCK, age 28 (b. ca. 1847).[1310]
 ii DANIEL HARRIS, b. Canaan, Conn., 10 Oct. 1860,[1311] perhaps the Danny Harris, age 10, whose undated gravestone is in Grassy Hill Cemetery in Canaan.
 iii DEFORREST HARRIS, b. b. Conn. ca. 1864, with parents in 1870.
 iv JESSE HARRIS, b. Conn. ca. 1866, with parents 1870, her father in 1880.
 v   GEORGEANNA HARRIS, b. Conn. ca. 1868, with parents 1870, her father in 1880.

63 MILES[6] HARRIS (*Mylo[5], John[4], Daniel[3], Walter[2], John[1]*), born in Connecticut about 1816, was living in Lake County, Ohio, in 1880, age 64.[1312] He was "of Salisbury, Conn.," when he married first at Becket, Massachusetts, on 21 December 1842 **ELIZA JANE AMES**, born there on 6 January 1823, died in Ohio in 1850s (perhaps at the birth of their child in 1853), daughter of Pliny and Abigail K. (Nichols) Ames.[1313] Milo married second, after 1860, **MATILDA COOKINGHAM**, born in New York in October 1826, who was living as his widow in Hyde Park, New York, in 1900 and 1910.[1314]

In 1840 and 1842, Miles and his brother Martin mortgaged and conveyed 200 acres in Salisbury "near Chapinville."[1315] On 2 July 1843, Mrs. Eliza Jane Harris was admitted from Becket to the church in Salisbury, then dismissed by general letter dated 21 October 1849, the same day that Miles's cousin William Jay and wife Sarah Harris were dismissed.[1316] They obviously left immediately for Ohio, as Miles and Eliza were farming there in Lorain County in 1850,[1317] and where Miles was living alone in 1860.[1318]

By 1870, Miles had married Matilda and they were residing in Lansing, Michigan, where he was "manufacturing lumber." Their household then included [his daughter] Florence Harris, age 16 (who was not with him in

---

[1309] 1860, 1870 U.S. Census, Canaan, Litchfield Co., Conn., pp. 885, 12, respectively. An unidentified Charles Harris, b. Mass. ca. 1848, was in their home both in 1860 and 1870.

[1310] Canaan, Conn., Town Records.

[1311] Canaan, Conn., Town Records.

[1312] 1880 U.S. Census, Willoughby, Lake Co., Ohio, p. E.D. 89, p. 15.

[1313] *Vital Records of Becket, Massachusetts, to the Year 1850* (Boston: NEHGS, 1903), p. 10 (birth), p. 40 (marriage).

[1314] 1900, 1910 U.S. Census, Hyde Park, Dutchess Co., N.Y., E.D. 11, sheet 12A, and E.D. 54, sheet 1A, respectively. Matilda's household in both years included "sister" Cornelia LeRoy, b. Aug. 1831.

[1315] Salisbury, Conn., Deeds, 21:314, 315, 22:536.

[1316] Salisbury Congregational Church Records, 2:113, 138, 210, 227.

[1317] 1850 U.S. Census, Huntington, Lorain Co., Ohio, p. 641.

[1318] 1860 U.S. Census, Huntington, Lorain Co., Ohio, p. 127.

1860), and [niece] Carrie Cleveland, age 13.[1319] By 1880, they were in Lake County, Ohio.

Child of Miles[6] and Eliza Jane (Ames) Harris:

    i FLORENCE[7] HARRIS, b. Ohio 26 July 1853, d. 19 Aug. 1935, bur. Waite Hill Village Cemetery, Lake Co., Ohio.[1320] She m. Lake Co. 16 April 1879 MARK W. JUDD, Rev. W. A. Robinson presiding,[1321] b. Willoughby, Ohio, 28 July 1845, d. Lakewood, Cuyahoga Co., Ohio, 12 Dec. 1926 [*sic*: before 1910 if the reported status of Florence then as a widow is correct], son of Freeman and Delia (Smalling) Judd.[1322] Mark W. Judd, age 32, a miller, wife Florence, age 25, and one-month-old female "baby" were residing in Willoughby, Ohio, in 1880.[1323] In 1910, Florence Judd, widow, age 56, was listed as a "boarder" in the home of [her stepmother] Matilda Harris in Hyde Park, N.Y.[1324]

64 HARLOW PECK[6] HARRIS (*Mylo[5], John[4], Daniel[3], Walter[2], John[1]*), born on 30 July 1830, died 10 July 1885 and buried in Salisbury Center Cemetery. He married at Salisbury, Connecticut, on 4 April 1854 **MARGARETTA A. SWEET**,[1325] born in New York on 31 March 1830, died on 26 January 1899, "wife of Col. Harlow Peck Harris."[1326] Harlow's biography identifies her as "daughter of L. B. Sweet of Copake, N.Y.,"[1327] evidently Lewis B. and Samantha (____) Sweet, whose household in Salisbury included her with other children in 1850.[1328]

The biography mentions that Harlow became the superintendant of the Richmond [Mass."] Iron Works in 1865, purchased 12,000 acres in Iowa in 1868 as a member of a land company, passed the winter of 1868–69 in Vermont, and returned to Salisbury in 1871 where he became superintendant of Chatfield Mining Company at Ore Hill.

[1319] 1870 U.S. Census, Ward 4, Lansing, Ingham Co., Mich., p. 18.

[1320] Data online at <www.findagrave.com>, accessed Sept. 2012. The dates given are assumed correct for Florence, but the dates for her husband's death (1926) and the identity of her mother as Mathilda Cookingham are not consistent with evidence reviewed for this article.

[1321] Ohio County Marriages, 1789–1994, online at <www.FamilySearch.org>, accessed Sept. 2012.

[1322] Data online at <www.findagrave.com>, accessed Sept. 2012.

[1323] 1880 U.S. Census, Willoughby, Lake Co., Ohio, E.D. 89, p. 23.

[1324] 1910 U.S. Census, Hyde Park, Dutchess Co., N.Y., E.D. 54, sheet 1A. The record that Florence was the mother of three children, all then living, and that both of her parents were born in Conn.

[1325] Salisbury Episcopal Church Records, 1:97.

[1326] Inscription Salisbury Center Cemetery.

[1327] *History of Litchfield County,* 558.

[1328] 1850 U.S. Census, Salisbury, Litchfield Co., Conn., p. 27.

Children of Harlow Peck[6] and Margaretta A. (Sweet) Harris:

    i   MAGGIE[7] HARRIS, b. 1863, d. 1865.[1329]

    ii HARLOW PECK HARRIS JR., b. Richmond, Mass., 12 Aug. 1866, son of H. P. Harris,[1330] d. 16 June 1883, three days after he was bp. at home as an adult.[1331]

SEVENTH GENERATION

65 FRANCIS HOSEA[7] HARRIS (*Hosea[6], John[5], Hosea[4], Thomas[3], Walter[2], John[1]*), born in Wethersfield on 24 January 1829, was living in New Haven, Connecticut, in 1900, occupation "wholesale liquor."[1332] He married on 22 October 1856 **EMELINE WILLOUGHBY BRADLEY**, born in Connecticut about February 1835, who was with Francis in 1900. They were in New Haven in 1880, when he was a cutlery manufacturer.[1333]

Children of Francis H.[7] and Emeline W. (Bradley) Harris:[1334]

    i   EMMA FRANCES[8] HARRIS, b. 16 Oct. 1857; m. 2 Sept. 1885 BENJAMIN H. COBB.

    ii RICHMOND RUSSELL HARRIS, b. 27 Dec. 1859; m. 23 Nov. 1886 JANE R. PERKINS, b. Conn. in June 1860, d. before 1910. He was a "wholesaler" residing in New Haven in 1920 with his daughter Marguerite Peck.[1335]
          Children of Richmond Russell[8] and Jane R. (Perkins) Harris:[1336]
            1 *Dorothy P.[9] Harris*, b. 29 May 1888, d. 5 March 1891.
            2 *Marguerite Harris*, b. Conn. 30 April 1891; m. Elliot M. Peck, b. Conn. ca. 1891, with whom she was living in New Haven in 1920.

    iii CHARLES HOSEA HARRIS, b. 11 March 1863; m. 13 Oct. 1894 MINNIE C. EARLE, b. May 1873. Charles was a liquor dealer in New Haven in 1900 and 1910.[1337]
          Children of Charles Hosea[8] and Minnie C. (Earle) Harris:
            1 *Mildred E.[9] Harris*, b. 24 May 1902.
            2 *Francis E. Harris*, b. ca. 1905.

    iv FRANK BRADLEY HARRIS, b. 18 Nov. 1870; m. 30 June 1898 SUSIE H. WRIS-LEY, but he was living separately with his parents on the 1900 census date.
          Child of Frank Bradley[8] and Susie H. (Wrisley) Harris:
            1 *Ruth H.[9] Harris*, b. 8 May 1899.

[1329] Inscription Salisbury Center Cemetery.

[1330] Massachusetts Vital Records, 1841–1910, 186:68. The child's name was left blank in this record.

[1331] Salisbury Congregational Church Records, 3:236, 271.

[1332] 1880 U.S. Census, New Haven, New Haven Co., Conn., E.D. 78, p. 44.

[1333] 1880 U.S. Census, New Haven, New Haven Co., Conn., E.D. 78, p. 44.

[1334] Stiles, *Ancient Wethersfield*, 2:416.

[1335] 1920 U.S. Census, Ward 9, New Haven, New Haven Co., Conn., E.D. 365, sheet 9A.

[1336] Stiles, *Ancient Wethersfield*, 2:416.

[1337] 1900, 1910 U.S. Census, New Haven, New Haven Co., Conn., E.D. 356, sheet 2B, E.D. 416, sheet 6A, respectively.

66 RANSOM ADDISON[7] HARRIS (*Harvey[6]*, *Elisha[5]*, *Jeremiah[4]*, *Daniel[3]*, *Walter[2]*, *John[1]*), born in Troy, Geauga County, Ohio, on 9 July 1832, died in Colchester, Branch County, Michigan, on 12 January 1897;[1338] married in Wood County, Ohio, on 7 October 1854 **SUSANNAH M. SAUNDERS**,[1339] born in Ohio in July 1835, died in Coldwater on 8 January 1904.

On 8 September 1857, Ransom purchased from his parents a plot of land in Troy Township, Wood County, Ohio.[1340] He probably was residing there on 24 August 1861, when he enlisted at Freedom, Ohio, for three years service in Co. K, 21st Regiment, Ohio Volunteers, for the Civil War. He was injured in February 1862 at Bacon Creek, Kentucky, while loading timbers in a wagon, and was discharged by surgeon's certificate at Athens, Georgia, on 14 July 1862. His pension file describes him as 5' 9⅞" tall, with light complexion, blue eyes, auburn hair, and a farmer at enlistment.

After his return, he purchased on 22 September 1862 an additional 40 acres from his parents in Wood County. On the same day, Ransom and Sarah sold an acre back to his parents, probably their home lot.[1341] However, it is evident from his pension declaration that Ransom could not do the labor required for farming because of his war injury (a rupture), and in January 1863 he moved his family to Coldwater, Michigan. On 19 March 1866, he sold his property in Wood County, Ohio, to Samantha Dinius.[1342]

Random stated in his pension application that he had "lived continuously (in Coldwater) except in 1872 and 1873, when he lived in Allegan County, Michigan. "I have," he stated, "teamed, tended bar, peddled, and first year did a little farming since my discharge." At the time of the 1870 and 1880 censuses, he was residing on Harrison St., 3rd Ward, in Coldwater. In 1893, he was listed as a resident of Coldwater in an *Atlas of Branch County*.

His obituary states that Ransom died at his home at 3 o'clock Tuesday afternoon of typhoid pneumonia after an illness of about two weeks. He was a carpenter by trade, a soldier in the late war, and for the past two years was in the employ of S. I. Treat and Son. His widow and three children survive. He was buried in the Oak Grove Cemetery, Coldwater.[1343]

Ransom's widow, Susannah, applied for her pension on 1 February 1897, stating that she had only a house and lot in the First Ward of Colchester and that she was a cripple using a crutch. Ransom's brother Sherburn Harris of

---

[1338] Ransom Harris, Civil War Pension File, 188707, WC648031, National Archives, Washington, D.C.

[1339] Ohio County Marriages, 1789–1994, online at <www.FamilySearch.org>.

[1340] Wood Co., Ohio, Deeds, P307.

[1341] Wood Co., Ohio, Deeds, V:370.

[1342] Wood Co., Ohio, Deeds, 26:597.

[1343] *Coldwater Weekly Reporter*, 16 Jan. 1897.

Lemoyne, Troy Township, Wood County, Ohio, filed an affidavit on her behalf.

Children of Ransom Addison[7] and Susannah M. (Saunders) Harris:

    i   GEORGE A.[8] HARRIS, b. Ohio ca. 1855; m. (1) LAURA ____, b. Ind. ca. 1861. They were residing with his parents in Colchester in 1880. He m. (2) Grand Rapids, Kent Co., Mich., 14 Feb. 1915 MARY JOHANNA DE RYKE REYNOLDS,[1344] b. Mich. ca. 1870. They were in Grand Rapids in 1920, where George was a shipping clerk in a retail store.[1345]

   ii WILLIAM R. HARRIS, b. Mich. ca. 1864; m. Coldwater, Mich., 24 Dec. 1886 TENA F. FIELDS, b. Bethel, Mich., ca. 1866.[1346]

  iii A child that died before 1897.

   iv CORA M. HARRIS, b. Mich. in July 1870; m. Coldwater, Mich., 25 Sept. 1895 HARRY L. BOOSINGER, b. Ind. in Oct. 1873, son of William and Rosa (Hoan) Boosinger.[1347] They were residing with her mother in Coldwater in 1900.

   v DORA Y. HARRIS, b. Mich. ca. 1874, d. before 1897, prob. the mother of Dora M., b. Jan. 1893, described as "granddaughter" in Susannah M. Harris's household in Coldwater in 1900.

77 ALBERT S.[7] HARRIS (*John Sheldon[6], Elisha[5], Jeremiah[4], Daniel[3], Walter[2], John[1]*), born in Ohio on 14 October 1828, died in Troy Township, Geauga County, Ohio, in June 1894. He married in Geauga County on 22 December 1859 **MARIAN E. CANFIELD**,[1348] born in Portage County, Ohio, about 1838, daughter of Charles G. and Laura (____) Canfield of Troy Township. They were living with his parents in Hiram Township in 1860.

Albert's will, dated 30 December 1891 and proved in Portage County on 23 June 1894, names his wife Marion E. and the four children below. He made provisions for the care of his father and stepmother.[1349]

Children of Albert S.[7] and Marian E. (Canfield) Harris:

    i   GEORGE LEWIS[8] HARRIS, b. Hiram, Ohio, 1 Oct. 1861, d. at his home in Hiram Village 9 March 1925; m. (1) Portage Co. 27 Jan. 1883 ALBERTA ALLEN,[1350] (2) Geauga Co. 19 Jan. 1903 BLANCH PONTIUS of Hudson Twp., Summit Co., Ohio.[1351] According to his obituary, "he was the only son and oldest

[1344] Michigan Marriages, 1868–1925, online at <www.FamilySearch.org>.

[1345] 1920 U.S. Census, Grand Rapids City, Kent Co., Mich., E.D. 67, sheet 3A.

[1346] Michigan Marriages, 1868–1925, online at <www.FamilySearch.org>.

[1347] Michigan Marriages, 1868–1925, online at <www.FamilySearch.org>.

[1348] Ohio County Marriages, 1789–1994, online at <www.FamilySearch.org>.

[1349] Portage Co., Ohio, Estate No. 7185, Administration Docket 14:451.

[1350] Ohio County Marriages, 1789–1994, online at <www.FamilySearch.org>.

[1351] Ohio County Marriages, 1789–1994, online at <www.FamilySearch.org>.

child of Albert and Marian Canfield Harris, the fourth generation of both paternal and maternal sides of residents in and about Maple Grove and Auburn. He was a cattle and livestock dealer as well as a farmer. For four years he was in the Northwest, in the states of North Dakota and Montana, and over the line into Canada, buying horses to ship east."[1352] They were in Troy, Geauga Co., Ohio, in 1910.[1353]

    Child of George Lewis[8] and Alberta (Allen) Harris:
      1 *Charles Lynn[9] Harris*, b. Ohio ca. 1894, living in Cleveland in 1925.
    Children of George Lewis[8] and Blanch (Pontius) Harris:
      2 *Henrietta Harris*, b. Ohio ca. 1905.
      3 *Hope Harris*, b. Ohio ca. 1908.

  ii HENRIETTA HARRIS, b. Troy, Ohio, 17 Aug. 1864; m. Geauga Co. 31 May 1900 WILLIAM FLUX.[1354]

  iii GERTRUDE HARRIS, b. Ohio in Dec. 1865; m. Geauga Co. 21 April 1892 CARL J. SMITH, b. Ohio in Sept. 1865.[1355] They were in Troy, Geauga Co., in 1900.[1356] She was in Cleveland in 1925.

  iv MABEL E. HARRIS, b. Troy, Ohio, 23 Sept. 1871; m. (1) Geauga Co. 3 July 1900 FERD DAYTON,[1357] (2) Cuyahoga Co., Ohio, 10 Jan. 1925 GEORGE RANKER.[1358]

68 LUCIUS O.[7] HARRIS (*Philo[6], Elisha[5], Jeremiah[4], Daniel[3], Walter[2], John[1]*), born in Hiram, Ohio, on 25 June 1837, died in Chagrin Falls, Ohio, on 28 May 1912 and buried in Evergreen Hill Cemetery.[1359] He married in Geauga County, Ohio, on 29 June 1858 **ESTHER C. HICKCOX**[1360] "of Newbury Township," born in Michigan in February 1844, died in 1916 and buried beside him.

    Lucius and Esther were in Chagrin Falls, Ohio, in 1870, 1880, and 1900, where he was a house carpenter.[1361]

    Children of Lucius O.[7] and Esther C. (Hickcox) Harris:

  i ANNA P.[8] HARRIS, b. Ohio ca. 1862, with parents 1870, 1880.
  ii SHERIDAN HARRIS, b. Ohio ca. 1866, with parents 1870, 1880.
  iii LUCIUS F. HARRIS, b. Ohio in Feb. 1874, with parents 1880, 1900.

[1352] Obituary, Hiram College Library, copy courtesy of Mrs. Betty J. Widger of Ravenna, Ohio, 1977.
[1353] 1910 U.S. Census, Troy Twp., Geauga Co., Ohio, E.D. 68, sheets 7B, 8A.
[1354] Ohio County Marriages, 1789–1994, online at <www.FamilySearch.org>.
[1355] Ohio County Marriages, 1789–1994, online at <www.FamilySearch.org>.
[1356] 1900 U.S. Census, Troy Twp., Geauga Co., Ohio, E.D. 56, sheet 9A.
[1357] Ohio County Marriages, 1789–1994, online at <www.FamilySearch.org>.
[1358] Ohio County Marriages, 1789–1994, online at <www.FamilySearch.org>.
[1359] Gravestone photo online at <www.findagrave.com>, accessed Sept. 2012.
[1360] Ohio County Marriages, 1789–1994, online at <www.FamilySearch.org>. Lucius's uncle Henry H. Harris, a J.P. in Chester, performed the marriage.
[1361] 1870, 1880, 1900 U.S. Census, Chagrin Falls., Cuyahoga Co., Ohio, p. 2, E.D. 59, p. 5, and E.D. 6, sheet 1B, respectively.

69 JOSEPH ROSWELL[7] HARRIS (*Edwin*[6], *Joseph*[5], *Jeremiah*[4], *Daniel*[3], *Walter*[2], *John*[1]) was born in Illinois, probably at Durand (then Howard), Winnebago County, on 17 November 1840. He died near Big Cabin, Craig County, Oklahoma, on 23 May 1921 and was buried at Vinita, Oklahoma.[1362] He married at Durand on 27 August 1865 **RACHEL HANNAH MARIA ("NELLIE") PUTNEY**,[1363] born in New York on 2 March 1851, who died on 23 November 1911 and buried beside her husband.

Joseph R. Harris appears at age nineteen in John F. Pettingill's home at Durand in 1860.[1364] The Pettingill farm, at the south edge of Durand Village, was nearby to the west of Joseph's uncle Elisha Harris's farm (no. 51). The Pettingills had erected a 42-room hotel in Durand in 1856.[1365] Joseph enlisted at Durand on 6 August 1862 in Company H, 74th Regiment, Illinois Infantry, in which he served as a private throughout the Civil War, the same company in which his cousin Erastus P. Harris (no. 51 ii) served and died in 1863 at Murfreesboro, Tennessee. On 20 June 1864, Joseph was shot in the right knee at Kennesaw Mountain, Georgia. It was later reinjured by a falling ambulance-team mule. The "condition of his said injured knee grew worse gradually until the 9th day of December A.D. 1872 when amputation of his right leg above the knee became necessary to save his life."[1366]

Joseph was discharged at Nashville, Tennessee, on 22 June 1865, returned to Durand, married within three months, and was enumerated there in 1870 with his wife and two children.[1367] By December 1872 he had moved to Osceola, Clark County, Iowa, where his leg was amputated "at his residence." In April 1875 he and his wife, "Maria H. Harris," were in Smith County, Kansas, where, as heirs of his mother, they acknowledged their release of interest in her Durand property.[1368] A census taken in Kansas that spring shows J. R. Harris in Oak Township, Smith County, with wife "Nellie," age 23, son John, 8, daughter Ulala, 6, and Arthur Harris, age 9. He had farming implements valued at $50, and had sown in Fall of 1874 five acres of spring wheat and 15 acres of corn. He had planted that spring a one-acre crop of Irish potatoes.[1369]

[1362] Inscription, Fairview Cemetery (viewed Sept. 1981), and Civil War pension file, cited below.

[1363] Winnebago Co., Ill., Marriage Records, Rockford, Ill.

[1364] 1860 U.S. Census, Durand Village, Winnebago Co., Ill., p. 369, house 2727.

[1365] *Changing Ways*, 6, 74.

[1366] Civil War pension file 112173, National Archives, Washington, D.C.

[1367] 1870 U.S. Census, Town of Durand, Winnebago Co., Ill., fam. 165.

[1368] Winnebago Co., Ill., Deeds, 93D:449-51.

[1369] 1875 Kansas State Census, Oak Twp., P.O. Stone Mound, Smith Co., p. 10, and agricultural schedule, p. 5. The family had come to Kansas "from Iowa."

In 1880 Joseph, his wife "Nellie," and children John and "Illah" were enumerated as residents of St. Joseph, Missouri, where Nellie was keeping a restaurant.[1370] However, a letter to his "Dear Wife" (no address) shows that Joseph was visiting with relatives in Durand that June:

Durand, Ill., June 29, 1880

I arrived here the 25th and found uncles folks [Elisha Harris, no. 6] all well and am enjoying myself first rate. Intend to go over and see Zelia [his half-sister] this week. She still lives at Pecatonica. Uncle's Boys have grown so that I did not know any of them but Charlie. I find a great many of the old (setlers?) that used to be here and also quite a number of Strange faces. Durand is verry much as it was when we lived here although there are some changes in the village for instance a fine town hall & School house—will write You at greater length in the near future. From Your affectionate Husband.   /s/ Joseph R. Harris.[1371]

On 12 March 1883, their son John Wesley Harris, then only fifteen, had been working in St. Joseph as a "salesman" for two and a half years.[1372] John moved soon after 1883 to Indian Territory (now Craig County, Oklahoma) where on 6 December 1892 he obtained a permit to employ his father "to labor as a useful Laborer within the district" for three months.[1373]

In June 1900, the household of Joseph R. Harris, farmer, in Cherokee County, Indian Territory, included his wife, then recorded as "Nellie M.," and granddaughter Susie "Lukinbill," age 12. The record shows that they had been married 34 years and that Nellie was the mother of two children, only one then living.[1374] Joseph R. and "Nellie M." were living in a rented home in Craig County in 1910.[1375] Joseph's Civil War pension file shows that he was living with his son John near Big Cabin in 1917, and he was in John's home in January 1920, a widower.[1376]

[1370] 1880 U.S. Census, St. Joseph, Buchanan Co., Mo., p. 9A.

[1371] I thank Joseph R. Harris's great grandson Raymond Nelson Harris of Vinita, Okla., and the latter's son R. Wesley Harris for the copy of this letter and much of the material summarized below for this family.

[1372] Letter of Recommendation, J. M. Easton Co., 12 March 1883, copy courtesy of R. Wesley Harris, Heber Springs, Ark.

[1373] Cherokee Nation Permit, Cooweekoowee District.

[1374] 1900 U.S. Census, Cherokee Co., Indian Territory, E.D. 18, sheet 11.

[1375] 1910 U.S. Census, Twp. 8, Craig Co., Okla., E.D. 36, sheet 2A.

[1376] 1920 U.S. Census, Twp. 8, Craig Co., Okla., E.D. 15, sheet 3B.

Children of Joseph Roswell[7] and Rachel Hannah Maria (Putney) Harris:[1377]

81 i JOHN WESLEY[8] HARRIS, b. Durand, Ill., 23 June 1867; m. IDA JOSEPHINE JENKINS.

  ii ULALAH MAY HARRIS, b. Durand, Ill., 24 Sept. 1869, d. before June 1900 and bur. at Vinita, Okla.;[1378] m. by 1887 ____ LUCKENBILL, b. Iowa according to the 1910 census entry for daughter Susie.

    Child of ____ and Ulalah May[8] (Harris) Luckenbill:

    1 *Susie I. Luckenbill*, b. Indian Territory in July 1887, was living with her Harris grandparents in June 1900, age 12, and as "niece" in the home of her uncle John W. Harris in 1910, age 22. In 1910 she was surnamed *Shupert* and had been married 2 years, apparently as a 2nd marriage.[1379]

70 FLOYD O.[7] HARRIS (*Erwin[6]*, *Joseph[5]*, *Jeremiah[4]*, *Daniel[3]*, *Walter[2]*, *John[1]*), born in Ohio on 4 April 1846, died "at his residence in north-east Hiram," Portage County, Ohio, on 29 September 1917 and buried beside his wife in his parents' lot in the Park Cemetery at Garrettsville.[1380] He married in Portage County on 4 January 1870 **ELLEN H. PAINE**,[1381] born in Hiram, Ohio on 29 December 1846, died at Chagrin Falls, Ohio, on 17 June 1932, a daughter of Lewis C. and Eveline (Udall) Paine of Hiram.[1382]

The 1850 through 1910 censuses for Hiram Township show that Floyd settled there on or near his father's farm. The entries for 1900 and 1910 show that Ellen was mother of four children, all then living. Their son Melvin Jay and his wife, Hattie, then married "½ year," were residing with them in 1900.[1383] Floyd's widow Ellen H. Harris was granted administration of his estate on 12 November 1917; the application names their four children and states their residences at that time.[1384]

[1377] These children's names and birth dates are included on a page headed "Family Record," showing also their parents' birth and marriage dates, once in possession of their son John Wesley Harris. This record also lists Arthur Harris, b. 10 Aug. 1865, who is said by a descendant of John Wesley not to be "a relative, just a child they took in for awhile." He was in Joseph Roswell Harris's household in 1875 at age 9, but not there in 1870 or 1880, nor is he accounted for as a child of this family in the 1900 census.

[1378] Inscription, Fairview Cemetery, no date inscribed.

[1379] 1910 U.S. Census, Twp. 8, Craig Co., Okla., E.D. 36, sheet 9A.

[1380] *Ravenna Republican*, 11 Oct. 1917, and tombstone inscriptions.

[1381] Ohio, County Marriages, 1790–1950, online at <www.FamilySearch.org>, accessed Aug. 2011; 1870 U.S. Census, Hiram Twp., Portage Co., Ohio, 334B.

[1382] Certificate of Death, Ohio Dept. of Health, Division of Vital Statistics, file no. 24890 (informant, Carl B. Harris of Cleveland); 1860 U.S. Census, Hiram Twp., Portage Co., Ohio, p. 114 (Lewis C. Paine household); 1920 U.S. Census, Hiram Twp., Portage Co., Ohio, E.D. 98, sheet 11B (Ellen H. Harris household).

[1383] 1900 U.S. Census, Hiram Twp., Portage Co., Ohio, E.D. 84, sheet 9.

[1384] Portage Co. Probate, Ravenna, Ohio.

Children of Floyd O.[7] and Ellen H. (Paine) Harris, all b. Ohio:

    i   CARL B.[8] HARRIS, b. Hiram, Ohio, 4 Nov. 1871, d. Cleveland, Ohio, 8 Sept. 1953, a supervisor for the U.S. Postal Department.[1385] He m. Cuyahoga Co., Ohio, 4 Nov. 1897 ANNETTIE A. SEARS,[1386] b. N.Y. in May 1864, and living in 1953 when she was the informant for Carl's death certificate. In 1900, they were residing at 161 Chestnut Street in Cleveland, when Carl was a fritter carrier in a foundry.[1387] By Jan. 1920, they had moved to 12347 Forest Ave. in Cleveland, where Carl was a "Mail Carrier."[1388] The 1900 through 1920 censuses list no children for them.

    ii LEWIS ERWIN HARRIS, b. Hiram, Ohio, 1 Nov. 1873, was living in Los Angeles in 1920, age 46; m. (1) in Troy, Geauga Co., Ohio, 18 Oct. 1899 ETHEL MAY WEBSTER,[1389] b. Mich. in May 1880. In 1900, Lewis's widowed "mother-in-law" Olive Webster, b. Mich. in Dec. 1843, was living in his home in Hiram Twp., Portage Co., Ohio.[1390] Lewis was in Los Angeles by 1918[1391] and had m. (2) CLARA ADDIE PRINCE, b. Calif., ca. 1894, dau. of George S. and Addie (___) Prince of Los Angeles.[1392]

    iii LAURA BELLE HARRIS, b. in Sept. 1876 and living at Hiram in 1917; m. Portage Co. 18 Dec. 1905 NELSON H. BECKWITH, b. Mich. 13 Oct. 1884, son of C. D. and Mary (Udall) Beckwith.[1393] In 1910, Nelson and Laura were residing with her parents in Hiram Twp.[1394] By 1920, Nelson and Laura had divorced and he and their two young children were residing in Hiram with Laura's widowed mother.[1395]

        Children of Nelson H. and Laura Belle[8] (Harris) Beckwith, from 1910 and 1920 census:

        1 *Evaline M. Beckwith*, b. Ohio ca. 1908.

        2 *Corral Beckwith*, b. Ohio ca. 1911.

    iv MELVIN JAY HARRIS, b. 21 July 1878, was living in Chagrin Falls, Ohio, in 1917, in Bainbridge Twp., Geauga Co., Ohio, in 1920,[1396] and Chagrin Falls Village in 1930.[1397] He m. Troy, Geauga Co., 25 April 1900 HATTIE A. WILLIAMS,[1398]

[1385] Certificate of Death, Ohio Dept. of Health, Division of Vital Statistics, file no. 58163 (informant, Nettie A. Harris).

[1386] Ohio Marriages, 1899–1958, online at <www.FamilySearch.org>, accessed Aug. 2011.

[1387] 1900 U.S. Census, 5th Ward, City of Cleveland, Cuyahoga Co., Ohio, E.D. 22, sheet 2.

[1388] 1920 U.S. Census, City of Cleveland, Cuyahoga Co., Ohio, E.D 610, sheet 2.

[1389] Geauga Co., Ohio, Marriage Records, 5:35.

[1390] 1900 U.S. Census, Hiram Twp., Portage Co., Ohio, E.D. 84, sheet 12.

[1391] World War I Draft Registration Card, no. 500-72, age 44, residing Los Angeles, a motorman, nearest relative "wife Clara Addie Harris" of same address.

[1392] 1920 U.S. Census, Los Angeles City, Los Angeles Co., Calif., E.D. 103, sheet 1A (household of George S. Prince including "son-in-law" Lewis E. Harris and "daughter" Clara A. Harris).

[1393] Portage Co., Ohio, Marriages, license no. 10494.

[1394] 1910 U.S. Census, Hiram Twp., Portage Co., Ohio, E.D 101, sheet 5B.

[1395] 1920 U.S. Census, Hiram Twp., Portage Co., Ohio, E.D 98, sheet 11B.

[1396] 1920 U.S. Census, Bainbridge Twp., Geauga Co., E.D 60, sheet 7A.

[1397] 1930 U.S. Census, Chagrin Falls Village, Chagrin Falls Twp., Cuyahoga Co., Ohio, E.D. 18-553, sheet 13B. Perhaps the actual location was the same in all cases. Maps show Chagrin Falls in Cuyahoga Co., but very near the northwest corner of Bainbridge in Geauga Co.

b. Ohio in Oct. 1881, living Chagrin Falls 1930, prob. the Hattie Harris b. 7 Oct. 1881 who d. in Willoughby, Lake Co., Ohio, in Oct. 1974.[1399] They were residing with Melvin's parents at the time of the 1900 census in Hiram Twp. By 1910 they had a separate household in Hiram, where he was "farming."[1400] Melvin was residing in Chagrin Falls on 12 Sept. 1918, when he registered at age 40 for the draft during World War I, giving his occupation as farming and Mrs. Hattie Harris of same address as his nearest relative.[1401] Melvin was an oil-truck driver at Chagrin Falls in 1930.

Children of Melvin Jay[8] and Hattie A. (Williams) Harris, from 1910, 1920, and 1930 census entries:

1 *Cass[ius?] L.*[9] *Harris*, b. Ohio ca. 1901.
2 *Mildred F. Harris*, b. Hiram, Ohio, 24 Jan. 1905.[1402]
3 *Maxine B. Harris*, b. Ohio ca. 1922, with parents 1930.

71 JOSEPH E.[7] **HARRIS** (*Eli*[6], *Joseph*[5], *Jeremiah*[4], *Daniel*[3], *Walter*[2], *John*[1]), was born about 1834 as indicated by the 1860 census (born Ohio) or in September 1833 as indicated by the 1900 census (born New York). Perhaps his birthplace was in Geauga or Portage County, Ohio, where his parents may have resided briefly with relatives before returning to Steuben County, New York. He was living alone in Steuben County in June 1900.[1403] He married first in 1854, probably in Steuben County, **EMELINE AMANDA WHITNEY**, who was born in Danby, New York, on 5 February 1836, and died in Salamanca, Cattaraugus County, on 19 April 1866, where she is buried, a daughter of James Lewis and Lucy Maria (Hall) Whitney of Danby and of Canton, Steuben County.[1404] He married second by 1870 **FRANCIS** ____, born in Canada about 1844,[1405] and third by about 1877 **JENNIE** ____, born in Pennsylvania about 1853, who was his "wife" in Allegany in 1880.

On 21 August 1860, Joseph E. Harris of Portville, Cattaraugus County, acknowledged a release to his uncle Charles Mulford that he and his sisters Julia Whitney and Laura Whitney had executed a month before in Steuben County as heirs of their deceased mother, Mary (Mulford) Harris.[1406] Birth-

---

[1398] Geauga Co., Ohio, Marriage Records, 5:65.

[1399] Social Security Death Index, SSN 274-62-1538.

[1400] 1910 U.S. Census, Hiram Twp., Portage Co., Ohio, E.D. 101, sheet 6. The 1910 census schedule for Hiram is difficult to read; the name of the son looks like *Cassius* in 1920.

[1401] World War I Draft Registration Card, serial no. illegible, local board Chardon, Geauga Co., Ohio.

[1402] Geauga Co., Ohio, Birth Records, 2:52, no. 7490.

[1403] 1900 U.S. Census, Caton Twp., Steuben Co., N.Y., E.D. 70, sheet 12.

[1404] *Whitney Family of Connecticut*, 2:1551-52. The will of James L. Whitney, dated at Canton, Steuben Co., 16 Jan. 1877, leaves all real and personal property to "my wife Maria Whitney" and names no heirs (Steuben Co. Wills, 14:339, file 11675).

[1405] 1870 U.S. Census, Town of Salamanca, Cattaraugus Co., N.Y., p. 541 (Joseph "works on saw mill").

[1406] Steuben Co. Deeds, 89:542.

places stated for children indicate that Joseph probably resided at different times across the state line in Pennsylvania.

Joseph was a "sawyer" when he was residing in Portville in 1860.[1407] In 1870 he was working "on a sawmill" in Salamanca,[1408] and he was in Allegany, Cattaraugus County, in 1880, where he was working at that time in a shingle mill.[1409] In 1900, at age 66, he was styled "mechanic."

Children of Joseph E.[7] and Emeline Amanda (Whitney) Harris, as indicated by the 1860 and 1870 censuses:

    i   CHARLES[8] HARRIS, b. Pa. ca. 1855, at home 1870.
    ii WILLIE HARRIS, b. N.Y. ca. 1857, at home 1870.

Child of Joseph E.[7] and Jennie (____) Harris, from 1880 census:

    iii KITTY HARRIS, b. Pa., ca. 1877.

72 EDWARD W.[7] HARRIS (*Eli[6]*, *Joseph[5]*, *Jeremiah[4]*, *Daniel[3]*, *Walter[2]*, *John[1]*), born in Steuben County, New York, 4 June 1843, died at Hubbard, Hubbard County, Minnesota, on 6 March 1913, where he is buried.[1410] He married in Fayette County, Iowa, 6 July 1872, **MERCY JANE ROBERTS**,[1411] born in New York on 27 February 1848 (or 1850?), died at Hubbard on 14 March 1929, daughter of John H. and Matilda (Hill) Roberts of Eden Township, Fayette County.[1412]

Edward W. Harris first appears at age seven in 1850 in his uncle Charles Mulford's home in Lindley, Steuben County, while his mother, Mary (Mulford) Harris, and sister Laura Harris were nearby in his grandfather Jeremiah Mulford's home.[1413] His father Eli Harris had died a short time before. At age fifteen and an orphan, he went in 1858 to Winnebago County, Illinois, where "he worked on a farm until 1861 when he enlisted."[1414] His military record shows that he served from Durand, Winnebago County. The date he

---

[1407] 1860 U.S. Census, Town of Portville, Cattaraugus Co., N.Y., house 530.

[1408] 1870 U.S. Census, Town of Salamanca, Cattaraugus Co., N.Y., p. 541.

[1409] 1880 U.S. Census, Allegany, Cattaraugus Co., N.Y., p. 33A (his birthplace is "N.Y." in this census).

[1410] Tombstone, Hubbard Cemetery, with Civil War marker, and Death Certificate, State of Minnesota Division of Vital Statistics, naming his parents Eli Harris and Mary Mulford and his occupation as "Rural Carrier."

[1411] Marriage record included in Edward's Civil War pension file, Cert. no. 828228, National Archives, Washington, D.C.

[1412] Tombstone, Hubbard Cemetery; Hubbard Co. Death Records. Mercy's death record states that she was born in Pa. on 27 Feb. 1850, but when she was enumerated in her parents' home in 1870, she was listed as age 22 and born in "N.Y." (1870 U.S. Census, Eden Twp., Fayette Co., Iowa, p. 8).

[1413] 1850 U.S. Census, Town of Lindley, Steuben Co., N.Y., families 78 and 79.

[1414] Obituary of Edward W. Harris, included with his Civil War pension file.

claimed to have arrived there, 1858, is within a year of the date that his uncle Edgar Eggleston Harris (no. 54) arrived in Durand from Binghamton, New York.

Edward enlisted twice, the first time at age eighteen on 9 September 1861 in the 55th Regiment, Illinois Infantry. With that unit, he "participated in the battles of Shiloh, Corinth, Chickasaw Bayou, Haines Bluff, Arkansas Post, Raymond, Edwards Station, Champion Hills, Charge and Siege of Vicksburg, Jackson, Mission Ridge, and Lookout Mountain." His disability claim was based on wounds received during the retreat at Shiloh. After his discharge at Chattanooga on 31 October 1864, he reenlisted in the 153rd Illinois Infantry, in which he served as a sergeant until mustered out at Memphis on 21 September 1865. His name is inscribed on the monument to Civil War veterans in Durand.

In 1868, Edward went to Fayette County, Iowa, where he married in 1872 and appears in Eden Township in 1880 renting a farm with wife Mercy and three daughters.[1415] His uncle Erastus Harris (no. 42) was residing nearby in Illyria Township. In the "Fall of 1880" [*sic*: probably 1886 according to children's birth places], Edward moved to Wadena County, Minnesota. His uncle Erastus apparently arrived there about the same time. In 1895, Edward and Maria, with six children at home, were residing in Shell River Township, Wadena County.[1416] By 1900 Edward was a "farm laborer" nearby in Hubbard Township; his wife, "Mercie J." Harris, was mother of seven children, all then living.[1417] From 1903 to his death there in 1913, Edward "faithfully discharged the duties of Rural mail carrier, Route no. 1, Hubbard, and has endeared himself to all the patrons of the route."[1418] In 1920, widow Mercy J. Harris was living with her daughter Laura E. Doane and husband in the Village of Hubbard.[1419]

Children of Edward W.[7] and Mercy Jane (Roberts) Harris from obituary, census, and county records:

 i   BLANCHE G.[8] HARRIS, b. Iowa ca. 1873 and living at Menahga, Wadena Co., Minn., in 1920; m. in Wadena Co., 15 Dec. 1895, HENRY E. GARZEE, "both of Wadena County," at the "house of E. Harris by J.P."[1420] Mrs. H. E.

[1415] 1880 U.S. Census, Eden Twp., Fayette Co., Iowa, E.D. 197, fam. 159.

[1416] 1895 Minnesota State Census, Shell River Twp., Wadena Co., p. 6, online at <www.FamilySearch.org>.

[1417] 1900 U.S. Census, Hubbard Twp., Hubbard Co., Minn., E.D. 72, sheet 9.

[1418] Obituary of Edward W. Harris.

[1419] 1920 U.S. Census, Hubbard Village, Hubbard Co., Minn., E.D. 142, house 35.

[1420] Wadena Co. Marriage Records, Wadena, Minn. Possibly her parents were living at that time near Shell City, just over the county line from Hubbard, where her great uncle Erastus Harris had settled.

Garzee of Menahga provided the information for her father's death certificate in March 1913. If Henry E. Garzee's age was correctly recorded in Jan. 1920, he was about thirty years older than Blanche. The census at Menahga shows that his birthplace was in Vt. and that he was 76 years old, thus born ca. 1844.[1421] No children for them are listed in 1920.

ii   LAURA ELENA HARRIS, b. Eden, Iowa, 27 Aug. 1877, d. "of Stroke" in Hubbard, Minn., 15 Nov. 1946 and buried Hubbard Cemetery, aged 69, "daughter of Edward W. and Mercy Jane Harris";[1422] m. Hubbard Co., 8 Dec. 1893, DON A. DOANE,[1423] b. Mich. in Dec. 1865, d. 1955 and buried Hubbard Cemetery. In 1900, Don and Laura Doane were residing in her parents' home in Hubbard Township, the census stating that she was mother of one child, then living. They were residing in the Village of Hubbard in 1920 and in 1930.[1424]

Child of Don A. and Laura Elena[8] (Harris) Doane, from the 1900 and 1920 censuses:

     1 *Frederick H. Doane*, b. Minn. in Oct. 1894, d. 1944 and buried with parents in Hubbard Cemetery.

iii   MATILDA MARY HARRIS, b. Eden, Fayette Co., Iowa, 4 Aug. 1879, d. Neosho, Mo., 29 Dec. 1906, but buried in Hubbard Cemetery;[1425] m. Hubbard Co., 6 Nov. 1898, "both of Hubbard County," ORVILLE E. WEIKEL,[1426] b. Mich. in Feb. 1871, d. 1945 and buried Hubbard Cemetery.[1427] Their Hubbard Co. marriage record was signed by E. W. Harris and witnessed by Don A. Doane and Blanche Garzee. Their household in Hubbard Twp. in 1900 was listed next to her parents' home. They had no children by the date of that census, but Orville's "widowed" mother, (Pauline?) Weikel, b. New York in June 1845, was living with them. In 1910, Orville E. Weikel, widower and farmer, was living alone in Hubbard Twp.[1428]

iv   ZOE A. HARRIS, b. Iowa in June 1881, living Hubbard Twp. in 1905;[1429] m. Hubbard Co., 6 Nov. 1898 (same date and witnesses as her sister Matilda above) GEORGE A. MCNAMER, b. Iowa in May 1877, "both of Hubbard

---

[1421] 1920 U.S. Census, Menahga, Wadena Co., Minn., E.D. 245, sheet 4A.

[1422] Obituary, undated newspaper clipping transcribed by Darryl Hensel, Hubbard County Genealogical Society; Inscription, Hubbard Cemetery. The obituary says she was survived by four sisters and one brother (unnamed).

[1423] Hubbard Co., Minn., Marriage Records (witnesses: Blanche Harris and Clarence Roberts).

[1424] 1920, 1930 U.S. Census, Hubbard Village, Hubbard Co., Minn., E.D. 142, house 35, and E.D. 29-16, sheet 4B, respectively.

[1425] Obituary, undated newspaper clipping transcribed by Darryl Hensel, Hubbard County Genealogical Society; Inscription, Hubbard Town Cemetery; birthplace from 1900 census. The obituary states that Matilda was survived by her husband, her father and mother, and five sisters and one brother: Mrs. Blanche Garzee of Menahga, Mrs. Laura Doane, Mrs. Ruby Reed, Miss Zina Harris, and Hiram Harris, all of Hubbard. Sister Zoe McNamer apparently was omitted in transcription.

[1426] Hubbard Co., Minn., Marriage Records.

[1427] Birth data from 1900 census; death from inscription, which reads "1870–1945."

[1428] 1910 U.S. Census, Hubbard Twp., Hubbard Co., Minn., E.D. 78, sheet 1A.

[1429] Named with husband in a 1905 census index, Hubbard County Genealogical Society.

County."[1430] George, a day laborer, and wife Zoe were residing in Hubbard in 1900, the census entry showing that she was at that time the mother of one child, not living.[1431]

        Children of George A. and Zoe A.[8] (Harris) McNamer:

        1 Child who d. before 1900 census date.

        2 *Arkley L. McNamer*, b. Hubbard Co. 4 Jan. 1901.[1432]

  v RUBY HARRIS, b. Iowa in June 1883, living Jersey Shore, Lycoming Co., Pa., 1920;[1433] m. Hubbard Co., 11 Nov. 1902 CLAUDE H. REED,[1434] b. Pa. ca. 1881, a railroad brakeman in Jersey Shore in 1920. They were in Clinton Co., Pa., in 1910, when Claude was a locomotive fireman.[1435]

        Child of Claude H. and Ruby[8] (Harris) Reed:

        1 *Maxwell Reed*, b. Minn. ca. 1905, with parents 1910, 1920.

  vi ZINA GRACE HARRIS, b. Iowa in Feb. 1885; m. Hubbard Co., 30 Oct. 1907, JOHN W. KEE "of Todd County," Minn. Edward W. Harris, "father of Z. Grace Harris of Hubbard County," procured the license.[1436] She was "Virginia" in the 1900 census, "Zina" in her sister Matilda's Jan. 1907 obituary, and "Grace" in her father's 1913 obituary.

 vii HIRAM OTTMER HARRIS, b. Shell City, Minn., 20 May 1887, d. in Hubbard, Minn., on 12 April 1954; m. in Hubbard Co., 21 Nov. 1915, ROSE LEE IRWIN, b. Belle Plaine, Minn., 14 March 1895, d. in Everett, Wash., 23 Aug. 1956, daughter of Andrew Gould and Kathryn (Costello) Irwin. Hiram and Rose are buried in the Hubbard Cemetery.[1437] At the time of the 1910 census, Hiram, aged 22, was living with his parents in Hubbard Twp.

        Children of Hiram Ottmer[8] and Rose Lee (Irwin) Harris:

        1 *Lenore Adair[9] Harris*, b. 27 Nov. 1916, d. 14 Dec. 1970.

        2 *Jane Kathryn Harris*, b. 15 March 1918.

        3 *Bertice Florence Harris*, b. 31 Oct. 1919.

        4 *Robert Edward Harris*, b. 16 Sept. 1921, d. 11 Sept. 1974.

        5 *Ruth Evelyn Harris*, b. 16 Sept. 1921.

        6 *Harold Dean Harris*, b. 6 July 1923, d. 17 Nov. 1988.

        7 *Richard Frederick Harris*, b. 3 Jan. 1926.

        8 *Donald Eugene Harris*, b. 8 Aug. 1931.

        9 *Jack Russell Harris*, b. 26 March 1934.

        10 *Lora Dale Harris*, b. 11 June 1936, d. 11 Sept. 1943.[1438]

        11 *Darrel Dwayne Harris*, b. 2 Dec. 1938.

[1430] Hubbard Co., Minn., Marriage Records.

[1431] 1900 U.S. Census, Hubbard Twp., Hubbard Co., Minn., dwelling 214.

[1432] Hubbard Co., Minn., Birth Records, stating her parents' ages and birthplaces.

[1433] 1920 U.S. Census, Jersey Shore Borough, Lycoming Co., Pa., E.D. 44, sheet 1A.

[1434] Hubbard Co., Minn., Marriage Records, witnesses, Lelia Louise Loring and Chas. F. Campton.

[1435] 1910 U.S. Census, Beech Creek Borough, Clinton Co., Pa., E.D. 2, sheet 13B.

[1436] Hubbard Co., Minn., Marriage Records.

[1437] Data for this family, including the children, are from a family Bible, information provided by Mrs. Carole A. Heuer of Longmont, Colo., 1995. Hiram and Rose Harris's ages and birthplaces are also stated in Hubbard Co. birth records of some of their children.

[1438] Gravestone, Hubbard Cemetery.

73 HENRY EDWARD[7] HARRIS (*Elisha[6], Joseph[5], Jeremiah[4], Daniel[3], Walter[2], John[1]*), born "in the old log house on the home farm" at Durand (then Howard), Winnebago County, Illinois, on 27 November 1842,[1439] died in a veteran's hospital at Port Orchard, Washington, on 14 March 1917.[1440] He married first at Durand on 29 December 1864 **ANN CECELIA FRITZ**, born there on 20 July 1842, who died there on 14 November 1892 and is buried in Durand Cemetery. She was a daughter ("adopted," 1870 census) of George and Cornelia Jane (Cleveland) Fritz of Durand.[1441] He married secondly, at the home of her mother Mrs. Burton in Chicago, 18 January 1899, **FREDERICA ANNA (JACKSON) REA**, born Buffalo, New York, on 4 January 1851, widow of Lester Rea (died 9 February 1897) whom she had married on 30 March 1892. Frederica married third at Bremerton, Washington, 24 July 1917, Rinaldo H. Brown.[1442] A Durand newspaper item (name of paper missing) dated 26 January 1899 expresses the town's surprise that their "genial postmaster . . . Henry E. Harris . . . one of our most popular citizens," on an ostensible business trip to Chicago brought back with him a bride, but wished them "every happiness in life."[1443]

On 10 August 1861, Henry E. Harris joined the 11th Illinois Infantry Regiment at Rockford, Illinois, and was engaged in the battles of Port Henry, Fort Donelson, Shiloh, Corinth, Jackson (Tennessee), Padueah, and the Siege of Vicksburg. Following his discharge at Vicksburg on 17 August 1864, he returned to Durand, where he appears in the 1865 Illinois State Census with a household consisting only of a male and a female, both age 20-29.[1444] He appears there in the 1870 U.S. Census, a "carpenter," with his wife, Ann C., and first child, Freddie M.[1445] His household was listed next but one from his uncle Edgar Eggleston Harris (no. 54), whose wife Maria Louisa later became his stepmother. In 1889, according to his biography, Henry became the Postmaster of Durand. That position for him is also stated in the 1900 census for Durand, when his household included his second wife, his daughter Lillian J. Harris—"1st Asst. Postmaster"—and his "niece" Matie E. Harris, aged 29.[1446] The "niece" was in fact his stepsister and half

---

[1439] Biography of Henry E. Harris, *Portrait and Biographical Record of Winnebago and Boone Counties*, 652-53.

[1440] Civil War pension file 707003, National Archives, Washington, D.C.

[1441] *Cleveland and Cleaveland Families*, 1341-42; biography of George A. Fritz in Church, *Past and Present of the City of Rockford and Winnebago County*, 246.

[1442] Henry Edward Harris pension file.

[1443] Item provided by Barbara Winchester, Durand, Ill.

[1444] 1865 Ill. State Census, Howard, Winnebago Co., Ill., p. 47.

[1445] 1870 U.S. Census, Durand Twp., Winnebago Co., Ill., p. 270.

[1446] 1900 U.S. Census, Durand, Winnebago Co., Ill., E.D. 121, sheet 13.

first-cousin, Marietta Elnora Harris (no. 54 vii), who had returned to Durand from Beatrice, Nebraska.

Next year, to the town's amazement, Henry E. Harris was replaced as Postmaster by his daughter Lillian because of an alleged "defalcation." He acknowledged it on 22 August 1901 and was taken to Chicago, but the outcome of his case is not stated.[1447] It appears, however, that with the assistance of his daughter and the town's sympathy, he made restitution. By 1905, he was residing in Seattle, Washington,[1448] where his younger brother William Eugene Harris had arrived about 1903. Henry's address in 1910 and for pension matters in 1915 was 651 5th Street, Bremerton, Washington.[1449]

Children of Henry Edward[7] and Ann Cecelia (Fritz) Harris:[1450]

    i   FREDERICK MELVIN[8] HARRIS, b. Ill. 16 April 1866, d. before the 1910 census date and buried in Durand Cemetery.[1451] He m. Rock Co., Wis., 30 Oct. 1892 NELLIE L. MILLER,[1452] b. Ill. in Jan. 1868, daughter of William H. and (Aurilla?) (___) Miller with whom she was living as a widow at Durand in 1910.[1453] Frederick was elected Durand Township Clerk in April 1899, appears there in 1900, and was a rural mail carrier there in 1905.[1454]

       Children of Frederick Melvin[8] and Nellie L. (Miller) Harris, from 1900 and 1910 censuses:

       1 *Vernon M.[9] Harris*, b. Ill. in June 1893, living with mother in 1910.

       2 *Mildred C. Harris*, b. Ill. in Aug. 1894.

       3 A child who died before the 1900 census.

   ii LEWIS HENRY HARRIS, b. Ill. 12 June 1870, was living near his uncle Elmer E. Harris in Grand Junction, Colo., in Jan. 1920, farmer, aged 49, and single.[1455] He was in Seattle in 1905,[1456] but had returned to Durand by 1910, when he was a drayman residing at Cora Felt's boarding house, aged 39 and single.[1457]

[1447] Durand newspaper clipping, 24 Aug. 1901.

[1448] Biography of Elmer E. Harris in Church, *Past and Present of the City of Rockford and Winnebago County*, 291-92.

[1449] 1910 U.S. Census, 3rd Ward, Bremerton, Kitsap Co., Wash., E.D. 227, sheet 3A.

[1450] Henry Edward Harris pension file (affidavit dated in 1915); *Cleveland and Cleaveland Families*, 1341-42.

[1451] Gravestone, no dates inscribed.

[1452] Wisconsin Marriages, 1836–1930, online at <www.FamilySearch.org>, accessed Aug. 2011.

[1453] 1910 U.S. Census, Durand Twp., Winnebago Co., Ill., E.D. 142, sheet 7B.

[1454] 1900 U.S. Census, Durand Twp., Winnebago Co., Ill., E.D. 121, sheet 5; biography of George A. Fritz in Church, *Past and Present of the City of Rockford and Winnebago County*, 246.

[1455] 1920 U.S. Census, Grand Ave. Road, Precinct 1, Mesa Co., Colo., E.D. 86, sheet 4A.

[1456] Biography of George A. Fritz in Church, *Past and Present of the City of Rockford and Winnebago County*, 246.

[1457] 1910 U.S. Census, Durand Village, Winnebago Co., Ill., E.D. 142, sheet 10A.

iii RAYMOND FRITZ HARRIS, b. Ill. 5 Nov. 1872, d. Cook Co., Ill., 12 Jan. 1942, bur. West Point Cemetery, Liberty, Union Co., Ind.[1458] He was "of Chicago" when he m. at Oak Park, Cook Co., Ill., 7 Sept. 1912 KATHERYN LANDIS "of Oak Park,"[1459] b. Liberty, Ind., 1875, d. Oak Park 2 Jan. 1919, bur. West Point Cemetery, dau. of Joseph and Prudence (Hughes) Landis.[1460] In 1900, Raymond was a "grocery salesman" and residing at Sycamore, DeKalb Co., Ill., with his uncle Willis Spencer Harris (no. 51 x). In 1910, aged 37 and still single, Raymond F. Harris was a "roomer" on Prairie Avenue in Chicago, where he was employed as a "Bookkeeper with Cigar Company."[1461] He was an accountant at Oak Park, Ill., on 12 Sept. 1918, when he registered at age 45 for the draft during World War I.[1462]

iv LILLIAN JULIA HARRIS, b. Ill. 21 Sept. 1874, was living in Durand in 1920, unmarried. Lillian Harris was in Mrs. W. H. McClintock's Durand High School "Class of 1891."[1463] She was the Assistant Postmaster of Durand in 1900 and her father's replacement as Postmaster in Aug. 1901. As a "highly thought of young lady," the "citizens generally have signed a petition that she be appointed postmistress."[1464] For some years, she kept house in Durand for Edward E. Edwards, widowered brother-in-law of her step grandmother Maria Louisa (Fassett) Harris.[1465] At age 35 and single, Lillian was "keeper, Post Office," there in 1910.[1466] A decade later, in 1920, she was still living there, aged 45 and single, but unemployed.[1467]

[1458] Data online at <www.findagrave.com>, accessed July 2010 ("Lot 100, Sec. 1, No Stone").

[1459] Cook Co., Ill., Marriages, license no. 606004.

[1460] West Point Cemetery transcription data and her gravestone photo online at <www.findagrave. com>, accessed July 2010 ("Sec. 1 Lot 100 E1/2").

[1461] 1910 U.S. Census, City of Chicago, Cook Co., Ill., E.D. 404, dwelling 73, where he was rooming with Thomas R. Walker, a "Candy Store Keeper," and his wife Nelle.

[1462] World War I Draft Registration Card, no. 4722-A6574, stamped 12-3-7C.

[1463] Letter of Barbara Winchester of Durand, 30 Sept. 1985.

[1464] Durand newspaper clipping, 24 Aug. 1901.

[1465] Edward E. Edwards, carpenter (b. Utica, N.Y., 27 July 1836, d. Durand 27 May 1924), and his wife Anna (Fassett) were living in Durand in 1870 (census) but moved to Spencer, Iowa, before her sister Maria Louisa (Fassett) Harris and husband Edgar E. Harris, where they all appear in the 1880 census. Edwards' Civil War pension application (no. 556136, National Archives), dated at Durand 23 Sept. 1920, claims that he had resided at Durand from 1865 to 1871, in Spencer from 1871 to 1884, and in Orleans, Nebr., from 1884 to 1893, when he returned to Durand. Anna d. at Durand in July 1893 and he m. there second, in May 1899, Elizabeth, widow of L. V. Cleveland, who d. in 1905. In 1937, Guy Earl Wescott of Alma, Nebr., wrote that his "uncle" Ed Edwards had built three houses then standing in Orleans. "It seems," he continued, "that Mary Louise [his grandmother Maria Louisa (Fassett) Harris], who had a town property at Durand, Ill., where she lived, traded it to Edwards for a farm near Orleans and Edwards and wife went back to Durand. His wife [Anna] died quite a few years before his death I believe because a niece Lillian Harris kept house for him for years." (Guy Wescott to Mrs. Fred Fassett, March 1937.)

[1466] 1910 U.S. Census, Durand Village, Winnebago Co., Ill., E.D. 142, sheet 10A.

[1467] 1920 U.S. Census, Durand Village, Winnebago Co., Ill., E.D. 162, sheet 11B. Except for her uncle Willis Spencer Harris buried there in 1936, Lillian Julia Harris is the last known person of this family group to preserve the surname in Durand.

74 WILLIAM EUGENE[7] HARRIS (*Elisha[6], Joseph[5], Jeremiah[4], Daniel[3], Walter[2], John[1]*) was born at Durand (then Howard), Winnebago County, Illinois, on 14 May 1847 and died of arteriosclerosis at his home at 7757 32nd Avenue N.W., Seattle, Washington, on 20 March 1927, age 79y 10m 6d.[1468] He married in Winnebago County on 9 September 1869 **CORA A. HURD**,[1469] daughter of Dillazon S. and Harriet Eliza (Manchester) Hurd of Durand village, born in Wisconsin on 12 March 1851[1470] and died in Bellingham, Washington, on 20 January 1936, age 84y 10m 8d,[1471] probably at the home of her son Elisha D. Harris with whom she was living there in 1930, age 79.[1472]

At age 13, William E. Harris was residing with his widowed maternal grandmother Lovina Robb in 1860, whose farm was a short distance northeast of his father's place, and adjacent north of the D. S. Hurd farm.[1473] In 1870, William and his bride were living nearby, their household then including Abigail Hurd, aged 78, born in Connecticut, apparently Cora's grandmother and widow of Zera Hurd.[1474]

By 1875, William had joined his brother Lewis Frederick Harris in Greenwood County, Kansas,[1475] where he appears in 1880 with his wife Cora A. and two sons.[1476] In September 1881, William recorded a Patent in Greenwood County for the NE¼, Section 4, Township 36, Range 12, near the village of Neal. Next month, William bought the NE¼ of Section 34 from Austin Corlin.[1477] The 1903 Platt of Neal Village shows that the latter quarter section comprised about all of the east half of the village, while most of the rest was owned by W. E. Robb, T. N. Robb, and W. B. Hurd, with Robb Street crossing the railroad to the southwest of town. "T. N." Robb no doubt was William and Lewis Harris's uncle Thomas Newell Robb who

---

[1468] William E. Harris Certificate of Death, Washington State Board of Health, Bureau of Vital Statistics, Record no. 815, which states that William, b. in "Illinois," was husband of Cora A. Harris, the "Informant," who was residing at 7757 32nd Ave., N.W., and son of Elisa [*sic*] Harris, b. "New York," and Celista Robb, b. "Ohio." William Eugene's birth date is given as 8 May 1847 in the 1905 biography of his brother Elmer E. Harris (Church, *Past and Present of the City of Rockford and Winnebago County*, 291-92).

[1469] Winnebago Co., Ill., Marriage Records; 1870 U.S. Census, Town of Durand, fam. no. 96 ("married within year—Sept.").

[1470] 1900 U.S. Census, Quincy Twp., Greenwood Co., Kans., E.D. 58, sheet 3.

[1471] Washington Death Certificates, 1907–1960, online at <www.FamilySearch.org>, giving parents' names as Dillizon Hurd and Elizabeth Manchester, spouse's name as William Harris.

[1472] 1930 U.S. Census, Bellingham City, Ward 2, Whatcom Co., Wash., E.D. 37-18, sheet 1B ("mother" in Elisha Harris household).

[1473] *Changing Ways*, 74.

[1474] Rowland, *Pioneers of Winnebago and Boone Counties, Illinois*, 228-29.

[1475] 1875 Kansas State Census, Pleasant Grove Twp., P.O. Quincy, Greenwood Co., p. 15.

[1476] 1880 U.S. Census, Salem Twp., Greenwood Co., Kans., E.D. 97, sheet 1.

[1477] Greenwood Co., Kans., Deeds, A:32; 19:487.

died at Neal in 1907.[1478] Plainly, this related family group had come out from Durand in the mid-1870s and acquired the property which, today, makes up almost the entire town of Neal, Kansas.

W[illiam] E. Harris was a "railroader" in Quincy Township, Greenwood County in 1885.[1479] In 1900, his household there included his wife Cora, two children, his mother-in-law Eliza Hurd (born in "Canada" in October 1825), and boarder David W. Basham, aged 45, born in Kentucky. This census, enumerated incidentally by William's brother Lewis F. Harris, reports that Cora was mother of four children, all then living.[1480] On 14 February 1903, William E. Harris and his wife Cora sold their properties at Neal to Sam Newbold, Homer V. Harrington, and Susan N. Otis.[1481] They probably moved at that time to Seattle, where they were said to be residing in 1905 and 1916.[1482]

In 1910 they were at 2814 15th Avenue South in Seattle, where their household consisted of William and Cora and their daughter Pearle aged 27, son Walter, aged 24, grandson Zera Harris, aged 15, and granddaughter Muryl Harris, aged 11. The adjoining household was that of their widowed son Henry A. Harris, aged 39.[1483] In 1920, William and Cora were residing in Bellingham, Washington, when he was listed as a vegetable gardener.[1484] The biography of William's brother Elmer E. Harris states without naming them that William had three sons and one daughter; all are found in the censuses mentioned.

Children of William Eugene[7] and Cora A. (Hurd) Harris:

    i   HENRY A.[8] HARRIS, b. Ill. in April 1871, living in Seattle in 1920, a "laborer" for Standard Oil Company.[1485] Henry m. (1) ca. 1894 KATE B. [KAIN?], b. Ill. in Nov. 1870, with whom he was living in Ogden, Utah, in 1900, where he was a teamster for Continental Oil Company, the census indicating that Kate was the mother of three children, two then living.[1486] Kate d. before 1910, when his household in Seattle included "brother-in-law" Frank Kain, aged 33, born Ill., and three "lodgers" surnamed Forsyth.[1487] Henry m. (2)

[1478] Rowland, *Pioneers of Winnebago and Boone Counties, Illinois*, 368.

[1479] 1885 Kansas State Census, Quincy Twp., P.O. Neal, Greenwood Co., p. 23.

[1480] 1900 U.S. Census, Quincy Twp., Greenwood Co., Kans., E.D. 58, sheet 3.

[1481] Greenwood Co., Kans., Deeds, 60:370, 371, 373.

[1482] Biography of Elmer E. Harris, in Church, *Past and Present of the City of Rockford and Winnebago County*; 291-92; *Historical Encyclopedia of Illinois and History of Winnebago County*, 2:1081.

[1483] 1910 U.S. Census, 2nd Ward, Seattle, King Co., Wash., E.D. 76, sheet 5B.

[1484] 1920 U.S. Census, 2nd Ward, Bellingham City, Whatcom Co., Wash., E.D. 21, sheet 6A.

[1485] 1920 U.S. Census, Seattle, Precinct 276, King Co., Wash, E.D. 339, sheet 1A.

[1486] 1900 U.S. Census, 2nd Ward, Ogden City, Weber Co., Utah, E.D. 187, sheet 12.

[1487] 1910 U.S. Census, 2nd Ward, Seattle, King Co., Wash., E.D. 76, sheet 5B.

by 1913 ETHEL MOREY, b. Detroit, Mich., ca. 1879,[1488] who was living with him in 1920, dau. of Edward S. Morey, listed as "father-in-law" in the same household, a "druggist."

Children of Henry A.[8] and Kate B. (Kain?) Harris, from 1900 and 1910 census entries (another child had died before 1900):

    1 *Zera G.*[9] *Harris* (son), b. Neal, Kans., 3 Nov. 1894, living with his Harris grandparents in 1910. In June 1917, Zera was single, a pipe fitter for Standard Oil Co., and residing at 2802 15th Ave. South in Seattle when he registered for the draft in World War I.[1489]

    2 *Muryl C. L. Harris* (dau.), b. Utah in Sept. 1898, living with Harris grandparents in 1910.

Child of Henry A.[8] and Ethel (Morey) Harris, from 1920 census:

    3 *Norma Harris*, b. Wash. ca. 1913.

  ii ELISHA DILLAZON HARRIS, b. Kans. 29 Nov. 1877, d. 1956, bur. Greenacres Memorial Park, Ferndale, Wash.[1490] He m. ca. 1901 ANNA JENSEN, b. Denmark ca. 1880,[1491] living with Elisha 1940. They were in King Co., Wash., in 1910, when Elisha was working in a saw mill.[1492] On 12 Sept. 1918, he registered at age 40 for the draft during World War II, giving his address as P.O. Winslow, Kitsap Co., Wash., and occupation as "dentist."[1493] By 1920 they had moved to Bellingham, where he had a belt making shop.[1494] In 1930 he had "his own business" as a "belt maker" in Bellingham,[1495] and in 1940 he was a "belt man" there in a lumber mill.[1496]

Children of Elisha Dillazon[8] and Anna (Jensen) Harris:

    1 *Julia*[9] *Harris*, b. Mo. ca. 1903, nurse in a hospital 1930.

    2 *Louise Harris*, b. Utah ca. 1906, public school teacher in 1930.

    3 *Leonora Harris*, b. Utah ca. 1907, stenographer with parents in 1940.

    4 *James Willard Harris*, b. Utah ca. 1909, belt maker "for his father" in 1930.

    5 *Naomi Harris*, b. King Co., Wash., 14 Sept. 1911,[1497] at home 1930.

    6 *Frances Harris*, b. Wash. ca. 1914, bookkeeper with parents in 1940.

    7 *Eliot David Harris*, b. Wash. ca. 1922, janitor with parents in 1940.

  iii JULIA PEARLE HARRIS, b. Kans. in April 1883, single and at home in 1910.

[1488] 1880 U.S. Census, Detroit, Wayne Co., Mich., E.D. 281, p. 33 (Ethel, age 1, in Edward S. and Ella M. Morey household).

[1489] World War I Draft Registration Card, no. 3666-52.

[1490] Inscription online at <www.findagrave.com>, accessed July 2010.

[1491] Anna's birthplace and date from census, surname from daughter Naomi's birth record.

[1492] 1910 U.S. Census, Tanner Precinct, Kings Co., Wash., E.D. 47, sheet 4B ("Alisha D. Harris," the entry indicating that Anna was the mother of four children, all then living).

[1493] World War I Draft Registration Card, no. 3072-A3018, stamped 46-1-8C, listing Anna Harris at same address as his nearest relative.

[1494] 1920 U.S. Census, Bellingham City, Ward 2, Whatcom Co., Wash., E.D. 221, sheet 1B.

[1495] 1930 U.S. Census, Bellingham City, Ward 2, Whatcom Co., Wash., E.D. 37-18, sheet 1B.

[1496] 1940 U.S. Census, Bellingham City, Whatcom Co., Wash., E.D. 37-10, sheet 1A.

[1497] Washington Births, 1907–1919, online at <www.Ancestry.com> (parents: Elisha Harris, Anna Jensen).

iv WALTER LESLIE HARRIS, b. Kans. 26 Nov. 1885, d. Kirkland, King Co., Wash., 25 Jan. 1937.[1498] He m. ca. 1912 FLORENCE M. ____, b. Minn. ca. 1887, living as widow in King Co. in 1940.[1499] Walter was single and with his parents in 1910, a "solderer" for Standard Oil Company. On 12 Sept. 1918, he registered at age 32 for the draft during World War II, giving his address as 5420 Barnes, Seattle, and occupation "belt maker."[1500] By 1920, he had his wife, Florence, and moved to Bellingham and, like his brother Elisha, had become a belt maker in his "own store."[1501] He was a carpenter for a belting company in Bellingham in 1930.[1502]

Children of Walter Leslie[8] and Florence M. (____) Harris, from 1920 and 1930 census:

1 *Robert R.[9] Harris*, "adopted son," b. Wash. ca. 1916 (age 14 in 1930).
2 *Warren E. Harris*, b. Wash. ca. 1917. In 1940, at age 23, he was working for a logging company at a camp in Polk Co., Oreg.[1503]

75 LEWIS FREDERICK[7] HARRIS (*Elisha[6], Joseph[5], Jeremiah[4], Daniel[3], Walter[2], John[1]*), born in Illinois 10 October 1848, died at Neal, Greenwood County, Kansas, on 2 August 1909 and buried in Neal Cemetery.[1504] He married in Greenwood County on 9 November 1872 **MYRA AMINA TURNEY**,[1505] born in Durand, Illinois, on 23 December 1855, who died in a Wichita, Kansas, hospital on 10 September 1919, but last residing in Eureka, Kansas. She was buried at Neal beside her husband. Her parents were Edwin and Martha J. (Caldwell) Turney of Durand,[1506] but living in Greenwood County in 1900.

At age 21, Lewis was still with his parents near Durand in 1870. By 1872 he moved to Greenwood County, where he appears in 1875,[1507] and in 1880 with his wife "Mira" and daughters Mattie and Lula Harris.[1508] On 14 January 1879, he had acquired title from the County to the SW¼ of Section 27, Township 25, Range 12, just north of Neal,[1509] where his brother William

---

[1498] Washington Death Certificates, 1907–1960, online at <www.FamilySearch.org>, giving parents' names as William E. Harris and Cora Heard, and spouse as Frances V. Harris.

[1499] 1940 U.S. Census, Cleveland Election Precinct, King Co., Wash., E.D.17-49, sheet 61A, stating that she had been living in Redmond, King Co., in 1935.

[1500] World War I Draft Registration Card, no. 240-914, stamped 46-1-10C, listing Florence Harris at same address as his nearest relative.

[1501] 1920 U.S. Census, Bellingham City, Ward 1, Whatcom Co., Wash., E.D. 209, sheet 4B.

[1502] 1930 U.S. Census, Bellingham City, Ward 1, Whatcom Co., Wash., E.D. 37-3, sheet 4A.

[1503] 1940 U.S. Census, Willamette Camp, Polk Co., Oreg., E.D. 27-48, sheet 2A, stating that he had been living in King Co., Wash., in 1935.

[1504] Gravestone inscription, Neal Cemetery.

[1505] Greenwood Co., Kans., Marriage Records, B:34.

[1506] Kansas State Death Certificate, Topeka, Kans.

[1507] 1875 Kansas State Census, Pleasant Grove Twp., P.O. Quincy, Greenwood Co., p. 15.

[1508] 1880 U.S. Census, Quincy Twp., Greenwood Co., Kans., E.D. 96, sheet 14.

[1509] Greenwood Co., Kans., Deeds, 15:964.

Eugene Harris and uncle Thomas Newell Robb settled.[1510] Lewis's household there in 1885 included his wife and three eldest children.[1511]

The 1900 census for Quincy Township, Neal Precinct, enumerated in a very legible hand by Lewis F. Harris himself, shows him with his wife Myra A. and daughter Hazel I. Harris, states that they had been married 27 years, and reports that Myra was mother of five children, all then living.[1512] In 1910, widow Myra A. Harris, "Postmistress, U.S. Post Office," and her daughter Hazel I. Harris were living in Quincy Township.[1513] The biography of Lewis's brother Elmer E. Harris states that Lewis had four daughters and a son.[1514] An obituary of his widow, Myra Harris, dated 18 September 1919, names five children: Mattie Boone of Glendale, California; Lulu Harris of Virgil, Kansas; Roy Harris of Seattle, Washington; Jessie Waddill of Colton, California; and Hazel Boone of Cartago, California.[1515]

Children of Lewis Frederick[7] and Myra Amina (Turney) Harris:

    i   MARTHA CHRISTINE ("MATTIE")[8] HARRIS, b. Ill. 23 Jan. 1874, d. San Bernardino, Calif., 15 March 1957;[1516] m. ca. 1908, as her 2nd husband,[1517] ISAAC MORGAN BOONE,[1518] b. Kans. 24 July 1880, d. San Bernardino 31 Dec. 1959.[1519] He was a rancher at Victorville in 1910 (when Mattie's sister Jessie was in their home), a carpenter at Glendale in 1920,[1520] and a carpenter in the motion picture industry in Los Angeles in 1930.[1521]

          Children of Isaac Morgan and Martha Christine[8] (Harris) Boone:

             1 *Lewis E. Boone*, b. Kans. ca. May 1909, still with parents in 1930, a bank filing clerk.

             2 *Leah L. Boone*, b. Kans. [*sic*] ca. 1911, still with parents in 1930.

    ii LULA B. HARRIS, b. Kans. in April 1876 and living in Virgil, Greenwood Co., Kans., in Jan. 1920;[1522] m. Neal, Greenwood Co., 23 Sept. 1896 EDWIN S.

[1510] Rowland, *Pioneers of Winnebago and Boone Counties*, 368.

[1511] 1885 Kansas State Census, Quincy Twp., P.O. Neal, Greenwood Co., p. 20.

[1512] 1900 U.S. Census, Neal Precinct, Quincy Twp., Greenwood Co., Kans., E.D. 58, sheet 1.

[1513] 1910 U.S. Census, Quincy Twp., Greenwood Co., Kans., E.D. 33, sheet 10A.

[1514] Church, *Past and Present of the City of Rockford and Winnebago County*, 291-92.

[1515] Gravestone photo and obituary transcription online at <www.findagrave.com>, accessed July 2010, citing *Eureka Herald*, 18 Sept. 1919, p. 1.

[1516] California Death Index, 1940–1997, online at <www.Ancestry.com>, accessed July 2010.

[1517] 1910 U.S. Census, Victorville, San Bernardino Co., Calif., E.D. 100, sheet 6B.

[1518] The 1910 census indicates that this was a second marriage for both Isaac and Mattie. Isaac M. Boone had m. Agnes L. McCready in Greenwood Co., Kans., on 29 Feb. 1904 (Greenwood Co., Kans., Marriage Records, F:138), but a prior marriage record for Mattie has not been found.

[1519] California Death Index, 1940–1997, online at <www.Ancestry.com>, accessed July 2010.

[1520] 1920 U.S. Census, Glendale City, Los Angeles Co., Calif., E.D. 22, sheet 10B.

[1521] 1930 U.S. Census, Los Angeles City, Los Angeles Co., Calif., E.D. 19-205, sheet 1B.

[1522] 1920 U.S. Census, Virgil, Lane Twp., Greenwood Co., Kans., E.D. 30, sheet 4.

HARRIS[1523] (unrelated), b. Kans. in Jan. 1867 and living at Virgil in 1920, son of George W. and Sarah (___) Harris of Greenwood Co.[1524] Edwin and Lula had moved to Virgil in Lane Twp. by 1910, where, in Sept. 1919, he provided information for his mother-in-law Myra A. Harris's death certificate.

Children of Edwin S. and Lula B.[8] (Harris) Harris, from 1900, 1910, 1915, and 1920 censuses, all b. in Kans.:

1 *Norma M. Harris*, b. April 1898.
2 *Iona E. Harris*, b. ca. 1905.
3 *Arthur S. Harris*, b. ca. 1913.

iii ROY M. HARRIS, b. Kans. 20 March 1882 (calc.), d. Seattle, Wash., 16 Feb. 1920, age 37y 10m 27d,[1525] bur. Sunset Hills Memorial Park, Bellevue, King Co., Wash.;[1526] m. ca. 1906 ESTELLA C. ____, b. Kans. ca. 1889, a widowed "lunch room manager" in 1930 residing in the Seattle home of her daughter Helen Bartee.

Child of Roy M.[8] and Estella C. (___) Harris, from census:

1 *Helen H.[9] Harris*, b. Wash. ca. 1908; m. ca. 1927 James W. Bartee, b. Tex. ca. 1903, living 1930.[1527]

iv JESSIE E. HARRIS, b. Kans. ca. 1890, d. before 1930 census date; m. ca. 1911 JAMES E. WADDILL, b. Tex. 6 June 1883, d. Los Angeles 12 Aug. 1965.[1528] Jessie was single, age 20, and a "law stenographer" boarding with her sister Mattie Boone's family in San Bernardino in 1910. She was with her husband Waddill at Colton, Calif., in 1919, but not found in 1920 census. In 1930, James Waddill, widower, age 47, was residing as "brother-in-law" in the home of Jessie's sister Hazel Boone in Tehama Co., Calif.[1529]

Child of James E. and Jessie E.[8] (Harris) Waddill:

1 *Leroy D. Waddill*, b. Calif. ca. 1912, with his father in 1930, age 18.

v HAZEL IRENE HARRIS, b. Kans. 18 July 1892, d. Tehama Co., Calif., 9 Dec. 1979;[1530] m. Greenwood Co. 1 May 1912 FRANK G. BOONE,[1531] b. Kans. 13

[1523] Greenwood Co., Kans., Marriage Records, E:91.

[1524] Edwin S. and Lula B. Harris are listed in the 1900 census on the same page and eleven doors away from Lewis Frederick Harris's household in Quincy Twp. Edwin's father George W. Harris (b. in Ill., parents b. in Tenn.) and his mother Sarah (b. in Mo.) came from Cowley Co., Kans., after 1880 and were living in Bachelor Twp., Greenwood Co., in 1900. Their children, as listed in 1880 and 1900 censuses, were: Mary A. Harris, b. Mo. in Nov. 1860; Finace W. Harris (a son), b. Kans. ca. 1862; Ida Harris, b. Kans. ca. 1863; Edwin S. Harris, b. Kans. in Jan. 1867; Eugene W. Harris, b. Kans. in June 1870; Jessie Harris (a dau.), b. Kans. in Aug. 1872; Hattie C. Harris, b. Kans. in Nov. 1874; Nettie P. Harris, b. Kans., in May 1877. Members of this Harris family owned land in Quincy Twp. adjoining properties owned by the unrelated brothers William Eugene and Lewis Frederick Harris considered in the present account.

[1525] Washington Death Certificates, 1907–1960, online at <www.FamilySearch.org>, accessed July 2010.

[1526] Inscription data online at <www.findagrave.com>, accessed July 2010.

[1527] 1930 U.S. Census, Seattle, King Co., Wash., E.D. 17-57, sheet 4A.

[1528] California Death Index, 1940–1997, online at <www.Ancestry.com>, accessed July 2010.

[1529] 1930 U.S. Census, Red Bluff Twp., Tehama Co., Calif., E.D. 52-20, sheet 4B (Frank G. Boone household).

[1530] California Death Index, 1940–1997, online at <www.Ancestry.com>, accessed July 2010.

May 1889, d. Tehama Co. 26 Sept. 1966.[1532] They were in Cartago, Calif.,
in 1919, but by 1930 had moved to Tehama Co. in northern Calif.[1533]
Children of Frank G. and Hazel Irene[8] (Harris) Boone (1930 census):
1 *Shirley M. Boone*, b. Kans. ca. 1914.
2 *Melvin F. Boone*, b. Kans. ca. 1915.
3 *Richard H. Boone*, b. Calif. ca. 1919.

76 ELMER E.[7] HARRIS (*Elisha⁶, Joseph⁵, Jeremiah⁴, Daniel³, Walter², John¹*),
born in Winnebago County, Illinois, on 23 July 1862, died in Bremerton,
Washington, on 3 December 1928.[1534] He married first on 11 April 1888
EVA A. PLACE, born 16 October 1868, who died on 23 December 1898,
daughter of John R. and Amanda (Morris) Place,[1535] whose farm was a half-
mile east of the farm of Elmer's father near Durand. He married second in
Winnebago County on 20 June 1900 **LOIS M. INGEBRITSON**,[1536] born in
Illinois on 14 January 1882 (calculated), who died at Bremerton on 7 April
1959, age 77y 2m 24d,[1537] daughter of Hawkins (or Haakon) and Lydia
(Gillam) Ingebritson of Durand.[1538] In April 1940, widow Lois Harris, age
58, was a housekeeper in a private home at Chico, Washington.[1539]

Elmer was at home with his parents in 1870 and 1880, but by 1892 he
was living with his young family on his father's "homestead." He was
chosen as Commissioner of Highways in the April 1899 Durand Township
election. He was still residing there in November 1907, when he buried a
son, but had moved to his Colorado fruit farm before April 1910, when his
household included "brother-in-law" Sherman Engebritson, a carpenter.[1540]
Elmer was living near Grand Junction, Colorado, in 1920, where he was a

---

[1531] Greenwood Co., Kans., Marriage Records, G:226.

[1532] California Death Index, 1940–1997, online at <www.Ancestry.com>, accessed July 2010.

[1533] 1930 U.S. Census, Red Bluff Twp., Tehama Co., Calif., E.D. 52-20, sheet 4B (Frank G. Boone household).

[1534] Washington Death Certificates, 1907–1960, online at <www.FamilySearch.org>, accessed July 2010.

[1535] Elmer E. Harris and John R. Place biographies in Church, *Past and Present of the City of Rockford and Winnebago County*, 291-92, 662.

[1536] Winnebago Co., Ill., Marriage Records, license no. 235.

[1537] Washington Death Certificates, 1907–1960, online at <www.FamilySearch.org>, accessed July 2010.

[1538] Elmer E. Harris biography in Church, *Past and Present of the City of Rockford and Winnebago County*, 291-92; and data from Barbara Winchester of Durand, 23 Jan. 1984.

[1539] 1940 U.S. Census, Chico, Kitsap Co., Wash., E.D. 18-29, sheet 11A (Eugene Fahey household), stating that she had been residing in Bremerton in 1935.

[1540] 1910 U.S. Census, Precinct 1, Mesa Co., Colo., E.D. 89, sheet 3B.

fruit farmer.[1541] He apparently was still in Colorado about 1925 (birthplace of youngest child, Shirley), but in 1930 his widow, Lois M. Harris, then an "ironer" at a laundry, was residing with the children in Bremerton.[1542]

Children of Elmer E.[7] and Eva A. (Place) Harris, from his 1905 biography:

    i   BESSIE A. L.[8] HARRIS, b. Ill. 18 Sept. 1889, with father in Colo. in 1910, age 19.

    ii LLOYD E. HARRIS, b. Ill. 28 Feb. 1893, d. 2 Nov. 1907, bur. Durand Cemetery.

    iii EVA IRENE HARRIS, b. 26 Nov. 1897, d. of "cholera infantum" 11 Sept. 1898, bur. Durand Cemetery.[1543]

Children of Elmer E.[7] and Lois M. (Ingebritson) Harris, from the 1910, 1920, and 1930 census entries:

    iv WAYNE JESSE HARRIS, b. Ill. 8 Sept. 1903, d. Bremerton, Wash., 7 Oct. 1978, age 75.[1544] He was a "clerk" in a Post Office at Bremerton, Wash., in 1930, when he and his wife were residing in his mother's home. He had m. ca. 1926 MAUDE BROUSE, b. Colo. ca. 1906.

         On 27 Jan. 1939, Wayne Jesse Harris, a resident of Bremerton, Wash., occupation "clerk," was arrested in Denver for postal embezzlement. He was convicted in Seattle on 13 March 1939 and sentenced to 15 months in the U.S. Penitentiary on McNeil Island.[1545] He was released and was working as a rigger in dry-dock construction by April 1940, when he and his wife Maude's household in Bremerton included daughter Patricia, age 8, and brother-in-law Alfred Brouse, age 26, b. Colo.[1546]

    v   EDNA H. HARRIS, b. Ill. ca. 1907, at home in Jan. 1920, aged 13, not with mother in 1930.

    vi MARY F. HARRIS, b. Colo. ca. 1910, with mother in 1930, aged 20, "bookkeeper" in a bakery. She m. by ca. 1933 (birth of first child) JACK SAMALA, b. Wash. ca. 1906, a baker with whom she was living in Chico, Wash., in 1940. Their household then included children Donald N., age 7, Anita J., age 4, Mary Lou, age 2, and "sister-in-law" Shirley A. Harris, age 15, b. Colo.[1547]

[1541] 1920 U.S. Census, Grand Ave. Road, Precinct 1, Mesa Co., Colo., E.D. 86, sheet 4A. See also biography of Elmer's brother Jessie F. Harris, in *Historical Encyclopedia of Illinois and History of Winnebago County*, 2:1081.

[1542] 1930 U.S. Census, Bremerton City, Kitsap Co., Wash., E.D. 18-8, sheet 15A. A letter of Guy Earl Wescott, of Alma, Nebr., to Mrs. Fred Fassett, Stevensville, Pa., 19 Feb. 1937 states: "I am writing to this half brother [step brother] and cousin of mother's in Colorado to find out what I can of the Harrises." Apparently, Guy was not informed that this cousin [probably Elmer] had died a decade before.

[1543] Letter of Barbara Winchester, 23 Jan. 1984.

[1544] Social Security Death Index, SSN 533-14-7513.

[1545] McNeil Island Penitentiary Records of Prisoners Received, 1887–1951, National Archives Microfilm Publication M1619, Records of the Bureau of Prisons, Record Group 129, roll 4, register no. 14069.

[1546] 1940 U.S. Census, Bremerton, Kitsap Co., Wash., E.D. 18-25, sheet 11A, stating that they had been residing in the "same place" in 1935.

[1547] 1940 U.S. Census, Chico, Kitsap Co., Wash., E.D. 18-29, sheet 11A, stating that they had been residing in Bremerton in 1935.

vii ELMER E. HARRIS Jr., b. Colo. ca. 1913, d. Bremerton, Kitsap Co., Wash., 19 Aug. 1970.[1548] He was with his mother in 1930, aged 17, apprentice in a navy yard. He m. ca. 1934 MARGARET ____, b. Wash. ca. 1915, d. Bremerton 25 April 1976, age 61.[1549] She was with him in Kitsap Co. in 1940, when he was working as a pipe fitter in a navy yard. Their household then included a son Jerry, age 5, and daughter Susan age 2m.[1550]

viii GLENN W. HARRIS, b. Colo. ca. 1914, with mother in 1930, aged 16. In 1940, Glenn W. Harris, age 26, b. Colo., no. 10787, was in the Washington State Reformatory, the record indicating that he was living in Bremerton in 1935.[1551]

ix LYDIA HARRIS, b. Colo. ca. 1916, with mother in 1930, aged 14.

x SHIRLEY A. HARRIS, b. Colo. ca. 1925, with mother in April 1930, aged 5. In 1940, at age 15, she was listed as "sister-in-law" in her sister Mary F. Samala's home in Chico, Wash.

77 CHAUNCY E.[7] HARRIS (*Erastus*[6], *Joseph*[5], *Jeremiah*[4], *Daniel*[3], *Walter*[2], *John*[1]), born in Iowa in 1856, died in 1925 and is buried in Shell City Cemetery, Wadena County, Minnesota. He married first at Park Rapids, Hubbard County, Minnesota, 2 September 1883, **LOUCIA A. (STOMBAUGH) CARTER**, Justice Buck presiding.[1552] She was born in Wisconsin on 2 September 1849 and died in Wadena County on 7 November 1900, daughter of Jacob and Sarah (Stewart) Stombaugh.[1553] Chauncy married secondly in Hubbard County on 30 June 1910 **SUSAN (____) SMITH**, born in Wisconsin about 1857 and living in Park Rapids, Hubbard County, in January 1920, when she was residing in a rented house with her unmarried "son" Clarence A. Smith, born in Wisconsin about 1883.[1554]

Chauncy may have been the first one of this Harris family group to settle in Minnesota. No doubt he was the Chauncy Harris, aged 22 [*sic*], born in "Iowa," who in 1880 was working on the farm of William E. Kindred in Wing River Township, Wadena County.[1555] The 1900 census for Shell River Township, Wadena County, shows Chauncy's household next to that of his brother Plinn Erastus, that he was a farmer, and that his wife Loucia was

---

[1548] Washington Death Index, 1940–1996, online at <www.Ancestry.com>.

[1549] Washington Death Index, 1940–1996, online at <www.Ancestry.com>.

[1550] 1940 U.S. Census, Snyder Election Precinct, Kitsap Co., Wash., E.D. 18-63, sheet 16B, stating that they had been residing in Bremerton in 1935.

[1551] 1940 U.S. Census, Washington State Reformatory, Park Place, Snohomish Co., Wash., E.D. 31-138, sheet 2B.

[1552] *Park Rapids Enterprise*, 7 Sept. 1883 (she was "Mrs. Lou Carter"; her prior husband has not been identified).

[1553] Gravestone, Shell City Cemetery; Wadena Co. Death Records, Wadena, Minn. Her death record states the year of her birth as 1850, but it appears as 1849 on her gravestone and in the 1900 census.

[1554] 1920 U.S. Census, Park Rapids Village, Hubbard Co., Minn., E.D. 145, sheet 12B.

[1555] 1880 U.S. Census, Wing River Twp., Wadena Co., Minn., E.D. 180, house 35; Chauncy's parents were both reportedly born in "N.Y."

mother of five children, four then living.[1556] In 1910, Chauncy E. Harris, "bother-in-law," and his son Adrian E. Harris, "nephew," were residing in Hubbard with Chauncy's sister Julia B. Wynn and husband. Chauncy's occupation at that time was "Salesman-Traveling."[1557] He is said to have "peddled Watkins Remedy for many years."[1558]

In January 1920, Chauncy Harris, described as a widower, was residing on a "rented farm" in Griggs County, North Dakota, with his son Adrian Harris and family.[1559]

Children of Chauncy E.[7] and Lucia A. (Stombaugh) (Carter) Harris, listed in 1900:[1560]

    i   LIZZIE A.[8] HARRIS, b. Iowa in Dec. 1883, living in 1900.[1561]
   ii   LOUANA MARIE HARRIS, b. Wadena Co., Minn., 1 April 1886, living with her parents in 1900.
  iii   ADRIAN EARL HARRIS, b. Wadena Co., Minn., 27 May 1890, living Bemidji, Minn., in 1940, age 49;[1562] m. by 1914 GLADYS E. JOHNSON, b. Minn. ca. 1897, living with Adrian in 1940. In 1910, Adrian and his father were residing in Hubbard with Adrian's aunt Julia B. Wynn and family. On 5 June 1918, Adrian registered for the draft, giving his address as Huntersville, Minn., married with three children, and engaged in farming.[1563]

        In 1920, Adrian, his wife, and their first four children were farming with his father in Griggs Co., N.Dak. By 1930, they were back in Minn., where he was working in Bemidji as a carpenter in an electric plant.[1564] They were still there in 1940, when he was a laborer working in "WPA building construction."[1565]

        Children of Adrian Earl[8] and Gladys E. (Johnson) Harris, nos. 1, 2, 3, and 5 recorded Hubbard Co., others based on census entries cited above:

    1 *Edna Mae*[9] *Harris*, b. 11 June 1914, with parents 1920, 1930.
    2 *Harvey Chauncy Harris*, b. 23 Sept. 1915, with parents 1920, 1930, 1940.
    3 *Woodrow Earl Harris*, b. 7 April 1917, with parents 1920, 1930.
    4 *Willis A. Harris*, b. ca. 1819, with parents 1820, 1830, 1840.

[1556] 1900 U.S. Census, Shell River Twp., Wadena Co., Minn., E.D. 210, sheet 3.

[1557] 1910 U.S. Census, Hubbard Twp., Hubbard Co., Minn., E.D. 78, sheet 4B.

[1558] As related to the writer by Mr. Bill Branham of Hubbard, 1978.

[1559] 1920 U.S. Census, Rosendal Twp., Griggs Co., N.Dak., E.D. 124, sheet 5B.

[1560] The census indicates that Lucia was the mother of two other children, one living and one dead, but their father could as well have been her former husband, Carter.

[1561] This child was listed in the next-door household of Chauncy's brother Plinn Erastus Harris in 1900, plainly not his daughter and with "occupation" listed as "labor" (1900 U.S. Census, Shell River Twp., Wadena Co., Minn., E.D. 210, sheet 3).

[1562] 1940 U.S. Census, Bemidji, Beltrami Co., Minn., E.D. 4-7, sheet 3A-3B.

[1563] World War I Draft Registration Card, no. 411, Shell River Precinct, Wadena Co.

[1564] 1930 U.S. Census, Bemidji, Beltrami Co., Minn., E.D. 4-7, sheet 4B.

[1565] 1940 U.S. Census, Bemidji, Beltrami Co., Minn., E.D. 4-7, sheet 3A-3B.

5 *Veda May Harris*, b. Beltrami Co. 5 Sept. 1920,[1566] with parents 1930.
6 A daughter, b. 17 Feb. 1922, prob. *Evelyn E. Harris*, b. ca. 1922, with parents 1930, 1940.
7 *Mildred Lucille Harris*, b. Beltrami Co. 4 April 1924,[1567] with parents 1930, 1940.
8 *Nyna Marie Harris*, b. Beltrami Co. 28 Oct. 1926,[1568] with parents 1940.
9 *Henry L. Harris*, b. ca. 1930, with parents 1940.
10 *Darlene Luana Harris*, b. Beltrami Co. 4 July 1933, with parents 1940.
11 *Clarence D. Harris*, b. ca. 1936, with parents 1940.
12 *Silvey J. Harris*, b. ca. 1938, with parents 1940.

78 PLINN ERASTUS[7] HARRIS (*Erastus[6], Joseph[5], Jeremiah[4], Daniel[3], Walter[2], John[1]*), born in Iowa (1860 census) or in Illinois (later censuses and death record) on 3 November 1858, died on 7 July 1933 and is buried in Shell City Cemetery, Wadena County, Minnesota. He married in Hubbard County, Minnesota, on 20 February 1887, **MARY MUNISTER** (also Minster), born in Minnesota on 11 October 1870, who died on 10 February 1924, daughter of Martin and Olive (Campbell) Munister.[1569]

Plinn E. Harris was in Hubbard County by September 1886, when he purchased property from Angus R. Macfarlane.[1570] He later lived "one-half mile south of Shell City [in Wadena County] on the west side of the road."[1571] Plinn's household is found in Shell River Township, Wadena County, at the time of the 1895 (State), and 1900, 1910, 1920, and 1930 U.S. censuses. In 1900, his wife Mary was stated to be mother of six children, all then living,[1572] and in 1910 the mother of nine children, all living.[1573] In 1930, the household in Shell River of the widower "Flynn" Harris, age 69 [*sic*], included four children still at home and was enumerated between those of his sons-in-law Walter Wynn and Henry Wynn.[1574]

Children of Plinn Erastus[7] and Mary (Munister) Harris, all born in Minnesota, as read from the 1895 through 1930 census schedules:

i   DORA BELLE[8] HARRIS, b. Minn. 2 Feb. 1888, d. 24 Sept. 1918.[1575]

[1566] Birth Certificate Index, Minnesota Historical Soc., online at <http://people.mnhs.org/bci/Results. cfm>.
[1567] Birth Certificate Index, Minnesota Historical Soc., online at <http://people.mnhs.org/bci/Results. cfm>.
[1568] Birth Certificate Index, Minnesota Historical Soc., online at <http://people.mnhs.org/bci/Results. cfm>.
[1569] Wadena Co., Minn., Death Records.
[1570] Hubbard Co., Minn., Deeds, D2:237.
[1571] Mr. Bill Branham of Hubbard, 1978.
[1572] 1900 U.S. Census, Shell River Twp., Wadena Co., Minn., E.D. 210, sheet 3.
[1573] 1910 U.S. Census, Shell River Twp., Wadena Co., Minn., p. 21, house 141.
[1574] 1930 U.S. Census, Shell River Twp., Wadena Co., Minn., E.D. 80-14, sheet 1A.
[1575] Gravestone, Shell City Cemetery, and Wadena Co. Death Records.

ii OLIVE M. HARRIS, b. Minn. 23 July 1890, d. 28 May 1965, bur. Shell City Cemetery, Wadena Co.;[1576] m. Wadena Co. 14 Dec. 1908 WALTER EDWARD WYNN,[1577] b. Minn. 24 April 1888, d. 19 March 1947, bur. beside Olive.

Children of Walter Edward and Olive M.[8] (Harris) Wynn, b. Minn.:[1578]

1 *James Clinton Wynn*, b. Wadena Co. 2 Oct. 1909, d. Hubbard Co. 28 Nov. 1929,[1579] with parents 1910, 1920.

2 *Verlina Maria Wynn*, b. Wadena Co. 5 July 1912,[1580] with parents 1920, 1930.

3 *Edward Plinn Wynn*, b. 12 July 1919, d. Wadena Co., 12 March 1992,[1581] with parents 1920, 1930.

4 *Walter Wynn*, b. ca. 1921, with parents 1930.

5 *Laurel Wynn*, b. ca. 1926, with parents 1930.

iii LULA AMIDA HARRIS, b. Minn. Oct. 1893, d. 1971, bur. Pine Ridge Cemetery, Pine River, Minn.;[1582] m. Wadena Co. 23 March 1911, JOHN HENRY WYNN,[1583] b. Minn. 6 May 1886, d. 22 Feb. 1961, bur Pine Ridge Cemetery.

Children of John Henry and Lula Amida[8] (Harris) Wynn, b. Minn.:[1584]

1 *Evelyn Lavinia Wynn*, b. Wadena Co. 5 Jan. 1912,[1585] with parents 1920, 1930.

2 *Jessie May Wynn*, b. Wadena Co. 28 April 1914,[1586] with parents 1920.

3 *Mary Wynn*, b. ca. 1917, with parents 1920, 1930.

4 *[name unclear]*, "daughter," b. ca. 1920, with parents 1930.

5 *Lloyd Wynn*, b. ca. 1922, with parents 1930.

6 *Margaret Wynn*, b. ca. 1925, with parents 1930.

7 *Allen Wynn*, b. ca. 1827, with parents 1930.

8 *Grant Wynn*, b. ca. 1828, with parents 1930.

9 *Robert Wynn*, b. ca. Nov. 1929, with parents 1930.

iv WILLIAM E. HARRIS, b. Minn. 10 Dec. 1894, d. 29 April 1968,[1587] living with his father in 1930, age 35.

v DELLA E. HARRIS, b. 1897 and living with parents in 1920.[1588]

vi LURIDA M. HARRIS, b. April 1900, living with parents in 1920.

[1576] Gravestone, Shell City Cemetery.

[1577] Wadena Co., Minn., Marriage Records.

[1578] From 1910 and 1920 Orton Twp., and 1930 Shell River Twp. census entries, Wadena Co., Minn., except where indicated.

[1579] Birth and Death Certificate Indexes, Minnesota Historical Society, online at <http://people. mnhs.org>.

[1580] Birth Certificate Index, Minnesota Historical Soc., online at <http://people.mnhs.org/bci/Results. cfm>.

[1581] Death Certificate Index, Minnesota Historical Soc., online at <http://people.mnhs.org/dci/Results.cfm>.

[1582] Gravestone photo online at <www.findagrave.com>, accessed July 2010.

[1583] Wadena Co., Minn., Marriage Records.

[1584] From 1920 Orton Twp. and 1930 Shell River Twp. census entries, Wadena Co., Minn., except where indicated.

[1585] Birth Certificate Index, Minnesota Historical Soc., online at http://people.mnhs.org/bci/Results.cfm>.

[1586] Birth Certificate Index, Minnesota Historical Soc., online at <http://people.mnhs.org/bci/Results.cfm>.

[1587] Gravestone, Shell City Cemetery, with marker: "PFC COM 363 Infantry, W.W. I."

[1588] 1920 U.S. Census, Shell River Twp., Wadena Co., Minn., E.D. 245, sheet 12A.

    vii   LAUREL ASHTON HARRIS, b. 28 Aug. 1902, living with his father in 1930, age 27, d. 20 Oct. 1969 and buried beside his brothers William E. and Harry Ulysses Harris in Shell City Cemetery, his stone inscribed "PVT U.S. Army, W.W. II."

   viii   HARRY ULYSSES HARRIS, b. 25 Aug. 1905, living with father in 1930, age 24, d. 31 Jan. 1935.[1589]

    ix   CORA LUELLA HARRIS, b. 9 Nov. 1907,[1590] living with parents in 1920.

     x   PEARL LAVERTTA HARRIS, b. 19 May 1910,[1591] living with parents in 1920.

    xi   BLANCHE HARRIS, b. 17 Aug. 1912,[1592] living with father in 1930, age 17.

79 ERWIN EUGENE[7] HARRIS (*Erastus[6], Joseph[5], Jeremiah[4], Daniel[3], Walter[2], John[1]*), sometimes "Irwin," born in Wisconsin in October 1868, was living in Los Angeles, California, in 1930, age 62.[1593] He was "of Wadena County" when he married at Hubbard, Minnesota, on 26 August 1893 **ALIDA S. BENHAM** "of Hubbard," born in Quebec, Canada, in July 1872,[1594] living in Los Angeles, California, in 1932, daughter of Solomon R. and Sophia (Persons) Benham.[1595]

In 1895, Erwin and Alida were residing in Shell River Township, Wadena County.[1596] On 25 October 1899, Erwin bought property from Ira Benham in Todd's Addition in Brighton (later named Hubbard). In 1906, he bought land in Section 29 from Mark and Rose E. Wynn, which he sold in 1908 to C. H. Smith.[1597] The 1900 census for Hubbard Township shows that Erwin was then a "farm laborer" and that his wife Alida was mother of two children, both living.[1598] They had moved to Park Rapids, Hubbard County, by 1910, where it was recorded that Alida was mother of five children, all then living.[1599] By 1920 they had moved about 40 miles north to Bemidji, Minnesota, where he was working in a box factory.[1600] Erwin was unem-

---

[1589] Gravestone, Shell City Cemetery, and Wadena Co. Birth and Death Records.

[1590] Wadena Co., Minn., Birth Records, probably the female child whose name appears as "Daisy" (?), aged 4, in the 1910 census.

[1591] Wadena Co., Minn., Birth Records.

[1592] Wadena Co., Minn., Birth Records.

[1593] 1930 U.S. Census, Montebello Twp., Los Angeles Co., Calif., E.D. 10-1186, sheet 19A.

[1594] *Park Rapids Enterprise*, 8 Sept. 1893; Hubbard Co., Minn., Marriage Records, showing that they also witnessed there in June 1910 the second marriage of Erwin's brother Chauncy E. Harris.

[1595] Obituary of Solomon R. Benham, who died in Hubbard on 22 Jan. 1932, names, among others, his deceased wife Sophia (Persons) and surviving daughter, "Mrs. Alida Harris of Los Angeles, California" (undated newspaper clipping transcribed by Darryl Hensel, Hubbard County Genealogical Society).

[1596] 1895 Minnesota State Census, Shell River Twp., Wadena Co., p. 5, online at <www.FamilySearch.org>.

[1597] Hubbard Co., Minn., Deeds, D11:363; D17:366; D22:562.

[1598] 1900 U.S. Census, Hubbard Twp., Hubbard Co., Minn., E.D. 72, sheet 9.

[1599] 1910 U.S. Census, Park Rapids Village, Hubbard Co., Minn., E.D. 80, sheet 15.

[1600] 1920 U.S. Census, Bemidji, Beltrami Co., Minn., E.D. 27, sheet 2B.

ployed in Los Angeles at the time of the 1930 census, but Alida was working there as a cook in a restaurant.

Children of Erwin Eugene[7] and Alida S. (Benham) Harris, b. Minn.:[1601]

   i VERA MERLE[8] HARRIS, b. 26 March 1894; m. LAURENCE MCKEE, b. "N.S." ca. 1893. They were living with her parents at Bemidji in 1920.
   ii BIRDIE HARRIS, b. Feb. 1896, with parents 1900, 1910.
   iii LETHA E. HARRIS, b. 21 May 1901, with parents 1910.
   iv ELNA/ALNA JANE HARRIS, b. 7 June 1907, with parents 1910, 1920.
   v JUNE E. HARRIS, b. ca. June 1909, with parents in 1910 (age 10m that April), 1920, and 1930.

80 ERNEST VICTOR[7] HARRIS (*Edgar Eggleston[6], Joseph[5], Jeremiah[4], Daniel[3], Walter[2], John[1]*), born in Durand, Winnebago County, Illinois, on 15 August 1865 (possibly 1866),[1602] died in Stroud, Lincoln County, Oklahoma, on 20 January 1933.[1603] He married at Opal, Woodward County, Oklahoma Territory, on 8 February 1903, **LAURA APALINE PIKE**,[1604] born in Arkansas City, Kansas, on 26 October 1885,[1605] who died in Baxter Springs, Kansas, on 10 August 1964,[1606] but buried in her parents' lot in Stroud Cemetery. She was a daughter of Francis Ion and Emma Lisa (Spruill) Pike of Tangier, Woodward County, Oklahoma Territory. Laura married second on 11 January 1946 Fred Bigelo Long,[1607] born Tenfield [*sic*: Penfield Township, Lorain County], Ohio, 8 December 1873, died in Woodward, Oklahoma, on

---

[1601] Hubbard Co., Minn., Birth Records (first 4 children), and 1895 through 1930 census entries cited. Their household in Los Angeles in 1930 included a "granddaughter" Elsie L. H. Kidder, age 9, b. Minn.

[1602] A handwritten family record kept by Ernest's wife Laura (provided by their son Delbert Leonard Harris of Oklahoma City) shows Ernest's year of birth as 1873, the year implied also in their marriage record. That date is plainly wrong, however. Ernest V. Harris appears at age four in his parents' home at Durand at the time of the 1870 census, at age fourteen in his sister Ida's home in Beatrice, Nebr., in 1880, at age 18 in Orleans, Nebr., in 1885, and his own affidavit in Feb. 1901 at Orleans in support of his great-uncle Calvin Bowman's Civil War pension application states that he was then aged 35. The derived year 1865 is consistent with his obvious relative age—a small lad—in a photograph (undated but near 1870) of his parents' elder children, the two youngest born in 1870 and 1872 not included. Ernest evidently was not yet born at the time of an enumeration of his parents' household taken at Durand on 3 July 1865 (1865 Ill. State Census, Howard, Winnebago Co., Ill., p. 44).

[1603] State of Oklahoma Death Certificate; Gravestone, Stroud Cemetery.

[1604] Woodward Co., Okla., Marriage License, Woodward, Okla. Laura's parents signed as witnesses; she gave her age as 17 years and Ernest, 29 years, understating it by eight years. Oklahoma Territory attained statehood four years later, in 1907.

[1605] Family record of Laura Apaline (Pike) Harris.

[1606] Obituary, Mrs. Laura Long, *The Joplin [Missouri] Globe*, 11 Aug. 1964. She d. in Baxter Springs, Kans., and "had lived in Columbus, Kan., after moving there from Woodward, Okla., earlier this year."

[1607] The year is 1944 in Holt, "Francis Ion Pike–Emma Liza Spruill Family Record," but 1946 in Laura' own family record.

23 October 1963, buried McLung Cemetery, May, Oklahoma,[1608] son of
Samuel and Sarah M. (—) Long.[1609]

"When he was 14 years old"—about 1879—Ernest Victor Harris "went to
Omaha and Orleans, Nebraska, were he grew to manhood."[1610] At the time
of the 1880 census he was residing at age 14 with his sister Ida Pemberton in
Beatrice, Nebraska.[1611] Ernest arrived in Orleans, Nebraska, about 1883,
perhaps at or about the same time his father arrived there after his divorce
from Ernest's mother in Spencer, Iowa, in September 1882. An uncle of
Ernest's mother, Calvin Bowman, had homesteaded near Orleans in 1872,
but since 1880 he had been engaged in the manufacture of plows and
wagons in a building that he and a partner, Michael Manning, had erected
for that purpose in Orleans.[1612]

In June 1885, his age then stated as eighteen years, Ernest was residing
near Orleans with the Charles A. Bennett family, his occupation listed as
"Works in Stable."[1613] Bennett, a livery keeper, was his younger sister
Maud's future father-in-law. Ernest was "farming" near Orleans in 1897
when his sister Addie Wescott came from Chicago to briefly reside with
him.[1614] On 23 February 1901, E. V. Harris, stating his age as 35 years and
that he had "lived in Orleans, Nebraska, 18 years," signed an affidavit supporting Calvin Bowman's Civil War pension claim.[1615]

On 13 September 1902, Ernest V. Harris, then "of Woodward, O.T.,"
filed application for a homestead near Tangier, Woodward County, Oklahoma Territory.[1616] Next February, he married his neighbor's seventeen-
year-old daughter, Laura A. Pike. He "proved" his claim on 8 April 1909,
his father-in-law Francis I. Pike witnessing. The drought of 1910, however,
caused crop failures sufficient to force Ernest and Laura to abandon the
homestead venture. By deeds dated 16 and 18 July 1910, Ernest V. and
Laura A. Harris traded their 160-acre homestead for a lot in "the Town of

[1608] Fred B. Long obituary clipping, newspaper not indicated.
[1609] 1880 U.S. Census, Oberlin Village, Lorain Co., Ohio, E.D. 181, p. 24.
[1610] Notes from obituary of Ernest Victor Harris, provided by Miss Bess V. Gleason, Manhattan, Kans. Ernest was with his parents at Durand in 1870, aged 4, but missing from the census of their household at Spencer, Iowa, in 1880, and found instead, age 14, in his sister Ida's home in Beatrice, Nebr.
[1611] 1880 U.S. Census, Beatrice, Gage Co., Nebr., E.D. 347, p. 86A (Leander Pemberton household).
[1612] Biographical sketch, Calvin Bowman, in A. T. Andreas, *History of the State of Nebraska* (Chicago: Western Historical Co., 1882), transcription by Connie Snyder online at <www.kancoll.org/books/-andreas_ne/harlan/harlan-p3.htma#orbios>, accessed 7 May 2006).
[1613] 1885 Nebraska State Census, Orleans Twp., Harlan Co., E.D. 392, p. 13.
[1614] Correspondence from Addie's granddaughter, Gwen Alice (Gleason) Haney of Concordia, Kans.
[1615] Pension file WC-528-211, National Archives, Washington, D.C.
[1616] Homestead Application no. 13014, National Archives and Records Administration.

Woodward."[1617] They moved to Stroud, Lincoln County, Oklahoma, by October 1912 (birthplace of fifth child), their residence in March 1914 when they sold their lot in Woodward.[1618]

On 12 September 1918, during World War I, Ernest registered for the draft at Chandler, Oklahoma, giving his birth date as 15 August 1873 [*sic*], height "tall," build "medium," eyes "blue," hair "brown," present address as Stroud, Oklahoma, and occupation as "farmer."[1619] In January 1920, Ernest, a "farmer," his wife Laura, and their first six sons were residing in a "rented" house in Lincoln County.[1620] In 1940, widow Laura Harris, age 54, was residing in a rented house in Stroud with her three youngest children.[1621] Through Laura, the descendants of Ernest and Laura Harris have a traceable descent from Edward I of England and his wife Marguerite of France.[1622]

Children of Ernest Victor[7] and Laura Apaline (Pike) Harris, the first three born at Tangier, the fourth probably at Woodward, and the rest at Stroud, Okla.:[1623]

   i   CLARENCE LINLEY[8] HARRIS, b. 22 May 1904, d. Columbus, Kans., 17 Feb. 1983; m. Stroud, Okla., 19 Nov. 1924 THELMA ELIZABETH NEWTON, b. Stroud, Okla., 11 Aug. 1905, d. Columbus, Kans., 29 June 2003. Clarence was employed in Stroud in 1940 as a roustabout in an asphalt refinery.[1624]

      Child of Clarence Linley[8] and Thelma Elizabeth (Newton) Harris:

        1 *Wilma Marie[9] Harris*, b. Stroud, Okla., 16 Jan. 1930; m. Columbus, Kans., 24 Jan. 1951 Robert E. Howard, b. 16 March 1930, d. Joplin, Mo., 1 April 1997.

   ii ERNEST FRANCIS HARRIS, b. 2 Oct. 1906, d. Upland, Calif., 27 Aug. 1998; m. (1) MARY GIBBS, (2) by 1935 ELMA KAISER, (3) Yuma, Ariz., 14 March 1940 NAOMI HUNTER, b. near Tulsa, Okla., 22 Nov. 1919. Ernest was employed in El Centro, Calif., in 1940 as a truck driver for a trucking company, the record showing that he was in Riverside, Calif., in 1935.[1625]

      Children of Ernest Francis[7] and Naomi (Hunter) Harris:

        1 *Gail Frances[9] Harris*, b. 16 Oct. 1940; m. (1) Walter Don Cracroft, (2) Pascual Sarabousquis Bailon, b. 18 Jan. 1945.

[1617] Woodward Co., Okla., Deeds, 25:198, 199.

[1618] Woodward Co., Okla., Deeds, 32:532. A map provided by Delbert Leonard Harris shows the locations of thirteen different houses occupied by this family in and around Stroud from about 1911 to 1933.

[1619] World War I Draft Registration Card, no. 3488-A1744, stamped 35-3-23-C, listing Laura A. Harris of Stroud as nearest relative.

[1620] 1920 U.S. Census, North Keokuk Twp., Lincoln Co., Okla., E.D. 116, sheet 5B.

[1621] 1940 U.S. Census, Stroud City, Lincoln Co., Okla., E.D. 41-39, sheet 14A.

[1622] Leaman Don Harris, "Historic Ancestors: John Paulet," *The Genealogist* 17 (2003):65-67, and references cited therein.

[1623] Unless otherwise stated, data are from the family record of Laura Apaline (Pike) Harris, provided by Delbert Leonard Harris. Additional details may be found in Shuster, *The Fassett Genealogy*, 205-7.

[1624] 1940 U.S. Census, Stroud City, Lincoln Co., Okla., E.D. 41-39, sheet 19A.

[1625] 1940 U.S. Census, El Centro City, Imperial Co., Calif., E.D. 13-16, sheet 2B.

        2 *Diane Mildred Harris*, b. 4 Oct. 1941; m. Larry Dale Elenburg, b. 1
        June 1940, divorced.
        3 *Sandra Joyce Harris*, b. b. 16 Oct. 1944; m. (1) Joseph Michael
        Lynch, b. 11 Jan. 1943, (2) Frank Mead, b. 28 Aug. 1938, (3) Los
        Angeles 23 Dec. 1979 Norman C. Gere, b. ca. 1940.[1626]
        4 *Victoria Noreen Harris*, b. 28 Feb. 1950, d. Aug. 2005; m. (1) ____ ____,
        (2) ____ Fox.
iii ALBERT ION HARRIS, b. 29 Aug. 1908, d. Cunningham, Kans., 5 Aug. 1966; m.
    Kingman, Kans., 29 April 1934 CARMEN ANGELINE WATERS, b. Preston,
    Kans., 31 July 1913, d. Oklahoma City., Okla., 10 Jan. 2000, dau. of Isaac
    Pingry and Della Alaretta (Crick) Waters. She m. (2) Newkirk, Okla., 18
    Nov. 1969 Ercel G. Reed, b. Benton, Kans., 12 Nov. 1913, d. Towanda,
    Kans., by his own hand 22 April 1989, son of Ruby C. and Jennie E. (____)
    Reed. Albert was employed in Cunningham in 1940, the record showing
    that he was in Riverside, Calif., in 1935.[1627]
        Children of Albert Ion[8] and Carmen Angeline (Waters) Harris:
        1 *Gale Ion[9] Harris*, b. Arlington, Calif., 7 Aug. 1935; m. Cunningham,
        Kans., 31 March 1956 Bonnie Jean Hazlett, b. Alva, Okla., 19 Oct.
        1936.
        2 *Leaman Don Harris*, b. Cunningham, Kans., 31 Dec. 1937; m. St.
        Paul, Minn., 20 Aug. 1966 Judith Louise Komives, b. St. Paul 28
        Sept. 1941.
        3 *Rex Layne Harris*, b. Cunningham, Kans., 3 Jan. 1950, d. Pratt, Kans.,
        29 March 2004; m. Cunningham 23 April 1978 Carol Louise Parry.
iv LEWIS MONROE HARRIS, b. 20 Sept. 1910, d. Stroud, Okla., 28 Oct. 1920.
v EMMA MARIE HARRIS, b. 22 Oct. 1912, d. Stroud, Okla., 27 Sept. 1915.
v LAUREN VICTOR HARRIS, b. 29 Jan. 1915, d. auto accident Porterville, Calif., 5
    Aug. 1997;[1628] m. (1) in England 2 Aug. 1944 ANNETTE BRADLEY, (2) in U.S.
    ROSE ____, b. 20 May 1914, d. Saratoga Springs, N.Y., 8 Feb. 1993.[1629]
    Lauren was employed in Arcadia, Calif., in 1940 as a trimmer for the forest
    service, the record showing that he was in Riverside, Calif., in 1935.[1630] He
    enlisted in Los Angeles on 8 April 1941, was assigned to the Army Air
    Corps,[1631] and served in England throughout World War II.
vii DELBERT LEONARD HARRIS, b. 15 Oct. 1918, d. Oklahoma City 22 Aug. 2003;
    m. Welston, Okla., 22 Nov. 1949 JoANN MILLS, b. Earlsboro, Okla., 8 Dec.
    1931, d. Oklahoma City 3 Nov. 2012, dau. of Clarence and Josephine (Cal-
    vard) Mills.[1632] Delbert enlisted in the Regular Army in Chandler, Okla., on

---

[1626] California Marriage Index, 1960–1985, online at <www.Ancestry.com>.
[1627] 1940 U.S. Census, Cunningham City, Rural Twp., Kingman Co., Kans., E.D. 48-29, sheet 1A.
[1628] Buried Hillcrest Memorial Park, 1013 East Olive Ave., Porterville, Calif.
[1629] Social Security Death Index, SSN 075-01-1629.
[1630] 1940 U.S. Census, Arcadia City, Monrovia Twp., Los Angeles Co., Calif., E.D. 19-359, sheet 1B.
[1631] Enlistment card record, Electronic Army Serial Number Merged File, ca. 1938–1946, Record Group 64, NARA, serial no. 39232282.
[1632] Obituary, JoAnn Harris.

29 June 1940, was assigned to the Army Air Corps, and served mainly in Texas throughout World War II.[1633]

Children of Delbert Leonard[7] and JoAnn (Mills) Harris:

1 *Stephen Wayne*[9] *Harris*, b. Wichita, Kans., 11 March 1951, d. by own hand in Oklahoma City on 12 Dec. 1992; m. Beverly Lynn Christopher, b. 5 Nov. 1953, divorced.

2 *Mark Leonard Harris*, b. Oklahoma City 19 Dec. 1955; m. (1) Susan Gail Stukey, b. 26 Nov. 1955, divorced, (2) Patricia/Trisha Gail Kopycinski, b. 31 July 1962.

viii GUY RONALD HARRIS, b. 8 Dec. 1920, d. Joplin, Mo., 1 Aug. 2000; m. Stroud, Okla., 27 June 1945 VIVIAN BERNIECE RAINS, b. Stroud 10 July 1923, d. Afton, Okla., 23 May 1996. On 20 May 1943, Guy was inducted in the army in Oklahoma City "for the duration of the War."[1634] He flew 42 missions as an engineer-gunner on B-24 bombers from southern Italy with the 15th Air Force between Sept. 1944 and the end of the war in Europe.

Children of Guy Ronald[8] and Vivian Berniece (Rains) Harris:

1 *Paula Guyann*[9] *Harris*, b. Galena, Kans., 31 Oct. 1950; m. Richard Alan Wyczynski, b. 3 June 1946.

2 *Tina Annette Harris*, b. Riverton, Kans., 10 Aug. 1956; m. Stanley Eugene Sanders, b. 10 April 1949.

ix MARJORIE ELLEN HARRIS, b. 31 March 1925, d. Point Roberts, Whatcom Co., Wash., 6 Feb. 2011;[1635] m. (1) 18 Dec. 1943 BOB HARMON,[1636] (2) by 1947 ____ MEDVED, (3) by 1951 LOTICE HARGER, (4) 17 Nov. 1954 BOB SCANTLIN, and (5) HARRY H. SHIER, b. 16 July 1918, d. Highland, Calif., 23 Dec. 2003.[1637]

Child of ____ and Marjorie Ellen[8] (Harris) (Harmon) Medved:

1 *Johnnie Richard Medved*, b. 5 May 1946, drowned in Fla. 15 April 1967.

Child of Lotice and Marjorie Ellen[8] (Harris) (Harmon) (Medved) Harger:

2 *Delbert Ronald Harger*, b. 25 Dec. 1949.

EIGHTH GENERATION

81 JOHN WESLEY[8] HARRIS (*Joseph Roswell*[7], *Edwin*[6], *Joseph*[5], *Jeremiah*[4], *Daniel*[3], *Walter*[2], *John*[1]), born in Durand, Winnebago County, Illinois, on 23 June 1867, died near Big Cabin, Craig County, Oklahoma, on 16 January 1938. He married at Siloam Springs, Benton County, Arkansas, on 10 July

[1633] Enlistment card record, Electronic Army Serial Number Merged File, ca. 1938–1946, Record Group 64, NARA, serial no. 7010405.

[1634] Form, Enlisted Record and Report of Separation: Honorable Discharge; Enlistment card record, Electronic Army Serial Number Merged File, ca. 1938–46, Record Group 64, NARA, serial no. 38405180.

[1635] Social Security Death Index, SSN not stated.

[1636] Date from letter, Guy Harris, Keesler Field, Miss., to Berniece Rains, 13 Jan. 1944 ("Did I tell you that Marjorie, my sis, got married. Anyway she did, Dec. 18. Of course he is a soldier"). Guy's personal notebook kept during his service includes an address: "Sis. Harmon, 4474 Magnolia, Riverside, Calif."

[1637] Social Security Death Index, SSN not stated.

1886 **IDA JOSEPHINE JENKINS**, born in Cooweeskoowee District, Cherokee Nation, 4 July 1870, who died near Big Cabin on 30 September 1947. Both are buried in Fairview Cemetery at Vinita, Oklahoma.[1638] She was a daughter of Elias H. Jenkins and his wife Arminda Jane (England), the latter a quarter-blood Cherokee whose parents, David and Susannah A. (Conner) England, were living on Tu Squ Li Ti Creek in North Carolina at the time of an 1835 census.[1639]

At age fifteen in March 1883, John Wesley Harris had been working for 2½ years in St. Joseph, Missouri, for the J. M. Easton Co., a retail firm.[1640] By 1886, he was in Indian Territory and had married across the border in Arkansas. A second marriage was performed about 1888 in a Federal Courthouse in Indian Territory because of some doubt about the legality of an Indian's marriage outside the Territory. He is said to have participated in the Sooner rush near Guthrie, Oklahoma, in 1889. In 1892, "J. Wesley Harris, recognized as a citizen of the Cherokee Nation," was permitted to employ his father for three months.[1641] He was appointed in July 1903 as the "First Director of the Harris School, located in Cooweeskoowee District," and was elected County Commissioner in 1907. John's household in 1910 included his wife Ida J., sons Roy C. and John W., and "niece" Susie I. Shupert. His married daughters Gertrude and Ulalah were living nearby.[1642] In January 1920 John's household included his wife Ida J. and his father, Joseph R. Harris, age 82; his married daughters Gertrude and Ulalah were in adjacent households.[1643] In 1921 John was a "farmer and stock raiser near Vinita."[1644]

Children of John Wesley[8] and Ida Josephine (Jenkins) Harris, "all born in Indian Territory near Big Cabin," Okla.:[1645]

    i   FLORA MAY[9] HARRIS, b. 25 July 1887, d. Vinita, Okla., in Sept. 1935; m. TIP CICERO MAYES. No children.

[1638] Transcription notes from the writer's visit there in Sept. 1981.

[1639] Eastern Cherokees Claims Application no. 1132, Commissioner of Indian Affairs, Washington, D.C.

[1640] Recommendation dated St. Joseph, Mo., 12 March 1883, on letterhead of J. M. Easton & Co., Toys, Fancy Goods, Picture Frames, Cutlery, Queensware and Glassware: "The bearer Wesley Harris was in our employ for two years and a half, and we always found him faithful, Energetic, a good salesman and strictly honest and reliable, and will prove a valuable addition to anyone requiring help in the mercantile line. Give him a trial and you'll secure a good worker. Resp'ct, J. M. Easton & Co."

[1641] "Permit, Cherokee Nation, Cooweeskoowee District," 6 Dec. 1892.

[1642] 1910 U.S. Census, Twp. 8, Craig Co., Okla., E.D. 36, sheets 9A, 9B.

[1643] 1920 U.S. Census, Twp. 8, Craig Co., Okla., E.D. 15, sheet 3B.

[1644] Emmet Starr, *History of the Cherokee Indians and Their Legends and Folk Lore* (Oklahoma City: The Warden Co., 1921).

[1645] Names and birth dates from "Eastern Cherokees Supplemental Application of Ida J. Harris for Minor Children," no. 1132, dated 1 June 1907, Commissioner of Indian Affairs, Washington, D.C.

ii Gᴇʀᴛʀᴜᴅᴇ Nᴇʟʟɪᴇ Hᴀʀʀɪs, b. 13 Jan. 1889, d. Big Cabin, Okla., 15 Nov. 1972;[1646] m. Neosho, Mo., 15 Jan. 1908, Jᴏʜɴ Gᴏʀᴅᴏɴ Cᴇᴀʀʟᴇʏ, b. Ga. ca. 1882.[1647]

Children of John Gordon and Gertrude Nellie[9] (Harris) Cearley, ages from 1910 and 1920 census:

1 *Howard Luther Cearley*, b. Okla. ca. 1908 (age 1y in April 1910, 12y in Jan. 1920).

2 *Kenneth Raymond Cearley*, b. Okla. ca. Dec. 1909 (age 4m in April 1910, age 10 in Jan. 1920).

3 *John Gordon Cearley*, b. Okla. ca. 1814, age 5 in Jan. 1920.

iii Uʟᴀʟᴀʜ Sᴏᴘʜʀᴏɴɪᴀ Hᴀʀʀɪs, b. 5 Sept. 1890, d. Vinita 27 Sept. 1962; m. Vinita 6 Nov. 1909 Oscᴀʀ Bʟᴏᴜɴᴛ, b. Mo. 7 April 1885, d. Okla. in Oct. 1963.[1648]

Children of Oscar and Ulalah Sophronia[9] (Harris) Blount:

1 *Beulah Ethel Blount*, b. Okla. ca. 1910 (age 9 in Jan. 1920).

2 *Patty Cornelia Blount*, b. Okla. ca. 1912 (age 7 in Jan. 1920, when she was entered as "Flora C.").

3 *Harris Oscar Blount*, b. Okla. ca. 1913 (age 6 in Jan. 1920).

4 *Julian Webster Blount*, not listed in 1920.

iv Rᴏʏ Cʟᴀᴜᴅᴇ Hᴀʀʀɪs, b. 20 April 1892, d. Vinita 10 April 1979; m. 24 Dec. 1914 Mᴀʀʏ Aɢɴᴇs Nᴀɪʀ, b. Vinita, Indian Territory, 1 Feb. 1897, who survived him, daughter of John Edgar and Margaret Nancy Belle (Noblitt) Nair. Roy Claude and Mary Agnes Harris "made their home 11 miles northwest of Vinita where he farmed until his retirement in 1971."[1649]

Children of Roy Claude[9] and Mary Agnes (Nair) Harris, all b. Vinita:[1650]

1 *Raymond Nelson[10] Harris*, b. 28 Dec. 1915.

2 *Pauline Marie Harris*, b. 20 Nov. 1921.

3 *Roy Norman Harris*, b. 4 Nov. 1933.

v Jᴏʜɴ Wᴇsʟᴇʏ Hᴀʀʀɪs, b. 3 June 1897, d. Pryor, Okla., 23 Jan. 1967; m. in May 1919 Lʏᴅɪᴀ Mᴀᴅɪsᴏɴ, b. 6 April 1894, d. Pryor in Sept. 1969.[1651]

Children of John Wesley[9] and Lydia (Madison) Harris:

1 *Grace Cornelia[10] Harris*, b. 19 March 1920.

2 *Robert Wesley Harris*, b. 11 March 1923.

3 *Ollie Jean Harris*, b. 14 May 1932.

4 *John Madison Harris*, b. 31 Aug. 1935.

[1646] Social Security Death Index, SSN 445-20-4543.

[1647] 1910 U.S. Census, Twp. 8, Craig Co., Okla., E.D. 36, sheet 9B.

[1648] Social Security Death Index, SSN 440-20-0157.

[1649] Obituary, *Vinita Daily Journal*, 10 April 1979.

[1650] Family Bible of J. E. and Belle (Noblett) Nair, page copies courtesy of R. Wesley Harris.

[1651] Social Security Death Index, SSN 441-26-6120.

APPENDIX I: THOMAS[1] HARRIS, SAWMILLER

As discussed in the preface to this book, the tradition still preserved in Wethersfield at the beginning of the twentieth century was that two brothers, John and Thomas, came up from New London in a boat as far as Middletown and traded their boat for land in Wethersfield. There were in fact two men of those names in seventeenth-century Wethersfield; the bulk of this book deals with John and his descendants. We have no contemporary evidence other than favorable circumstances to confirm that they were brothers, or even related, but it will be useful to include here a summary of "brother" Thomas and early generations of his descendants.[1652]

1 THOMAS[1] HARRIS, born probably in the 1630s (assuming he was about age 25 at the birth of his first known child), died between 1682 (when he was distributed a share of land in Hartford's Five Mile Lots, now in modern Manchester, Connecticut), and May 1688 (when the town of Hartford agreed to provide assistance with the cost of medical care for his minor son Thomas). He married by 1664 (birth of first child) **SARAH WRIGHT**, daughter of Capt. Richard Wright of Twelve-Mile Island (a large farm down the Connecticut River in present East Haddam, Connecticut).[1653] The marriage probably took place in or near Twelve-Mile Island, although no record of it exists.

Thomas's origins are unknown except that he probably had been in or near Twelve-Mile Island in Connecticut in the early 1660s before appearing in January 1666/7 with his wife Sarah and her father, Capt. Wright, on the east side of the Connecticut River in what is now East Hartford. On 11 January 1666/7, Governor Winthrop in Hartford recorded in his medical journal a prescription for "Harris Tho: his wife at sawmill capt: Wrights daughter."[1654] A series of similar entries in the journal shows that the Harrises and Captain Wright had come upriver from Twelve-Mile Island

---

[1652] The main source for this summary is my research article, "Thomas Harris, Sawmiller of Hartford, Connecticut," *National Genealogical Society Quarterly* [NGSQ] 78 (1990):182-203, which may be consulted for additional detail not repeated here. More recent work related to this Thomas or his wife is cited where appropriate in this summary.

[1653] "Thomas Harris, Sawmiller," NGSQ 78 (1990):189-90. For the identity of Capt. Wright, see Gale Ion Harris, "Captain Richard Wright of Twelve-Mile Island and the Burnhams of Podunk: Two Seventeenth Century Connecticut River Families," TAG 67 (1992):32-46; 68 (1993):83; and Robert Charles Anderson, *The Winthrop Fleet: Massachusetts Bay Company, Immigrants to New England, 1629–1630* (Boston: NEHGS, 2012), 696-98.

[1654] Medical Records of John Winthrop, 697.

and were residing, as a temporary arrangement, with the Thomas Burnham family in [modern] East Hartford. Burnham's wife, Ann, apparently was an older half sister of Thomas Harris's wife Sarah. About 1668, Thomas acquired a tract of land on Pewter Pott Brook in Hockanum, where he, with his young family and father-in-law Captain Wright, established a residence near the line that divides modern East Hartford from Glastonbury (then part of Wethersfield).

In October 1667, the Connecticut General Assembly, meeting in Hartford, had granted Thomas Harris "liberty to build a sawe mill on the Brooke beyond the bounds between Hartford and Wethersfield on the east side of the Great River provided it be accomplished within two years."[1655] Thomas met the deadline, but at great cost. On 15 October 1669, signing by mark *H*, he petitioned the Assembly for assistance, stating that he "did there erect a Sawmill by the expense of much Labour and Cash." He had to borrow heavily, his creditors were pressing him for payment, and he thereby "became a burthen to the town of Hartford and finally was necessitated to sell the said mill and tract of land." As a result of uncertain town boundaries at the time Thomas built it, the mill and its tract of land were found to be "within the Lotts of Weathersfield which extend three miles into the woods and particularly into Mr. Samuel Wells his Lott."[1656]

A proposed solution had fallen through. A nearby property owner, Samuel Smith, had promised to buy the portion of Wells's property on which the mill encroached and reconvey it to Thomas's buyers. Joseph Bull and John Bidwell Jr. Smith made the purchase, but then refused to sell, insisting instead on a one-third partnership in the mill. Bull and Bidwell agreed, Smith still stalled, and Thomas's buyers refused to pay on the grounds that the property was "litigious and incumbered." Thus Thomas's petition; he prayed that the Assembly would order Smith to reconvey the Wells tract, which they did. The deed in 1669 from Wells to Smith provides the additional evidence needed to conclude that this earliest known mill at Wethersfield was in Naubuc [in present Glastonbury], at the east end of the three mile lot originally granted to William Swayne.[1657]

It is clear that Thomas Harris never fully recovered financially from the loss of his sawmill venture in Naubuc. Sporadic references to him or members of his family appear in Winthrop's medical journal or in records at Hartford and Wethersfield through 1682.[1658] He apparently had died before

---

[1655] *The Public Records of the Colony of Connecticut* 2 (Hartford, 1852):78.

[1656] Connecticut Archives: Private Controversies, Series I, 1:72, Connecticut State Library.

[1657] For a detailed map of the neighborhood, see "Thomas Harris, Sawmiller," NGSQ 78 (1990):186-87.

[1658] "Thomas Harris, Sawmiller," NGSQ 78 (1990):188-89.

21 May 1688, when it was resolved at a town meeting in Hartford to provide assistance to the boy Thomas Harris [Thomas's son] who had a "lameness" in his leg. They agreed to pay Mr. John Hull of Derby, Connecticut, £10 "out of the next Town Rate" and £10 "to be added when he hath made a cure besides what he hath already receaved of the Town by a former agreement about the said Lad."[1659]

Sarah survived Thomas at least until 8 March 1690/1, when, as "Sara Harris widow," she and her eldest son William Harris sold a tract of land east of the Connecticut River in [present] East Hartford. It was described as 42 acres of upland, with "edifaces and fences." It lay on the north bank of the Hockanum (Saw Mill) River and adjoined sawmill properties developed as early as 1639 by John Crow. Thomas's widow has not been traced past 1691. Although not considered likely, she could have been the Sarah Harris who, by mark, witnessed John Seymour's will at Hartford on 12 December 1712.[1660]

Children of Thomas[1] and Sarah (Wright) Harris:

   i   THOMAS[2] HARRIS, b. between Aug. 1664 and March 1665, based on entries in the medical journal of John Winthrop, who treated him five times in the period 1667–1669.[1661] This Thomas was probably the "child" of Thomas Harris who drowned in John Pratt's well in East Hartford on 22 May 1669.[1662]

2 ii   WILLIAM HARRIS, b. Jan. 1667/8; m. ELIZABETH BRUNSON.

3 iii ROBERT HARRIS, b. prob. in early 1670s; m. (1) EXPERIENCE CHAPPELL, (2) ELIZABETH ____.

   iv EPHRAIM HARRIS, b. prob. in the 1670s, d. at Hartford before 3 March 1712/3, when "his brother William Harris of Wethersfield" was appointed administrator of his estate.[1663] In 1709, Ephraim Harris was in Captain Williamson's company "on the late expedition formed against Canada."[1664] Soon after, on 2 April 1710, he owned the covenant at the First Church in adjoining Farmington,[1665] but was back in Hartford when he died, apparently unmarried and without children.

   v   THOMAS HARRIS (again), presumably a younger son named for the Thomas who drowned in 1669, was identified as a "lad" in May 1688 when it was

---

[1659] *Hartford Town Votes, Vol. 1, 1635–1716*, vol. 6. Coll. Conn. Hist. Soc. (Hartford, 1897), 225-26.

[1660] Manwaring, *Early Connecticut Probate Records*, 2:290. For another possible identification of this Sarah, see the daughter of John[2] Harris (p. 16, no. 4 i in the present book).

[1661] Medical Records of John Winthrop, 716, 793, 832, 838, 902.

[1662] Helen Schatvet Ullmann, *Hartford County, Connecticut, County Court Minutes, Volumes 3 and 4, 1663–1697, 1697* (Boston: NEHGS, 2005), 106-7.

[1663] Hartford County Probate Records, 8:121, 140, Connecticut State Library.

[1664] *Wyllys Papers*, 371.

[1665] "Records of the First Church of Christ (Congregational) of Farmington, Connecticut, 1652–1938," 9 vols. (manuscript, Connecticut State Library), 1:238.

voted at a Hartford town meeting voted to provide assistance with his medical bills.[1666] Nothing further is known about this Thomas.

vi   A child (possibly Thomas above), "credited "to ye widow Harris," on a list of baptisms at Hartford's First Church in Oct. 1691.[1667] The only Harris widow found then at Hartford was Thomas's widow Sarah; and the First Church, on Hartford's north side, was attended by her sons William and Robert.

2 WILLIAM² HARRIS (*Thomas¹*), born at Hockanum in the south part of (modern) East Hartford in January 1667/8, probably was the "aged Mr. Harris" whose death in July 1759 was recorded in Meriden Parish at Wallingford, Connecticut.[1668] His birth date is closely fixed by Winthrop, who treated him three times as an infant, calling him "son of Thomas at Hockanum."[1669] William married by 1695 **ELIZABETH BRUNSON**, born about 1676/7, who died at Woodbury, Connecticut, on 3 September 1733, a daughter of Jacob Brunson of Farmington, Connecticut.[1670]

William was "of Hartford" in 1691 when he and his mother sold the property on Saw Mill River in (present) East Hartford. He had six children recorded at Hartford between 1695 and 1709,[1671] although other records place him in adjacent Wethersfield during part of that period (a child recorded at Hartford in August 1700 was baptized that month in Wethersfield, where William had been admitted as an inhabitant in the prior May).

William Harris, a carpenter, appears in records at Hartford through August 1711, before residing again at Wethersfield several years before settling in Woodbury, Connecticut. In 1717, Elizabeth Harris, "wife of Corpl. William Harris, recommended from Wethersfield," was included in a membership list of a New Milford church that included residents of Woodbury.[1672] On 18 November 1718, "William Harris at present residing in Woodbury" entered into an agreement "respecting ye building of a grist mill" near the mouth of Jack's Brook. Harris was to bring in the necessary ironwork and millstones, then provide the labor needed to put the mill into

[1666] *Hartford Town Votes*, 225-26.
[1667] *Historical Catalogue of the First Church in Hartford*, 1633–1885 (Hartford: Case, Lockwood Brainard Co., 1885), 169.
[1668] Donald Lines Jacobus, *Families of Ancient New Haven*, 8 vols. (1923–31; repr. Baltimore: Genealogical Publishing Co., 1974), 3:719.
[1669] Medical Records of John Winthrop, 790, 838.
[1670] John Insley Coddington, "Brownson, Bronson, Brunson Family of Earl's Colne, Essex, England, Connecticut, and South Carolina," TAG 38 (1962):193, and TAG 39 (1963):113.
[1671] Barbour Collection, citing Hartford FFS:68.
[1672] Samuel Orcutt, *History of the Towns of New Milford and Bridgewater, Connecticut* (Hartford: Case, Lockwood, Brainard & Co., 1882), 66.

operation by the end of the next March. In return, he and his heirs were to have the mill and lot as long as they maintained it.[1673]

On 5 June 1746, William, then age 78, sold to his "son William Harris Jr. of said Woodbury" several parcels of land, his corn mill, and all his carpenter tools "of what sort soever."[1674] Five years later, in 1751, he released his interest in the property at Manchester that had been distributed in 1682 on the right of his father.[1675] William appears to have lived another eight years at Wallingford, where his youngest daughter had married— assuming he was the "aged Mr. Harris" who died there in 1759.

Children of William[2] and Elizabeth (Brunson) Harris:[1676]

  i ELIZABETH[3] HARRIS, b. Hartford 17 Dec. 1695, probably the otherwise unplaced Elizabeth Harris bp. at the First Church in Hartford on 29 June 1712.
  ii SARAH HARRIS, recorded at Hartford in Aug. 1700, bp. Wethersfield on 4 Aug. 1700, d. Woodbury, Conn., 3 Sept. 1749. She m. (1) 18 Aug. 1718 JOSEPH MARTIN, who d. 3 Sept. 174[–]. By Jan. 1745/6, she had m. (2), as his 3rd wife, JOHN MITCHELL, bp. Feb. 1688/9, who d. 22 April 1758, son of John Mitchell. On 2 Oct. 1749, Asahel Martin, "eldest son of yᵉ late Widow Sarah Mitchell," was named administrator of her estate. Her property, valued at £409, was distributed to eight heirs [named below], called "yᵉ natural children of yᵉ deceased widow Sarah."
    Children of Joseph and Sarah[3] (Harris) Martin:
    1 *Abigail Martin*; m. Henry Gibbs.
    2 *Abijah Martin*, b. 18 Sept. 1720.
    3 *Hannah Martin*, bp. 2 July 1722; m. Nathan Warner.
    4 *Asahel Martin*, b. 2 July 1724.
    5 *Andrew Martin*, b. Oct. 1726.
    6 *Amos Martin*, bp. 8 Oct. 1728.
    7 *Joseph Martin*, b. 5 Aug. 1730.
    8 *Gideon Martin*, b. 28 July 1736.
  iii REBECKAH HARRIS, b. Hartford 12 July 1703, bp. First Church, Hartford, 18 July 1703.
  iv MARY HARRIS, b. Hartford 2 July 1705, bp. First Church 4 July 1705.
  v WILLIAM HARRIS, b. Hartford 14 Jan. 1707/8, bp. First Church 25 Jan. 1707/8, was living in Bedford, Westchester Co., N.Y., in Oct. 1747. He m. (1) prob. ca. 1727 TABITHA ____, who d. at Woodbury on 7 May 1728, and (2) SARAH ____, with whom he had six children at Woodbury between 1732 and 1744. William lived on land adjoining his father's property in Woodbury, and in June 1746 he bought his father's lands, corn mill, and carpenter's tools for £150. He did not remain in Woodbury, however, to run his

---

[1673] Woodbury, Conn., Deeds, 2:182.
[1674] Woodbury, Conn., Deeds, 7:149.
[1675] Hartford, Conn., Deeds, 8:423.
[1676] For these children, see "Thomas Harris, Sawmiller," NGSQ 78 (1990):192-94 and references there.

father's business. In Oct. 1746, he sold the mill and water rights for £300, and a year later, in 1747 he disposed of his remaining Woodbury property, identifying himself then as a resident of Bedford, N.Y.

    Child of William[3] and Tabitha (___) Harris, born Woodbury:

    1 *Tabitha*[4] *Harris*, b. 6 May 1728.

    Children of William[3] and Sarah (___) Harris, born Woodbury:

    2 *Sarah Harris*, b. 1 Aug. 1732.

    3 *Elizabeth Harris*, bp. 25 Sept. 1734.

    4 *Elizabeth Harris* (again), b. 2 May 1736.

    5 *Ann Harris*, b. 20 March 1740.

    6 *Daniel Harris*, bp. 26 Jan. 1742/3.

    7 *Mercy Harris*, b. 29 Feb. 1743/4.

vi THANKFUL HARRIS, b. Hartford 27 Dec. 1709; m. Woodbury, Conn., 28 April 1740 JOHN RUMRILL.

    Children of John and Thankful[3] (Harris) Rumrill, recorded or bp. at Woodbury:

    1 *Eunice Rumrill*, b. 13 May 1742.

    2 *Rachel Rumrill*, b. 29 Aug. 1743.

    3 *Tabitha Rumrill*, bp. 3 March 1745.

    4 *John Rumrill*, bp. 24 April 1748.

vii EUNICE HARRIS, b. Wethersfield 1 March 1711/2, d. at Wallingford on 16 or 17 Oct. 1747; m. at the Meriden Parish Church in Wallingford on 26 June 1739, as his 1st wife, EPHRAIM ROYCE, b. Wallingford 9 Feb. 1717/8, d. there on 14 Sept. 1762, son of Nehemiah and Keziah (Hall) Royce. Ephraim m. (2) 19 April 1749 Eunice Root, with whom he had another four children.

    Children of Ephraim and Eunice[3] (Harris) Royce, recorded Wallingford:

    1 *Mindwell Royce*, b. 12 Aug. 1740.

    2 *Keziah Royce*, b. 12 May 1742.

    3 *Ephraim Royce*, b. 30 June 1744.

    4 *Ebenezer Royce*, b. 8 Dec. 1745.

    5 *Eunice Royce*, b. 2 Oct. 1747.

3 ROBERT[2] **HARRIS** (*Thomas*[1]), was born probably at Hockanum in the south part of what is now East Hartford, Connecticut, in the early 1670s and apparently was living in Bedford, Westchester County, New York, in March 1742[/3?].[1677] He married first at Wethersfield, Connecticut, in David Sage's house at Dividend (near the Wethersfield-Middletown line), in 1700, **EXPERIENCE CHAPPELL**, James Treat, J.P., presiding.[1678] She was baptized

---

[1677] *Historical Records* (Town of Bedford, Westchester Co., N.Y.), 7 vols. (Bedford Hills: By the town, 1966–), 4:17. This summary for Robert is based mainly on my article, "Robert Harris of Connecticut and Descendants in the Hudson Valley," NYGBR 130 (1999):183-96, 269-82, 131 (2000):297-98, which may be consulted for some detail not repeated here.

[1678] Testimony of witness John Taylor, 31 May 1728, Connecticut Archives: Crimes and Misdemeanors, 3:329, Connecticut State Library.

in New London on 20 June 1675[1679] and was living in Farmington, Connecticut, in 1747, daughter of John and Elizabeth (Carpenter) (Jones) Chappell.[1680] Experience married secondly, probably not long after 23 May 1728, John Cowles of Farmington, born there 28 January 1670/1, who died there on 9 October 1748, son of Samuel and Abigail (Stanley) Cowles.[1681] Long before Experience petitioned for a divorce from Robert in 1728,[1682] he married secondly **ELIZABETH** ____, the mother of his eight children recorded at Stamford, Connecticut, from 1714 to 1730.

On 15 March 1695/6, Robert Harris and sixteen other young East Hartford residents owned the covenant at Hartford's First Church,[1683] the same attended by his mother Sarah and his brother William. Robert's marriage four years later in Wethersfield to Experience Chappell began under circumstances portending trouble. In April 1701, about four months after the Wethersfield townsmen agreed to allow Robert to dwell there for "half a year [but] at the end of that time to depart if the town shall see cause,"[1684] he and his wife were before the court on a charge of fornication before marriage. Robert denied the charge.[1685] According to Experience's long-delayed petition for a divorce at Farmington on 23 May 1728, Robert had deserted her in 1709 and "lived from her in total neglect of all matrimonial duties ever since till this day."

No local records place Robert and Experience in Wethersfield after 1701; the town's temporary permission to dwell there apparently was not renewed. They were in East Hampton, Long Island, by 27 June 1708, when the "wife of Rob[ert] Harris" owned the covenant, and Mercy, a "child of Rob[ert] Harris," was baptized by the Reverend Nathaniel Huntting at the same church attended by the widow and daughter of Robert's older cousin Thomas Harris.[1686] After Robert and Experience separated in 1709, she returned to her mother's relatives in Farmington.

Josiah Churchill and Prudence Goodrich of Wethersfield testified at Experience's divorce proceeding in 1728 that Robert was "in ye town" about

---

[1679] New London First Congregational Church Records, 6 vols. (FHL microfilm 5131), 1:60.

[1680] Gale Ion Harris, "George Chappell of Windsor, Wethersfield, and New London, Connecticut," NEHGR 150 (1996):59-60.

[1681] Cowles, *Genealogy of the Cowles Families*, 1:41-42.

[1682] Connecticut Archives: Crimes and Misdemeanors, 3:328-31, Connecticut State Library.

[1683] *First Church in Hartford,* 24.

[1684] Wethersfield Town Votes, 1:262, Town Clerk's Office.

[1685] Hartford County Court Records, 6:172, Connecticut State Library.

[1686] *Records of the Town of East Hampton,* 5:427, 454; Harris, "Thomas Harris of East Hampton," NYGBR 128 (1997):13-15, 24.

"12 or 13 yeares ago and we never see him since."[1687] Their estimate places Robert in Wethersfield on some visit about 1715 or 1716, or near the time his cousin Walter died and his brother William left there to build a gristmill in Woodbury.[1688] William's son, William Harris Jr., moved on to Bedford in Westchester County, New York, not far across the line from the Town of Stamford in Connecticut. He arrived in Bedford before October 1747,[1689] where, as shown below, his uncle Robert Harris of Stamford had settled some years before.

Robert Harris arrived in Stamford "about 1710,"[1690] closely following, according to Experience's later claim, the date that Robert deserted. Robert was a saw miller, carpenter, and grist miller in Stamford, the occupations of his father, Thomas, his brother William, his cousins Walter and Thomas, and his maternal grandfather, Richard Wright.[1691] All indications are that Robert remarried and reared a family in Stamford without benefit of a divorce from Experience Chappell.

Robert operated or owned shares in at least two grist mills and a saw mill in Stamford. One was mentioned in December 1716, when the Town designated a committee to report on Mr. Robert Harris's request for a half acre "southerly of the New Tide grist mill . . . to sett a house thereon."[1692] He probably operated that mill for several years, but had ceased operations there some years before 1727 when Peter and Anthony Demill were granted rights to build a grist mill at the mouth of Mill River, twenty rods below where "Harriss's old mill was."[1693]

In November 1724, Robert, then styled "carpenter" of Stamford, bought from Nathaniel Newman four acres on Mianus River including a half interest in "a grist or corn mill now erected . . . joyning to [Newman's] land on the west side of my now dwelling house," and a "privilege to buld a fulling

---

[1687] Connecticut Archives: Crimes and Misdemeanors, 3:328-31, Connecticut State Library.

[1688] Harris, "Walter Harris of Wethersfield," NEHGR 142 (1988):325; "Thomas Harris, Sawmiller," NGSQ 78 (1990):191-92.

[1689] Woodbury, Conn., Deeds, 7:271; Bedford Town Book, 3:2a, in *Historical Records* (Town of Bedford), 4:5. No trace of William Harris Jr. or his family is found after he recorded an earmark at Bedford in Oct. 1747 unless his son Daniel, who was bp. at Woodbury on 26 Jan. 1742/3, was later the Daniel Harris, a carpenter, aged 33, 5'8" tall, and born in "America," who enlisted on 6 Jan. 1777 as a private and was discharged on 2 March 1780 from the New Eleventh Pennsylvania Regiment, apparently a unit from the vicinity of Sunbury on the Susquehanna River (*Pennsylvania Archives*, 5th Ser., 3:645).

[1690] E. B. Huntington, *History of Stamford, Connecticut* (Stamford: By the author, 1868), 184.

[1691] Harris, "Captain Richard Wright of Twelve-Mile Island and the Burnhams of Podunk," TAG 67 (1992):34-39.

[1692] "Stamford Town Meeting Records, 1640–1806" (Stamford Genealogical Society, microfilm Reel 1), 2:428.

[1693] Huntington, *History of Stamford*, 183.

mill."[1694] By a separately recorded agreement, Robert was to have "full use of one half of that part of the Stream of Mianus River that passeth through the land of said Numan." In addition, Robert "may buld a fulling mill if he see cause, provided [it] shall not obstruct . . . any mill or stream that shall be in partnership between [Harris and Newman]," and have use of a way "to transport graine or logs . . . advantageous to said Harris." A few years later, in July 1728, Robert bought from Edmond Lockwood two acres that had been laid out nearby to Daniel Lockwood on Mianus River.[1695]

On 1 December 1729, Robert Harris, Daniel Briggs, John Newman, Jonathan Newman, Thomas Newman, and Nathaniel Newman of Stamford, all signing by name except Nathaniel Newman, agreed to build a saw mill on Mianus River west of Nathaniel's dwelling house. Robert was to have "one quarter and a half quarter" interest "for his part in Bulding said mill," and the others "one half quarter apiece." Harris and John Newman agreed to provide land needed for "a yard to lay logs in order for sawing and also for a highway," provided the property revert to them "after said mill shall fail and cease to be under improvement."[1696] On 6 February 1730/1, by a deed indexed as "Harris Ezekiel Sale from his father harres," Robert Harris of Stamford, for £250, conveyed to his sixteen-year-old eldest son a half part of his grist mill and three-eights part of his saw mill "together with three acres of land joyning to said saw mill on the west side of Mianus River [and] on the west side of Nathaniell Numans now dwelling house."[1697]

Sometime during the 1730s, Robert moved across the line into Bedford, New York, where, on 26 March 1740, his property on the west side of Beaver Dam River and Davids Brook about two miles north of Bedford village was cited as the north bounds of land surveyed for Anthony Demill, the gristmiller of Stamford mentioned above.[1698] On 1 March 1742[/3?], a white oak tree standing in the corner of Robert's fence was a bounds marker of land laid out to Thomas Chambers.[1699] Robert may have constructed the saw mill that his son Ezekiel owned near this property on Beaver Dam River in 1756. A century later, from 1833 to 1841, several of Robert's grandsons and great grandsons were assessed for work on the "highway"—now Harris Road—that runs near the west side of Robert's old property.[1700]

[1694] Stamford, Conn., Deeds, C:91, 93.
[1695] Stamford, Conn., Deeds, C:85, 150.
[1696] Stamford, Conn., Deeds, D:259.
[1697] Stamford, Conn., Deeds, C:288.
[1698] Bedford Town Book, 2:371, in *Historical Records* (Town of Bedford), 3:249.
[1699] *Historical Records* (Town of Bedford), 4:17, 154.
[1700] *Historical Records* (Town of Bedford), 5:149, 190-91.

Children of Robert[2] and Experience (Chappell) Harris:

    i   Perhaps a child[3] b. Wethersfield soon before 10 April 1701, but whose paternity is placed in doubt by Robert's denial on that date.[1701]

    ii   MERCY HARRIS, b. ca. 1704, bp. East Hampton, L.I., 27 June 1708,[1702] d. at Farmington on 7 Feb. 1799, aged 94.[1703] She m. at Farmington on 26 Oct. 1728 HEZEKIAH SCOTT, b. there in Sept. 1703, who d. there on 17 Jan. 1765, son of Samuel and Mary (Orvis) Scott.

        Children of Hezekiah and Mercy[3] (Harris) Scott, all but no. 5 recorded at Farmington:[1704]

        1 *Hezekiah Scott*, b. 7 Oct. 1729.

        2 *Elisha Scott*, b. 26 July 1732.

        3 *Elizabeth Scott*, b. 12 Nov. 1734; m. William Lewis of Southington.

        4 *Ezekiel Scott*, b. 26 June 1738.

        5 *Rhoda Scott*, named in both parents' wills; m. (1) Ezekiel Humphries of Farmington, (2) by 1805 Asa North.

        6 *Samuel Scott*, b. 12 March 1746.

Children of Robert[2] and Elizabeth (—) Harris, all recorded at Stamford:[1705]

4   iii   EZEKIEL HARRIS, b. 19 Oct. 1714; m. MARTHA ____.

    iv   MARY HARRIS, b. 16 Nov. 1716.

5   v   THOMAS HARRIS, b. 15 June 1718; m. ____ ____.

6   vi   ROBERT HARRIS, b. 31 Oct. 1720; m. ____ ____.

    vii   SARAH HARRIS, b. 28 Feb. 1722/3.

7   viii   EPHRAIM HARRIS, b. 31 July 1725; m. ____ ____.

    ix   ELIZABETH HARRIS, b. 7 Sept. 1727.

    x   JAMES HARRIS, b. 10 Nov. 1730, and his brother Ephraim appear in the Crum Elbow Precinct, Dutchess Co., N.Y., tax lists in Feb. and June 1760.[1706] No Dutchess Co. deeds or mortgages are found for James. A claim that he joined Ephraim in Rensselaer Co., N.Y., confuses him with his nephew James, son of Robert (no. 6 ii).[1707]

4 EZEKIEL[3] HARRIS (*Robert[2], Thomas[1]*), born in Stamford, Connecticut, on 19 October 1714,[1708] died at Bedford, Westchester County, New York between 3 May 1783 and 28 May 1784, the dates of his will and its proof.[1709] His wife, **MARTHA ____**, is mentioned twice, once on a Bedford

[1701] Hartford County Court Records, 6:172, Connecticut State Library.

[1702] *Records of the Town of East Hampton*, 5:427, 454.

[1703] *Connecticut Courant* [Hartford], 11 Feb. 1799.

[1704] "Thomas Harris, Sawmiller," NGSQ 78 (1990):195-96.

[1705] Barbour Collection, citing Stamford VR1:10. No more is known of the three daughters.

[1706] Clifford M. Buck, *Crum Elbow Tax Lists* (Salt Point, N.Y.: By the author, [1976?]), 18.

[1707] Roderick Bissell Jones, "The Harris Family of Block Island and Dutchess County, N.Y.," NYGBR 84 (1953):144n.

[1708] Barbour Collection, citing Stamford VR1:10.

[1709] New York County Wills 37:9, WNYHS 12:319-20.

gravestone as the mother of his son Ezekiel Jr., who was born in 1756,[1710] and again in his 1783 will.

When he was only sixteen years old, Ezekiel acquired in February 1730/1 a part interest in his father's grist and saw mills on Mianus River in Stamford. Ezekiel, then "of Bedford," sold it over a decade later, on 3 January 1743/4, to Jonathan Dann of North Castle, Westchester County.[1711] Ezekiel plainly had continued in his father's trade, as, in February 1756, he owned a saw mill in Bedford on Beaver Dam River.[1712] Styled "Yeoman," Ezekiel was the only Harris listed as a freeholder at Bedford in 1763. In December 1779, the County of Westchester paid him "for making assessments in Bedford in March last." As Ezekiel Harris, "Esq.," he administered an oath at Bedford in April 1780.[1713]

In his 1783 will, Ezekiel styled himself a "carpenter, being aged and infirm of body," and left to "my dearly beloved wife Martha, and my daughter, Reuamy Harris, the sole privilege and use of the west room and bedroom of my house, also the west chambers and equal privilege in the kitchen during the said Martha's widowhood, or for Reuamy's use so long as unmarried and no longer." Martha was to have all movable estate except carpenter's tools and farming utensils, which were to go "to my son Ezekiel." After Martha's decease, the movable estate was to go "to my three daughters, Martha, wife of Silas Miller; Dorcas, wife of Lemuel Light; and Sarah, wife of Zephaniah Miller." Daughter Reuamy was to have land "on the west side of the highway, which I purchased of Richard Honeywell," but son Ezekiel could have it if he would pay her £100. Ezekiel was to have the remainder of "my lands on the east side of the highway, except for the temporary reserve above mentioned for his mother and sister." Wife Martha, Lemuel Light, and Lott Sarlls were named executors; David Holmes, Abraham Berritt, and Lott Sarlls witnessed.

Children of Ezekiel[3] and Martha (____) Harris, order not certain:

    i   MARTHA[4] HARRIS, b. prob. in the early 1740s and living in Bedford in May 1800;[1714] m. prob. by 1763 SILAS MILLER, who d. at Bedford not long before 7 June 1785, when Martha was granted administration on his estate.[1715] Silas was probably a son of Martha's father's neighbor Abner Miller. Silas Miller,

---

[1710] William A. Korroch, *Some old Gravestones of Westchester Co. N.Y.* (Lansing, Mi., 1987), no. 3463.

[1711] Stamford, Conn., Deeds, D:452, 453.

[1712] *Historical Records* (Town of Bedford), 4:154, citing the Katharine B. Clark Collection.

[1713] *Historical Records* (Town of Bedford), 4:89, 5:254, 281.

[1714] *Historical Records* (Town of Bedford), 4:192.

[1715] New York County Letters of Administration, July 11 – Dec. 30, 1785, WNYHS 13:387.

"Yeoman," was a Bedford freeholder in Feb. 1763 and was assessed for real and personal property there in 1779.[1716] During the Revolution he became, on 29 May 1776, 2nd Lt. of the Grenadier Company, and on 28 May 1778, 1st Lt. of the Bedford New Purchase Company, both in Col. Thomas Thomas's 2nd Regiment of Westchester Co. Militia.[1717] He was one of the officers in 1781 who signed a petition seeking protection of the frontiers of that county and was a highway master at Bedford in 1784.[1718]

On 29 Dec. 1787, Martha Miller, "administratrix of Silas Miller, late of Bedford," sold to Lemuel Light 65 acres on Broad Brook and Beaver Dam River, "bounded on the west by the land of Timothy Miller and that formerly belonged to Abner Miller." In April 1792, "land occupied by the Widow Martha Miller" adjoined property sold to David Haight by Justus and Jemima (Miller) Harris, and Jemima Miller "widow of Abner Miller." Martha's adjoining property evidently was the 11-acre parcel adjoining lands of Lemuel Light and David Haight that she sold to Moses St. John on 6 May 1800, her brother Ezekiel Harris witnessing.[1719]

In 1790, the Bedford household of "Miller, Martha (Wid° of Silas)," consisted of two males over age 16, one male under 16, and two females,[1720] but no children are identified.

ii   DORCAS HARRIS, living in Bedford in 1800; m. prob. in the 1760s LEMUEL LIGHT, living there in 1800, both aged 45 or over.[1721] Lemuel Light and Justus Harris were among the Bedford men in April 1778 who petitioned the Governor to provide guards for the town's jail.[1722] Lemuel was assessed for real and personal property at Bedford in 1779 and is credited with service during the Revolution in the 1st, 2nd, and 4th Regiments, New York Line. He served the Town of Bedford as constable from 1784 to 1789, and was assessed there for highway work in 1797.[1723] On 5 May 1788, Lemuel Light, farmer, and his wife, Dorcas, of Bedford sold to John Jay of New York City—who next year became the first Chief Justice of the U.S. Supreme Court—a 41-acre portion of the 65-acre property on Broad Brook and Beaver Dam River that they had purchased from Dorcas's sister Martha in Dec. 1787. In July 1792, Lemuel and Dorcas sold 24 acres on David's Brook to Henry Clapp.[1724] Lemuel's household at Bedford in 1790 consisted of four males aged 16 or over, one male under 16, six females, and one slave.[1725] No children have been identified.

[1716] *Historical Records* (Town of Bedford), 5:254, 257.

[1717] Berthold Fernow, ed., *New York State Archives: New York in the Revolution*, Vol. I, in *Documents Relating to the Colonial History of the State of New York*, 15 (Albany, 1887):305.

[1718] *Historical Records* (Town of Bedford), 5:245, 278; 7:28.

[1719] *Historical Records* (Town of Bedford), 4:192, 290-91, 293-94, 385-86.

[1720] 1790 U.S. Census, Township of Bedford, Westchester Co., N.Y., p. 183.

[1721] 1800 U.S. Census, Bedford, Westchester Co., N.Y., p. 139.

[1722] *Public Papers of George Clinton, First Governor of New York*, 10 vols. (Albany, 1900–14), 3:157-59.

[1723] *Historical Records* (Town of Bedford), 5:38, 229, 257; 7:22.

[1724] *Historical Records* (Town of Bedford), 4:330-31.

[1725] 1790 U.S. Census, Township of Bedford, Westchester Co., N.Y., p. 182.

iii REUAMY HARRIS, b. ca. 1748, d. at Bedford on 5 July 1830, aged 82; m. prob. ca. 1785 her first cousin ABIJAH HARRIS and had with him at least two children (see no. 6 iv).

iv SARAH HARRIS, living in Bedford in 1788; m. ZEPHANIAH MILLER, living there in 1790, apparently a son of Sarah's father's neighbors Abner and Jemima Miller. On 4 April 1768 Justus Harris and Zephaniah Miller witnessed Silas Miller's sale of a house and property adjoining "land of Zephaniah Miller." On 28 May 1778, Zephaniah Miller was appointed 1st Lt. of a company in Col. Thomas Thomas's 2nd Regiment of Westchester County Militia.[1726] He was assessed at Bedford in 1779 for real and personal property, and served the town as Highway Master in 1785.[1727] On 24 April 1788, Zephaniah and his wife, Sarah, of Bedford sold to John Banks Jr. 90 acres on Beaver Dam River.[1728] Zephaniah's household at Bedford in 1790 consisted of one male aged 16 or over and six females.[1729] No children have been identified.

v EZEKIEL HARRIS JR., b. in Bedford on 20 Sept. 1756, d. there on 26 June 1837 as "son of Ezekiel and Martha."[1730] Ezekiel, his wife, and some of their children are buried in the Buxton Cemetery about three miles northwest of Bedford Village. He is said to have had an early wife, MARY BASSETT,[1731] but he certainly m. in June 1781 ELIZABETH HAMILTON, b. 31 Dec. 1760 (calc.), d. 23 April 1853, aged 92y 3m 23d, dau. of Mercer and Elizabeth (Belden) Hamilton.[1732]

Ezekiel served in the Revolution as a private with Abijah Harris in Capt. Josiah Miller's Company (with Ezekiel's brother-in-law Zephaniah Miller as 1st Lt.), and with Sgt. Justus Harris in Capt. Marcus Moseman's Bedford New Purchase Company (with Ezekiel's brother-in-law Silas Miller as 1st Lt.), all in Col. Thomas Thomas's 2nd Regiment, Westchester Co. Militia.[1733] Ezekiel's pension application, dated at Bedford on 3 Oct. 1832, states his birth date and place, and names Abijah Harris and Abner Miller as witnesses to his service. Ezekiel and Abijah Harris were present at Elizabeth Harris's wedding in Bedford in Dec. 1777 (no. 6 vi).

In July 1791, Ezekiel Harris of Bedford, farmer, and his wife, Elizabeth, were dwelling on a 116-acre farm bounded by Beaver Dam River and a highway leading from Bedford village to Vecol's ford on Croton River,[1734] apparently the land that Ezekiel had received by his father's will in 1783. Ezekiel was still living there, "on the east side of the highway" (now Harris Road), in May 1826, when he quitclaimed a 20-acre portion of that land to

---

[1726] Fernow, *New York in the Revolution*, 305.

[1727] *Historical Records* (Town of Bedford), 5:33, 245.

[1728] *Historical Records* (Town of Bedford), 4:117.

[1729] 1790 U.S. Census, Township of Bedford, Westchester Co., N.Y., p. 182.

[1730] Korroch, *Some old Gravestones*, no. 3463; *Historical Records* (Town of Bedford), 8:154.

[1731] *DAR Patriot Index* (Washington, D.C.: National Society of the Daughters of the American Revolution, 1966), 306, not confirmed.

[1732] Revolutionary War pension files S6191 and W17978, National Archives; Korroch, *Some Old Gravestones*, no. 3461; *Historical Records* (Town of Bedford), 8:154.

[1733] Fernow, *New York in the Revolution*, 305, 389.

[1734] Westchester Co., N.Y., Mortgages, D:491.

his son Abijah Harris Jr. The parcel abutted north on his son Nathaniel's land and was "opposite" the dwelling house of [his cousin and brother-in-law] "Abijah Harris, Esqr.," on the west side of the highway. In May 1835, for "love and affection," Ezekiel gave his son Lemuel Harris, "late of the City and County of New York," 15 acres on Beaver Dam River.[1735]

Ezekiel's will, dated at Bedford 11 March 1836, gave wife Betsey household items, a cow, and a heifer, son Frederick Harris $50, dau. Charlotte Harris $200 and "a home in my house so long as she remains unmarried," dau. Mary Seely $100, dau. Betsey Sniffin $100, son Abijah Harris two parcels of land, son Nathaniel Harris part of the farm adjoining Beaver Dam River, son James M. Harris the upper garden and half the "dwelling house in which I now live . . . subject to the use as a house for my daughter Charlotte," and the remainder to be sold with proceeds to sons Thomas J. Harris and James M. Harris equally. Son Nathaniel and friend Jabez Robertson were named executors; William Lyon and Squire W. Smith witnessed.[1736]

Recorded with Ezekiel's will is a "citation" for his widow, heirs, and next-of-kin to appear before the Surrogate's Court at White Plains in Dec. 1837. It lists in addition to those mentioned in his will: Nathaniel Sniffin and his wife Elizabeth at North Castle, Westchester Co.; Herbert Hall and his wife Phebe M. in the City of New York; "grandson" Samuel Harris at Ithaca, Tompkins Co., N.Y.; William Harris (with James M. Harris) at Natchez, Miss.; Ezekiel Harris in Mississippi, place unknown; and Lemuel Harris, John H. Harris, and Morris Seely and wife Mary at Tremont, Tazewell Co., Ill.; all over age 21. Ezekiel's executors in March 1838 sold to Thomas J. Harris of Bedford 38 acres on Beaver Dam River adjoining lands of Lemuel Harris and Abijah Harris Jr., subject to dower rights of widow Elizabeth Harris.[1737] In Aug. 1850, Elizabeth Harris, aged 89, was living with her son Nathaniel Harris in Bedford.[1738]

Children of Ezekiel[4] and Elizabeth (Hamilton) Harris:

1 *Frederick[5] Harris*, b. N.Y. ca. 1782, living in Bedford with his brother Abijah Jr. in 1850.[1739]

2 *Abijah Harris Jr.*, b. N.Y. prob. ca. 1784, d. Bedford 25 Feb. 1864, aged 82 [*sic*: 80?]; m. Mary ____.[1740]

3 a son b. prob. near 1785; m. Elizabeth ____, b. N.Y. ca. 1783.[1741]

[1735] Westchester Co., N.Y., Deeds, 28:292-94, 60:59-60.

[1736] Westchester Co., N.Y., Wills, U:219-30.

[1737] Westchester Co., N.Y., Deeds, 79:422-26.

[1738] 1850 U.S. Census, Bedford, Westchester Co., N.Y., p. 104.

[1739] 1850 U.S. Census, Bedford, Westchester Co., N.Y., p. 103.

[1740] Korroch, *Some Old Gravestones*, no. 3452; Abijah's age was given at Bedford as 66 years in 1850 and 74 years in 1860 (U.S. Censuses, pp. 103, 312).

[1741] This son is accounted for in Ezekiel Harris's household in 1790 and 1800, and seems by elimination to be the father of Samuel Harris (age 30-39) at Ithaca, N.Y., in 1840 (U.S. Census, p. 255); of Phebe M. Hall (b. N.Y. ca. 1811), wife of Herbert Hall and living at Poughkeepsie, N.Y., in 1850 and Sing Sing, N.Y., in 1860 (U.S. Censuses, pp. 174 and 37, respectively); and prob. of Ezekiel Harris of Mississippi in 1837. Elizabeth Harris, aged 67, b. N.Y., was living with Herbert and Phebe Hall at Poughkeepsie in 1850. The

4 *James M. Harris,* b. by 1790, living Natchez, Miss., in 1837.

5 *Mary Harris,* b. 1785–1790, living Tazewell Co., Ill., in 1840;[1742] m. Morris Seely.

6 *Lemuel Harris,* b. N.Y. ca. 1790, living Tazewell Co. in 1850;[1743] m. [as 2nd wife?] Mary ____.[1744]

7 *John H. Harris,* b. N.Y. ca. 1792, living Tremont, Tazewell Co., in 1860;[1745] m. Sarah F. ____.

8 *Nathaniel Harris,* b. N.Y. 8 Sept. 1794 (calc.), d. Bedford 26 July 1859, aged 64y 10m 18d; m. Thankful Jones.[1746]

9 *William Mercer Harris,* b. 1799 [*sic*: 1797?], d. Natchez, Miss., 1848; m. Caroline Harrison.[1747]

10 *Elizabeth Harris,* b. 27 June 1799, d. Bedford 5 Dec. 1885; m. Nathaniel Sniffin.[1748]

11 *Thomas J. Harris,* b. 13 Aug. 1800, d. Bedford 23 Oct. 1877; m. Sarah ____.[1749]

12 *Charlotte G. Harris,* b. ca. 1801, d. Bedford 17 Oct. 1846, aged 45, unm.[1750]

13 *Caroline Harris,* b. ca. 1806, "youngest daughter of Ezekiel of Bedford," d. Natchez, Miss., 15 Dec. 1828, aged 22, unm.[1751]

5 THOMAS³ HARRIS (*Robert²*, *Thomas¹*), born in Stamford, Connecticut, on 15 June 1718,[1752] was living in Cortlandt Manor, Westchester County, New York, in May 1762. He apparently was married and residing at Bedford in 1746, but his wife remains unidentified and little more is known about him. He probably was the Thomas Harris listed in 1760 as a soldier in Captain Hackaliah Brown's Sixth Company, Upper Battalion, of Westchester County militia.[1753] In April 1762, "Thomas Harriss of Cortlandts Manor"— apparently that part of it just north of Bedford and later named Stephentown,

---

International Genealogical Index lists marriages in Adams Co., Miss. (Natchez, county seat), of Ezekiel Harris to Hester Ann Gibson on 27 June 1827 and to Ann Weekes on 15 July 1837.

[1742] 1840 U.S. Census, Tazewell Co., Ill. (no twp. listed), p. 17.

[1743] 1850 U.S. Census, Tazewell Co., Ill. (no twp. listed), p. 43.

[1744] Lemuel was assessed for taxes on Bedford property in 1815 (*Historical Records* (Town of Bedford), 5:271) and had a household adjoining his brother Thomas J. in New York City, 6th Ward, in 1830 (U.S. Census, p. 381).

[1745] 1860 U.S. Census, Tremont Twp., Tazewell Co., Ill., p. 97.

[1746] *Historical Records* (Town of Bedford), 8:154.

[1747] *Lineage Book[s]*, National Society of the Daughters of the American Revolution, 8 (1899):279, 96 (1927):175.

[1748] *Historical Records* (Town of Bedford), 8:154.

[1749] *Historical Records* (Town of Bedford), 8:155. Ezekiel Harris's Revolutionary Pension file mentions son Thomas J. Harris living at 53 Chatham St., N.Y. City, in 1843.

[1750] *Historical Records* (Town of Bedford), 8:154.

[1751] Fred Q. Bowman, *10,000 Vital Records of Eastern New York, 1777–1834* (Baltimore, 1987), 112.

[1752] Barbour Collection, citing Stamford VR1:10.

[1753] Catherine A. Verplanck, "Colonial Muster Rolls," NYGBR 38 (1907):87.

now Somers, where Hackaliah Brown lived—bought 138 acres there on Croton's River from Joseph Willson of Greenwich, Connecticut. Willson had purchased the property in 1753 from Stephen Van Cortlandt, for whom Stephentown was named.[1754] Thomas mortgaged the property in May 1762 to James Brown, probably the man who had been the Lieutenant of his company two years before. Thomas's subsequent forfeiture of the property is implied by Brown's sale of it to Benjamin Kniffen of Rye sometime before February 1776.[1755]

Based on locality, associations, and the absence of alternatives, Thomas had at least two children: Justus born at Bedford in 1746/7 and Elizabeth who married Lemuel Peatt nearby at Salem in 1767. Others may be the Robert, Zebulon, and Anne included below.[1756]

Apparent children of Thomas[3] and ____ (____) Harris:[1757]

    i   JUSTUS[4] HARRIS, b. at Bedford on 22 Jan. 1746[/7], d. prob. either at Galway, Saratoga Co., N.Y., or in Genesee (now Wyoming) Co., N.Y., on 5 Oct. 1817. He m. 29 Oct. 1767 JEMIMA MILLER, b. Bedford 16 Dec. 1751, who d. in her son Thomas Harris's home at Covington, Wyoming Co., N.Y., on 22 Sept. 1841, dau. of Abner and Jemima (____) Miller of Bedford.[1758] In April 1768, Justus witnessed his brother-in-law Silas Miller's sale of a house and land on Beaver Dam and Cross Rivers (see no. 4 i).

       Justus served in the Revolution as Sergeant (with privates Ezekiel and Zebulon Harris) in Capt. Marcus Moseman's Bedford New Purchase Company, and with privates Ezekiel, Robert, and William Harris in Capt. Moses St. John's Company, all in Col. Thomas Thomas's 2nd Regiment, Westchester Co. Militia.[1759] Justus was assessed for real and personal property at

---

[1754] J. H. French, *Gazetteer of the State of New York* (Syracuse: R. Pearsall Smith, 1860), 705-6.

[1755] Westchester Co., N.Y., Deeds, K:392, 394; Westchester Co., N.Y., Mortgages, A:73-74.

[1756] The Benjamin "Harace" who m. Phebe Wright at the Salem Church on 4 Oct. 1781 may be related someway, but more evidence is needed to place him in any family ("Records of the Church of Christ in Salem, Westchester Co., N.Y.," NYGBR 31 [1900]:177). He may be the Benjamin Harris whose household in North Castle, Westchester Co., in 1790 included a male aged 16 or over, four males under 16, and one female.

[1757] A Thomas Harris "of Westchester County," relationship if any not determined, "fled from home and joined the [British] army in 1779 doing duty until the peace" when he went to New Brunswick and "plied trade as [a] carpenter." There, "through fatigue," he had "lost use of eyes and is now useless" on 4 March 1786 when he entered a claim at St. John. He claimed as losses a "house bought from Hezekiah Ward at Morrisiana," horses, and three years of service, but all were rejected. (Peter Wilson Coldham, *American Loyalist Claims* [Washington, D.C.: National Genealogical Society, 1980], 1:219.)

[1758] Widow Jemima Harris's Revolutionary War pension file W15909, National Archives; DAR Application no. 603246. Jemima's pension file mentions her "brother" Timothy Miller, a son of Abner and Jemima Miller.

[1759] Fernow, *New York in the Revolution*, 305, 389; no evidence is seen for the claim that he served as a Captain in the same regiment (*Historical Records* (Town of Bedford), 7:16).

Bedford in March 1779.[1760] He and his apparent cousins Abijah and Ezekiel Harris had the only listed Harris households at Bedford in 1790.[1761] Recorded dates indicate that Justus's duties as a highway master in 1791 probably were assumed next year by his younger cousin Abijah Harris.[1762] In April 1792, Justus, his wife, Jemima, and mother-in-law, Jemima Miller, widow of Abner Miller, all of Bedford, sold to David Haight a "messuage" of 39 acres adjoining land of widow Martha Miller (no. 4 i) by the "highway that leads from Bedford to Elijah Buckbees."[1763] Probably about that time Justus and Jemima moved to Schenectady, N.Y., where their son Harvey is said to have been born in Jan. 1794. By 1800, however, they were residing at Halfmoon, Saratoga Co., N.Y.,[1764] where he was appointed Justice of the Peace in 1803 and named as executor of David Schauber's estate in April 1804. He became a member of the Presbyterian Church at Galway by Feb. 1807, and was residing at Galway in 1810.[1765]

Children of Justus[4] and Jemima (Miller) Harris:[1766]

1 *Elizabeth*[5] Harris, b. 18 Sept. 1768, d. 29 Dec. 1792.

2 *Sarah Harris*, b. 21 March 1770, d. 6 June 1808.

3 *Isaac Harris*, b. 8 March 1772, d. 13 Oct. 1810.

4 *Justus Harris*, b. 13 May 1774, d. 13 July 1836.

5 *Jemima Harris*, b. 10 Aug. 1776, d. 22 Nov. 1818.

6 *Hannah Harris*, b. 5 Aug. 1781, d. Wyoming Co., N.Y., 1850; m. _____ Bantes or Bantis.

7 *Stephen Harris*, b. 16 Jan. 1785, d. 25 May 1812.

8 *Nancy Harris*, b. 30 Sept. 1787, d. 26 Nov. 1823.

9 *Thomas Harris*, b. 26 Dec. 1791, a "carpenter," d. prob. Manlius Twp., LaSalle Co., Ill., 27 Nov. 1870.

10 *Harvey Harris*, b. Schenectady, N.Y., 21 Jan. 1794, d. Odell, Livingston Co., Ill., 17 Feb. 1880.

ii ELIZABETH HARRIS, b. prob. by 1750 based on her marriage date, was living in South Salem, Westchester Co., in 1810.[1767] She m. at Salem Church of Christ, 11 Nov. 1767, LEMUEL PEATT, b. ca. 1745, who d. at Salem 29 Aug.

[1760] *Historical Records* (Town of Bedford), 5:256.

[1761] 1790 U.S. Census, Town of Bedford, Westchester Co., N.Y., pp. 182, 188.

[1762] *Historical Records* (Town of Bedford), 5:242.

[1763] Westchester Co., N.Y., Deeds, P:261-62. A list of eight persons assessed for highway work and assigned to path master Nicholas Haight at Bedford in 1797 includes David Haight (6 days), Elijah Buckbee (7 days), and an unidentified John Harris (1 day) (*Historical Records* (Town of Bedford), 5:34). John's exceptionally light assessment suggests that he was a young man with little property.

[1764] 1800 U.S. Census, Halfmoon, Saratoga Co., N.Y., p. 4a.

[1765] Nathaniel Bartlett Sylvester, *History of Saratoga County, New York* (Philadelphia: Everts & Ensign, 1878), 83, 364; Saratoga Co., N.Y., Wills, 1:256, abstract on FHL microfilm 17,937, p. 18; 1810 U.S. Census, Galway, Saratoga Co., N.Y., p. 232.

[1766] Sydney Mike Gardner, *Some Descendants of Justus Harris* (Chicago: Adams Press, 1974), 1-2; DAR Application no. 603246. At p. 2, Gardner mentions that Jemima, Hannah, and Stephen, children of Justus Harris, were bp. 9 July 1786 by the Reverend John Davenport of the Bedford Presbyterian Church, and that his daughter Nancy was bp. there on 15 June 1788.

[1767] 1810 U.S. Census, South Salem, Westchester Co., N.Y., p. 204.

1795,[1768] a private from New York during the Revolution.[1769] The Lemuel "Pyatt" household at Salem (now Lewisboro) in 1790[1770] was near those of William and Gilbert Reynolds who owned land in 1781 adjoining Elizabeth's apparent uncle Robert Harris's property across and on the Bedford side of Cross River. Lemuel's household in 1790 consisted of three males aged 16 or over, four males under 16, and one female. "Elizabeth, the wife of Lemuel Peatt" was admitted and baptized at the Salem Church on 7 Oct. 1792.[1771] She appears as a widow, aged 45 or over, with children at South Salem (Lewisboro) in 1800 and 1810. In Nov. 1825, Thomas Peatt, evidently her son, purchased property in Poundridge adjoining "land formerly occupied by Enoch Harris" (no. 6 i 1).[1772]

Children of Lemuel and Elizabeth[4] (Harris) Peatt, all bp. Salem Church 17 Oct. 1792:[1773]

1 *Ruben Peatt.*

2 *Isaac Peatt.*

3 *Thomas Peatt.*

4 *Stephen Peatt.*

5 *Henry Peatt*, b. ca. 1784, d. Poundridge 20 June 1851, age 67; m. Sarah _____.[1774]

6 *Doctor Peatt.*

7 *John Peatt*, b. ca. 1790, d. Poundridge 6 March 1876, age 87 [*sic*: 87th year?]; m. Phebe _____.[1775]

iii (poss.) ROBERT HARRIS, b. by 1755 and living in Huntington (now Shelton), Conn., in 1800, aged 45 or over.[1776] Robert was of Weston, Conn. (not far across the line from Westchester Co., N.Y.), on 26 Oct. 1775 when he m. (1) at Fairfield, Conn., MARY BULKLEY, b. there 3 April 1757, prob. dau. of James and Elizabeth (Whitehead) Bulkley. Robert m. (2) at Weston 15 Nov. 1778 EUNICE GRAY, b. Fairfield 19 Jan. 1756, living in March 1800, dau. of Nathan and Mary (Hurlbut) Gray. With Mary, Robert had a son Stephen baptized with him at Weston on 12 July 1777. A son of Robert, name not reported, was baptized at Easton in Aug. 1789.[1777] Robert's household at Weston in 1790 included three males under 16 and three females.[1778] By

---

[1768] "Church of Christ in Salem," NYGBR 31 (1900):88, 33 (1902):116.

[1769] *DAR Patriot Index*, 533.

[1770] 1790 U.S. Census, Salem Twp., Westchester Co., N.Y., p. 199.

[1771] "Church of Christ in Salem," NYGBR 31 (1900):85, 33 (1902):88.

[1772] Westchester Co., N.Y., Deeds, 26:302.

[1773] "Church of Christ in Salem," NYGBR 33 (1902):88.

[1774] Korroch, *Some Old Gravestones*, nos. 6175, 6178.

[1775] Korroch, *Some Old Gravestones*, nos. 6176, 6177. John Peatt probably was born soon after the 1790 census date and appears in Bedford in Sept. 1860, aged 70, in the William and Jerusha Hull household (U.S. Census, p. 277).

[1776] 1800 U.S. Census, Huntington, Fairfield Co., Conn., p. 162.

[1777] Donald Lines Jacobus, *History and Genealogy of the Families of Old Fairfield*, 2 vols. in 3 (1930; repr. Baltimore, 1976), 2 (pt. 1):168, 403, 537.

[1778] 1790 U.S. Census, Weston, Fairfield Co., Conn., p. 242.

1800 his household was in adjacent Huntington and included six children, none of whom have been identified.

iv (poss.) ZEBULON HARRIS, b. prob. by 1760, the private who served about 1778 or 1779 with Pvt. Ezekiel Harris and Sgt. Justus Harris in Capt. Marcus Moseman's Bedford New Purchase Company in Col. Thomas Thomas's 2nd Regiment, Westchester Co. Militia.[1779] No further record found.

v (poss.) ANNE [HARRIS], (surname unrecorded) who m. WILLIAM BROWN (Jr.) of Salem Town (now Lewisboro), adjoining the east and north sides of Somers and Bedford. "Anne, the wife of William Brown," was admitted to the Salem Church on 21 July 1790 and on that day they had several children baptized there, the first transcribed as "William Harris."[1780] Their household in Salem Town about that time consisted of three males aged 16 or over, one male under 16, and five females.[1781] William Harris (no. 6 v) had leased the confiscated loyalist property of William Brown (Sr. or Jr.?) about 1780.

Children bp. at Salem Church on 21 July 1790: 1. *William Harris Brown* (or poss. a William and a Harris). 2. *Mary Brown*. 3. *James Brown*. 4. *Eunice Brown*.

6 ROBERT³ HARRIS (*Robert²*, *Thomas¹*) was born at Stamford, Connecticut, on 31 October 1720[1782] and was living at Nassau (then Stephentown), Rensselaer County, New York, in 1800.[1783] He had married by 1748, probably at Bedford, Westchester County (birthplace of son James). His unidentified wife could be the female aged 45 or over in his home at Nassau in 1800.

A statement by Robert's son Abijah Harris that he, Abijah, was born in 1755 at "Cortlandt Manor (now Somers)"[1784] suggests that Robert may have resided for some time there near his brother Thomas (no. 5). In July 1774, however, Robert was styled "of Bedford" when he mortgaged 204 acres on Cross River to Augustus Van Cortlandt of the City of New York. Gilbert Browne and Edward Courtright witnessed. The deed mentions adjoining lands of William and Gilbert Reynolds, James Lord, and Ebenezer Ward. On 22 April 1781, Robert Harris "late of the Town of Bedford" sold that property to John Banks of Bedford. The witness Ezra Wilson deposed in March 1784 that he had seen Robert Harris sign and deliver the deed, and that he had seen Abijah Harris sign "as the other witness."[1785]

[1779] Fernow, *New York in the Revolution*, 305, 389.

[1780] "Church of Christ in Salem," NYGBR 31 (1900):85, 33 (1902):38. The "William Harris" possibly was intended for two boys, a *William* and a *Harris*. For comparison, see the children of Anne's possible cousin Elizabeth (Harris) Trowbridge (no. 6 vi) who gave a son the name *Harris* in 1783.

[1781] 1790 U.S. Census, Salem Twp., Westchester Co., N.Y., p. 198.

[1782] Barbour Collection, citing Stamford VR1:10.

[1783] 1800 U.S. Census, Stephentown, Rensselaer Co., N.Y., p. 935.

[1784] Revolutionary War pension file S32286, National Archives.

[1785] Westchester Co., N.Y., Mortgages, C:41; Westchester Co., N.Y., Deeds, I:211.

Robert may have been leasing that property from the widow of Frederick Van Cortlandt Sr. before buying it from Frederick's son Augustus.[1786] The tract was located in the northeast part of the Town of Bedford and less than a mile across the town line from Salem (later South Salem and Lewisboro) where, as shown below, some of his older children married at the Salem Church in and after 1770.

Robert's removal from Bedford sometime between 1774 and 1781 gives cause to believe that he was the first of this family group to move up the Hudson River to Rensselaer County, where he may have been operating a "large grist mill" at East Nassau about 1778.[1787] His brother Ephraim (no. 7) arrived nearby in Rensselaerwyck (now Schodack) in 1777. Robert's son James Harris moved from Bedford to Nassau in 1781, the year that Robert sold his Bedford property. Robert would be the older one of two Robert Harrises, styled "Robert" and "Robert Jr.," whose households appear at Nassau (then part of Stephentown) in 1790 and 1800.[1788] Robert's home in 1800 consisted of a male and a female aged 45 or over, and a male aged 16-25.

No deeds are found in Rensselaer County for these Roberts, but it is said that "near the opening of the [nineteenth] century" Robert Harris, Robert Harris Jr., and James Harris had lots in the "south portion" of Nassau, and William Harris had a lot nearby in the western part of Stephentown.[1789] The Van Rensselaer papers contain a receipt dated 28 February 1803 from Thomas Mayhew for £2 "of Eliphalet Reed for rent for farm leased to Robert Harris" and another for release of rents "on [a] farm leased, April 6, 1801, to James Harris."[1790] All children below except no. ix are identified as brothers or sisters in the will and probate papers of Robert's youngest son, Orry Harris, of Stephentown.[1791]

[1786] *Historical Records* (Town of Bedford), 4:viii, 410.

[1787] Charles Baker Anderson, *Landmarks of Rensselaer County, New York* (Syracuse: D. Mason & Co., 1897), 549. Anderson's comment that this mill was operated at that time by Morgan Harris is plainly in error as Morgan, b. ca. 1789, was Robert's grandson (see no. 6 v 3).

[1788] 1790 U.S. Census, Stephentown, Rensselaer Co., N.Y., pp. 285, 292.; 1800 U.S. Census, Stephentown, Rensselaer Co., N.Y., p. 935.

[1789] Nathaniel Bartlett Sylvester, *History of Rensselaer County, New York* (Philadelphia: Everts & Peck, 1880), 422, 494. We are confronted with twelve Harris households at Stephentown in 1790 (then including the south and east parts of Nassau). In addition to Robert and his sons James, William, Robert Jr., John, Daniel, and Arie [Orry] identified below, they include two Josephs, of whom one may be Robert's son, a Thomas, a David, and the unrelated Nicholas Harris, b. in R.I. in 1749 and d. in 1819, who m. Phebe Tibbits (Mrs. Thomas H. Ham, *A Genealogy of the Descendants of Nicholas Harris, M.D.* [Albany: C. I. F. Ham, 1904], 7-9).

[1790] "Van Rensselaer Manor Papers," FHL microfilm 1,697,716, Item 1, pp. 60, 107.

[1791] Rensselaer Co., N.Y., Wills, 53:314-16, and probate file no. 138 (FHL microfilms 550,685 and 1,452,328). Most importantly, file 138 contains the 27 Dec. 1859 petition of Orry Harris's administrator

Children of Robert[3] and _____ (___) Harris, order not certain:

i ENOCH[4] HARRIS, b. prob. in the mid-1740s (based on marriage); m. at Salem Church in Westchester Co., N.Y., 31 May 1770, JUDE AVERY.[1792] He served in the Revolution after June 1778 as a private with his cousins Ezekiel and Justus Harris in Col. Samuel Drake's 3rd, also "Manor of Cortlandt," Regiment of Westchester County Militia.[1793] Orry Harris was said in 1859 to have had a "brother whose name was Enoch Harris who died & left children whose names and places of residence are unknown."[1794] Enoch's household is not found in the 1790 or 1800 censuses, but he is probably the father of Enoch Harris and Betsey Harris whose marriages in the early 1790s were recorded at Salem Church.

Children of Enoch[4] and Jude (Avery) Harris, perhaps others:

1 *Enoch[5] Harris*, b. 4 Jan. 1771 (calc.), d. Poundridge, Westchester Co., 25 Jan. 1818, aged 47y 21d;[1795] m. Salem Church, 9 Oct. 1792, Hannah Knapp.[1796]

2 *Betsey Harris*, b. say 1773; m. Salem Church 11 Aug. 1791 [Isaac?] Avery.[1797]

ii JAMES HARRIS, b. Bedford, N.Y., 18 July 1748, "was accidentally killed by being run over by a team" in New Lisbon, Otsego Co., N.Y., on 19 Feb. 1835, "aged eighty-six years and seven months."[1798] He m. at Salem

---

Richard Smith, which also names a number of Robert Harris's grandchildren and great grandchildren as Orry's next-of-kin.

[1792] "Church of Christ in Salem," NYGBR 31 (1900):88.

[1793] Virgil D. White, *Index to Revolutionary War Service Records*, 4 vols. (Waynesboro, Tenn., 1995), 2:1206-7. Col. Samuel Drake replaced Col. Pierre Van Cortlandt in command of the 3rd Regiment, 25 June 1778 (Fernow, *New York in the Revolution*, 306).

[1794] Rensselaer Co., N.Y., Probates, file 138 (petition of Richard Smith).

[1795] Korroch, *Some Old Gravestones*, nos. 3462, 3465. Philip Van Cortlandt, in a letter dated at Croton, 24 Dec. 1817, mentions that he had "writen to the man who wishes to purchase the farm in Pound Ridge where Enoch Harris Resides" (Jacob Judd, ed., *The Van Cortlandt Family Papers*, 4 vols. [Tarrytown: Sleepy Hollow Restorations, 1976–81], 4:62).

[1796] "Church of Christ in Salem," NYGBR 31 (1900):241. Enoch and Hannah's children apparently included Avery Harris, b. ca. 1794, no doubt the "Awry" Harris who served in 1816 as Ensign of Lt. Col. Abijah Harris's 38th Regiment in Westchester Co. (see no. 6 iv). Avery Harris, whose name also variously appears as "Awre," "Owry," "Orin," and "Orre," is found in censuses for Poundridge and Lewisboro from 1820 through 1850, but he was assessed for highway work in Bedford in 1841 (*Historical Records* (Town of Bedford), 5:155).

[1797] "Church of Christ in Salem," NYGBR 31 (1900):241.

[1798] Dates and age from a biography of James's grandson Albert Harris (misprinting James as "Joseph") in *Biographical Review . . . Otsego County, New York* (Boston: Biographical Review Pub. Co., 1893), 589-90. The precisely stated dates suggest that the family had a Bible or similar record available in 1893, but James's Revolutionary War pension application at New Lisbon (R4658), dated 19 Feb. 1833, states that he was "born in the town of Bedford in the County of Westchester . . . in the year 1749 in the month of July." A newspaper reported the death at New Lisbon on 19 Feb. 1835 of "James Harris, 87," probably meaning in his 87th year (Gertrude A. Barber, "Deaths Taken from the Otsego Herald and Western Advertiser and Freeman's Journal, Otsego County, N.Y.", 3 vols. in 1 [[Cooperstown?], 1932–], 1:77).

Church, Westchester Co., 27 March 1772 ELIZABETH RUNDLE,[1799] b. 27 Nov. 1753, d. Nassau, Rensselaer Co., N.Y., 25 Aug. 1808 "after a union of thirty-six and a half years."[1800]

James Harris's rejected Revolutionary War pension application, dated at New Lisbon 19 Feb. 1833, states that he first enlisted at Bedford in Aug. 1776, that he moved to "Nassau formerly Stephentown," Rensselaer Co., in 1781 [the year his father sold Bedford property, which James may have been farming], and that "for 16 years past he has lived in New Lisbon." He claimed that after his arrival in Stephentown he had continued his service in 1782 by volunteering in Capt. John W. Samerhorns [*sic*] Company. His name in fact appears as a private on the roll of Capt. Schermerhorn's Company of Col. Killian Van Rensselaer's 4th Regiment (2nd Rensselaerwyck Battalion) of Albany County Militia with cousins Ephraim and Ezekiel Harris (nos. 7 i and 7 ii), and John Harris (probably a brother).[1801]

James Harris's household is found at Stephentown in 1790, 1800, and 1810, then at New Lisbon in 1820 and 1830. His home at New Lisbon in 1830 consisted of himself, aged 80-89, and a female aged 40-49 (probably his unmarried daughter Sally).[1802] It is said that he brought to New Lisbon "three of his younger children" and that he was "a Justice of the Peace for many years."[1803] In 1833, James could name "no living witness except his Daughter Elizabeth Marks" to support his military service claim, but [his son-in-law] Solomon Davis and [daughter] Bethiah Church of New Lisbon swore that they were "well acquainted" with him and that they "believe him to be eighty three years of age."

The will of James Harris "of New Lisbon," dated 4 Feb. 1831 and proved 31 Oct. 1835, mentions sons James, Enoch, John, and Orry Harris, and daughters Elizabeth Marks, Bethiah Church, Charlotte Davis, and Sally Harris. Son Orry Harris was named executor.[1804] In 1859, eight children (all except Sally below) and several grandchildren of James Harris were named in the probate of James's brother Orry Harris's estate at Stephentown, Rensselaer County.[1805]

Children of James[4] and Elizabeth (Rundle) Harris, not including two sons who "died in infancy":[1806]

1 *Mary*[5] *Harris*, b. N.Y. ca. 1773, living New Lebanon, Columbia Co., N.Y., in 1860, aged 87;[1807] m. John Smith.[1808]

[1799] "Church of Christ in Salem," NYGBR 31 (1900):174.

[1800] *Biographical Review . . . Otsego County*, 589.

[1801] Fernow, *New York in the Revolution*, 264-65, 389.

[1802] 1830 U.S. Census, New Lisbon, Otsego Co., N.Y., p. 273.

[1803] *Biographical Review . . . Otsego County*, 589.

[1804] Otsego Co., N.Y., Wills, H:512, abstracted in Gertrude A. Barber, "Abstracts of Wills of Otsego County, N.Y.," 3 vols. (n.p., 1946), 3:38.

[1805] Rensselaer Co., N.Y., Probates, file 138 (petition of Richard Smith).

[1806] *Biographical Review . . . Otsego County*, 589, unless otherwise indicated.

[1807] 1860 U.S. Census, New Lebanon, Columbia Co., N.Y., p. 586.

[1808] Rensselaer Co., N.Y., Probates, file 138 (petition of Richard Smith).

2 *Elizabeth Harris,* b. ca. 1775-1780, deceased in 1859; m. Cornelius Marks.[1809]

3 *Bethiah Harris*, b. ca. 1778, d. in 1853, aged 75; m. ____ Church.

4 *James Harris*, b. ca. 1780, prob. living in St. Johnsville, Montgomery Co., N.Y., in 1840,[1810] "reared a large family in the Mohawk Valley, and died in old age."

5 *Sally Harris*, b. N.Y. ca. 1784, d. unm. at New Lisbon 13 Sept. 1855, in her 72nd yr.[1811]

6 *John R. Harris*, b. N.Y. ca. Aug. 1787, d. 16 Feb. 1870, age 82y 6m, bur. Spring Forest Cemetery, Binghamton, Broome Co., N.Y.[1812] He was in Binghamton in 1860, aged 73.[1813]

7 *Enoch Harris*, b. N.Y. ca. 1790, bur. Fort Hill Cemetery, Auburn, Cayuga Co., N.Y., 31 Aug. 1871, age 81;[1814] m. Julia Swift, b. Pa. ca. 1803, bur. beside Enoch 1 Jan. 1882, age 79, dau. of Reuben and Mary (Stephens) Swift. Enoch was a retired farmer in Auburn in 1870, age 80.[1815]

8 *Orra Harris*, b. Nassau, Rensselaer Co., N.Y., ca. 1794, d. New Lisbon 23 April 1862, age 68;[1816] m. Jane E. Mather.

9 *Charlotte H. Harris*, b. N.Y. ca. 1797, living Garrattsville, Otsego Co., in 1860, aged 63,[1817] where she d. at age 68; m. Solomon Davis.

iii JOSEPH HARRIS, a "brother" of Orry Harris, "who died & left children in Canada whose names are unknown."[1818] This Joseph is possibly one of the two Joseph Harrises with households including several children in Stephentown, Rensselaer Co., in 1790.[1819]

iv ABIJAH HARRIS, b. Cortlandt Manor (now Somers), N.Y., in 1755,[1820] d. at his residence in Bedford on 6 Jan. 1843, in his 88th year.[1821] He m. prob. ca.

[1809] In 1859, the "children of Elizabeth Marks deceased, a daughter of James Harris," were Benoni Marks, Electa Marks late Electa Van Deusen widow of John Van Deusen, James Marks, Nelson Marks, Sally widow of Charles Thomas, William Marks, Clarissa Marks, and Elizabeth Ismond, "all of Cherry Valley, Otsego County, N.Y." (Rensselaer Co., N.Y., Probates, file 138 [petition of Richard Smith, and citation for appearance]).

[1810] This James Harris's household can be traced in U.S. Censuses from Nassau, Rensselaer Co., in 1810 (p. 113), through Palatine, Montgomery Co., in 1820 (p. 418) and 1830 (p. 156), to St. Johnsville in 1840 (p. 342). He apparently had a wife b. ca. 1785–80, plus two boys and six or seven girls born from about 1804 to about 1820. A younger James with a household listed on the same page at Nassau in 1810 was probably his cousin James W. Harris, son of William (no. 6 v 2).

[1811] Barber, "Deaths Taken from the Otsego Herald and Western Advertiser and Freeman's Journal," 2:71.

[1812] Gravestone photo online at <www.findagrave.com>, accessed Oct. 2012.

[1813] 1860 U.S. Census, Village of Binghamton, 5th Ward, Broome Co., N.Y., p. 419 (household of James and Clemenia McElroy).

[1814] Data online at <www.findagrave.com> (lot 50, graves 2 and 3), accessed Oct. 2012.

[1815] 1870 U.S. Census, City of Auburn, 2nd Ward, Cayuga Co., N.Y., p. 12.

[1816] Barber, "Deaths Taken from the Otsego Herald and Western Advertiser and Freeman's Journal," 2:98.

[1817] 1860 U.S. Census, Garrattsville, Otsego Co., N.Y., p. 424.

[1818] Rensselaer Co., N.Y., Probates, file 138 (petition of Richard Smith).

[1819] 1790 U.S. Census, Stephentown, Rensselaer Co., N.Y., pp. 288, 291.

[1820] Revolutionary War pension file S32286, National Archives.

1785 (see children) his cousin REUAMY HARRIS, b. ca. 1748, d. 5 July 1830, age 82,[1822] dau. of Ezekiel and Martha Harris (no. 4 iii). Abijah and Reuamy were buried in St. Matthew's Cemetery near Harris Road about two miles north of Bedford village. Abijah's pension application, dated at Bedford on 4 Oct. 1832, states that he was aged 77 and was born at "Cortlandt Manor (now Somers)" in 1755.

Abijah and his cousin Ezekiel Harris Jr. (no. 4 v) had served in the Revolution as privates in Capt. Miller's Company of Col. Thomas Thomas's 2nd Regiment;[1823] then, evidently later, Abijah was a Lieutenant in the 4th Regiment (formed Oct. 1779) of Westchester County Militia (see brother William, no. 6 v). Abijah and Ezekiel Harris had been present at Abijah's sister Elizabeth Harris's wedding at Bedford in Dec. 1777 (no. 6 vi). Abijah was assessed for personal property only at Bedford in March 1779[1824] and witnessed a deed there for his father in April 1781. His household there in 1790 consisted of a male aged 16 or over, one under 16, and two females.[1825] He was promoted in 1809 to Lt. Colonel and commandant of the 38th Regiment, Westchester County Infantry, and resigned in 1816.[1826] In May 1826, the "dwelling house" of Abijah Harris, Esq., on the west side of the "highway" (now Harris Road), was opposite the dwelling of his cousin Ezekiel Harris (Jr.) on the east side.[1827] This description indicates that Abijah and Reuamy were living on property that her father, Ezekiel Harris (Sr.), had given her in his 1783 will (see no. 4). Abijah's household at Bedford in 1830[1828] consisted of himself, aged 70-79, and a female aged 80-89, who is not accounted for in his home there in 1840.

Abijah's will, dated at Bedford on 25 Oct. 1838 and proved on 5 May 1843, gave equal undivided half parts of "the lands which belonged to my wife Rumah Harris" to son Henry Harris and granddaughters Elmira, Ann Eliza, and Sarah H. Palmer. Daughter Sarah Palmer was to have $600 payable in annual installments of $100 each, son-in-law Samuel Palmer two bonds or mortgages "which I hold against his estate," and granddaughter Sarah H. Palmer $500 with personal and household items; son Henry Harris

---

[1821] Obituary of Col. Abijah Harris, in Natalie M. Seth, comp., Obituary Notices from The Hudson River Chronicle, Sing Sing, N.Y., Sept. 24, 1839 to April 16, 1850, typescript (n.p., 1946), p. 4 (issue of 10 Jan. 1843) [FHL microfilm 982,409]. A transcription of Abijah's tombstone states his age as 86 years, thus b. ca. 1757 (*Historical Records* (Town of Bedford), 8:153), but he was 45 or over at the time of the 1800 U.S. Census in Bedford (p. 141) and aged 85 in the census of pensioners there in 1840 (p. 254), consistent with his own statement in his pension application that he was born in 1755 and with "88th year" at death as stated in his obituary.

[1822] *Historical Records* (Town of Bedford), 8:153. Korroch transcribed her name as "Ruamy" but wrongly prints 1850 as her year of death (*Some Old Gravestones*, no. 3470).

[1823] Fernow, *New York in the Revolution*, 389.

[1824] *Historical Records* (Town of Bedford), 5:258.

[1825] 1790 U.S. Census, Bedford Twp., Westchester Co., N.Y., p. 188.

[1826] Hugh Hastings, ed., *Military Minutes of the Council of Appointment of the State of New York, 1783–1821*, 4 vols. (Albany, 1901–2), 1042, 1401, 1671. "Awry Harris" was Ensign in this regiment in 1816.

[1827] Westchester Co., N.Y., Deeds, 28:292-94.

[1828] 1830 U.S. Census, Bedford, Westchester Co., N.Y., p. 143.

and friend Jabez Robertson executors. Jarvis Bouton, Daniel Light, and Samuel H. Miller of Bedford witnessed.[1829]

On 25 April 1850, Henry Harris, aged 63, deposed that his father, Abijah, d. on 4 Jan. 1843 leaving daughter Sarah, widow of Samuel Palmer, and himself as only heirs.[1830] "Henry Harris & Sally Harris of Sing Sing N.Y." were mentioned in 1859 as "children of Abijah Harris a deceased brother" of Orry Harris.[1831]

Children of Abijah[4] and Reuamy (Harris) Harris:

    1 *Henry*[5] *Harris*, b. N.Y. ca. 1786, a "merchant" in Ossining, West-chester Co., in July 1850,[1832] where his aunt Elizabeth (Harris) Trowbridge had died two years before.

    2 *Sarah Harris*, b. 27 April 1789 (calc.), d. Bedford 14 April 1867, age 77y 11m 17d;[1833] m. Samuel Palmer whose home at Bedford in 1830 and 1840 was listed near Sarah's elderly father.

v   WILLIAM HARRIS, b. say 1757, but after 1755 (age 26–44 in 1800), d. Ham-burg, Erie Co., N.Y., 24 Sept. 1840; m. at Bedford 17 April 1782 RACHEL RUNDLE, b. ca. 1765, d. at Hamburg on 28 Feb. 1844,[1834] dau. of John and Rachel (Finch) Rundle.[1835] Rachel Harris, aged 77, applied for a widow's pension at Hamburg on 16 May 1842; her file includes a declaration signed by her husband, William Harris, at Buffalo, N.Y., on 16 Aug. 1830 stating that he had served in the Revolution from 1775 to 1781 under Westchester Co. officers, including "his brother" Lt. Abijah Harris.

William is said to have been taken prisoner by the British and confined for six months in the "Old Sugar House" prison in New York City.[1836] About 1780, William leased confiscated loyalist property at Bedford, "late the property of Wm Brown."[1837] By 1790, William had joined his father in Stephentown, Rensselaer Co., N.Y.,[1838] where he leased 61 acres from Stephen Van Rensselaer in April 1793.[1839] He resided briefly in the mid-1790s at Litchfield, Conn.,[1840] but returned to Rensselaer Co. by 1800,[1841]

[1829] Westchester Co., N.Y., Wills, Z:150-54.

[1830] Pension file S32286, National Archives.

[1831] Rensselaer Co., N.Y., Probates, file 138 (petition of Richard Smith).

[1832] 1850 U.S. Census, Ossining, Westchester Co., N.Y., p. 24.

[1833] *Historical Records* (Town of Bedford), 8:276.

[1834] Widow Rachel Harris's Revolutionary War pension file W17052, National Archives.

[1835] Frederick W. Kates, *Patriot Soldiers of 1775–1783 . . . of Chautauqua County, New York*, 2 vols. (Albion, N.Y.: Jamestown Chapter, National Society, Daughters of the American Revolution, 1981–87), 2:427-28. Kates cites Mrs. Harriet Faust for information that Rachel's father John Rundle, b. Greenwich, Conn., 12 Sept. 1743, was killed on 16 July 1779 while serving with Connecticut troops at Stony Point, N.Y. His widow appears to be the Rachel Rundle b. 16 Nov. 1745, "wife of John," who d. on 25 April 1839, aged 93y 5m 9d and buried in Lewisboro, Westchester Co. (Korroch, *Some Old Gravestones*, no. 7064).

[1836] Kates, *Patriot Soldiers*, 2:428.

[1837] Anita A. Lustenberger, "Tenants of Commissioners of Sequestration in Westchester County 1778–1783," NYGBR 124 (1993):32.

[1838] 1790 U.S. Census, Stephentown, Rensselaer Co., N.Y., p. 285.

[1839] Rensselaer Co., N.Y., Deeds, 77:447.

[1840] Litchfield, Conn., Deeds, 15:609, 16:134.

where he leased another 69 acres in Nassau from Van Rensselaer in April 1801.[1842] He moved to Portland, Chautauqua Co., N.Y., in 1814, where he kept a tavern for several years.[1843] He had been residing in Buffalo "for the space of nine months" on 16 Aug. 1830, when he signed his pension declaration.

Rachel's estate at Hamburg was administered by her son James W. Harris of Buffalo; children and heirs named: James Harris, William Harris, Joseph Harris, George Harris, Hannah Dusenbury, Rachel Andrus, and Loretta (wife of Joel S. Smith).[1844] Rachel's pension file mentions sons-in-law Joel S. Smith and Sylvester Andrus, and sons John and Morgan Harris who survived her in 1847. In Feb. 1837, Morgan Harris and his wife Betsey of Stephentown conveyed to an unplaced Orry G. Harris two parcels of 47 acres and 76 acres in Stephentown, the latter parcel subject to terms of a lease executed by Stephen Van Rensselaer on 6 Aug. 1806 to "James Harris Junior."[1845] Relationships are unstated, but James Jr. is probably Morgan's older brother James W. Harris who would have been styled "Junior" in 1806 to distinguish him from his uncle James Harris (no. 6 ii) then residing in Stephentown. In 1859, John Harris, Morgan Harris, Hannah wife of Benjamin Dusenbury, and Rachel Andrus were mentioned as children of "Wm Harris a deceased brother of . . . Orry Harris."[1846]

Children of William[4] and Rachel (Rundle) Harris:

1 *John*[5] *Harris*, b. ca. 1782-84, deceased in 1859.[1847]

2 *James W. Harris*, b. say 1785, but between 1785 and 1790, living Buffalo, N.Y., in 1844; m. Elizabeth Dusenbury, dau. of Enoch of Nassau.[1848]

3 *Morgan Harris*, b. N.Y., ca. 1789, living in Troy, N.Y., in July 1850, aged 61,[1849] but deceased in 1859; m. (another) Elizabeth Dusenbury.[1850]

4 *Hannah Harris*, b. ca. 1790-94; m. Benjamin Dusenbury.

5 *Rachel Harris*, b. Litchfield, Conn., 21 Jan. 1795; m. Nassau, N.Y., 14 June 1814, Sylvester Andrus.[1851]

[1841] 1800 U.S. Census, Stephentown, Rensselaer Co., N.Y., p. 936.

[1842] Rensselaer Co., N.Y., Deeds, 77:403.

[1843] Kates, *Patriot Soldiers*, 2:427-28. William is not found in Rensselaer Co. in the 1810 census.

[1844] Erie Co., N.Y., Probates, file 9231.

[1845] Rensselaer Co., N.Y., Deeds, 42:292, 77:435.

[1846] Rensselaer Co., N.Y., Probates, file 138 (petition of Richard Smith).

[1847] In 1859 William Harris "of Texas" and Hiram and Edmund Harris "of Troy N.Y." were mentioned as "children of John Harris a deceased son of Wm Harris a deceased brother" of Orry Harris (Rensselaer Co., N.Y., Probates, file 138 [petition of Richard Smith]).

[1848] Phillips, "Abstracts of Wills of Rensselaer County," no. 838.

[1849] 1850 U.S. Census, City of Troy, 6th Ward, Rensselaer Co., N.Y., p. 206.

[1850] In 1859, William H. Harris of East Nassau, George Harris of Stephentown, Rachel Arnold of Providence, R.I., Catharine the widow of Anson Barnes of Troy, Caroline the wife of [Julius F.] Quimby of Troy, and Deborah J[ane] wife of [Harlan J.] Bennett of Troy were named as "children of Morgan Harris a deceased son of Wm Harris a deceased brother of . . . Orry Harris" (Rensselaer Co., N.Y., Probates, file 138 [petition of Richard Smith]).

6 *Joseph* Harris, b. 1795-1800; m. Flora Beach.

7 *George Harris,* b. 1795-1800; m. Marilla Hill.

8 *William Harris,* b. Rensselaer Co. ca. 1804;[1852] m. Sophia Williams.

9 *Loretta Harris,* b. ca. 1805; m. Joel S. Smith.

vi ELIZABETH HARRIS, b. Bedford, N.Y., 29 Jan. 1759, d. Ossining, Westchester Co., N.Y., 18 Nov. 1848; m. Bedford 29 Dec. 1777 JAMES TROWBRIDGE, b. there ca. 1754, who d. in Ossining 30 April 1821, son of Samuel and Anna (Eells) Trowbridge.[1853] Elizabeth's Revolutionary War widow's pension application, dated 4 Jan. 1837, states that Abijah Harris and Ezekiel Harris of Bedford were present at her marriage there in 1777.[1854] It was said in 1859 that Orry Harris "had a sister Betsey Trowbridge who died & left children whose names and places of residence are unknown."[1855]

Children of James and Elizabeth[4] (Harris) Trowbridge, b. at Bedford:[1856]

1 *Samuel Trowbridge,* b. 25 Jan. 1779.

2 *John Trowbridge,* b. 26 March 1781.

3 *Harris Trowbridge,* b. 13 Sept. 1783.

4 *James Trowbridge,* b. 17 July 1785.

5 *Stephen Trowbridge,* b. 22 Feb. 1787.

6 *George Trowbridge,* b. 6 Dec. 1789.

7 *Polly Trowbridge,* b. 16 Jan. 1792.

8 *Betsey Trowbridge,* b. 11 April 1794.

9 *Sarah Trowbridge,* b. 14 April 1796.

10 *Ann Trowbridge,* b. 2 Dec. 1798.

11 *Catharine Trowbridge,* b. 2 Aug. 1802.

vii MARY HARRIS, b. ca. 1760, d. Nassau, Rensselaer Co., 10 May 1839, age 79, bur. in East Nassau Cemetery near her brother Daniel Harris.[1857] She m. PETER BROWN, b. Nine Partners, Dutchess Co., N.Y., ca. 1756, who d. at Nassau after 9 Aug. 1832, when he applied for a pension,[1858] and before 30 March 1835 when his will was proved. Peter's pension application states his birthplace and age (77 years), and claims that he had enlisted at Nassau and served in the New York Line during the Revolution. His household is found at Stephentown in 1790 and 1800, and at Nassau in 1810 and 1820 (the east part of Nassau was formed from Stephentown in 1808). These censuses indicate that he probably had four children—two boys and two girls—born in the 1780s. His will dated at Nassau on 19 Feb. 1831 names wife Mary, daughter Polly Hicks, sons Peter Jr. and David "now upwards of 40 years of age," and appoints son David Brown and son-in-law Bernard Hicks execu-

---

[1851] Kates, *Patriot Soldiers,* 2:428.

[1852] 1855 New York State Census, Hamburg, Erie Co.

[1853] Francis Bacon Trowbridge, *The Trowbridge Genealogy* (New Haven: Tuttle, Morehouse & Taylor, 1908), 133, 153.

[1854] White, *Abstracts of Revolutionary War Pension Files,* 3:3541 (file no. W16763).

[1855] Rensselaer Co., N.Y., Probates, file 138 (petition of Richard Smith).

[1856] *Trowbridge Genealogy,* 153.

[1857] Charles Shepard II and Milton Thomas, *Some Rensselaer County Gravestone Inscriptions* (Washington, D.C.: C. Shepard, 1923), 32.

[1858] White, *Abstracts of Revolutionary War Pension Files,* 1:428 (file no. S28652).

tors.[1859] It was said in 1859 that Orry Harris had a "sister by the name of Mary wife of Peter Brown who died and left a son David Brown of Illinois & another son Peter Brown residence unknown and a daughter Mary Hicks of Nassau N.Y. widow of Bernard Hicks."[1860]

Children of Peter and Mary[4] (Harris) Brown, order not certain:
1 prob. a daughter[5] b. by 1784 and living in 1800.
2 *David Brown*, b. ca. 1785-90, who resided sometime in Illinois.
3 *Peter Brown Jr.*, b. ca. 1785-90, living Nassau, N.Y., in 1830.[1861]
4 *Mary Brown*, b. prob. ca. 1790; m. Bernard Hicks.

viii ROBERT HARRIS JR., b. say 1762 (between 1755 and 1765), was living in Sherburne, Chenango Co., N.Y., in 1820.[1862] Based on his children's apparent ages, he m. probably by about 1785, but his wife remains unidentified. He seems to be the Robert Harris who served after Sept. 1780 as a private with Ezekiel, Justus, and William Harris in Capt. Moses St. John's Grenadier Company of Col. Thomas Thomas's 2nd Regiment, Westchester Co. Militia.[1863] Robert was with his father at Nassau by 1790, however, when his household consisted of a male aged 16 or over, one under 16, and two females.[1864] In 1800, his home there included himself aged 26-44, a male aged 16-25, a female aged 45 or over, a female aged 26-44, and a female aged 10-15.[1865] He may be, instead of his father, the Robert Harris who was released in Feb. 1803 from rent due on a farm leased from Stephen Van Rensselaer.[1866] Robert had moved to Sherburne by 1810, when his household consisted of himself and a female both aged 45 or over.[1867] They were still there in 1820, probably as renters since no deeds are found for him in Chenango Co. It was said in 1859 that Orry Harris had "a brother Robert Harris who died and left a son Grove Harris and a daughter Betsey whose places of residence are unknown."[1868]

Children of Robert Jr.[4] and _____ (_____) Harris:
1 *Grove D.[5] Harris*, b. prob. near 1785, was residing near his father at Sherburne, Chenango Co., in 1810, and was living in Sempronius, Cayuga Co., in 1830.[1869]
2 *Betsey Harris*, b. 1785-90, at home in 1800.

ix (prob.) JOHN W. HARRIS, b. N.Y. 21 June 1764 (calc.), who d. at Greenfield, Saratoga Co., N.Y., 10 June 1851, age 86y 11m 19d, and buried in a ceme-

---

[1859] Ralph David Phillips, "Abstracts of Wills of Rensselaer County, N.Y., 1787–1850" (Nassau, N.Y., 1938), no. 988.

[1860] Rensselaer Co., N.Y., Probates, file 138 (petition of Richard Smith).

[1861] 1830 U.S. Census, Nassau, Rensselaer Co., N.Y., p. 302.

[1862] 1820 U.S. Census, Sherburne, Chenango Co., N.Y., p. 354.

[1863] Fernow, *New York in the Revolution*, 305, 389.

[1864] 1790 U.S. Census, Stephentown, Rensselaer Co., N.Y., p. 292.

[1865] 1800 U.S. Census, Stephentown, Rensselaer Co., N.Y., p. 935.

[1866] "Van Rensselaer Manor Papers," p. 107.

[1867] 1810 U.S. Census, Sherburne, Chenango Co., N.Y., p. 358.

[1868] Rensselaer Co., N.Y., Probates, file 138 (petition of Richard Smith).

[1869] 1830 U.S. Census, Sempronius, Cayuga Co., N.Y., p. 311.

tery off the South Greenfield Road.[1870] His wife HANNAH ____, b. ca. 1770, d. 15 May 1841, aged 71, is buried beside him.

John W. is presumably the John Harris, a single man in Nassau (then Stephentown), Rensselaer Co., N.Y., in 1790, when his household was listed in sequence with his presumed father Robert and brothers Daniel, Orry, and James Harris.[1871] He would be the John Harris who about 1782 served as a private with [his older brother] James Harris and [cousins] Ezekiel and Ephraim Harris (nos. 7 i and 7 ii) in Capt. John Schermerhorn's Company of Col. Killian Van Rensselaer's 4th Regiment (2nd Rensselaerwyck Battalion) of Albany Co. Militia.[1872] John W. was in Greenfield by 1800, where his cousins Ezekiel and Ephraim Harris had settled a decade before. He was residing there in 1850 at age 86 in the home of Nathan G. Willsee, aged 38, and apparent wife Sharlott Willsee, aged 32.[1873] John W. is not found in 1810, but he appears in all later U.S. Censuses at Greenfield through 1850. The early censuses suggest that he may have had at least a daughter b. in the 1790s, who was at home in 1800, but he probably died without descendants as he is not mentioned with other siblings in his brother Orry Harris's probate in 1860.

x   DANIEL HARRIS, b. N.Y. ca. 1767, d. Nassau, Rensselaer Co., on 1 June 1855, age 88, where he is buried in East Nassau Cemetery.[1874] He m. by about 1798 (see children) BETHIAH ____, b. Conn. ca. 1773, who d. 1 July 1857, age 84, and buried in the same cemetery. In 1790, Daniel Harris, then single, was separately listed in the census for Nassau (then Stephentown) near his father and brothers James, Robert Jr., William, and Orry Harris. Daniel's household appears there in all later U.S. Censuses through 1850, when he was a "farmer," aged 83, and "blind."[1875]

On 7 March 1836, Daniel Harris "of Nassau," by mark, quitclaimed to his son Seth a 150-acre "farm . . . in the Town of Nassau" subject to a lease executed by Seth the same day to "Daniel Harris and Bethiah his wife" for their natural lives or the "longest liver" of them. The property was as described in a "Lease executed to Ezekiel Thomas by Stephen Van Rensselaer" on 27 Aug. 1790. Next year, on 7 Oct. 1837, Seth assigned the property back to Daniel. When Seth acknowledged the deed that day, the commissioner noted that Seth was "made known to me on oath of [the witness] Henry Harris of the City of Troy."[1876] Subsequently, in March 1843, Daniel reassigned the same property to Seth, who, with his wife, Adelia Ann, quit-

---

[1870] Elizabeth Prather Ellsberry, "Cemetery Records of Saratoga County, New York," typescript, 2 vols. (Chillicothe, Mo., 197–), 1:12, 13.

[1871] 1790 U.S. Census, Stephentown, Rensselaer Co., N.Y., p. 285.

[1872] Fernow, *New York in the Revolution*, 264, 389. Ezekiel and Ephraim Harris's brother John (no. 7 iv) was too young (about age 12 in 1782) to be the private in Capt. Schermerhorn's Company.

[1873] 1850 U.S. Census, Greenfield, Saratoga Co., N.Y., p. 305.

[1874] Shepard and Thomas, *Rensselaer County Gravestone Inscriptions*, 29, 32. The 1855 state census, which could have provided the county of Daniel's birth, was taken 19 days after he died. His "widow" Bethiah's birth place is stated "Conn." (Dwelling no. 71).

[1875] 1850 U.S. Census, Nassau, Rensselaer Co., N.Y., p. 377.

[1876] Rensselaer Co., N.Y., Deeds, 44:327; 64:488.

claimed it to his brother Robert R. Harris of Nassau on 4 Nov. 1843 and soon thereafter moved to Wisconsin.[1877] On 25 Aug. 1846, Daniel Harris conveyed his "undivided half" (except 10 acres "this day conveyed to Samuel G. Harris") of the 150-acre farm "formerly owned by Robert R. Harris" to Robert's widow, Lurena Harris, and four minor children.[1878]

Eight of the following children are named in their uncle Orry Harris's will dated at Stephentown on 23 April 1850 (no. 6 xi below). Another child seems to be the Henry Harris of Troy in 1837 who could be the "Rev. H. Harris," b. 1807, d. 1846, who is buried near Daniel and Bethiah in East Nassau Cemetery.[1879]

Children of Daniel[4] and Bethiah (____) Harris:

1 *Polly[5] Harris*, b. N.Y. ca. 1798, living at Nassau in 1860, age 62;[1880] m. Jacob Van Hoesen.

2 *Abigail Harris*, b. N.Y. ca. 1799, living at Nassau in 1850, age 51;[1881] m. Reynolds Knapp.

3 *Betsey Harris*, b. Rensselaer Co. ca. 1802, living at Nassau in 1860, unm.

4 *Pamelia Harris*, b. N.Y. ca. 1804, living at Nassau in 1860;[1882] m. Jason Belknap.

5 *Robert R. Harris*, b. ca. 1807, d. Nassau 16 June 18[4]6, age 39;[1883] m. Lurena ____.[1884]

6 (prob. Rev.) *Henry Harris*, b. 1807, d. 1846.

7 *Daniel Harris Jr.*, said to have been residing at Vandalia, Fayette Co., Ill., in 1859.[1885]

8 *Seth Harris*, b. N.Y. ca. 1812, living in Winnebago Co., Wis., in 1860, age 48;[1886] m. Adelia Ann ____.[1887]

9 *Samuel G. Harris*, b. Rensselaer Co. ca. 1813, living in Nassau in 1880;[1888] m. ca. 1835 Charity Dusenbury.[1889]

[1877] Rensselaer Co., N.Y., Deeds, 58:8-9; 64:58-59.

[1878] Rensselaer Co., N.Y., Deeds, 66:22.

[1879] Shepard and Thomas, *Rensselaer County Gravestone Inscriptions*, 34.

[1880] 1860 U.S. Census, Nassau, Rensselaer Co., N.Y., p. 404.

[1881] 1850 U.S. Census, Nassau, Rensselaer Co., N.Y., p. 354.

[1882] 1860 U.S. Census, Nassau, Rensselaer Co., N.Y., p. 403.

[1883] Robert R. Harris is buried beside his mother in East Nassau Cemetery, his year of death wrongly transcribed from his tombstone as 1816 (Shepard and Thomas, *Rensselaer County Gravestone Inscriptions*, 29). Robert R. was age 30-39 at the time of the 1840 U.S. Census in Nassau (p. 189), when his household included, beside himself, a male and a female each under 5, a female 30-39, and a female 15-19.

[1884] "Widow" Lurena Harris, b. ca. 1806, was living with her children in Daniel Harris's home at Nassau in 1850 and 1855, and with her sister-in-law Betsey Harris there in 1860. "Laura Harris," age 74, was called "mother-in-law" in the home of Jay and Pamelia Bingtton (age 34) of Nassau in 1880 (U.S. Census, p. 28).

[1885] Rensselaer Co., N.Y., Probates, file 138 (petition of Richard Smith).

[1886] 1860 U.S. Census, Utica Township, Winnebago Co., Wis., p. 785.

[1887] Rensselaer Co., N.Y., Deeds, 64:58-59.

[1888] 1880 U.S. Census, Nassau, Rensselaer Co., N.Y., p. 15.

[1889] Samuel G. Harris's household was near his father Daniel's home in 1850 (U.S. Census, p. 374) and included wife Charity and nine children, one named "Daniel R.," age 12. Charity's surname is from the IGI.

xi ORRY HARRIS, b. Conn. [*sic*] ca. 1769 (1850 census), d. Stephentown 13 Dec. 1859, age 90, but buried beside his wife, Deborah, in Winslow Road Cemetery nearby at New Lebanon, Columbia Co., N.Y.[1890] "Oorey Harris" m. at the Reformed Protestant Dutch Church in Nassau, 23 Feb. 1815, DEBORAH PADDOCK,[1891] who d. 2 March 1818. In 1790, "Arie" Harris, then single, was separately listed near his father and older brothers in Stephentown. He is not found in 1800, but his household appears in all later U.S. Censuses at Stephentown through 1850, and in the state census of 1855 when he was a "farmer," age 86, "widowed," and residing in the home of his niece Pamelia and her husband Jason Belknap.[1892]

 The will of Orry Harris of Stephentown, dated 23 April 1850 and proved 26 March 1860, gave equal undivided halves of his real estate and livestock to Jason Belknap and his wife, Pamelia, "the daughter of my brother Daniel Harris." To brother Daniel and his wife Bethiah, Orry gave $125 each, and to the rest of their children he gave legacies as follows: Daniel Harris Jr. and Samuel Harris $200 each; Seth Harris, Polly the widow of Jacob Van Hoesen, and Abigail the wife of Reynolds Knapp $100 each; Betty Harris $300; and the minor children of Robert Harris deceased (Mary Louisa, John S., Sarah Elizabeth, and Amelia Caroline Harris) $37.50 each. Orry appointed Richard Smith and Meshach Strait executors; the witnesses were Horatio N. Hand and Jonathan N. Fellows.[1893] The petition of the executor Richard Smith of New Lebanon, Columbia Co., presented on 27 Dec. 1859, states that Orry had died at Stephentown on 13 Dec. 1859 leaving "no widow or descendants."[1894] Cited frequently above, this petition identifies many of Orry's brothers and sisters, nephews and nieces, living and deceased.

7 EPHRAIM[3] HARRIS (*Robert[2]*, *Thomas[1]*) was born at Stamford, Connecticut, on 31 July 1725[1895] and was living in Rensselaer County, New York, in 1790. He had married and was residing at Bedford, New York, in November 1754 (birth of son Ezekiel), but his wife is not identified.

 Ephraim and his brother James Harris moved by 1760 to Dutchess County, New York, where they were assessed for taxes in Crum Elbow Precinct that February and June, apparently in that part of it that soon became Charlotte Precinct.[1896] Ephraim was selected at Charlotte Precinct meetings in April 1774 and April 1775 as highway overseer for a section of road running southerly from Stephen Wood's land past his own property and on

---

[1890] *Tree Talks*, Columbia Co., p. 2. In 1855 Orry's birthplace was given as Rensselaer Co., surely in error.

[1891] Reyden W. Vosburgh, "New York Church Records" (microfilm Reel 8, no. 5), p. 65.

[1892] 1855 New York State Census, Stephentown, Rensselaer Co., dwelling 436.

[1893] Rensselaer Co., N.Y., Wills, 53:314-16; original in file 138.

[1894] Rensselaer Co., N.Y., Probates, file 138.

[1895] Barbour Collection, citing Stamford VR1:10.

[1896] Buck, *Crum Elbow Tax Lists*, 18; see also Jones, "Harris Family of Block Island and Dutchess County," NYGBR 84 (1953):144n.

to the south side of Israel Deuel's land.[1897] He was assessed there through 1777, when he moved on up the Hudson to Schodack, Rensselaer County (then Rensselaerwyck or Phillipstown, Albany County), near his brother Robert (no. 6) in adjoining Nassau. Robert apparently had come up from Bedford about that time. Ephraim and a son of that name account for the two Ephraim Harris households at Rensselaerwyck in 1790.[1898] The older Ephraim's household consisted of a male aged sixteen or over, one under sixteen, and two females.

By that time, three other sons—Ezekiel (born in Bedford), Stephen, and John (born in Dutchess County)—had moved on upriver to Greenfield, Saratoga County (then Ballstown, Albany County), where they were adjacently listed in 1790 and where in 1817 they owned adjoining properties in Lot No. 1 of Great Lot No. 4 of the 22nd allotment of the Patent of Kayaderosseras.[1899] They all named sons *Ephraim*, born from about 1786 to 1793, who are styled 1st, 2nd, and 3rd in Saratoga County records.

Children of Ephraim³ and ____ (____) Harris, perhaps there were others:[1900]

    i   EZEKIEL⁴ HARRIS, b. Bedford, N.Y., 26 Nov. 1754, was living in Greenfield, Saratoga Co., in 1834[1901] and probably was the male aged 80-89 in his son Lewis's home there in 1840.[1902] His unidentified wife, b. 1755–60, is traced through the censuses there from 1790 through 1830 and would be the female aged 80-89 in Lewis's home in 1840.

        Ezekiel served during the Revolution as a private with his brother Ephraim and cousins James and John Harris (nos. 6 ii and 6 ix) in Capt. John Schermerhorn's Company of Col. Killian Van Rensselaer's 4th Regi-

---

[1897] Franklin D. Roosevelt, ed., *Records of Crum Elbow Precinct, Dutchess County, New York, 1738–1761*, Dutchess Co. Hist. Soc. Coll., 7 (1940):81, 86.

[1898] 1790 U.S. Census, Rensselaerwyck, Rensselaer Co., N.Y., pp. 267, 274.

[1899] Saratoga Co., N.Y., Deeds, H:119.

[1900] Ephraim's children possibly included the Robert and Seth Harris who appear with households listed adjacent to each other at Rensselaerwyck in 1790 (census, p. 267) but gone by 1800. They could be, however, sons of the unrelated sythemaker Joseph⁵ Harris (*Daniel*⁴⁻³⁻², *Thomas*¹) who lived near Pine Plains in Dutchess Co., N.Y. Joseph's son Seth, b. ca. 1763, is known to have resided several places including Burlington, Vt., and Kingsbury, Washington Co., N.Y., before returning about 1810 to Pine Plains, where he d. in 1842 (Gale Ion Harris and Margaret Harris Stover, "The First Daniel Harris of Goshen, Connecticut, and his Descendants in Dutchess and Washington Counties, New York," NYGBR 119 [1988]:151-53, 223-25). A brother Robert of this Seth is not known, but the next-door neighbor of the Seth at Rensselaerwyck could be the Robert Herris with wife Elizabeth who had a son John Smit Herris b. 7 Sept. 1786 and bp. 15 Oct. 1786 in the Round Top Lutheran Church at Pine Plains (Vosburgh, "New York Church Records," microfilm Reel 8, p. 28) and not found there at the time of the 1790 census.

[1901] Revolutionary War pension file S9914, National Archives, wife and children not mentioned.

[1902] 1840 U.S. Census, Greenfield, Saratoga Co., N.Y., p. 188, which, however, does not list Ezekiel in the household as a Revolutionary War veteran as would be expected from his pension record.

ment (2nd Rensselaerwyck Battalion) of Albany Co. Militia.[1903] Ezekiel's pension application, dated at Greenfield 9 April 1834, states his birth date and place, and claims that he served during and after 1777 from Phillipstown, Albany (now Rensselaer) Co., N.Y., and that he had been living in Greenfield since 1789. On 27 Dec. 1788, Ezekiel Harris, then a "farmer of Phillipstown," had purchased 116 acres in the Kayaderosseras Patent, Albany (later Saratoga) Co., from James and John Beekman of the City of Albany.[1904] On 4 June 1832, Ezekiel Harris of Greenfield sold to Lewis Harris 72 acres "being the farm on which . . . Ezekiel Harris now lives." The property was in Lewis's "actual possession now being" and adjoined the "home" farms of John Harris and Joseph Mitchell.[1905]

Children of Ezekiel[4] and ____ (____) Harris; the early censuses indicate another male and five female children b. by 1804:

> 1 *Ezekiel[5] Harris Jr.*, b. 1775-80, living Greenfield in Oct. 1825; m. Keziah ____.[1906]
> 2 *Ephraim Harris 1st*, b. Albany Co. ca. 1786,[1907] d. 30 Nov. 1857, age 71; m. Betsey ____.[1908]
> 3 *James Harris*, b. ca. 1790, living 1830; m. Lois ____.[1909]
> 4 *Lewis Harris*, b. Saratoga Co. ca. 1801,[1910] living Greenfield in 1880, age 79;[1911] m. Amy ____.

ii EPHRAIM HARRIS, b. say 1760 (between 1755 and 1765), was living in Schodack, Rensselaer Co., in 1790, 1800, and 1810, where he d. between 14 April and 10 May 1813 (will and probate) leaving widow ABIGAIL ____,[1912] b. in R.I. ca. 1763, and nine named children. Abigail was living in her daughter Phebe Waterbury's home nearby at Nassau in 1850, age 87.[1913]

Ephraim served in the Revolution with his brother Ezekiel (see above) in Capt. John Schermerhorn's Company from Phillipstown (later Schodack). In Sept. 1794, Ephraim leased 110 acres in Nassau from Stephen Van Rensselaer for an annual rent of twelve bushels of wheat.[1914] Ephraim's will appoints his wife Abigail, son John, and Joseph Cain as executors. Thomas

---

[1903] Fernow, *New York in the Revolution*, 264, 389.

[1904] Albany Co., N.Y., Deeds, 12:91.

[1905] Saratoga Co., N.Y., Deeds, DD:44-45.

[1906] Saratoga Co., N.Y., Deeds, K:385, M:412. Ezekiel Jr. may be the male age 50-59 in the home of (his son?) Israel Harris, b. ca. 1805, in the 1830 U.S. Census for Greenfield (p. 224).

[1907] 1855 New York State Census, Town of Greenfield, Saratoga Co., Fam. 176. Ephraim had been living in Greenfield for "66 years" in agreement with his father Ezekiel's statement in 1834 that he, Ezekiel, had moved there from Phillipstown in Albany (later Rensselaer) Co. in 1789.

[1908] Ephraim Harris and his wife Betsey (d. 9 Sept. 1858, aged 68) are buried in the Mitchell Cemetery "located about 2 miles south from Porters Corners" in Saratoga Co. (C. E. Durkee, "Some of Ye Epitaphs in Saratoga County" [1876], FHL microfilm 17,932, p. 564).

[1909] Saratoga Co., N.Y., Deeds, R:409, S:49, T:90.

[1910] 1855 New York State Census, Town of Greenfield, Saratoga Co., Fam. 149.

[1911] 1880 U.S. Census, Greenfield, Saratoga Co., N.Y., E.D. 72, p. 1.

[1912] Phillips, "Abstracts of Wills of Rensselaer County," no. 289.

[1913] 1850 U.S. Census, Nassau, Rensselaer Co., N.Y., p. 393.

[1914] Rensselaer Co., N.Y., Deeds, 77:402.

Frost, Joseph Cain, and Levi Lobdell witnessed. By indenture dated 7 Feb. 1831, John and Ruth Mickel of Cayuga Co., Richard and Mary Caine of Saratoga Co., Henry and Cynthia Rowland of Onondaga Co., and Robert and Mary Bullis, David E. and Phebe H. Waterbury, and John and Sarah Harris of Rensselaer Co., "heirs and legatees of Ephraim Harris deceased," quitclaimed to their brother William Harris of Nassau in Rensselaer Co. their shares of Ephraim Harris's land in Schodack and Nassau. The grantors all signed their names except Eunice Garrison, who signed by mark. John Harris and his wife Sarah were "cotenants" of the land with William Harris. The conveyance was subject to annual rents payable in winter wheat according to "the original lease from Stephen Van Rensselaer Esq."[1915]

Children of Ephraim[4] and Abigail (____) Harris:[1916]

    1 *Ruth[5] Harris*, "eldest daughter" in 1813, living Cayuga Co., N.Y., in 1831; m. John Mickel.

    2 *Eunice Harris*, b. 1780-90, living Schodack, Rensselaer Co., in 1840;[1917] m. Daniel D. Garrison.

    3 *Mary Harris*, living Saratoga Co., N.Y., in 1831; m. Richard Caine.

    4 *John Harris*, b. ca. 1790; m. Nassau 2 April 1812 Sarah Waterbury.[1918]

    5 *Hannah Harris*, living 1813, d. prob. before 1831.

    6 *Thirza Harris*, b. N.Y. ca. 1793, living Stillwater, Saratoga Co., in 1850, age 57; m. Robert Bullis.

    7 *Cynthia Harris*, living Onondaga Co., N.Y., in 1831, but apparently d. there before 1840;[1919] m. Henry Rowland.

    8 *William Harris*, b. ca. 1801, d. Schodack, N.Y., 11 March 1848, age 47;[1920] m. Lucinda Waterbury.[1921]

    9 *Phebe H. Harris*, b. Rensselaer Co. ca. 1807, living Nassau, N.Y., in 1855, age 48;[1922] m. David E. Waterbury.

iii   STEPHEN HARRIS, b. in 1760s, probably in Dutchess Co., N.Y., was living in Saratoga, Saratoga Co., N.Y., in 1840.[1923] He m. SARAH ____, b. 1760s, who consented to his land deeds in 1821, 1825, and 1829, and presumably the female age 70-79 in his home in 1840. He was in Ballstown by 1790 when adjacently listed with Ezekiel and John Harris, his own household then including a male age 16 or over, one under 16, and five females.[1924] At

---

[1915] Rensselaer Co., N.Y., Deeds, 26:29-31.

[1916] Phillips, "Abstracts of Wills of Rensselaer County," no. 289; Rensselaer Co., N.Y., Deeds, 26:29-31.

[1917] 1840 U.S. Census, Schodack, Rensselaer Co., N.Y., p. 128.

[1918] "Records of the Reformed Protestant Dutch Church in the Town of Nassau, Rensselaer County, N.Y.," Vosburgh Collection, Reel 8, no. 5, p. 62.

[1919] 1840 U.S. Census, Onondaga Co., N.Y., p. 122.

[1920] Milton Thomas, ed., *Vital Records of Rensselaer County, New York, Deaths 1847–1851* (Troy, N.Y., 1923), 17.

[1921] Lucinda Waterbury Harris, "wife of William Harris," d. 13 Aug. 1855, aged 50, and buried in Clark's Chapel Cemetery at Nassau (Shepard and Thomas, *Rensselaer County Gravestone Inscriptions*, 46).

[1922] 1855 New York State Census, Nassau, Rensselaer Co., p. 21.

[1923] 1840 U.S. Census, Town of Saratoga, Saratoga Co., N.Y., p. 270.

[1924] 1790 U.S. Census, Ballstown, Saratoga Co., N.Y., p. 305.

age 26-44, he was enumerated in Greenfield with a family in 1800,[1925] and is found there in 1820 and 1830.

In April 1815, Stephen Harris "of Greenfield . . . farmer" bought 98½ acres "now in [his] possession" in the "22nd allotment of the Patent of Kayaderosseras."[1926] In Oct. 1821, Stephen Harris Jr. witnessed when Stephen and his wife Sarah, both signing by marks, sold a 50-acre portion of this property to John E. Harris of Greenfield, it "being part of [their] homestead farm" and in John E. Harris's "actual possession now being."[1927] In April 1825, Stephen and Sarah sold another 44-acre portion to John Harris of Greenfield, probably Stephen's brother (no. 7 iv).[1928] In April 1829, they sold the remaining portion of that property to Ephraim Harris "the 2nd" of Greenfield, "in his actual possession now being."[1929] The relationships are unstated, but the first and third of these three deeds are of the kind one would expect from parents to sons. In Oct. 1830, Ephraim Harris 2nd and wife Hannah, then "of the Town of Halfmoon," sold his portion to John Harris and Lewis Harris of Greenfield, apparently his uncle John (no. 7 iv) and cousin Lewis (no. 7 i 4).[1930]

Apparent children of Stephen[4] and Sarah (____) Harris; the early censuses also include several unidentified female children:

1 *Ephraim[5] Harris 2nd*, b. near 1790, living in Milton, Saratoga Co., in April 1836; m. (1) by Nov. 1817 Polly (prob. Mary Hendricks), (2) by Oct. 1830 Hannah ____.[1931]

2 *Stephen Harris Jr.*, b. in 1790s, a witness in 1821.

3 *John E. Harris*, b. 1795–1800, living 1830.

4 (prob.) *Thomas Harris,* b. 1805-10, whose household adjoined his apparent father in 1830.

iv JOHN HARRIS, b. Dutchess Co., N.Y., ca. 1770,[1932] d. Saratoga Co. 8 Feb. 1859, age 89, where he is buried at Greenfield in the Harris Cemetery beside his wife, KAZIA ____, b. ca. 1767, who d. 12 May 1841, age 74.[1933] John's household appears in census entries for Ballstown and Greenfield

[1925] 1800 U.S. Census, Greenfield, Saratoga Co., N.Y., p. 57.

[1926] Saratoga Co., N.Y., Deeds, O:119.

[1927] Saratoga Co., N.Y., Deeds, O:15.

[1928] Saratoga Co., N.Y., Deeds, L:322.

[1929] Saratoga Co., N.Y., Deeds, R:513. In 1820 the household of Ephraim Harris 2nd, his age wrongly marked as 45 years or over, was listed adjacent to that of Stephen Harris at Greenfield (U.S. Census, p. 174a).

[1930] Saratoga Co., N.Y., Deeds, S:352. John Harris seems to have provided the purchase price of $172. In Aug. 1832 he conveyed his interest in it, for the same consideration, to Lewis Harris "in his actual possession now being" (ibid., AA:544).

[1931] Saratoga Co., N.Y., Deeds, H:11, 119, S:352, BB:306. Ephraim 2nd appears to be the "Ephrium Harris" said to have had with wife Mary Hendricks three sons b. in Saratoga Co.: Justice in 1823, Isaac in 1825, and Wellington in 1827 ("Harris-Hendricks-Fitzsimmons," NYGBR 100 [1969]:180).

[1932] 1855 New York State Census, Town of Greenfield, Saratoga Co., Fam. 150. John was "widowed" and had been living in Greenfield for "65 years."

[1933] This cemetery is "a small private enclosure located on the Harris estate, about one-half mile east of Schoolhouse No. 3" (Durkee, "Epitaphs in Saratoga County," p. 557, inscriptions read on 9 Dec. 1876).

from 1790 through 1855. John Harris and Ezekiel Harris "were residents of the Town [Greenfield] previous to 1795"[1934] and their households are adjacently listed in all U.S. censuses there from 1790 through 1820. In April 1817, John Harris and Ezekiel Harris "of Greenfield, Farmers," bought 136 acres adjoining the "east bank of Kayaderosseras Creek" and "land that John Harris first bought where he now lives."[1935] In April 1825, John Harris of Greenfield bought 44 acres there from Stephen and Sarah Harris (no. 7 iii).[1936] In July 1850 John Harris, "farmer," then age 80, was residing in Greenfield with his apparent sons Ephraim and Aaron Harris.[1937]

Children of John[4] and Kazia (____) Harris, probably others including two boys indicated in the early censuses:

    1 *Ephraim[5] Harris 3rd*, b. Saratoga Co. 20 Nov. 1793 (calc.), d. 5 Nov. 18[6]6, aged 72y 11m 15d; m. Margaret Saiben.[1938]
    2 *William Harris*, b. Saratoga Co. ca. 1798, living in Greenfield in 1860; m. Betsey ____.
    3 *Aaron Harris*, b. N.Y. ca. 1800, a widower living in Greenfield in 1880, age 80, with his nephew Charles, son of Ephraim Harris 3rd.[1939]

[1934] Sylvester, *History of Saratoga County*, 439.

[1935] Saratoga Co., N.Y., Deeds, S:135.

[1936] Saratoga Co., N.Y., Deeds, L:322.

[1937] 1850 U.S. Census, Greenfield, Saratoga Co., N.Y., p. 322.

[1938] Sylvester, *History of Saratoga County*, 512, naming them as parents of Chester and Charles Harris of Porter's Corner in Greenfield. Ephraim and Margaret (d. 16 Jan. 1870) are buried in the "Harris Cemetery" near Ephraim's parents. He was age 61 in Greenfield in 1855 (State Census, Fam. 151) and 66 there in 1860 (U.S. Census, p. 25), so his year of death could not be "1856" as read from his tombstone.

[1939] 1880 U.S. Census, Greenfield, Saratoga Co., N.Y., E.D. 72, p. 1.

APPENDIX II: OTHER HARRISES IN CONNECTICUT BEFORE 1700

A detailed study of all early Harrises in Connecticut was a necessary part of the research conducted for this book. The Harris families included in the following sketches have no known relationship to the Harrises already discussed. It is assumed, however, that basic information for them would be of interest for anyone whose ancestry includes early Harrises in Connecticut. The sketches are limited here to the first two generations; references cited in the footnotes should be consulted for additional information about descendants. The sketches are presented in order of first appearance in Connecticut sources.

Walter Harris of New London[1940] (1652)

1 **WALTER[1] HARRIS** was born in the 1590s, as estimated from the dates of his children's baptisms, and died at New London on 6 November 1654.[1941] He married by 1621 (baptism of first child) **MARY FRY**,[1942] perhaps from Axminster, Devonshire, England, who died at New London on 24 January 1655[/6].[1943]

Data presented below show that Walter and Mary's seven children were baptized at Honiton, Devonshire, at regular intervals from 1621 to 1636. Thus he was not as sometimes claimed the Walter Harris who appears as one of sixteen names on a passenger list dated at the port of London on 7 March 1631[/2].[1944] He must have been, instead, the Walter on the passenger

---

[1940] The sketch presented here is based on the article by the present author, "Walter and Mary (Fry) Harris of New London, Connecticut," NEHGR 156 (2002):145-58, 262-79, 357-72, 392, which should be consulted for information not included here.

[1941] New London Births, Marriages, and Deaths, [vol.] 1C, p. 2, FHL microfilm 1312157, Item 1 (sometimes referred to as "Vol. 1" or "first book," it is a transcript "made by the authority of the Court of Common Council, June 1st 1896").

[1942] Mary's family name is inferred from these facts: In 1643 Walter Harris was an appraiser of the estate in Weymouth, Mass., of William Fry who, by his nuncupative will, devised "a kid" each to "Thomas Harris, Thomas Rawlens & John Meggs his three sisters youngest children" (William Blake Trask, "Abstracts of the Earliest Wills upon Record in the County of Suffolk, Mass.," NEHGR 2 [1848]:385).

[1943] New London Births, Marriages, and Deaths, "first book," 2. For comments on Mary's possible home, see Burton W. Spear, *Search for the Passengers of the Mary and John, 1630*, 16 (1991):39.

[1944] John Camden Hotten, *The Original Lists of Persons of Quality . . . 1600–1700* (New York and London: J. W. Bouton, 1874), 149; Robert Charles Anderson, *The Great Migration Begins[:] Immigrants to New England 1620–1633*, 3 vols. (Boston: NEHGS, 1995), 2:866. Anderson points out that nothing is seen of the London passenger after 8 April 1633 when, as an indentured servant, he gave consent for an assignment of his service in New Plymouth. For discussion of a third Walter Harris in New England, a younger man of no known relationship to the other two, see Harris, "Walter Harris of Wethersfield, Connecticut," NEHGR 142 (1988): 323-49.

list for the ship *Speedwell* sailing from Weymouth, England, on 22 April 1637 with "his wife, six children & three servants."[1945] Soon thereafter, he was in Weymouth, Massachusetts, where he was granted land in the "west Field," eight acres in "Harrises Raing," and eight acres in the "mill fur-longe."[1946] Walter was an appraiser at Weymouth of the estate of William Fry, his brother-in-law, in December 1643,[1947] but he had moved to Dorchester by December 1648.[1948] A list of debts annexed to the will of Edward Bullock of Dorchester dated 25 July 1649 includes an item: "To Walter Harris, a pecke of Rye, for tryming for a hatt 7ᵈ or 8ⁱ."[1949]

On 20 May 1652, "Water [*sic*] Harries of Dorchester desires a house lott" at the south end of New London "by plot of land by Jno Coites."[1950] He was still at Dorchester in March 1652/3.[1951] However, he had arrived in New London before 5 December 1653, when "Goodman Harris for his son Gabriell hath given him six ackers of upland for an house lot joyning next to his fathers'." The following June, the town chose Goodman Harris as ordinary keeper. On the day Walter died, "Widdo Harris was granted by voat to keep an ordinary if she will," but she seems to have declined as the town chose John Elderkin as Walter's successor.[1952]

The will of Mary Harries [*sic*], signed by mark at New London on 19 January 1655[/6], names "my eldest daughter Sarah Lane" and Sarah's daughters Mary and Sarah, "my daughter Mary Lawrence" and Mary's "eldest sone," "second sonne," and "yongest sonne," "my yongest daughter Elizabeth Weekes," "my sonne Thomas" (ten shillings, if he doe come home or be alive), and "my sonne Gabriell" (my house, land, cattle and swine,

[1945] Peter Wilson Coldham, *The Complete Book of Emigrants, 1607–1660* (Baltimore: Genealogical Publishing Co., 1988), 185.
[1946] George Walter Chamberlain, *History of Weymouth, Massachusetts*, 4 vols. (Boston: Weymouth Historical Soc., 1923), 3:255–56, citing Weymouth Land Grants, 255.
[1947] Trask, "Abstracts of the Earliest Wills," NEHGR 2 (1848):385.
[1948] *Dorchester Town Records, Fourth Report of the Record Commissioners of the City of Boston*, 2ⁿᵈ ed. (Boston, 1883), 302 ("for br[other] Harris buildinge we haue opposed it as not knowing him to haue sufficient ground to set it vp without further Leaue from the Towne").
[1949] Trask, "Abstracts of the Earliest Wills," NEHGR 6 (1852):355-56. For Edward Bullock, see Robert Charles Anderson, George F. Sanborn Jr., and Melinde Lutz Sanborn, *The Great Migration: Immigrants to New England, 1634–1635, Volume I, A–B* (Boston: NEHGS, 1999), 476-77.
[1950] New London Deeds, 2:37; Frances Manwaring Caulkins, *History of New London, Connecticut, from the First Survey of the Coast in 1612, to 1860* (1860; repr. New London, 1895), 84. The quotations here are from transcriptions provided by Norman W. Ingham from "New London Town Records 1651–1660," 15, in hand of Obadiah Bruen, in City Clerk's vault, New London.
[1951] *Dorchester Town Records*, 315 ("It is voted [14 day of the 1 mo: 52 or 53] that whereas Walter Harris desireth a little p'cell of land, p'cill of the garden belonging to Pristes howse, and which he form'ly haue enjoyed, to by the same, it is by vote left vnto the select men").
[1952] Caulkins, *History of New London*, 86, 88.

with all other goodes reall and p[er]sonall in Pequet or any other place). Mary's will also mentions "my sister Migges, "my cosen Calib Rawlyns," "my two cosens Mary and Elizabeth ffry," Mary Barnet, "my sister Hannah Rawlin," "my brother Rawlin," "my two kinswomen Elizabeth Hubbard and Mary Steevens," and "my brother Migges his three youngest children." In addition, Mary gave Rebekah Bruen "a pynt pott of pewter, a new petticoate and wascote w[hi]ch she is to spin herselfe; alsoe an old byble, and a hatt w[hi]ch was my sonn Thomas his hatt." She appointed son Gabriel as sole executor. Mary died not long after Walter, so one inventory dated 14 April 1656 sufficed for both.[1953]

Children of Walter[1] and Mary (Fry) Harris, all baptized in Honiton, Devonshire:[1954]

    i   MARY[2] HARRIS, bp. 4 Nov. 1621, died young.
    ii SARAH HARRIS, bp. 13 March 1624[/5], d. Hingham, Mass., 27 March 1695.[1955] She m. by 1638 (first child) GEORGE[2] LANE of Hingham, b. ca. 1613, who d. there 4 June 1689,[1956] son of William[1] and Agnes (Farnsworth) Lane of Dorchester.[1957] The will of Mary Harris of New London in Jan. 1655[/6] gave "to my eldest daughter, Sarah Lane, the bigest brass pan, and to her daughter Mary, a silver spoone. And to her daughter Sarah, the bigest pewter dish and one silken riben. Likewise I give to her daughter Mary, a pewter candlesticke."[1958] The will of George Lane, dated 16 Oct. 1688, proved 20 Aug. 1689, names his wife Sarah, sons Josiah, Ebenezer, and Peter, daughters Sarah Luis, Elizabeth Poor, and Mary Ellis, and grandchildren Thomas Robbart, George Umphrey, William Umphrey, Ebenezer Umphrey, and Joseph Umphrey, and Mary Lane, daughter of his son Josiah.[1959]

[1953] New London Deeds, 3:47, 49. For a transcription and comments on Mary Harris's will, see Caulkins, *History of New London*, 269-70.

[1954] A. J. P. Skinner, "Honiton Parish Register, Baptisms, 1562–1734," (1919), 73, 84, 89, 94, 101, 109, 115 [FHL microfilm 917147]. The discovery of these baptisms is credited to Douglas Richardson in Spear, *Passengers of the Mary and John*, 16:8, 44, although the list of children given there (p. 44) omits a daughter Susannah and has some dates differing slightly from those found in Skinner's transcriptions.

[1955] C. Edward Egan, Jr., "The Hobart Journal," NEHGR 121 (1967):282 ("y[e] widow Sarah Lane died"). The date is printed 26 March 1694/5 [*sic*] in *History of the Town of Hingham, Massachusetts*, 3 vols. in 4 (Hingham: By the Town, 1893), 2:411. Sarah's birth was probably well before her baptism, considering how young she was when her first child was born.

[1956] Hobart Journal, 274.

[1957] James Hill Fitts, *Lane Genealogies*, 3 vols. (Exeter, N.H.: News-letter Press, 1897–1902), 2:6-8. For the Lane's origins in Beaminster, Dorsetshire, England, see Frederick J. Nicholson, "A Clue to the English Origin of Thomas[1] Lincoln (the cooper) and William[1] Lane of Hingham, Mass.," TAG 64 (1989):214-15, and "Note by the Editors," TAG 65 (1990):106.

[1958] New London, Conn., Deeds, 3:47; see also Caulkins, *History of New London*, 270.

[1959] Ellen Jeannette Lane, "Parentage of John Lane of Hingham and Norton, Mass.," NEHGR 83 (1929): 466-67, citing "Suffolk Probate Records." See also Belle Preston, *Bassett-Preston Ancestors* (New Haven: Tuttle, Morehouse & Taylor Co., 1930), 171.

iii MARY HARRIS (again), bp. 4 Feb. 1626[/7]; m. by 1652 (birth of 1st known child) NICHOLAS LAWRENCE of Charlestown and Dorchester, who d. between 26 Jan. 1684[/5] and 20 Feb. 1684[/5], the dates of his will and inventory.[1960] Nicholas's widow Mary was living on 21 May 1685, when she deposed to the inventory in Boston.[1961]

The will of Nicholas Lawrence, "sick and weake of body," left to his "loveing and kind wife Mary" all of his estate for her natural life with provisions in case "she dye before my two youngest children be brought up able to get their living." He left to his "eldest son [unnamed] one fourth part of my sheep" and to "my four other children Mary, Rebecca, Nicholas, and Benjamin" each one sheep or lamb. His inventory included carpenter's tools.

iv GABRIEL HARRIS, bp. 8 March 1628[/9], d. in New London on 16 March 1683/4.[1962] Gabriel Harris "of Pequot," the early name for New London, m. at Guilford, Conn., on 3 March 1653[/4], ELIZABETH ABBOTT, "of Guilford,"[1963] who d. as "widdow" Elizabeth Harris in New London on 17 Aug. 1702.[1964] In November 1691, Gabriel's widow was listed among members of New London First Congregational Church as "Mrs. Elizabeth Harris."[1965] The descendants of Gabriel and Elizabeth are numerous.

v ELIZABETH HARRIS, bp. 28 Aug. 1631, d. Dorchester 10 April 1723 in her 90th year according to a transcription of her gravestone inscription,[1966] though her date of death in Dorchester records is "March the [*blank*] 1722/3."[1967] She m. before 19 Jan. 1655/6 (date of her mother's will) AMIEL[2] WEEKES, bp. Seaton, Devonshire, England, 6 Nov. 1631, who d. as "Serg^{t}" at Dorchester 20 April 1679, aged 46 [*sic*],[1968] son of George[1] and Jane (Clapp) Weekes.[1969]

The will of Mary Harris of New London in Jan. 1655[/6] gave "to my youngest daughter, Elizabeth Weekes, a peece of red broad cloth, being about two yards, alsoe a damask livery cloth, a gold ring, a silver spoone, a

---

[1960] Suffolk Co., Mass., Probate, 6:490 (repaged 796–97, will), 9:119 (repaged 229, inventory), file 1406.

[1961] Suffolk Co., Mass., Probate, 9:119 (repaged 229, inventory), file 1406. It is assumed here that Nicholas's widow Mary was his only wife and the mother of his children. However, the possibility is not entirely excluded that he, instead of his son of the same name, was the Nicholas Lawrence recorded at Dorchester, strangely enough, as having married a "Mary Harice" there on 3 Nov. 1681.

[1962] Sydney H. Miner and George D. Stanton, Jr., *The Diary of Thomas Minor, Stonington, Connecticut, 1653–1684* (New London: Press of the Day Publishing Co., 1899), 182 ("gabrill Harice departed this life").

[1963] Barbour Collection of Connecticut Vital Records, citing Guilford VR A:122.

[1964] New London Births, Marriages, and Deaths, "first book," 28.

[1965] New London First Congregational Church Records, 6 vols., 1:7, FHL microfilm 5131.

[1966] William B. Trask, "Inscriptions from the Old Burial Ground in Dorchester, M[ass.], 1638–1699," NEHGR 5 (1851):255; see also *History of Weymouth*, 3:255, and Robert Dobbs Weeks, *Genealogy of the Family of George Weekes of Dorchester, Mass., 1635–1650*, 2 vols. (Newark, N.J.: Press of L. J. Hardham, 1885), 1:69-71.

[1967] *Dorchester Births, Marriages, and Deaths*, 132.

[1968] *Dorchester Births, Marriages, and Deaths*, 30 (for title and date); Trask, "Inscriptions . . . in Dorchester," NEHGR 4 (1850):167 (for date and age).

[1969] Herbert F. Seversmith, "George Weekes of Dorchester, Mass.," TAG 23 (1946):82 (baptism).

fether bed and a boulster [and] my best hatt, my gowne, a brass kettle, and a woolen jacket for her husband."[1970] The will of Jane (Clapp) (Weekes) Humphrey of Dorchester in Jan. 1666/7 gave several articles of clothing "to my sonn Amiells wife" and various items to grandchildren, including Amiel's children Elizabeth, Thankfull, Amiel, and Ebenezer Weekes.[1971]

vi   SUSANNA HARRIS, bp. 31 May 1634. She is accounted for as one of the "six children" with her parents on the *Speedwell* from Weymouth, England, in April 1637, but she is not mentioned in her mother's Jan. 1655[/6] will.

vii THOMAS HARRIS, bp. 10 Jan. 1635[/6]. In her Jan. 1655[/6] will, Mary Harris gave "my sonne Thomas, ten shillings, if he doe come home or be alive."[1972] The will of Mary's brother William Fry, who d. at Weymouth, Mass., on 26 Oct. 1642, left legacies to "his three sisters youngest children" Thomas Harris, Thomas Rawlens, and John Meggs.[1973] By her own will, Mary gave "to Rebeckah Bruen . . . a hatt w[hi]ch was my sonn Thomas his hatt." Rebecca m. in 1663, as his second wife, Thomas Post of Norwich, and d. there in 1721.[1974]

William and Daniel Harris of Middletown[1975] *(1653)*

These brothers were sons of Thomas[1] Williams *alias* Harris, who came with his wife Elizabeth, five sons, and a daughter to the Massachusetts Bay Colony in 1630 with the Winthrop fleet, possibly on the *Lyon*, which sailed from Bristol, England.[1976] Daniel was in Middletown by 16 July 1653, when his second child was recorded. William and his brother Daniel both owned lands there before June 1654.[1977]

WILLIAM[2] HARRIS (*Thomas*[1]), born say 1620,[1978] died in Middletown or Wethersfield, Connecticut, before 4 February 1688[/9], when "heirs of the widow Harris" were mentioned as in possession of adjoining land in a deed

[1970] New London, Conn., Deeds, 3:47; see also Caulkins, *History of New London*, 270.

[1971] Trask, "Abstracts of the Earliest Wills," NEHGR 18 (1864):328-30.

[1972] New London, Conn., Deeds, 3:47; see also Caulkins, *History of New London*, 270.

[1973] Trask, "Abstracts of the Earliest Wills," NEHGR 2 (1848):385.

[1974] *Vital Records of Norwich, 1649–1848*, 2 parts (Hartford: Society of Colonial Wars in the State of Connecticut, 1913), 1:22.

[1975] The sketch presented here is based on the article by the present author, "The Brothers William[2] and Daniel[2] Harris of Middletown, Connecticut," NEHGR 164 (2010):165-74, 281-91; 165 (2011):62-67; "Additions and Corrections" at 164 (2010):297. It should be consulted for further information on descendants.

[1976] Walter Goodwin Davis, *The Ancestry of Bethia Harris, 1748–1833, Wife of Dudley Wildes of Topsfield, Massachusetts* (Portland, Maine, 1934), 5–6; Robert Charles Anderson, *The Winthrop Fleet: Massachusetts Bay Company Immigrants to New England, 1629–1630* (Boston: Great Migration Study Project, NEHGS, 2012), 364-66.

[1977] Middletown, Conn., Deeds, 1:9.

[1978] Anderson, *Great Migration Begins*, 2:865.

from Thomas Williams to son John Williams in Wethersfield,[1979] apparently in the neighborhood called Dividend in what is now the town of Rocky Hill. Contrary to early and repeated statements that William "died in 1717, at an advanced age,"[1980] Middletown land records explicitly state that he was "dead" on 1 April 1689, when his son-in-law and administrator, Francis Whitmore, took a deed from Samuel and Mary Bow in favor of William's estate.[1981] William's inventory had been presented in court on 7 March and administration was granted to Whitmore on the same day.[1982]

William married first, by 1642, **EDITH** ____, who died at Middletown on 5 August 1685.[1983] She had been admitted as "Eedy Harris" to the First Church in Charlestown, Massachusetts, on 30 9m [November] 1642.[1984] William married second, by 3 May 1687,[1985] **LYDIA (WRIGHT) SMITH**, living in Wethersfield in February 1688[/9], but deceased in 1692,[1986] widow of Joseph[2] Smith (*Richard*[1]) and daughter of Thomas[1] Wright of Wethersfield.[1987] With her former husband, Lydia had five children: Lydia Smith, born about 1654; Elizabeth Smith, born in 1656; Joseph Smith, born

---

[1979] Wethersfield, Conn., Deeds, 3:285. See also Gale Ion Harris and Norman W. Ingham, "Thomas[1] and Rebecca (Waterhouse) Williams of Wethersfield, Connecticut," TAG 79 (2004):38-56, at 42. William was presumed to be alive on 12 April 1688, when his stepfather, William Stitson of Charlestown, left him 5*s*. in his will (Anderson, *Great Migration Begins*, 1765).

[1980] "Will of Richard Hills," 219; James Savage, *Genealogical Dictionary of the First Settlers of New England* (Boston, 1860–62), 2:365.

[1981] Middletown, Conn., Deeds, 1:106; 2:68, 299.

[1982] [Annie Eliot Trumbull], *Records of the Particular Court of the Colony of Connecticut: Administration of Sir Edmond Andros, Royal Governor, 1687–1688* (Hartford: Case, Lockwood & Brainard Co., 1935), 32.

[1983] Donald Lines Jacobus, "Middletown (Conn.) Vital Records In Land Records, Volume I," TAG 12 (1935–6): 155-70, 210-22; 13 (1936–7): 32-45; at 12:156 ("Eudith").

[1984] James F. Hunnewell, "The First Record-Book of the First Church in Charlestown, Massachusetts," NEHGR 23 (1869):280; Thomas Bellows Wyman, *The Genealogies and Estates of Charlestown . . . 1629–1818*, 2 vols. (Boston: D. Clapp and Son, 1879), 1:467.

[1985] The date of a court held at Hartford where "Lydia Harris relict of Joseph Smith late of Rocky Hill" asked for a settlement of Joseph's estate (Helen Schatvet Ullmann, *Hartford County, Connecticut, County Court Minutes, Volumes 3 and 4, 1663–1667, 1697* [Boston: NEHGS, 2005], 434).

[1986] On 4 Feb. 1688[/9], Thomas Williams conveyed to son John Williams seven acres at Rockie Hill bounded by "land of the heires of Joseph Smith Deceased north, and heirs of the widow Harris west." An appended note in 1692 mentions the same property then bounded on Lydia Cole south, Jonathan Smith north, Samuell Smith west. (Wethersfield, Conn., Deeds, 3:285.) Apparently, widow Harris had died and the bounding property then was in the hands of her three surviving Smith children.

[1987] Donald Lines Jacobus, "Richard Smith of Wethersfield," TAG 25 (1949):128. On 21 Feb. 1652[/3], Richard Smith wrote from Wethersfield to John Winthrop Jr. in New London describing the strange symptoms of "[m]y sons wife Lidia Wright," who was suffering from an ailment modernly diagnosed as pulmonary echinococcosis (Malcolm Freiberg, ed., *Winthrop Papers, Volume VI, 1650–1654* [Boston: Massachusetts Historical Society, 1992], 251-52, note 3). The editor unfortunately followed superseded accounts in Stiles, *History of Ancient Wethersfield*, 1:299, 2:645, for remarks about the identity of this Richard Smith.

in March 1659/60; Jonathan Smith, born in August 1663; and Samuel Smith, born in August 1666.[1988]

William moved from Charlestown to Rowley, Massachusetts, about 1643, where he was granted a house lot that year[1989] and where he recorded a daughter Mary in July 1645.[1990] He returned soon to Charlestown where, on 12 June 1652 as "yeoman, Inhabitant in Charltowne," he and his wife "Edee" sold property in Malden adjoining [his brother-in-law] Elias Maverick, which he had purchased from his stepfather, William Stitson.[1991]

William had moved to Middletown before May 1654,[1992] when he already owned properties there adjoining those of his brother Daniel.[1993] Although one might wish for a better account of the circumstances behind a ruling of a Court of Magistrates at Hartford on 13 October that year, the brief record states only that "William Harris of middletowne" was fined 40[l]

for the breach of an Order by Intermeddling to the Intangling of the Affectyons of Thomas Ossmores Daughter.[1994]

[1988] Jacobus, "Richard Smith of Wethersfield," 128; Gale Ion Harris, "The Doubtful English Ancestry of Richard Smith of Wethersfield, Connecticut," NEHGR 143 (1989):245. Follow-up by Neil D. Thompson, "Isaac Buswell and Rebecca (Buswell) Smith of Husbands Bosworth, co. Leicester, and New England," NEHGR 158 (2004):33-39.

[1989] *The Early Records of the Town of Rowley, Massachusetts, 1639–1672, Being Volume One of the Printed Records of the Town* (Rowley, 1894), 5.

[1990] *Vital Records of Rowley, Massachusetts, To the End of the Year 1849*, 2 vols. (Salem: The Essex Institute, 1928–31), 1:89.

[1991] *[Third] Report of the Record Commissioners Containing Charlestown Land Records, 1636–1802*, 2nd ed. (Boston, 1883), 127.

[1992] When he was made freeman (*Public Records of the Colony*, 1:256).

[1993] Middletown, Conn., Deeds, 1:3, 8, 9. An early statement that William bought a house and land in Hartford from William Williams in 1659 before settling in Middletown ("Will of Richard Hills," 219, and repeated in some later works) confuses him with a different person, William Ayres. For a discussion, see Gale Ion Harris, "William[1] and Goodwife Ayres of Hartford, Connecticut: Witches Who Got Away," TAG 75 (2000): 197-205.

[1994] *Records of the Particular Court of Connecticut, 1639–1663*, Coll. Conn. Hist. Soc. 22 (Hartford, 1928):138. The wording of this entry shows that the fine was based on an order of the General Court of Connecticut on 5 July 1643 (and included verbatim in the Code of 1650) concerning the "government and ordering" of families. It provided that persons, male or female, "that remaineth under the government of parents, masters or guardians, or such like," are forbidden to "make, or give interteinment to, any motion or sute in way of marriage without the knowledge and consent of those they stand in such relation to," and moreover, "nor shall any third person or persons intermeddle in making any motion to any such, without the knowledge and consent of those under whose government they are, under the same penalty" (*Public Records of the Colony*, 1:92, 540). It seems that William Harris was such a "third person" in this case. "Thomas Ossmores Daughter" apparently was Hannah Hosmer, b. say 1636, daughter of Thomas Hosmer/Osmore of Cambridge and Hartford, who m. Josiah Willard at Concord, Mass., on 20 March 1656/7 (Anderson, *Great Migration Begins*, 2:1004).

It was agreed at a Middletown town meeting on 10 March 1654[/5?] that the meadow fence should be set up "in the old place where it stood the last year." The work-assignment list included William Harris for "one day" and Daniel Harris for "halfe a day."[1995] In July 1662 William provided hay at Middletown to feed horses that John Pynchon of Springfield, Massachusetts, was shipping to Barbados.[1996] On 22 August 1669, it "[b]eing the Lords Day Lieutenant [Daniel] Harris with the wife of our Bro: William Harris [was] recommended to us from the Church of Christ at Rowley."[1997]

William's property valuation of £200 at Middletown in March 1670 exceeded those of all fifty-one other householders and proprietors except £225 for Mr. Nathaniel Collins, the minister.[1998] The record of the Middle-town town meeting on 18 November 1679 includes a list of 64 "proprietors of the bell," inhabitants who had contributed to the purchase of a bell for the meeting house. William Harris's contribution, £1, was exceeded only by the merchant-mariner Mr. Giles Hamlin (£3), George Phillips (£2), and Sgt. William Ward (£1 6s.).[1999]

On 30 June 1685, nine men including William Harris and his brother Daniel were selected "to procuer a paten for the towne," which was granted by the Governor and General Court of Connecticut on 11 March 1685/6. Next year, about the time of his second marriage, William was a deputy from Middletown at the October 1687 session of the General Court.[2000]

On 6 October 1687, William Harris traded the Middletown lot "where his house standeth" and other parcels to William Sumner for Sumner's "house and land" in Boston's North End, and another lot "neare Charlstowne fery."[2001] In December 1692, William Harris's daughter Patience and husband Daniel Markham "of Middletowne" released their interest in this Boston property to Francis Whitmore, who appeared in Boston on 28 June 1693 to sell it to William Phipps.[2002] Perhaps William Harris had intended to retire to Boston with his second wife, Lydia, but he died soon afterward and

---

[1995] From a transcription of the town record in "Settlement of Middletown," *History of Middlesex County, Connecticut* (New York: J. B. Beers & Co., 1884), 66.

[1996] Carl Bridenbaugh and Juliette Tomlinson, *The Pynchon Papers, Volume II: Selections from the Account Books of John Pynchon, 1651–1697* (Boston: Colonial Society of Massachusetts, 1985), 157. Large ships could not sail up the Connecticut River beyond Mattabesett, the early name for Middletown.

[1997] Middletown First Congregational Church Records, 1:31, FHL microfilm 4848.

[1998] "Settlement of Middletown," 67-68.

[1999] "Settlement of Middletown," 68-69. The list also includes William's brother Capt. Daniel Harris (16s.), and nephews Daniel Harris Jr. (10s.), and Thomas Harris (4s.).

[2000] "Settlement of Middletown," 69, 73; *Public Records of the Colony*, 3:239 ("Capt. Wm Harris").

[2001] Middletown, Conn., Deeds, 1:138.

[2002] Suffolk Co., Mass., Deeds, 15:53; 16:125, 242.

there is no evidence that they ever established residence there. William had no sons, in particular not a Thomas who sometimes has been supposed to be the second husband of Sarah (Nettleton) Miller, widow of Thomas Miller of Middletown.[2003]

Children of William[2] and Edith (____) Harris:

    i   MARY[3] HARRIS, b. Rowley, Mass., 1 July 1645,[2004] was living in Middletown in April 1716,[2005] but was "lately deceased" on 1 Sept. 1721.[2006] She m. (1) there 18 April 1664, JOHN[2] WARD,[2007] b. say 1637, who d. there before 22 Feb. 1683/4, the date of his inventory,[2008] son of Andrew[1] and Hester (Sherman) Ward of Fairfield, Deputy Governor of Connecticut in 1634.[2009] She m. (2) in Jan. 1687/8, as his 2nd wife, JOSIAH[2] GILBERT,[2010] bp. Yardley, Worcestershire, England, 27 Nov. 1625,[2011] d. Wethersfield 22 Aug. 1688,[2012] son of Thomas[1] Gilbert of Braintree, Mass., and Glastonbury. Josiah had m. (1) Elizabeth Belcher, dau. of Gregory and Catherine (____) Belcher of Braintree, with whom he had ten children.[2013]

   ii   MARTHA HARRIS, b. say 1647, d. New London, Conn., 14 July 1713.[2014] Joshua Hempstead's diary entries for that day include: "old Mr [*sic*] Coit died Last night . . . I went to yᵉ funerall of Ms Coit."[2015] Martha m. there 17 July 1667 JOSEPH[2] COIT,[2016] bp. Salem, Mass., 30 July 1643, a ship

---

[2003] For more on this point, see Harris, "Walter Harris of Wethersfield," 326, and Gale Ion Harris, "Thomas Herris, Merchant of New England: Reassembling a 'Split Identity,'" NGSQ 80 (1992):50.

[2004] *Vital Records of Rowley*, 1:89.

[2005] Connecticut Archives: Private Controversies, Series I, 6:453, Conn. State Library.

[2006] Manwaring, *Early Connecticut Probate*, 1:451 (settlement of Josiah Gilbert's estate in Wethersfield).

[2007] "Middletown Vital Records, Volume 1," 12:163.

[2008] Manwaring, *Early Connecticut Probate*, 1:373-74; Ullmann, *Court Minutes*, 368.

[2009] Donald Lines Jacobus, *History and Genealogy of the Families of Old Fairfield*, 3 vols. in 2 (1930–32; repr. Baltimore, 1976), 1:645-46.

[2010] Manwaring, *Early Connecticut Probate*, 1:450. The transcribed "Ante-Nuptial Agreement on File" for Josiah Gilbert and Mary Ward, widow (ibid., 448), is dated 18 Oct. *1681*, almost certainly a misreading or misprint for *1687*, as it is indicated in the court records of March 1696/7 that they did not marry until Jan. 1687/8.

[2011] Douglas Richardson, "The English Origin of Thomas[1] Gilbert of Braintree, Mass., and Wethersfield, Conn., With a Note on Lydia Gilbert Executed for Witchcraft in 1654," TAG 67 (1992):161-66, at 162, citing Yardley parish register on FHL microfilm 1520013.

[2012] Homer Worthington Brainard, Harold Simeon Gilbert, and Clarence Almon Torrey, *The Gilbert Family, Descendants of Thomas Gilbert, 1582(?)–1659, of Mt. Wollaston (Braintree), Windsor, and Wethersfield* (New Haven: A. C. Gilbert, Jr., 1953), 63.

[2013] For the Gilberts, see *Gilbert Family*, 9, 19, 24, 63-69, and Richardson, "Thomas[1] Gilbert."

[2014] Barbour Collection, Conn. Vital Records, citing New London VR1:20.

[2015] *Diary of Joshua Hempstead of New London, Connecticut, Covering a Period of Forty-Seven Years from September, 1711, to November, 1758*, Coll. New London Co. Hist. Soc. 1 (New London, 1901):25.

[2016] Barbour Collection, Conn. Vital Records, citing New London VR1:5.

carpenter,[2017] who d. New London 27 March 1704,[2018] son of John[1] and Mary (____) Coit of Gloucester, Mass., and New London.[2019] The New London town record of Martha's marriage identifies her as daughter of William Harris "of Wethersfield," but no other record found suggests that he resided there until 1688, after he had married Joseph Smith's widow of that town. In 1716 John, Joseph, and Solomon Coite, and the "orphans of William Coit of New London, deceased," belatedly petitioned the General Assembly as "coheirs of Mrs. Martha Coit late of New London, deceased, one of the five of y[e] Daughters of Mr. William Harris, late of Middletown, deceased" for settlement of William's estate. Their petition asserted that William had "no sons," and sought "their fifth part" of the estate.[2020]

iii   ELIZABETH HARRIS, b. say 1650, d. Middletown 7 Oct. 1684; m. there 20 June 1670 EDWARD FOSTER,[2021] b. Kingsware, England, ca. 1644,[2022] who d. Guilford, Conn., 14 June 1712,[2023] son of John Foster of Kingsware. Edward apparently had a wife after Elizabeth, as he is recorded in Middletown as father of Tamsen and John Foster b. 26 Aug. 1688 and 10 Feb. 1691/2.[2024] A mariner, Foster resided at Marblehead, Mass., in Middletown, and in Guilford. In April 1716, in response to a petition, the Middletown constable was ordered to "give notice unto Mary Gilbert, Hannah Whitmore, & Patience Marcum all of Middletown Widows; and Thomas Foster, Edward Foster, Joseph Rockwell and Elizabeth his wife, [and] Robert Collins and Mary his wife all of s[d] Middletown," to appear at the next General Court at Hartford "to answer to the petition of John Coite and Solomon Coite of New London, and Joseph Coite of Plainfield."[2025]

iv   HANNAH HARRIS, b. say 1652, was living in Aug. 1722 when the court ordered distribution of her father's estate.[2026] She m. Middletown 8 Feb. 1674 FRANCIS[3] WHITMORE,[2027] b. Cambridge, Mass., 12 Oct. 1650, who d. Middletown 9 Sept. 1700,[2028] son of Francis[2] (*John[1]*) and Isabel (____) Whitmore of Cambridge.[2029] Francis Whitmore was the administrator of his

[2017] Caulkins, *History of New London*, 250, 275.

[2018] Barbour Collection, Conn. Vital Records, citing New London VR1:20.

[2019] Mary Walton Ferris, *Dawes-Gates Ancestral Lines*, 2 vols. (n.p.: By the author, 1931–43), 191-93, citing Vital Records of Salem, 1:377, for Joseph's baptism.

[2020] Connecticut Archives: Private Controversies, Series I, 6:452a, Conn. State Library; see also Manwaring, *Early Connecticut Probate*, 2:396-98.

[2021] "Middletown Vital Records, Volume 1," 13:41 (Elizabeth's marriage and death).

[2022] Frederick Clifton Pierce, *Foster Genealogy; Being the Record of the Posterity of Reginald Foster, an Early Inhabitant of Ipswich, in New England* (Chicago: W. B. Conkey Co., 1899), 1015.

[2023] "Middletown Vital Records, Volume 1," 13:41.

[2024] "Middletown Vital Records, Volume 1," 13:41 (both entries name only the father).

[2025] Connecticut Archives: Private Controversies, Series I, 6:453, Conn. State Library.

[2026] Manwaring, *Early Connecticut Probate*, 2:398.

[2027] "Middletown Vital Records, Volume 1," 13:45.

[2028] Manwaring, *Early Connecticut Probate*, 2:135; "Middletown Vital Records, Volume 1," 13:45 ("Leftenant ffrancis").

[2029] For discussion, see Owen S. Hart, *Hart Genealogy; With Collateral Family Lines* (West Hartford: By the author, 1970), 468ff.

father-in-law's estate; its settlement seems to have been delayed many years by Francis's death. The inventory of the estate of Francis "Wetmore" taken at Middletown 4 Dec. 1700, lists children Francis, age 25, Hannah, 23, Elizabeth, 21, Abigail, 19, Martha, 17, Joseph, 14, William, 12, Edith, 10, Isabell, 6, and John, 3. Administration was set 16 Dec. 1700 to "Hannah the widow, relict, and Francis, eldest son."[2030]

v   PATIENCE HARRIS, b. say 1654, d. Middletown 19 March 1732/3.[2031] On 24 July 1678, "Patience the Daughter of Wm. Harris," appeared before a court in Hartford "to Answer for her committing fornication." She accused John Orton "for begetting her with Child which child was born march last." Orton admitted "that he was at the house of Wm Harris & kept there sometime about the time he was charged with begetting her with child." The court ordered Patience to pay a fine of £5 and Orton, adjudged "to be the reputed father," was ordered to pay 2s. per week as maintenance for the child "till it shall attayne the age of Three yeares if it shall liue so long."[2032]

The court record refers to Patience as though she were still single in March and July 1678, but Middletown vital records and land records both indicate that a few months before, on 2 Jan. 1677[/8], she had m. there, as his 2nd wife, Deacon DANIEL MARKHAM, who d. there 6 Feb. 1712/3.[2033] The date given for their marriage is consistent with a deed dated 20 Jan. 1677[/8] whereby William Harris of Middletown conveyed lands to "Daniel Marcom his son-in-law sumtims of Cambridg in Massachusetts Colony but now of Middletown . . . and his Daughter petience Wife to the sayd Danill Markham."[2034]

Daniel Markham had m. (1) 3 Nov. 1669, Elizabeth Whitmore, elder sister of Francis Whitmore, husband of Patience's sister Hannah,[2035] with whom he had the children Daniel, James, and Elizabeth named in his will at Middletown on 23 Nov. 1708.[2036] Appended to William Harris's deed of 2 Jan. 1677[/8], mentioned above, is a caveat dated 8 March 1711/2 by Daniel Markham "son to Decon Daniel Markham late of Middletown dec[ease]d," against sale of the property before trial. On 12 March 1712/3, James Markham of Middletown mortgaged property "which descends . . . by deed of gift from his father Deacon Daniel Markham having date January 23, 1701/2."[2037] Daniel Markham's 1708 will also names "my daughters Martha and Edith," to whom he gave £20 each. In a subsequent clause, he gave his "daughter Martha Center . . . 4 or 5 rods of ground where Jonathan Center's house standeth." On 1 March 1722/3, by mark, Patience Markham of Middletown, "widow and relict of Mr. Daniel Markham," gave her "loving daughters Martha Center of Middletown and Editha Arnold of Haddam" all her

[2030] Manwaring, *Early Connecticut Probate*, 2:135-36.
[2031] "Middletown Vital Records, Volume 1," 13:45.
[2032] Ullmann, *Court Minutes*, 238-39.
[2033] "Middletown Vital Records, Volume 1," 13:45 (marriage and death for Daniel).
[2034] Middletown, Conn., Deeds, 1:139.
[2035] W. H. Whitmore, "The Wilcox Family," NEHGR 29 (1875):27; *Hart Genealogy*, 468.
[2036] Manwaring, *Early Connecticut Probate*, 2:256-57; 3:xvii, 83.
[2037] Middletown, Conn., Deeds, 3:39.

Middletown property and mentioned "my loving sons in law Jonathan Center and John Arnold husbands of s^d Martha and Editha."[2038]

2 DANIEL^2 HARRIS (*Thomas^1*), born say 1626,[2039] died at Middletown on 30 November 1701.[2040] He married by 1651 (birth of first child) **MARY WELD**, baptized at All Saint's Parish, Sudbury, co. Suffolk, England, 1 July 1629, who died at Middletown on 5 September 1711,[2041] daughter of Joseph and Elizabeth (Wise) Weld of Roxbury, Massachusetts.[2042] On 27 May 1660, John Winthrop Jr. recorded a prescription at Middletown for "Harris Eliz: 1¼ y: Daught of Dan: he maried Mary Weld."[2043]

A wheelwright, Daniel was granted a house lot at Rowley, Massachusetts, after 1643, where he took the freeman's oath on 30 September 1651.[2044] He was in Middletown by 16 July 1653, when his second child was recorded. Daniel and his brother William Harris owned lands there before June 1654.[2045]

The account books of John Pynchon at Springfield contain an entry dated October 1659: "To 1 barall of Porke at Mattabeset [Middletown] from Dan Harris & Tho Rayny," £3 15*s*.[2046] In February 1659/60, the Connecticut General Court "approved [Daniel] for an Ordnary keeper in Middle Towne."[2047] On 11 March 1659[/60], on a page headed "Middletown," Winthrop entered a prescription for William Markham, age "almost 3y," who had measles, adding that he was "so[n] of William who married Mr Websters daughter he now lives at Harriss." On the same day, Winthrop entered a prescription for Daniel Harris "his wife."[2048] Daniel's wife apparently was the "Mary Harris of Middletowne" who was to share equally with "Grace Clarke the wife of Thomas Clark of Ipswich" and "Anne Clap wife of Nicholas Clap of Dorchester" in bequests of wearing apparel by the will,

---

[2038] Middletown, Conn., Deeds, 4:197.

[2039] Anderson, *Great Migration Begins*, 2:865.

[2040] "Middletown Vital Records, Volume 1," 12:211 ("Last day of Nov. 1701").

[2041] "Middletown Vital Records, Volume 1," 12:211 ("widdow of Cap^n Daniel").

[2042] Douglas Richardson, "New England Weld Family," TAG 55 (1979):148.

[2043] "Medical Records of John Winthrop," 395.

[2044] Davis, *Ancestry of Bethia Harris*, 9.

[2045] Middletown, Conn., Deeds, 1:9.

[2046] *Pynchon Papers*, 152.

[2047] *Public Records of the Colony*, 1:344.

[2048] "Medical Records of John Winthrop," 383. The father, William Markham of Hartford and Hadley, had married, as his 2nd wife, Elizabeth Webster, daughter of Gov. John Webster (Lucius Barnes Barbour, *Families of Early Hartford, Connecticut* [Baltimore: Genealogical Pub. Co., 1982], 379, 645-46).

dated 20 August 1677, of "Mary Norton of Boston," the widow of "Mr. John Norton sometime teacher of the Church of Christ in said Boston."[2049]

"Lieutenant [Daniel] Harris" was admitted on 22 August 1669 to the First Congregational Church in Middletown by recommendation "from the Church of Christ at Rowley.[2050] He is counted among the earliest settlers of Middletown Upper Houses (now Cromwell) and had an estate valued at £132 on 22 March 1670.[2051] He was appointed Captain of the Middletown militia company in 1677 and served from there as Deputy to the General Court in 1678, 1684, 1687, and 1689.[2052] He was one of the deputies present in 1687 when Connecticut's Charter was hidden from Governor Andros and, so tradition holds, secreted by Capt. Joseph Wadsworth in the charter-oak tree.

Daniel Harris's will, executed at Middletown on 13 March 1698/9, gave land to his sons Daniel, Thomas, William, and John Harris. John was to have the dwelling house, barn, etc, "now belonging to my home," and "my negro Mengo," on condition that he "shall provide for myself and my wife all such comfortable and convenient maintenance . . . during our natural lives." Daniel also gave land to his daughters Mary Johnson, Elizabeth ("land in Middletown which I bought of Joseph Bull of Hartford"), and Hannah Cook. His grandchildren Thankfull Bidwell and Abiell were to receive land when age 18 or married, or if they die before age 18, then to "their parents, that is, Abiell's to her mother (my daughter Elizabeth), and Thankfull Bidwell's to her father (my son-in-law), Samuel Bidwell." Abiell was to be placed in "custody of my son John Harris" until 18 or married. Son John and son-in-law Samuel Bidwell were appointed joint executors, "hereby giving . . . to my s[ai]d son-in-law Samuel Bidwell what in reversion was to have been my daughter Sarah's." The will was proved on 1 January 1701/2, but in November 1711 Isaac Johnson and Daniel Harris complained that the executors had neglected to set out their legacies according to the will.[2053]

[2049] Robert Charles Anderson, *The Great Migration: Immigrants to New England 1634–1635*, 7 vols. (Boston: NEHGS, 1999–2011), 5:276-77, citing Suffolk, Mass., Probate Records, 6:222-24.

[2050] Middletown First Congregational Church Records [*supra* note 32], 1:31.

[2051] David D. Field, *Centennial Address; With Historical Sketches of Cromwell, Portland, Chatham, Middle-Haddam, Middletown, and its Parishes* (Middletown, 1853), 40, 149, 295; "Settlement of Middletown," 67-68.

[2052] *Public Records of the Colony*, 2:304; 3:16, 155, 248, 254.

[2053] Manwaring, *Early Connecticut Probate*, 2:72-74.

Children of Daniel[2] and Mary (Weld) Harris, the first recorded at Rowley, Mass.,[2054] and the others at Middletown:[2055]

    i   MARY[3] HARRIS, b. Rowley 2 April 1651, d. Middletown 1 Aug. 1740.[2056] She m. Roxbury, Mass., 26 Oct. 1669,[2057] ISAAC[3] JOHNSON, bp. there 7 Jan. 1643[/4],[2058] who d. Middletown 23 Feb. 1719/20,[2059] son of Isaac[2] Johnson (*John[1]*) and his wife Elizabeth (Porter).[2060] On 8 June 1667, Winthrop treated "Harris Mary, 15 or 16 yr: breaking out" and referred to a note by her father "Daniel Harris at Middletown."[2061] Two years later, on 22 Aug. 1669, "Mary Harris daughter of Lieutenant Harris, being shortly about to remove from us, was called upon to and did publickly and solemnly owned her fathers Covenant in the face of the Assembly."[2062] On 26 Nov. 1672, Isaac Johnson was admitted to the church at Middletown by recommendation from the Church of Christ at Roxbury.[2063]

        The will of Isaac Johnson Sr., dated Middletown 13 Jan. 1719/20 and proved 5 April 1720, gave his wife Mary half "of my household stuff, all my stock and tools, and 15 acres of land which came by her brother Thomas," and named son Isaac, "son Nathaniel's heirs" (mentions his sons Nathaniel and Jonathan), sons Daniel and Joseph, and daughters Elizabeth and Mary. He appointed "my three sons, Isaac, Daniel, and Joseph" as his executors; William Russell, William Harris, and John Harris witnessed.[2064]

   ii DANIEL HARRIS, b. 16 July 1653,[2065] d. Middletown 18 Oct. 1735 and was bur. in McDonough Cemetery.[2066] He m. (1) Middletown 14 Dec. 1680 ABIGAIL BARNES,[2067] b. prob. at New Haven on 16 March 1656/7, who d. at Middletown on 22 May 1723[2068] and was bur. beside Daniel, dau. of

---

[2054] *Vital Records of Rowley*, 1:90;

[2055] "Middletown Vital Records, Volume 1," 12:211 (all of "danill & mary").

[2056] "Middletown Vital Records, Volume 1," 13:40 ("the Widow Mary" Johnson).

[2057] *Vital Records of Roxbury, Massachusetts, To the End of the Year 1849*, 2 vols. (Salem: The Essex Institute, 1925–26), 2:223.

[2058] *[Sixth] Report of the Record Commissioners Containing the Roxbury Land and Church Records*, 2nd ed. (Boston, 1884), 115.

[2059] Jennie Henderson Porter, *Hannah Johnson and Polly Palmer with Some of their Kinsfolk* (Kansas City, Mo., 1930), 11, citing cemetery record ("He is buried under a tree near the railroad track."). This record is not included in Connecticut Headstone Inscriptions, Hale Collection, Conn. State Library.

[2060] Porter, *Hannah Johnson and Polly Palmer*, 11,12; Mary Lovering Holman, *Ancestry of Colonel John Harrington Stevens and His wife Frances Helen Miller*, 2 vols. (Concord, N.H., 1948–52), 1:324. See also Douglas Richardson, "The Heath Connection . . . ," NEHGR 146 (1992):274.

[2061] "Medical Records of John Winthrop," 733.

[2062] Middletown First Congregational Church Records, 1:31.

[2063] Middletown First Congregational Church Records, 1:7.

[2064] Manwaring, *Early Connecticut Probate*, 2:406-7.

[2065] "Middletown Vital Records, Volume 1," 12:211.

[2066] Connecticut Headstone Inscriptions, Hale Collection, Conn. State Library, 28:639.

[2067] "Middletown Vital Records, Volume 1," 12:211.

[2068] "Middletown Vital Records, Volume 1," 12:211.

Thomas and Mary (____) Barnes.[2069] "Sargt." Daniel m. (2) at Middletown 5 Jan. 1726/7 ELIZABETH (SHARP) (BEADLES) COOK,[2070] living in March 1734/5 (Daniel's will),[2071] widow of Nathaniel Beadles of Boston and of Samuel³ Cook (*Samuel²*, *Henry¹*) of Wallingford, Conn.[2072]

While a young single man in April 1677, Daniel was fined in Hartford County court for "living alone contrary to law."[2073] His will, dated at Middletown 22 March 1734/5, gave wife Elizabeth "household stuff she brought to my house when I marryed her," and names sons Daniel and Joseph (deceased), daughters Abigail Cornell (deceased), Mary Ward, and Patience Gilbert, and grandchildren Abigail (Cornell) Miller, Elizabeth Cornell, Joseph Cornell, Daniel Cornell, Nathaniel Cornell, "my grandsons, sons of my daughter Mary Ward," Jonathan Gilbert, Daniel Harris, Moses Harris, Joseph Harris, Abigail Harris ("daughter of my son Joseph Harris deceased"), and sons-in-law Ezekiel Gilbert, Joseph Cornell, and William Ward.[2074]

iii   JOSEPH HARRIS, b. 12 Feb. 1654[/5], was age 12 on 8 June 1667, when Winthrop recorded prescriptions for him and for his sister Mary.[2075] He was living in Oct. 1675, when ordered to serve as a guard for a supply vessel at Middletown in King Philip's War,[2076] but died without issue before the date of his father's will in 1698/9.

iv   THOMAS HARRIS, b. 20 May 1657,[2077] d. Middletown 22 Aug. 1700.[2078] He m. (1) ZIPPORAH ____, born about 1667, who d. there on 8 Jan. 1688/9, aged 21, and bur. McDonough Cemetery.[2079] He m. (2) by 1695 TABITHA WARD, who d. there on 23 Jan. 1711/2,[2080] a dau. of Samuel Ward who d. at Middletown in 1715; his inventory included lands in Branford, Conn.[2081]

Thomas Harris's inventory was taken on 4 Sept. 1700 by John Hall and William Ward; it listed "one daughter, Mary 5 years of age." Next day, administration was granted to "Mrs. Tabithy Harris, the relict," with Isaac Johnson Sr. as surety.[2082]

[2069] Myrtle Melona Morris, *Joseph and Philena (Elton) Fellows, and, Their Ancestry and Descendants; also the Ancestry of Reuben Fairchild, John and Dorothy (Waldorf) Turner and George Morris* (Washington, D.C., 1940), 168, 170.

[2070] "Middletown Vital Records, Volume 1," 12:211.

[2071] Manwaring, *Early Connecticut Probate*, 3:164.

[2072] Donald Lines Jacobus, *New Haven Genealogical Magazine* 2 (1923–24):435; Davis, *Ancestry of Bethia Harris*, 9. Elizabeth m. first at Boston, 30 Jan. 1694, Nathaniel Beedle (*Boston Births, Baptisms, Marriages, and Deaths, 1630–1699*, 217).

[2073] Connecticut Colonial Probate Records, "Court Side," 3:162 (Conn. State Library).

[2074] Manwaring, *Early Connecticut Probate*, 3:164-65.

[2075] "Medical Records of John Winthrop," 733.

[2076] *Public Records of the Colony*, 2:374.

[2077] "Middletown Vital Records, Volume 1," 12:211.

[2078] "Middletown Vital Records, Volume 1," 12:211.

[2079] "Middletown Vital Records, Volume 1," 12:211; Connecticut Headstone Inscriptions, Hale Collection, 28:637.

[2080] "Middletown Vital Records, Volume 1," 12:211.

[2081] Manwaring, *Early Connecticut Probate*, 2:446-47.

[2082] Manwaring, *Early Connecticut Probate*, 2:74.

    v   ELIZABETH HARRIS, b. 22 March 1659[/60], d. Middletown before 4 Dec. 1710, when her son John Hunnewell was granted administration of her estate.[2083] She m. after Aug. 1683, but before about 1687, JOHN HUNNEWELL, who d. before 5 Aug. 1706, when Bridget Hunnewell, aged 15, "daughter of John Hunewell, late of Middletown, made choice of her uncle Isaac Johnson to be her guardian."[2084] Hunnewell had m. (1) at Wethersfield 1 Jan. 1679/80 Lydia ____, who d. there 10 Aug. 1683, probably Lydia² Edwards (*John¹*), b. there in July 1650. With Lydia, John Hunnewell had a child Mary b. at Wethersfield 10 June 1682.[2085] In July 1712, the son John Hunnewell, being "absent at sea," had not finished the administration of his mother's estate, so the court granted administration "unto Samuel Williams of Wethersfield, who married one of the daughters of s[ai]d dec[ease]d." In Aug. 1713, Elizabeth's estate was distributed to John Hunnewell, eldest son, a double portion, to daughter Elizabeth Williams, and to "youngest daughter" Bridget Hunnewell.[2086] Before her marriage to Hunnewell, Elizabeth had the daughter Abiell mentioned in the will of Elizabeth's father and placed in custody of Elizabeth's brother John.[2087] As an illegitimate child, Abiell was not entitled under prevailing law to an intestate share of her mother's estate.

    vi   SARAH HARRIS, b. 17 Feb. 1660[/1], d. Middletown 15 March 1661.[2088]

    vii   SARAH HARRIS (again), b. 30 Sept. 1663, d. Middletown after 8 Dec. 1695 but before the date of her father's will in 1698/9. She m. by 1695 SAMUEL² BIDWELL, b. Hartford ca. 1651, who d. Middletown 5 April 1715, aged 65,[2089] son of John¹ and Sarah (Wilcock) Bidwell. He m. (1) Middletown 14 Nov. 1672 Elizabeth Stow, and (3) by Jan. 1698/9 Abigail ____, who d. 8 March 1732/3.[2090] On 2 Jan. 1665/6, Winthrop noted a prescription for "Harris Sarah 2¼ y: daughter of Daniel yᵗ Middletown."[2091] On 7 Feb. 1674, Samuel Bidwell of Middletown, his brother John Bidwell Jr. of Hartford, and Thomas Miller of Middletown agreed to build a saw mill "not far above the Corne Mill now standing which is Thomas Miller's" in Middletown.[2092] The will of Samuel Bidwell Sr., dated at Middletown 23 March 1715, was witnessed by Daniel Harris Sr. and Samuel Miller. He mentioned his sons Samuel, Nathaniel, and Moses Bidwell, daughters Sarah Brainard, Elizabeth Brainard, Abigail Sumner, Mary Bidwell, Hannah Bidwell, and Thankful Bidwell, and appointed wife Abigail sole executrix.

[2083] Manwaring, *Early Connecticut Probate*, 2:236-37.

[2084] Manwaring, *Early Connecticut Probate*, 2:237.

[2085] Gale Ion Harris, "John Edwards of Wethersfield, Connecticut," NEHGR 145 (1991):339-41.

[2086] Manwaring, *Early Connecticut Probate*, 2:237.

[2087] See also Stiles, *Ancient Wethersfield*, 2:456, who, however, mistakenly lists Abiell as a child by John Hunnewell.

[2088] "Middletown Vital Records, Volume 1," 12:211.

[2089] "Middletown Vital Records, Volume 1," 13:42. Age and birth date estimate from Jacobus and Waterman, *Hale, House, and Related Families*, 470-71.

[2090] *Hale, House*, 470-71.

[2091] "Medical Records of John Winthrop," 614.

[2092] Middletown, Conn., Deeds, 2:532.

His inventory, valued at £977, was taken on 25 April 1715 by John Hamlin, Joseph Rockwell, and William Harris.[2093]

viii WILLIAM HARRIS, b. 17 July 1665, d. Middletown as "Capt. William Harris" in Feb. 1751[/2], aged 87, and bur. in Old Farm Hill Cemetery.[2094] He m. Middletown 8 Jan. 1689/90 MARTHA[3] COLLINS,[2095] b. there 3 March 1666,[2096] who d. there on 14 Aug. 1750, aged 85, and bur. next to her husband, dau. of Samuel[2] (*Edward*[1]) and Mary (Marvin) Collins of Cambridge, Saybrook, and Middletown.[2097]

Sergeant William Harris was one of the three listers of estates at Middletown for the year 1710.[2098] As "Mr. William Harris of Midletown," he was commissioned Lieutenant of the south company or trainband in Oct. 1716.[2099] Jonathan Yeomans was granted administration of his estate on 7 March 1750/1, with William Rockwell as bondsman. The distribution, exhibited on 9 March 1754, names eldest daughter Mary Lay, Sibbil, wife of Jonathan Yeomans, Prudence, wife of Daniel Brown, and heirs of William Harris Jr., deceased, only son of Capt. William Harris.[2100]

ix JOHN HARRIS, b. 4 Jan. 1667[/8], d. Middletown 29 Nov. 1754, aged 88, and bur. Old Farm Hill Cemetery.[2101] On 23 Jan. 1667/8, Winthrop noted a prescription for "Harris John, 3 weekes old son of Daniell at Middletown."[2102] John m. at Middletown on 18 March 1702/3 SUSANNAH (HENCHMAN) COLLINS,[2103] b. in Boston on 7 June 1667,[2104] who d. in Middletown on 10 Feb. 1747/8,[2105] aged 80, and bur. beside her husband. She was a daughter of Daniel and Sarah (Woodward) Henchman of Boston and Worcester, Mass., and widow of Samuel[3] Collins Jr. (*Samuel*[2], *Edward*[1]) of Middletown, with whom she had a daughter, Susannah Collins, b. in 1694.[2106] In his old age, John m. at Middletown on 11 May 1749 MINDWELL (___) LYMAN "of Durham," Conn., who d. at Middletown on 6 Feb. 1758.[2107]

[2093] Manwaring, *Early Connecticut Probate*, 2:356-57.

[2094] Connecticut Headstone Inscriptions, Hale Collection, 28:346.

[2095] "Middletown Vital Records, Volume 1," 12:157.

[2096] "Middletown Vital Records, Volume 1," 12:168.

[2097] Smyth, "Edward and John Collins," NEHGR 61 (1907):282; and corrections by Frank Farnsworth Starr, NEHGR 62 (1908):304.

[2098] Connecticut Archives: Finance and Currency, First Series, 1:51.

[2099] *Public Records of the Colony*, 5:573.

[2100] Hartford District Probate, file 2594, cited by Jacobus in "Early Harris Families," 155.

[2101] "Middletown Vital Records, Volume 1," 13:38; Connecticut Headstone Inscriptions, Hale Collection, 28:338.

[2102] Medical Records of John Winthrop," 778.

[2103] "Middletown Vital Records, Volume 1," 13:38.

[2104] *Boston Births, Baptisms, Marriages, and Deaths, 1630–1699*, 104.

[2105] "Middletown Vital Records, Volume 1," 13:38.

[2106] Smyth, "Edward and John Collins," NEHGR 61 (1907):282; and corrections by Frank Farnsworth Starr, NEHGR 62 (1908):305.

[2107] "Middletown Vital Records, Volume 1," 13:38 (marriage and her death).

In Feb. 1698/9, the town of Middletown granted John Harris a parcel of land "to run from the east end of his house westward . . . to John Stows Lott."[2108] Presumably, "his house" at that time was his parents' home, which was formally given to him a few weeks later by his father's will in return for their maintenance. In Nov. 1728, Sergeant John Harris of Middletown took a mortgage from James Johnson for land with a house and barn on the east side of the Connecticut River, adjoining west on Benjamin Harris's land, north on land originally belonging to John Cornwall, deceased, and south on Philip Goff's land. Benjamin Harris witnessed.[2109] John's will, dated 30 April 1754 and proved next 30 Nov., names his wife Mindwell (estate she brought at marriage), eldest daughter Sarah (wife of Nathaniel Baker), grandson Harris Jones, only son of daughter Jane (sometime the wife of Timothy Jones) deceased, granddaughters Elizabeth, Deborah, and Susannah (children of Jane), youngest daughter Rachel (wife of William Prout), Susannah Robberds (eldest daughter of my first wife, which she had by her former husband), John Harris son of Deacon Benjamin Harris, and grandson John Prout.[2110] There is no known evidence that the Benjamin Harris mentioned in John's will and in the land records was related.[2111]

x   HANNAH HARRIS, b. 11 Feb. 1669[/70], was living in 1714 but probably had died before May 1719. She m. (1) ca. 1690, as his 2nd wife, JOHN[2] COOKE, b. Warwick, R.I., ca. 1650, who d. at Middletown 16 Jan. 1704/5,[2112] son of John[1] and Mary (____) Cooke of Warwick. She m. (2), by 1714, as his 2nd wife, JONATHAN[3] SPRAGUE (*William[2], Edward[1]*) of Providence, R.I.[2113] John and Hannah Cooke resided for several years in Potopaug quarter at Saybrook, Conn., but settled in Middletown about 1695. The will of John Cooke, dated Middletown 15 Aug. 1698, gave wife Hannah the use and improvement of the house and homelott "till my son Daniel come to age, and after, if she bears my name." He named children John and Mary [by former wife, Phebe (Weeden)], Daniel ("house and homestead where I now live"), Sarah ("the choice and best of my feather beds"), and child "my wife is now with" (100 acres, "being the remainder of my lott in Cockingchauge"). Daniel Harris and Alexander Rollo witnessed; the inventory, taken 5 March 1704/5, included "60 acres of land that his father Harris gave him out of his farm," and lists children John and Mary, both of age, Daniel, age 14, Sarah, age 12, and Ebenezer, age 7.[2114]

[2108] Middletown, Conn., Deeds, 2:39.

[2109] Middletown, Conn., Deeds, 1:333; 2:528.

[2110] Middletown Probate District, file 1678, as abstracted in Jacobus, "Early Harris Families," 155.

[2111] Benjamin Harris, b. ca. 1701, son of Isaac[2] Harris (*Arthur[1]*) and his wife Mary (Dunbar) of Bridgewater, Mass., came to Middletown before Aug. 1727 and d. at East Hampton, Conn., 11 April 1775, aged 74 (Harris, "Arthur[1] Harris of Duxbury, Bridgewater, and Boston," NEHGR 159 [2005]:351-53).

[2112] Manwaring, *Early Connecticut Probate*, 2:45.

[2113] Jacobus, "Early Harris Families," 154; Jane Fletcher Fiske, "John Cooke of Warwick, R.I., and Middletown, Conn.," TAG 52 (1976):5-10.

[2114] Manwaring, *Early Connecticut Probate*, 2:45.

Oliver Harris of Wethersfield (1655)

At a quarter court held in Hartford on 6 September 1655, "Oliver Harriss for his misdimenor in selling strong water to the Indians the Courte adjudgeth that he be put in security for his good behavior and make his appearance at the next Courte if he be living in the Country. Oliver Harriss is bound in a recognissce of 20 pound according to the censure of he Courte. Jn° Knott [and] Will Pa[l]mer [Wethersfield residents] are bound in a recognissce of 10 pound a peece for Harris."[2115]

There is no further record of Oliver Harris; the implication is that he took the opportunity to leave the colony.

James Harris of Boston and New London[2116] (before 1668?)

James Harris's place in the sequence of these sketches is debatable. His more prominent son of the same name had come from Boston to New London, Connecticut, in 1695 and his parents followed in about 1704. However, there are reasons to suspect that the elder James had been in Connecticut earlier, before the first evidence of his presence in Boston in 1668. The reasons include his association in the south end of Boston for many years after 1668 with Capt. (later Governor) John Leverett, the same who owned the large Twelve-Mile Island farm in Connecticut, lying between what later became the towns of Lyme and East Haddam in the lower Connecticut River Valley. As more fully discussed elsewhere,[2117] the first lessee, or manager, of this farm was Capt. Richard Wright, father-in-law of the sawmiller Thomas Harris discussed in Appendix I. This circumstance, coupled with the fact that James and the sawmiller both gave the name *Ephraim* to sons, suggests that they were related, but no definitive evidence is found.

[2115] *Records of the Particular Court of Connecticut, 1639–1663*, Coll. Conn. Hist. Soc, 22 (Hartford, 1928):152.

[2116] The sketch presented here is based on the article by the present author, "James and Sarah (Eliot?) Harris of Boston and New London," NEHGR 154 (2000):3-32. It should be consulted for further information on descendants.

[2117] Harris, "James and Sarah (Eliot?) Harris of Boston and New London," NEHGR 154 (2000):12-14; Harris, "Captain Richard Wright of Twelve-Mile Island and the Burnhams of Podunk: Two Seventeenth Century Connecticut River Families," TAG 67 (1992):32-46; 68 (1993):83.

1 JAMES[1] HARRIS was born say 1642, presuming that he was about 25 when he married.[2118] His birthplace may have been in Connecticut, although no definite proof is found there. He died on 9 June 1714, probably at his son James Harris's home in Mohegan (North Parish of New London, now Montville), Connecticut.[2119] His wife by March 1667/8 (birth of first child) was Sarah, probably **SARAH ELIOT** who was baptized in Boston on 5 December 1647, "about 6 Dayes old,"[2120] daughter of Deacon Jacob and Margery (____) Eliot.[2121] Sarah was living in New London, probably North Parish, in June 1714, when James left his whole estate to her for life and appointed her and his son James as executrix and executor of his will.[2122]

The first notice of James's presence in Boston is the record of his daughter Sarah's birth there in March 1667/8. James never owned recorded property in Boston, but, in June 1670, he witnessed when William Talmadge, a carpenter, transferred his house and pasture to his father-in-law John Pierce, a bricklayer. In January 1672/3, James again witnessed when Pierce sold the property to Thomas Walker, a brick maker.[2123] This property, now crossed by Common Street, was remotely located southwest of Deacon Jacob Eliot's house in Boston's "neck" of that period on the west side of the Road to Roxbury (modern Washington Street) and adjoined Eliot's pastures to the west.[2124] On the south, it adjoined a pasture held by John Leverett, who also owned a large farm in Connecticut called *Twelve-Mile-Island*.

A careful comparison of Boston tax lists with a lot-by-lot reconstruction of property ownership in the South End shows that James probably resided on leased property directly across Essex Street from the Eliots until about 1691, then about two blocks north until sometime after 1696.[2125] Sometime before 1687, probably before Governor Leverett sold his land in the neck to

---

[2118] Although Nathaniel Harris Morgan, *Harris Genealogy, A History of James Harris of New London, Connecticut* (Hartford: Case, Lockwood & Brainard Co., 1878) states, p. 17, that James was born "about 1640," he gives no evidence and in some other cases provides specific dates with no indication that they are his estimates and not based on a recorded age or the equivalent.

[2119] *Diary of Joshua Hempstead*, 35.

[2120] Richard D. Pierce, *The Records of the First Church in Boston, 1630–1868*, 3 Vols. (Boston, 1961), 1:309 (vols. 39–41, Publications of the Colonial Society of Massachusetts.

[2121] Anderson, *The Great Migration Begins*, 1:629.

[2122] New London District Probate, B:142-43.

[2123] Thomas T. Temple, ed., *Suffolk [Mass.] Deeds* (Boston: Rockwell and Churchill, 1880–1906), 7:243; 8:48-50.

[2124] See Annie Haven Thwing, *The Crooked and Narrow Streets of the Town of Boston, 1630–1822* (Boston: C. H. Simonds Co., 1920), 240–41, and map between pp. 228–29.

[2125] *First Report of the Record Commissioners of the City of Boston, 1876*, 2nd ed. (Boston, 1881), 75, 126, 144, 156. The surviving lists for 1674 and 1676 are missing the section of town designated as Division Eight in later tax assessments.

John Bennett in 1675,[2126] or when Leverett died in March 1678/9,[2127] James moved onto the rental lot owned in that period by Leverett's nephew Isaac Addington at the northeast corner of Washington and Essex Streets.[2128]

Standing south just across Essex Street from James Harris, on the Jacob Eliot property, was the "Liberty Tree," said to have been planted in 1646, which became famous in the Stamp-Act era of the next century and was cut down by Tories in 1775.[2129] Possibly, James and Sarah lived part of the time before 1687 on the various Eliot properties in that neighborhood, but no formal distribution of the older Eliot estate was recorded.[2130] In 1687, however, James apparently was still, or again, a tenant of the Leverett in-laws.

The elder James Harris appears in Boston records through 1700. In November 1676, he brought a complaint against John Williams and Richard Hake, butchers in Boston's North End, "for abuseing of him in bad language and throwing theire offal out of theire shop into his wheelebarrow among his meate as hee was driving it through the Town for sale." The court admonished Williams and required Hake to pay Harris five shillings.[2131] In January 1676/7, James witnessed "schoolmaster" John Sanford's will and proved it in court next April. Sanford left his schoolhouse to the Old South Church in Boston, and his remaining estate, after his wife's decease, to children of his brother Robert Sanford of Boston and of his brother-in-law Edward Turner of Middletown on the Connecticut River, a few miles north of Twelve-Mile Island.[2132] In November 1678, James Harris was among those who took the oath of allegiance.[2133] At the March 1682/3 selectmen's

---

[2126] Thwing, *Streets of the Town of Boston*, 240-41.

[2127] C. Edward Egan, Jr., "The Hobart Journal," NEHGR 121 (1967):203; see also Nathaniel B. Shurtleff, "Genealogical Notice of the Family of Elder Thomas Leverett," NEHGR 4 (1850):128.

[2128] Addington was not residing there, but at a location farther north in town (*First Report of the Record Commissioners*, 49, 54, 117, 141, 158).

[2129] *Second Report of the Record Commissioners of the City of Boston, containing the Boston Records 1634–1660, and the Book of Possessions*, 3rd ed. (Boston, 1902), 87. For a sketch of this tree and property at a later date, see Thwing, *Streets of the Town of Boston*, between pp. 234-35, where it is depicted on the southeast corner of Washington and Essex Streets.

[2130] *Book of Possessions*, 63-64; the analyst, William H. Whitmore, remarked that he was "obliged to assume various unrecorded divisions of the Eliot lands among the various branches of the family, in order to make any sense out of the existing deeds."

[2131] Allyn Bailey Forbes, ed., *Records of the Suffolk County Court, 1671–1680*, vols. 29-30, *Publications of the Colonial Society of Massachusetts* (Boston: John Wilson and Son, 1933), 30:756.

[2132] Suffolk Co., Mass., Probate, 6:181, repaged 273-76. Lt. Theophilus Frary, apparently James Harris's brother-in-law, was one of the overseers. Edward and Mary (Sanford) Turner's daughter Elizabeth of Middletown subsequently m. in 1688 Thomas Miller. Miller was a stepson of the mariner John Herris, whose sister Hannah and her husband Enoch Hobart in 1691 bought the inn by Wheeler's Pond managed at that time by James Harris (see following sketch, *Thomas Herris of Hartford*).

[2133] Forbes, *Records of the Suffolk County Court*, 30:963.

meeting, James was chosen as a hog reeve, a duty he performed again for the year following March 1693/4.[2134] In 1688, he was short the cow listed for him in the 1687 tax assessment in Division Eight.[2135]

Innkeeper Nehemiah Pierce died before 29 August 1690, when his widow Anne, Governor Leverett's niece, obtained a license to retail "out of dores."[2136] Anne soon leased Nehemiah's inn, located between Washington Street and Wheeler's Pond (second lot north of modern Bedford Street), to James Harris. Perhaps under the widow's newly granted license, James already was the proprietor by next 21 October, when neighbor Samuel Sewell noted "a rumor in Town that Sir Edmund [Andros] is to come Governour of New York, and Col. Slater our Governour. Tories are flush'd, and 'tis said were drinking Sir Edmund's Health last night at Neh[emiah] Pierce's."[2137] In any case, James must have been in charge there five months later, on 26 March 1691, when he witnessed John Hurd's sale of property next south of Sewall's lot and about 100 feet north of the inn.[2138]

In December 1691, Isaac Addington, acting as agent for his sister Anne Pierce, sold the inn to Enoch and Hannah (Herris) Hobart from Hingham, Massachusetts.[2139] James was still in "present occupation and tenure" when Enoch and Hannah sold it to Florence Mackarty in July 1694 and moved on to join Hannah's father in Philadelphia. (See sketch, *Thomas Herris of Hartford*, next following.) When Mackarty sold it in July 1696 to Capt. George Rescarricke, mariner, of the City of New York, it was still in the possession of "James Harris Inholder."[2140] But James had lost his lease before December 1698, when Rescarricke sold it to Gyles Dyer of Boston, a merchant, who leased it to John Briggs.[2141]

[2134] *[Seventh] Report of the Record Commissioners of the City of Boston, Containing the Boston Records from 1660–1701* (Boston, 1881), 159, 217.

[2135] *First Report of the Record Commissioners*, 126; William Blake Trask, transcriber, "Boston Tax Valuation of 1688," Boston Public Library, Catalog No. Ms Bos 5 (1688), Sheet 8, p. 44.

[2136] *Boston Records from 1660 to 1701*, 204.

[2137] M. Halsey Thomas, ed., *The Diary of Samuel Sewall, 1674–1729*, 2 vols. (New York: Farrar, Straus and Giroux, 1973), 1:268.

[2138] Suffolk Co., Mass., Deeds, 15:80.

[2139] Suffolk Co., Mass., Deeds, 15:160-61; Hannah Herris, daughter of the merchant Thomas Herris of London, Boston, Hartford, and Philadelphia, was unrelated to James Harris (see following sketch, *Thomas Herris of Hartford*).

[2140] Suffolk Co., Mass., Deeds, 16:66–67; 17:282–84. Not long before 22 Jan. 1697/8, Lt. John Christophers, constable at New London, Conn., arrested George Rescarricke in New York, "who behaved himselfe in a violent manner in the town of Newlondon." New York authorities fined Christophers for acting outside his jurisdiction, but the Connecticut General Court reimbursed him (*Public Records of the Colony of Connecticut, 1689–1706*, 4:239).

[2141] Suffolk Co., Mass., Deeds, 19:50. The identity of this John Briggs is not certain, but it is likely that he was the brother-in-law of John[1] Harris, whose descendants are the subject of the main part of this

Sometime after 1696, James had moved his family farther north in town to Division Four, where, in 1700, he appears in Constable Billings tax-abatement list with three "Polls," two under "Watch," and with "Houses" but no "Personall Estate."[2142] The two standing for watch duty were most likely James and his nineteen-year-old son Asaph.[2143]

James and Sarah Harris moved to Mohegan in Connecticut about April 1704, where they probably moved in with their eldest son, James Jr., who had arrived several years before. The latter was not distinguished as "Jr." in New London deeds through March 1704, but he was beginning next May.[2144] No deeds attributable to the elder James have been found in New London, but his younger sons Asaph and Ephraim witnessed deeds there for their brother James Jr. in September 1706.[2145]

Children of James[1] and Sarah (Eliot?) Harris, all but ii, vi, and vii from the Boston town records,[2146] and all but ii and iv baptized in Old South Church:[2147]

   i   SARAH[2] HARRIS, b. 2 March 1667[/8] and bp. 12 Aug. 1683. A Sarah Harris, probably the same, recorded the birth of a daughter Martha in Boston on 20 Jan. 1688[/9], the father named as HENRY LILLY.[2148] Henry was entered in the unalphabetized 1687 tax list between James Harris and Theophilus Frary; that is, apparently between Sarah's father and her aunt Hannah Eliot's husband.[2149] Lilly was a glover noted several times in Boston town records between 1682 and 1687 for entertaining strangers, including one Jonathan Franklin "suspected to be a very dangerous person to reside in ye Towne."[2150] Lilly came to Boston with his wife Anne on the *Unity* from

---

book (Harris, "William[1] and Mary Briggs of Boston and the Connecticut Valley," NEHGR 151 (1997): 87-91, 98-101).

[2142] *[Tenth] Report of the Record Commissioners of the City of Boston, Containing Miscellaneous Papers* (Boston, 1886), 102.

[2143] The Record Commissioners dated Constable Billings' list as "1700?" with an explanation that it may belong in 1702 (*Miscellaneous Papers*, 90). It can be positively assigned to 1700, however, as Joseph Billings was Tithingman in Division Four in March 1698/9 and was chosen constable for a single one-year term beginning 11 March 1699/1700 (*Boston Records from 1660 to 1701*, 229, 239; *[Eighth] Report of the Record Commissioners of the City of Boston, Containing the Boston Records from 1700 to 1728* [Boston, 1883], 5, 22).

[2144] New London, Conn., Deeds, 6:212; 9:112.

[2145] New London, Conn., Deeds, 6:138.

[2146] *Boston Births, Baptisms, Marriages, and Deaths, 1630–1699*, 104, 114, 128, 132, 138, 152, 157, 163, 169, 180.

[2147] Records of the Old South Church, Baptisms, 1669–1875, pp. 33, 38, 47, 55, FHL microfilm 856694.

[2148] *Boston Births, Baptisms, Marriages, and Deaths, 1630–1699*, 180.

[2149] *First Report of the Record Commissioners*, 126. The sequential order of their names almost certainly means that Henry Lilly was residing very near the Harrises and Eliots at the corner of Essex and Washington Streets in 1687, little more than a year before Sarah's child was born.

[2150] *Miscellaneous Papers*, 55, 60, 75, 80.

London in 1680.[2151] Marriage intentions for an unplaced Sarah Harris and one Stephen White were published in Boston on 25 Sept. 1695.[2152]

ii   MARY HARRIS b. ca. June 1669, d. 25 Sept. 1670, as "daughter of James and Sarah Harres," aged 15 months.[2153]

iii   JAMES HARRIS, b. 4 April 1673 and bp. 12 Aug. 1683, d. Colchester, Conn., 10 Feb. 1757.[2154] Two days later, Hempstead noted that "Lt James Harris was buried the 10th aged 80 odd, he formerly lived in the North Parish and laterly with a son Lebbeus at Poagwonk where he died."[2155] *Poagwonk* was the section of Colchester, Lyme, and Mohegan that eventually became the Town of Salem in 1819. James was bur. at Mohegan (North Parish, now Montville) between his two wives, both named *Sarah*, and near the traditional burial place and monument to Uncas.[2156]

James m. (1) by 1697 (first child) SARAH[3] ROGERS, born in New London on 9 Aug. 1676,[2157] dau. of Samuel[2] Rogers (*James[1]*) and his wife Mary (Stanton) of New London and Mohegan, and younger sister of his brother Asa Harris's wife Elizabeth.[2158] Reverend David Jewett, Montville's second minister, in his "Memoranda Relating to the Families of First Settlers," recorded in his account of James[2] Harris's family that "Old Miss Harris Died 13 Nov 1748."[2159] Hempstead noted the event next day: "the wife of Lt. James Harris aged 70 died."[2160] In his old age James "marrd [intentions published 27 Aug. 1749][2161] the Wid° Sary Harris, his second wife [who] died 9 Oct. 1752."[2162] She was SARAH (HARRIS) JACKSON, b. in New London on 1 Jan. 1704/5,[2163] dau. of the unrelated Joseph[3] Harris (*Gabriel[2]*,

---

[2151] Henry F. Waters, "Voyage of the Ship Unity, 1680," NEHGR 33 (1879):307-10, citing "Essex County Court Papers."

[2152] *Boston Marriages from 1700 to 1751, [Twenty-Eighth] Report of the Record Commissioners of the City of Boston* (Boston, 1898), 348.

[2153] *Gravestone Inscriptions and Records of Tomb Burials in the Granary Burying Ground, Boston, Mass.* (Salem: The Essex Institute, 1918), 121.

[2154] Montville Congregational Church Records, Formerly New London North Parish, 4 vols. (FHL microfilm 4863), 3:15.

[2155] *Diary of Joshua Hempstead*, 681.

[2156] Morgan, *Harris Genealogy*, 20, whose transcriptions of the wives' gravestone inscriptions show dates slightly different from more reliable records, cited below.

[2157] Barbour Collection, Conn. Vital Records, citing New London VR1:11.

[2158] James Swift Rogers, *Ja*Error! Bookmark not defined.*mes Rogers of New London, Connecticut* (Boston: By the author, 1902), 41, 49.

[2159] Montville Congregational Church Records, 3:15.

[2160] *Diary of Joshua Hempstead*, 508-9.

[2161] Hempstead noted on 27 Aug. 1749: "Lt James Harris & Sarah the wife of Samll Jackson (who hath been gone to N Caralina several years) were published" (*Diary of Joshua Hempstead*, 534).

[2162] Reverend Jewett's "Memoranda," Montville Congregational Church Records, 3:15. Hempstead noted on 10 Oct. 1752: "Sarah the wife of Lt James Harris (Lately Sarah Jackson the Daughter of Lt Joseph Harris Dec[ease]d) was buried in the North Parish. Died Yesterday aged about 48" (*Diary of Joshua Hempstead*, 596).

[2163] Barbour Collection, Conn. Vital Records, citing New London VR1:30.

Walter[1]) and widow of Samuel Jackson, whom she had married in New London on 16 Sept. 1730.[2164]

James left home in Boston by 1696, so he possibly was the man of that name who witnessed at Windham, Connecticut, on 9 July 1695 when John Fitch conveyed land.[2165] He was in New London within the year and by Nov. 1698 had settled on Mohegan lands granted to his wife by Uncas's son Owaneco, then Sachem of the Mohegans.[2166] A year later, he was styled "weaver, sometime of New London" when he and Thomas Jones exchanged a hundred acres on the bounds of New London and Norwich.[2167] Apparently, Harris's residence was regarded at that time to be within the bounds of Norwich, adjoining New London's North Parish, but he recorded a cattle earmark in New London on 10 Sept. 1700.[2168]

James was soon dealing with men in Wethersfield and Glastonbury, Connecticut. In Nov. 1704, James Harris "of New London" appealed a Hartford Co. judgment in favor of Ebenezer Smith of Glastonbury on a debt by assignment for £4 10s.[2169] Three years later, "James Harris of New London" was sued by James Wright of Wethersfield for a debt of £5.[2170]

James had returned to Boston by Nov. 1707, when, as "husbandman of New London, now resident in Boston," he was adjudged bound on a debt to Eliah Adams, a Boston shopkeeper. He was back in New London in Nov. 1711 when the shopkeeper's widow Rebeckah prosecuted the action.[2171] Concurrent events suggest that James Harris's temporary residence in Boston may have been connected with the settlement of the estate of Connecticut's Governor Fitz-John Winthrop who died at Boston in Nov. 1707. Unless it was by assignment, the debt was not Harris's, but one owing to the shopkeeper in right of the latter's earlier wife, Priscilla (Winthrop), Fitz-John's cousin, who had d. in Boston in 1702 or 1703.[2172]

James had in fact returned to New London earlier, by Jan. 1708/9, when he witnessed arrangements by George and Caleb Chappell for care of their

[2164] New London First Congregational Church Records, 6 vols., Connecticut State Library, Hartford (FHL microfilm 5131), 1:158.

[2165] Windham, Conn., Deeds, CC:50. This witness, however, could have been the James Harris of undetermined parentage who m. (1) at Bridgewater, Mass., 14 Feb. 1692/3, Elizabeth Bayley, and (2) there 11 March 1695/6, Elizabeth Fry (*Vital Records of Bridgewater, Massachusetts, to the Year 1850*, 2 vols. [Boston, 1916], 2:157, 159). In Oct. 1697, James Harris of Bridgewater bought land in the North Purchase of Taunton, Mass., and was resident there in 1700 (F. C. Warner, "Probable Identity of the Daughters of Roger Chandler of Duxbury, Mass.," TAG 27 [1951]:1).

[2166] New London, Conn., Deeds, 6:4, 48.

[2167] New London, Conn., Deeds, 6:19.

[2168] New London, Conn., Deeds, 4:398.

[2169] Records of the Court of Assistants and Superior Court, Hartford, 1687–1715, 58:39, Conn. State Library.

[2170] Hartford County Court Records, 1:39. No relationship is known between James Wright of Wethersfield and the Capt. Richard Wright mentioned above in connection with James[1] Harris.

[2171] Hartford County Superior Court Files, 1711–1764, Folder 1711–1712, Conn. State Library.

[2172] *[Twenty-Fourth] Report of the Record Commissioners of the City of Boston, containing Boston Births from A.D. 1700 to A.D. 1800* (Boston, 1894), 13, 26; *Boston Marriages from 1700 to 1751*, 6.

mother, Mrs. Margaret Chappell, the aged widow of George Chappell of New London. He witnessed further arrangements for her in Oct. 1714.[2173]

In May 1710, James purchased Mohegan land from John Livingston and his wife Madam Mary, Fitz-John Winthrop's only daughter.[2174] Also in that year, by a "conveyance of great import," Owaneco gave "no less than a general deed of the Mohegan lands between Norwich and the old town-line of New London [reserving the section occupied by the tribe] to Major John Livingston, Lt. Robert Denison, Samuel Rogers Jr., and James Harris Jr."[2175] Numerous later deeds for these lands associate James Harris Jr. with Livingston, Madam Winthrop (Fitz-John's widow), Mrs. Sarah Knight (Livingston's mother-in-law), and others of that family group.

James Harris was commissioned Lieutenant of the North Parish militia in May 1714,[2176] but by May 1718 his residence was in the south part of Colchester, when he gave deeds for Mohegan lands to Joseph Bradford of New London. James was then styled "Gentleman."[2177] In Oct. 1725, Lt. James Harris, in behalf of the "New Parish, being the north part of Lyme and south part of Colchester [modern Salem]," petitioned the General Assembly to approve a tax to support a minister.[2178] Many deeds in New London, Colchester, and Lyme reveal wide-ranging connections with men in Boston, Salem, and Weston, Massachusetts; and Portsmouth and Newport, Rhode Island. Between 1730 and 1745, he was styled "of New London" in Colchester land records. He had returned to Mohegan (then part of New London), where the Reverend Jewett noted that James and Sarah Harris were "present when I came 1739."[2179]

In that period, James was closely involved with the Mohegan Sachem, Ben Uncas, in the complex maneuvering between Capt. John Mason of Norwich, the Mohegans, and Connecticut authorities over lands granted as much as eight decades earlier by Uncas and his son Owaneco. In Jan. 1735/6, Governor Talcott notified the Massachusetts governor that "Mr. Saltinstall, Lieut. James Harriss, and Mr. Hallum of Newlondon" had informed the Governor of Rhode Island about "a late underhanded intrigue of Capt. Mason's . . . that Mahomett was the lawful heir to the Mohegan crown." Next month Talcott sent an apology to Lt. James Harris—"I should have spoken to you sooner after you came to Hartford"—and requested

---

[2173] New London, Conn., Deeds, 6:167; 347–48; Gale Ion Harris, "George Chappell of Windsor, Wethersfield, and New London, Connecticut," NEHGR 150 (1996)48-73, at 53.

[2174] New London, Conn., Deeds, 6:241.

[2175] New London, Conn., Deeds, 6:205; *Public Records of the Colony of Connecticut, from May, 1717, to October, 1725, with the Council Journal from May, 1717, to April, 1726*, 6 (Hartford, 1872):321, 388, 458; Caulkins, *History of New London*, 428.

[2176] *Public Records of the Colony of Connecticut, from October, 1706, to October, 1716, with the Council Journal from October, 1710, to February, 1717*, 5 (Hartford, 1870):433.

[2177] New London, Conn., Deeds, 7:225-27.

[2178] *Public Records of the Colony, 1717–1725*, 6:577.

[2179] Montville Congregational Church Records, 3:20, 21.

Harris's "best help [with] our defense against Capt. Mason's complaints." Later, James presented an account of his efforts and expenses.[2180]

In April 1739, John Reed of Boston informed Governor Talcott that "Mr. James Harris came to this Town about a fortnight ago with Ben Uncas, Sachem of Mohegan, went to Col. Brown, Mr. Dolbeare and Mr. Allen, to raise money in defense of the Gov^t against Mason. [He] applied to Col. Winthrop for the copys out of the Commissioners book for the Indian affairs, to prove Ben Uncas always to have been the reputed Sachem of the Mohegans." Winthrop refused the request because he had earlier refused Captain Mason, but James managed somehow to persuade the Massachusetts governor to call a meeting of the Commissioners, who voted that he should have them. He also "got an Address in Ben's name to the King" and other papers to send to Wilks, the Connecticut agent in London. Reed added that "Mr. Harris hath been indefatigable in the affair, and I doubt not but it has been very expensive to live here so long in ye pursuit of ye affair." Reed's transmittal to Wilks included Ben Uncas's Address to the King, dated 4 May 1739, congratulating His Majesty the Prince of Wales on the birth of his second son, Edward Augustus, Duke of York and Albany.[2181] Next Oct., on motion of Ben Uncas, the Connecticut governor ordered delivery of firearms to Ben, "taking James Harris's bond for their safe return."[2182]

Notwithstanding Harris's indefatigable efforts, five years later, in May 1745, the Mohegans complained to the General Assembly that "Mr. James Harris of New London [and] one Asa Harris [James's nephew]" had obtained twenty-year leases on their lands, "of which none of ye Indeans knew any thing till after said Leas was obtained but Ben our Sachem who we think hath no Right to Leas our Lands without our Leave . . . and by all which Doings of ye said Harrises we are Exceedingly Distressed impoverished and allmost undone."[2183]

James eventually returned to Colchester to live with his son Lebbeus. In 1756, he sold sixteen acres there to his son Jonathan, adjoining the latter's "land where he now dwells."[2184] On 7 March 1757, administration was granted to Lebbeus "on ye estate of Capt. James Harris late of Colchester, dec'd." The inventory, valued at £52, was exhibited next June, and in Sept. Lebbeus showed the estate to be insolvent.[2185] James had initiated a suit on a bond against Gershom Breed of Norwich. In March 1757, Lebbeus successfully prosecuted that action on behalf of the estate. But in Oct. 1758

[2180] Mary Kingsbury Talcott, ed., *The Talcott Papers*, 2 vols. (Hartford, 1892–96), 1:331-33, 344-47, (Vols. 4–5, *Collections of the Connecticut Historical Society*).

[2181] *The Talcott Papers*, 2:98-99, 102-103.

[2182] *Public Records of the Colony of Connecticut, from October, 1735, to October, 1743, Inclusive*, 8 (Hartford, 1874):254, 262.

[2183] *The Law Papers: Correspondence and Documents during Jonathan Law's Governorship of the Colony of Connecticut, 1741–1750*, 2 vols. (Hartford, 1907–11), 1:287 (Vols. 11 and 13, *Collections of the Connecticut Historical Society*).

[2184] Colchester, Conn., Deeds, 7:31.

[2185] East Haddam District Probate, 2:418, 434, 435, 444, 465, 467.

Breed successfully petitioned the General Assembly for reversal and retrial, pleading "the condition of the bond . . . and circumstances of two certain carroons in the City of London [showing that] nothing was due on said bond."[2186] A record of adjusted creditor's claims to Mr. James Harris's estate, dated at Colchester 2 April 1759, shows items owing to Thomas Gustin, Joshua Ransom, James Hamilton, Daniel Hamilton, Elpheus Rogers, Lebbeus Harris, Alexander Whaley, Stephen Hempsted, James Harris, Ephraim Harris, Jonathan & Lebbeus Harris, Jonathan Harris (again), John Richard, Asa Harris, and Lebbeus Harris (again).[2187]

iv   MARGARET HARRIS, b. 16 Jan. 1674[/5], but not bp. with other children in 1683.

v   MARY HARRIS (again), b. 3 Feb. 1676[/7] and bp. 12 Aug. 1683, evidently d. by Oct. 1686 when a third child was given the same name.

vi   DEBORAH HARRIS, b. say 1678,[2188] birth unrecorded but bp. 12 Aug. 1683. Deborah and her sister Elizabeth next below are placed according to their sequence in the 1683 baptism list—Sarah, James, Mary, Deborah, Elizabeth, Asa, and Hannah. No further record of Deborah is found.

vii   ELIZABETH HARRIS, b. say 1679, bp. 12 Aug. 1683. No further record of her is found. She was not, as Morgan wrote, the Elizabeth who m. in New London, 27 Aug. 1713, William Rogers, b. 1693.[2189] Rogers' wife was the unrelated Elizabeth Harris b. in New London on 10 Aug. 1693, daughter of Peter[3] Harris (*Gabriel[2], Walter[1]*)[2190] as shown by Peter's will and sales by his heirs of lands in Mansfield, Conn.[2191]

viii   ASAPH/ASA HARRIS, b. 10 Nov. 1680, d. at Preston, Conn., 20 Aug. 1715.[2192] He was bp. as *Asa*, the form subsequently used by his family and descendants, but it probably came from his uncle Asaph Eliot of Boston. He m. New London 17 March 1709 ELIZABETH (ROGERS) STANTON,[2193] b. there 8 May 1673, who d. before Dec. 1753, when her sons sold her property at Alewife Brook, discussed below. She was daughter of Samuel[2] Rogers (*James[1]*) and Mary[2] Stanton (*Thomas[1]*), sister of his brother James's wife, and widow of Theophilus[3] Stanton (*John[2], Thomas[1]*) who d. at Preston in

---

[2186] *Public Records of the Colony of Connecticut, from May, 1757, to March, 1762, Inclusive*, 11 (Hartford, 1880):185-86; by footnote, Hoadly, the editor, defined a carroon as a "rent received for the privilege of driving a car or cart in the city of London."

[2187] East Haddam District Probate, 3:14, file 1574.

[2188] No proof has been found in Boston town or church records for Morgan's undocumented statement that Deborah was born in July 1670 (*Harris Genealogy*, 19). Perhaps he somehow confused her with the daughter *Mary* b. there on 4 July 1670 to James and Sarah *Hains* (*Boston Births, Baptisms, Marriages, and Deaths, 1630–1699*, 114).

[2189] Morgan, *Harris Genealogy*, 19. Morgan also states that James Harris's daughter Elizabeth was born in "June, 1678," but no record of her birth has been found.

[2190] Charles D. Parkhurst, "Manwaring Family Genealogy," NYGBR 51 (1920):308-9.

[2191] New London District Probate, B:295; Mansfield, Conn., Deeds, 3:838.

[2192] Morgan, *Harris Genealogy*, 30.

[2193] New London First Church Records, 1:142.

1705.[2194] Asa's wife is identified by deeds and the will of Samuel Rogers, "aged 72 and upwards," dated 20 Feb. 1712/3, which mentions his daughters Mary Gilbert, Sarah Harris [James's wife], and Elizabeth Harris; and his grandchildren "Elizabeth Stanton and her brother Theophilus."[2195] In April 1711, Asa Harris and his wife Elizabeth received 12 acres on Alewife Brook from "her father Samuel Rogers."[2196]

Asa apparently stood watch with his father in Boston's Division Four in 1700 and presumably came to Mohegan with him in 1704. In Sept. 1706, he and his younger brother Ephraim witnessed their brother James's sale of a saw mill and ten acres on Alewife Brook.[2197] Asa also witnessed eight months later when brother James and his wife Sarah sold land lying at the bounds of New London and Colchester.[2198] After he married Sarah's widowed sister in 1709, Asa settled in Preston where she had been living with her former husband. They recorded four children there between 1709 and 1714. On 13 Sept. 1715, the same day his father's will was approved for probate, administration of Asa's estate was granted to his widow Elizabeth Harris. Robert Denison and Asa's elder brother James gave bond. Next month, Elizabeth exhibited the inventory, valued at £109.[2199]

ix   ANNA HARRIS, b. 22 April 1682 and bp. as *Hannah* 12 Aug. 1683. Morgan commented that Hannah and her sister Mary (below) "probably came to N.L." with their parents, but no trace of them is seen there.[2200]

x   EPHRAIM HARRIS, b. 17 Dec. 1684 and bp. 21 Dec. 1684, evidently d. by July 1688, when his name was given to another child.

xi   MARY HARRIS (again), b. 11 Oct. 1686 and bp. 17 Oct. 1686.

xii   EPHRAIM HARRIS (again), b. 11 July 1688 and bp. 15 July 1688. On 4 Sept. 1706, Ephraim and Asa Harris witnessed their brother James's sale of a saw mill near the boundary of Mohegan, Lyme, and Colchester, Conn.[2201] No further record of Ephraim is found.

Thomas Herris of Hartford[2202] *(1681)*

Thomas Herris was a merchant from London and Boston who first appears in Connecticut records in December 1681, when the town of Hart-

---

[2194] Richard Anson Wheeler, *History of the Town of Stonington, County of New London, Connecticut, from its first Settlement in 1649 to 1900, with a Genealogical Register of Stonington Families* (New London: Press of the Day Publishing Co., 1900), 582.

[2195] New London District Probate, B:51.

[2196] New London, Conn., Deeds, 8:93.

[2197] New London, Conn., Deeds, 6:138.

[2198] Colchester, Conn., Deeds, 2:97.

[2199] New London District Probate, B:142–43.

[2200] Morgan, *Harris Genealogy*, 19.

[2201] New London, Conn., Deeds, 6:138.

[2202] The sketch presented here is based on the article by the present author, "Thomas Herris, Merchant of New England: Reassembling a 'Split Identity'," NGSQ 80 (1992):36-56. It should be consulted for details not repeated here.

ford denied him legal status as an inhabitant,[2203] although he continued to reside there for several years. He signed his name in documents in a practiced hand as *Thomas Herris*, thus distinguishing himself from the sawmiller, Thomas Harris, discussed in Appendix I, who signed by mark.

Thomas[1] **Herris**, born probably in England in the 1620s, assuming that he was in his mid-20s at the apparent time of his son John's birth, died "of old age" at Philadelphia, Pennsylvania, shortly before 14 September 1713.[2204] By an unknown wife or wives, he had children—all born before 1660. Soon after 26 June 1678, he married, probably in Boston, Mrs. **Rebecca (___) Willis**, widow of Mr. William Willis and apparent daughter of Edmund and Elizabeth (Cotton) Sheafe of London.[2205] Rebecca subsequently appears in Hartford on 30 March 1684 and 10 March 1685/5,[2206] and possibly at Boston in July 1692.[2207]

Thomas Herris was mentioned in Boston in May 1667 as a "Londiner" in a business transaction,[2208] but the earliest clear notice that he had actually arrived there was in July 1676.[2209] For the next two years, his activities in and around Boston are chronicled in documents consistently using the distinctive spelling of his surname. On 26 November 1676, he confessed judgment on a debt of £27 owed to Duncan Maclouthland. In July 1677, he was fined £5 for selling liquor to the Indians and for the "entertaining of them Contrary to Law."[2210] In June 1678, after his arrangement to marry Mrs. Willis, he appeared as witness when Sampson Sheafe claimed the forfeited property of Eneas and Joane Salter in the south part of Boston.[2211] In November 1678 and April 1679, respectively, Thomas Herris and Sheafe took the oath of allegiance in Boston.[2212]

Thomas Herris, his son John, and the merchant Richard Harris [*sic*], probably a relative, appear in the 1681 tax list for Division Seven of Boston.

[2203] *Hartford Town Votes*, Coll. Conn. Hist. Soc. 6 (Hartford, 1897):196.

[2204] *Boston Newsletter*, 14–21 Sept. 1713.

[2205] Thomas T. Temple, ed., *Suffolk [Massachusetts] Deeds*, 14 vols. (Boston: Rockwell & Churchill, 1880–1906), 11:66.

[2206] Parker, *History of the Second Church of Christ in Hartford*, 292; Middletown, Conn., Deeds, 1:45.

[2207] Roderick Bissell Jones, "Harrises in Boston before 1700," NEHGR 106 (1952):22.

[2208] Temple, *Suffolk [Mass.] Deeds*, 5:471.

[2209] Forbes, *Records of the Suffolk County Court*, 30:709.

[2210] Forbes, *Records of the Suffolk County Court*, 30:756, 837. This matter in Boston might provide an explanation for Hartford's refusal four years later to grant Thomas the privilege of inhabitancy there.

[2211] Temple, *Suffolk [Mass.] Deeds*, 10:120. Sheafe was acting on behalf of his wife, Mehitable (Sheafe) Sheafe, his 2nd cousin and granddaughter of Boston's wealthy merchant Henry Webb.

[2212] Forbes, *Records of the Suffolk County Court*, 30:964, 968.

Thomas and John were absent in the tax lists thereafter, except for a cameo appearance in 1688.[2213]

By December 1681, Thomas was in Hartford, where his wife Rebecca apparently kept their home while his business seems to have taken him away more often than he was present. On 17 February 1682/3, as "Thomas Herris of Hartford," he purchased from Walter Davis a 20-acre parcel on land on Lieutenant's River in Lyme, Connecticut, along the inlet where the Connecticut River empties into Long Island Sound.[2214] The acquisition apparently was made for business purposes, probably as a warehouse site for trade goods.

On 10 June 1684, the court at New London, Connecticut, initiated probate on the will of Susannah Westall, widow of a previous owner of Thomas's Lyme property, the innkeeper John Westall of Saybrook. Thomas had witnessed a codicil to the will in which a bequest was made to one John Page.[2215] Ten days after the exhibition of the will, Page gave power of attorney to the New London merchant John Wheeler to recover an alleged debt from "Thomas Harris (late) of Hartford ... Merchant."[2216] On the following 16 September, a judgment was issued in favor of Page against the property of "Thomas Herris, late of Hartford, merchant," for £150 due on account.[2217] To satisfy the judgment, Herris's Lyme tract was seized; and on 10 February 1684/5, the constable there sold the land of "Mr. Thomas Harresis [at] beat of drum and out cry."[2218]

On 10 March 1685/5, "Thomas Harris of Hartford, Merchant," executed an agreement in Middletown, Connecticut, with Samuel Ward, master and part owner of the sloop *Endeavor*. At "the first opportunity of Wind," Ward was to be with his sloop at "the usual landing place at Windsor [upriver from Hartford], then to proceed to the warehouses at Hartford ... giving notice at the dwelling house of said Thomas Harris if requested by his wife there." Subsequently, if his vessel was not fully laden with goods, Ward might again stop at Middletown; by then, "without any sayling to seabrook [Saybrook]," he was to sail for New York and deliver those goods "to Thomas Harris or in his absence to Mr. Pinhorne, merchant."[2219] En route to New York, apparently by different transportation, Thomas attended other business in New Jersey. Six days after the agreement with Ward in Middle-

---

[2213] For discussion, see Harris, "Thomas Herris, Merchant of New England," NGSQ 80 (1992):39.

[2214] Lyme, Conn., Deeds, 1:124-25.

[2215] New London Court Records, Trials, 4:76, Connecticut State Library.

[2216] Connecticut Archives: Private Controversies, Series I, 3:151, Connecticut State Library.

[2217] New London Court Records, 4:85, 88.

[2218] Lyme, Conn., Deeds, 1:148.

[2219] Middletown, Conn., Deeds, 1:45.

town, "Thomas Harris of Connecticut" bought 450 acres on the Cohansey River in West Jersey.[2220]

Thomas Herris reappeared in Connecticut on 17 June 1685, buying a gray mare at Saybrook from Walter Davis,[2221] the man from whom he had purchased the Lyme property two years before. Returning to Hartford by October, Thomas appealed the Page-Wheeler action. His petition, boldly signed *Thomas Herris*, began by asserting that he was "last yeare by his business Called out of this Collony to Pensilvania: where he was necessarily detained longer than expected." During that time Page's attorney, John Wheeler, had filed suit against him—an action that had, Herris avowed," "exposed by estate both land and provisions and goods; and sheep; to sayle by outcry . . . to my great oppression . . . the effects whereof or things themselves are chiefly in sayd Wheelers Hands." Thomas asked for a rehearing of the matter at the next county court at New London, for an interim injunction against any disposal of the property, and for an order that Daniel Raymond—"who hath bough my land (having yet payd little)"—should not complete those payments until the issue was decided. The plea was mostly granted, with the hearing set for May in the General Court itself.[2222]

At Saybrook on 13 January 1685/6, [Thomas's son] John Herris witnessed Thomas's release of William Spencer from an indenture the latter had previously made to him.[2223] John appears again with Thomas the following spring, amid the Page-Wheeler proceedings. On 12 March, in the presence of the New London County marshal, Thomas served on Wheeler a copy of the October order; and a similar copy was served on Raymond's wife by William Measure. The following day, the marshal prepared a list of the Herris property sold at auction—i.e., land, "a sloop as ye estate of Thomas Herris," six barrels of powder, pork, whalebone, sixteen sheep, and various other items totaling £58 10s. 11d. On 20 April, according to a note bearing the autograph signatures *Tho Herris* and *John Herris*, a copy of the October court order was served on Page at his Saybrook house.[2224] Meanwhile at Hartford, a distribution of the estate of Sgt. Richard Smith on 20 March 1685/6 included an item for "Mr. Tho: Harris," £1 4s. 11d.[2225]

Litigation on the Page-Wheeler case continued through May and June 1686. Thomas presented a document at Hartford charging Wheeler with the

[2220] Sheppard and Cook, "Harris of Cumberland County," PGM 17 (1949):103.
[2221] Saybrook, Conn., Deeds, 1:270.
[2222] Connecticut Archives: Private Controversies, Series I, 3:152, 154a.
[2223] Saybrook, Conn., Deeds, 1:169.
[2224] Connecticut Archives: Private Controversies, Series I, 3:153, 154b, 155.
[2225] Estate of Richard Smith, Hartford Probate District, 1685/6, No. 5016.

"foule practises" of "maintaince" and using of his client in a corrupt action. That client, he averred, "goes off the stage and acts no more." Herris asked for the return of his estate and reimbursement of his costs, including expenses for "two Journeys to New London" and for the business that was said to be "urgent on [him] in Delaware." Indeed, the client Page failed to appear at the final hearing; Wheeler came to court "speaking little . . . and making no allegation to clear up the righteousness of his case."[2226]

The General Court ruled against Wheeler, authorizing Herris to proceed against Page under common law at the next New London County court. On 26 May 1686, Herris read this order to Raymond at the latter's house; but when he attempted to serve the order on Page, in company with [his son] John Herris and John Reilean, Page's wife appeared "at ye window [and] would not open ye doore nor give any answer." The June court also decided for Thomas—except for its opinion that the sloop was not his in the first place. A year later, Wheeler cited this exception in a petition asking for compensation in the form of a grant of land for his "disappointment" in his loss of the sloop, *Johns Adventure*.[2227]

With this controversy settled, Thomas appears to have left immediately on a trip to London, after which he returned briefly to his former residence in Boston before moving on to Philadelphia. No further record of his presence at Hartford is found. On 24 August 1686, Governor Robert Treat wrote to William Whiting, the Hartford agent who represented in London the interests of Connecticut and its charter. The letter begins: "You are in the first place to enquire after a former Address to his Maj^{tie} sent by one Mr. Thomas Harris of this Colonie or one Capt^{in} Fairwether whither presented to his Maj^{tie} or not, by either of them."[2228] Captain Fairwether, a Boston mariner bound for England in the summer of 1686 with a duplicate copy, had returned from a voyage to England the year before.[2229] Thomas Herris and his son John (who probably accompanied his father to London), had returned to Boston before 27 August 1688, when they were sequentially

---

[2226] Connecticut Archives: Private Controversies, Series I, 3 (unnumbered page following 155). The business in Delaware probably involved the tobacco trade at New Castle, as inferred from a petition by Herris four years later in Philadelphia.

[2227] Connecticut Archives: Private Controversies, Series I, 3:154c, 160-61. The Herris-Wheeler controversy appears to have begun in Philadelphia where, at the time of Herris's appeal, the distiller Wheeler was building a brick house that he was forced to sell to Edward Shippin, a Philadelphian with business connections to Boston's Richard Harris, probably a relative of Thomas Herris (Philadelphia Deeds, E1:441, 443; Temple, *Suffolk [Mass.] Deeds*, 7:148-49, 12:285-86).

[2228] *The Public Records of the Colony of Connecticut* 3 (Hartford, 1859):368.

[2229] John B. Carney, "In Search of Fayerweather: The Fayerweather Family of Boston," NEHGR 144 (1990):16-18.

listed on the tax assessment for Division Two. Each was charged with one male "from sixteen yeares old and upwards." Listed next after them was Thomas Willis, apparently Thomas's stepson, his wife Rebecca's son.[2230]

Thomas and John's stay in Boston this time was brief. Thomas was in Philadelphia by 1689, when he owed quitrents to William Penn for property he had purchased there from James [Gardfrine?].[2231] In April 1690, he petitioned the Provincial Council, complaining against the county court at New Castle (modern Delaware) in a case against a Boston tobacco trader, Oliver Perry [Berry]. The council ordered the case heard at the next provincial court in September, provided that the matter was not settled before then.[2232] In May 1690, "Thomas Herris of Philadelphia, merchant," bought a lot and its brick houses—described as lying between Front and Second Streets, with Chestnut Street on the south, and adjoining Alexander Parker and the widow Culcupp. The following October—with the signed consent of "his son John," who obviously had become a partner in the venture—Thomas mortgaged "his part" of that lot to two London merchants for £110. This second transaction most likely financed the stock of goods to be sold from a shop on the premises.[2233]

Under the sundry spellings *Harris, Herries,* and *Herris,* Thomas's name appears amid witnesses to documents executed in Philadelphia in March 1690/1, October, 1691, February 1691/2, and August 1694.[2234] The Philadelphia tax list of 1693 clusters the entries for Thomas Harris (a £50 estate), John Harris (no valuation), and "Wid: Culcup" (£40 estate).[2235] In May 1695, as Thomas Herris, he presented another petition to the Provincial Council; it nature is not recorded, only the fact that the council refused to hear it on grounds that "hee might have had an appeall to the County Court in equity."[2236] Two weeks later, in an apparently connected incident, the man

---

[2230] *First Report of the Record Commissioners of the City of Boston, Second Edition* (Boston: Rockwell and Churchill, 1881), 136.

[2231] "The Blackwell Rent Roll, 1689–1690," in Marianne S. Wolkeck, Joy Wiltenburg, Alison Duncan Hirsch, and Craig W. Horle, eds., The *Papers of William Penn,* 5 vols. (Philadelphia: Univ. of Penn. Press, 1986), 3:706.

[2232] *Minutes of the Provincial Council of Pennsylvania* (Philadelphia: Jo. Severns & Co., 1852), 1:325, 329-30. Oliver Berry, master of the ketch *Unity,* came in to Boston from Newcastle on 29 Sept. 1689 with sixty hogshead of uncertified tobacco (Tappan, *Edward Randolph, Letters and Papers,* 28:40-41, 49).

[2233] Philadelphia Deeds, E2:140, F1:145; Hannah Benner Roach, "Philadelphia Business Directory, 1690," *Pennsylvania Genealogical Magazine* 23 (1963):102.

[2234] Philadelphia Deeds, E2:161, 212-13, 278; William H. Egle, ed., *Minutes of the Board of Property of the Province of Pennsylvania, Minute Book F., Pennsylvania Archives, 2nd Ser.,* 19 (Harrisburg, 1890):120-22.

[2235] William Brooke Rawle, "The First Tax List for Philadelphia County, A.D. 1693," *Pennsylvania Magazine of History and Biography* 8 (1884):87.

[2236] *Minutes of the Provincial Council,* 1:478-79.

from whom Herris had purchased the property on Cohansey River in New Jersey (Joshua Berkstead or Barkstead), acknowledged their deed.[2237]

On 12 March 1696/7, 116 persons signed a "remonstrance" against the contemporary Quaker government.[2238] Amid the signatures are three consecutive names: *Thomas Herris, Jno. Herris,* and *Enoch Hobart*; i.e., Thomas, his son John, and son-in-law Enoch Hobart who had married his daughter Hannah in Hingham, Massachusetts, on 7 August 1676.[2239]

Two months after the above remonstrance, the Provincial Court rejected a petition of "Tho. Herris" regarding the "clerk of ye market." On the same day, the Council considered favorably two proposals by Andrew Hamilton "for encourage[e]m[en]t to support ye post, both by ye publick and upon private Letters." It then enacted the law by which Pennsylvania officially recognized the colonial post-office system.[2240] Ten days later, on 1 June 1697, "Thomas Harris of Philadelphia, Merchant," sold his Cohansey River property to Hamilton,[2241] who subsequently became "Post Master General in America."[2242] Thus, the stage was apparently set for Thomas's final occupation.

On 1 March 1699/1700, Thomas sold his lot with its brick houses on Chestnut street to his neighbor Patrick Robinson, Gentleman, for £300. Thomas was still called "merchant of Philadelphia" in May 1700, when he sold an adjacent lot to the brick maker Thomas Sison for £34, and again in February 1700/1 when he sold a "tract of land" on Chestnut Street (near the later site of Independence Hall) to William Carter for £50.[2243] Apparently it was after this date when Thomas became the Philadelphia postmaster; he was described in the 1713 newspaper report of his death as "former postmaster" of Philadelphia.

Children of Thomas[1] and ____ (____) Herris, perhaps there were others:

i JOHN[2] HERRIS, b. prob. in England before 1650, was living in Philadelphia in Nov. 1715, when, as "only son and heir of Thomas Herris late of the said city Merchant dec[ease]d," he relinquished his interest in his father's property on Second Street.[2244] He possibly was living in Middletown, Conn., as

---

[2237] Sheppard and Cook, "Harris of Cumberland County," PGM 17 (1949):103.

[2238] Wokeck et al., *Papers of William Penn*, 3:499-502. The editors note (ibid., 502): "the signors represented a growing opposition movement which included Anglicans and other disaffected non-Quakers, along with some Keithian Quakers, all of whom resented the Quaker domination of Pennsylvania government."

[2239] George Lincoln, *History of the Town of Hingham*, Massachusetts, 3 vols. (Cambridge: John Wilson and Son, 1893), 2:339.

[2240] *Minutes of the Provincial Council*, 1:524.

[2241] Walter Lee Sheppard, Jr., "Harris of Cumberland County, N.J.," NEHGR 105 (1951):56.

[2242] *Minutes of the Provincial Council*, 2:32-33.

[2243] Philadelphia Deeds, C2:159-60, F1:143-45, 113, 119-21.

[2244] Philadelphia Deeds, E7:326-27.

late as Sept. 1723, assuming he was the man of that name who made an appearance there.[2245] His only known wife was SARAH (NETTLETON) MILLER, with whom he executed a contract of marriage at Middletown on 16 May, 1684.[2246] Sarah, b. ca. 1642, daughter of Samuel and Mary (___) Nettleton of Branford, Conn., d. as John's widow at Middletown on 20 March 1727/8, age 86y.[2247] With her former husband, Thomas Miller who d. in 1680, she had eight children recorded at Middletown between 1666 and 1680.[2248]

In June 1682, six months after his father first appeared in records at Hartford, "Mr. John Harris" appeared there as attorney for Mary Houghton, widow of Richard Houghton of Beverly, Massachusetts.[2249] Houghton had died that May in Wethersfield while supervising the construction of a sloop, *Endeavor*, at Middletown, in which John had an interest with several businessmen in Boston. In July 1683, still acting as attorney for Mary, John entered a caveat at Middletown barring the disposal of any property belonging to the shipwright George Phillips.[2250] The sloop was completed and was hired by John's father in March 1684/5 to ship goods to New York.

In April 1686, John obtained title to a home lot in Middletown adjacent to the property that his wife had inherited from her former husband.[2251] From Middletown, John returned to the Sound, where he appeared at Saybrook to help his father serve court orders in the Page-Wheeler controversy in late April and on 26 May 1686.[2252] After the close of that affair, John probably accompanied his father on his trip to London, discussed above, and returned with him to Boston, where they appear together in Aug. 1688.

During John's absence, his wife Sarah appears in Middletown records in the spring of 1688. Redeeming the corn mill she had mortgaged to Giles Hamlin, she immediately gave it to her eldest son, Thomas Miller, as a wedding gift—on condition that he pay her £6 per year during her natural life "if shee need or require it."[2253]

John followed his father to Philadelphia, where in Oct. 1690 they jointly owned a lot and brick buildings. From a mortgage they gave to two London merchants, it may be inferred that they were importing goods for his father's shop.[2254] John also appears there in March 1696/7, when he joined

---

[2245] Middletown, Conn., Deeds, 3:261-62, 5:3.

[2246] Middletown, Conn., Deeds, 1:131.

[2247] Barbour Collection, Conn. Vital Records, citing Middletown LR1:17; inscription, Old Farm Hill Cemetery, Middletown.

[2248] Spencer Miller, "The Millers of Bishop's Stortford, co. Herts, England," NYGBR 70 (1939):144ff; Mary Lovering Holman, *Ancestry of Colonel John Harrington Stevens and His Wife Frances Helen Miller*, 2 vols. (Concord, N.H.: Rumford Press, 1948), 1:301.

[2249] Manwaring, *Early Connecticut Probate*, 1:317.

[2250] Middletown, Conn., Deeds, 1:29, 126.

[2251] Middletown, Conn., Deeds, 1:71, 109.

[2252] Connecticut Archives: Private Controversies, Series I, 3:153, 154b, 155.

[2253] Middletown, Conn., Deeds, 1:52, 60.

[2254] Philadelphia Deeds, E2:140, F1:145.

his father and his brother-in-law Enoch Hobart in signing a remonstrance against the colonial government.[2255] John was still there in Nov. 1715, when he relinquished his interest in the Second Street lot left by his deceased father, and may have returned to Middletown. He apparently had died before 28 March 1724, when "Sarah Harris . . . widow and sole executrix to the estate of Thomas Miller her former husband, dec[ease]d," appointed William Whitmore of Middletown to act as her agent for the remainder of her life in the collection of debts, rents, and other income.[2256]

No evidence is found that John had any children of his own.

ii   HANNAH HERRIS, b. presumably in England not long after 1650, was living in Boston in 1695 and presumably was with her husband at Philadelphia in 1697. As "daughter of Thomas Harris," she m. at Hingham, Mass., 7 Aug. 1676 ENOCH HOBART, bp. there 28 May 1654, son of Joshua and Ellen (Ibrook) Hobart.[2257] As residents of Hingham on 5 Aug. 1691, they sold two acres of Broad Cove meadow land. By that October, they were in Boston, where Enoch, described as "yeoman and boatman," mortgaged a 20-acre parcel of the Broad Cove tract he had received from his parents and bought property at the "southward end of Boston." The house with its "little garden," an inn, and other buildings stood near Boston Common and the junction of modern Bedford and Washington streets. In July 1694, they sold the property and—still in Boston—acknowledged the conveyance in April 1695.[2258] They evidently moved soon after that to Philadelphia, where, on 12 March 1696/7, Enoch joined Thomas and John Herris in signing a "Remonstrance of Philadelphia Inhabitants" critical of the current Quaker government.[2259] Enoch and Hannah had six children recorded at Hingham.[2260]

iii ELIZABETH HERRIS, b. ca. 1656, not a native of New England, d. at Stratford, Conn. (a port town), in July 1725, aged 69y.[2261] She had four husbands, all merchants. On 29 May 1678, a month before [her father] Thomas Herris announced his intention to marry Rebecca Willis at Boston, Elizabeth m. at Stratford (1) SAMUEL WHEELER,[2262] b. there 28 April 1649, who d. there in 1699, son of Moses Wheeler. Samuel's will in Nov. 1698 left Elizabeth his entire estate, with the right to dispose of it or bequeath it; however, "if she [should] see good to remove her selfe out of this Country towards her

---

[2255] Wokeck et al., *Papers of William Penn*, 3:499-502.

[2256] Middletown, Conn., Deeds, 5:14.

[2257] Lincoln, *History of the Town of Hingham*, 2:339.

[2258] Suffolk Co., Mass., Deeds, 15:126, 129, 160-61. The deed in 1694 states that their inn was "in the present tenure and occupation of James Harris Inholder." Despite this odd circumstance, no relationship is known or suspected between this James Harris—whose sketch appears separately next above—and the Herris family considered here.

[2259] Wokeck et al., *Papers of William Penn*, 3:499-502.

[2260] Lincoln, *History of the Town of Hingham*, 2:339.

[2261] William Howard Wilcoxson, *History of Stratford, Connecticut* (Stratford: Stratford Tercentenary Commission, 1939), 205, which, however, repeats an earlier misidentification of this Elizabeth (see Jacobus, *Families of Old Fairfield*, 1:80, 677).

[2262] Stratford, Conn., Deeds, 1:225.

Native Land," then Samuel's brother Moses Wheeler would have the right of first refusal.[2263] She stayed—on 16 Sept. 1703, as "Mis^ت Elizabeth Wheeler," she m. at Stratford (2) Mr. HUGH NESBITT, of whom little more is known. On 20 Nov. 1712, she m. there (3) Mr. EDWARD POISSON, a merchant who had resided in Wethersfield, Middletown, and Derby, Conn.[2264] As Elizabeth Wheeler "alias Delaporte Poisson of Stratford," she signed with her mark, *E*, a deed to her "brother Moses Wheeler" for an acre of land and a one-fourth interest in a sawmill near the house of her former husband, "Mr. Samuel Wheeler."[2265] Finally, at Stratford on 27 Aug. 1717, as "Mrs. Elizabeth de la Porte alias Poisson," she m. (4) Mr. RICHARD BLACKLEACH, b. ca. 1654, who d. at Stratford 4 Sept. 1731.[2266] A prominent West Indies trader and Stratford official, Blackleach's connections with Hartford relatives, and the Sheafe and Herris families, have been discussed elsewhere.[2267]

Although Elizabeth had four husbands, she died childless.

William Harris of Block Island and Lyme (1691)

This William Harris appears in Connecticut on 11 June 1691, when he bought from Christopher Swayne "a certine Smith Shoop and small parcel of land" adjoining Edward DeWolfe's house in Lyme.[2268] He had been a blacksmith in New Shoreham (now Block Island), Rhode Island, since May 1664, when he was admitted there as freeman.[2269]

William[1] **Harris** was born probably in the mid-1640s, assuming he was in his mid-20s when he married. He died in Lyme, Connecticut, after 12 June 1693 and before the following September, the dates when he and his wife Elizabeth sold a dwelling house on Block Island, Rhode Island, to John Rodman, and of a record of his estate.[2270] As "William harass black smith," he married at Block Island on 24 July 1672[2271] ELIZABETH INNES (or *Enos*) who died at Lyme on 6 July 1729, aged 66 [*sic*: age apparently understated

---

[2263] Jacobus, *Families of Old Fairfield*, 1:80, 677.

[2264] Stiles, *History of Ancient Wethersfield*, 1:290, 2:523; Harris, "Walter Harris's Widow and the Blinns of Wethersfield," NEHGR 143 (1989):306, 323.

[2265] Stratford, Conn., Deeds, 2:279.

[2266] Jacobus, *Families of Old Fairfield*, 1:80.

[2267] See, e.g., Gale Ion Harris, "John Blackleach, Merchant, of London and New England," NEHGR 148 (1994):7-44, 189.

[2268] Lyme, Conn., Deeds, 2:90.

[2269] John Russell Bartlett, ed., *Records of the Colony of Rhode Island and Providence Plantation* (Providence, 1857), 2:58.

[2270] New Shoreham Deeds, 2:250A, abstract by Nellie M. C. Beaman, *Rhode Island Genealogical Register* [RIGR] 10 (1987):333; Roderick Bissell Jones, "The Harris Family of Block Island and Dutchess County, N.Y.," NYGBR 84 (1953):134.

[2271] New Shoreham Town Book, 1:51 (p. 66 in typescript copy at Rhode Island Historical Society).

or misread from tombstone],[2272] daughter of Alexander and Catharine (___) Innes of Taunton, Massachusetts, and Block Island.[2273] The marriage record does not state her name, but on their marriage date William Harris of New Shoreham gave property to "Elisabeth Enos of New Shoreham my supposed wife & her first child lawfully begotten."[2274] On 8 December 1680, William Harris received from Robert and Margaret Guthrey land at Block Island "in behalf of his wife Elizabeth for the love we bear her . . . for the hayres of her body."[2275] The reason for this gift is not evident.

Elizabeth married second, before February 1694/5, Richard Smith Jr. of Lancaster, Massachusetts, and Lyme. She married third at Lyme in March 1711/2 Roger Alger, who died before July 1729.[2276] With her second husband, Elizabeth had three children: Carley Smith, born February 1694/5; Margaret Smith, born June 1697; and Phebe Smith, born in December 1699.[2277]

The first definite record of William is in May 1664 when he was among the seventeen "inhabitants and housekeepers at Block Island" admitted as freeman of Rhode Island.[2278] He was recorded as a blacksmith when he married there in 1672. He signed his name to deeds,[2279] though his son William used marks *W* and *WH*. No further evidence is found to confirm a speculation by G. Andrews Moriarty that William "probably came from Braintree [the prior residence of many early Block Islanders] and may be a kinsman of Mr. Richard Harris of that town."[2280] He clearly was not the William "Haires" who sold a house lot at Hartford sometime before 18 April 1659 to William Williams, as Jones speculated in 1951.[2281]

William was "of Block Island" as late as 11 June 1691 when he bought from Christopher Swayne "a certine Smith Shoop and small parcel of land"

[2272] Old Meeting House Hill Cemetery, Old Lyme (Hale Collection: Conn. Headstone Inscriptions, 39:83). In Lyme Deeds (2:364), it is recorded: "Elizabeth widow of Roger Alger – Late of Lyme Dec^d – formerly ye wife of William Haris – Dyed – in July in ye year – 1729."

[2273] William B. Saxbe, Jr., "Four Fathers for William Ennis of Kingston: A Collective Review," NYGBR 129 (1998):232-38.

[2274] New Shoreham Deeds, 2:212, abstract by Beaman, RIGR 10 (1987):332. I thank Robert H. Bowerman of Middletown, R.I., for bringing this record to my attention; it eliminates a nonexistent first wife Elizabeth proposed by Jones in his "Harris Family of Block Island and Dutchess County," NYGBR 84 (1953):134-35. See also NYGBR 124 (1993):222.

[2275] Jones, "Harris Family of Block Island and Dutchess County," NYGBR 84 (1953):134-35.

[2276] Lyme, Conn., Deeds, 2:57, 364.

[2277] Donald Lines Jacobus, "Richard Smith of Lyme," TAG 25 (1949):141.

[2278] Bartlett, *Records of the Colony of Rhode Island and Providence Plantation*, 2:58.

[2279] See, e.g., Lyme, Conn., Deeds, 2:109.

[2280] G. Andrews Moriarty, "Some Notes on Block Islanders of the Seventeenth Century," NEHGR 105 (1951):174.

[2281] Jones, "Harrises in Boston before 1700," NEHGR 105 (1951):243. See Gale Ion Harris, "William[1] and Goodwife Ayres of Hartford, Connecticut: Witches who Got Away," TAG 75 (2000):197-205.

in Lyme adjoining Edward DeWolfe's house.[2282] He recorded an earmark "for all sorts of creaters" at Lyme on 12 September 1692, but the entry is followed by a note transferring it to "John Harui Junr" (probably John Harvey Jr.) because "Willim harriss hath [refused?] the towne."[2283] On 19 December 1692, "William Haris of Lyme" sold his shop and land to Daniel Comstock.[2284] William's estate was open until 1718 when his son William sued Roger Alger and his wife Elizabeth, "late widow of William Harris," for its settlement.[2285]

Moriarty stated that William had two sons and two daughters.[2286] Jones showed five more, however, and provided convincing evidence for a total of at least seven children. Rachel, whom Jones listed as "perhaps," is included below for reasons given, though more definite proof is desired.

Children of William[1] and Elizabeth (Innes) Harris:

    i   WILLIAM[2] HARRIS, b. Block Island, R.I., 10 Feb. 1675,[2287] was "of Colchester" as late as 8 Dec. 1762 when he acknowledged by mark at Fairfield, Conn., a deed for Colchester land.[2288] He m. at Block Island 30 Nov. 1697 ELIZABETH BROCKWAY,[2289] b. at Lyme 24 May 1676, dau. of Wolston and Hannah (Briggs) (Harris) Brockway. (See this book, pp. 2-3) Elizabeth was living at Colchester 30 Aug. 1754 when, by mark, she consented to her husband's gift of land to their daughter Esther, but probably had died by 25 April 1757 when the record of a similar transaction does not show her consent.[2290]

        William was on Block Island as late as 1702, when he served on a coroner's jury.[2291] In that same year (May 1702) he recorded a child at Lyme, and he was "of Lyme" 23 Jan. 1705/6 when Wolston Brockway gave two parcels of upland at Tantum Morantum "to my well beloved son-in-law William Harris that married my daughter Elizabeth Brockway." On the same day, William bought an adjacent 14-acre parcel from his brother-in-law Samuel Mott.[2292] By mark *WH*, he witnessed in Dec. 1707 an agreement between Mott and his father-in-law to divide some Lyme

[2282] Lyme, Conn., Deeds, 2:90.
[2283] Lyme Grants and Earmarks, EM:4, in Lyme, Conn., Deeds, Vol. 39.
[2284] Lyme, Conn., Deeds, 2:109.
[2285] Jones, "Harris Family of Block Island and Dutchess County," NYGBR 84 (1953):136.
[2286] Moriarty, "Some Notes on Block Islanders of the Seventeenth Century," NEHGR 105 (1951):174.
[2287] Jones, "Harris Family of Block Island and Dutchess County," NYGBR 84 (1953):136, citing Block Island records, 1:89.
[2288] Colchester, Conn., Deeds, 7:531.
[2289] Jones, "Harris Family of Block Island and Dutchess County," NYGBR 84 (1953):136, citing Block Island records, 1:263.
[2290] Colchester, Conn., Deeds, 6:283; 7:73.
[2291] Jones, "Harris Family of Block Island and Dutchess County," NYGBR 84 (1953):137, citing Block Island records, 1:51, 263.
[2292] Lyme, Conn., Deeds, 2:346, 382.

land.[2293] He was still residing at Lyme in Oct. and Dec. 1713 when, by marks *W*, he sold to William Rathbon the Tantum Morantum property received from his father-in-law, and sold back to Mott the adjoining parcel he had received from him earlier.[2294] Elizabeth eventually released her right of dower in the former deed at Colchester in 1732.

In Nov. 1713, between the dates of his sales at Lyme, William bought from Robert Ransom 50 acres in Colchester, called the latter's "rights in land he bought of Shubul Rowlee Senr." Three years later, the Colchester proprietors laid out to Harris and Ransom an adjoining small parcel, "they giving up to commons."[2295] William was in Colchester in 1718 when he sued for settlement of his father's estate. Subsequent deeds at Colchester and Lyme chronicle William and Elizabeth's land accumulations and eventual transfer to their daughters and others.[2296] In their seventh decade of life, William and Elizabeth finally joined the Congregational Church at Colchester. She joined 3 July 1737; William was baptized as an "adult" on 22 Aug. 1742 and admitted as member next Jan.[2297]

An account of their seven daughters is given elsewhere.

ii THOMAS HARRIS, b. Block Island 22 March 1677, d. in Dutchess Co., N.Y., between 27 Dec. 1725 and 22 Feb. 1725/6, the dates of execution and proof of his will.[2298] He m. by 1700 MIRIAM WILLIE, b. at New London 1 Nov. 1677, dau. of John and Miriam (Moore) Willie of New London and East Haddam.[2299] She is not mentioned in Thomas's will.

Thomas was in Lyme by 7 March 1701/2, when he witnessed the will of his mother Elizabeth's second husband, Richard Smith.[2300] The given name is now unreadable, but Thomas almost certainly was the Harris whose earmark entry at Lyme on 14 Jan. 1702/3 follows one recorded that day for his brother William Harris. Thomas's entry is followed by a note transferring his earmark to "Isack Watters [Waterhouse] of Black Hall."[2301] Thomas seems to have moved across the Connecticut River into Saybrook where he recorded a cattle earmark on 28 May 1704.[2302]

This Thomas probably was the Thomas Harris in Ulster Co., N.Y., by Sept. 1709, where he was taxed in Jan. 1714/5 in the locality now included in the towns of Marlborough and Plattekill.[2303] Also, he seems to be the

[2293] Lyme, Conn., Deeds, 2:364.
[2294] Lyme, Conn., Deeds, 2:444; 3:18.
[2295] Colchester, Conn., Deeds, 1:109-10; 2:21.
[2296] Lyme, Conn., Deeds, 4:174; Colchester, Conn., Deeds, 2:352, 4:346, 5:312, 6:283, 7:73, 531.
[2297] Erwin, "First Society Church Records," DSGRM 48 (1984):80; Jones, "Harris Family of Block Island and Dutchess County," NYGBR 84 (1953):136-37.
[2298] *Old Miscellaneous Records of Dutchess County (The Second Book of the Supervisors and Assessors)* (Poughkeepsie, N.Y.: Vassar Brothers' Institute, 1909), 184-85.
[2299] For Miriam's parents, see Lyme, Conn., Deeds, 3:92, and Manwaring, *Early Connecticut Probate*, 1:520; 2:116-17.
[2300] Donald Lines Jacobus, abstracts, "New London Probate Records," TAG 18 (1941):124.
[2301] Lyme Grants and Earmarks, 1665-1948, EM:8, in Lyme, Conn., Deeds, Vol. 39.
[2302] Saybrook, Conn., Deeds, 1:238.
[2303] C. M. Woolsey, *History of the Town of Marlborough, Ulster County, New York* (Albany: J. B. Lyon Co., 1908), 83.

Thomas who appears in tax lists of nearby Fishkill, Dutchess Co., from 1719 to 1725 when his will there names a daughter in Lyme.[2304]

Thomas's interest in New York lands may have been generated by the Rathbone family. His father, as noted, sold his house on Block Island in 1693 to John Rodman, late of that place. Rodman and William Huddlestone bought land at Poughkeepsie from Henry Ten Eyck. In May 1699, being then of New York City, they sold it to Thomas Rathbone of Block Island, a close associate of Thomas Harris's father and brother William.[2305] For example, it was Rathbone's brother or nephew William Rathbone who bought brother William Harris's property at Lyme in 1713.[2306]

The above cited article by Jones is mainly an effort to trace Dutchess County descendants of this Thomas Harris, but it is highly speculative and of uneven quality. Several supposed relationships and identities are disproved elsewhere.[2307] Jones proposed eight children for Thomas and Miriam Harris, but proof is available only for one—the Miriam born about 1703. She is the only legatee named in Thomas's brief will: "my Loving Daughter Maryam, house wife to Benjamin Colt at Lime in Connecticut Collony, Three Pound of Current money of New York."[2308]

iii ELIZABETH HARRIS, b. ca. 1680, d. New London, Conn., 28 Feb. 1713, aged 32 years.[2309] She m. by 1699, as his 1st wife, JAMES ROGERS, b. at New London 2 Feb. 1675, who d. at Norwalk, Conn., 9 July 1735, son of James and Mary (Jordon) Rogers. He m. (2) 29 June 1713 (int. pub.) Freelove Hurlburt, b. Norwalk ca. 1693, who d. there 26 Jan. 1738.[2310] James Rogers Jr. was admitted to the bar in 1708, was "taken into the church" at New London on 15 March 1713, lived on a farm at the Great Neck, and moved to Norwalk about 1726. Elizabeth is not certainly identified by the prior writers cited, but no other reasonable place for her has been discovered. It is significant that her presumed sister Mary below was in New London in 1714 and her presumed brother William had interests in Norwalk where his youngest daughter, Margaret, married in 1732/3.[2311]

iv MARY HARRIS, b. ca. 1682, d. Lebanon, Conn., in Aug. 1748, aged 66, where she was buried in the "Old Cemetery."[2312] She m. by 8 July 1701 JAMES

[2304] Jones, "Harris Family of Block Island and Dutchess County," NYGBR 84 (1953):138-39.

[2305] G. Andrews Moriarty, "Additions and Corrections to Austin's Genealogical Dictionary of Rhode Island," TAG 20 (1943):55.

[2306] John Osborne Austin, *The Genealogical Dictionary of Rhode Island* (1887; repr. Baltimore, 1969), 159.

[2307] Gale Ion Harris, "The Supposed Children of Thomas Harris of Dutchess County, New York: Re-evaluation and Revisions," NYGBR 133 (2002):3-18.

[2308] *Old Miscellaneous Records of Dutchess County*, 184-85.

[2309] Headstone Inscriptions, Hale Collection, 35:355.

[2310] Rogers, *JaError! Bookmark not defined.mes Rogers of New London*, 71; Henry A. Baker, *History of Montville, Connecticut* (Hartford: Case, Lockwood & Brainard Co., 1896), 186-87; Charles M. Selleck, *Norwalk* (Norwalk: By the author, 1896), 162.

[2311] Gale Ion Harris, "William² and Elizabeth (Brockway) Harris of Lyme and Colchester, Connecticut: With Notes on their Seven Daughters," TAG 70 (1995):233-39, at 238.

[2312] Headstone Inscriptions, Hale Collection, 23:69.

DANIELSON JR.,[2313] b. at Block Island and d. at Lebanon 16 Jan. 1752, aged 64 [*sic*],[2314] son of the Scot James Danielson and his wife Hannah (George) Rose.[2315] He m. (2) widow Irene Fisher who subsequently m. Caleb Hyde. James Danielson, yeoman, and his wife Mary were "of New London" in Nov. 1714.[2316] It is said that a diary kept by Mary's great-nephew Peter Coult/Colt of Hartford, Treasurer of Connecticut from 1789 to 1794, refers to "James Danielson of Lebanon, who married our aunt" who later married "the wicked widow Fisher."[2317]

v CATHERINE HARRIS, b. ca. 1682 and aged about 11 years when her father d. in 1693, was living at Lyme with her mother and stepfather, Richard Smith, when he d. in March 1701/2. In 1718, upon her brother William's suit for settlement of their father's estate, £9 reverted from William Harris's estate to Smith's estate to compensate for Catherine's maintenance for eight years.[2318]

vi RICHARD HARRIS, b. say 1684, was a minor in March 1701/2 when his stepfather gave a bequest to "my wife's son Richard Harise if he continue with his mother until he be of age." He was old enough on 4 April 1705 to witness the will of Wolston Brockway's son-in-law Thomas Champion at Lyme.[2319]

vii ALEXANDER HARRIS, b. at Block Island 22 July 1685, d. there next 5 Sept.[2320] No doubt he and his sister Catherine were named for their maternal grandparents, Alexander and Catharine Innes.

viii (prob.) RACHEL HARRIS, b. say 1687; m. at Lyme 21 Jan. 1706/7, MOSES HUNTLEY JR.[2321] b. there 23 May 1681, who d. at East Haddam, Conn., about 1746, son of Moses and Abigail (Chappell) (Comstock) Huntley.[2322] Jones tentatively placed Rachel in this family as "perhaps,"[2323] citing Huntley's comment that she "may have been a sister of Richard Harris who was mentioned in the will of Richard Smith as son of his wife Elizabeth, widow of John [*sic*: William] Harris. The name Richard Harris persists through all the descendants of this family" (meaning Moses Huntley's descendants).[2324] Recent studies have suggested no other place for Rachel. Other associations are evident; for example, lands laid out to her husband's

[2313] Mary was "now wife" of James Danielson of New Shoreham on 8 July 1701; see New Shoreham Deeds, 1:357-58, abstract by Beaman, RIGR 4 (1981):126.

[2314] Headstone Inscriptions, Hale Collection, 23:69. His age probably is understated or misread from the tombstone.

[2315] Moriarty, "Some Notes on Block Islanders of the Seventeenth Century," NEHGR 105 (1951):180.

[2316] New Shoreham Deeds, 1:460-61, abstract by Beaman, RIGR 9 (1987):340.

[2317] Jones, "Harris Family of Block Island and Dutchess County," NYGBR 84 (1953):136, 141.

[2318] Jones, "Harris Family of Block Island and Dutchess County," NYGBR 84 (1953):136.

[2319] Donald Lines Jacobus, abstracts, "New London Probate Records," TAG 10 (1934):167; 18 (1941):124.

[2320] Jones, "Harris Family of Block Island and Dutchess County," NYGBR 84 (1953):136, citing Block Island records, 1:117.

[2321] Lyme, Conn., Deeds, 2:230.

[2322] AliError! Bookmark not defined.ce P. Huntley, "John Huntley and Some of his Descendants," in *Genealogies of Connecticut Families from the New England Historical and Genealogical Register*, 3 vols. (Baltimore: Genealogical Pub. Co., 1983), 2:226-29.

[2323] JoError! Bookmark not defined.nes, "Harris Family of Block Island and Dutchess County," NYGBR 84 (1953):136.

[2324] Huntley, "John Huntley and some of his Descendants," 228.

grandfather, John[1] Huntley, in 1687/8, included parcels adjoining Richard Smith and Wolston Brockway's son-in-law Thomas Champion. Moses Huntley lived in Lyme until at least 1726, and later in East Haddam where his home was on the west side of Eight-Mile River. Administration on his estate there was granted to his son William in 1746.[2325]

Ebenezer Harris of Plainfield[2326] (1695)

Ebenezer[3] Harris, the youngest known child of Thomas[2] (*Thomas[1]*) and Martha (Lake) Harris of Ipswich, Massachusetts, was a nephew of brothers William and Daniel Harris of Middletown, whose sketches appear above.[2327] His children's recorded birth places show that he moved from Ipswich to Plainfield, Connecticut, about 1695. His maternal grandmother Margaret (Reade) Lake, sister-in-law of John Winthrop Jr., had lived at Saybrook and with the Winthrops on Fisher's Island and at New London many years before.[2328] Ebenezer's sister Elizabeth Harris, wife of John Gallop Jr., had been living at Stonington, Connecticut, for over a decade.

The most comprehensive account of Ebenezer Harris and descendants is the well-documented book by Edythe L. and David C. Haskell, cited above. It is generally followed here except where noted otherwise.

EBENEZER[3] HARRIS (*Thomas[2-1]*), born about 1662, no doubt at Ipswich, died at Plainfield on 12 February 1751.[2329] He married first at Ipswich 15 September 1690 **REBECCA CLARKE**, who died at Plainfield on 16 June 1699. He married second about 1701 **CHRISTOBEL CRARY**, born in February 1678/9, who died at Plainfield on 17 September 1754, daughter of Peter and Christobel (Gallop) Crary of Groton, Connecticut, and Plainfield.[2330]

In October 1701, Mr. John Gallop brought to the Connecticut General Assembly a complaint against Major James Fitch on behalf of John Fellows, Ebenezer Harris, and John Gallop Jr. He alleged that they had quietly entered on land in Plainfield and raised a crop of English grain, but Fitch forced them off, "not suffering them to inne the crop that was on [the land],

---

[2325] Huntley, "John Huntley and some of his Descendants," 228-29.

[2326] The sketch presented here is based mainly on a section about Ebenezer in the book by Edythe L. and David C. Haskell, *Capt. Seers Harris of Plainfield in Connecticut* (Stony Creek, N.Y.: By the authors, 1987), 25-80.

[2327] Davis, *Ancestry of Bethia Harris*, 11ff.

[2328] Robert C. Black III, *The Younger John Winthrop* (New York and London: Columbia University Press, 1966), 138, 328, 384.

[2329] Haskell, *Capt. Seers Harris*, 29, 33, citing Plainfield Church record.

[2330] Louis Marinus Dewey, "Peter Crary of Groton, Conn., and some of his Descendants," NEHGR 60 (1906):350.

and also arresting and imprisoning them and extorting a considerable summe of money from them for their freedome." The Assembly held that Major Fitch's proceedings had been "very erroneous and illegall."[2331]

On 11 September 1702, Ebenezer Harris bought land in "the town of Plainfield in the Quinabogue country" from John and Wait Winthrop of Boston. His home farm in the southern part of Plainfield was on the "Country Road," now Route 12, just south of modern Lillibrige Road. In June 1728, he was one of the several men injured when a bridge under construction over Shetucket River in Norwich collapsed. In 1738, he gave to his eldest son, Thomas, a 65-acre farm on Mill Brook. Five years later in 1743, he divided the rest of his lands among his younger sons: Ebenezer, Daniel, Peter, and Nathan. Joshua Hempstead of New London was in Plainfield on 17 August 1744 "to look after Mr. Winthrop's Lands." He "went to the S.E. Quarter of the Town after wee had a Conference with old Ebenezer Harris & John Fellows, 2 of ye first settlers."[2332] Ebenezer's will, dated 21 June 1750, disposed of his personal property.[2333]

Children of Ebenezer[3] and Rebecca (Clarke) Harris:[2334]

     i   THOMAS[4] HARRIS, b. Ipswich, Mass., 22 March 1692, d. at Cornwall, Conn., between June and Dec. 1744.[2335] He m. at Plainfield 11 Feb. 1713/4, ELIZABETH CHURCH, "dau. of Samuel,"[2336] who d. before April 1770, evidently daughter of Samuel[2] Church (*Garrett*[1]) of Voluntown, Conn.[2337] Thomas was one of the original proprietors of the Town of Cornwall in 1739. His estate was settled and distributed to his heirs in the long period between 1745 and 1770. In May 1745, his administrators Matthew Millard and widow Elizabeth Harris petitioned the Conn. General Assembly for permission to sell land to pay debts.[2338] The remaining estate was finally distributed to son Thomas and daughters Elizabeth, Rebecca, Martha, Sarah, and Esther. On 29 Nov. 1769, Richard and Rebeckah Lovejoy of Plainfield, Thomas and Sarah Rose of Norwich, Joseph and Martha Geer of

---

[2331] Hoadly, *Public Records of the Colony, 1689–1706*, 4:370, 391.

[2332] *Diary of Joshua Hempstead*, 429.

[2333] Haskell, *Capt. Seers Harris*, 27-29.

[2334] Haskell, *Capt. Seers Harris*, 29-30.

[2335] Cornwall, Conn., Deeds, 1:21, 114, 177; Litchfield District Probate Records, 2:237, file 2691. See Gale Ion Harris and Margaret Harris Stover, "Thomas Harris of Plainfield and Cornwall, Ct.," TAG 63 (1988):154-60, for Thomas's migration from Plainfield to Cornwall and further information about his descendants.

[2336] Barbour Collection, Conn., Vital Records, citing Plainfield VR, 1:24.

[2337] Fredric C., Robert M., and Helen C. Search, "Samuel Church of Stonington, Conn.," NEHGR 118 (1964):263; Robert M. and Helen C. Search, "Garrett Church of Watertown, Mass.," NEHGR 123 (1969):182.

[2338] Hoadly, *Public Records of the Colony, 1744–1750*, 9:135-36.

Stonington, and Elijah and Esther Bennet of Canterbury, all in Connecticut, conveyed to the Cornwall selectmen all their interest in land there that "Thomas Harris late of said Cornwall died seized and possesset of."[2339]

ii   EBENEZER HARRIS, b. Ipswich 11 July 1694.

iii MARTHA HARRIS, b. Plainfield 26 Nov. 1696, d. Voluntown, Conn., 4 Jan. 1791, aged 95. She m. there 29 Dec. 1720 EBENEZER DOW, b. Ipswich, Mass., 26 May 1692, who d. at Voluntown 2 Oct. 1755.[2340]

Children of Ebenezer[3] and Christobel (Crary) Harris, all b. Plainfield:

iv   SARAH HARRIS, b. 10 Aug. 1702, d. Plainfield 16 Dec. 1791 in her 90th year. She m. JOSIAH BUMPAS, b. Bristol, R.I., 9 April 1698, d. at Plainfield 3 Sept. 1757, son of Philip[2] Bumpas (*Edward[1]*) and his wife Sarah Eaton.[2341] Josiah and Sarah are bur. in the "Old Yard" at Plainfield; his will dated there 20 Aug. 1757 shows that they had no children.[2342] It names Josiah's wife Sarah and, oddly, also left a £5 bequest to "my Sister Sarah Harris." See the following sketch, "Thomas Harris of Plainfield," for the likely identity of the Harris husband of Josiah's sister Sarah.

v   CHRISTOBEL HARRIS, b. 22 March 1703/4, d. 1 April 170[ ].

vi   EBENEZER HARRIS, b. 6 July 1705, d. at Stafford, Conn., in 1778 or early 1779. He m. (1) in Plainfield 5 June 1732 SARAH TRULL, b. Billerica, Mass., 22 Oct. 1698, who d. in Plainfield 29 March 1751, dau. of John and Elizabeth (Hooper) Trull. Ebenezer m. (2) in Plainfield 29 Oct. 1751, ANNA BENJAMIN, who survived him and was probably the widow Harris at Stafford in 1790 with a male age 16 or over and three females in her household.[2343] They sold their Plainfield land in 1767 and moved to Monson, Mass., where they bought a farm in Jan. 1768. In 1775 and 1776, Ebenezer sold his property at Monson and moved south across the Mass.-Conn. line into Stafford, Conn. His estate, in probate there in April 1779, was distributed to his widow Anna, eldest son Ebenezer, "second son" Robert, and daughters Anne, wife of Joseph Butler; Betty, wife of Seers Harris, Sarah, wife of Samuel Butler, Asenath Harris, Sylvania Harris, and Eunice Harris.[2344]

vii ELIZABETH HARRIS, b. 16 Jan. 1708, d. in Becket, Mass., 5 Nov. 1792 in her 84th year and bur. in the cemetery at Becket Center. She m. (1) before 1744 (____) SEARS, as she was a widow Sears when she m. (2) at Canterbury, Conn., 11 Oct. 1744 EBENEZER ADAMS, b. ca. 1707, who d. at Becket 28 Sept. 1775 in his 69th year and bur. beside Elizabeth. They moved from Canterbury to Suffield, Conn., about 1752 and from there to Becket soon after May 1759. In April 1771, Ebenezer sold his home farm and other lands there to his sons Barnabas Adams and Ebenezer Adams Jr.[2345]

2339 Cornwall, Conn., Deeds, 3:23.

2340 Haskell, *Capt. Seers Harris*, 31-32.

2341 Mrs. John E. Barclay, "The Bumpas Family of New England," TAG 43 (1967):150-51.

2342 Haskell, *Capt. Seers Harris*, 29, 94.

2343 1790 U.S. Census, Stafford, Tolland Co., Conn., p. 190.

2344 Haskell, *Capt. Seers Harris*, 32-34.

2345 Haskell, *Capt. Seers Harris*, 34-37.

viii CHRISTOBEL HARRIS (again), b. in Nov. 1710, was living in Oct. 1782. She m. at Plainfield 5 Nov. 1729 WILLIAM PARKE JR., who d. in Plainfield "by a fall from his horse" on 6 Feb. 1781. They lived for a period during the 1770s in the Wyoming Valley of Pennsylvania, but returned to Plainfield. His will, dated 29 Jan. 1779 and exhibited 6 March 1781, mentioned his wife Christobel, daughter Cynthia, heirs of daughter Rachel Satterlee, heirs of daughter Christobel, deceased daughter Alice's daughter Hannah, and sons Nehemiah, Elias and William. Nehemiah was named executor.[2346]

ix DANIEL HARRIS, b. 13 April 1712, d. in French and Indian War service at Ft. Edward, N.Y., 9 Sept. 1758. He m. Plainfield 25 May 1744 ANNE WELCH, b. Voluntown, Conn., 23 June 1716, who d. at Shaftsbury, Vt., 28 Feb. 1799 in her 84th year, dau. of Thomas and Ann (Edwards) Welch.[2347] An inventory of Daniel's estate was filed on 9 Oct. 1758; next day his brother Peter posted bond for widow Ann Harris, administrator. She twice petitioned the General Assembly for permission to sell land in order to pay debts. She and her co-administrator William Parke sold 35 acres to Thomas Fanning of Norwich in Sept. 1765. She sold other property in Oct. 1768, Jan. 1769, and in April 1770, "probably constituting the last of the holdings of Daniel's estate and her widow's dower."[2348] On 3 May 1763, the probate court in Plainfield appointed Mrs. Anna Harris guardian for Ebenezer, Thomas, and Zilpha Harris, minor sons and daughter of Mr. Daniel Harris late of Plainfield, deceased.[2349] No doubt Anne went to Shaftsbury with her son Ebenezer who moved there sometime between Sept. 1777 and March 1781.[2350] The Haskells mentioned a "vexing" problem that one Daniel Harris Jr. also was in Shaftsbury, who may have been Daniel and Anne's son Daniel b. in Plainfield in 1749.[2351] A more extensive analysis shows, however, that Daniel Jr. of Shaftsbury was a distant relative, son of Daniel[5] Harris (*Daniel*[4-2], *Thomas*[1]) from Dutchess Co., N.Y.[2352]

x ANN HARRIS, b. 23 Oct. 1714.

xi PETER HARRIS, b. 15 March 1716/7, d. Westmoreland Co., Pa., between 26 Dec. 1778 and 26 April 1779, the dates of his will and its presentation for probate at Westmoreland. He m. ca. 1742 MARY WELCH, b. Plainfield 16 July 1723, who survived him, dau. of John and Abigail (Dibble) Welch. Peter sold his land at Plainfield in Feb. 1767. In 1769, he was listed among the "First Forty" settlers in the Wyoming Valley of Pennsylvania. He is often mentioned in the early settlement of that region as a settler in Kingston. His will made bequests to his wife Mary, sons Seers Harris, Elijah

[2346] Haskell, *Capt. Seers Harris*, 37-39.

[2347] Alexander McMillan Welch, *Philip Welch of Ipswich, Massachusetts, 1654, and His Descendants* (Richmond, Va.: W. Byrd Press, 1947), 299.

[2348] Haskell, *Capt. Seers Harris*, 39-42.

[2349] Welch, *Philip Welch of Ipswich*, 299ff.

[2350] Shaftsbury, Vt., Deeds, 1:29, 30.

[2351] Haskell, *Capt. Seers Harris*, 41.

[2352] Harris and Stover, "The First Daniel Harris of Goshen," 156-57.

Harris, Peter Harris, and daughters Abigail Harris and Lydia Shay. Son Peter was named sole executor.[2353]

xi   MARY HARRIS, b. 3 March 1718/9, d. Plainfield 11 Nov. 1754. She m. STEPHEN RUDE, b. Preston, Conn., 10 Nov. 1717, who d. before May 1790, son of Jacob and Jemima (Park) Rude. He m. (2) 2 Dec. 1755 Mary Richardson by whom he had children recorded in Plainfield. Stephen and Mary (Harris) Rude lived in Plainfield where in Jan. 1748/9 he bought from his brother-in-law Nathan Harris eleven acres on Mill Brook and (modern) Flat Rock Road.

xiii   NATHAN HARRIS, b. 18 Dec. 1721, d. Plainfield 12 or 15 April 1700. He m. there 5 July 1749 SUSANNAH RUDE, b. 11 Sept. 1729, who probably was the "Mrs. Widow Harris" who d. there 11 May 1808. She was sister of Stephen Rude, husband of Nathan's sister Mary. Her sister Dorothy married Nathan Harris's relative Daniel[5] Harris (*Daniel[4]*, *John[3]*, *Thomas[2-1]*) of Preston.

Nathan received his father's home farm and several other lots, and was named residuary legatee and sole executor. In May 1790, Nathan conveyed all his Plainfield property to his son Jeptha, who leased it back to his father in 1797. The same property, as Nathan's estate, was distributed in 1801 to Mrs. Susannah Harris; "to sons Nathan, eldest heir; Daniel, second son; Jeptha, third son; Joseph, fourth son; Zadock; Jemimah, eldest daughter; Christable, second and youngest daughter." The personal property distribution lists Zadock as fifth and youngest son and omits Nathan and Jeptha. Administration of widow Susannah Harris's estate was granted to son Jeptha on 1 Nov. 1808. The distribution in 1811 names heirs Nathan, Daniel, Joseph, Jeptha, Jemimah, and Christable. "Zadoc had his full share previous to the distribution."[2354]

Thomas Harris of Plainfield[2355] (1700/1)

This Thomas Harris, probably a son of Isaac[2] Harris (*Arthur[1]*) of Bridgewater, Massachusetts,[2356] arrived in Connecticut from Stow, Massachusetts, probably very near our cut-off date (1700) for these sketches.

3 **THOMAS[3] HARRIS** (prob. *Isaac[2]*, *Arthur[1]*), born probably in the late 1660s, died in Plainfield, Connecticut, on 29 December 1751, where the record includes a notation, "O man," probably meaning "old man."[2357] He married first in Concord, Massachusetts, on 17 September 1688 **MARY**

[2353] Haskell, *Capt. Seers Harris*, 42-47.

[2354] Haskell, *Capt. Seers Harris*, 48-50.

[2355] The sketch presented here is based on the article by the present author, "Arthur[1] Harris of Duxbury, Bridgewater, and Boston: With an Account of his Apparent Grandson Thomas Harris of Plainfield, Connecticut," NEHGR 159 (2005):261-73, 349-59. It should be consulted for further information on descendants and probable ancestry.

[2356] Harris, "Arthur[1] Harris of Duxbury, Bridgewater, and Boston," NEHGR 159 (2005):350, 353.

[2357] Mary Kingsbury Talcott, "Records of the First Congregational Church, Plainfield, Conn.," NEHGR 70 (1916):310.

SHEPARD,[2358] born probably at Concord about 1669–1671 and living in Stow, Massachusetts, in March 1695, daughter of Isaac[2] and Mary (Smedley) Shepard of Weymouth and Concord.[2359] Thomas married second at Windham, Connecticut, on 5 March 1700[/1] **JANE EDWARDS**,[2360] born in Stonington, Connecticut, on 8 November 1675,[2361] daughter of Thomas and Marie (Birch) Edwards of Dorchester, Massachusetts, and Stonington.[2362] Jane died before 1715, by which time Thomas had married, as his third wife, **SARAH** ___, presumably the "Sarah Harras" who died in Plainfield on 17 June 1748.[2363] "Sarah, wife of Thomas Harris, from Plainfield," was admitted to the church in adjoining Killingly, Connecticut, on 14 September 1740.[2364]

On 5 March 1695, Thomas Harris of Stow, Massachusetts, farmer, with his wife Mary's consent, sold to Walter Power of Concord a third of a tract at Nashobey (Littleton), Massachusetts, "being part of lands granted to the three surviving children of Isaac Shepard deceased (viz. Isaac Shepard, Mary 'my now married wife,' and Samuel Shepard) by their grandfather Ralph Shepard deceased."[2365]

On 15 January 1727/8, "for parental love and affection," Thomas Harris of Plainfield conveyed to his "loving son John Harris of Plainfield" a half of his housing and land to be divided "after my death by the judgment of disinterested persons." Thomas reserved to himself use of the "east end of my now dwelling house so long as I shall live." John was to pay to his father yearly a half of the grain, fruit, and hay raised on the farm, "and in case I dye before my wife Sarah" John was to pay the same to her "so long as she remains my [widow]."[2366] Something about this arrangement proved unsatisfactory, for on 29 January 1730/1 John conveyed the half-interest back to his father in exchange for a deed to a 10-acre parcel "in the common field."[2367]

On 25 September 1734, "for parental love and affection," Thomas conveyed to his "son" Silvenas Harris of Plainfield a 30-acre tract bounded by

[2358] *Concord, Massachusetts, Births, Marriages, and Deaths, 1635–1850* (Boston: Todd, 1895), 27.

[2359] Gerald Faulkner Shepard (Donald Lines Jacobus, ed.), *The Shepard Families of New England*, 3 vols. (New Haven: New Haven Colony Historical Society, 1971–73), 1:12.

[2360] Barbour Collection, Conn. Vital Records, citing Windham Vital Records, A:8.

[2361] Barbour Collection, Conn. Vital Records, citing Stonington Vital Records, 1:136.

[2362] Frederick C. Church, and Robert M. and Helen C. Search, "Samuel Church of Stonington, Conn.," NEHGR 118 (1964):265.

[2363] Talcott, "Records of the First Congregational Church, Plainfield," NEHGR 70 (1916):309.

[2364] E. D. Larned, trans., "Killingly, Conn., Church Records," *Putnam's Historical Magazine*, N.S. 3 (1895):225.

[2365] *Shepard Families*, 1:12, citing Middlesex Co., Mass., Deeds, 12:193.

[2366] Plainfield, Conn., Deeds, 3:5.

[2367] Plainfield, Conn., Deeds, 3:92-93.

the country road and lands of Joseph Coit, John Harris, and John Douglas. Silvenas sold the same 30 acres to John Douglas on 23 July 1737.[2368]

Thomas Harris's will, signed by mark and dated at Plainfield on 22 November 1748, describes him as "being now advanced unto old age." It does not mention his wife, evidently deceased, but it names all children listed below except the first Thomas. His "friend" Eleazer Cady, named as sole executor, exhibited the will in court on 14 January 1752. The inventory, dated three days before, lists personal and household items, tools, one cow, and 14 sheep.[2369] On 11 February 1752, the court made allowances totaling £79 15s. to John Harris "out of his father Harrises estate" for "wintering one cow" for the years 1747 through 1751, "provisions for my father & tendance" for the years 1749 through 1751, for costs of nursing and "rhum in his last sickness," and for Dr. [Ebenezer] Robison's bills.[2370] John's receipt to the executor, Eleazer Cady, for these costs was witnessed on 18 February 1752 by David Harris, presumably John's young son, and by the mark of Mary Downing, unidentified.[2371]

Children of Thomas[3] and Mary (Shepard) Harris, recorded in Concord:[2372]

i   THOMAS[4] HARRIS, b. 22 Nov. 1689, apparently d. before 1715, when his name was given to another child.

ii STEPHEN HARRIS, b. 9 Jan. 1691/2, d. Plainfield 26 April 1749.[2373] His wife SARAH, mother of his son Stephen b. in Plainfield in 1738 and living as his widow in 1749, was probably SARAH BUMPAS, b. ca. 1702, daughter of Philip and Sarah (Eaton) Bumpas of Plainfield, and the "sister Sarah Harris" mentioned in the will of Josiah Bumpas at Plainfield in Aug. 1757.[2374] The undated record of a birth of a child Olive to Stephen and Sarah Harris at Stafford, Conn., indicates that they may have briefly resided there.

On 19 June 1749, the court in Plainfield granted letters of administration on the estate of Mr. Stephen Harris to Mrs. Sarah Harris and Mr. Isaac Coit of Plainfield. The inventory taken next 20 May lists personal and household items, a brown cow, smith's bellows and tools, meat and "bear" barrels, a gun, and a bayonet, with a total valuation of £224 16s. The balance of the

---

[2368] Plainfield, Conn., Deeds, 3:180, 301.

[2369] Plainfield District Probate, 2:202-4.

[2370] Plainfield District Probate, 1:114.

[2371] Plainfield District Probate, 2:231. The physician, Ebenezer Robison, also gave a receipt.

[2372] *Concord Births, Marriages, and Deaths*, 31. Thomas's children ii through xi are listed in the order they are named in his will.

[2373] Barbour Collection, Conn. Vital Records, citing Plainfield VR 2:8.

[2374] Confusingly, as pointed out in Haskell, *Capt. Seers Harris*, 29, 94, Josiah Bumpas's wife also was a Sarah Harris, daughter of Ebenezer Harris of Plainfield. The Harris husband of Josiah's sister "Sarah Harris" was unknown to the authors of *Capt. Seers Harris* and also to Mrs. John E. Barclay, "The Bumpas Family of New England," TAG 43 (1967):150-51.

estate after debts and charges (£150) was distributed on 26 Sept. 1749 to Sarah "the widow and Relick," one third, and to Stephen "the only son," two thirds. On 19 June 1749, the court appointed Isaac Coit as guardian for Stephen Harris, minor son.[2375]

Children of Thomas³ and Jane (Edwards) Harris:

   iii   MARY HARRIS, b. say 1702, living 1748 (father's will), prob. the daughter of Thomas Harris who m. by 1735, as his 1ˢᵗ wife, JOHN BACON, b. Newton, Mass., 30 July 1704,[2376] who was living in Voluntown, Conn., as late as 18 May 1779,[2377] son of Jacob and Dorothy (Bradhurst) Bacon of Newton and Voluntown.[2378]

   iv   JOHN HARRIS, was of age for his father to convey land to him in 1727 and is prob. the John Harris of Plainfield whose will, dated 15 May 1773, was presented in court there on 7 Dec. 1773.[2379] He apparently had four wives; the first, mother of his four children listed below, may have been the "[*blank*] Harris" who died in Plainfield on 3 April 1752 of "Cons[ump-tion]."[2380] He m. (2) in Preston (Griswold Parish) 30 Nov. 1752 ABIGAIL MACWITHY,[2381] prob. a daughter of David and Abigail (Park) Macwithy of Preston.[2382] Based on his petition dated 17 Sept. 1759, John was granted a divorce from Abigail in March 1760 on grounds that she had deserted him after three years when she "went to yᵉ Place called Batemans Patent in Dutchys [Dutchess] County in New York Province" and "hath lived and cohabited with another man for yᵉ space of more than three years last past."[2383] John m. (3) in Hopkinton, R.I., 15 June 1760 ELIZABETH GOOD-WILL "of Stonington" (as recorded in Plainfield).[2384] John m. (4) in Hopkinton 2 June 1770 HANNAH BABCOCK of Hopkinton (recorded in Plain-field),[2385] who was named in his will in 1773.

[2375] Plainfield District Probate, 1:36, 40, 47, 2:74. In March 1752, after achieving legal capacity to do so at age 14, Stephen made his own choice of Mr. Isaac Coit as guardian (ibid., 1:118).

[2376] *Vital Records of Newton, Massachusetts, to the Year 1850* (Boston: NEHGS, 1905), 14; Thomas W. Baldwin, *Bacon Genealogy: Michael Bacon of Dedham, 1640, and His Descendants* (Cambridge, Massachusetts: Murray and Emory Co., 1915), 124.

[2377] Voluntown, Conn., Deeds, 6:142.

[2378] Gale Ion Harris, "The Estate of Martha Harris and Early Bacon Families of Eastern Connecticut," scheduled for publication in NEHGR in 2013.

[2379] Plainfield District Probate, 6:81, 89-90.

[2380] Talcott, "Records of the First Congregational Church, Plainfield," NEHGR 70 (1916):310.

[2381] Frederic W. Bailey, *Early Connecticut Marriages as Found on Ancient Church Records Prior to 1800*, 6 vols. (New Haven, 1896–1904), 4:38.

[2382] Kendall P. Hayward, "Plainfield, Connecticut: Miscellaneous Items from Land Records," TAG 28 (1952):52. This marriage and the next one are incorrectly attributed in Haskell, *Capt. Seers Harris*, 92, to John's son of the same name, listed below.

[2383] John's petition and the decree are recorded in Plainfield, Conn., Deeds, 5:19; see also Gale Ion Harris, "Lieutenant John and Irene (Griffing) Harris of Lyme, Connecticut," *The Genealogist* 11 (1997): 54-62, at 55, 59.

[2384] Barbour Collection, Conn. Vital Records, citing Plainfield Vital Records, 2:50.

[2385] Barbour Collection, Conn. Vital Records, citing Plainfield Vital Records, 2:72.

John's will names his "well beloved wife" Hannah (house and personal items), son John, "my oldest daughter" Martha, and "my youngest daughter" Priscilla.[2386] Another child, David, is proven by records in other towns. In 1760 David's "brother" John Harris "of Lyme" was appointed administrator on his estate at New Milford, Conn.[2387] On 7 May 1761, John Harris of Lyme and Martha and Priscilla Harris of Plainfield sold David's New Milford land. David was called "former Apprentice" to Peter Brownson.[2388]

v   SILVANAS HARRIS, living Voluntown, Conn., 1755; m. Griswold Parish, Preston, Conn., 15 Dec. 1731 DOROTH[Y] _____.[2389] Silvanas received 30 acres in Plainfield from his father in Sept. 1734, which he sold to John Douglas in July 1737,[2390] and was mentioned in his father's will in 1748. Silvanas and "his son Thomas Harris" were Voluntown residents on 28 Feb. 1753, when they jointly purchased 50 acres there on the Preston line from Enoch Ballard. On 6 June 1755, Silvanas Harris, who signed by mark, of Voluntown and his son Thomas Harris, then of Stonington, Conn., conveyed the same property back to Ballard.[2391]

vi   HANNAH HARRIS, living 1748 (father's will).

vii   JANE HARRIS, living Coventry, Conn., March 1771;[2392] m. there 14 Aug. 1728, her cousin WILLIAM[3] EDWARDS,[2393] b. Windham, Conn., 12 Nov. 1703,[2394] d. Coventry 7 July 1752,[2395] son of Daniel[2] Edwards (*Thomas*[1]) and his wife Elizabeth (More). On 11 March 1771, Jane Edwards of Coventry quitclaimed her dowry rights in the house and land of "my late husband and their father William Edwards" to "my sons" Eliphalet, Joshua, Wareham, John, and James Edwards, and to "daughter Anne Edwards," all of Coventry.[2396] Coventry church records show deaths of "widow Edwards" in March 1769 and Oct. 1786, and of "Aged Widow Edwards" in Dec. 1791.[2397]

Children of Thomas[3] and Sarah (_____) Harris:

viii   THOMAS HARRIS "3d", b. Plainfield 19 April 1715,[2398] living 1748 (father's will). It seems that his wife by 1739 was MARY _____, the mother of Phebe Harris, daughter of "Thomas Jr. and Mary," whose birth on 14 Feb. 1739/40

[2386] Plainfield District Probate, 6:89-90.

[2387] Woodbury District Probate, 5:36.

[2388] New Milford, Conn., Deeds, 9:570, 659.

[2389] Bailey, *Early Connecticut Marriages*, 4:34.

[2390] Plainfield, Conn., Deeds, 3:180, 301.

[2391] Voluntown, Conn., Deeds, 4:35, 147-48.

[2392] Coventry, Conn., Deeds, 5:530.

[2393] Susan Whitney Dimock, comp., *Births, Marriages, Baptisms, and Deaths from the Records of the Town and Churches in Coventry, Connecticut, 1711–1844* (New York, 1897), 139.

[2394] Barbour Collection, Conn. Vital Records, citing Windham Vital Records, A:7, 1:25.

[2395] Dimock, *Records of the Town and Churches in Coventry*, 180.

[2396] Coventry, Conn., Deeds, 5:530.

[2397] Dimock, *Records of the Town and Churches in Coventry*, 220, 226, 228.

[2398] Barbour Collection, Conn. Vital Records, citing Plainfield Vital Records, 1:94.

was recorded in Killingly, Conn.[2399] On 12 April 1739, "Thomas Harris of Plainfield . . . yeoman" sold to John Douglas 5½ acres there with a house, barn, orchard, and fences.[2400] On the same day, Thomas a bought a 50-acre parcel in Killingly from John Church and John Church Jr.[2401] On 16 Feb. 1740/1, Thomas was "of Killingly, husbandman," when, signing by mark, he sold that parcel, apparently after building a house on it.[2402]

Thomas seems to have died in Newport, R.I. On 11 Aug. 1761, William Harris, minor son of Thomas Harris, deceased, appeared in Plainfield court where he chose Mr. James Dixon of Voluntown to be his guardian. Later, on 5 Feb. 1765, Sarah Harris, "a minor daughter to Mr. Thomas Harris late of Newport deceased," chose the same guardian.[2403] When the estate of Thomas's younger sister Martha Harris was distributed in 1798, it was noted that she had no brothers or sisters then living.[2404]

ix SARAH HARRIS, b. Plainfield 3 March 1716/7,[2405] living 1748 (father's will).

x CATHERINE HARRIS, b. Plainfield 3 June 1722,[2406] living 1748 (father's will).

xi MARTHA HARRIS, birth unrecorded, was residuary legatee in her father's will in 1748. On 14 Aug. 1756, Martha was "of Plainfield, single woman," when John Harris, presumably her brother, was appointed guardian for her minor daughter "Susanah Harris alias Dow."[2407] Martha d. before 5 April 1796, unmarried, when administration on her estate was granted to Calvin Goddard Esq. of Plainfield. Her inventory, dated 9 June 1796 and valued at £50 7s. 9d., included clothing, "a bark box with sundry trifles," furniture, and notes "against" Isaac Morgan, Samuel Hall, Stephen Clark, and James Bradford; Anthony Bradford and Walter Palmer were the appraisers.[2408] On 27 Nov. 1798, the court ordered distribution of the estate, valued at $130.13 after debts, to her nephews and nieces, "there being no brothers and sisters to the s[ai]d deceased living."[2409]

[2399] Barbour Collection, Conn. Vital Records, citing Killingly Vital Records, 1:24. The suffix "3d" appended to Thomas's name in the Plainfield town record in 1715 no doubt was the clerk's way to distinguish him from Ebenezer[3] Harris's son Thomas[4], b. Ipswich, Mass., 22 March 1692, who was denoted "Jr." in the record of birth of his son Thomas[5] there in 1725 (Barbour Collection, Conn. Vital Records, citing Plainfield Vital Records, 1:92). By 1739, Ebenezer's son Thomas[4] had moved to Cornwall, Conn. (Harris and Stover, "Thomas Harris of Plainfield and Cornwall," TAG 63 (1988):154-60); thus by that date "Thomas 3d" would have become "Jr." in Plainfield, the scheme seemingly followed by the clerk in adjacent Killingly.

[2400] Plainfield, Conn., Deeds, 3:293-94 (Thomas acknowledged in Killingly on 19 April 1739).

[2401] Killingly, Conn., Deeds, 4:107-8.

[2402] Killingly, Conn., Deeds, 4:176.

[2403] Plainfield District Probate, 4:219, 5:284.

[2404] Plainfield District Probate, 10:211.

[2405] Barbour Collection, Conn. Vital Records, citing Plainfield VR, 1:96.

[2406] Barbour Collection, Conn. Vital Records, citing Plainfield VR, 1:96.

[2407] Plainfield District Probate, 4:62.

[2408] Plainfield District Probate, 9:640.

[2409] Plainfield District Probate, 10:211.

INDEX OF NAMES WITH PAGE NUMBERS

Authors are indexed only at the first citation of a reference.

BEEKMAN
James 219
John 219
BELCHER
Catherine (—) 231
Elizabeth 231
Gregory 231
BELDEN
Elizabeth 43, 199
Infant 43
Joseph 43
Lois (Curtis) 43
Marianna (Phelps) 43
Mary 43
Mehitable (Harris) 43
Thomas Jr. 43
Thomas 43
BELKNAP
Jason 216, 217
Pamelia (Harris) 216, 217
BENEDICT
Alice 64
Francis Knapp 49
Hepsibah 49
Levi 49
Phebe (Northrop) 49
BENHAM
Alida S. 125, 178, 179
Ira 178
Solomon R. 178
Sophia (Persons) 178
BENJAMIN
Abigail (Eddy) 4
Abigail 4
Anna 268
Caleb 3, 4
John 4
Martha 4
Mary (Hale) 3, 5
Samuel 4
Sarah 4

BENNET
Elijah 267
Esther (Harris) 267
Basil Henry 137
Bess G. 137
Charles A. 137, 180
Deborah Jane (—) 212
Elmus Clark 137
Emma (—) 137
Grace P. 137
Harlan J. 212
John 243
Madeline/Matie 138
Maud Luella (Harris) 137, 180
Phyllis O. 137
BERKSEAD/BARKSTEAD
Joshua 257
BERRITT
Abraham 197
BERRY
Oliver 256
BERRYMAN
Mary 36
BIDWELL
Abigail (—) 238
Elizabeth (Stow) 238
Hannah 238
Hiram H. 84
John Jr. 188, 238
John 238
Laura Eliza (Harris) 84
Mary 238
Moses 238
Nathaniel 238
Samuel W. 92
Samuel 235, 238
Sarah (Harris) 238
Sarah (Wilcock) 238
Sarah Alice 92
Thankful 238
Thankfull 235
Thomas Jr. 58
BIERCE
Mary E. 87

BILLINGS
Constable 245
Joseph 245
BINGTTON
Jay 216
Pamelia (—) 216
BIRCH
Marie 271
BIRDSALL
Benjamin Jr. 72
BLACK
Robert C. III 266
BLACKLEACH
Elizabeth (Herris) (Wheeler) (Nesbitt) (Poisson) 260
Elizabeth 8
John 8
Richard, Mr. 260
BLAKESLY
Rhoda 127
BLAND
Charles 31
Hannah (Alderman) 31
James 31
Rachel (Alderman) 31
BLINN
Ann *alias* Harriss 26
Anna (Coultman) 25
Anne 11, 25, 26
Delia R. 45
Deliverance 10
John 62
Martha (Harris) 62
Mary (Hollister) (Harris) 5, 10
Peter 5, 10, 22, 25
William Jr. 25
William 20, 25, 26
BLOUNT
Beulah Ethel 185
Harris Oscar 185
Julian Webster 185
Oscar 185
Patty Cornelia 185

GEORGE
Hannah 265
GERE
Norman C. 182
Sandra Joyce
(Harris) (Lynch)
(Mead) 182
GIBBS
Abigail (Martin) 191
Henry 191
Jerusha 45
Mary 181
GIBSON
Hester Ann 201
GILBERT
Elizabeth (Belcher)
231
Ezekiel 237
Harold Simeon 231
Jonathan 237
Josiah 231
Lydia (—) 231
Mary (Harris)
(Ward) 231
Mary (Harris) 232
Mary (Rogers) 251
Patience (Harris)
237
Thomas 231
GILL
Ebenezer 18
Joshua 18
GILLAM
Lydia 172
GILLESPIE
Samuel 128
GILSON
Leonard 73
Sarah (Morse)
(Harris) 73
GIST
Christopher 38
GLEASON
Alice Bessie Leone
(Wescott) 135
Bess V. 129-131,
135, 180

Elizabeth (Demond)
16, 40
Gwen Alice 133,
135, 136
Olin Stanley 135
Thomas 40
GLOVER
Mr. 14
Pelatiah, Rev. 15
GODDARD
Calvin, Esq. 275
GOFF
Philip 240
GOFFE
Aaron 8
David 24
Lydia (Boardman),
24
Moses 8
Philip 8
GOLDWAITHE
Charlotte 43
GOODLAXEN
Maria B. 140
GOODRICH
Honor 95
Mehitable 92
Prudence 193
GOODWILL
Elizabeth 273
GOODWIN
Joseph, Sgt. 57
GRAY
Eunice 204
Mary (Hurlbut) 204
Nathan 204
Susannah 47
Warren 49, 70
GREEN
Statira 88
GRIDLEY
Harriet Cornelius 67,
105
Julia E. (Harris)
(Mowbray) 111
Leonard A. 111
Leonard C. 112

Leonard, 112
Mercy (Finney) 112
GRINNELL
Hannah/Anna 47
GRISWOLD
Abigail (Harris) 45
Annie 95
Charlotte 43
Daniel 45
Delia R. (Blinn) 45
Elizabeth R. (—) 45
Glenn E. 45
Harris 45
Jacob 45
Jerusha (Gibbs) 45
Jerusha 45
John 12
Josiah 45
Lydia 21
Prudence 21
Thomas Harris 45
GROAT
Adeline 82
Charles W. 81, 82
Charles 82
Ellen 82
Frances Mariah 82
Lydia (—) 81
Martha Matilda 82
Mary (Harris) 81
Mary Jane 81
Philip 81
Samuel D. 81, 143
Sarah 81, 142, 143
GROSVENOR
Jeannette 115
GUNN
Minnie L. 105
GUSTIN
Thomas 250
GUTHREY
Margaret (—) 261
Robert 261
GWINN
Edna J. (Sprague)
92, 93
Oliver H. 92, 93

Rebeckah (Pulver)
146
William 146
KNIFFEN
Benjamin 202
KNIGHT
Sarah, Mrs. 248
KNOTT
John 241
KNOWLTON
James 73
KOMIVES
Judith Louise 182
KOPYCINSKI
Patricia/Tricia Gail
183
KORROCH
William A. 197
KRESBOUGH
Anna 141
Joseph 141
LAKE
Margaret (Reade)
266
Martha 266
LANDIS
Joseph 165
Katheryn 165
Prudence (Hughes)
165
LANDON
David 84
Frederick C. 84
Johannah (—) 84
Laura Eliza (Harris)
(Bidwell) 84
LANE
Agnes (Farnsworth)
225
Ebenezer 225
Ellen Jeannette 225
Elvira A. 76, 138,
139
George 225
Josiah 225
Mary 224, 225
Peter 225

Sarah (Harris) 224,
225
Sarah 224
William 225
LANGLEY
Esther 34
LARNED
E. D. 271
LATIMER
Rhoda 21
LATTIMER
Elizabeth 5
John 10
LAVIERS
Barbara (Purple) 75
LAWRENCE
Abigail (Ogden) 55
Benjamin 226
Daniel 54
Elizabeth 53
Jonathan 55
Mary (Harris)
224-226
Mary 55, 226
Nicholas 225, 226
Rebecca 226
Ruth (Ogden)
(Harris) 54
LAY
Mary (Harris) 239
LEEDS
Anna (Harris) 44
Cary Jr. 44
Gideon 44
Joseph Harris 44
Lavina 44
Lucy 44
Mary Elizabeth
(Weed) 44
LEEK
Abigail 32
Recompense 33
LEITCH
Lizzy B. 82
LEROY
Cornelia
(Cookingham) 148

LEVERETT
John, Capt. and Gov.
241-244
LEWIS
Elizabeth (Scott),
196
Fanny A. (Harris) 95
William 196
LIGHT
Daniel 211
Dorcas (Harris) 197
Lemuel 197, 198
LILLY
Anne (—) 245
Henry 245
Martha 245
LINCOLN
"Abe" 69
George 257
LIVERMORE
Leonard 48
LIVINGSTON
John 248
Mary (Winthrop)
248
LOBDELL
Levi 220
LOCKWOOD
Almira (Pardee) 42
Daniel 195
Edmond 195
James, Rev. 21, 22
Lewis 42
Rev. 22
LONG
Fred Bigelo 179, 180
Laura Apaline (Pike)
(Harris) 179
Samuel 180
Sarah M. (—) 180
LONGESPÉE
William 13
LONGLEY
Artie T. 141, 142
Esther (Murdock)
141
William 141

Sarah (Harris) 191
MARVIN
Mary 239
MASON
John, Capt. 248, 249
Levi 80
MASTEN
Anna 42
MATHER
Jane E. 209
MAVERICK
Elias 229
MAYER
Pauline A.
(Pemberton) 131
Wyley B. 131
MAYES
Flora May (Harris)
184
Tip Cicero 184
MAYHEW
Thomas 206
MCCLINTOCK
W. H., Mrs. 165
MCCRACKEN
George E. 40
MCCURDY
Anna (Harris) 32
Elijah 32
MCELROY
Clemenia (—) 209
James 209
MCKEAN
Thomas Lincoln 69
Elizabeth Minerva
(Harris) 68
Emma Jane
(Darling) 68
Emma Marie
(Brown) 69
Emma May 69
John Spencer 68
John, Rev. 68
Joseph 68
Laura V. (—) 69
Minnie J. 68
Thomas, Prof. 68

William 68
MCKEE
Laurence 179
Vera Merle (Harris)
179
MCLAUGHLIN
Marian Eliza
(Merritt) 133
MCMURRAY
Sarah 142
MCMUSTEE
Angeline 136
MCNAMER
Arkley L. 162
George A. 161, 162
Zoe A. (Harris) 161,
162
MCNIGHT
Mary (Lawrence)
(Harris) 55
MEAD
Angeline
(McMustee) 136
Frank 182
Harry Monroe 136
Howell Clarence 136
Maude Blanche
(Wescott) 136
Sandra Joyce
(Harris) (Lynch),
182
MEASURE
William 254
MEDVED
Johnnie Richard 183
Marjorie Ellen
(Harris) (Harmon)
183
MEGGS
John, 223, 227
MELVOIN
Richard I. 37
MERCHANT
Denah Temperance
136
MEREDITH
John 12

MERRITT
Alice (Jolley) 133
Ariel D. 133
Edgar Lindley 133
Goldie Alice 133
Ida Louisa 133, 134
Jacob 132
Julia Alverette
(Harris) 132, 133
Linley S. 132, 133
Marian Eliza 133
Merilynn 133
Ronald D. 133
Ronald 133
Sarah J. (Sutton) 132
MEYERS
Merrible E. 66
MICKEL
John 220
Ruth (Harris) 220
Daniel J. 82
Elizabeth (—) 82
Frances Mariah
(Groat) 82
John 82
MIGGES
sister 225
MILLARD
Matthew 267
MILLER
Abigail (Cornell)
237
Abner 197-199, 202,
203
Aurilla (—) 164
Capt. 210
Jemima (—) 198,
199, 202, 203
Jemima 198, 202
John Sr. 12
Josiah, Capt. 199
Martha (Harris) 197,
198, 203
Nellie L. 164
Patience 20
Samuel H. 211

170
W. E. 166
ROBBART
  Thomas 225
ROBBERDS
  Susannah (Collins)
  240
ROBBINS
  Abigail 22, 44, 45
  Daniel 21
  Elisha 21
  Frances 62, 94, 95
  Hezekiah 21
  Joshua 44
  Julia Ann 44
  Julia 62
  Lucy (Wolcott) 21
  Martha 21, 44
  Mary (Welles) 44
  Mehitabel (Harris)
  21
  Mehitabel 21
  Prudence (Griswold)
  21
  Rebecca (Crane) 94
  Robert 62
  Samuel 21
  Sarah (Harris) 21
  Sarah 21
  Wido Hez[a] 21
  William, 94
ROBERTS
  John H. 159
  Matilda (Hill) 159
  Mercy Jane 115,
  159, 160
ROBERTSON
  Jabez 200, 211
ROBINSON
  Harriet Evelina
  (Francis) 92
  Marcus E. 92
  Patrick 257
  Peter 19
  Sarah (Buck) 19
  W. A., Rev. 149

ROBISON
  [Ebenezer], Dr. 272
ROCKWELL
  Elizabeth (Foster)
  232
  Joseph 232, 239
  William 239
RODMAN
  John 260, 264
ROGERS
  Amanda 105
  Elizabeth (Harris)
  250, 264
  Elizabeth 246, 250
  Elpheus 250
  Freelove (Hurlburt)
  264
  James Swift 246
  James 264
  Mary (Jordon) 264
  Mary (Stanton) 246,
  250
  Philip M. 50, 65
  Samuel Jr. 248
  Samuel 246, 250,
  250
  Sarah 246
  William 250
ROGGEN
  Ann 42
  Anna (Masten) 42
  Petrus 42
ROLLO
  Alexander 240
ROOD
  J. 128
ROORK
  Hannah (Harris)
  (Whitacar) 53
  Thomas 53
ROOSEVELT
  Franklin D. 218
ROOT
  Deborah (Buck) 19
  Ebenezer Jr. 19
  Eunice 192
  Lovina (Preston) 118

ROSE
  Hannah (George)
  265
  Samuel 22
  Sarah (Harris) 267
  Thomas 267
ROWE
  Alice Josephine 97
  Henry 97
ROWLAND
  Cynthia (Harris) 220
  Henry 220
  Katherine E. 118
ROWLEE
  Shubul, Sr. 263
ROYCE
  Carrie T. (Harris) 95
  Ebenezer 192
  Ephraim 192
  Eunice (Harris) 192
  Eunice (Root) 192
  Eunice 192
  George 95
  Keziah (Hall) 192
  Keziah 192
  Mindwell 192
  Nehemiah 192
RUDE
  Dorothy 270
  Jacob 270
  Jemima (Park) 270
  Mary (Harris) 270
  Mary (Richardson)
  270
  Stephen 270
  Susannah 270
RUEDI
  Jacob M. 104
  Jennie A. (Wells)
  104
RUMRILL
  Eunice 192
  John 192
  Rachel 192
  Tabitha 192
  Thankful (Harris)
  192

WHITMORE
Abigail 233
Edith 233
Elizabeth 233
Francis 228, 230, 232, 233
Hannah (Harris) 232, 233
Hannah 233
Isabel (—) 232
Isabell 233
John 233
Joseph 233
Martha 233
W. H. 233
William H. 243
William 233, 259
WHITNEY
Anna 127
Asa 70, 127
Edgar Mortimer 114, 115
Emeline Amanda 114, 158, 159
Harriett (Westcott) 114
James Lewis 114, 158
Julia (Harris) 158
Julia A. (Harris) 113, 114
Laura (Harris) 113, 114, 115, 158
Lucy Maria (Hall) 158
Maria (—) 158
Mary Frances 115
Nellie (—) 115
WHITTACAR
Ambrose 34
Ruth (Harris) 30, 34
WHITTLESEY
Eliphalet 83
WIARD
John, 20
Phebe (—) 20
WICKHAM

Gertrude Van Rensselaer 107
Mary 23
WIDGER
Betty J. 66, 73, 111
WIDGER
Betty J., Mrs. 153
WILCOCK
Sarah 238
WILCOCKS *ALIAS* HARRIS
Rhoda 57
WILCOCKS
Ephraim 57
Ezra 57
WILCOX
Elijah 58
Elizabeth (Humphrey) 58
Francis C. 91
Hepzibah (Humphrey) 58
Inez 98
James 58
Lucy (Harris) 91
Reynold Webb 56
Rhoda 58
Rhoda, Mrs. 56
WILCOXSON
Abigail (Thrall) 56
Ezra 56
Giles 56
Hezekiah 56
John 56
Joseph 56
Rhoda (Alford) (Harris) 56
Rhoda 56
William Howard 259
Zeruiah 56
WILKS
Conn. Agent 249
WILLARD
Anna (Harris) 21
Anne 21
Ephraim 21
Hannah (Wolcott) 22
John 21

Josiah 229
Lydia (Griswold) 21
Martha (Robbins) 21
Mary/Polly 21
Rhoda (Latimer) 21
Stephen 21
Thomas 21
Wealthy 21, 22
William 21, 22
WILLCOCK
Francis 17
WILLIAMS *ALIAS* HARRIS
Thomas 227
WILLIAMS
Abraham 6, 22
Adeline (Cooley) 112
Cornelia (—) 146
Elijah H. 42
Elisha Jr. 20, 22
Elizabeth (Hunnewell) 238
Eunice (Boardman) 6, 22
Hattie A. 157, 158
Jefferson 112
John 7, 146, 228, 243
John, Rev. 37
Julia Alice 112
Mary E. 146
Miranda (Pardee) 42
Rebecca (Waterhouse) 6
Rebecca 6, 11, 22, 23
Samuel 238
Sophia 213
Thomas 228
William 229, 261
WILLIAMSON
Capt. 189
WILLIE
John 263
Miriam (Moore) 263
Miriam 263

WYMAN
  Thomas Bellows 228
WYNN
  Allen 177
  Charles V. 123
  Edward Plinn 177
  Evelyn Lavinia 177
  Grant 177
  Henry 176
  James Clinton 177
  esse E. Jr. 124
  Jessie Edward 124
  Jessie May 177
  John Henry 177
  Josie 124
  Julia B. (Harris) 175
  Julia Betsey (Harris)
   124
  Laurel 177
  Lloyd 177
  Lula Amida (Harris)
   177
  Margaret 177
  Mark 178
  Mary 177
  Olive M. (Harris)
   177
  Robert 177
  Rose E. (—) 178
  Verlina Maria 177
  Vietta Maria
   (Downer) 123
  Walter Edward 177
  Walter 176
  Walter 177
YATES
  Clarissa Antoinette
   (Cleaveland) 83
  Horatio Rev. 83
  Jacob Peter 83
  Marilla (Woodruff)
   83
YEOMANS
  Jonathan 239
  Sibbil (Harris) 239

YOUNG
  Denah Temperance
   (Merchant) 136
  Elizabeth (Harris) 36
  Frank Jr. 95
  Frank Merchant 136,
   137
  Frank 95
  George Washington
   136
  Joseph 36
  Lucelia 66, 104
  Marietta Elnora
   (Harris) 136, 137
  Martha R. (Harris)
   95